Interventions is produced on the land of the Wurundjeri people of the Kulin Nation. We acknowledge the Traditional Owners of country throughout Australia and recognise their continuing connection to land, waters and culture. We pay our respects to their Elders past, present and emerging. Their land was stolen, never ceded. It always was and always will be Aboriginal land.

First published 2023 by Interventions Inc

Interventions Inc is a not-for-profit, independent, radical book publisher.
For further information:

www.interventions.org.au
info@interventions.org.au
PO Box 963 Coffs Harbour
NSW Australia 2450

Layout by Leigh Milward

Cover illustration by Audrey Eberhard

Editors: Alex Ettling and Iain McIntyre

Title: **Knocking The Top Off:
A People's History of Alcohol in Australia**

ISBN: 978-0-6452535-9-7: Paperback
ISBN: 978-0-6452535-8-0: eBook

© Alex Ettling and Iain McIntyre 2023

Individual chapters remain the property of their respective authors.

The moral rights of the author have been asserted.

All rights reserved. Except as permitted under the Australian Copyright Act 1968 (for example, a fair dealing for the purposes of study, research, criticism or review), no part of this book may be reproduced, stored in a retrieval system, communicated or transmitted in any form or by any means without prior written permission.

The editors and the publishers wish to thank all those who supplied images and gave permission to reproduce copyright material in this book. Every effort has been made to contact all copyright holders, and the publishers welcome communication from any copyright owners from whom permission was inadvertently not obtained. In such cases, we will be pleased to obtain appropriate permission and provide suitable acknowledgment in future editions.

All inquiries should be made to the publisher.

 A catalogue record for this book is available from the National Library of Australia

Knocking The Top Off:
A People's History of Alcohol in Australia

Alex Ettling & Iain McIntyre

CONTENTS

Introduction Alex Ettling and Iain McIntyre ii
Chapter 1   'Grog for Me': Convicts and Alcohol   Michael Quinlan and Hamish Maxwell-Stewart 1
Chapter 2   The Life of Matthew Brady, Gentleman Bushranger   Alex Ettling 11
Chapter 3   A Cheeky Few: Early Socialism and Alcohol   Alex Ettling 19
Chapter 4   Pubs and the Formation of Unions in Australia   Iain McIntyre 35
Chapter 5   Disturbing the Peace: The 1851 Rocks Riot   Iain McIntyre 37
Chapter 6   The Dunmore Arms and Brisbane's 'Blood or Bread' Riots   Iain McIntyre 43
Chapter 7   Pay The Rent!: Wombeetch Puyuun   Alex Ettling 45
Chapter 8   'Manhood… drowned out of them with liquor': William Lane's Teetotal Utopia   Jeff Sparrow 47
Chapter 9   Alcohol and Celebrations of the Eight Hour Day   Iain McIntyre 59
Chapter 10   Anti-Chinese Racism and the Life of Publicans Jimmy and Evelina Ah Foo   Alex Ettling and Iain McIntyre 61
Chapter 11   'Stubborn Struggles': Beer Strikes in Western Australia, 1901–1925   Iain McIntyre 65
Chapter 12   'Champagne is Not Reserved for the Stomachs of the Rich': Chummy Fleming and a Donation to the Unemployed   Iain McIntyre 75
Chapter 13   The Communists Meet the Bohemians: Drinking at the Margins, from the 1900s to the 1930s   Alex Ettling 77
Chapter 14   The 1912 Broken Hill Hotel and Restaurant Strike   Iain McIntyre 91
Chapter 15   State Control of Liquor in the Northern Territory: A Brave but Unpopular Experiment   Maggie Brady 93
Chapter 16   'Thirsty Days': The 1918 Brisbane Beer Strike   Iain McIntyre 97
Chapter 17   Christmas and Beer   Chris McConville 99
Chapter 18   Pub Boycotts, Loyalism, and Unions in Queensland   Iain McIntyre 111
Chapter 19   Cecilia Shelley: Feminist, Activist, Trailblazer   Daniel A. Elias 113
Chapter 20   Communist Jocka Burns and Grape Picking   Alex Ettling and Iain McIntyre 121
Chapter 21   The Matteotti Club   Iain McIntyre 123
Chapter 22   'What Should We Do…': Maritime Workers and Drinking   Alex Ettling 125
Chapter 23   'Valour among the Vats': 1937 Castlemaine Brewery Dispute   Carol Corless 131
Chapter 24   The Battle of Australian Modernism   Alex Ettling 141
Chapter 25   Gold Diggings and Company Towns: From the Buckland Race Riot to the Rostrevor Hops Farm   Alex Ettling and Iain McIntyre 153
Chapter 26   Folk, Jazz and Booze: Moral Panics from the 1940s to the 1970s   Alex Ettling 161
Chapter 27   Before, After and During Work: Alcohol and the Development of Noel Counihan as an Artist   Alex Ettling 169
Chapter 28   'The Inns are Out': The Pub, the People and the Post-War New Order   Tanja Luckins 175
Chapter 29   For Aboriginal Humanity: The Social Justice Agenda of the Woman's Christian Temperance Union in Australia   Alison Holland 187
Chapter 30   Drink Deep: The Long Life of Jack Clancy   Alex Ettling 195
Chapter 31   A Cold War Shirtfronting   Rowan Cahill 197
Chapter 32   George Seelaf: A Political Life Around Booze   Alex Ettling 201
Chapter 33   Critical Drinking with the Sydney Push   Wendy Bacon 207
Chapter 34   The 1962 Victorian Beer Ban   Iain McIntyre 223
Chapter 35   Education In Reverse? The Drinking Culture of Brisbane's Student Radicals   Alex Ettling 225

Chapter 36	Colour Bar – the Freedom Ride and the Walgett RSL Lisa Milner	237
Chapter 37	Balmain and the Politics of Draught Terry Irving	241
Chapter 38	Jean Young, Kath Williams and the Fight for Equal Pay Iain McIntyre	247
Chapter 39	Counterculture Carlton and the Pubs Alex Ettling	253
Chapter 40	Black and White Solidarity in the Pubs of Brisbane Alex Ettling	259
Chapter 41	'Alk!': Pubs, Communities, and a Brotherhood in its Cups David Nichols	271
Chapter 42	Alcohol and the Law: The 1979 Frankston Riot and Other Stories John Finlayson in conversation with Alex Ettling	281
Chapter 43	Black Power and Alcohol: An Oral History with Gary Foley Gary Foley in conversation with Alex Ettling	291
Chapter 44	'We are going to blacklist this hotel': Alcohol and the Activism of Chicka Dixon Alex Ettling	307
Chapter 45	'Rough As Guts': The Summerhill and The Maoists Alex Ettling	309
Chapter 46	Liberating the Local: Women Demand Access to the Public Bar Diane Kirkby	321
Chapter 47	A Sunken Ship and its Sunken Beer: The Tragedy of the Blythe Star Alex Ettling	327
Chapter 48	Whitlam and the Gurindji Land Rights Ceremony Alex Ettling	331
Chapter 49	Farewell Frothies? Global Heating and Disappearing Kelp Alex Ettling	333
Chapter 50	'We Found Our Own Way': Talking with Gay Liberation Activists Bruce Carter	335
Chapter 51	Folk, Politics and the Law at The Rainbow Hotel Alex Ettling	349
Chapter 52	The Woolshed Kiss-In Graham Willett	353
Chapter 53	'Drink and Go To Work': The Saints and the Brisbane Punks Alex Ettling	355
Chapter 54	The Star Hotel Graham Willett	367
Chapter 55	Triple Zed's Joint Efforts: Beer, Bands, and Breaking The News Alex Ettling	369
Chapter 56	'A Pub of our Own!': The Kingston Hotel, Melbourne's Women's Pub Janey Stone	383
Chapter 57	The Oxford Hotel 'Riot', Wollongong, 1981 Nick Southall	387
Chapter 58	A Pub at the End of the World: Making Something Meaningful in Tasmania's Wild West Alex Ettling	393
Chapter 59	Confrontational Temperance Activism Among Indigenous Women Maggie Brady	405
Chapter 60	The Changing Face of Alcohol Consumption & Culture from the 1970s Alex Ettling	415
Chapter 61	Funding the Cause: Benefit Gigs at the Empress of India Hotel Iain McIntyre	429
Chapter 62	The Singing Syrup: Melbourne's Trades Hall Gets a Bar Alex Ettling	431
Chapter 63	Stopping AIDEX '91 Iain McIntyre	445
Chapter 64	Workplace Politics at the West End Brewery in Adelaide Phoebe Kelloway	447
Chapter 65	Rockhampton Accessible Pub Crawls, 1989–2022 Alex Ettling and Iain McIntyre	453
Chapter 66	Choke Point: Inside a Wildcat Strike in the Melbourne Liquor Distribution Centre Simon Burns in conversation with Alex Ettling	455
Chapter 67	Spitting In a Fascist's Beer: The Far Right and Pubs Alex Ettling and Iain McIntyre	467
Further Reading		473
Contributors		491
Acknowledgements		497
About Interventions		498

The Hop Picker, Ovens Valley, 1957 (Jeff Carter Archive/National Library of Australia)

Sydney drinkers, late 1960s (Jacinta Elliott Collection)

Amos Hotel barmaids march for equal pay as part of a Newcastle stopwork, 1967 (*Tribune*/Search Foundation, State Library of NSW)

INTRODUCTION

Alex Ettling and Iain McIntyre

In the summer of 2019/20, the world's attention was focused on Australia, as a scale of bushfires never seen before scorched the continent. Hundreds of lives, including those of firefighters were lost, along with thousands of homes. The flames incinerated forests and with them billions of native animals, the emblems of the continent. Cities were choked with the smell of devastation. This brought home the reality of climate change and its impact on country towns and the bush, places where so much of the Australian mythos is located, but which generally exist out of mind for the urban majority.

Media coverage of the disaster veered towards human interest stories. One iconic figure who emerged from this catastrophe was a volunteer firefighter, Paul Parker. When approached by a Channel 7 news team he yelled from his fire truck, 'Are you from the media? Tell the Prime Minister to go and get fucked from Nelligen. We really enjoy doing this shit, fuckhead.'

Charles A. Doudiet watercolour of the burning of the Eureka Hotel, a key event that led to the subsequent rebellion in Ballarat, 1854 (Art Gallery of Ballarat)

The interaction went viral, with many wanting to show their appreciation to the person who had given the PM a serve. The licensee of the Steampacket Hotel in Nelligen, Joel Alvey, told the *Sydney Morning Herald*, 'We've had people ringing up from all around Australia, wanting to transfer money so Paul doesn't need to pay for his own beers.' It was reported that his bar tab became a shout for all his mates whenever he was in the pub, 'You've got to share things around', the firefighter said.

Parker's spray formed part of a broad and furious response to the conservative Prime Minister Scott Morrison's decision to go on a Christmas holiday, and overseas to boot, during the catastrophe. Morrison's trip came on the back of decades of government decisions which had fuelled climate change, including dismissal of the dangers involved and hostility towards those calling for solutions. It also highlighted a yawning gap between public expectations of how people should be supported during a crisis, and what the government was prepared to deliver. Morrison's hubris and lack of sympathy was summed up in a quip during a radio interview in which he claimed he couldn't be of help because, 'I don't hold a hose, mate.'

An Australian tourist who happened to be staying at the same resort in Hawaii took a photo of the PM with a drink. Interviewed by *10 News First*, Craig Way said, 'He was quite happy to sit here and have cocktails served to him whilst our firefighters are doing it really hard.' The image went viral, having been shared on Twitter by the photographer's nephew, who happened to be a politically savvy trade unionist and knew how damaging it would be. Street artist Scott Marsh painted a mural based on the photo, depicting the prime minister and his cocktail, with the title 'Merry

Illustration of the Kelly gang's last stand at the Glenrowan Inn during which Ned Kelly was captured and Dan Kelly, Joseph Byrne and Steve Hart killed, 1880 (*Australian Pictorial Weekly*)

Crisis'. The potency of the image was measured both in its popularity on social media as well as by the $50 000 it made for charity via t-shirts and prints.

Morrison was the archetypal politician of the modern age and acquired the derisive nickname #ScottyFromMarketing. On the election campaign trail in 2022 he sought to fix his problems of relatability. Visits to pubs have long been used for politicians to display a 'common touch' and so an appearance was duly arranged inside Newcastle's Edgeworth Tavern.

As a media stunt it was not nearly stage-managed closely enough. A 73 year old disability pensioner, Ray Dury, grabbed the headlines after confronting the prime minister. Dury had been a miner for 30 years. Stricken with dust disease and asbestos tumours, he complained about the circumstances of his low income and the government's failure to introduce an Integrity Commission. Jabbing his finger at Morrison, he told him, 'You better fucking do something. I'm sick of your bullshit!'

A bad day for the PM was capped off during a selfie with Kamilaroi woman Chantelle Howlett. As he looked towards the camera, she told him: 'Congratulations on being the worst prime minister we've ever had.' There's an expression in Australian political chatter, 'the pub test', and it was clear that this prime minister had failed it. Not long after his government was voted out, suffering a major loss in the 2022 election.

These events tell us much about how Australian social understandings and conflict continue to play out through recreational culture, and the alcohol consumption that regularly accompanies it. There are clear meanings associated with being accepted, or not, into social spaces. There are others regarding drinking unearned cocktails and receiving well deserved beers.

This book is a collection of histories and insights into the role alcohol has played in Australians' lives. From the early days of colonisation through to the contemporary moment, alcohol has featured in every stage of Australia's history. It was part of iconic events and attainments, such as the Ned Kelly story, Eureka Stockade rebellion, and the Eight Hour Day, as well as lesser-known occurrences and movements.

As a people's history this anthology looks at developments in Australian life from the vantage point of workers and marginalised communities, the exploited and oppressed. Chronologically structured and featuring hundreds of images, it brings together chapters from more than 20 historians and activists, and weaves contributions from the editors around them. Via short expositions and deep dives into incidents, periods, groups and individuals, it sheds light on a number of themes to do with alcohol consumption and the society in which it has taken place.

There is a mythic quality to Australian drinking culture, as represented in advertising that has amplified, or good naturedly made fun of, depictions of the average drinker as a white, hardworking, blue collar, masculine beer swiller. From the creation of Vegemite as a by-product of brewing, and claims that the national accent was in part the result of drunkenly slurred speech during the early years of colonisation, alcohol has played a core part in branding of Australia™.

Many of this book's chapters separate the image from the reality. Drinking is not important to everyone. Neither has it been a feature of all communities. Drinking rates have varied greatly over Australian history. In the 1830s they hit a peak of 13.6 litres annually per capita of population. This dipped to 5.8 litres in the 1890s and then 2.5 during the 1930s. Following World War Two consumption steadily rose until it reached 13.1 litres per capita in 1974. By 1995 it was down to 9.8 litres per adult and remained steady until a slight rise in the late 2010s.

Although these measures track broad patterns, alcohol consumption has always been uneven across demographics and played diverse social roles for different groups of people. Many of these defy received ideas. The average Aboriginal Australian drinks less than non-Aboriginal Australians, but instances of problem drinking amongst Aboriginal populations are significantly amplified in the media. Other stereotypes have been challenged by studies which indicate that wealthy people consume the most alcohol in Australia, and that rates of drinking amongst youth are falling rather than rising.

Shifts in drinking trends have related to a variety of factors. These include, but are not limited to, changing work and recreation patterns, economic booms and busts, the arrival of the motor car, legislative and regulatory reforms, forms of urban development, and the availability and popularity of other intoxicants. The presence of alcohol, and its absence, has left a mark in many unexpected ways.

Alcohol existed on the Australian continent prior to colonisation but there appears to have been no large-scale production. The national reputation for heavy drinking began with colonists and was established almost immediately after invasion. Some have claimed that the first European settlers in Australia drank more alcohol per head of population than any other community in the history of humanity. There is a contrary view though, expressed by historian Noel Butlin, that consumption of spirits and wine in Sydney was little different to that in England.

In *A Short History of Drunkenness*, author Mark Forsyth makes a case that few settlers were drunk all the time. This is in part evidenced by another set of themes explored within this collection, the use of alcohol as a means of exercising social control and expressing power.

Gertrude Street, Melbourne, late 1970s (John Corker)

From the beginning of colonisation limitation was used as a tool to compel people to work, discipline the workforce, and establish dominance for those who controlled its flow. Functionally alcohol also became a form of currency, and it was an attempt at breaking this economic control that led to the infamous Rum Rebellion of 1808, and a period of military dictatorship during which Australia was described as a 'rum state'. It follows that those at the bottom of society, workers who in most cases had been forcibly brought to an unfamiliar land as convicts, would seek to exercise their own agency over supply through flouting rules and engaging in forms of workplace resistance.

The history of alcohol in Australia includes many instances of concern and condemnation. A number of contributions to this book explore how public perceptions, government policies and individual and group behaviours have been shaped and interpreted according to views regarding the role alcohol should, and does, play in society. These have often reflected trends in ideas concerning morality and health, both of which have been the subject of much dissension and debate.

Measures to curtail alcohol consumption have included education campaigns, restrictions on pubs and retailers, bans, reduced opening hours, and increased taxes. Although specific forms, and the communities targeted, have varied and changed over time, these methods remain in use today. These have shaped the culture of drinking and had implications for workers and communities beyond the point of production, sale and consumption.

The arrival of the temperance movement in the nineteenth century added particular force to calls for reform. Political activity to limit or abolish alcohol use throughout society

Street advertising for Liquor Referendum Polling Day on Riley Street, Darlinghurst, 1916 (City of Sydney)

was largely pursued via electoral forums. Campaigns for individual abstinence created social spaces without alcohol, from giant coffee palaces to alcohol-free dances. In doing so they changed the nature of public activities as the movement strengthened a trend towards the use of municipal and non-alcohol-based venues for unions and sporting clubs, as well as civic events and meetings.

The high point of success for the anti-alcohol movement was during the era of the 'wowsers'. 'Wowserism' as a derogatory label and concept was applied to a variety of crusades for social reform in the late nineteenth and early twentieth centuries. The strength of these is evident in state-based legislation that led to a reduction in the number and type of alcohol-based venues, opening hours being limited, and restrictions placed on women owning and working in pubs, as well as drinking in sections of them. Such changes were accompanied by new restrictions on gambling and the operation of theatres and dance halls, greater censorship, and stricter policing of sex work, public bathing, young people smoking, and other activities.

Unsurprisingly, sections of society have regularly opposed and defied such changes, and their application has been varied and uneven. In regard to alcohol, campaigns against prohibition and restrictions have generally been run by the liquor industry. In times when labour movements had a strong presence in the industry, this was often in alliance with unions.

On an informal level some consumer responses to regulation have fuelled the negative consequences of alcohol intake. Most famously, early closing led to the 'six o'clock swill', a practice in which drinkers downed as much alcohol as possible in the short period between knocking off work and the pub

Painting by H Glover of the Norfolk Arms Inn, Adelaide, 1854 (State Library of SA)

closing. Bans on select communities have at times increased the ingestion of cheaper and stronger drinks, and alcohol-based substances, in unregulated and unsupervised spaces. Such responses, counter-responses, and outcomes are discussed and dissected by various contributors, along with paths less often taken, for example governments experimenting with ownership of pubs during the early decades of the twentieth century.

Many temperance advocates had an overarching commitment to social change and were commonly active in other causes. The ways in which their ethics changed and challenged the approaches and activities of labour and social movements feature throughout a number of chapters. The role that organisations such as the Woman's Christian Temperance Union played in groundbreaking campaigns regarding human rights and other issues is also discussed.

Drunkenness has long been depicted as a moral failing and a sinful behaviour linked to poverty and crime. Over time an acceptance of a 'medical' model of problem drinking has emerged. This has shifted blame away from the individual and focused on social factors while arguing that alcoholism is more akin to a disease or mental health issue. Such approaches have often depicted a contrast between 'problem' and 'normal' drinkers, and defined alcoholism in terms of cravings and loss of control. The role and differing approaches that community-based organisations, unions and individual activists have played in ameliorating harms in the workplace, home and public spaces, forms a further subject of this book.

Licensing laws and those targeting public drunkenness have channelled drinking into certain places and forms. Combined with

Australian Hotel, Roma, 1915 (State Library of Queensland)

vagrancy acts they have regularly been employed to harass First Nations communities, the unemployed, homeless and poor, as well as to remove what are seen as sources of social disorder. As seen in events covered in this collection policing has recurringly led to riotous reactions expressing deeper economic and social fractures.

Experiences of oppression, and responses to it, have had complex implications for alcohol use. Marginalised groups have regularly demanded the right to engage in the social worlds open to others – including consuming the same products and participating in the same institutions. Contributors cover the many means used by communities and movements to challenge laws, rules and customs designed to restrict First Nations Australians, women and others' access to alcohol and venues. They also explore the contradictory and vexed nature of intoxication and the places in which it takes place, as well as the way in which these can variously symbolise and facilitate comfort, lateral violence, control, and freedom.

Through law and custom the history of alcohol in Australia is entwined with that of the venues licensed to sell it. The practice of drinking in company within designated venues was directly imported from Britain. It was construction of the Roman road network that developed the first public houses, or pubs, called tabernae (taverns). After the departure of Roman authority, Anglo-Saxons established alehouses, most likely a side-hustle for the domestic dwellings of those who carried out farming and brewed alcohol from their produce. These alehouses evolved into regular meeting places where people would congregate, gossip and arrange mutual aid within their communities, an important social function in a class society without a welfare system.

When British capitalism was forcibly introduced to Australia, the tradition of pubs accompanied it, and these venues have endured to this day with surprisingly few adaptations. In the eighteenth and nineteenth centuries the pub was commonly the first structure built for community use in a new settlement. Towns would grow up around them, with pubs serving multiple functions in addition to the sale and consumption of alcohol: providing accommodation and meals, and serving as a post office, bank or general store, a secure location to stable your horse, and a place to store your corpse (as the cold cellars were often the only facility that could function as a morgue).

Such economic and practical functions are relatively easy to quantify from historical records. A more challenging task, taken up by this volume's contributors, is to grasp the social and economic impact and evolution of pubs, clubs, and other venues. The nature of who congregated in these places, and the factors that determined access to them, are surveyed, along with the way in which drinking, both in venues and at home, has shaped and expressed elements of gender, sexuality, class and ethnicity.

In doing so the broader history of a range of communities is explored, not least those who have sought to challenge the status quo. Alcohol-based venues are shown to have played a major role in the emergence of a range of movements, scenes and institutions, from the very first unions through to those associated with experimental and alternative forms of art and music. They have served as formal and informal performance, debating and organising spaces for a range of people and initiatives with reforming, radical and revolutionary intentions. For cash-strapped campaigns and groups, 'whip arounds', raffles, gigs and other events within pubs, and alcohol sales at gatherings outside them, have been a common means of raising funds. The regular mixing of alcohol with political and artistic activities is also shown to have at times had profoundly negative impacts for movements and individuals.

Commercial imperatives are widely evident in the ways and places Australians have interacted with alcohol. As profit making enterprises venues, breweries, and other alcohol related industries have traditionally been, and remain, a major economic sector. Developments within sections of the industry are connected throughout the book to wider changes in the national and global economy. These include the rise and fall of specific companies and products, types of businesses, patterns of employment, and balances of power in terms of deciding who profits and how profits are achieved. Similarly, the use of strikes, boycotts and other forms of contention are linked to everyday experiences of working life and the conditions under which people have laboured.

A number of interventions by unions and community movements in issues affecting consumers are also documented. These have included cost, safety, quality, government and company policies, heritage protection and other issues. Such campaigns further demonstrate how certain products and places have served as vehicles through which to exercise pressure and express power.

Over time alcohol has maintained its place alongside other commodities – such as oil, coffee, fertiliser and sugar – as a product with an outsized impact on political economy and social life at a global, national and local level. This book is in a tradition of scholarship which focuses on one aspect of society, as a way of looking at the totality.

The oral historian Wendy Lowenstein knew the value of following where the liquor flowed. When travelling around Australia recording people's recollections and life stories, she would go into pubs, and ask who the best yarn teller was. She'd then buy a jug, go up to them and record what they had to say. Each of the following chapters in this book welcomes you to pull a chair up to the table, and enter a dialogue with the history of Australian culture and politics as seen from below.

Banners and placards during a picket of Tooheys Brewery, Sydney, 1980 (*Tribune*/Search Foundation)

CHAPTER 1
'GROG FOR ME': CONVICTS AND ALCOHOL

Michael Quinlan and Hamish Maxwell-Stewart

On 22 February 1844 the convict William Bray was charged in the Bothwell police office with 'not reporting himself on arrival in the Township, tippling in a public house & being found disguised in soldiers clothes.' It was an offence for a convict to cross the threshold of a licensed house, let alone to be discovered quaffing ale or spirits. The wording of Bray's charge suggests that he had been drinking with the local garrison. When the borrowed jacket of a soldier failed to prevent his identification as a convict, he was arrested and sentenced to five days solitary. His conviction was subsequently transcribed into the 'black books' – a Vandemonian record series that contains summary information for over 400 000 convict encounters with lower courts. The purpose of this voluminous administrative record was to keep track of offending across an entire workforce. It was a crucial tool of labour management that ensured that the stain of conviction history would obscure the realities

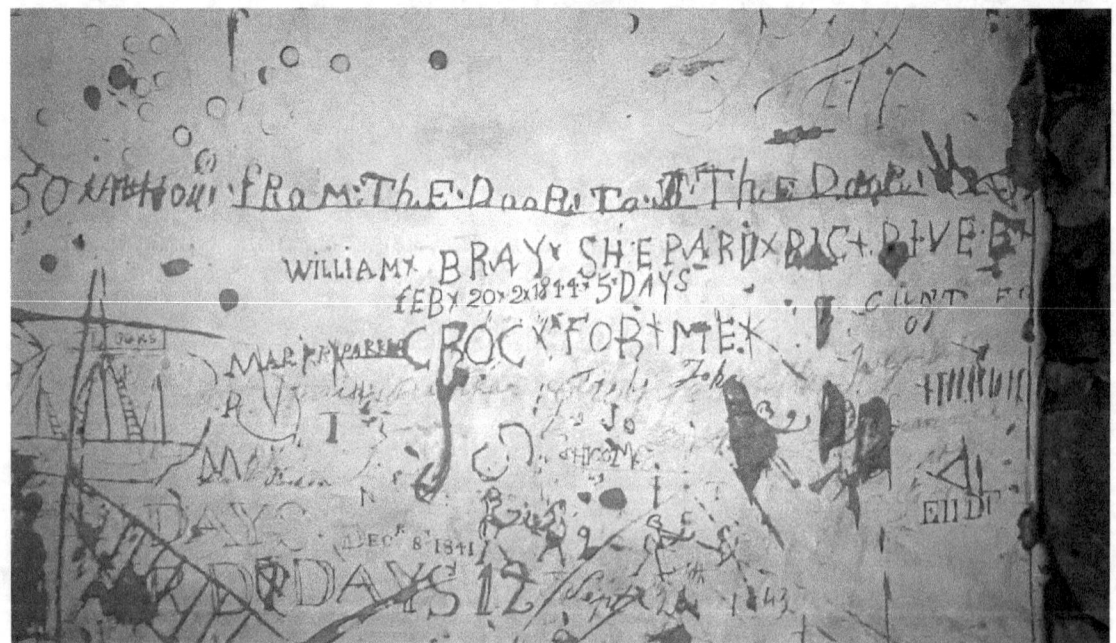

Graffiti in Solitary Cell, Bothwell (Hamish Maxwell-Stewart)

of workplace labour exploitation. By the time his offence had been officially recorded Bray had left an indelible record of his own. He scratched the following into the plaster of the Bothwell solitary cell:

> WILLIAM BRAY x SHEPARD x BIG + RIVER x
> fEB x 20 x 2 x 1844 x 5 DAYS
> GROG x FOR x ME *

It would be easy to dismiss this event as a frolic – symptomatic of the many alcohol-infused moments that disrupted attempts to correct the behaviour of those who had 'left their country for their county's good.' Yet, an alternative reading is possible. Bray was working as an iron moulder when he was sentenced to 15 years transportation at the Suffolk Assizes for 'burglariously breaking and entering the dwelling-house of Richard Elmer, of Barham, and stealing therefrom a silver watch.' While he had four prior convictions for poaching, there is no evidence that he had ever worked as a shepherd before his arrival in a remote British penal colony. If Bray was occupationally reinvented by transportation, he appears to have embraced the change – proclaiming his new calling on the interior of the Bothwell solitary cell. He also attached himself to the landscape of work. The 'Big River' was the colonial lower-order name for the Derwent River. It was also the appellation used to describe the Aboriginal people who had adapted the region through mosaic burning. It was these lands, originally cleared to increase carrying capacity for Palawa hunters, that had been expropriated by colonial capital and hitched to the international wool market. Bray's 'high density micro narrative' illustrates the process by which state and private landholders used the labour of thieves to steal a continent. As he added, grog played a central role in that process.

Exchange of alcohol lubricated negotiations between masters and their assigned servants, helping to close deals by coaxing labour from otherwise unwilling bodies. While its supply to serving convicts was banned by the government, this rule was honoured in the breach. Many masters preferred the supply of grog as an incentive over cash, the payment of which was also prohibited prior to the introduction of the probation system in 1840. Yet, while both forms of incentive were proscribed, one had advantages over the other. The odds were that alcohol would be consumed on property, cash on the other hand would be spent in the external economy – usually on alcohol purchased elsewhere. In short, cash incentives encouraged absenteeism. Their supply could also result in embarrassment, as masters were ordered to collect wayward charges from local lock-ups. This risked exposing estate management practices to outside scrutiny but was also inconvenient for other reasons.

Masters and mistresses exercised power over their assigned servants while they remained 'on property' but lost much of that control once their charges wandered off. While a drunken worker could be forgiven by an estate manager, the local magistrate might impose a sentence. This could lead to temporary, or even permanent loss of labour. During harvest and

Convicts embarking for Botany Bay, circa 1800 (Thomas Rowlandson, National Library of Australia)

shearing the loss of any worker could impact the balance sheet – the loss of critical skills could halt production altogether.

In the case of some tasks, masters had little say. By the 1820s the supply of a daily grog allowance to convicts employed washing sheep had become an established norm. On James Mudie's New South Wales property, Castle Forbes, two or three glasses were provided to men engaged in this work. Refusal by landholders to provide alcohol during sheep-washing was a common trigger for disputes. In January 1835 Oatlands landholder William Foord paid a visit to his men while they were sheep-washing. Edward Smith, a farm labourer from Lancashire, used the appearance of his master to demand a quart of wine. When this was refused, he called Foord a 'bloody scoundrel' shouting that 'every man and every mother cries shame on you for treating your servants as you do.' He then refused to work, threatening to knock Foord's head off with an axe. The court extended his sentence by three years 'being a most violent and dangerous character' and sent him to the Constitution Hill Road Party.

Alcohol was also often provided to convict agricultural workers as a reward for completing the harvest or for working in bad weather, Sundays or other public holidays. Convict harvest workers at Yass in New South Wales were routinely supplied with two glasses of rum daily, in addition to other incentives. In February 1825 the Van Diemen's Land master James Cubbitson Sutherland supplied his convict reapers with 'an abundance of lifting

Convict-driven tramway, 1854 (Godfrey Mundy, National Library of Australia)

beer', while Edward Archer gave his men a pint of London Stout each day during the 1837 harvest and William Brumby a bottle of wine per man.

Rain could bring labour on the public works to a standstill. It was an established convention that government convicts could not be put to work at outside tasks in inclement weather. Convicts in the private sector battled to extend these provisions to assigned labour and would often refuse to work in wet conditions unless an incentive was provided – usually alcohol. The provision of such inducements was sometimes recorded in diaries or revealed in court proceedings. Mrs. Bailey of Broadmarsh prosecuted three servants for indecent language, one having called her a 'bloody old whore'. It emerged in court that all three were the worse for wear, having been provided with 'a little extra to drink' as an inducement to toil in the wet on a Sunday. The implication was that a considerable amount of grog had been provided to get the three men to labour in foul weather on their day off. Two were ordered to a road gang for six months with a recommendation that they should not be returned to her service, while the third was let off with a warning.

Post-harvest celebrations were also common and these invariably involved the provision of beer, rum or wine. The editor of the *Colonist* – an organ critical of the administration in Van Diemen's Land – complained of political interference in 1836 when they were deprived of their assigned servants 'because some of our men had got drunk at a harvest supper.'

Convicts were charged with being found in drinking establishments including the Brown Bear Inn (Tasmanian Archives)

Alcohol was widely used to reward all kinds of behaviour. James Mudie supplied a bottle of wine for every two men following a visit by the governor in 1834. One suspects that this reward had been pre-advertised and was in effect a bribe designed to illicit good behaviour over the course of the regal visit. Others were rewarded for meritorious service. Longford farmer William Brown's assigned servants Thomas Leake and Thomas Williams received drink in 1854 for helping extinguish a hay fire suspected to be the result of incendiarism of two free men (although the latter were both discharged for want of evidence).

As some masters discovered, conceding to demands to increase incentives could trigger further requests. Peter Roberts, a landholder in the same district, charged four convict sheep washers with insubordination in December 1841. In court he stated that, while he had promised the men spirits, they had demanded additional tea and sugar. When these were provided, they bargained for an even greater supply of spirits.

Disputes exposed the differing ways in which convicts and masters viewed such perks. In the eyes of employers they were 'indulgences' supplied out of the kindness of the employer's heart. Convicts, on the other hand, argued that payments in-kind were earned through work and constituted a right, rather than a perk. Court cases provide evidence of how such differing interpretations could give rise to workplace disputes. Matthew Mitchell, for example, charged two of his assigned servants in 1834 with 'mutinous and disrespectful conduct' after they refused a bottle of rum on Christmas Eve as 'it was not enough.'

Some masters supplied their assigned servants with liberal quantities of alcohol on festive occasions – a reminder of the considerable savings that accrued from hiring bond workers over free. Sutherland served up roast meat, a pudding and a bottle of rum to his men for Christmas in 1825. On New Year's Day in 1827 he provided a bottle of rum to each man during their work and a second with their dinner. Those that celebrated with their servants risked censure, as George Meredith discovered when he held a New Year's party for the convicts in the neighbourhood. While the colonial secretary was prepared to overlook this transgression, seeing it as 'merely a little merry-making on the first of the year', Lieutenant-Governor Arthur differed. As he put it, 'any master who can be found at 2 or 3 o'clock on Sunday morning carousing with his servants, is, in my opinion, very unworthy of the trust reposed in him by the Government.' In Arthur's view the maintenance of penal discipline required an appropriate separation between master and servant. He also took a dim view of celebrations when they led to acts of public disorder. Gilbert Roberson had his servants withdrawn in 1835 after they became

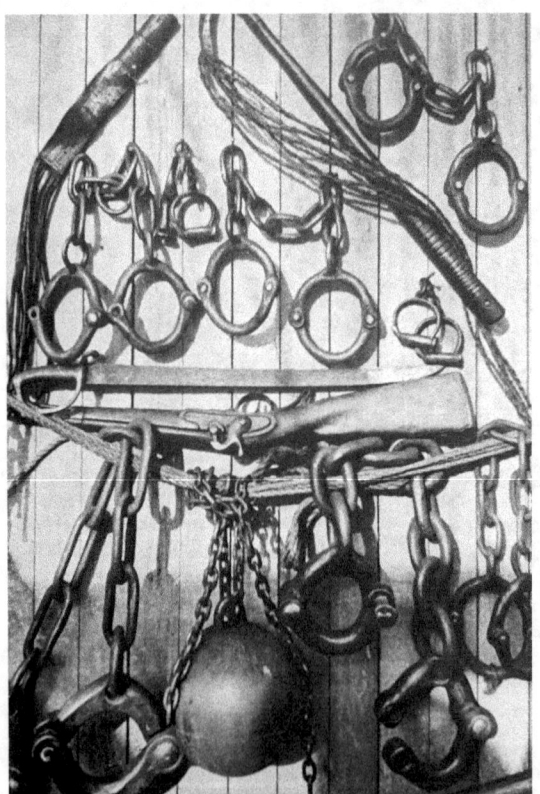

Convict leg irons.

riotous following a harvest supper and were accused of tipping the district flagellator over the parapet of the Richmond bridge.

Several other riots occurred when Christmas festivities got out of hand. In December 1844 a detachment of soldiers were called to assist the constables with restoring order in Liverpool Street, Hobart, when alcohol infused celebrations by the inmates in the Prison Barracks got out of control, spilling out into the centre of town. At least three convicts were charged in Hobart in 1828 with 'Disobedience of orders & being absent without leave the whole of the 1st January (a holiday) and returning at night in a state of intoxication & using abusive language and with mutinous conduct generally.' A 'very serious affray' took place on Christmas day 1834 when the Ross District Constable attempted to 'remove' some public works prisoners from the tap-room of an inn where they were drinking. The prisoners 'beset the constabulary with stones and palings', which they tore up from an adjoining fence until 'the lives of the police being in danger', the military marched to their assistance. They too were set upon and 'much abused and beaten.' This 'outrage', which lasted for a considerable length of time, shocked the administration. Lieutenant-Governor Arthur and the Acting Police Magistrate travelled to the district to conduct a full investigation as soon as news reached Hobart. Ten convicts were flogged for participating in the riot. In addition their sentences were extended and they were retransported to Port Arthur penal station and the Hulk Chain Gang.

Other gatherings were more peaceful but could still result in prosecution. On Christmas Day 1834 Joseph Archer's servant Joseph Senior held a Christmas party in his hut, inviting fellow servants Richard Thomas, William Perkins, Aaron Dodd and William Butler and two female servants. The two women, Rachel Holmes and Ellen Butler were assigned to neighbouring properties. When two convict tailors were charged in Sydney with being absent from their master and drunk and disorderly on 26 December 1825, one claimed that as an Irishman, he 'must be excused working on St. Stephen's Day (Monday) as by doing so he would be guilty of a great sin.' The magistrate replied that 'it was considered a greater sin to be drunk than to work.' Both were sentenced to be flogged. Despite the moralising, those charged with maintaining law and order were on occasion themselves prosecuted for festive revelry. Convict Alexander Adams, a five foot nine three quarter inch butcher from Montrose in Scotland, was fined five shillings for being drunk in Oatlands on Christmas Day 1830 while employed in the field police.

Analysis at scale reveals a surge in the number of charges brought against male and female convicts in the days immediately following Christmas, although not New Year (see Figure 1). A similar technique can be used to look at weekly prosecution patterns (Figure 2). Charges for being found in a public house were more likely to be brought on a Monday. Many of these arrests occurred on Sunday, the day that public works convicts were exempt from labour, although Sunday drinking inevitably spilled over into Monday. Colonial papers railed at the extent to which 'Saint Monday' was honoured in the colony – a reference to the British artisanal tradition of taking an additional day's leave to recover from Sunday excess. As the Molesworth Report put it, convict mechanics were 'generally the worst behaved and the most drunken.'

Convict consumption of alcohol implies access to cash. Like publicans everywhere, it seems unlikely that the colonial purveyors of spirits and beer were in the habit of giving away their merchandise. As the *Tasmanian* put it, a general issue facing employers of skilled unfree labour was that convict mechanics 'claim to themselves all the rights and privileges of free men, and quote the hours of labour and the wages paid to similar persons in London and elsewhere in the mother country, unmindful that they are expiating the crimes which sent them out.' As the paper continued, it was precisely this species of convict worker who cluttered up the courtroom 'on the Monday morning habited in their Sunday garments, charged with every species of Sabbath breaking.' The number of alcohol related convictions stand testimony to the degree to which many convicts succeeded in wrangling cash in exchange for labour services – despite the fact that such payments were prohibited by the rules governing assignment.

There is a twist to this particular tale. Although the *Tasmanian* claimed that it was convicts that broke the Sabbath, many private sector masters and mistresses ordered their assigned servants to labour on the 'Lord's day'. In the public works convicts were exempt from labour on Saturday afternoons and Sunday. Even in penal stations convicts were not worked on the Sabbath. Male assigned servants, however, were commonly tasked with Sunday labour during harvest and shearing and for female convicts the threat was omnipresent. Almost all assigned convict women performed domestic work. As grates needed cleaning, meals prepared and sheets washed regardless of the day of the week, they were often commanded to break the Sabbath. As with drink-related offending, charges for being absent were frequently brought on a Sunday – despite the fact that this was a day of rest. For many convicts, a Sunday tipple formed part of a wider protest aimed at delineating the limits of work. Such actions were motivated by convict desires to ensure that the sentence imposed upon them by British and Irish courts had daily limits. These

	Number of Charges	Number of co-related alcohol charges	Percentage of co-related alcohol charges
Assault	1683	50	2.97
Larceny	4974	56	1.13
Indecent and riotous conduct	1057	116	10.97
Insolence	7206	800	11.10
Insubordination	952	27	2.84
Idleness	1824	3	0.16
Neglect of Work	5805	486	8.37
Refusing to Work	2451	37	1.51
Disobedience of orders	7214	193	2.68
Misconduct otherwise unspecified	12703	786	6.19
Absconding	24766	562	2.27
Absent	21614	2287	10.58
Out after hours	7437	1847	24.84
All offences	110287	21757	19.73

Table 1: Charges Brought Against Convicts Involving Being Drunk or Drinking.

were forms of protest that were designed to loosen the shackles imposed upon them by limiting the power of a sentence to command all of their time. The state and private sector masters, on the other hand, sought to restrict convict socialising, containing their bond workers to the confines of the property they were assigned.

As might be expected alcohol on occasion acted as an accelerant – fuelling workplace dissent. Yet, overall surprisingly few convicts were charged with being drunk and committing violent offences. Mary Milligan was one of a handful of assigned servants in Van Diemen's Land charged with being drunk and assaulting her mistress. She was sentenced to two weeks solitary confinement and thereafter to six calendar months hard labour in the female factory. Hannah Miller was also sentenced to solitary confinement when she was charged with 'Absenting herself from her Master's House without leave' and remaining absent until apprehended by her Master in Macquarie Street about 2 o'clock, when she was intoxicated and abusive. Yet, only three percent of 1683 common assault charges brought against convicts in Van Diemen's Land involved additional charges for being drunk.

The evidence that convict attacks on others stemmed from excessive drinking is limited (see Table 1).

The same could be said for other prosecutions. While 20 percent of all charges brought against convicts were for acts involving drinking, few of these directly related to the process of labour extraction. Although 11 percent of charges for insolence and indecent and riotous conduct involved additional charges for being drunk, this applied to less than three percent of 952 prosecutions brought for the more serious offence of insubordinate or mutinous conduct. Surprisingly, less than 1 percent of charges for being idle involved alcohol consumption, suggesting that alcohol impairment contributed little to convict unwillingness to perform work. By contrast, movement offences often centred around drinking. 11 percent of convicts charged with being absent and 25 percent of those out after curfew were also charged with being drunk. As we argue above, access to alcohol formed an important part of convict leisure.

Many alcohol-related prosecutions reflect convict determination to exercise rights over the end of the working day and the freedom to socialise in their own time away from

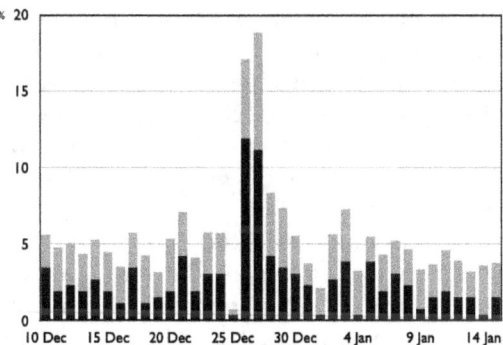

Figure 1: Drink related charges brought against male and female convicts in Van Diemen's Land in the period 10 December –15 January.

Sources: Con 31, 32, 33, 40 and 41. Total count of all female conduct record, four percent longitudinal sample for male. N = 2227.

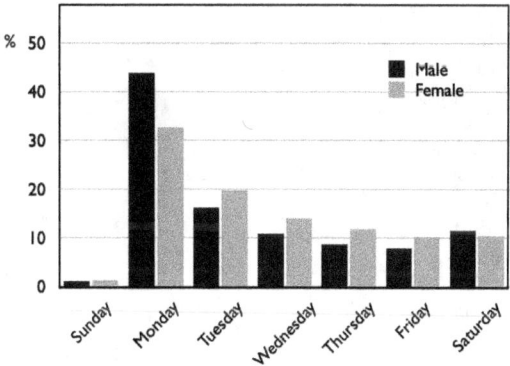

Figure 2: Day of the Week Convicts Were Prosecuted for Being in a Public House

Sources: Same as Figure 01.1. N = 1522.

their place of work. A record of individual prosecutions is matched by prosecutions for collective withdrawals of labour for leisure-related purposes, of which there were literally thousands of instances. On 3 March 1829 thirteen members of the Launceston chain gang were charged with 'disobedience of orders, lawless and drunk and absenting themselves by remaining behind their party in the town.' John Denner and James Lawley were adjudged as ringleaders and were flogged, but the rest were simply reprimanded suggesting a recognition of the everyday nature of such offending. In March 1834 dealer Samuel Mckeay charged Rachel Leach and Eliza Wynne with being disobedient, absent and drunk, the prosecution stating one of the women got drunk every time she 'goes out Saturday', highlighting the connections between alcohol consumption and the exercise of rights over leisure.

Even convicts assigned to hotels and breweries, places with ready access to alcohol, preferred to drink elsewhere. On 4 November 1834 three convicts assigned to brewer J.T. Hughes were charged with being found drinking at Herd's public house in Sussex Street. As with individual cases collective absences clustered on weekends, Monday and public holidays. In all, the evidence suggests that charges for drinking related offences brought against convicts reflect the struggle over access to free leisure time – traits that could also be used to describe the actions of Australia's burgeoning free working class. We find little to support the alternative view that drink-related offending confirms that lumpen-proletarian convicts lacked the organisational skills to mount effective political opposition.

Alcohol was occasionally linked to other instances of collective action, most typically insolence but even this was associated with recreational activities, either on the employers' premises or after convicts had returned from an absence. Aside from bargaining for grog allowances by rural workers, strikes rarely entailed alcohol. Seldom was it linked to group absconding for the obvious reason that being drunk hindered escape. In September 1834 Henry Davis, Bridget Dagherty, William Popham and Jonathon Wilson were charged with absconding and being drunk by New South Wales Southern Highlands landholder, William Hutchinson. However, the difference between absence and absconding depended merely on the length of time the prisoner was away. In this case the absconding charge probably reflected Hutchinson's desire to impose a more severe penalty – the men got 50 lashes while Dagherty was sentenced to 60 days in the female factory.

On 27 February 1833 the *Sydney Monitor* published an editorial entitled 'Stills, Drunkeness and Murder' where it linked secret illicit stills to social breakdown in the Bathurst region and more widely as well to convict insubordination, though the *Monitor* then inconsistently stated illicit distilling on farms and the like affected both convict and free. It overlooked the fact that the Bathurst revolt in

Convict description of Thomas Randall, transported in 1828. Randall was tattooed with bottles and glasses, a testimony to the role that alcohol played in convict leisure (Tasmanian Archives)

1830 that had so frightened authorities was driven by starvation and ill-treatment, not alcohol. Indeed the causes of convict dissent overwhelmingly stemmed from complaints over working conditions and the resulting struggle over the terms and conditions of employment. Instances of an interconnection between alcohol, violent crime and convicts are to be found, but whether this was higher than in the working class community more generally has yet to be demonstrated. In contrast, the vast judicial record we have examined indicates alcohol was far more typically linked to struggles over leisure time or pseudo-wage bargaining for additional rewards by convict workers. These were emblematic of behaviour in the working class more generally where alcohol was heavily linked to recreation, as indeed it still is. It also needs to be recognised that convicts were denied other recreational options like joining clubs or playing sport. The latter option only became common amongst the working class as unions slowly began to secure a half-holiday (the precursor to the weekend) after 1850 and more especially the 1870s (coinciding with the rise of organised sport).

The convict period left a tangible legacy. As Allen argues, the policing of alcohol in Australia owes much to convict origins. Early concerns about labour control and social and geographical mobility in convict Australia laid the foundation for later discretionary legislation which could be used to exert respectable control. Colonial newspapers continued to rail about the frequency with which workers adhered to the traditions of Saint Monday long after the abolition of transportation. Much could be said for other alcohol related norms established by unfree workers. Convict demands for alcohol to complete seasonal pastoral and agricultural tasks, for example, carried over to the free labour market. These included demands for grog and other rewards during harvest and shearing – one of a large number of indications that the transition to a free labour market did not mark the beginning of industrial struggle in Australia. Mass conflict over the terms and conditions of work had established itself many decades earlier, alcohol played a critical role in this process. But this should be seen as part of a wider connection between the working-class organisation and drinking that predated convict transportation to Australia and lived on long past the arrival of the last convict vessel. Pubs and hotels were the traditional meeting places of the working class in the United Kingdom and this carried over to Australia. Both convicts and ex-convicts drank in working class hotels alongside free-emigrants and the native born – there were no social divides on this score. Many working class-pubs had trade or vocation-based clienteles which became, as in Europe, the springboard for forming the first unions composed of former convicts, free emigrant and native born workers. Many of these were formed in licensed establishments and public houses and these remained the meeting place for unions until gradually replaced by trades-halls in the half century after 1870.

CHAPTER 2
THE LIFE OF MATTHEW BRADY, GENTLEMAN BUSHRANGER
Alex Ettling

Sketch of Matthew Brady, 1826 (Thomas Bock, Libraries Tasmania)

The outlaw Matthew Brady (1799–1826), often styled as 'The Gentleman Bushranger', is a romantic figure in a period of Australian history otherwise known for rough justice and violence. There are degrees of exaggeration and apocryphal stories built up around Brady's mythology but we do know his rebel story began in northern England.

One of the most significant events in the emerging workers movement in Britain was the Peterloo Massacre of 1819, an historic moment when the masses moved into resistance against chronic inequality and economic hardship. In response to 60 000 rallying at St Peter's Field in Manchester to demand suffrage, the authorities sent in police and soldiers, resulting in the deaths of at least 18 civilians and the wounding of hundreds. In the aftermath of the event came a crackdown which saw arrests and trials for sedition, the shutting of the radical *Manchester Observer*, and the passing of new anti-protest laws.

The poet Percy Bysshe Shelley took inspiration and wrote the famous lines: 'Rise like Lions after slumber, In unvanquishable number, Shake your chains to earth like dew, Which in sleep had fallen on you – Ye are many – they are few.' However, it is unlikely that Matthew Brady ever heard these rousing words from 'The Masque of Anarchy'. Only days after witnessing the Peterloo Massacre he was in gaol and well on his way to experiencing the enduring horrors of the British legal system.

Brady was a young working class man, categorised at this time as a 'servant'. His specific role was as a groom – working with horses. He would have seen first-hand the poverty and deprivations of industrial capitalism, and after witnessing the hand-of-law at Peterloo perhaps likely had an even more diminished respect for the order of the system. Brady felt compelled to steal some basic food supplies – butter, sugar, rice and a flitch of bacon – which he is noted to have shared with two women. He was caught, tried in Lancaster on 17 April 1820, and given a seven-year sentence of transportation. He arrived in Australia in chains on the convict ship *Juliana* on 29 December 1820.

In Matthew Brady's criminal papers we gain a sense of the human behind the myth. He was 22 years old, with dark brown hair and blue eyes. He was 'stout, square-built', and slightly marked with smallpox. He had tattoos, a man and woman on his left arm, 'tb' and a fish on his right. These same papers also detail the punishments he endured as a prisoner, including 350 lashes, a long list of insubordination and attempts to escape.

At this time in history, if you did something considered bad you got sent to Australia. If you were considered really bad then you got sent to Tasmania (then known as Van Diemen's Land). And if you were considered *really* really bad, you got put on Sarah Island. This is where Brady ended up. It would seem that amongst the worst crimes one could commit were those of insubordination. In effect it was the refusal to accept the logic of the new economics where hungry people went without, as well as having the temerity to fight back against state discipline which maintained social control through ever more punishing institutions.

On Sarah Island conditions were unsparing and escape considered impossible. It was a relatively new prison, established at the beginning of 1822 as part of the Macquarie Harbour Penal Station. Lieutenant-Governor William Sorell had wanted a penal settlement that would be economically viable enough to cover the costs of having set it up in the first place. Sarah Island was the base, and like all the land surrounding Macquarie Harbour had a valuable natural resource in Huon pine. Convicts spent their days cutting timber, usually in chains, often in the miserable cold and rain of Tasmania's west coast. At night the cells were so crowded that the inmates could not even sleep on their backs. Scurvy and dysentery were rampant.

Brady did not willingly accept his confinement and these brutal conditions. Historian Charles White recorded in 1900 that, 'Soon after his arrival, however, he set about forming a secret league among his fellow convicts, of whom his size and strength made him undisputed leader.' The only way of escape was seaward through a treacherous narrow channel known as Hells Gates, navigating 20 metre high waves and musket shots

Satirical illustration of Peterloo Massacre, 1821 (George Cruikshank, British Museum)

from prison guards. In 1824, Brady and 13 other convicts managed to break out, stealing a whaling boat and sailing to freedom down the Derwent River. Notably, a decade later another group would make a similar bid, requisitioning a ship they had built on the island, the *Frederick*, and sailing it to South America. Those that managed to get off the island knew that this was only the beginning of their struggle for freedom.

Making a life on the run was not easy. Hiding out in the Tasmanian bush, with the particularly damp conditions of the west coast, was wearying. Brady and his fellow escapees could only maintain a low fire of coals so as not to give away their presence with rising smoke. On 20 November 1825 the *Gazette* published the testimony of a man named Mr R. Denne who spent six days with the gang:

> They lead a miserable and terror struck life. They are constantly on guard during the night, and not a creature can stir or a sound be heard, than they are instantly filled with alarm. They frequently debate and quarrel for hours together, about their future proceedings. The guard is relieved every two hours. They are constantly expressing disgust at their mode of life, and the certainty of being speedily apprehended.

The historian J.E. Calder wrote the most detailed and reliable history of Brady's activities, which this account will be largely based on. The prospects for escaped convicts were slim in Tasmania, so it is unsurprising that Brady turned to bushranging to materially support himself. He was involved in a series of heists that mostly targeted homesteads and inns, and he also carried out highway robberies. In total, Brady and his compatriots carried out an estimated 300 appropriations. Their illegal activities were some of the most daring escapades seen on the island, featuring a certain tactical nous and use of psychological tricks to overcome numerical weakness.

Historian of the early settlement, D.A.C.G. Lempriere, resided in Brady's bushranging territory and recorded the following observations of his conduct:

> It is, however, complained of him that he was too fond of fun and practical jesting to have been quite agreeable, and that he too often made all the menials of the household helplessly drunk when he left, which looked like carrying frolic too far. But this conduct, which was mistaken for mischievous fun,

Macquarie Harbour, 1833 (W.B. Gould, State Library of NSW)

was in reality a piece of policy only; for he well knew that it was from the convict class of servants, and hardly any others, that treachery was to be feared, and that they were the men and not their masters, who were in league with the police, and by leaving them hopelessly drunk, he had nothing to fear from them till he was far enough away.

An example of this occurred at the home of Mr Lawrence of the Lake River, where the bushrangers displayed their convivial approach to crime. In Calder's account of Brady and company entering this house:

> Some of his men got to the cellar, and drank till they were half stupified, and behaved very grossly. Bird and the fiendish Murphy, the most mischievous and intractable of all of them, were the authors of much unnecessary outrage. The owner of the estate was absent, but a son and several servants were about, and all the latter were made helplessly drunk by these two fellows. Having robbed the house, they next burned it to the ground.

Although such reports ascribe compulsion and perfidy to Brady's actions, it is quite possible that the servants willingly imbibed and that the distribution of their masters' alcohol was a gift.

As the weeks went on, the original gang of escapees declined, with members leaving only to be caught and executed shortly thereafter. New members were easily recruited as there was no shortage of dissatisfied people in Van Diemen's Land enduring a life of semi-slavery under the Masters and Servants Act. The gang that Brady was part of was distinct because it was said to have 'no fixed leader'. Exactly how things operated within this set-up is unclear. Brady was called 'Mat' by his comrades. Denne included in his observations of his time with the gang that 'they frequently debate and quarrel for hours together, about their future proceedings.' This suggests a participatory decision making structure in stark contrast to the hierarchical discipline they were generally accustomed to. Denne also noted that 'the opinions of Brady or Dunne are generally listened to', indicating that qualities of leadership earned respect.

It is generally accepted that the gang held quite distinct values about how they conducted their unlawful business, avoiding unnecessary suffering and being particularly considerate of women. In White's account, one gang member, McCabe was disciplined: 'For offering violence to a woman Brady shot him through the hand, disarmed and thrashed him, and expelled him finally from the gang.' On another occasion, 'One man, who had asked a servant girl for a kiss, was at once knocked down by his leader.' The only killing generally agreed to have been committed by Brady was the execution of Tom Kenton, a former friend who betrayed him.

Brady conducted himself with his own distinct framework of morality. He was known for his kindness to animals, and amongst the horses in his gang were two white stallions. His experience with horses in Manchester no doubt was useful to life as a bushranger.

Accounts of Brady's activities present a dashing hero, particularly fond of carousing, and with an affinity for acquiring the hats of those with elevated status. Calder describes one robbery where upon encountering one of his wealthy victims he:

> Snatched off his hat, a new Panama, presenting him with his own old one in return, saying he hoped that both of them would be benefited by the exchange ... Then with a shew of politeness, he raised his stolen hat to Mr. Flexmore, and jumping into the stolen saddle, galloped off with all his grim looking followers at his heels, to the nearest public house of Green Ponds.

In another confrontation, the gang fired guns into the air which caused a colonel to lose his cap. It was 'picked up and afterwards worn by Brady in triumph.' Wearing this military headdress is consistent with Brady's fondness of ridicule towards social hierarchies. Another gang member, Murphy, was described as a 'little man', with 'a piece of gold lace, with a precious stone, round his cap.' With all these delightful hats, and two white stallions in their gang, the image of these gentlemen bushrangers was certainly enigmatic.

Brady targeted the rich in his robberies. It may be a stretch to say this amounted to a Robin Hood situation, although Brady had a network of supporters in legitimate society and these working class people may have been the recipients of his generosity. Of course, robbing the rich just makes good business sense. On one occasion Brady became aware of the well-stocked Meredith homestead, and as told by Calder:

> Possessed as this gentleman was of ample means, and a well stocked house, Brady marked it for plunder. They made prize of a large quantity of plate, provisions and spirits of all kinds, and a larger selection of choice wines than I care to enumerate.

This heist, with its particularly large bounty of alcohol, led to a curious development in the story of the Brady gang. The bushrangers commandeered a boat but finding it leaking abandoned their intended destination and landed on a sand beach. In Calder's account:

> Strife soon arose amongst themselves, which Brady was powerless to repress. The abundance of wines and spirits they had with them soon set them quarrelling ... a desperate brawl was the result of this debauch, which some of the others joined in as well as McCabe. While it was at its height the boatman Hunt was shot dead, and his body buried in the sand. Heated with wine and rioting, most of them were soon too drunk to continue further disturbance. Then it was that Brady and another man named McKenny, seeing the evil that must come of this state of things, determined that it should go no farther; and before their companions recovered consciousness, they demolished every bottle that remained; a procedure that was ultimately approved by all the others, except the ungovernable McCabe, who was absolutely furious when he awoke.

One of the most frequently recounted exploits of the Brady gang, and an example backed with more rigorous evidence, was their remarkable seizure of an entire town with a military garrison. During the brazen escapade they turned the tables on the state by leading the redcoats, British soldiers, into their own cells. Calder's account quotes from reporting in the *Colonial Times* of 2 December 1825, and describes the proceedings of their foray into Sorrell:

> The gentlemen were treated with the utmost civility. Dinner was prepared and every attention paid them. But after sitting at their wine for an hour or two, the weary visitors asked to be shown to their bedrooms, pleading fatigue as their reason for wishing to break up so early. But Brady shook his

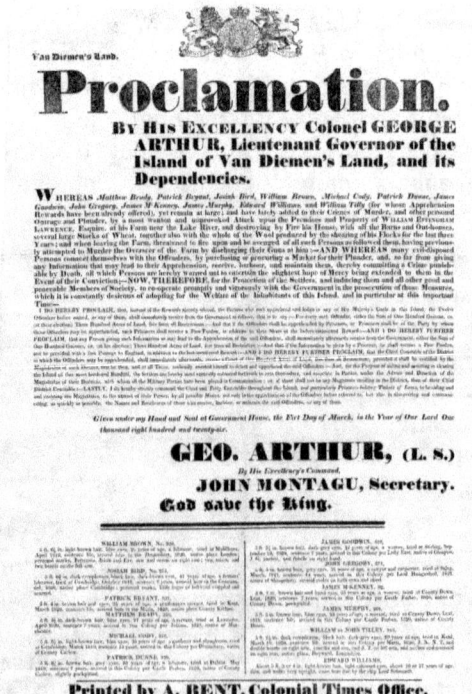

Proclamation regarding Matthew Brady and other escaped convicts, 1826 (Libraries Tasmania)

head at this proposal, and surprised them by telling them with a slightly altered look, that they must not think of retiring just yet, for though it was now ten o'clock and the day near closing, its real business was not yet begun, and, in time informed them that he meant to attack the gaol and guardhouse immediately, 'and you gentlemen,' he continued with polite solemnity, 'must all accompany me down to the township, as I mean to liberate all the prisoners now in gaol, and to put you in, in their places.'

There are two accounts of what happened with prisoners found in the town. In one, the gang released all present, whom they then led in raucous celebration. Another, from the *Gazette*, is that 'the criminals who were in the gaol when Brady took it, refused the liberation that he offered them.'

One of the bushranger's heists in a hotel seems to be a further contributor to his 'Gentleman Brady' title. The gang had bailed-up the Duke of York Inn, and among the hostages was a man whom Brady misidentified as Colonel Balfour, owner of the aforementioned hat. Brady had low regard for the colonel and knocked him down. Having realised that he was the wrong person, he 'apologised like a man.'

Brady's hatred seems to have been directed at officers and redcoats, and he maintained a sense of justice that was divided between the ruling class and the exploited. An interesting incident involved a tragic encounter when Brady tried to compel a servant, now freed, to join his gang. When the timid man refused to pursue his freedom by becoming an outlaw, Brady poured him out a full glass of rum. Perhaps, it was for Dutch courage, forced relaxation, or as a gateway into the equalising culture of drink. An article about Brady by Bernard Cronin and Arthur Russell in *The Queensland Times* on 26 January 1932 provides the most detailed account:

British military officers, the 'Red Coats', 1809 (Thomas Rowlandson, Met Museum)

Brady ordered an assigned servant to join his band of rascals. The servant, very properly refused, whereupon Brady walked to the sideboard, poured out a large glass of raw rum and ordered the man to drink it upon pain of death. The poor wretch, who protested that he was a teetotaller, had no resource but to obey. As he staggered away, gasping from the shock of the spirits in his unaccustomed throat, Brady laughed heartily. It was a good joke. Not so, however for the victim. Next morning, he was found lying in the bushes some distance from the house, still intoxicated and evidently in great agony. The raw spirit had done its work only too well. He muttered: 'Water, for God's sake give me some water,' as they lifted him; and almost immediately died. When Brady heard of this he confessed to great sorrow. He declared that he had acted without any desire to injure the man, still less to cause his death. From what is known of him, this can be readily believed. His was not a hard, calculating character. He was susceptible to the weakness and sentiment of human nature, and really had a very decent side to him.

The version of events narrated here suggest that Brady may have had a built up frustration with the internalised self-discipline of the prisoners and workers he encountered who would rather be bonded in servitude than take the chance at freedom that he himself had readily seized.

Matthew Brady never experienced Australian pub culture as a free man, only as an escaped convict. This was a curious time in the history of the colony. During the convict era, pubs became a crossroads where the broadest extremes of colonial society could meet. Until the late 1820s all ranks were free to mingle. In *The Australian Pub*, Kirkby, Luckins and McConville write, 'Male and female, bonded and free, sailor and settled, policemen and prisoner – got drunk together, usually on rum imported from India.' In historian James Boyce's view this is 'one of the most remarkable aspects of early Van Diemen's Land.' In the historical accounts of Brady's time on the run, he is frequently in hotels, often robbing them. The context of the time suggests that Brady would not have had trouble fitting in with the mixed setting if he could pass without being identified (not impossible in a time before photography).

As Brady's activities gained more and more notoriety, and some degree of sympathy, the authorities increased the inducements for someone within the bushranger's trust to betray him. After hearing of the reward being offered by Governor Arthur for his capture, Brady in reply cheekily announced a reward of 20 gallons of rum for the capture of the Governor:

> Mountain Home, April 20th, 1825.
>
> It has caused Matthew Brady much concern that such a person known as Sir George Arthur is at large. Twenty gallons of rum will be given to any person that will deliver his person unto me. I also caution John Priest that I will hang him for his ill-treatment of Mrs. Blackwell, at Newtown.
>
> M. BRADY.

This notice was posted on the door of the Royal Oak Inn at Crossmarch, Oatlands, ostensibly so that rum thirsty would-be bounty hunters would see it. But more likely, as pubs were the social centres of these communities, it was placed so that the humorous riposte would find its audience. With these appealing gestures, it is not difficult to see how Brady established a sympathetic reputation amongst the underclass of Van Diemen's Land.

After another of the gang's successful robberies, they made their way to a nearby public house. In good spirits, according to Calder, they:

> Offered to treat everyone who liked to drink for nothing, which was of course all of them; and the first suspicion they had that all was not quite right was when they saw Brady take charge of the bar (pushing the landlord out altogether) and of premises generally, and

handing the beer and spirits about like water, greatly to the satisfaction of all present except the deposed landlord, who saw with ill-concealed displeasure the liberal disbursement of his liquors, which everybody drank and nobody paid for. Pot after pot, and nip after nip, were handed across the counter by the officious Brady as fast as they were called for, till all the company except his own party and the landlord were as drunk as fiddlers at a fair.

The gang, which at this time numbered 14, rode on, stopping off at a homestead occupied by a woman whose name is recorded only as 'Ransome'. She was a supporter whom Brady felt confident to ask that 'each of them might be supplied with a glass of wine, for which he thanked her respectfully and rode off.' The day had become something of a bender.

The bushrangers roamed the southern districts of Van Diemen's Land until February 1826. After 21 months of freedom, but unsatisfied with their future prospects, Brady had the ambition to reach the Australian mainland. He attempted to pirate several ships, including the *Duke of York* and *Glory*, in order to make it over the Bass Strait. After commandeering one vessel and starting the voyage, treacherous conditions and inexperience with sailing forced him to turn back.

As Brady's exploits further enraged the colonial authorities, the rewards escalated, and the tactic to bring the bushrangers to heel turned to internal betrayal. There was the promise of a pardon and return ticket back to England for an informer, a strongly appealing offer for the many who were resigned to never seeing their loved ones again. It is a curious form of justice when the state would send one criminal back into the community just to make an example of another. The authorities enlisted three police spies to penetrate the gang, and the man who successfully betrayed Brady was named Cowan. Following an encounter with soldiers and armed convicts, Brady scuppered into the bush a wounded man. There he was eventually captured by the famous bounty hunter, and soon to be founder of Melbourne, John Batman.

Brady had acquired such a notorious reputation, and popularity, that there was great interest in his trial. He offered one final gesture of contempt for establishment justice when he expressed to the court his intention of pleading guilty to every charge brought against him, whether he was guilty of it or not. A writer in the *Colonial Magazine* recorded the exchange: 'Guilty, your honour; I shall plead guilty to all, and much more than you can bring against me. It would, therefore, be only wasting your honour's time, and that of the gentlemen of the jury, to proceed.' As the trial progressed, Brady was firm in this position, offered no explanations to satisfy the court he had no respect for, and to every charge 'smilingly answered "Guilty".'

There were multiple unsuccessful petitions to halt Brady's execution, and 'his cell was filled with wine, fruit, cakes, confectionary and flowers from the ladies of Hobart Town.' On 4 May 1826 Matthew Brady was executed at the age of 27.

Old Hobart Gaol, where Matthew Brady was hanged.

CHAPTER 3

A CHEEKY FEW: EARLY SOCIALISM AND ALCOHOL

Alex Ettling

During the nineteenth century, idealistic people around the world looked upon the new society forming in Australia with curiosity. Seeking an alternative to the 'dark satanic mills of Europe', some even made the long journey to start a new life. But it was not the 'workingman's paradise' they had been led to believe, with the experience of free labour a variation on that which they had previously known – grinding and hardly free at all.

Life for workers in the new colony involved many of the same concerns as today: inadequate pay to meet the cost of living; insecure work; stress over housing and healthcare; and worries about providing for those in their care. Critics had begun theorising these relatively new social relations of capitalism – variously assessing it as inefficient, immoral, unjust.

The early socialists were in the process of developing ideas on alternative ways of living – and working out strategies to get there. For most, the task was to grow from a small group to a mass movement. This led to an orientation to the working class, which socialists understand to hold a particularly strategic power to remake the world. It is due to the unique role workers hold in the economic production which all capitalist societies are formed by and which the culture of these societies is shaped around.

But stepping back from this abstraction, activists needed to relate to the present-day culture of the community they were organising within to find an audience. It follows that, in Australia, drinking was often a considered element – or purposeful absence – from radical social spaces. The venues involved might be pubs but also included temperance halls. Fundraising with sales of alcohol has long been a feature of political organising, but it is also the case that events could be supported more earnestly when they were situated *away* from drinking. Socialist publications provided space for abstaining views, just as they sold advertising space for drinking venues. A number of socialist organisations received donations from those in the alcohol industry, revenue derived from everything from wine sales to cork manufacture.

This chapter looks at the rise of socialism in Australia and a few key moments when the presence of alcohol – or its inverse – asserted itself. It traces some of the transnational influences on drinking culture and anti-capitalist organising – an interrelated phenomena that helped shape early socialism in Australia.

Beginnings

Just as the political economy of the new society was imported, so were a number of traditions of resistance. Following invasion, a militarised penal colony was established that for years engaged in frontier wars with First Nations. The imported European population was mostly comprised of those who did not conform to the orderly running of capitalism in the British-Irish Isles, so the colonial settler outpost was from its very beginnings the home of dissatisfied people holding a grievance with the state. As an example, in 1830 the Swing Rioters reacted to intensified exploitation by destroying new agricultural technology in a coordinated attack. The state sent 322 of the offenders to Australia. As prison labourers, they commonly engaged in acts of defiance through drinking, including gestures of solidarity such as taking alcohol to other workers and prisoners. Significantly, as historian Bruce W Brown has detailed, a small number of them engaged in the most powerful act of worker's resistance – the withdrawal of labour. However, the fate of most political prisoners sent to Australia was not dissimilar to that of the iconic Tolpuddle Martyrs, English farm workers transported to Tasmania in 1834 for their union activity. They were split up and brutalised, often sent to isolated farms where there were few opportunities to connect with other workers.

As a public sphere developed in Australia, and the ruling class opened up to the beginnings of representative democracy, socialist agitators sought to push change even further. Sharing ideas often involved stump oratory on street corners and gatherings at pubs. There are accounts of socialists hanging out of pub balconies to deliver speeches to crowds gathered below on the street. Seeking receptive audiences, many socialists travelled the same circuits as regional workers. Another option was to establish a locale that could draw an audience in. This could be a bookshop,

William Cuffay in Newgate Prison, 1848 (William Paul Dowling, National Portrait Gallery, London)

reading room, gymnasium, boarding house, ethno-cultural club, or any kind of venue for conviviality.

Finding the audience was one thing, but there was always an onus on the skill of the activist to attract attention and make their case. Socialist agitators tended to be somewhat flamboyant and theatrical, and used these traits to their advantage. A notable example is William Cuffay, the famous Black leader of the Chartists, considered the world's first mass movement of the working class. In London, state spies had infiltrated the rebels' meetings at the Orange Tree tavern and obstructed their plans to overthrow the existing government and establish a republic. What is now known as the 'Orange Tree Conspiracy' saw Cuffay arrested and sent in chains to Australia in 1848. He numbered among the last batches of convicts sent to Australia's eastern coast. Although the practice would continue in Western Australia until 1867, the final shipload of convicts arrived in Tasmania in 1853.

Cartoon of Karl Marx as Prometheus, bound to a printing press while the royal eagle of Prussian censorship rips out his liver, 1843

With the waning of transportation, the dynamics of class struggle changed greatly in Australia. After serving his sentence Cuffay remained in Hobart and returned to working class politics, campaigning against the repressive Masters and Servants Act. Having received donations from supporters, he obtained the licence of the Albert Theatre and used the venue to host entertainment and political events. This included his own comedic performances, which seem likely to have been a vehicle for theatrical political messaging. The advantage of a performance space over a bar was the focus being directed to the stage, as well as a more sober audience.

Cuffay himself was not a drinker, but this is not to say that such venues were free of alcohol. The Albert Theatre had only recently been prosecuted for the sly grogging of gin. It is possible that this illegal trade may have been the only successful business model for such a venue as the theatre did not last long under Cuffay's tenure. Even the efforts of a talented political leader were not enough to conjure up any sort of insurgent workers movement. Tasmania had a small urban proletariat, and the island was not a preferred destination for labour activists arriving free of chains. It was the only colony where no significant socialist organisation formed, suggesting that these sorts of objective factors could be decisive.

Concentrated populations of workers with grievances were presenting themselves in other places around the country. The collective experience of labouring was enough to compel many workers towards banding together – with unions proliferating in the mid-1800s. The most powerful weapon workers had against their exploiters was to withdraw their labour. However, strikes tended to involve only a section of the working class. There was a need for a political movement to unite workers across industries and change the system which was oppressing all. It was not until boot-makers and printers in Collingwood engaged in collective struggle that the first socialist organisation was formed in Australia. Here, the influence of migrants who brought with them German socialist ideas was a game changer.

The German Radicals

Germany was one of the more advanced capitalist economies, with one of the most advanced working class movements. The persecution of rebels there contributed to two significant waves of migration to Australia. An anonymous Melbourne correspondent, 'E.B.', writing for the German socialist journal *Neue Zeit*, claimed in 1909 that German social democrats were 'the Sauerteig' (the yeast or ferment) that started the socialist movement in Australian cities. The first wave of arrivals arose from the 1848 revolution, with the second coming in the years after 1878 when the German state sought to exile all socialists.

As well as the organisational capacity provided by these activists, the other German influence was on the level of theory. In the major study of early socialism in Australia, *In Our Time: Socialism and the Rise of Labor, 1885-1905*, political scientist Verity Burgmann asserts that 'if any single idea could be isolated and designated as the driving force of the socialist movement in this period, it would be the notion of surplus value.' Karl Marx, the German philosopher behind this concept, had initially been politicised by the economic hardship of wine producers in the Mosel region where he grew up. His family had a vineyard in Mertesdorf and he was a keen consumer of wines (at one stage president of the Trier Tavern Club). In 1842, the 24 year old became the editor of a start-up newspaper that reported on the economic conditions in the Mosel Valley. According to Marx's collaborator Friedrich Engels, it was the economic hardship of these wine producers, instigated by the Prussian state, that led Marx 'from pure politics to economic relationships and so to socialism.'

The story of the German socialists and their relationship to Australia takes form in London. After being exiled, Marx was advised by communist Heinrich Baur to make a home in Soho, the centre of the German refugee community. The socialists met in the Red Lion pub and discussed the way forward for their international movement. Baur, one of the first 'revolutionary proletarians' that Engels ever met, took experience and knowledge from these gatherings with him when he migrated to Australia in 1851.

Baur was a leader of several significant left-wing organisations, including the organisation that commissioned Marx and Engels to write the *Communist Manifesto*. Its concluding statement famously exhorted: 'Workers of the world, unite! You have nothing to lose but your chains!', and so it is only to be expected that Marx maintained an interest in the activities of his German associates as they dispersed around the globe. One contact was Gustav Techow, who had led the revolutionary army in Baden in 1848 before migrating to Australia four years later. In 1860, Marx received a letter addressed from a pub in St Kilda, the Royal Hotel, where Techow was residing. Unfortunately, most of the potentially subversive written material of the Germans in Australia has been lost to history.

Australia's First Socialist Organisation

Along with some of these German radicals, the first supporters of Marxism in Australia were militant workers in Collingwood. They were organising broad support for a local cabinet-makers' strike, and in the process of this struggle formed the country's first socialist organisation, the Democratic Association of Victoria (DAV) in February 1872. This group aligned themselves to the International Working Men's Association, and their manifesto quoted the preamble to the provisional rules of the First International as written by Marx. The DAV manifesto declared that the emancipation of the working classes must be achieved by the working classes themselves, further indication of the influence of Marxist ideas.

In its short life, the DAV supported striking workers, held regular meetings to discuss political affairs, and established two co-ops. Its existence seems to have largely corresponded with their publications. For 10 months, they put out the paper *The Internationalist* where, amongst other things, they addressed questions around alcohol. In the first issue on 24 February 1872, a contributor under the pseudonym 'Anvil' offered a critique of colonialism and the missionaries who brought 'strong drink' and a 'keg of spirits'. The second issue of *The Internationalist* made a case against drunkenness being posed as a problem exclusive to the working class:

> People may answer at the idea of the 'Emancipation of the working classes,' and say, that the working classes should emancipate themselves from their habits of sensuous indulgence in the form of beer drinking – so they should; and so also should the upper classes, for they are quite as bad in this respect, and are more extravagant with it.

The DAV addressed the issue of alcohol in a lengthy rumination on the question of liberty, in the 11 May 1872 issue of *The Internationalist*. It challenged:

> What? Would you 'rob the poor man of his beer?' Would you, who are believers in the sacred figment of personal liberty, actually proscribe the Bacchanal the enjoyment of his privilege (time honoured and vested) to get gloriously drunk and ineffably silly when he personally chooses?

The German emigres likely brought their continental approach towards drinking to the social milieu around the DAV, but they were not the only members of the organisation to take an interest in alcohol. The secretary George Scammel Manns, after becoming a school teacher in Wodonga, cultivated a vineyard and founded the Wodonga Wine and Fruitgrowers' Association. Shortly after moving to the Murray, 'he was the ruling spirit in the social life of the community.' Manns produced a prize-winning wine, a light dry red, and was well appreciated for the parties he organised in the community.

DAV: Publications

George Leonard Vogt was a key figure behind the DAV publications. Simultaneous to his political commitments to the working class, he was also a leading business figure in cork manufacturing. Sadly, he spent much of his life popping the cork on new newspapers he established (only for them to fall flat). His ultimate goal was to establish a wide-circulation paper for the workers movement, and he invested significant capital to pursue those ends. The high point was the establishment of the *Peoples Daily*, a publication that existed for 106 issues between 1903-04. Although it did not last, it did play a part in the election of a socialist MP, William 'The Little Doctor' Maloney. The investigative journalism of Vogt uncovered a ballot counting room scandalously strewn with loose ballot papers and whisky, enough evidence to see the initial election result voided, which cleared the path for Maloney's ascendency.

Maloney is a figure we will return to in this piece. He was an activist who had concerns about the unfavourable media for the workers movement. At one public event he set fire to a copy of *The Age*, exclaiming: 'Boys, we will light such a spark of freedom tonight as will not be put out until the whole colony is ablaze.' Socialists had a difficult relationship with *The Age*, then as now. It was seen as being in the service of what are today described as 'small l' liberals, and functioned to subdue any left pressure from the labour movement on the Labor Party. Socialists were desperate for a more sympathetic organ that could be a voice for the workers. It was destined to be an unrealised dream, with a number of aborted attempts, or worthy publications that never managed to achieve a wide readership.

To drive engagement with only minimal resources, there was a temptation to publish provocative commentary. Burgmann details how a newspaper of a later era, the *Socialist*, put into print on 6 June 1896 that the director of the State Labour Bureau, Joseph Creer, 'owed his position to political corruption and that before he was connected with the temperance movement he had been an inveterate drunkard, being many times hurled out of hotels by irate publicans.' The editors Tom Batho and Harry Holland were charged with criminal libel and even though Creer was proved to be a liar in court, it did not stop the judge from handing out jail sentences. They were not the only socialist publishers to be crushed by the repressive arm of the state.

DAV: Finances

Another challenge for socialists and their publications was securing enough money to function. Revenue came from sales, donations, union patronage, and advertising. It was inevitably a more difficult task for publications hostile to business to secure advertising. *The Internationalist* had done their bit to endorse the local wine trade by advertising the 'luncheon rooms and Scotch pie shop' of L. Langlois, promoting the availability of 'Colonial Wine per glass 3d'. The first president of the DAV, John Ross, was from 1866 a merchant selling colonial wine. Like Vogt, Ross also carried with him a lifelong interest in media, being a leading figure in the proposed Labor daily, *Progress*, in 1906. Socialist organisations with stronger connections to unions, and possibly more social democratic than revolutionary, were more likely to receive advertising for liquor brands. *The Tocsin*, a socialist Labor aligned paper at the turn of the century, featured prominent liquor ads for Carlton Ale and Wolfe's schnapps. The seditious organisations were more likely to receive funding from supporters who operated small bars.

As seen with Vogt, some proportion of revenue from the trade in liquor went towards establishing the DAV and subsequent projects. There is a curious pattern of figures associated with the wine industry who have supported socialist projects. Others included the elder of the famous Aarons family of the Communist Party of Australia (CPA), Louis Aarons, who was a wine merchant. J.S. Fidler, was a member of the socialist Y Club, which he supplied with wine from his store. Harry

William Maloney (National Library of Australia)

Samuel Taylor, a member of the family behind the Yalumba winery, convalesced at the vineyard between forays into building socialist communes in Paraguay, as well as at Murtho on the Murray River.

John Moir Alexander operated a vineyard at Yering and cellars at Melbourne's Eastern Market, becoming one of the Australian far left's most significant benefactors. He bailed out a number of Victorian Socialist Party (VSP) activists who were arrested during free speech campaigns, and regularly donated to the party. He made a £5 weekly donation to the Communist Party throughout the Depression, which his son-in-law Ralph Gibson described as a 'veritable goldmine'. In the years to come, Alexander's commercial wine operations would also help fund the establishment of Camp Eureka, the party's retreat near Warburton. It is notable that when the Communist Party was banned, party member Amirah Inglis recounts that there was an immediate police raid on Alexander's wine cellars. Clearly the river of money from wine into the far left had not gone unnoticed.

DAV: Co-ops

Returning to the much earlier era of the DAV, it is notable that John Ross, a socialist business figure in the wine industry, also took an interest in promoting the co-operative movement. It was one of the more favoured schemes of the early socialist movement, although critiqued for being piecemeal and not tackling the system as a whole. The DAV signalled in their first issue of *The Internationalist* their interest in the Rochdale co-op principles. The Rochdale Pioneers in 1844 had established cooperative stores, self-managed by a committee selected by their working class members. One feature was that they applied a percentage of their profits to educational purposes. In the 1860 version of their rules they also had temperance clauses. Ross was aware of the perception of the DAV as imbibers, so it is notable that he put on meetings to spruik co-ops at the Temperance Hall. *The Internationalist* on 20 April 1872 records one meeting where it was assured to the audience: 'Though the promoters as a body were not exactly teetotallers, they were determined not to sell intoxicating drinks from their stores, and not to introduce them to their reading rooms.' Any workers wanting booze had to pursue this liberty at the *for-profit* grog shop next door, which as a matter of observation would not have bothered Ross's own business interests.

DAV: Death is not the End

If these contradictions were of any concern, they were not the reason for the demise of the group. The aforementioned *Communist Manifesto* opens with the line: 'A spectre is haunting Europe – the spectre of communism.' However, it was a disagreement about literal spectres that played a part in the DAV's demise. There was division amongst the leaders of the

J.M. Alexander

group on whether to promote spiritualism, a 19th century fad that maintained it was possible to communicate with the dead.

In some respects this movement, with its flat hierarchy of mediums holding the ability to talk to ghosts, was an extension of the reform mindset. It critiqued the dogma of established religion and applied a rationalism based on what was communicated through the seances. One of the most talented mediums in Melbourne, and the leader of the movement in that city was William Terry. He held many progressive views, and for a time ran a popular Progressive Spiritualist Lyceum and Sunday school. In these endeavours he received little support from his wife Martha, who held conventional Christian views. A vegetarian and anti-alcohol, Terry blamed his wife's ill temper on 'pork and porter'.

Vogt could not abide the nonsense of his collaborators taking an interest in the dead. He wound up *The Internationalist* but in the decades that followed continued to pursue his successful cork business alongside his unsuccessful left-wing media initiatives, until the laws of capitalism – a glut of new competitors in the cork industry – drove down his profits.

German Migration and German Cultural Groups

Following the demise of the DAV, it would be several years before any other socialist groups were launched. There continued to be union organisation, as well as further migration into Australia of people with sympathy for working class movements. Between the late 1870s and the mid-1880s, the Australian Government induced migration from Germany via cheap fares and promises of land. Material conditions were a major factor. As Burgmann explains:

> The decades around the turn of the century marked a period of international capitalist development that in turn fostered an international labour market. During the Indian summer of free trade and imperial expansion, the European-settler economies of the New World offered higher wages than were available at home.

Germans were considered 'sound' migrants, although the Australian ruling class do not seem to have considered their homeland's burgeoning socialist movement in their calculations. On one occasion, a passenger ship *RMS Osterley*, carrying German migrants to Australia, was observed flying a red flag on the third class deck. There was scaremongering in the newspapers out of this, with talk of 'red hot... seething socialists... armed to the teeth'. However, the value of educated white migrants far outweighed the need for scapegoats, so the controversy was effectively doused.

As noted earlier, an added impetus for migration was repression. In 1878, the Reichstag passed the anti-socialist law known as the Sozialistengesetz. This included Paragraph 28, which enabled the banishment

The Golden Fleece Hotel in Melbourne was a popular meeting venue for left-wing political radicals (City of Melbourne Art and Heritage Collection)

of party supporters from their hometown without any legal recourse. Amongst the cohort of political refugees that ended up in Australia was Hans Heinrich Diercks and Louis Gross, described as 'an earbasher for socialism', both of whom were expelled from Hamburg in the 1880s.

Joseph Schellenberg was also a refugee from Germany in this period. He became a member of the Australian Socialist League (ASL) before forming the Communist-Anarchist Group of Central Cumberland, setting up an 'operations centre' at a farm at Smithfield in 1891, about an hour from Sydney. The impact of this flower farm of radical hue is uncertain, it appears to have primarily functioned as a distribution centre for literature. It may have also functioned as a queer social space for the many unmarried socialist men in the scene.

At any rate, we know that fun was had. Ernest Lane in *Dawn To Dusk* records a heavy drinking session involving two prominent comrades:

> A local vineyard was explored and E.J. Brady was overcome by the wine and lay down on a stretcher by the window to sleep. However, he took part in a barricade revolution in his dreams, as was natural, when with a shout of 'Fire!' he flung his arms up and smashed the window. Andrews, with primitive faith, gathered sprays of gum trees to cover Brady's body.

Despite the number of radicals peppered amongst them, the majority of German migrants were not at all political. Indeed many were hostile to the socialists, including those connected to the Lutheran church. Nevertheless, there were enough people with experience of the social democrats of Europe to sustain something of this politics in Australia.

A social evening at the Melbourne Turn Verein, 1880 (*The Australasian Sketcher*, State Library of Victoria)

Class Distinction in the German Clubs

The migrant experience could be somewhat insular with people gravitating towards social clubs based around their ethnic background. In Europe, repression had also encouraged a tradition of joining social clubs and this too was transferred to Australia. The beleaguered German radicals in London, drinking in the Red Lion pub, had been scheming a way forward for the socialist movement. Friedrich Engels, in his essay 'On the History of the Communist League' stated, 'Where workers' associations could be founded, they were utilised in like manner. Where this was forbidden by law, one joined choral societies, athletic clubs, and the like.'

In Australia, clubs such as these became home for a number of German socialists. In Adelaide and Melbourne, where there were large German migrant populations, there was a class divide in the social club scene with more explicitly left-wing clubs forming in both cities. In Adelaide, the Deutsche Club formed in 1854. Members sought to promote 'deutschtum' (German language, culture and customs). This became institutionalised as the middle class club once working class Germans founded the Allgemeiner Deutscher Verein (ADV) in 1886. We know that the ADV served alcohol in their club because of newspaper reports on police seizure of their supplies in 1892. In response the ADV argued that as a club they were allowed to serve alcohol to their members, and pointed out their other services, such as a library of 1200 books.

The historian Ian Harmstorf makes the case that despite appearances the ADV did not function as a socialist organisation, but rather as an umbrella organisation for a whole raft of pre-existing German clubs, many apolitical. As such, the ADV became a significant node within the network of 'democratic societies' operating in Adelaide. The Deutsche Club simply considered the ADV to be a den of communism. Relations between the two organisations were frosty.

In Melbourne, the main German club, the Turn Verein, established in 1860, was not especially radical, or even working class. Dissatisfaction with this prompted the formation of the Socialistischer Verein Vorwärts in July 1887. They held fortnightly meetings at Durgarten's Hotel, near the Turn Verein in La Trobe Street. Carl Mitscherlich described the object of the club as:

> Buying different socialistic books. We used to receive books from Germany and America, and we used to buy the *Labor Call*, [and] if we had a credit balance we would subscribe to various social movements [and support justified strikes] ... we believe

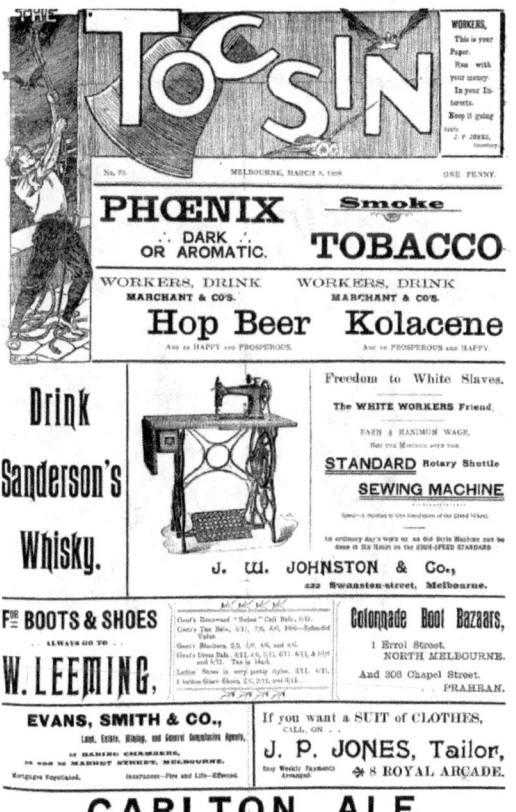

Tocsin newspaper, 1898 (National Library of Australia)

in no war, or creed, or nationality, our religion is 'the brotherhood of man'.

However, organisations like the Turn Verein did not have to be assertive in activism to play a role in Australian socialism. An example is found in the life story of the aforementioned socialist parliamentarian William Maloney. He was sent on his political journey after coming off second best in a fight. His response was not to pursue justice through the instruments of the state, but rather to bulk up and seek revenge. He joined the Turn Verein where he became an accomplished gymnast, and developed 'the greatest chest expansion of anyone connected with [the Turn Verein]', a boast he later made in parliament.

The Turn Verein offered opportunities to develop one's physique, but also the attractions of sausages and beer. One might end up arm-in-arm, singing German drinking songs with acquaintances of Marx and Engels. One of these was Hermann Puttman, a central figure in revolutionary socialist German literature who moved to Australia in 1855. In his new home he published *Deutsches Liederbuch für Australien* in 1862, which included drinking songs intended to be of use to the Turn Verein choir.

Amongst all this pumping iron and bonhomie, Maloney, a local born in Melbourne in 1854, was introduced to socialist ideas by German migrants. Thus we can say that the schemes of Engels and co, hatched in the Red Lion, came to fruition at least once. Maloney regarded himself as a socialist in the tradition of German social democracy, although he never acquired much of a knowledge of Marx. He remained a member of the Turn Verein for decades. His association with the organisation, his bohemian appearance and his eclectic approach to socialism were no impediment to being voted into parliament, where in a fifty-one-year stint as a (mostly Labor) parliamentarian, he had the distinction of being the first person in any of the Commonwealth nations to introduce a parliamentary bill to extend the vote to women.

Police pose at a mock grave for Tom Mann during a strike in Broken Hill, a beer taunts the abstainer, 1909 (Broken Hill City Library)

If Maloney was an example of the possibilities of such an organisation to politicise, there was also the potential for the inverse. A flat political climate, and waning motivations to engage in activism, could render social clubs pacifying. Gustav Techow, the former revolutionary leader, was said to have left his radical past behind him after moving to Melbourne where he became committed to gymnastic instruction, publishing a book on the subject in 1886.

British Socialist Traditions

We have so far focussed on the German 'yeast' to Australian socialism, but now shift back to the British influence, which was far and away the more pervasive. The Social Democratic Party of Germany had embraced a full social infrastructure within the sphere of party life and this approach was similarly promoted by figures in the British socialist scene.

An interesting period of socialism to examine in this respect is that which follows the collapse of the Australian workers movement with the defeat of the Great Strikes during the depression of the 1890s. In response many socialists followed a path into reformism through the establishment of the Labor Party (and its various precursors). Those organisations that did not fold directly into the Labor project mostly attempted the difficult task of being Labor's 'socialist conscience'. Attempts to push the party towards social transformation generally lead to disappointment.

Bernard O'Dowd, editor of *The Tocsin* (1897-1906), was part of this trend, following a peripatetic journey across the Australian progressive scene. What is notable in this period is the Tocsinner's organisational plurality and emphasis on social organising at the periphery. O'Dowd was inspired by English journalist and socialist Robert Blatchford, believing that socialists need to create their own 'social atmosphere'. He set about creating a counter-culture characterised by a 'full-blooded, full-minded, morally-balanced' approach to living. Drinking was allowed but would not have a favoured place in this uplifted lifestyle. Its adherents presented themselves as distinct from their austere rivals under the sway of the Church, as well as the other sections of the Left who they viewed as being too bookish. *The Tocsin* declared a determination to avoid the pitfall of:

> The divorce of Labour from life. The labourer loves, sorrows, aspires, sins, dreams, reveres. In a word he is living. ... He is not the sexless automaton of the political economy books.

This appears to have been a dig at those grappling with Marx's *Capital*. It also corresponded with the ethical socialist understanding of 'the inextricable interrelationship between social and individual regeneration', as historian Paul Strangio describes it. For these socialists it would be moral enterprise, not merely depersonalised material forces, that drove social change. Historian Roger Coates provides some further context, noting 'British socialism tended to draw quite heavily on both an evangelical, dissenting and non-conformist Christianity and a secular rationalism for its social and personal ethics.' An editorial in *The Tocsin* provides an example:

> We will never get salvation till we deserve it, that we must socialise the community, and most of all that nobody can save ourselves. Before we can reach the Promised Land of the social commonwealth each one of us must be fit to be the Moses.

Sober Socialists

Most of the English socialist leaders that visited Australia and had an impact on local politics were anti-alcohol. Keir Hardie's first cause was temperance, and Ben Tillett had once complained of workers: 'drink killed their ambition and their self-respect.' The most significant English socialist to spend time in Australia was Tom Mann, who described himself as 'a whole souled advocate of total abstinence.' However, Mann also argued that socialists had a duty to demonstrate their capacity for enjoyment, so he was a supporter of the 'total social life' approach to socialist organising – just one that passed on the beers.

When Mann founded the Victorian Socialist Party (VSP) in 1905, its rapid growth was likely helped along by the broad periphery that had developed around The Tocsinners in the previous decade. This included anti-capitalist social clubs, an example being the Hegemony group which held 'smoke nights' that likely did involve alcohol on the sly (they pointedly set themselves up opposite the Temperance Hall).

The social schedule of the VSP went beyond previous efforts, with mostly non-drinking groups and events. These included socialist Sunday school, dances, singing groups, Australian Rules football teams, drama clubs, orchestras, and regular picnic excursions. Their approach to alcohol seemed to be about providing alternative activities rather than pursuing an overt temperance policy. Mann also had reason to keep his head down on that question. The Victorian Premier Thomas Bent had reminded the local polity that the socialist had been prosecuted for selling watered down beer when he ran a pub in England. This reputation damaging crime has never been fully explained. Most proprietors charged with such a thing are motivated by maximising profits, for Mann it is possible he practiced it on worker welfare grounds.

The Victorian Socialist Party also had a material interest in not condemning alcohol – they were receiving financial support from those in the alcohol industry, including the aforementioned J.M. Alexander. In 1918, when the organisation had reached the end of its political relevance, some particularly keen members ended up facilitating a social drinking circle, the Y Club. J.S. Fidler kindly donated wine and cheese from his store to these gatherings. The existence of a gentlemanly drinking club – including such members as Alf Foster, R.S. Ross, Guido Baracchi and Peter Simonoff – is odd in the history of Australian socialism. It also represents something of the organisational inertia between the great rupture of the Russian Revolution in 1917 and the leisurely pace at which an Australian communist party was formed in 1920.

The Germ of Revolution

Things had seemed far more promising during the previous decade. The year 1907 was an auspicious year, as Carlton & United Breweries (CUB) was formed, and the Harvester Judgement on the living wage handed down. It has also been described as 'a magic year in Australian socialism.' For radicals the arrival of the Industrial Workers of the World (IWW) provided a seed of revolutionary politics that would have a transformative effect on the Australian political scene.

This current of revolutionary strategy came out of organisations with a strong association with drinking culture. The mysterious Horace J Hawkins had encountered American syndicalist ideas in England before emigrating to Australia. He found himself in Broken Hill where he managed to interest members of the working class mining community in the politics of the IWW.

Just how and why these ideas took shape in this remote community is difficult to pinpoint. The difficult conditions of mining and the existence of a terrible boss (BHP) were necessary preconditions for widespread worker dissatisfaction, but these were common throughout Australia. To Hawkins' advantage there was a sizeable and concentrated working class community, and one whose industrial culture was potentially fruitful. Burgmann offers an explanation in her study *Revolutionary Industrial Unionism: The Industrial Workers of the World in Australia*:

> Class consciousness and its manifestations have flourished in mining communities the world over. ... The one-industry based social structure of the community has

tended to create a duplication in civic life of the class relations in the industry itself, and hence a heightened awareness of the significance of these relations.

It seems quite possible that the hot-house atmosphere of this mining town, which extended into workers' drinking venues, played a role. The Barrier Socialist Propaganda Group where IWW ideas took root, was formed out of the Barrier Social Democratic Club. On the surface, it seemed like most other social clubs of the era. Having formed in 1903, the following year it opened clubrooms which featured a bar, billiard room and library. The Club's stated aims were to 'educate people in the principles of Social-Democracy' and 'to impart information, arouse sympathy, encourage activity, and inspire enthusiasm in the cause of human betterment.' These lofty ambitions did not inspire the conservative establishment of Broken Hill and the club came under fire from both Protestant and Catholic leaders. It was described by opponents as 'a veritable drinking and gambling hell.' As Burgmann explains:

> This 'Social Democratic Clique' was held responsible by the clergy of Broken Hill for the lamentable decline in the public morals of the townsfolk. ... The socialism

The club rooms of the Barrier Social Democratic Club in Broken Hill, 1906 (*Tocsin*, National Library of Australia)

it expounded was the socialism of the devil and not of the New Testament.

The Barrier Social Democratic Club had been in the sights of the police who successfully managed to remove their licence to sell liquor on Sundays. This caused their membership to decline from a recorded 1350 members in its early years, to 417 members in November 1907. It is possible that this loss of members due most likely to the reduced availability of alcohol had an effect of sharpening the political culture of those that remained, and that this extended to the Barrier Socialist Propaganda Group. The latter organisation was more politically assertive. It also opposed racism and was prepared to engage in direct action. A more strident political lead appears to have resonated at a time when so many members had been familiar with the passive 'parliamentary road to socialism', if not just focused on drinking their troubles away.

In June 1907, during a meeting of socialist groups in Melbourne, Hawkins had represented the Barrier Socialist Propaganda Group and made his case 'that the time has arrived for the re-organisation of the Australian working-class on the lines of the Industrial Workers of the World.' The conference of seven socialist groups voted to endorse the statement, representing a watershed moment in Australian socialist politics.

Bar Sales for the Revolution

The International Socialist Club (ISC) were one of the organisations in attendance. They had been reformist but became enthusiasts for the IWW. This group had once meekly described revolution as being like a 'calm sunset', but now came to revolutionary socialism in earnest. The ISC included veterans of the Paris Commune, and was also led by political exiles, including the prominent Italian socialist Francis Sceusa and the aforementioned Heinrich Dierks. As well as being a leader of the ISC, 'Henry' Dierks was a liquor and hospitality trade unionist.

The ISC had formed in 1898, after splitting from the Australian Socialist League. It held a commitment to organising the working class as a whole, regardless of race. This was in direct opposition to much of the labour movement, which was engaged in exclusionary strategies, including advocating a 'White Australia'. Historian Roger Coates contends that, 'in 1907 the ISC was one of the important centres of the socialist second wave.' The presence of socialists with continental European drinking traditions within the group may partly account for how it operated, including holding convivial activities in their Sydney club rooms

Socialists holding their publications, including *International Socialist*.

at 1 Willmott Street. Burgmann, speaking at the *Communists and the Labour Movement Conference* in 1980, observed:

> EJ Brady describes this club as a good meeting place where draught lager was always available and eclectic discussion could be carried on in most continental languages. So it's really a social club for displaced European cosmopolitan-minded socialists. Now they didn't actually do much other than drink until about 1907 when their finances were so solid as a result of this imbibing that they launched a review, the *International Socialist Review*.

Maintaining finances in this way could be difficult. In 1906 their bar was raided, although they managed to get off the charges. In 1910, Dierks was again prosecuted for selling liquor at an ISC event without a license. Undercover police had infiltrated the ISC's 'bazaar' at the Manchester Unity Hall and purchased lager beer using a coupon system. This trick attempts to bypass licencing restrictions by technically cutting out direct exchanges of alcohol for money. Instead, punters are only able to buy coupons, which in turn can be redeemed for a drink. Despite being used well into the late twentieth century, this ruse has rarely passed close inspection by the authorities. In the ISC's case the *Sydney Morning Herald* reported the enterprise was busted only after a 'brisk trade had been done.'

An intriguing political aspect in the evolution of the ISC is that they were one of the few socialist organisations of the time that opposed World War One in its entirety (rather than just military conscription). The socialism of the ISC was thoroughly internationalist. This can be put down to the role of anti-racism in their formation, possibly a more rigorous commitment to reading theory, and maybe even the culture of convivial internationalism promoted by their clubhouse drinking.

Given that both went from being something of a drinking talk-shop to more radical and focused positions, it is worth considering the similarities and differences of the ISC and the Barrier Socialist Propaganda Group. The former was urban and cosmopolitan in character, whereas the Broken Hill group was a blue-collar rural formation. Both valued political debate and made radical literature available. Emerging alongside their prominent drinking culture, the politics of the two organisations contributed significant elements that were often absent in early forms of socialism, respectively anti-racism and revolution. The ISC, like so many of the early socialist formations, initially fuzzy on the question of how to get where they wanted to go, took influence from the revolutionary industrial unionism of the Broken Hill miners and came to declare: 'there's only one road to socialism, through revolution.'

Conclusion

The period covered in this chapter was one of deepening class consciousness, with intensified workplace and community conflict followed by cycles of retreat and revival. Many of the political actions and groups involved were small in scale, a stark fact given the scale of their ambitions. However, as historian Bruce Scates has observed, 'size is a poor criterion of significance. The challenge of 19th century radicalism was its very existence.' A through line exists from some of these modest groups, grappling with core issues of politics and organisation, to the more significant players in Australian politics, not least of all the Labor Party and Communist Party. There was much at stake and these early radicals, for better or worse, were putting in the groundwork for much of what would come later. With cheers, jeers, clinking of glasses, celebration and commiseration, the debates would continue as more chapters were added to the ongoing story of Australian socialism.

CHAPTER 4
PUBS AND THE FORMATION OF UNIONS IN AUSTRALIA
Iain McIntyre

Workplace resistance and organisation was carried out on a largely ad hoc and unofficial basis in the first decades following the invasion of Australia. Depending on one's status the illegality of forming and belonging to 'combinations' carried with it the threat of prison or the lash. Only from the 1820s onwards did formal labour associations begin to come together, often in the guise of societies for mutual aid.

An example of this was in Western Australia, where the Shepherds Club and Mutual Protection Society formed in 1843. By pooling resources it promised that each member would be looked after 'if attacked by sickness and other casualties, or where dismissed from service by caprice.' As with similar groups it also had an overtly political dimension in seeking 'the due protection' of members against 'the dangerous powers conferred on magistrates by a late Act of the Legislative Council respecting contracts between masters and servants.'

Like most workers organisations of the time these shepherds, who hailed from areas around the Avon Valley, used a pub, the York Hotel, for their meetings. The hotel also served as a point where members could leave union dues for delegates to collect.

Such activity in pubs flowed on from earlier informal efforts as well as the basic fact that hotels were where many gathered for pleasure and relief at the end of the working day. Further to this, pub based organising also reflected a simple lack of alternatives since, from colonisation onwards, few indoor places outside of hotels were readily available for use by the working classes. As such, alcohol based venues hosted gatherings of all sorts of secular groups, from sporting clubs through to political parties.

Hundreds of organisations were formed and met in pubs during the nineteenth century. These venues played a major role in the rise of early trade unions and in campaigns for the eight hour day. In Sydney and its surrounds unions regularly held meetings and events from the 1840s to 1860s at places such as the Lighthouse, the Pelican, the Oddfellows' Arms, and the Rose of Australia. Quarrymen in Melbourne met at Fitzroy's Labour In Vain while the nearby Belvidere Hotel not only provided a meeting space but also a mailing address for building unions. Trades societies and unions covering stonemasons, carpenters, tailors and others met at Adelaide pubs such as the Port Admiral, Norfolk, Prince of Wales and Hotel

Belvidere Hotel, corner of Brunswick Street and Victoria Parade, Fitzroy, 1864 (State Library of Victoria)

Europe, while advocates for reduced hours in the city's retail trade regularly gathered at the Gresham and Blenheim hotels. In Hobart the Free Labour Movement met at the Jolly Hatter, describing it in 1847 as 'the headquarters of freedom.'

Towards the end of the century the opening of Trades Halls, mechanics institutes, and other venues meant that the use of pubs for official purposes declined. In part this reflected an ambition for independence from non-member controlled enterprises. Some organisations also expressed a desire to meet away from the immediate influence of alcohol, a point particularly emphasised by abstinent members.

In this regard Melbourne's Early Closing Association led the way, holding its meetings during the 1850s at John Tankard's Temperance Hotel, the first non-alcohol based venue of its kind in the city. Largely led by business owners, religious figures, and prominent liberals the association also numbered former and current retail workers. Having a bet each way, Brisbane's eight hours movement split its early meetings between the North Australia Hotel, which served alcoholic beverages, and Day's Temperance Hotel, which did not.

Amidst changing patterns of organisation, pubs continued to serve as a forum for informal discussion, lobbying, and scheming. With hotels one of the first, if not the first, form of public infrastructure to be built, unionists in remote and regional areas would continue to also use them in an official capacity into the early years of the twentieth century.

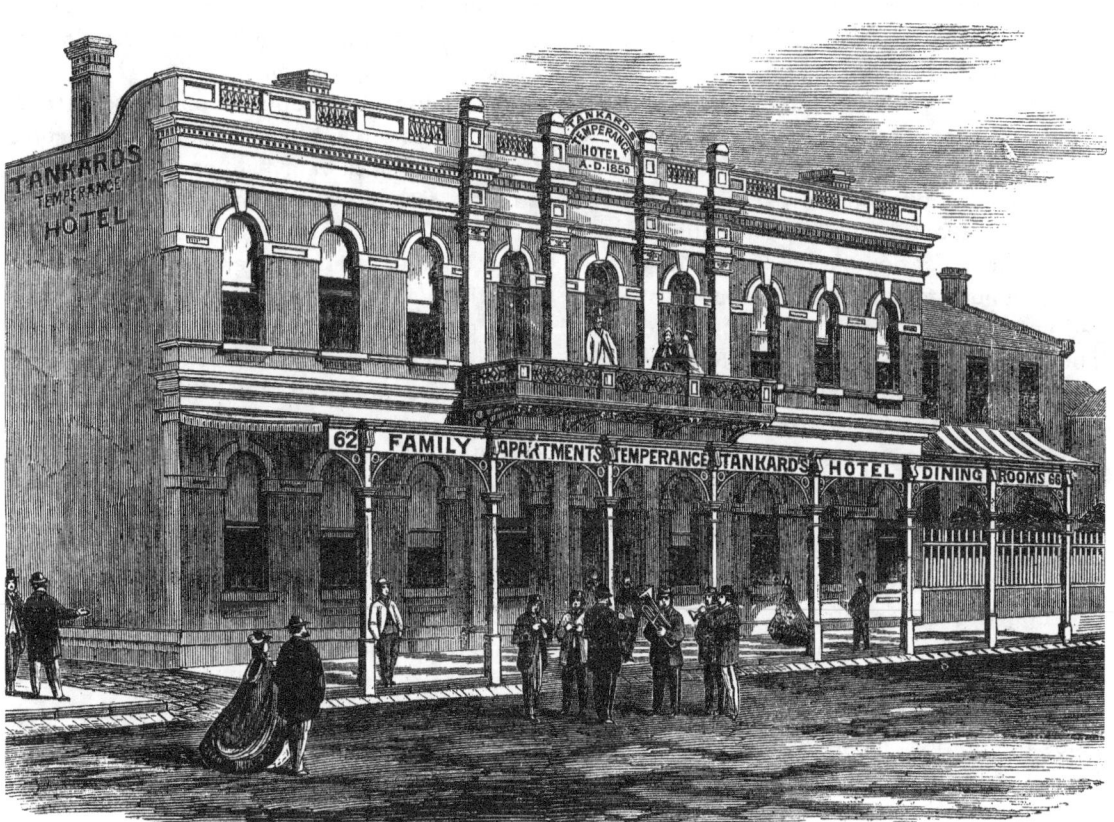

Tankard's Temperance Hotel, Lonsdale Street Melbourne, 1863 (*Illustrated Melbourne Post*, State Library of Victoria)

CHAPTER 5
DISTURBING THE PEACE: THE 1851 ROCKS RIOT
Iain McIntyre

In August 1851 a hard fought riot broke out in Sydney's Rocks district. Such disturbances were far from unknown at the time, but this particular event was unique in that it was sparked by the arrest of a sailor for a combination of breaches including drunkenness, wearing women's clothing, and disrupting a church service. As such the riot provides us with insights into the interplay of class, alcohol, gender roles, and policing amongst the colony's 'lower orders'.

Situated on the western side of Sydney cove, the Rocks district was originally known by its traditional owners, the Gadigal people, as Tallawoladah. Following invasion and dispossession it initially provided living quarters for Sydney's convict population. By the 1840s the area continued to house the city's poorest, who had come to include a mix of former unfree labourers, the generations born to them, and recent immigrants. Adjacent to the harbour, and bounded by water on three sides, it also provided accommodation and entertainment for sailors who freely mixed with long term residents, many of whom worked in maritime industries. While much of Sydney had been rebuilt around a grid-like system of roads, the rugged geography of the Rocks meant it retained winding thoroughfares and warren like structures.

In their survey of Rocks' riots during the 1840s the authors of *Radical Sydney: Places, Portraits and Unruly Episodes*, Terry Irving and Rowan Cahill, observe that in the area 'working people hated the police ... [they] were slow to come to the aid of members of the public and cowardly in the face of resistance.' Such antipathy was unsurprising given the direct or familial convict pasts of many residents. A fair proportion of police were former convicts themselves, adding to their reputation as 'traitors' to some and 'good-for-nothings' to others. Although antagonism was sharpest amongst Sydney's most deprived, it extended across classes due to the force's reputation for indiscipline, thuggery and ineptitude.

The colony had long struggled to attract talent to the force, in part because of the job's low status. A lack of investment by the colonial administration meant that police were barely trained, poorly supervised, and received little direct compensation for their efforts. Combined with the power to arrest members of the public and deal out state sanctioned violence this was a recipe for abuse and corruption, behaviours which were amplified by the fact that officers got to keep half of any fine levied against those they had charged.

Weaved into this situation was the role of alcohol. A central complaint amongst both members of the lower and middle classes was that the crime of 'drunkenness' had long been used as a catch-all charge. It could serve as the prime reason for an arrest or easily be added to other breaches of the law. Heavy drinking was widespread across all classes but arrests among the elite were rare.

Police had the arbitrary power to define whether a person was over-intoxicated. When facing court some arrestees challenged their accuser's version of events. This rarely worked as magistrates tended to unquestioningly accept police testimony. Not only did this situation enable the punishment of anyone who crossed the police but, as already noted, it also offered officers a quick and simple way to generate personal income.

As with drug and alcohol offences today, some critics questioned whether the state should be using criminal law to deal with what could be characterised as health and moral matters. Even for those who thought it should, the poor reputation of the police raised questions about their role in the process, as did their lack of education in matters of the law. The editor of *Bell's Life in Sydney* argued in 1847 that 'It is ridiculous in the last degree to elevate a police force into a conservator of morals ... they are about as ignorant a class of individuals as can possibly be found within the limits of the colony.'

Most galling for many was the fact that members of the police were regularly observed drunk themselves, on and off duty. A number, including a Commissioner and Inspector, were dismissed during the 1840s and early 1850s for such behaviour, adding to what was already a high turnover and lack of experience amongst the force.

The old Cumberland Street Watch-house, 1886 (State Library of NSW)

In terms of direct resistance to policing, arrests for drunkenness regularly generated opportunities for conflict. Alcohol itself also likely fuelled the bravado needed to confront authorities. Defiance mainly played out in attempts, sometimes successful, by individuals and small groups to contest, evade and escape arrest. On occasion clashes escalated into large scale riots, as can be seen in the case described below.

At 8 pm on Sunday 23 August 1851, a Constable McEwan was called out to the Church Hill area of the Rocks where two sailors had been reported as being drunk and acting disorderly. They were both described to him as men, and one was dressed in 'female apparel'.

At this time – especially when compared to later in the nineteenth century – many categories, understandings and concepts regarding the nature and connection of gender and sexual identity were relatively unfixed. Terms such as 'transgender', 'cross-dressing', 'homosexual', and 'heterosexual' had yet to be invented. Nevertheless, specific activities, including wearing clothing that did not conform to a designated gender, were already crimes under British law.

Arriving at the scene McEwan was advised that the sailors had moved on to the Black Boy pub, located on the corner of George and King Street. When he proceeded there and attempted to tackle the one in women's

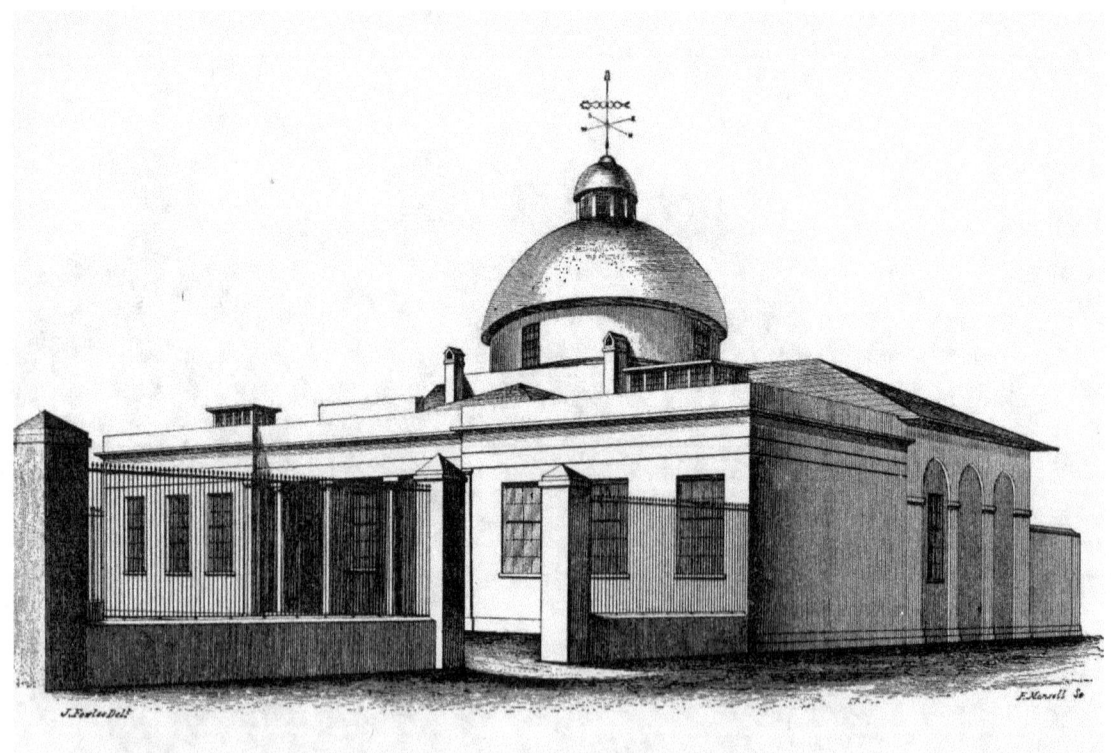

The George Street Police Office where the arrestees faced court, 1848 (Joseph Fowles, State Library of NSW)

clothing he found himself in trouble, and the two exchanged blows. The sailor, to the cheers of other drinkers, got the better of the constable, knocking him down and running away.

McEwan ran for help and after mustering another officer, returned to the area. By this time, the sailor had returned to Church Hill and was found disturbing the evening service at St Philip's. The constables overpowered the sailor and dragged them to the watch-house in Cumberland Street. From there they were sent on to the main watch-house in Druitt Street.

On hearing of their comrade's arrest, several sailors from the military ships Caliope and Pandora raised a crowd of around 60 people from across the Rocks. They marched on the Cumberland Street watch-house, attacking police along the way. The crowd obtained entry after overpowering a gaoler who had opened the door in response to their knocking. Armed with bludgeons and iron fence palings they demanded the release of all prisoners. One gaoler, Sergeant Palmer, later stated, 'They threatened that they would pull down the watch-house and knock out my brains ... I could offer no resistance, and therefore unlocked the cell.' The only prisoner present, a different sailor who had been arrested for being drunk, was freed.

Although police soon arrived most held off taking action, except for Constable McEwan, who ran in and was smashed in the head with a paling. A constable claimed that one of the crowd's more vociferous members, a sailor named John Down, had threatened, 'You ____, you had better keep back or we'll cut the ____ heads off you [deletions in original text].' At the behest of the women present the crowd soon left the police behind and made their way to the female watch-house in Clarence Street. More people joined along the way, with numbers swelling to 600.

Upon arrival at Clarence Street, the crowd demanded the release of all prisoners. Sergeant Moss, who was on duty, 'perceived that they was bent on mischief, [due to] several persons being armed with bludgeons.' He quickly ran inside and secured the entrance. Despite the crowd threatening him and battering the door for 15 minutes he was successful in keeping them out, thereby preventing the rescue of 14 prisoners.

In the meantime the police had caught up to the crowd and, despite coming under a hail of stones and sticks, distracted their attention. Moss held that had they not done so the entrance would have been breached.

This fracas lasted for only a short time as the police officers withdrew to their barracks. One constable related that 'the civilians present were far worse than the seamen, inciting the latter as much as possible against us – many saying, "Go at them- we'll take your part – we'll stand with you."'

The crowd now proceeded to the central watch-house at Druitt Street. There they rang the gate bell and rushed into an entry area, demanding access to the gaol and the release of the person arrested for wearing female apparel, as well as all other prisoners. A number of police secured an inner gate and prevented their admittance to the main gaol.

With the crowd assembled outside, one prisoner, named Kidney, tried to escape. Having left his cell he tackled one of the constables at the gate. He was struck to the ground by another constable who subsequently claimed that he was forced to continue hitting him as 'he was very violent after he was knocked down.' Kidney was in a bad state when he later faced court, with his head bandaged, clothes saturated in blood, and arm in a sling. As the beating was carried out, rioters continued to attempt to breach the gates but failed to do so.

By this point mounted police and other reinforcements had been mobilised. Upon their arrival they forced their way through to the front of the crowd, ordering them to disperse in the name of the Queen. When they refused, the police attacked, this time successfully driving them back.

Once the crowd had been dispersed, arrests began. Some resisted bitterly. One policeman reported that 'I apprehended the prisoner Wakeman, armed with a paling with which he struck me two or three blows.' Another related that 'I saw Stewart get over the wall near George Street [after escaping the scene] and took him into custody; he bit my hand most severely. I was knocked down by someone and lost my gloves and the key to my handcuffs.'

The rough night continued for both jailers and jailed. Some prisoners were so troublesome that the Provincial Inspector ordered them put in leg irons. Many injuries had been incurred and the Police Surgeon, Mr Rutter, reported that he spent most of the night and the following morning attending to police and prisoners' wounds.

The next day 22 people, many of them described as 'clerks of respectable appearance', were brought before the Central court. Nearly all of them complained of having been arbitrarily arrested and beaten for no reason. In a letter to the Sydney Morning Herald one correspondent complained of a friend being scooped up when he stepped outside his house to observe matters. It was further alleged that having been unfairly arrested he was made subject to the further indignity of having his 'hair and whiskers cropped' before facing court.

Another arrestee complained of being attacked and arrested by jumpy constables after he rushed from his bed to check out the source of a noise. Badly injured, he was told by the Police Magistrate that 'You should have stayed in bed and you would not now have been here.' A third protested that he had copped it from all sides as his attendance at St Philip's had been disrupted by the initial fracas and he had subsequently been arrested while walking home from the church.

All prisoners were found guilty as charged. Most were sentenced for drunkenness, disorderly conduct, incitement, 'heading a mob', and assault. Most of the sentences only amounted to a small fine or a caution, with more serious cases receiving fines of up to five pounds or one month in gaol. The sailor at the centre of events was additionally fined for 'having been dressed in female apparel' and bound over with two sureties of 10 pounds in default of a month in jail. One of the magistrate's main complaints was that none of the ships' officers whose men had ignited the riot had bothered to attend the hearings.

On the same day as these cases were heard a small group of sailors once more attempted to free prisoners. Armed with bludgeons, most were later described as drunk by authorities. Having run into a naval officer and constable collecting stragglers due back on ship, the group, supported by Rocks' residents, exhorted an arrestee to escape and began harassing his keepers. Hotly pursued, the officer and constable ran down to Circular Quay where they made their way onto a ship.

Now numbered at 200, the crowd made their way through the Rocks to the Clarence Street watch-house where they 'endeavoured to force in the door ... [and] demanded admittance.' Within a short time a marine arrived and convinced the majority of sailors to disperse. At this point police arrested some remaining sailors and civilians for obstruction and 'riotous conduct.' One woman was also detained for yelling, 'Let the sailors go, you set of wretches.' Most went on to receive fines of five pounds, in default of a month's jail.

In the week after the riot *Bell's Life in Sydney* claimed that 'the presence of a British vessel of war in Port Jackson has almost always been accompanied by the most disgraceful scenes of blackguardism and riot.' Issuing another of its regular calls for reform it observed that despite the regularity of such events 'the police have cut but a sorry figure' having 'yet never managed to check and prevent these disturbances, however effective [they] may have been in apprehending "some" of the rioters after all the mischief had been done.'

No testimony from the sailor involved in the arrest that sparked the riot was ever recorded. As a result we do not know the reason why they wore the clothes they did and why they chose to fight their captors. As for those who initiated the attempt to free them from detention, it may be that they only knew that an arrest had taken place and not what the person involved had been arrested for. Nevertheless, these events suggest the possibility that the breaking of gender codes was condoned and supported by at least some sailors. The initial fight in the pub also demonstrates that civilian onlookers were willing to encourage resistance to arrest from someone in non-conforming and illegal dress. Certainly none of the reports include evidence of physical or moral support for the constable involved.

More broadly, the riot demonstrates that a sizeable body of military sailors held civilian authorities and society in contempt to the point of attacking police and freeing prisoners. It also shows that a good number of Sydney residents, particularly from the Rocks, were willing, and indeed, raring to get involved in such disturbances.

CHAPTER 6
THE DUNMORE ARMS AND BRISBANE'S 'BLOOD OR BREAD' RIOTS
Iain McIntyre

During mid-1866 the recently formed colony of Queensland was enduring an economic and political crisis. This had been brought on by a confluence of developments, including the collapse of the Bank of Queensland in the wake of a major international financial downturn. Diminishing agricultural production due to drought had already led to high unemployment. This was compounded by the inability of the government to fund infrastructure via its favoured method of borrowing from British banks, shutting down key projects and sending more than 150 businesses bankrupt.

Key levels of government were respectively dominated by pastoral interests (parliament) and the merchant class (Brisbane council). These were mired in contests for power and construction, railway and other projects were regularly dogged by conflicts of interest. The malaise within public institutions was such that they were unable to swiftly and effectively deal with economic turmoil, deepening its impacts and leading to a series of political resignations and ministerial collapses.

Poverty had already been widespread in the colony and there were few forms of support for the jobless. Agitation concerning unemployment increased throughout this period, coming to a head in Brisbane on 11 September 1866 when around 500 unemployed people and supporters gathered outside the Dunmore Arms hotel (later known as the Treasury hotel) in George Street. In previous weeks railway stores had been raided in Laidley and groups of unemployed labourers from around the state had hopped trains and met in Ipswich before marching on Brisbane. Upon arrival these had joined local unemployed people to hold a public meeting and send a deputation to the government, which resulted in offers of limited rations, some work at reduced wages, and transport to other parts of the state.

Many had been placated by these concessions, but on the morning of 11 September a more militant deputation attempted to put the case for full wages and relief before the Governor. They were fobbed off and sent to the Secretary for Public Works instead. During a rowdy meeting of around 50 people a rally was called for that evening. Although some argued for another site, the Dunmore Arms was chosen as it was close to a number of key government sites as well as, according to one militant, 'plenty of stones'. It also had a balcony from which speakers could address the crowd. This feature would make pubs around Australia a regular rallying point for outdoor strike meetings and protests into the early Twentieth century.

From 8 pm a large crowd heard incendiary speeches, including one which declared:

> We did not come here to be paupers, nor to accept of charity, but to work and work we cannot get, and bread we cannot do without – and bread we will have – if we don't

get bread we will have blood. And bread or blood we will have tonight - let us do it now.

Following this call, the group immediately rushed from the pub to the city's Commissariat Store on William Street where stones were thrown and attempts made to break in the door. Authorities had already stationed artillery outside Government house and sworn in hundreds of government officials as special constables. These were not called on, but regular police read the Riot Act twice and repeatedly charged the crowd. During the fracas key activists were arrested, one for calling the Police Commissioner a 'damned scoundrel' to his face. An intervention by a Roman Catholic priest failed to move the crowd, who began to disperse after officers fixed bayonets and loaded live ammunition. It would not be until 11.30 pm that the police were able to fully regain control of the streets.

Dunmore Arms Hotel, Brisbane, 1886 (State Library Queensland)

CHAPTER 7
PAY THE RENT!: WOMBEETCH PUYUUN
Alex Ettling

In an otherwise ordinary cemetery, rises a commanding monument, a memorial obelisk for Wombeetch Puyuun, from the Leehura Gunditj Clan of the Djargurd Wurrong.

Wombeetch Puyuun, who was also known as 'Camperdown George', died of bronchitis on 26 February 26 1883, aged approximately 63. His body had been tossed into a wet bog outside of the whites-only cemetery. A white sympathiser James Dawson appealed to land owners for money for a grave stone and was disgusted at the insulting replies he received. Dawson, having dug up the body himself and placed it within the cemetery without permission, finally paid for the stone obelisk over Wombeetch's grave himself. It now serves as a memorial to all the dispossessed First Nations of Victoria's west.

Dawson had long known the man and opposed the treatment he faced. In 1872, when Wombeetch was sentenced to prison and hard labour, Dawson was so appalled that he wrote a letter to the *Camperdown Chronicle*. He remonstrated about the unfairness of a punishment doled out:

> Simply because he is black, gets drunk on spirits supplied by his Christian [sic] white brethren, makes a noise in imitation of men who under similar circumstance would be admonished by the Bench, and considered wronged by a quarter of George's sentence, without the hard labour.

Alcohol had long existed on the Australian continent prior to British colonisation. However, any large-scale production and consumption of alcohol is not in evidence. It was produced variously from fermented honey, intoxicating roots, coconut palms, soaked and pounded cones, and other sources. In contemporary times, artisanal alcohol producers exploiting First Nations knowledge, and the inappropriate use of sacred plants, has led to grievances. After a distillery in Margaret River infused a batch of gin with Moojar tree flowers, Wadandi Bibbulmun elder Sandra Hill told the

Unknown man standing beside the monument to Wombeetch Puyuun, 1885 (Davis Brothers, State Library of Victoria)

ABC, 'I think it's absolutely culturally inappropriate and absolutely rude to not consult with the elders and custodians about the use of this tree, which is our most revered tree. It's like going into a church and desecrating the idols in there.' Menang man Larry Blight added, 'If they'd have spoken to any Noongar elder they would have told them to leave that tree alone.'

The relationship between Aboriginal people and alcohol has been highly politicised since invasion, and this has continued to this day. Heavy drinking was a key feature at all levels of colonial society but racist stereotypes rapidly emerged regarding its effects on, and use by, Aboriginal people. A pattern was soon set through which laws targeting public drunkenness were regularly used to criminalise, harass, and disperse First Nations community members. In line with other racist laws, access to alcohol was eventually banned in many parts of Australia.

As with other sections of the population, prohibition and segregation – especially in the context of oppression, trauma and marginalisation – also fuelled the negative consequences of alcohol intake. Public health researcher Rob Moodie and others have argued that such bans shaped the drinking cultures that emerged in some Aboriginal communities. Rapid consumption, and resulting heavy intoxication, is more likely to occur when drinkers are trying to avoid harassment and arrest. Purchases of alcohol of varying quality, at elevated prices sometimes via the black market, are also encouraged, as well as the drinking of dangerous products containing alcohol (such as methylated spirits). As a result, restrictions can lead to an increased intake of stronger drinks in places where people are more vulnerable to violence from fellow drinkers, the police and others. Similar patterns have also arisen amongst other sections of society forced to furtively drink in non-regulated spaces.

Imprisoned on various occasions for alcohol related offences, Wombeetch felt the full brunt of social stigma and state harassment. In 1877, he fronted the magistrate's court. The offending behaviour, as reported by the *Hampden Guardian*, was 'being noisy and disagreeable, having ... been supplied with intoxicating liquor.'

The magistrate was Peter McArthur, a European migrant who had joined the lucrative ranks of the squattocracy, extracting profits from Aboriginal homelands that had been claimed as pastoral land. The magistrate was fulfilling his role in the colonial imperative to remove the traditional owners from their land and press them into missions. McArthur made a proposal to Wombeetch that he should join the Framlingham mission. Wombeetch was having none of this. It was reported that he pointedly retorted that as 'This was his country, [Wombeetch] offered to take sixpence as an instalment of the rent due by the white fellows, and the magistrate in particular.'

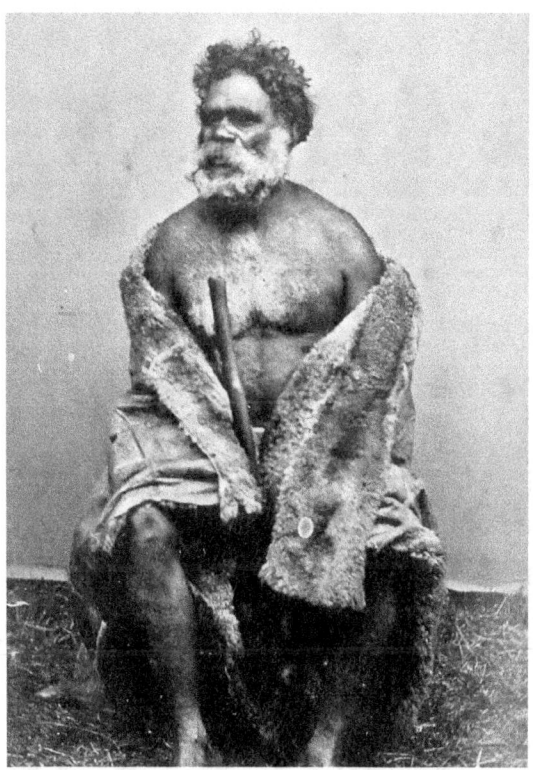

Wombeetch Puyuun, also known as Camperdown George, 1878 (Fred Kruger/State Library of Victoria)

CHAPTER 8
'MANHOOD... DROWNED OUT OF THEM WITH LIQUOR': WILLIAM LANE'S TEETOTAL UTOPIA

Jeff Sparrow

William Lane in the 1890s

> You are hereby notified that you have been expelled from the New Australia Co-operative Settlement Association for persistent and wilful violation of the clause in the mutual agreement signed by you relating to liquor drinking.

The notice posted by William Lane on Friday 15 December 1893 signalled the beginning of the end of his utopian settlement in Paraguay, at least as originally conceived.

The collapse of New Australia has been exhaustively studied ever since Lloyd Ross's 1935 account *William Lane and the Australian Labor Movement*. Yet surprisingly little attention has gone to the specific matter on which the colonists divided: namely, alcohol.

Lane, however, had no doubt as to its importance. 'Expelling drink clique,' he telegrammed back to Australia on 19 December as an explanation of his actions.

The three men he sought to exclude – Lewis Simon, a miner from Broken Hill; Thomas Westwood, a draper from South Australia; and Frederick White, a Queensland jackeroo – do not seem to have been chronic drunkards. On the voyage out, they returned 'a bit merry' from a shore visit in Montevideo; in Paraguay, they were accused of trading with locals for small quantities of spirits.

So why did their minor, drink-related infractions enrage Lane so much? What, precisely, did alcohol signify, to him and his antagonists?

William Lane was born in Bristol in 1861. The drunkenness of his father, a conservative nurseryman and florist, exposed the young William to the 'deterioration in external conditions, the frightful shattering of mental and physical health, the ruin of all domestic relations' that Engels, writing of Manchester in a slightly earlier period, attributed to drink.

In his *A Peculiar People: William Lane's Australian Utopians in Paraguay*, historian Gavin Souter suggests William, appalled at his father's behaviour, promised his mother not to indulge. That might be true, though familial alcoholism just as often produces the opposite effect. In any case, whatever the initial motivation for Lane's teetotalism, when he moved to America in 1877, his commitment became explicitly political.

Lane's arrival in the US coincided with the end of the Great Railway Strike, a shattering defeat that probably contributed to his lifelong dislike for industrial disputation. Employed as a typesetter and then as a journalist, Lane gravitated to the most significant working-class organisation of the era, the Noble and Holy Order of the Knights of Labor.

As their formal name suggests, the Knights originated as a secret fraternal order, committed to the elaborate hierarchies and rituals found in Freemasonry. Under the energetic leadership of Terence Powderly, they developed a membership of about 750 000 people, organised into a formation somewhere between a trade union and a political party.

Though the Knights played an important role in the agitation for an Eight Hour Day, they remained philosophically closer to Henry George than Karl Marx, eschewing class conflict to build 'cooperative institutions productive and distributive' that would end the hostility between capital and labour. To that end, they oriented to 'producers' – a category that included most employers – and excluded from membership only those they considered parasitical: lawyers, stockbrokers, bankers and saloonkeepers.

That last category reflected their hostility to alcohol. 'I have never touch[ed] a drop of intoxicating beverage,' explained Powderly, 'and [am] hoping I never will with the help of God.' For the Knights, drunkenness eroded the physical and mental discipline that 'producers' required to create a new society.

Some accounts suggest Lane helped organise Toronto branches for the Knights. Whatever his precise relationship with Powderly's group, the ideas Lane advocated when he emigrated to Queensland in 1885 clearly reflected the influence of the Knights of Labor.

In Brisbane, Lane quickly established himself as a journalist, while helping consolidate the newly-formed Trades and Labor Council, an organisation that, like the Knights, advocated arbitration 'to obviate, as far as possible, the necessity of "strikes".'

In 1887, Lane collaborated with the TLC secretary Alf Walker and James Drake, the future attorney-general, to launch a newspaper entitled *The Boomerang*. This described itself as 'racy of the soil' – that is, emerging from local circumstances. In particular, Lane saw the white, male workers of the Queensland bush as providing the basis for an 'Australianised' version of the Knights' co-operation, centred on what he described as 'mateship'.

For Lane, socialism could be extrapolated from bushmen's camaraderie. It was, he declared, simply 'the desire to be mates, the ideal of living together in harmony and brotherhood and loving kindness.'

In 1890, he became the founding editor of the TLC's publication *The Worker*, which he used to propagandise for a social system that would 'satisfy our desire to be mates all round.'

Yet he also worried that 'a strange apathy, the result of centuries of degradation, dulls the workers' wits and renders them powerless' – and he associated that degradation with alcohol.

In his first editorial for the *Boomerang*, Lane had declared Australia the place where 'human society will develop itself and the yet unanswered riddles of the Sphinx will be finally solved.' But an antipodean millenarian also had to confront the depressing propensity of Australians to drink.

'We are a nation of Drunkards,' explained Marcus Clarke in 1869. 'King Nobbler rules over us, and all classes bow down before him.'

Letters written by a woman called Julia Cross to her mother in Britain provide a rare glimpse of what King Nobbler did to a working class family in nineteenth century Queensland. Describing her husband George, a labourer, Cross writes how:

> when he is mad drunk which is very often I have no light in the front room and tis all benches and blocks in the kitchen so when I hear him coming I put things away and he kicks and smashes and has it all to himself only we have a peep now and then to see what he is up to, when I say we, I mean Lucy and Georgy [their children].

By the time Lane arrived in Australia, the consumption of alcohol – particularly spirits – was in decline. Nevertheless, in 1890, the Labor Electoral League's George Daniel Clark calculated that, on average, people in NSW spent far more on 'intoxicating liquors' than they did on meat, vegetables, milk, tea and other necessities (including education).

Perhaps not surprisingly, the NSW Legislative Council's Intoxicating Drink Inquiry Commission concluded 'that a large proportion of the population die prematurely from excessive drinking.'

Workers, of course, suffered the most, since the relationship to alcohol was so strongly mediated by class. Clark pointed out that, with the wealthy able to indulge in their own homes, hotels did not proliferate 'among the aristocracy of Potts Point.' In working class Miller's Point, however, grog shops abounded, as they did near wharves and factories and other workplaces. In 1887 an astonishing 855 public houses could be found within inner-metropolitan Sydney alone.

The hotels catering to working men were notorious for beverages that were either adulterated (sometimes toxically so) or low quality, or both. In 1894, Sub-Inspector Walther Lenthall, the officer responsible for monitoring alcohol quality in Sydney, explained that 'men stupefied with liquor are never seen about the clubs and first-class hotels, whose frequenters often drink double as much first-class liquor as many an unfortunate drunkard and who gets the rubbish.'

In 1885, the year he arrived in Australia, Lane wrote a widely-circulated article in which he disguised himself as an alcoholic to investigate the appalling conditions of the 'drunk cells' in the Brisbane watchhouse.

Then as now, alcohol was linked with criminality. In the 1880s and 1890s, around 30 to 40 per cent of arrests and criminal convictions were said to be drink related.

For Lane, that association made drinking an obvious threat to working class organisation.

In the *Worker*, he discussed the case of John Walsh, the longstanding secretary of the Rockhampton Wharf Labourers Union, who had been charged with drinking away union funds. Rather than simply denouncing Walsh, Lane chastised the membership for electing a known drinker, and thus providing Walsh with opportunities to ruin himself. Lane wrote:

> We must insist on temperance and stamp out drunkenness if we are ever going to do any good for ourselves – this none hold more strongly than many who drink to excess. And we can begin by blocking from all prominence in the Organisation of Labour those who cannot at all times be relied upon to be themselves, thus making the tone of the movement even more pronouncedly teetotal than it already is.

That later became part of the rationale for the alcohol ban in Paraguay, with Lane calling on moderate drinkers to abstain for the sake of those with an addiction. In the journal established by the settlement movement, he wrote:

> In New Australia we want an arena where the one-time victim of drink can fight the demon fairly, downed by none but helped by mately hands all round him. The man who is not willing, for the sake of a weaker brother or sister, to forego his own pleasure to the extent of an occasional glass, has never realised what mateship means and had better keep outside the New Australia ring fence.

Lane's position was far from unusual in the late nineteenth century labour movement where, for instance, the vast majority of the 35 men elected to the NSW parliament under the banner of the new Labor Party were public abstainers. Yet his preoccupation with mateship as the basis for co-operation gave his argument a distinctive twist, most apparent in his novel *The Workingman's Paradise*, which he wrote to raise funds for men imprisoned after the shearers' strike.

By the 1890s, alcohol consumption seems to have been considerably higher in the major population centres in other states than in Queensland. The ironic title of *The Workingman's Paradise* thus presents Sydney as, in Brien Kernan's words, 'the centre of the exploitative capitalism that is dominating the whole continent', deforming its inhabitants and preventing them from being 'mates'. When the socialist Nellie educates the Queensland bushman Ned about the reality of the city, she devotes considerable time to denouncing alcohol. In one passage, she describes a drinker as 'worse than a blackleg', explaining:

> it's drink that makes most of the blacklegs, anyway. Most of them are men whose manhood has been drowned out of them with liquor and the weak men in the unions are the drunkards who have no heart when the whisky's out of them.

Nellie's reference to 'manhood' extends the argument beyond a tactical concern about liquor's consequences for a strike, linking alcohol to the degeneration of essentialised traits of working-class men and women.

In a key scene, Nellie, whose face shows her 'intense womanliness', takes Ned, who exudes 'a dashing manliness in every motion', to Paddy's Market, where he is appalled at 'the crushing, hustling, pushing mass of humans, some buying, more bartering, most swept aimlessly along in the living currents that moved ceaselessly to and fro.'

> All around were like this. All! All! All! Everyone in this swarming multitude of working Sydney. On the faces of all was misery written. Buyers and sellers and passers-by alike were hateful of life. And if by chance he saw now and then a fat dame at a stall or a lusty huckster pushing his wares or a young couple, curious and loving, laughing and joking as they hustled along arm in arm, he seemed to see on their faces the dawning lines that in the future would stamp them also with the brand of despair.

For Lane, the metropolis destroyed an innate 'manliness' and 'womanliness', characteristics that, like the mateship they enabled, could not be legislated but arose from nature itself.

'[If] things were once fixed right,' he argued, 'we should no more need laws to make healthy men good mates than we need laws to make healthy women good mothers.'

Elsewhere, he put the same argument in reverse, claiming 'our civilisation is slaying us all, all that is best in us, all that is manly and brave and true.'

That was the basis for establishing New Australia: as its newsletter explained, the settlement would create 'a society where individually and severally as well as socially, every man and woman shall be able to live a straight, honest and manly or womanly life.'

Lane urged those 'who long to be manly, to be true, to be what men should be' to leave what he called 'this hateful life, the life that is full of unspoken misery, of heart-sickening longing, of evil habits growing with the years of sin and slavery that lead to nothing but death.'

Nellie's claim that 'a man who has a drink in him isn't a man' identified alcohol as a facet of the corrosion associated with the capitalist city. But it was not the only one.

In another passage Nellie discussed 'the round-cheeked, bland-faced Chinaman', explaining that 'this yellow man and such men as he were watching them all slowly going down lower and lower, were waiting to leap upon them in their last helplessness and enslave them all...'

Race was a key theme for Lane, for whom capitalism and eugenic decline went together. 'Our children,' he warned, 'must be white in order that they may take the lamp of progress from us and be able to keep it burning for the generation to come.'

The Knights of Labor had held contradictory ideas about race. They organised black members (at a time when that was vanishingly rare) yet argued for the exclusion of Chinese immigrants. When Lane 'Australianised' his politics, he abandoned the progressive elements of the Knights 'co-operativism' to champion the White Australia racism prevalent in the labour movement.

In his doctrine, the corruption that endangered bush mateship involved miscegenation as well as alcohol. If drink eroded

Cosme kindergarten in 1898

'manliness' and 'womanliness', it also facilitated eugenic degeneration. As the bohemian socialist Stratton explains in *The Workingman's Paradise*, 'let our women once become brutalised, masculinised, and there will be no hope for anything but a Chinese existence.'

In 1888, Lane published a serialised novel entitled *White or Yellow? A Story of the Race-War of AD 1908*, in which a certain Lord Stibbins conspires with the millionaire Sir Wong to let the Chinese take over Queensland. The last instalment of the text appeared on the same day a drunken mob launched a vicious anti-Chinese pogrom in Brisbane. David Crouch notes the presence of a certain 'Mr W Lane' among the jury that acquitted the only rioter arrested.

Lane's racism underpinned his New Australia colony, a project that Verity Burgmann suggests was conceived partly in reaction to the passage of the Polynesian Labourers' Bill in 1892. The refusal of the Queensland government to prevent indentured Islanders toiling in the cane fields rendered, he thought, the state – and, indeed, the nation – unfit for white men, with Lane vowing he would 'rather see his daughter dead in her coffin than kissing [a black man] on the mouth or nursing a little coffee-coloured brat that she was mother to.'

He planned his settlement explicitly as an ethno-state, where socialistic mateship and defined gender roles would flourish free of alcohol, non-whites and other corruptions.

The association Lane made between alcohol and racial decline explains his fury at the 'drink clique'. When the settlers' ship reached Montevideo, he had posted a notice forbidding colonists from going ashore, arguing that the locals might resent European immigrants. Lane and his supporters denounced the imbibers as 'scabs' (an insult that nearly provoked a knife fight) not merely because they were tipsy but because of the possibility they'd caroused with non-whites.

Similarly, the drinking that enraged Lane in Paraguay involved the men socialising with the locals. The New Australians were accused of trading communal tools for liquor – and, according to a Lane supporter, one of the drinkers 'openly announced his intention of bringing a native woman into the colony to live with him.'

For Lane, the infractions represented his worst fears. The men wanted alcohol and miscegenation, both of which threatened his understanding of 'mateship'. That was why he felt entirely justified in threatening to call the police unless the offenders departed.

After the incident, the split widened between an anti-Lane faction calling themselves the 'Rebels' and those known as the 'Royalists'. On 12 May 1894, Lane gathered his supporters and moved them to a new location, where they established a fresh colony known as Cosme. They described Cosme as a 'Commonhold of English speaking whites, who accept among their principles Life marriage, Teetotalism and the Color Line.'

But if Lane's doctrine explains his outrage over drink, how might we understand the behaviour of his opponents? They had knowingly signed onto the New Australia project. Why did they fall out with Lane over alcohol?

The relationship between drink and working-class Australia was, of course, far more complicated than Lane allowed.

Quentin Beresford argues that many workers in the late nineteenth-century retained an older attitude to alcohol as 'health-giving and a necessary adjunct to labour', with drinking a customary accompaniment for certain trades. Sailors, for instance, swore that grog helped them 'get through ten times the quantity of work that they would otherwise do.' In many trades, drinking was customary at lunch, as well as after work.

The reliance on alcohol also reflected an absence of other alternatives. Many working class neighbourhoods still lacked an adequate

Travelers to *New Australia* aboard the Royal Tar in 1893 (State Library of NSW)

Group photo of colonists at Cosme

supply of clear water. Milk was often contaminated; soft drinks were expensive, difficult to obtain and not necessarily very pleasant.

Most obviously, for all the devastation caused by alcohol, it also served as a relaxant and a source of pleasure for people enduring difficult lives. As Henry Lawson famously said, 'beer makes you feel the way you ought to feel without beer.'

The division between the drinking habits of the wealthy and the poor exacerbated the damage that alcohol did to workers. Yet it also meant drink was indelibly linked with working-class culture, particularly for men. Susan Doyle explains:

> Lower-class men did most of their drinking in pubs where a masculinist culture flourished. Here married men found a retreat from domestic squalor and demands in the companionship of other men. Single men living in boarding-houses found it more welcoming in the evenings than a comfortless room. Men could drink, smoke and swear freely. They could play at cards or dice and wager in a small way on the games. Bets on the races could be placed with SP bookmakers and race results received, delivered by lightning messengers within minutes of the event. Gossip could be exchanged, keeping one in touch not only with local goings-on but with stories and scuttlebutt which kept the entire city humming. Country visitors could get their bearings and 'receive proper elucidation'. Except in the poorest houses, free lunches were available for the price of a drink. Indeed the claim was made that 'publicans had done more for the working man, with their counter luncheons, than the combined efforts of teetotallers and parsons... It is the only meal they often have of a day.'

In other words, the masculine traits that Lane admired were, for most Australians, deeply entwined with the alcohol he condemned.

In one of the best-known passages from *The Workingman's Paradise*, Ned declaims about 'mateship', explaining that the very word 'mate' makes him 'feel good, just the sound of it.' He tells a story of a shearer named Bill, who defines 'mates' as 'them wot's got one pus [purse].'

> If I go to a shed with Jack an' we're mates an' I earn forty quid and Jack gets sick an' only earns ten or five or mebbe nothin' at all we put the whole lot in one pus, or if it's t'other way about an' Jack earns the forty it don't matter. There's one pus no matter how much each of earns an' it b'longs just the same to both of us alike. If Jack's got the pus and I want half-a-crown, I says to Jack, says I, 'Jack, gimme the pus.' And if Jack wants ten quid or twenty or the whole lot he just says to me, 'Bill,' says he, 'gimme the pus.' I don't ask wot he's goin' to take and I don't care. He can take it all if he wants to.

Ned is, however, a teetotaller and so does not acknowledge that the pooling of resources he describes most often took place in the pub. In the 1890s, solitary drinkers were frowned upon, with men expected to buy drinks (or 'shout') for others. Accordingly, a group of men drinking together behaved as if they were 'them wot's got one pus'. As Susan Doyle says, 'the practice of shouting... facilitated social bonding through reciprocity among peers... to avoid one's shout was one of the most unacceptable of all public acts and could result in social obloquy.'

For the rural workers Lane idealised, 'mateship' was also connected to what Robin Room calls 'the tradition of 'work and burst', in which they bonded on sprees 'often in town, at the end and on the proceeds of a hard spell of work in the bush.'

Henry Lawson thus defined 'mateship' in terms of a bushman's desire to have someone 'to comfort him and argue with him, and work and tramp and drink with him'. For Lawson, drinking was fundamental to the

Anglo-Australian identity that Lane sought to harness – it was, he argued, partly through drinking that a rural worker earned the title 'white man'.

We can see, then, why those committed to Lane's vision for a white settlement in Paraguay might still dispute with him over alcohol. They might join in the New Australia marching anthem, with its chorus:

> Shoulder to shoulder, mates,
> Shoulders together,
> Hand clasped in hand, my mates,
> Fair and foul weather,
> Hearts beating close, my mates,
> Each man a brother,
> Building a home, my mates,
> All for each other.

But the very mateship they celebrated could also mandate the masculine ritual of shouting each other drinks in Montevideo after a long voyage or celebrating the establishment of a new home in Paraguay with a few bottles.

In a sense, the principles the 'drink clique' shared with Lane fuelled the outrage with which the dissidents responded to his attempts to discipline them.

'In our opinion,' they wrote in response, 'we have been unjustly treated, and our individual liberties have been unduly interfered with. Hard words have been said and deeds have been done which, in our opinion, render reconciliation upon our existing basis absolutely impossible.'

The dispute among the New Australians represented, in microcosm, a broader argument playing out among the labour movement internationally.

In Britain, for instance, most of the key activists associated with the New Unionism – Ben Tillett, Tom Mann, Charles Fenwick, Thomas Burn, John Wilson and John Burns – publicly declared their opposition to alcohol, with Burns arguing that it represented 'the Circean cup that is offered by a callous dominant class to those whom otherwise they could not enslave.'

Yet, as the pioneer British Marxist Harry Quelch noted, the mainstream temperance movement sought to impose abstinence on workers from without, in ways that ordinary people saw as an intolerable infringement on customary liberties. He argued:

> Surely, if a workman is to have any freedom at all, it should be freedom to spend and enjoy in his own way the leisure and wages he has earned by his own labour. If his way and his tastes do not commend themselves to his 'betters,' let them show him a 'more excellent way,' and provide him with opportunities for the cultivation of higher tastes and for more rational pleasures.... The whole movement is based on the assumption

Cover of *The Worker* during Lane's time as editor

that the workingman is a vile, incorrigible, drunken beast, incapable of self-control.

On a similar basis, Karl Kautsky, the major theoretician of pre-war Marxism, deployed his considerable authority against a faction seeking to impose a temperance policy upon German social democracy.

Kautsky acknowledged the problems caused by alcohol abuse but rejected moralism in favour of a historical analysis. 'Like drink,' he argued, 'so has the drinker, so has the way to drink changed as a result of the revolution in the conditions of production.'

Modern capitalism fostered such misery that a certain percentage of the population sought to obliterate themselves with the intensely alcoholic *schnapps* distilled by the German landowners (or 'junkers') precisely for that purpose. But that did not alter the social significance of the taverns in which working class people gathered, both to socialise and to organise.

Kautsky argued:

> The only bulwark of the proletariat's political freedom that cannot be confiscated from it so easily is the tavern.... If the temperance movement were to succeed... in convincing German workers to stay away from the tavern en masse, they would have achieved what the anti-socialist laws never came close to: the destruction of the cohesion of the proletariat.

The SPD duly supported a *schnapps* boycott while continuing to meet in the working-class taverns.

Where Kautsky sought a dialectical and materialist response to the drink question, Lane employed a very different methodology.

In the late 1880s, Lane had published an edition of the *Communist Manifesto* from which he omitted the passages denouncing utopian socialist ventures as reactionary and 'doomed to failure', presumably because he recognised that Marx and Engels were polemicising against projects very much like his own. Michael Wilding claims that Lane's project should not be seen as 'utopian retreat' but rather 'an attempt to produce a vanguard for the revolution.' But the utopian socialism of the past was invariably presented in that way, too: imagined as an exemplar for others to follow.

Marx and Engels argued utopian colonies foundered because their architects built upon arbitrary moral principles that they sought to implement in isolation from the rest of society. Small-scale communities, no matter how carefully designed, could not escape the capitalism they claim to challenge. Geographical seclusion might enable subsistence farming but, almost by definition, atavistic modes of agriculture could not support social progress.

Accordingly, such communities either resigned themselves to material and cultural impoverishment or relied on the exchange of commodities for the products and services they could not supply themselves (or a combination of two). Commodity exchange meant they must (as per Marx's Law of Value) adopt the norms (in terms intensity of labour, productivity, technology, etc) set by other capitalists – for, if they did not, they went broke. Collective self-management usually gave way to collective self-exploitation, which created schisms between those who pragmatically adapted to capitalist norms and the more ideological members defending their original commitments through moral exhortation and authoritarianism.

That was more-or-less exactly how New Australia played out, with alcohol serving as a cypher for a more fundamental schism.

For the three men who shared a mately drink in Montevideo, the accusation of scabbery demonstrated the authoritarianism of an out-of-touch leader. In New Australia itself, the necessity of trade trumped, for the dissidents, Lane's dogma of racial isolation.

In his diary, Tom Westwood wrote of establishing friendly relations with the local people. 'At 11 o'clock had a good meal at the priest's house. He produced a bottle of wine of his own making and good wine too.' This was not the binge of a desperate alcoholic but a recognition that, to live any kind of life in Paraguay, the newcomers needed to ditch Lane's dogma of racial isolation.

For Lane, on the other hand, drinking constituted blacklegging – an egregious abandonment of principle. Yet, because the colony rested purely on ethical pledges, his only recourse lay in bureaucratic threats and shrill restatements of principle. Symptomatically, Lane's rhetoric became overtly religious as he started declaring communism 'part of God's law.'

The anti-Lane 'Rebels' eventually either returned to Australia or discarded co-operative principles to farm much as their neighbours did.

The Loyalists who followed Lane to Cosme maintained, by sheer effort, a white, teetotal community for some years. Yet it never really prospered. After failing to attract new members on a recruiting tour, in 1899 Lane moved his family to New Zealand where he reinvented himself as an overt reactionary. By 1909, the people remaining at Cosme had also abandoned collectivism in favour of private farming.

New Australia did not collapse because of alcohol. It failed because of the inherent contradictions of William Lane's utopianism – with the cultural ambiguities of alcohol providing the form in which those contradictions played out.

New Australia journal in 1893

CHAPTER 9
ALCOHOL AND CELEBRATIONS OF THE EIGHT HOUR DAY
Iain McIntyre

Pubs and alcohol played a major role in the early years of the eight hour movement and the commemorations that followed its attainment. In Melbourne the Operative Mason's Society was restarted, following a period of dormancy due to members leaving for the goldfields, at Clark's Hotel in Collingwood during 1853. Meetings of this and other unions were later held at Fitzroy's Belvidere Hotel. This would serve as the initial place where plans were made to campaign for the eight hour day. Subsequently it would be the place to which building workers marched to celebrate their successful strike for a shorter working week on 21 April 1856. The venue would later feature meetings to successfully send Victorian Eight Hours Labor League vice-president Charles Jardine Don to parliament.

Victories around working hours by individual trades in different cities, towns and suburbs were generally followed by celebratory dinners and other events held in pubs. Featuring speeches and numerous toasts, some of these became annual fixtures. The popularity of the movement was strong enough to see two Eight Hour hotels open at different times in Sydney, with a similarly named pub also trading in Melbourne.

Melbourne's first commemorative eight hour day street parade was held in May 1856 and yearly April events followed thereafter. The number of trades represented steadily swelled, as did the place of the anniversary in Victorian society. In 1879 a public holiday was won for people to attend the celebrations, which they were now doing in their tens of thousands. Public holidays were also gained in other places and marches held on locally significant dates.

Commemorations not only expressed pride in union achievements but were also vehicles for demonstrating support for their entrenchment and expansion. They also articulated and represented working class power more broadly.

During parades workers expressed pride in their work, and exhibited the materials, products, and skills involved, through depictions on banners and floats, as well as live demonstrations. This meant that representations of alcohol were displayed by brewery workers, bar staff, barrel and bottle makers, and others.

Marches were generally followed by carnivals incorporating picnics, sporting galas, concerts, lotteries, dances, and banquets. The provision and role of alcohol at these was sometimes controversial. This was in part because of the desire of movement leaders to project respectability and moderation.

Despite the risk that alcohol influenced behaviour posed, organisers did not typically ban intoxicants as to do so would have been highly unpopular and cut into fundraising. As a result they occasionally had to deal with contentious events, such as those that occurred in Adelaide in 1882 when a series of condemnatory articles and letters appeared in local newspapers. These claimed that during the anniversary's afternoon dance, 'drunken folks of both sexes' had been witnessed 'dancing, sweating, cursing, fighting, glass-smashing and indulging in other amusements of the like nature.' Reports regarding 'terminal orgies' by 'objectionable characters' and 'degraded looking males and females', as well as of 'men dancing with each other', reflected conservative fears regarding youth and the lower orders. They were also used to attack the eight hour system itself, with one correspondent claiming 'leisure means larrikinism.'

In contrast, an article in the *Adelaide Advertiser* argued 'considering that there were about 6000 or 7000 persons present, if, indeed, there were not more, the amount or drunkenness was remarkably small ... the crowd was as a rule more good humoured than fightable, and very few disturbances occurred.' Similarly an editorial in the *South Australian Register* held that the working people of Adelaide 'scored a conspicuous success in the manner in which they carried out Friday's demonstration.'

For its part the Eight Hours' Demonstration Committee claimed that there had only been three fights during the entire day and that glasses were broken due to 'a loose trestle being accidentally overturned.' Reports of 'hooting and yelling' and the venue 'being taken by storm' were dismissed as 'purely the work of imagination.' To ensure that future events would not be threatened a deputation visited the Colonial Secretary to lock in his support. They were successful in doing so and continued lobbying saw the government concede an Eight Hour Day holiday for the following year.

Worker from the Warracknabeal based EC Stevens Brewery and Aerated Waters Factory in their 8 Hours Day parade costume, circa 1910 (State Library of Victoria)

CHAPTER 10
ANTI-CHINESE RACISM AND THE LIFE OF PUBLICANS JIMMY AND EVELINA AH FOO
Alex Ettling and Iain McIntyre

Jimmy and Evelina Ah Foo, circa 1900

Jimmy Ah Foo, was a Queensland publican who ran a number of hotels with his wife in the late nineteenth century, becoming one of the state's best known Chinese immigrants in the process. Born in the Guangzhou district of China around 1843, he had travelled to Australia by the 1860s and based himself in the central highlands town of Springsure. Travelling to Rockhampton in 1866, he married Evelina Vessey (sometimes spelled Evelyna), an immigrant of Irish extraction who had been born in Lincolnshire, England.

In 1873 the couple gave up their store and market garden and moved to Queensland's northern goldfields, where they operated a series of pubs, including the Canton Hotel in Thornborough and another venue at Cooktown. It could be a dangerous profession. Jimmy was shot on 3 April 1876 after he tried to prevent a Chinese immigrant, who owed him money, from leaving his pub.

Many of Queensland's smaller rural towns were subject to economic volatility. Populations rapidly grew and collapsed depending on how long gold and other minerals lasted, as well as due to seasonal and price variations in agricultural products. As with many rural Queenslanders, the Ah Foos would regularly relocate over the coming decades in response to such changes.

In 1877 the family moved back to Springsure, where they ran the Post Office Hotel and the Carriers' Arms. At the time of their return, locals of Chinese descent also held the licenses for the Shearers' Arms and the Springsure Hotel. The latter would eventually come under the control of the Ah Foo family. As one of the few Chinese immigrants to become a naturalised British citizen, Jimmy was able to free select and buy land. He did so, acquiring and selling a series of farms and properties.

After Springsure entered a period of economic decline the family moved on to Barcaldine in the 1880s, where they took over the Terminus hotel. Their affection for their previous locale, and perhaps the hotel they'd kept there, was reflected in the choice of name for a new venue they built. Advertising for the pub in 1887 declared:

> When you come to town, whate'er you do,
> Call at the house kept by Jimmy Ah Foo;
> Accommodation, stabling and liquors
> of the best,
> In short, the Springsure Hotel
> is the travellers' rest.

An incident occurred in the following decade which reflected the strong current of racism present in Anglo-Australian society. Built on land seized from First Nations owners, the British colonies which came to be known as Australia were based on imperial racial hierarchies and ideas from the beginning. Although borders would become increasingly policed over time, initially access to the country was relatively open to a range of settlers and visitors. Nevertheless, on top of discrimination and stereotypes meted out to people hailing from different parts of the British-Irish Isles, people from other parts of the world were subject to ranking and racism on the basis of background and appearance.

As the nineteenth century unfolded a particularly virulent set of ideas and practices came to target people of Chinese descent. As with other forms of racism it evolved alongside, and interacted with, strains of oppression based on class, gender and other designated characteristics while simultaneously depicting the communities under attack as a homogenous mass.

By the latter decades of the nineteenth century much of Australia's union movement had adopted racist ideas and embraced a strategy of improving wages and conditions for those designated 'white' through the organised exclusion of those who were viewed as otherwise. Non-whites came to be positioned as innate class enemies destined to undermine prevailing labour standards. This was regardless of the fact that the overwhelming majority were working class themselves and that there were plenty of instances of them fighting bosses from all cultural backgrounds. Indeed, as related in an essay by socialist historian Liam Ward, in 1852 Chinese shepherds carried out the first ever recorded strike in what would eventually become Queensland. In doing so they employed many of the tactics that radical bush workers would use in the late 1880s and 1890s, including arming themselves and occupying employers' property.

Although there were exceptions, attempts by Chinese workers to join existing unions were generally denied. As a result, the radical voices of those who pointed to the interests and enemies that all workers shared were sidelined. In the context of rising racist action across society came an incident that specifically targeted the Ah Foo family as publicans. Writing in the *Western Champion's* Pencil Point column in 1907 Phil Harum claimed:

> During the [Barcaldine] shearing trouble
> of '91 Jimmy professed unlimited sympathy
> with the 'tall, western bushmen' that
> crowded into the strike camps of the West
> ... Naturally, like the big majority of western
> hostelries of the day, Jimmy employed a
> Chinese cook. This did not suit his union
> supporters, and they conveyed the fact to
> him in language that was as plain as it was
> forcible. If he wished to retain the support
> of the unionists, and the privilege of placing

many drinks upon the slate that would be settled when the cruel strike was over, he must dispense with the services of his chef ... Sacking the cook was an easy matter. Jimmy promptly complied with the request, and – went [to work in] the kitchen himself.

This version, including the Barcaldine location, unionists' fondness for the publican, and Jimmy taking over cooking duties in response to the boycott threat, would be repeated in recollections published in the *Australian Worker* in 1927, the *Sunday Mail* in 1933, and *The World News* in 1953. Reports carried in newspapers during the late 1890s included the same events but placed them in Longreach during 1896.

Regardless of their veracity, it was true that during the Ah Foos' time as publicans rural unions across Queensland carried out concerted and recurring campaigns to remove cooks and other workers of Asian descent from hotels and stations. On the back of mass recruiting drives and successes in forcing some pastoralists to only employ unionists in shearing in 1890, the labour movement moved to expand the closed shop. This could have been done on a non-racial basis. Instead, at the beginning of the shearer's strike in January 1891 Roma, Minnie Downs, Bowen Downs and other towns and districts saw stations and pubs targeted in what the *Barrier Miner* described as a 'crusade against Chinese cooks.'

In Barcaldine a torchlit march of up to 2000 unionists on 28 February took in stops at hotels, possibly including the Ah Foos' pub. Establishments employing Chinese kitchen staff were hooted, while those with Anglo-Saxon cooks were cheered. Subsequently, a state wide boycott of Chinese cooks and market gardeners was declared for 1 March.

Finding replacements beyond what was described as the 'Johnny-cake and salted cook' variety was difficult. A common response from hoteliers was that if unions wanted to dictate hiring practices then they would also need to ensure a flow of alternative labour. The licensee of the Commercial Hotel in Clermont, a Mrs Mullin, cited this, and the fact she had employed her current cook for 16 years, as reasons for resisting union demands. She was promptly boycotted. In Tambo two hotels went through six white cooks in four weeks before rehiring Chinese staff.

Photos of the Afoo Family Band, circa 1900s

Campaigns against cooks spread interstate, resulting in an incident in Molong, NSW where a Shearers' Union agent was booed and threatened during an April 1891 lecture after questioning revealed that he was staying at a hotel which employed a Chinese cook. The agent's attempt to build the Molong branch was brought to an end after attendees walked out en masse. Later in the year existing rules prohibiting union representatives from staying at pubs with Chinese employees were bolstered, with exceptions only allowed in cases where alternatives could not be accessed.

This strategy of exclusion, unsurprisingly, did not help the unions to avoid major defeat in 1891, nor during later shearers' strikes. Nevertheless it continued to be implemented. Boycotts, in areas such as Brisbane, Chillagoe and Cairns, were again used as a tactic to compel employers to remove Chinese and Japanese cooks from pubs and stations during the 1920s. Support for exclusionary practices in workplaces was regularly sought by union delegations to employers' associations and government ministers. It was also promoted through racist depictions and cartoons in labour and mainstream newspapers, including one in 1907 which referenced the Ah Foo incident. Such racism ultimately did no favours for the workers' cause, only creating unnecessary barriers towards industrial cooperation.

Although they undoubtedly faced racism, there does not appear to have been any overt or official move by unions to remove the Ah Foos from their position as proprietors of hotels. Indeed, with the household expanding to include 13 children, all of whom were given a musical education, the family broadened its involvement in the entertainment industry through the formation of what became known as 'Affoo Family' bands. Upon their arrival in Barcaldine in 1887 the eldest daughters had joined the local Ethiopic and Dramatic club, with one described in a local newspaper as having 'a soprano voice of peculiar sweetness.' In the coming years other family members would form brass and string acts. Beyond involvement in local societies and performances at fundraisers and concerts, the children supplied entertainment for patrons and music for dances at their parent's pubs.

By the end of 1896 the Ah Foos had once more relocated, this time to Longreach, where they built the two story Federal Hotel. Their children continued to perform within pubs and also headed up the town band. The family then engaged in what the Australian Chinese Museum describes as 'a brief and disastrous hotel venture in Rockhampton in 1899.'

Following this Jimmy and Evelina appear to have given up being licensees altogether. They returned to Barcaldine where they found stability, running a store and market garden until 1916. Retiring to Longreach, Jimmy passed away in 1918, followed shortly after by his wife. Some of their children married into local pastoral and business elites, while others continued to work in the entertainment industry, running pubs, performing and teaching music, and opening some of the first cinemas in the region.

CHAPTER 11

'STUBBORN STRUGGLES': BEER STRIKES IN WESTERN AUSTRALIA, 1901–1925

Iain McIntyre

The tactic of boycotting individuals, businesses and organisations by ostracising them, refusing to work for or supply them, or to purchase their products, dates back millennia. Mainly associated today with lifestyle choices and large scale environmental, union and anti-discrimination campaigns, historically boycotts in Australia were often grassroots campaigns focused on industrial disputes and the cost of living.

In the first half of the twentieth century one of the key places of organised disputation over consumption in Australia were pubs and other alcohol-based venues. Popularly known as 'beer strikes', hundreds of boycott campaigns saw drinkers refuse to patronise some or all of the hotels in a locality until their demands were met. Grievances were often focused on the cost of alcohol but, with pubs providing many services, issues such as the price and quality of accommodation and food, and the treatment of employees and patrons, also acted as a catalyst.

Sporadic beer strikes were recorded in the 1880s and a wave of union boycotts targeted pubs employing workers of Chinese descent in Queensland during the 1890s. It was not until the twentieth century that beer strikes began to occur on a regular and widespread basis.

Although unions were not often involved in an official capacity, many campaigns involved unionists and used forms of organisation, mobilisation and action commonly seen in industrial disputes. These included the establishment of committees, the drawing up of a log of claims, visits by deputations, the holding of public meetings, and formal votes on the outcome of negotiations. In some cases hotels were picketed and fines and other penalties meted out to campaign members who broke vows of temporary abstinence.

Beer strikes were overwhelmingly led by and involved Anglo-Celtic male drinkers. To some extent this cohort had always dominated pubs. However cultural and legal shifts, largely driven by the temperance movement and the White Australia Policy, further pushed female, Chinese, Aboriginal and other drinkers out of hotels during the late nineteenth and early twentieth centuries. Women were involved in boycotts on occasion, but usually as workers within pubs rather than consumers.

Western Australia experienced a wave of beer strikes in the early part of the twentieth century. The practice became particularly popular on the goldfields and the majority of disputes occurred in regional areas, in part because these were typically subject to monopoly and cartel-like behaviour. As one of the first forms of infrastructure to be built, pubs also played an outsized role in the life of newly established settlements.

Many of the WA districts involved in the earliest boycotts were dominated by mining and prospecting. These areas typically featured a concentration of unaccompanied males for whom pubs were a key source of entertainment and relief from gruelling work in harsh conditions. The practice of beer strikes likely spread between unionists and other workers via travel and networks. The involvement of alcohol also made these disputes a perennial favourite with newspapers and heavy media coverage further promoted and popularised the practice.

The following chronology traces the growth and spread of beer strikes in WA from the beginning of the twentieth century through to the first time a major wave extended across the most populous areas of the state's southwest. In providing a sample of the dozens of disputes which took place during this time it casts a light on the determination, wit and tactics of those involved in what one newspaper described as 'stubborn struggles.'

1901, Collie

In one of the first recorded instances of such action in Western Australia, members of the Collie River Districts Miners Association formed a committee which resolved to 'devise ways and means' of reducing 'the exorbitant charges made by the publicans' in the town. Living on wages of nine shillings a day locals claimed it was unfair to expect them to sustain the price of six pence (half a shilling) per pint. They also complained of profiteering. The price of other consumer items were barely above those in Perth, 160km to the north, while beer was double.

After public meetings and negotiations came to naught, publicans were given warning on 9 October 1901, via a letter and notices posted around the town, that a beer strike would ensue within a week. The Chairman of the Collie Licensed Victuallers Association, representing the town's seven pubs, dismissed the threat as 'most unreasonable.' Citing recently introduced federal excises, and costs associated with wages and rents, he offered to open his books to complainants. He further claimed in a newspaper interview with the *Collie Miner* that the beer strike was contrary to the committee's 'own principles of unionism' as 'if an organised attempt was made to reduce their rate of pay for coal-cutting to 3s 6d per ton they would be the first to complain.'

While some publicans dismissed strikers as 'beer swipers' in the press, claiming they would be unable to maintain the boycott, other businesspeople feared the spectre of collective action. Citing previous cases in which residents had threatened to establish a cooperative store, one retailer declared that it was the start of 'a reign of terrorism' against 'the trade of the town.' Claims that the action would cut off small business support for strikes in the future

Midland Junction Hotel, 1924 (Midland and Districts Historical Society)

The inside of Tattersalls Hotel in Boulder, date unknown (June O'Brien, Eastern Goldfields Historical Society)

were dismissed in a letter from a unionist which stated 'it would be easier for the miners to extract Bovril from blowflies.'

1902, Mulline

The first of many beer strikes to take place on the Western Australian goldfields saw concerted picketing of Mulline's two hotels to back demands that prices be reduced from one shilling to six pence per pint. The four month dispute was closely watched across the region and letters and telegrams of support sent from various towns. In late January two barrels of beer sent from nearby Menzies were loaded onto a dray and transported from hotel to hotel where strikers toasted the empty bars and sang 'For he's a jolly good fellow' to honour the anonymous donor. A few non-unionists who tried to sneak a drink in during proceedings were unceremoniously turned away.

Despite strikers singing temperance songs and wearing the movement's blue sash, attempts by the Young Men's Christian Association to convert them to long term abstention failed. For a period, miners instead ran their own bar on Saturday nights, charging only three pence a pint.

The eventual collapse of the strike was credited to the organising committee agreeing to a three-day suspension in hostilities during a visit by the state government's Minister for Mines. Having again tasted the pleasures of beer on demand in their usual haunts, the majority of strikers were unable to return to the fray.

Four years later locals called a second beer strike at an open-air meeting in the main street. An early attempt by a publican to lure them off the wagon by donating a keg of beer to celebrate a football match failed after players and the crowd drank it and then promptly swore off alcohol once more. Despite holding out for a further four months this boycott also collapsed. With prices still riding high, beer strikers would try once more in 1912.

1903, Kookynie

During a campaign for lower prices, posters were placed on hotel windows after a public meeting resolved to treat anyone found drinking in them as a 'blackleg.' Pickets carried out patrols, taking down the names of strike breakers, which they promised would be 'printed and broadcast throughout the state.' During the second week of the strike one letter writer claimed:

> Feeling here runs very high on the subject, and one person found drinking got a hiding, and had to seek police protection from the just fury of the multitude ... We are, in short, resolved to get sixpenny beers or die in the attempt or, worse still, join the cold water brigade.

With reports of Saturday pay days being 'the quietest ever seen', the gap in entertainment was filled by open air meetings of up to 200 people as well as the holding of football matches and other events. At one point strikers sang 'My drink is water bright, from the crystal springs', while parading up and down the main street with bank books tied into their buttonholes to demonstrate the amount of money publicans had lost. After spurning offers of compromise the campaign won after four weeks, gaining six pence pints.

1903, Burtville

In the course of a three week boycott, which successfully halved the price of beer, pickets regularly dunked would-be strike breakers in horse troughs outside pubs. At one point, a banner flown at a football game in nearby Laverton bore a cartoon of a blackleg in a trough with the warning 'Beware.'

1903, Mt Morgans

Following the win at Burtville, miners at nearby Mount Morgans refused to spend their earnings at the town's six hotels until the price of a pint was similarly reduced from a shilling to six pence. Holding their own 'smoker' at the Amalgamated Workers' Association hall they announced that all names of boycott breakers would be written down and publicly shared. Deputations to all the pubs and a procession through town, followed by drinks on the football oval, saw the town's hoteliers cave in within 72 hours.

1903, Feysville

With beer strikes extending across the Eastern goldfields, taking in Pig Well and Four Mile as well as other locales, members of the Feysville Miners Union became the next to foreswear their refreshments. Adopting the watchwords 'No Surrender' and 'Kalgoorlie Prices' they soon received a reduction in the price of pints.

1904, Sir Samuel

Demonstrating the centrality of hotels to all living in remote towns a coalition of bank clerks, civil servants and miners struck in the summer heat seeking six pence beers, counter meals at 9pm (to allow for late working hours), and the provision of newspapers for reading.

1904, Murrin

A two week beer strike saw publican opposition overcome after strikers repeatedly pelted patrons with eggs.

1905, Abbotts

During a strike for lower prices in this Murchison district town strikers placed advertisements stating they 'respectfully request all those travelling through Abbotts to kindly assist them by refraining from taking refreshments there.'

1907, Maninga Marley

Drinkers in this town of 250 people began a boycott campaign by congregating outside its sole pub after a football game. Lighting a bonfire they declared the town to be 'off juice' until prices were reduced. Around the clock picketing followed until the publican relented.

1907, Sandstone

Inspired by events at Maninga Marley, drinkers 20 kilometres away in Sandstone struck for six pence pints of locally brewed beer. Numerous incidents of violence occurred during the five month dispute, resulting in two pickets receiving heavy fines, before around 300 strikers were able to celebrate their success. A further boycott two years later, aimed at getting the cost of all types of beer in the town reduced, failed after two months.

1908, Wiluna

Having already experienced a beer strike in 1903, locals sought a reduction in the price of beer by boycotting hotels for six months from October 1908 onwards. Motions calling for total abstinence were rejected during meetings held at the local recreation reserve, with some strikers switching to drinking at home and on the street. Before the campaign ended in victory six new 'cool drink' stores selling non-alcoholic beverages had opened.

Allegations in regional media that the dispute was being run by 'beer chewers' and 'beer bummers', and had resulted in 'filthy and degrading exhibitions', were denied by members of the strike committee. The campaign ended in victory, but Wiluna saw further beer strikes in 1923, 1930 and 1931, followed by an all-out boycott in 1933 that extended to illegal 'sly-grog' sellers and chemists selling wine tonics.

1910, Nannup

Members of the local cricket club boycotted the timber town's lone hotel over prices, enlisting all of the local businesspeople – a butcher, blacksmith, baker, and bootmaker – in the campaign. Backsliders faced a one pound fine for their first offence and were kicked out of the club on their second. In 1922 the Nannup Hotel would find itself targeted again over prices, with pickets mounted and public meetings held on its doorstep.

1910, Northam

Displeased with local prices being much higher than those in similar towns, a committee of drinkers carried out inquiries in regards to production and transport expenses, coming to the conclusion that publicans were charging a 200 per cent mark up on the wholesale cost of beer. Correctly identifying that hotels could not survive without their custom, a boycott calling for three penny glasses and four penny pints was initiated in early May. Vigilance committees were formed, the town postered, and the break in usual entertainment bridged by campaign meetings and weekly social events featuring music from two brass bands. During one such event the campaign chairman declared:

> The worker was entitled to have a cheap drink. Some people said it was a luxury, but it was a luxury to which they were entitled. It was a case, pure and simple, of the worker fighting for himself against the capitalist.

In addition to black banning pubs, activists also formed a committee to create a long term alternative in the form of a workers' club. The threat of these were occasionally raised during beer strikes but, faced with numerous obstacles ranging from population turnover to raising capital and navigating bureaucratic planning and licensing processes, cooperatives rarely eventuated. In this case advice was sought from the Midland Workers' Club and after overcoming delays, stemming from police and publican opposition and a state-wide government freeze on licenses, Northam workers opened their own venue in late 1911. This was particularly welcomed by the hardy few who had stuck out the boycott for over 18 months.

1911, Marble Bar

Following completion of the rail line from this Pilbara town to Port Hedland, and a consequent lowering of transport costs, locals demanded a reduction in the price of beer. Although many successful campaigns were conducted in the heat of the summer, weather could still play a role in their defeat, as recounted in the following poem from the *Eastern Districts Chronicle*:

> They had a beer strike at the Bar; the workers 'twould appear,
>
> Object to pay a shilling for a single glass of beer.
>
> So they held a monster meeting, and they passed a motion that
>
> Bottled Swan and Emu should be jerked out for a sprat.
>
> Then they sent a startling message to the publicans in town
>
> That they'd put the blooming peg in if the price was not cut down.
>
> When they made this resolution the twinkling stars were out,
>
> And they weren't so much affected by the Great Australian Drought.
>
> But as the publicans stood firm, and day by day went by,
>
> They recognised the fact that things about the Bar were dry.
>
> And 'twas hard to keep a promise, in cooler moments made,
>
> When the temperature was something o'er a hundred in the shade.
>
> So one by one they faltered, till they all got on the job,
>
> Now the publicans are smiling and the beer is still a bob.

1911, Lawlers

Following a meeting of the Mines Medical Fund, 60 locals stayed on to organise a deputation which visited the town's pubs to demand prices be brought down in line with those charged in the rest of the goldfields. With this rejected, a boycott and several further public meetings ensued before two of the publicans caved in and halved prices to six pence a pint. The minutes of the meeting where this was announced read:

> Moved by Mr. McGhee, seconded by Mr. W. Taylor, that everyone in the meeting adjourns to [the first] pub and have a bob in and then go on to [the second] pub and do likewise; also that the winner of these two shakes should contribute 2/6 each for the hire of the hall. Carried unanimously.

1912, Laverton

Workers from the Ida H goldmine launched a beer strike after a publican refused to serve them following late shifts and outside of official hours. Backsliders were subject to a six shilling fine.

1914, Bullfinch

A year long beer strike began in March with a demand that the price of pints of beer be cut from six to four pence and 'nobblers' of spirits from a shilling to six pence. Despite tensions in other parts of the goldfields, Anglo-Celtic, Austrian and Italian workers joined together and notices in all their languages posted around town.

Nannup Hotel, circa 1910 (Nannup Historical Society)

Pickets were mounted outside of hotels and supplies of bottled beer brought in by train. The resulting loss of custom soon led publicans to request that arbitration be undertaken. This was rejected.

Summing up the state of events at this time the *Truth* published the following ditty:

> At Bullfinch they have banked their pay,
> They reckon beer too dear,
> The bungs with gloom survey each room
> That once held lots of beer.
> The pots on counters stand around,
> In empty gloom – there is no sound,
> Though brandy is demanded, biz is slack.
> The bung a tear sheds o`er the till,
> That will not fill with dough derived from beer,
> The blowflies on the ceiling hum –
> The bung is feeling very glum.

Following a decision by a single vote to continue the strike, confidence was maintained throughout April and moves made to found a workers' club. By mid-May however, a number of stalwarts had left town for work and strike numbers declined thereafter. A committee continued to fierily denounce publicans at open air meetings but by the following year even they admitted defeat and declared the strike officially over.

1915, Gwalia

Responding to pressure from socialists and temperance advocates (sometimes one and the same) various governments around Australia experimented with state owned hotels during the early decades of the twentieth century. For some campaigners these were viewed as a compromise, in the belief that state control could stem excesses associated with the trade. Others hoped it would be the first step in phasing out drinking, by persuasion or decree, altogether.

The first state hotel in WA was built on the eastern goldfields at Gwalia in 1903. As with similar venues it struggled to balance social and economic goals. On the one hand it was intended to help reduce the consumption of illegal and adulterated alcohol while providing a controlled and salubrious alternative to privately owned venues in nearby Leonora. On the other, it was expected to pay its way and not become a burden on the state.

By 1915 the pub was deemed to be generating insufficient revenue and the government ordered it to raise prices. Local drinkers clearly had their own ideas about the value of state ownership and these centred on maintaining what they considered fair charges. As a result they soon began picketing the pub.

The boycott was initially ridiculed by the state Labor Attorney General Thomas Walker. He declared that he hoped the strike would never end, arguing:

> State hotels are not built to encourage drinking, or to invite custom, but for the purpose of ensuring that the best qualities of liquor shall be provided to those who demand them, and that they shall be worked, as far as possible, to secure sobriety in the community where they exist.

Over the next three months the boycott held firm. Many strikers travelled to Leonora for a drink or imbibed at miners' camps, leading to raids by police. The Gwalia Miners Union lobbied various political and labour bodies for assistance and broadened their demands to include improved hygiene, standardisation of glass sizes, reinstatement of bar staff, and the purchase of alcohol from unionised breweries.

With the venue losing up to 200 pounds a month the government eventually caved in and restored prices. Grievances continued to accrue however and in 1919 patrons struck again, demanding price reductions, the rehiring of a popular manager, improvements in beer quality, and upgraded hygiene measures. The latter included the replacement of a septic tank and the installation of glass washing apparatus. This time around it would take six months before the dispute was resolved.

State ownership of venues did not become widespread but the Gwalia hotel weathered further beer strikes in 1920, 1930, 1940 and 1941 to remain open for decades. With the state government selling off many of the ventures it had acquired in earlier periods, the pub was taken over by a cooperative in 1960. Following the closure of the local mine it shut its doors four years later.

1918, Midland Junction

A beer strike in this heavily unionised community followed claims from publicans that they had no choice but to pass on the cost of increased taxes to consumers. A detailed circular attempted to appeal to the drinkers' sense of solidarity, arguing that 'the Association of Hotelkeepers is as legitimate a union as any other trade union, and its present action simply amounts to a demand for a fair living wage.' The one publican in the town who was holding out against the price rise was decried by his fellow victuallers as a 'scab'. Rejecting the likening of a business association to their own organisations, workers from the railway workshops successfully held out for a continuance of three penny pints.

1920, Boulder

Although illegal or 'sly grog' sales often increased during boycotts, any direct connection between them and boycott organisers could be highly damaging, as seen in the reputational blows that strikers suffered during a goldfields wide campaign. As members of the One Big Union (OBU) Propaganda League – a regroupment of militants following persecution during World War One – those involved in organising action against a price rise in pints of beer from six to seven pence were already susceptible to hostility from conservatives, the media, and police. The boycott also formed part of a broader challenge to the power of the Australian Workers Union (AWU).

The strike had some initial success in shutting down hotel trade in the 'Golden Mile', particularly in Boulder but also in smaller settlements such as Comet Vale, Kurrawang and Hampton Plains. Claims by publicans that 'throughout the whole of Australia prices have been increased without murmur', did not convince many. This was not least because newspapers had carried reports of dozens of other beer strikes taking place around the nation.

Responding to claims that price rises could not be avoided due to rising costs, one letter writer justified the boycott on the basis that:

> We have got tired of this cheerful game of the capitalist passing on, as the passing on increases each one it passes, so we decided to do a little passing on too – we have booted it back to the brewer.

Although strikers claimed that they were primarily opposed to the region's brewing monopoly, pubs, as the last link in the chain and the place at which profits could primarily be targeted, remained the focal point of consumer action.

Unusually for a beer strike, formal support was given by the local peak union body, the Eastern Goldfields District council of the Australian Labour Federation. For its part the OBU opened a cool drink store which served as a meeting hall and also raised funds for the cause. One newspaper reported that the publican across the street could 'generally be observed looking sullenly on, occasionally objecting when something unpalatable is dealt out.'

Selling non-alcoholic beverages was one thing, but engaging in the sly grog trade was another. Roughly six weeks after the boycott began two men, one of whom was a key boycott organiser, were arrested for illegally transporting and selling alcohol, as well as for attempting to bribe police. Initially claiming ignorance of the law, and that they had only been taking alcohol to share at no cost with fellow strikers camping in the bush,

The strike rapidly spread. Guildford and Bassendean residents voted on 1 May to begin their own bans after a meeting of 300 heard of the need to act 'in sympathy with Midland Junction' in order to secure price reductions. The following day, drinkers in Guildford elected to join them and within a week a meeting of 500 residents from Maylands and Bayswater also took up the challenge.

Further south, drinkers in St Ives walked out of local pubs while workers at the Mornington Mills began boycotting those in Wokalup and Harvey. Pubs also emptied in Collie, where names of boycott breakers were read out at public meetings and a resolution passed calling on the state government to nationalize all hotels. A similar resolution, as well as one demanding beer be brewed from pure malt and hops, was later passed in Midland Junction.

Publicans argued that they had little control over prices. The *Westralian Worker* chimed in on the theme, condemning monopolistic breweries and reporting that their owners were also major stakeholders in mining, financial, manufacturing, media and other industries. As such the newspaper argued that:

> The struggle for cheap beer or satisfactory industrial conditions is being waged, not against hotelkeepers, who appear in the foreground, but against one of the greatest and wealthiest of the Australian financial combines.

Although others similarly blamed suppliers, pubs remained in the front line as strikers, in the words of a Midland Junction boycott committee member, believed 'the only way of getting at the breweries was by putting pressure on the hotels.'

Bunbury's Rose Hotel, 1924 (State Library of WA)

Central Perth and Fremantle also saw boycotts, but these were focused on concurrent industrial action led by the Hotel, Club, Caterers, Tearoom and Restaurant Employees' Union [see chapter 19 about Cecilia Shelley]. Those eateries, hostels and pubs able to secure scab labour and stay open were plastered with notices declaring them black banned. Workplaces were occupied and placards waved accusing restaurants of selling 'stuffed cockroaches' and 'fly soup.' Due to the nature of the workforce women, as unionists and pickets, took a leading part in this boycott campaign, eventually winning increased wages and improved conditions.

Outside of the city, publicans largely avoided making threats and did not tackle pickets. Some aired complaints in the media but most sat events out in the hope that striker resolve would eventually break.

The strike continued to spread throughout May, with drinkers in Protheroe forming a mid-west bastion. This proved to be a peak and action eventually faltered area by area. Maylands was the first to see the boycott officially called off on 18 June, 'owing to inconsistency on the part of those who had begun the strike.'

The areas where the dispute first began remained staunch for a period, with meetings of up to 600 voting for continuance, but the boycott at Midland Junction eventually ended in mid-July. Organized opposition in the form of an Anti-Beer Strike Committee succeeded in Bunbury with a street meeting declaring the town's boycott off on 18 July. Having prevailed, the Bunbury Licensed Victuallers' Association declared two days later that they would lower the price of bottled beer.

Collie was the last to fall on 15 August. The question of fair prices for alcohol and decent conditions for workers were far from settled however. Beer strikes enjoying varying degrees of success would continue to regularly occur across the state over the coming decades. Bunbury, for example, would experience another strike over prices in 1933 and Fremantle and Collie ones in support of female bar staff in 1933 and 1935.

CHAPTER 12

'CHAMPAGNE IS NOT RESERVED FOR THE STOMACHS OF THE RICH': CHUMMY FLEMING AND A DONATION TO THE UNEMPLOYED

Iain McIntyre

Unemployment has long been an endemic part of life in Australia. Those who have found themselves without work have consistently been made to suffer for the economic and political decisions of others. In response they have regularly had to organise, protest and campaign for provisions, relief work and other forms of welfare. At times some have raised calls for more than the right to mere survival. In Melbourne during June 1902, such demands led to the unemployed receiving a taste of the good life in the form of 300 bottles of fine champagne.

This came about largely due to the activism of bootmaker, trade unionist and anarchist John 'Chummy' Fleming. Born into a radical family in 1863, Fleming had begun work in Leicester, England at the age of 10. By the time he emigrated to Melbourne in 1884 he had already attended secularist and free thought meetings. In Australia his radicalisation was to go much further.

Fleming endured his first arrest after a march of the unemployed was attacked in 1885 by police outside the Treasury building. As a public speaker and organizer he was regularly verbally and physically harassed due to his vehement opposition to oppression, whether based on class, race, gender, or religious views. He was jailed in 1890, for leading a procession of thousands to parliament to demand that public libraries and museums be opened on Sundays, the only day off that most workers had. Despite repression he continued his activism up until his death in 1950, helping to found the city's May Day marches along the way. Unemployed organizing remained a key theme and he regularly joined deputations to parliament and spoke at rallies and processions numbering from dozens to thousands.

In a May 1901 protest Fleming ran onto Princes Bridge, bringing the Governor-General's carriage, which was taking Lord John Hopetoun to open the first Federal Parliament, to a halt. Preventing the police from dragging the anarchist away, the aristocrat took time to listen to his views. Out of this grew an unlikely friendship with the Governor-General visiting Fleming's private cobbler shop in Argyle St Carlton, which he had set up due to difficulties in finding work.

Following disputes with his colonial employers, Hopetoun quit his position and returned to Britain in 1902. Having already met with a deputation of the unemployed, and lobbied the government to provide increased relief, he made parting gifts via his radical friend.

Alongside confrontational actions and protest, mutual aid was a key theme in unemployed organising and alternatives to patronising charities were created in the form of grassroots labour bureaus and soup kitchens, some of which also distributed furniture and clothing. Thanks to donations from Hopetoun, and others that followed his example, unemployed workers also received cash payments via Fleming's shop on 24 June 1902. Further to this six hogsheads of beer, donated by a sympathetic brewer, were provided to the assembled women and men, leading to scenes that were described as 'hilarious, and then uproarious.'

The following day 300 bottles of champagne, paid for by Hopetoun, were also distributed. This, and chaotic scenes during distribution, were mocked by mainstream newspapers but Fleming, a non-drinker, remained resolute. When quizzed by journalists as to why he hadn't sold the alcohol and distributed the takings, he responded, 'Why shouldn't the poor get champagne? Champagne is not reserved for the stomachs of the rich.' Furthermore, he asserted, 'It would have been a breach of faith to his Lordship to have sold the wine.'

Chummy Fleming hands over the first bottle of champagne, 1902 (*Australasian*)

CHAPTER 13

THE COMMUNISTS MEET THE BOHEMIANS: DRINKING AT THE MARGINS, FROM THE 1900S TO THE 1930S

Alex Ettling

Smoke Night, Victorian Artists Society, 1906 (Percy Lindsay, *The Story of Australian Art*)

For years, communism had only been an idea, mostly dreamed over by wide-eyed intellectuals. But with the wave of revolutionary upheaval sweeping through Europe between 1917 and 1923, there seemed a very real possibility of a new way of living. The promises of industrialisation swirled around a modernising Europe in political revolt, and the possibilities of a major social restructure was profoundly reshaping intellectual life around the world.

The politically minded in Australia were enthusiastic for any dispatches that could illuminate the success of Russian Marxism – an *actual* workers revolution after so much ink had been spilled on the possibility. The workers on the world stage were also enlivening the creative milieus that looked optimistically towards aesthetic, cultural and industrial modernity.

People searching for ideas, stimulation and active participation in social affairs sought out communal environments in which to meet other willing interlocutors. In many cases it was in the forums around drinking where the social exchange around these ideas were at their most vibrant. Conversations could of course happen almost anywhere, but certain venues of notoriety were an attraction. It was the bars and cafes around alcohol where bohemian life became visible in the public sphere, where progress seemed to be nourished. They were red pulsing beacons where intrigues were shared, ideas sharpened, friendships and rivalries formed, and occasionally, plans hatched that endured through the next day's hangover to become reality.

The accounts of radicals dousing revolutionary class consciousness into the bohemian pot are scant – just fleeting encounters revealed in letters, memoirs and oral histories. The words spoken in those alcohol-infused encounters have floated off amidst the chatter and clinking of glass, forever out of grasp of the historical record. Nevertheless, the meeting of Communists and other non-conformists sits like a red mist over the reputation of bohemian Melbourne.

The Roots of Bohemia

From the 1860s, Australian cities were being shaped by the first splutterings of industrialisation. Capital accumulation progressed at such speed after the Gold Rush that the excesses of colonial wealth was endowed into the city's cultural institutions. The philanthropic investment in galleries, public libraries, universities and art schools laid the ground work for the first generations of local writers and painters, whilst also educating a segment of moneyed Melbourne in arts consumption.

Not all members of the artistic/literary subculture are bohemians. People are bohemian to the extent that parts of their lives push at the edges of acceptability at any given time. By the time of the emergence of the Communist Party of Australia in 1920 there had been generations of bohemian artists in Melbourne. These bohemians had used the recreational city space in spectacular and creative ways: 'posing, partying, pubbing'. Some leaned towards the cause of the workers, but most generally played their allotted role in the expansion of the bourgeois state of affairs – at the margins, but a valuable spark for innovative thinking.

The city studio was a sanctuary of aesthetic pleasure, usually located in near-condemned, drafty buildings, but also with ready access to the world of bohemia. The studio arrangement stimulated a common hatred of landlords, contributing to the sentiment of disdain that many artists held about their predicament under capitalism. A studio was also a place to drink outside of the home, around the restrictions of early closing. Artist Ola Cohn remembered one particularly rowdy evening at the studios in Grosvenor Chambers, circa 1930s: 'They danced so hard that they shook dust upon me from the ceiling as I lay in bed not many feet below.' Of course Cohn got out of bed and joined the party.

Alcohol has been an enduring feature of Melbourne's artist communities, with some of the most evocative descriptions coming from those looking in, such as this prescription: 'the fire must be kept going. Beer stimulates and soothes them.' More commonly, the consumption of alcohol and laziness were associated together as a moral critique of the lifestyle: 'It seems to be the general idea that the average artist is a plant of the hothouse variety, living in a Bohemian atmosphere and lazing the day away, occasionally emerging from the beer and spaghetti festival to paint a picture.' There was little understanding for the irregular hours of the artist and the nature of the activity that drew creatives to late night drinking.

With the little money they had, bohemian artists generally patronised low-priced cafes, often run by immigrants, such as Belloti's, the Latin Café, Florence and Petrushka. These establishments tended to be open at later hours, especially Italian establishments which commonly served free wine with meals. The association of bohemians to Latinate cafes became well known, which was useful for attracting like-minded people together. It also lead to the curious situation of the patrons becoming something of spectacle. L.M. Camusso's Cafe Bohemia advertised in *The*

Socialist in 1909: 'if you like to amuse yourself, come along on Wednesday night – you have a chance to see the Melbourne Bohemians enjoy themselves a la Continentale.'

Wine was regarded by most Australians as foreign and decadent. In the bohemian cafes it was a standard accompaniment to food, and often served illegally, which contributed to an appealing atmosphere for the bohemian set.

A key venue bringing Melbourne's socialists and artists together in this era was Fasoli's. Vincent Fasoli opened the restaurant at 108 Lonsdale Street in 1897 before moving to King Street in 1907, where it survived into the 1930s. Fasoli had been involved in wine making before starting the cafe, having established a vineyard at Spring Creek in 1869 and taking home prizes for both his red and white wine varieties. His daughter, Katherine Maggia was also responsible for the café's operations.

The 'Fasolians', as its habitués cast themselves, would drink, smoke and discuss 'subjects ranging from the art of Conder to the supposed canals of Mars.' The more bohemian members of the Victorian Socialist Party also met here. So too would other leftists and artists including George Bell, Eric Thake, Jimmy Flett, Dominic Leon, and Bill Dolphin. On Friday nights in particular the young bohemians of Melbourne would gravitate to Fasoli's, and it is on one such occasion that the artist Herbert McClintock recalled making the acquaintance of likeminded communist bohemians Roy Dalgarno and Judah Waten.

Art and Commerce

The bohemian community of Melbourne was a refined ecosystem, with various establishments and economic circuits sustaining the community and nourishing the vitality of the culture. It was only in the 1910s and 1920s that a developed art industry began in Australia, but it would only support certain favoured salon artists and the acceptable styles for upper-class tastes. Significantly, it was not necessarily full-time fine artists, liberated from the 'depravity' of advertising culture, who produced the most progressive or avant-garde explorations of aesthetic and social meanings through art. The self-sustaining fine artists in fact seemed to be isolated in their practice, quite often removed from any communal gatherings or discussion in the pubs and cafes. This was perhaps a factor in the conservatism found in both their politics and the content of their art.

As the market for consumer goods expanded, the advertising sector around it grew, and so artists were attracted to paying work in commercial arts which had a need for their creative skills. Artists who did challenging work, and young emerging talents, were often compelled to divide their time between *art for art's sake*, and pure commercial illustration to pay the bills. Many of the significant Australian artists of the period have a commercial portfolio, and undoubtedly many did this kind of work in secret. Such associations were unpalatable to some. In periodic cycles, there were proclamations of the purported death of bohemia, as yesterday's rebels seemed to dissipate into the ordinary running of capitalism.

Whilst some creatives undoubtedly made good money, and entered a different class structure as they moved into advertising and

Sketch of Fasoli's, 1898-1905 (Herbert Moore, State Library of Victoria)

public relations, there was also a layer of workers in the industry that had no control over their labour and generally low incomes. The proletarianisation of these commercial artists fed into a more strident anti-capitalist expression of bohemianism. There was a curiously large cohort of Communists who found a home in commercial arts and advertising, and were part of the driving force of the political wing of bohemia. Communist artist Roy Dalgarno is said to have produced advertisements for Bulimba Breweries by day and cartoons for the brewery's striking workers at night.

It has been the class struggle in broader society that has most significantly influenced the development of art scenes with social critique. Artists who have been elevated out of the working class, or impoverished middle class, have understandably shifted in their concerns. However, out of step with economic crisis, the culture of bohemia has at times served as a self-sustaining scene of radical critique. This has included a regular history of closing doors in on itself. Bohemians commonly acted snootily towards others who lacked the creative skills to join, but nevertheless yearned for exposure to the idea of freedom associated with the bohemian scenes.

Socialist Vance Palmer was one of the first to voice his dissatisfaction with the well rehearsed tropes, rallying the Australian artistic community to 'break from the limiting shackles of bohemia' in his 1907 essay 'Australia and the Bohemian Ideal'. His claims against bohemia were numerous, arguing that its 'unconventionality is so drearily conventional' and its 'gaiety is so depressingly sad.' Palmer was clear on the main problem:

> If there is one thing that must be smashed before we can build up our national life on a new basis, it is the tyranny of commercial values. But the Bohemians do nothing towards this reorganisation. They profess to see the futility of the wild rush to the feet of the golden calf, but for the rest they are content to retire to their dens.

In the end, Palmer's exhortations were less impactful on affairs than the arrival of capitalist crisis. The war economy that began in 1914 had contradictory effects on bohemian communities. A reduction in consumption is generally followed by a scaling back on advertising and any discretionary spending for cultural philanthropy. But if networks of bohemia required some degree of economic support, they were also cohered by the grit of hard times and indignation at the system. The crisis of the war, and later the Great Depression, did not lead to a dismantling of bohemianism, but instead created a cohort within the scene that had a proletarian revolutionary consciousness.

Guido Baracchi

Foremost amongst these was Guido Baracchi who became a vibrant presence in the civic life of Melbourne after making a name for himself as a radical within the establishment enclaves of Melbourne University. He happily joined in with the carousing around bohemian circles. In the course of his life he was also a member of a succession of significant radical organisations in Australian history: the Victorian Socialist Party, the Industrial Workers of the World, the Communist Party of Australia, and finally the Trotskyist movement.

Baracchi's apprenticeship into revolutionary thought had taken place over a lengthy period. He particularly valued the economics classes run by Bill Smith, and ideas regarding surplus value were not undermined by the recognition that his tutor was 'a boozer.'

Temperance had been a dominating presence in Australian politics since the 1800s, but in the morally charged atmosphere of World War One it experienced a renewed wave of success. Anti-alcohol crusaders achieved the early closing of pubs in most parts of the country and there were a series of referendums held to consider banning alcohol entirely, ensuring the liquor question dominated in the press.

Baracchi expressed hostility to prohibition at his college debating club the Dialectic Society. Biographer Jeff Sparrow describes how, at the end of his speech, Baracchi produced 'a champagne bottle from the folds of his gown and brandished it in the air, with an exhortation to his followers to rally round the standard.' The radical took his seat to tempestuous applause.

Baracchi was a student activist in a period when university politics and campus debates were capable of drawing the attention of the media and police. After all, the next generation of civic leaders was being nurtured within its sandstone walls, including future conservative prime minister Robert Menzies. During World War One the men of Trinity and the staff of the university made a public declaration to shun liquor for the war effort and the young Menzies used the pages of *Melbourne University Magazine* (MUM) to rebuke those 'openly and unashamedly playing the drunken sot!' When the Law Students Society debated six o'clock closing, Baracchi spoke for the pro-alcohol 'Crème-de-Menthes', and invited his audience to 'forsake the teapot and get back to French claret and good beer.' Baracchi was establishing a *pro-joy* communist politics that rejected the bloodshed of imperialistic war, and welcomed the flow of alcohol and good cheer.

Despite the upheaval of the war years, and a successful campaign against conscription, the Australian left remained an assemblage of small socialist groups that were unable to replicate the mass parties of Europe. The project of communism was in a sense a revolutionary scheme to overcome the separation between the industrial and the political that had caused the Australian left so much difficulty in advancing. In this regard, organising amongst bohemians – very much at the margins – was unlikely to, in itself, significantly help any socialist group to rise to the top.

Baracchi continued to socialise in the bohemian milieu, but focused his political interventions on the conventional political spaces of the labour movement. He became a man of letters – on the far left. With Percy Laidler, he established an influential position as an editor of the *Proletarian Review*. Along with debating out the new developments from the Russian Revolution, Baracchi used this vehicle to advocate for an alternative to the surging temperance movement. This was an approach to politics that seemed informed by

Guido Baracchi, 1917 (State Library of NSW)

his lifestyle within bohemian Melbourne, along with his reading on classical philosophy and revolutionary thinkers.

Proletarian Review carried an article in its 7 October 1920 issue entitled 'Prohibition, Communism and the Joy of Life'. While defending a temporary ban on alcohol in Russia, on the basis of a need for revolutionary discipline in the face of concerted attack, the article, likely written by Baracchi, noted that the leading Bolshevik Nikolai Bukharin had declared that restrictions would soon be lifted and, 'fine wines introduced for the use of the workers.' The piece went on to critique capitalism's twisting of 'the human spirit', arguing that:

> The Communist program implies the emancipation of humanity from material oppression; but it equally implies emancipation from oppression of the spirit of man – freeing life from the fetters imposed upon its expression, its joy and its beauty.

The Melbourne Branch of the Communist Party of Australia

The same month that 'Prohibition, Communism and the Joy of Life' was published, Baracchi travelled to Sydney to join with a number of socialist and syndicalist organisations to found the Communist Party of Australia (CPA). The formation of the Melbourne branch occurred a month later inside a hotel at 198-200 Bourke Street. Parer's Crystal Café Hotel, opened in 1886 during the heigh of Marvellous Melbourne, and featured lavishly furnished dining rooms, a saloon, a café, clubrooms and billiard rooms. It was a salubrious choice of venue for a radical political party with world-making ambitions.

Unfortunately, the organisation had been formed too late. After 1920 strike levels fell, post-war radicalisation was on the ebb and CPA activists had to accept the less glamorous tasks of propaganda work: making a case for people to join their small organisation based on their ideas. There was no alternative – when there were strikes in the city, the tiny CPA were only too aware they had little presence in the industrial scene to offer any lead. However much they understood the necessity for this patient routine, it was inevitably demoralising as members seemed to be lost as soon as new ones were coming on board.

Only a minority of Melbourne bohemians, with an interest in radical developments, backed it up with membership cards to this new revolutionary organisation. Nevertheless, the visible bohemian participation was enough of a presence to warrant the retrospective observation in Jill and Jeff Sparrow's 2001 book *Radical Melbourne* that 'the group seemed as much Bohemian as Bolshevik.'

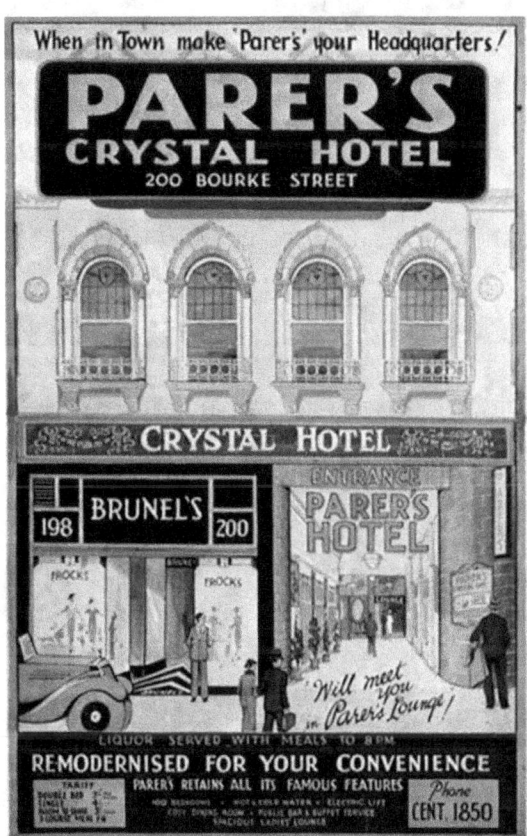

Parer's Hotel (Public Records Office of Victoria)

Bohemian creatives, who were effective at attracting people through their creativity, whether it was agitprop theatre or their writing, were an asset to building the party. Thin layers of intellectuals and artists were clearly not a sufficient base of recruitment for a mass workers party, but such a small organisation was not going to turn many away. However, in this early period of instability in the party's fortunes, they were often scapegoated for the failings of a movement not growing anywhere near fast enough. Guido Baracchi, wealthy and birthed out of the establishment, was one of the bohemian intellectuals who was soon targeted as being suspect.

Esmonde Higgins was another leading figure who would attract criticism for his absence of a working class background. In the early period, it was expressed mostly as self-recrimination. In Stuart Macintyre's *The Reds*, a description is made of Esmonde Higgins as a 'prisoner of the middle-class conscience.' In his letters he compared his own personal frailties with the sterling qualities of the British boilermaker Harry Pollitt: he was 'lazy, bookish, feckless, untrained in useful skills' and susceptible to 'fags, bed, booze.' Whereas, Pollitt was 'confident, shrewd, resourceful' and full of 'physical well-being.'

Esmonde Higgins came from a family where, according to biographer Terry Irving, 'The family values were typically bourgeois – hard-working, public-spirited, patriotic, prohibitionist and non-smoking – and Esmonde's early life seemed to embody them.' The teen rebellion that followed took a familiar trajectory: he smoked secretly in his last year at school, discovered alcohol while at Ormond College, and rejected his parents' Christianity. Irving, in his essay 'Modernity's Discontents: Esmonde Higgins and James Rawling as Labour Intellectuals' describes Higgins as:

> The indestructible reveller, the energetic dancer, the weekend cricketer and rambler, the breaker of female hearts, and the boozer who ended too many nights sleeping on the carpet at the Labor Research Department.

Higgins was a devoted party member for many years, but lost his position in the leadership in 1929 during the Stalinisation process.

Esmonde Higgins, 1919 (Oxford, Balliol College Archive)

Wowsers in the CPA

It would have been difficult to begin the CPA on a temperance footing given the composition of the party at this time. Along with founders like Baracchi and his well known advocacy against temperance, you also had John Moir Alexander (well known party member Dorothy Gibson's father), who was a successful vigneron and wine merchant. Alexander was a committed socialist who was known to donate to left-wing causes and organisations. Another early source of support came from Louis Aarons, scion of a generation of famous Aaronses in the party, who was a wine and spirit merchant in Prahran. There was clearly a section of the party that was sympathetic to the wowsers though, and prepared to scrutinise the drinking behaviour of its working class audience.

Although the Melbourne branch had formed in the drinking establishment of Parer's Hotel, it soon began using the Temperance Hall as its meeting place. In his history of the early CPA, Peter J Morrison writes that the CPA 'very often saw its failure to attract recruits as due to the moral degradation and/or insufficiency of the workers.' Its position as argued in the 7 September 1923 issue of Workers Weekly was that 'Communist propaganda depends upon workers with clear heads, not beer soaks.' Alcohol was a temptation that was feared to morally compromise any member of the labour movement, including Communists. Another issue of Workers Weekly on 3 July 1925 argued:

> It stands to reason that the man who cannot restrain himself from alcohol is always going to have a weak link in his composition ... and a man who drinks is always unreliable. Therefore it is the duty of every party member to wage an unceasing war against drink.

The party supported prohibition during a Queensland referendum in 1923, and once more came out to support prohibition when it was put to voters in NSW in 1929. With this platform, Morrison reveals that the CPA was even making minor inroads with temperance organisations, including the Women's Christian Temperance Union. It was also prepared to use alcohol and prohibition as a dividing line with rivals. The CPA accused the ALP of supporting brewers, lambasting a workers movement that 'reeks with the rottenness of drunken labour leaders who have sold out to the enemy.'

The message was clear about the CPA's attitude to alcohol. It appears, however, that the position was guidance rather than rules, with rarely any repercussions for members actually found drinking.

The CPA's growth through the 1920s remained slow and fitful. After the branch re-formed in 1924 there was more internal discord culminating in a damaging split in 1925 which saw the Melbourne membership drop to just 30 members. In 1927 the economy began to slow and unemployment began to rise. From 1928 there was a series of major industrial confrontations, which though they ended in defeat, presented a shift in the political climate which the Communists were finding a way to relate to. Membership in Melbourne crept back up to 48 members in 1928.

It was the Great Depression which saved the party from the fate of obscurity which had befallen the small socialist groups before it. The poverty that resulted from unemployment, with a minimal welfare state, compelled workers towards political resistance. The resulting growth in party members was enough to turn the CPA from a sect into a small party with an opportunity to make politics happen at its own instigation. The CPA launched the Unemployed Workers Movement and the Militant Minority Movement, becoming intensely involved in building workplace committees and community resistance. These sorts of activities restored the reputation of the Communist movement in the eyes of both workers and the radical intellectuals observing from outside the industrial arena.

At the same time, with the material basis for communism in Russia undermined by civil war and famine, Stalin had reconstituted the Communist project to put Russia first. It was now 'communist' and 'Marxist' for branding purposes rather than in any sense a political system of workers' control. In Australia, the Comintern threw its backing behind an obedient faction to the Stalinists. Party members, including Baracchi and Higgins, who did not fit into the new way of doing things were marginalised.

Opposition to alcohol consumption began to be wound back around 1930 due to the inevitable realisation that drinking was a rather common working class activity and could be useful in the recruitment process. Morrison explains:

> It would seem that the CPA came to accept a 'social drink' as something bordering upon revolutionary necessity, but it pursued the line of thinking with the same puritanical fervour. A token glass of 'shandy' became a mandatory prop at party socials or recruiting socials, and extremism of either colour – drunkard or teetotaller – was discouraged.

So drinking found a place, but was only morally defensible if it had a purpose in party activity. Heavy drinkers were still to be condemned, and the association of alcohol with sexual freedom or anything hinting of bohemianism was increasingly frowned upon. Historian Carole Ferrier writes that the CPA was 'subjected to a process of cleaning up and its bohemianism was replaced by what almost amounted to a wowseristic puritanism.' This would later come to include the expulsion of leading bohemian figures such as Baracchi and Judah Waten.

Workers Art Club

The Workers Art Club (WAC) was founded in 1931-32, proclaiming the indivisibility of aesthetic experimentation from social struggle with the rallying cry 'Art Is a Weapon'. Founding members included Alwyn Lee, Noel Counihan, Cyril Pearl, Jack Maughan, Itzak Gust, and Baracchi, who lectured at the club on 'Art and Marxism'. A writer in *Smith's Weekly* referred to the membership of the WAC as 'a collection of young men and women of pink political views and somewhat bohemian manners.'

The first theatrical production of the WAC was Ernst Toller's *Masses and Man*, staged at the Temperance Hall, which played to a large audience. We can see from the published material around this event that the WAC was positioning itself in a careful way, separate from bohemian concerns and with class struggle as the focus: 'Booze, sex-suppression, and money grubbing are the main themes about which the capitalist futilities of bourgeois art revolve.' Possibly it was fighting a rearguard action around perceptions of a suspicious bohemianism at its core. The performance was successful if attendance and press coverage is a measure, and the WAC was being put to other good uses with the commissioning of banners for May Day from its visual artists. But if these achievements were viewed with optimism by some, as Jeff Sparrow writes, 'the party simply considered art unimportant, and an interest in it as therefore suspicious.' One comrade simply declared that the WAC consisted of 'a pack of petit-bourgeois degenerates.' Even if the activity was scarcely bohemian, it inherited a weight of prejudices.

In the 1930s, known as the 'angry decade', historian Tony Moore argued that:

> The bourgeois privilege at its heart discredited the bohemian rebellion for a generation confronting the social upheavals of mass unemployment and war. The bohemians' celebration of individuality and personal development seemed inappropriate amidst the challenge of collective action and the promise of revolution.

Speaking to the Tenth Congress of the party, Lindsay Mountjoy forcefully declared that 'the Communist Party is not a bohemian club', and claimed that the sexual indiscretions of Communist women caused working class women to stop their husbands from joining. Stuart Macintyre in *The Reds* describes how on behalf of the entire district committee, Dinny Lovegrove and two other Victorians took a comprehensive list of accusations against the central committee to a plenum at the end of 1932. It accused the Sydney leaders of political failures but also of 'disgracing the party's reputation' with the Saturday night dances it held in the Sussex Street hall. The hall was described as 'little more than a brothel' that attracted the 'lumpen-proletariat, beer and prostitutes.'

It's not difficult to imagine that this wowserish atmosphere contributed to the high turnover in membership in the party. People were attracted to communist ideas, but not all were necessarily happy to be in *this* Communist Party.

The Swanston Family Hotel

The CPA attempted to confine its members to a narrow set of artistic and cultural activities, such as alcohol-free dances interspersed with political announcements. However, connections between artists within its ranks and bohemians outside continued. During the five years between 1934 and the outbreak of the Second World War the Swanston Family Hotel became a major social centre for Melbourne's radical intellectuals.

Nancy Wills provides an account of how the pub developed this scene in her memoir *Shades of Red*. For several years violin maker Bill Dolphin had encouraged artistic friends to call in for a chat at his city studio in the late afternoon, especially on Fridays. When enough companions had gathered, 'The Troops', as they became known, would depart for a favoured local pub. After this they would buy more beer and either go back to Dolphin's or continue on to the art studio of Nutter Buzzacott and Roy Dalgarno (where communist Noel Counihan also worked). The camaraderie of this drinking circle even resulted in a famous Counihan cartoon.

Dolphin moved his studio several times, and arrived at rooms above a shoe shop near the corner of Bourke and Swanston streets (272 Bourke St), thus necessitating a change of local. The Troops sought a drinking establishment only a short distance away with 'tram fares and shoe leather being important considerations in those years', as wryly noted by Dolphin. The group elected a committee – Dolphin, Counihan, Waten and one or two others – to approach nearby pubs to see if they could make a favourable arrangement for their regular custom. The proposal was that they had 20 to 30 people who would drink on a regular basis. They wanted a pub that would allow their women friends to join them in the bar. They also wanted the bar to provide credit on occasions when a member of their group was short on cash. And they required a degree of protection from harassment from those that might target them for their eccentricities.

They were met with flat refusal from The Royal Mail, the first establishment they approached. They lowered their standards, and next approached a venue described by

Swanston Family Hotel, 1911 (Algernon Darge, State Library of Victoria)

one as a 'blood house'. Again their proposal was rejected. Their next venture was to the Swanston Family Hotel.

The licensees of The Swanston Family Hotel during this period are listed as Robert and Valda Lewis. The approving decision was made by the 'charming old Irish woman', Ma Lewis, described by Counihan as 'a racy sort of woman'. She replied to the proposal: 'Entirely, entirely, come along boys, we'll make you welcome.' Not long after, management of the hotel was transferred to Mr and Mrs Bell Towers, who continued the arrangement with The Troops. The publican Henry Linacre Bell Towers was described as comporting himself like a Shakespearian actor with flowery language. He would activate his theatrical manner when ordering someone out of the bar. Journalist Zélie Pimlott recounted: 'He never laid hands on anyone ... simply advanced on them, one arm raised, finger pointing to the door and articulating like an enraged Lear.'

Shades of Red reveals that initially 'everyone who joined the group had to be creative in one way or another, there was no tolerance for "hangers-on".' It is not clear how firm or long-lasting this orientation was, or if it at any time affected interactions with leftists present who were not creative. The pub soon developed a self-sustaining reputation, and at the end of the working day, journalists, academics, novelists, librarians, school teachers, artists, and musicians converged at the corner of Little Bourke and Swanston Streets. The bar itself was described as dingy, dark and uninviting, but the talk 'intense, provocative and lively.' The manners, more often than not, 'rugged and crude.'

Accounts of the Swanston Family Hotel in Melbourne intellectual life emphasise openness, but the overall reputation as a left-wing haunt, and the colonising of a particular section of the hotel, indicates there was some degree of curation and gate keeping. Conservatives and reactionaries did not come to this establishment. Boorish drinkers with little to offer were not going to last long if they meandered into the corner where The Troops resided.

The historian Manning Clark described the Swanston Family Hotel as 'possibly the best university I have ever attended.' Philosopher Peter Herbst described the importance of these drinking communities:

> That I had access to them outside teaching hours was of the utmost importance for my intellectual development and I thought in later years that I learnt far more philosophy at dinner or having a drink in the pub with my philosophical friends and seniors than I could ever have acquired in formal lectures.

Cartoon of Bill Dolphin's studio, l-r Judah Waten, Bill Dolphin, Noel Counihan and Josl Bergner, 1942 (Noel Counihan, State Library of Victoria)

The artist Leonard French, referred to regular gatherings there as 'Len French's University'. It was where his vision of artistic practice was shaped by the debates he had with the various personalities who were responsible for setting the course of the Australian art scene in the period.

Waten introduced his artist friend Josl Bergner to Bill Dolphin, which brought him into the Swanston Family Hotel scene. The presence of a Jewish refugee within this group, no doubt added a resonance to the discussion of left politics. Not all the Communist artists participated in the scene however. Danilla Vassilieff never came to the Swanston Family Hotel. Albert Tucker, by far the most morally charged of the modernists, rarely drank there. Both of these figures were key to the development of Australian modernism in art, and also proved to be the most disruptive to the ambitions of the CPA within the local branch of the Contemporary Art Society.

Historian Sean Scalmer's view is that the hotel provided a loose, communal forum for political discussion and education, but that it was not a party front. It was difficult for a Communist to even get a license to run a pub. Don Thompson was refused a hotel

'The Troops' an illustration of Swanston Family Hotel regulars, 1939 (Noel Counihan, Estate of Mrs P Counihan)

license by the licensing court despite holding the legitimacy of being a former secretary of the Building Trades' Federation. The decision was attributed to anti-Communist bias. At any rate, it would appear that operating a bar was not necessary for the party, whose members could simply impose themselves on an establishment as their regular gathering point and make it work for them. Many who came regularly to the Swanston Family Hotel were members of the CPA or sympathisers. Scalmer ascribes the pub an important party political function, for 'it was within such forums that the unity between Communists and Labor Party supporters was championed and cemented.'

If Bill Dolphin was the more understated glue-guy of this scene, then the charismatic and impressive Brian Fitzpatrick played a complementary role. Fitzpatrick had been a founder of the Melbourne University Labour Club, and as a writer and academic historian went on to be a significant figure of reform in public life. As a protagonist in politics he was particularly influential with his work in the Council for Civil Liberties. On one occasion he helped secure the local distribution of Lenin's *State and Revolution* when the authorities attempted to ban its importation. Fitzpatrick's role as a political intermediary was complemented by his unique physiological ability to

Brian Fitzpatrick, 1928

Bertha Laidler, circa 1940s (Alan Walker Collection)

handle large quantities of alcohol. It meant that, according to philosopher Peter Herbst, he 'was able to dictate letters of extreme competence, letters beautifully structured and well-argued when he was too drunk to be able to sit upright in his chair at the table.' Fitzpatrick was therefore well suited to extended hours in the pub, while functioning as a useful foot soldier for the Communists inside the respectable world of politics and law.

Counihan noted that in initial negotiations, 'We had to be able to bring our womenfolk into the bar. They had to drink on even terms.' When the interviewer Barbara Blackman proposed the view to Noel Counihan that this arrangement represented an advancement for women, his reply confirmed that by 'the macho standards in Melbourne at the time, that's quite true.' It perhaps also reveals that Counihan was aware that it was a relative advance and not far enough.

The Troops who drank in the saloon bar of the hotel entered from Little Bourke Street. The women associated with the group were permitted by the hotel to drink at two or three small tables placed in a space at the end of the L-shaped bar which looked out into Swanston Street. Counihan's partner Zélie Pimlott held an enmity towards another female regular of the scene, Bertha 'Bubbles' Laidler, and so it was likely a frustration (for both) to be confined to the same table simply because of gender. Pimlott's assessment of the culture of pub is that, 'Women took no part in discussion. If we ventured an opinion we were either ignored or told to shut up as we knew nothing about what was being debated.' Nevertheless, elsewhere, Pimlott describes it as a 'great place' which they sometimes visited multiple times a day.

Two other women who were participants in the scene, the aforementioned Bertha Walker and Nancy Wills, did not include any criticism in their memoirs.

Another frustration was with how long patrons could drink due to the restrictions of six o'clock closing. In his biography of Noel Counihan, art historian and fellow Communist Bernard Smith details the solution the drinkers and publican came up with:

> They were shepherded up to rooms at the rear of the first floor where bare tables were laid with plates containing dry, empty oyster shells, putative evidence that anyone found drinking at those tables was a bona-fide traveller, legally permitted to drink after hours with a meal, a stratagem that could not possibly fool even the dullest policemen. Yet it worked. The dry oyster shells did splendid service for years.

Although the pub's heyday was in the 1930s it remained a key gathering place for leftists and bohemians, only shutting its doors in October 1959, with a large party of regulars commiserating its passing. On this final day of trading, the crowd spilled out onto the pavement where songs were sung including 'Auld Lang Syne' and 'A Pub With No Beer'. Arrests were made for offensive behaviour. When one defendant fronted up to the magistrate, he declared that the Swanston Family Hotel had 'a lot of sentiment attached to it' and he had nothing to be ashamed of. He declared he was celebrating the '*Bank* With No Beer', a sardonic commentary on the fact that a financial institution was replacing this legendary meeting place for Melbourne's bohemians and Communists.

CHAPTER 14
THE 1912 BROKEN HILL HOTEL AND RESTAURANT STRIKE
Iain McIntyre

Located on NSW's remote Barrier Range, Broken Hill established itself as a bastion of union militancy from the 1880s onwards via a series of bitter mining strikes. The Broken Hill Proprietary Company (BHP), the city's key employer, regularly strove to cut wages and resist any improvement in hazardous working conditions. Over the decades disputes saw lockouts and strikes last up to 18 months. Unionists were regularly jailed and blacklisted, and physical clashes between locals and squads of police and strike breakers imported from other parts of the country were common. Pubs were often dragged into disputes with pressure placed on them not to house and feed scabs or police. Despite some severe losses the region's miners were the first in Australia to win the 35 hour week. This came in 1920, 28 years before the 40 hour week was established as the national standard.

Union activism extended into other industries. In 1912, members of the Hotel, Restaurant and Employees' Union lodged a new log of claims with employers, seeking improvements in wages and a reduction in working hours, which were as many as 58 per week. Key to achieving these goals, and maintaining standards over time, was the demand that businesses should only employ union members. This was rejected with the result that 250 female and 100 male staff walked off the job on 26 February.

With two thirds of Broken Hill's bar staff, cooks and cleaners already in the union and now out on strike, the industry was hit hard. Support from the town's union peak body, the Barrier Labour Federation, came in the form of a call for all members to boycott offending establishments, with the names of those patronizing black banned premises to be publicly shared. On top of this, liquor unions cut off supplies of beer, sparkling water and spirits while the Bread Carters Union and others refused to deliver food. Municipal workers gave employers a week to comply with union demands or have their garbage collection cut off. More than 50 businesses were impacted with takings at formerly popular pubs rapidly reduced from 60 to 80 pounds a day to less than a pound. In the face of this, 15 employers immediately threw in the towel.

Those businesses which decided to test the strikers' mettle received extra attention on 27 February. After marching to various workplaces a group of female strikers gathered on the corner of Argent and Oxide streets. The crowd swelled from 50 to 1000, before marching on the Commercial Hotel. Finding the pub trading, women swept aside an attempt by the owner to lock them out, climbing on tables and sending customers scurrying amidst flying crockery. During this occupation of the dining room another group took over the kitchen, distributing food and dousing supplies in pepper, sugar and mustard.

The Centennial Hotel was also paid a visit. In this case strikebreakers were targeted with hundreds of people gathering outside the pub to hoot and yell. Female strikers chased two cooks onto the pub's balcony before removing them from the premises. Later that night 3000 attended a street meeting outside Trades Hall.

Telegrams were sent to Adelaide, Sydney and Melbourne requesting that unions prevent scab labour from being sent into town. In the end such assistance was not required as after three days of turmoil the strike was settled. Employers conceded all key demands and non-union staff were given seven days to join up. In some cases strikers were targeted with reprisals, necessitating further pressure to win their reinstatement. Further strikes in the hospitality industry, at times to defend standards and at others to gain improvements, were carried out in 1915, 1919, 1928 and 1931.

Commercial Hotel, circa 1920 (Noel Butlin Archives/ Australian National University)

Alcohol related humour from Broken Hill mine workers during five months of picketing and other action against pay cuts, 1909 (Noel Butlin Archives/Australian National University)

CHAPTER 15

STATE CONTROL OF LIQUOR IN THE NORTHERN TERRITORY: A BRAVE BUT UNPOPULAR EXPERIMENT

Maggie Brady

The Northern Territory has been no stranger to controversy when it comes to managing grog – particularly when the government intervenes in how, when and where the populace may consume it. With an ongoing history of heroic levels of consumption, irresponsible sales practices and associated high rates of physical and social harm, it's not surprising that the Territory has experimented with numerous alcohol regimes (especially since self-government in 1978). Each new regulation has provoked predictable outbursts of public comment. None, however, can quite match the controversy that was aroused in 1915 when the Northern Territory administration – then governed by the Commonwealth – nationalised the liquor supply in its northern region. It was the only instance of its kind in the history of Australian alcohol policies. The intervention lasted for six years, until 1921 when the State-owned hotels were quietly handed back to private enterprise.

The idea that the State should take control over what was commonly referred to at the time as the 'liquor traffic', seems to have been in the air since at least early in 1912. The Territory had an entrenched hard drinking culture and sly grog problems, and with general agreement that prohibition would be both undesirable and unattainable there was some popular support for greater regulation, the creation of State-owned hotels, and a crackdown on illegal sales. In March 1912 a Methodist minister J. Bennett had preached a sermon in Darwin on the need for State hotels; a few months later a Town Hall meeting discussed the matter, and several Christian ministers suggested a petition to bring the liquor traffic under proper State control. The pages of the *NT Times & Gazette* took up the debate, with objectors arguing that 'British Democracy' conferred the right to private and individual enterprise and that abolishing such a right was the doctrine of the 'extreme Socialistic party' (that is, Labor).

Indeed there was political support, because in October 1915, with a federal Labor government in power, an Ordinance was passed by the Federal Executive Council in Melbourne (located there until the move to Canberra in 1927) to take over the sale of liquor, both wholesale and retail, between the Katherine River and Darwin in the northern part of the Northern Territory. The desire of the administration was to keep down excessive drinking, improve the quality of the liquor and to suppress sly grog selling. The move would also provide much-needed revenue to Federal coffers, under strain partly because of World War One. Other underlying reasons included an ingrained racist antipathy towards Chinese people, who worked in hotel kitchens, and were allegedly involved in supplying sly grog. The Supervisor of Hotels, who arrived in August 1915, explicitly stated that part of the plan was to replace Chinese workers with Europeans.

The Darwin State Liquor Store, 1919 (Library and Archives NT)

Terminus Hotel, 1917 (Library and Archives NT)

It is highly significant that there was a federal Labor government in power, with Andrew Fisher (a Scot, from a sober Presbyterian background) as Prime Minister. Labor party policy at the time in Australia and in Britain was to nationalise monopolies in the interests of employees and the community, and the overall position of socialists when it came to alcohol was to improve the management of drinking places rather than abolish them. It was unfortunate though, that the decision made in Melbourne for liquor 'nationalisation' in the Territory, was to be administered by the federal government's Chief Executive Officer there, the newly appointed Dr J. A. Gilruth – who was both unpopular and autocratic.

The State compulsorily acquired four public hotels: three in Darwin (the Victoria Hotel, the Club and the Terminus), and one in Pine Creek (others were closed down) and it opened a State Liquor store at the back of the Victoria Hotel in Darwin. Compensation was paid to their private owners, and a 'Supervisor of Hotels' was appointed. Immediately after the acquisition, an industrial award raised costs, but alcohol sales initially made good profits for the government. However, there was a stream of other difficulties to deal with. The Australian Workers Union immediately demanded an increase in wages. The hotels acted as boarding houses as well as drinking places, but the accommodation was poor and needed repair and improvement at the time of the government takeover: customers complained about the unbearable tropical heat and unpalatable food. Darwin itself was ramshackle, lacking proper infrastructure such as sewage and running water. The entire non-Aboriginal population of the Territory was only 4000 (First Nations people were not counted) and materials and skilled workers were in short supply. As for the beer, the quality was poor and it was reported that drip-tray slops were tipped back in, with one drinker at a State hotel complaining of 'an aquarium of floating debris in his glass.'

Nevertheless, over time attempts were made at hotel improvement. The public bar at the Victoria Hotel had been closed in 1915 (causing much uproar), but after a few years a new lounge bar was opened there, with chairs and small tables 'to enable customers to partake of refreshments without the necessity of standing

Protest outside Government House, 1919 (State Library of South Australia)

up to the counter.' It was probably the Northern Territory's earliest effort to 'improve the public house'.

The Administrator Gilruth was attempting the challenging task of running hotels at a profit while simultaneously cutting down on drunkenness, but the hotels began to run at a loss and the sly grog situation did not improve. The population was incredulous that the administration could not make a profit out of Territory pubs and the hostility towards Gilruth increased, some of it undeserved. The State hotel enterprise was affected by many extenuating circumstances including a general dissatisfaction with wages, union agitation, and strikes, protests, and boycotts unrelated to the nationalisation of liquor.

A key factor underlying the general unrest had nothing to do with the State hotels nor with Gilruth himself. In 1911, Territorians had been disenfranchised as a result of the transfer of the administration of the NT from South Australia to the Commonwealth government: they were deprived of basic democratic rights, and had no elected representatives. Previously there had been an elected Territory member in the South Australian House of Assembly; the appointment of an Administrator in 1912 – answerable to the government in Melbourne – provoked widespread resentment and a sense that the people were not trusted with control over their own affairs. This distrust spilled over into attacks on Gilruth, including his management of the State hotel experiment, revealed in much sardonic correspondence to the local press. Describing the State takeover one contributor expostulated:

> Like the sudden eruption of a long-extinct volcano, a brain wave came over officialdom, a phenomena [sic.] hitherto unknown. The hotel-keepers were told that their businesses had been commandeered by Seizer Augustus. That was all, but it was quite sufficient. Protest was useless.

Gilruth left office in February 1919 following a 'rebellion' the previous December during which more than 1000 people demonstrated outside his home before roughing him up and burning him in effigy. Primarily caused by the factors discussed above, the protest was also stoked by a refusal to allow female state hotel staff an afternoon's leave to celebrate the Armistice, and the subsequently locking out of the workers after they took the time off anyway.

By the time the government relieved itself of (what it termed) the 'financial and administrative embarrassment' of the State hotels there was an operating loss of £6000, and the Administration seems to have lost heart. In November 1921 the premises owned by the State were relinquished, leased to private individuals licensed to carry on the trade.

In retrospect, this episode begs the question of why there was no exchange of ideas and experiences with Britain which, at the same time, during the period of alcohol austerity surrounding World War One, engaged in a successful government takeover of the liquor supply. In order to safeguard the war effort and control access to alcohol and the drinking behaviour of thousands of munitions workers in the north (in Carlisle and Gretna), a Liquor Control Board took over local breweries and nationalised 120 licensed premises. The State pubs introduced catering and recreational activities, strategies that ultimately contributed to the reform and overall improvement of pubs across Britain. Managers were encouraged to promote soft drinks and food and their income was not dependent on maximising alcohol sales (so-called 'disinterested management'). The Carlisle Scheme lasted until 1971. The Northern Territory failed to achieve reforms that bore any resemblance to the transformation brought about by the Carlisle Scheme. It was a missed opportunity, evidenced by the high levels of alcohol related harm in the Territory today, and the fact that monopolies are now accepted in many countries as one of the 'best buys' in international alcohol policy, acting as an instrument for public health and welfare.

CHAPTER 16
'THIRSTY DAYS': THE 1918 BRISBANE BEER STRIKE
Iain McIntyre

A decision by Brisbane hoteliers to pass the cost of a new federal alcohol excise onto drinkers saw the city's bars empty during the closing stages of World War One. This was one of the few Australian 'beer strikes' prior to the 1940s to involve a coordinated, city-wide campaign. It highlighted the difficulties associated with unions officially engaging in and maintaining such boycotts when huge numbers of drinkers and multiple parties with differing agendas were involved.

The dispute began with wharf labourers, painters and dockers, and other maritime workers calling for a boycott of pubs ahead of the price increase on 7 October. Come the day the price of pints rose from 4d to 6d with the result that waterside hotels emptied. In the evening a 'monster' meeting, presided over by trade union leader, military veteran, and ALP politician Hamilton Cuffe Jones, was held in William St, near Victoria bridge. The city's peak union body, the Brisbane Industrial Committee endorsed the campaign two days later, passing a resolution stating that it supported the 'strike wholeheartedly' and recommending 'every union to join.' Many did, with support pledged by union executives and branches covering a wide range of occupations.

State government owned railway refreshment rooms had initially followed private establishments in implementing the price rise. On 13 October the ALP Railways minister reversed this, claiming he had not been consulted. With bans lifted on government outlets Brisbane's Central Railway station was soon mobbed, leading Methodist and Presbyterian churches to pass motions condemning the venue as a 'common pot-house and brawl centre.'

By the time the campaign entered its second week temperance forces within the labour movement were pressing demands for the campaign to endorse six o'clock closing and/or the nationalization of pubs so that the state could take a direct hand in managing and moderating, if not eradicating, alcohol consumption. Following lengthy debate a resolution in favour of nationalisation and the continuance of the boycott was passed by the Industrial Committee on 24 October, but a decision regarding closing hours was tabled.

By late October internal police reports noted that 'hotel keepers are losing a great deal of their trade.' Despite this, the boycott was causing increased division amongst unions,

Kangaroo Point Hotel, 1915

branches and workplaces. In part this was due to differences regarding whether, and how hard, to push temperance as a long-term lifestyle choice. As further weeks went by, and discipline slowly faded in the face of hotelier resolve, tensions also rose between those who stuck firmly to the cause and the increasing number who didn't.

The boycott was never officially called off but according to a police report 'was finished in effect' by early December. Some beer strikers persisted, with the Furnishing Trades Union being one of the last hold outs. In response to queries from members regarding whether the campaign was still on, it resolved on 4 December to continue, censuring the Industrial Council for 'its apparent lack of interest in the beer strike through failing to maintain the firm stance adopted by it in the first place.'

Bar area of Vallely's Australian Hotel, circa 1910s (State Library of Queensland)

CHAPTER 17
CHRISTMAS AND BEER
Chris McConville

In December 2021, media networks tried to inject life into the corpse of a seasonal panic. Rifling through the tabloid world's stock of horrific images, and thus playing into the cultural memory of Australian drinkers, journalists warned of a Christmas beer shortage. Since at least Christmas 1940, Australians have panicked about these beer droughts, with fears for Yuletide supplies growing more frequent from war's end, 1945. In these increasingly sensational and ritualised alarms, the first hint of shortages generally surfaced towards the end of each November, before accelerating as the festive day drew near. In 2021 however, dread of a dry Christmas differed from fears about earlier droughts. Older moral panics had sheeted the beer drought home to that spectral folk devil, unionised workers. Journalists found no role for unions in the Great Christmas Beer Scare, 2021, since it arose because corporatised breweries had concentrated on mass-market rather than boutique lines. Just as they did, global capital's supply chains misjudged the number of timber pallets needed for deliveries. So, this particular panic proved short-lived. Nonetheless, the 2021 imaginary Christmas beer drought drew on deeply embedded uncertainties, many of them fanned by journalists each summer, from the 1940s onwards. These fears were well established by the 1960s, as Rohan Rivett pointed out:

> When Beer stops flowing from the Carlton and United Breweries in this year of grace 1965, many Victorians develop an interest in industrial arbitration, negotiation and court hearings far more conspicuous than when copper mining, postal services or the wharves are threatened with disruption.

How these interests arose, just what they had to do with the actual workers in breweries, and what they tell us about the media, and more significantly, changing class and gender relations in Australia, are the subjects of this chapter. As we will see, the pre-Christmas beer strike, an event more prominent in the imagination than in reality, can be explained in part by state wartime restrictions, and in the main, through changing structures within the twentieth-century brewing industry. As late-twentieth century brewing lost its localised diversity, monopolistic employers back-pedalled on negotiations with the varied unions covering workers in their plants. As the industry globalised, and drinkers turned away from beer, the pub lost its masculine ambience, so that Christmas strikes bothered few. At an

Tooths Brewery workers in Sydney, 1920 (Noel Butlin Archives/Australian National University)

historical moment when changing class and gender relations reshaped leisure, brewery managers, in thrall to neoliberal ideology, tried to reduce obligations to employees by defining them as sub-contractors. In the end, a short Festive Season strike could gain little for either 21st-century brewery workers, or their transnational employers.

Boycotts and Christmas Beer

As dramatic moments, moral panics about a dry Christmas disoriented drinkers in the years after World War One. Even then, the idea of a 'strike' hardly captures the reasons for beer shortages. One band of workers in 1919 found a way to co-ordinate a Christmas beer boycott with a production strike. Their dispute arose from a familiar workplace incident. On the NSW Central Coast, Castlemaine Brewery dismissed one of their workers, who just happened to be a returned soldier. Not only did workers go out on strike demanding the reinstatement of their war hero, Taylor, but miners took up his cause and refused to drink in Newcastle or Maitland hotels. O'Malley, Secretary of the Liquor Trades Employees Association, hinted that the brewers only adopted their hard line because they had imported the latest American managerial practices. If brewery owners succeeded in dismissing Taylor, then no worker was safe from the time-and-motion monitors. What's more, A.I.F. volunteer Taylor had gone to the front along with thousands of other brave Australians to make their new nation free, and incidentally, to protect property-owning capitalists, amongst them Castlemaine Brewery. As the union secretary pointed out to the local newspaper:

> Trade unionists of all organisations are asked now to remember that this is a case of victimisation and that if the brewery workers are defeated in the struggle not one of them will be safe.

Another 1919 stoppage, this time in Sydney, also halted beer supplies. Members of the Federated Engineers Drivers and Firemen's Union set up picket lines to block drays at Toohey's Brewery, forcing publicans to bid for beer deliveries allotted to bush pubs. Any entrenched strike was eventually 'averted' in time for Christmas drinks.

Even though short-lived and largely ineffectual, these 1919 strikes had brought together two resistances to brewers, both of them only incidentally linked to Christmas demand. Drinkers boycotted the public bar and brewery workers simultaneously blocked supplies to pubs still serving customers. The beer strike then was only infrequently caught up in problems of workplace militancy or Christmas demand. In these interwar years, in any case, and, as Iain McIntyre has made clear [in another chapter in this book], the term 'beer strike' was more often than not a substitute for 'beer boycott'.

Workers could enforce these boycotts most effectively in smaller more isolated industrial towns, typically where the local economy revolved around mining. On the regular occasions when publicans tried to raise beer prices in these union-dominated oases, often at the start of summer, union members resisted, sometimes going so far as to place black bans on both bars and beer itself.

The best remembered of these boycotts disrupted Mt Isa pubs in 1929. In the same year, workers in the national capital of Canberra also objected to local publicans' price rises, and declared beer black. As it turned out, the Mt Isa workers won more popular sympathy than their Canberra comrades. As one surprised journalist noted:

> While several miners have been declared 'black' by their stronger-minded fellows for having yielded to the temptation to drink the forbidden beer, a constable has been forgiven for a similar offence because his was deemed to be a special case. The only reasonable explanation of

this leniency is that the miners, perspiring and begrimed, recognise the policeman's lot is even more strenuous than their own.

The writer, likely speaking for readers as well, could only admire the miners' self-discipline. As Christmas approached and the inland town's summer heat intensified, they stuck to their pledge with 'sublime courage', insisting that beer be reduced to sixpence a glass, rather than the one shilling demanded by publicans.

Workers in one town in South Australia perfected these 'strikes' over decades. When publicans raised beer prices in 1902, unions in the shipping transit point of Port Pirie declared beer black, before following with a warning to members that they would be fined if they were seen in bars. Subsequent Port Pirie boycotts between 1912 and 1937 kept these threats alive. In one of many beer disputes, wharf labourers even gave up drinks that habitually accompanied morning 'smokos'. Work gangs typically sent their newest member 'running the rabbit', to buy from barrels on the docks, and bringing beer back by mid-morning, usually in jam jars. Momentarily, dock workers even decided to give up alcohol altogether, and instead shared apples for 'smokos'. So steadfastly did they stick to their boycott, that temperance campaigners turned up at union meetings, where they almost managed to persuade workers that Port Pirie should remain permanently 'dry'.

Insofar as union leaders could hold workers to a boycott, they knew their task would always be easier in winter, rather than in the heat of December and January. Occasionally workers stuck to their boycotts into early December, before rising temperatures quickly diminished the appeal of alternatives like apples at smoko time. The 1920 Port Pirie boycott did threaten to extend into a Christmas beer strike, before union organisers found a way to bring the bans to an end early in the month. And even before then, they had directed the bans towards the public bar, whilst saloon drinking continued on unhindered.

Celebrations following the conclusion of the Mt Isa beer strike, 1930

When disputes in the 1930s threatened Christmas beer, union leaders took the initiative and resolved differences with breweries. Strikes were routinely threatened, then imagined, and reified in the press, although in the event, rarely acted out. So, it was a very rare Christmas that had to be endured entirely without beer. Between the wars, newspaper editors confidently and solemnly predicted strikes, that then failed to eventuate, as was the case in Adelaide in 1933. Workers had threatened to walk out, but the brewery workers' union leaders hurriedly announced that they were on friendly terms with brewers. They had amicably resolved their dispute over a standard grievance of 'first on last off' in any workplace retrenchments as reported by the *Adelaide News*.

Another dispute in Brisbane in December 1936 threatened to slow bottling lines. The workers needed little persuasion to vote against direct action, and turned to arbitration instead. Union leaders were quick to dismiss any suggestion of a Sydney strike for Christmas 1937 as nothing more than 'brewery propaganda'. And in central Queensland, reporters blamed the 1936-37 Christmas beer shortages on a slow supply of malt.

Christmas Beer and World War Two

Wartime intensified these bottlenecks while giving employers new opportunities in enforcing workplace disciplines. In response, a summertime strike rather than winter boycott held new appeal for workers. Wartime restrictions also meant that Christmas had become a much curtailed celebration in Australian cities after 1939 so that beer shortages quickly came to symbolise restlessness about official intrusions into daily life. By 1942, brewers, for their part, were blaming state control of ingredients for beer shortages. In wartime Rockhampton, brewers had struggled to meet Christmas demand as malt supplies dried up. Then in 1944, brewers singled out drinkers hoarding empty beer bottles as the culprits behind reduced Christmas beer. In these and similar instances the press remained comfortable with announcing that beer droughts were 'AVERTED', a descriptor used with tedious familiarity each December from about 1940 onwards. Even then, fears of strikes could only be aroused because of the already straitened supplies ensured through Commonwealth restrictions aimed at cutting volumes of hops, malt, wheat or barley going to brewers. Only in 1946, according to Driscoll, did Commonwealth legislation allow for a 40 percent increase in brewery output.

Several unions had struck at Christmas during World War Two, with some disputes extended beyond December, disrupting beer deliveries after Christmas Day itself. Initially workers went along with these strikes as responses to employers' tactics, rather than challenges initiated from within the workforce, aimed at more humane conditions or higher wages. Once brewery workers realised that even the hint of a dry Christmas would bolster their bargaining power, they began to look more closely at the advantages of summer rather than winter stop-works.

This new form of industrial action at Christmas emerged more clearly in 1942, in one of Sydney's most important breweries.

Kent Brewery staff member in Sydney (Noel Butlin Archives/Australian National University)

Unions restricted their strike to Toohey's Brewery, with little call for wider solidarity, and with what seemed a fairly insignificant cause. Often an annual perk for brewery workers came in the form of a few dozen free bottles that brewery managers handed out each Christmas, and the 1942 dispute began as a relatively simple conflict over this free beer. Engineers at the Sydney brewery were denied their annual gift of a couple of dozen bottles for each driver. So 25 engine drivers decided to go out in December. The workers had already approached none other than the Minister for Customs, hoping he would intervene. Despite these efforts, and as an attack on Christmas conviviality, the walk-out remained largely ineffective. Toohey's workers closed the brewery before Christmas, staying out into January. By then, Toohey's had already shipped Christmas stocks out to pubs.

A Christmas strike followed in Cairns at the Northern Brewery in 1944, this time caused because management sacked four workers and refused to reinstate them. The strike continued over Christmas and, backed by the AWU, firemen in the brewery refused to stoke up boilers. The *Innisfail Evening Advocate*, reported that by 5 January 1945 the brewery was back running at full strength, with the Industrial Magistrate looking into the dismissal of the cellarmen, and the firemen agreeing to light boilers again.

Strategic Strikes and Christmas

This more intense focus on Christmas then, remained in the first instance coincidental rather than strategic, since managers persisted with their familiar and transparent subterfuge of slipping in dismissals a day or two before holidays began, and as January plant wind-downs distracted union leaders. The strikes of 1941-45 often came about because of these sudden sackings. In other words, these were defensive actions intended to protect informal workplace perks like free beer, or to support fellow workers. A more aggressive managerialism, probably as unions suspected before the war, built on American time-and-motion surveillance. It would eventually invite a similarly vigorous response through strike action.

In canvassing for a response to December sackings or to recover vanishing free beer, union leaders quickly realised that Christmas strikes might offer an ideal tactic, a means to improve conditions and wages rather than continuing as a defensive reaction. So, the Christmas beer drought, engineered through strikes, had emerged by the 1970s as one avenue through which brewery workers could challenge increasingly corporatised and monopolistic employers. When the Liquor Trades Union secretary T.J. Doyle remarked of Carlton and United's (CUB) hard-nosed managing director, Sir Reginald Fogarty, during the long 1952 strike, that 'we have him over one of his own barrels', he was giving voice to long suppressed workplace emotions. As it happened Sir Reginald escaped from his difficult position over the barrel with ease, and the strike fell away. Nonetheless, the union's temporary delight reflected accumulated frustrations that had arisen as brewery workers toiled through summer heat, counting off the days to their Christmas break, and all the while fending off demands from overbearing supervisors, insisting they work extra shifts to satisfy festive season demand.

The threat to Christmas beer in Melbourne in 1952 had begun earlier in the year with the brewery in dispute with one union after another. CUB staff had cleared blocked drains in the brewery rather than calling in unionised plumbers, and the conflict continued on into 1953, when the Plumbers Union banned any overtime at Melbourne breweries, outraged because managers had refused their cost-of-living adjustment, and holding up Christmas supplies from a new bottling plant. If unions saw Christmas as a moment in which they could press long-frustrated demands, managers still anticipated the festive season as a break in which they could get rid of staff, or reorganise work routines, whilst the rest of Australia headed off to the beach.

Strikers and Drinkers

Frequently after 1945, the histrionics of a beerless Christmas appeared as little more than a ghostly mirage, reflecting journalists' uncertainties about just where public sympathy might lie. Would drinkers side with fellow workers battling away in summer heat in what they might well have assumed was an essential service? Would the populace see strikes against monopolistic brewers happy to raise prices just before the festive season, as justified? In 1962 for example, Batman, columnist for *The Bulletin,* complained about damage to the Christmas spirit, not through workers blocking supplies, but because brewers were putting up prices. Even publicans took the side of brewery workers, at least in the early phases of strikes, as they reflected on their own struggles against penny-pinching, corporatised brewers, who exercised a monopoly over their public bar beer taps, and thus drinkers' choice. Sir Reginald Fogarty, for example, was content to inform the NSW Royal Commission of 1951 that problems with liquor laws revolved around publicans trying to manipulate their leases rather than breweries' price-gouging.

We could explain many beer shortages in the decade after World War II through a range of factors, most of which had nothing to do with workers or their unions. When Hobart faced an 'acute beer shortage' at Christmas 1951, publicans told *Mercury* reporters that this was nothing new, beer supplies were always low at holiday times.

The *Mercury* reporters put the expected drought down to a shortage of casks, because pubs would not send empties back to breweries; electricity power cuts had reduced bottling runs; a growing population in

Brewery workers leave a stop work meeting at the Sydney Town Hall, 1967 (*Tribune*/Search Foundation, State Library of NSW)

Tasmania with no new licenses or expanded bottling lines at breweries; increased tourism; and not least, the breweries outdated practice of delivering supplies no more than one week in advance of expected increased demand.

It took the Melbourne brewery strike more than one month out from Christmas 1952, to turn journalists to beer shortages caused by union action rather than managerial tactics. Workers in the Abbotsford plant had stopped work in June, to force wage negotiations on their employer, Australia's largest brewing corporation, CUB. No sooner had the workers returned to the Abbotsford Brewery than, in a pattern familiar from northern NSW and Queensland, managers sacked workers. The five dismissed boilerhouse workers admitted that they had gone into a room near to the boilers at the Abbotsford Brewery to drink beer. Under the firm hand of the 'tycoon's tycoon' Sir Reginald Fogarty, who had come to Melbourne after a rugged stint in brewing in Cairns, CUB fired, then refused to either negotiate with or reinstate the cellarmen. They did offer these sacked workers a 'gratuity' depending on length of service, which the indignant workers knocked back. Over one hundred brewery workers went out on strike and despite pressure from CUB, the Conciliation Commissioner refused to intervene. Buoyed by an obviously broad sympathy amongst Victorians, and with beer supplies guaranteed for Melbourne Cup Day, the brewery unions were able to maintain their strike and its picket lines into late-Spring. Spencer Douglas, one of the men dismissed, and for whom journalists sensed popular support, explained in one interview, that in rejecting any payment of 'gratuities', the men just wanted fair treatment. As he made clear to a sympathetic Argus industrial reporter:

> In my opinion I was treated worse than a criminal... even a criminal is given fair trial... I want my job back if it is possible to get it back. I worked for the tramways for 23 years and for the brewery for 12 without a black mark against me.

Although Spencer and his fellow workers could initially count on popular support, any enduring sympathy for the sacked men and for the union pickets, dissipated the closer it came to Christmas Day. Responding to the change, newspapers weighed in. 'Loyalty of unionists to fellow members is undoubtedly a commendable principle', asserted *The Age*, continuing to explain that 'if in turn the worker breaks his loyalty to both his employer in failing to do his duty for which he is paid, then he forfeits any right to be defended.' Unsurprisingly, when Trades Hall advised the pickets to return to work, union members took the hint. By 3 December they were back on the line, still dissatisfied, but agreeing to keep up Christmas supplies.

Even though these brewery employees had retreated before Christmas, their strike, far more than earlier disputes, established the trope of a union-initiated Christmas beer drought in the minds of newspaper writers and readers. Occasionally their worst fears were realised and beer vanished before Christmas. Strikes in Queensland and NSW in 1953, and later years, meant that pubs sold beer from Victoria's Richmond Brewery rather than local brands, but beer, although brewed in a Melbourne suburb, still flowed at Christmas. Even so, as shortages and strikes recurred with regularity between 1950 and 1990, they slowly wore down sympathy for brewery workers. For the most conservative of politicians, each strike was a godsend, and they could use popular panics about a dry Christmas to stoke underlying fears of their oft-proclaimed and rarely-discovered Red Menace.

From mid-century onwards, conservative politicians remained comfortable in using fears of communism to win votes. Whilst communist leadership in unions centred on the wharves, mines and transport, any attack on consumer goods, beer included, could be used to stimulate even greater fears. The radical communist union leader, destroying community harmony, whilst leading workers astray, had greatest currency and a lasting impact in Queensland during the Country Party's seemingly endless post-war regime. The Country Party's inimitable Russell Hinze, right-hand man to Premier Joh Bjelke-Petersen, and as it happens, a publican from the Gold Coast hinterland, delighted in labelling brewery workers' leaders as communists. And worse still, as southerners. In 1978, with a beer strike looking as if it might last through Christmas, Hinze presented the Queensland Parliament with a letter provided to him by 'sources'. Hinze proclaimed the brewery strike a fraud and he had proof that communists and their 'fellow-travellers' were orchestrating the stoppage. The strike leaders were not local radicals either, but rather, 'Communist elements in the south', in other words alien to Queensland. The brewery strike according to Hinze was simply a ploy to exert communist (and southern) authority over Queensland unions. What's more, alien manipulators had planned a strategy so they could end the whole action before it got too close to Christmas. As Hinze revealed to fellow parliamentarians:

> The stoppages were stage-managed and organised many weeks in advance. In fact my advice from these sources is that the date of the start of the strike, and its foreshadowed conclusion towards the end of October have been common knowledge among affiliated unionists since late June or early July.

Whatever we might think of 'Big Russ', ('The Colossus of Roads', or alternatively, Queensland's 'minister for just about everything'), Hinze touched on a growing

Sydney Tooheys demonstration and picket, 1980 (*Tribune*/Search Foundation, State Library of NSW)

sentiment; that workers were being manipulated as Christmas approached, and that conditions in breweries rarely caused industrial actions. Threatening a beer drought for Christmas in his account, and in the eyes of a growing number of drinkers, amounted to little more than a cynical tactic, intended to transform extraneous aspects of union structure and labour relations, rather than arising from genuine workplace grievances. In the long run, according to anyone persuaded by Russell Hinze's synthesis, an alien ideology was driving every dispute in the brewing industry. Once newspapers had caught onto this theme, media imagery of a 'stage-managed' Christmas beer strike, rather than any spontaneous reaction against the mistreatment of fellow workers, would become a ritualised narrative. As such, the Christmas beer strike, imagined or real, could only be resolved with the same theatricality with which Hinze had presented his inside knowledge about Southern Communists.

Beyond Beer

In the words of print, and by 1960, television journalists, the Christmas beer strike could be understood as both a political trope prefiguring threats of Australia's union-dominated future, and a folkloric emblem for an Australian masculinity they could see disappearing fast. There often remained a hint of melodrama, even nostalgia, in predictions of a dry Christmas. In the very same year as Hinze exposed a communist plot to Queensland parliament, other observers were noting that the media's negative imagery of unions in general had hardened, from legitimate though misguided defenders of honest toilers, to a clique of reckless individuals, promoting personal advantage, and driven by imported ideology. In that light, Russell Hinze's thesis on beer strikes, southerners and communism, needs to be set against new media imagery, especially that of television advertising, the changing roles of corporatised breweries, and dissipation of a masculine drinking culture. Beer advertising in fact kept the image of the stereotyped male worker alive long after technological and demographic changes had diversified the working class. This more diverse working class was to face an increasingly intrusive monitoring of traditional practices in the workplace.

The Taylorism alluded to by striking brewery unionists in Queensland in 1919 was to become familiar to other workers decades later. Port Pirie waterside workers, drinking beer as they laboured on the wharves, would have themselves been sacked had they continued on this way into the last decades of the twentieth century. An emphasis on workplace safety meant too that the breweries' customary handing of beer, gratis, to workers, came under suspicion.

Globalised capital and intensifying workplace surveillance went hand-in-hand. As they monitored for orderly and abstemious work practices, and in many ways a more Taylorist workplace, Australian brewing monopolies faced international competition. When Courage set up in Melbourne in 1967 and tried to cut into CUB's Melbourne monopoly, the sales and marketing structures solidified across the early twentieth century began to break down. For their part CUB had already taken over local rivals, expanding into Queensland and New Guinea, and were looking to breach the hold of Toohey's and Tooth's in Sydney. Brewers then found themselves the targets for takeovers, most spectacularly when a John Elliott-inspired Elders bought into, controlled, and then broke up the giant firm of CUB. The 1980s rivalries between CUB and Swan Brewery's dynamic new owner, Alan Bond, intensified once both conglomerates began to expand across state boundaries and into sporting sponsorship. Art connoisseur, occasional football club president, and failed television mogul, the former billboard-painter, Bond, may not have paid as much attention to his breweries as required by commercial probity and the need to remain solvent. He nonetheless did raise the stakes in restructuring the brewing industry. As Frank Bongiorno pointed out, 'With its ambition to "Fosterise" the world, CUB would do for beer what McDonald's had done for hamburgers and Colonel Sanders for fried chicken – but not if Bond had anything to do with it.' Bond eventually found himself confined to the beer-free environs of the West Australian prison system. Elliot's brilliant entrepreneurial star began to flame out, as financing transnational pub buy-outs, and challenging global beverage conglomerates undermined the security of regionalised markets.

Sydney drinkers in 1967 were aghast when they fronted up to local pubs in December to be offered Victorian beer and not only that, but Victorian beer sold to them in steel cans rather than bottles as the *Canberra Times* was quick to note. Coinciding with Courage's entry into the Australian market these parochial intransigences declined rapidly. If CUB could fall to a takeover, then smaller breweries could do little to avoid aggressive incorporation into transnational beverage conglomerates. CUB would come to stand for Carlton and United Beverages rather than Carlton and United Breweries, before relabelling as Foster's Brewing and finally returning, albeit with Japanese firm Asahi ownership, to its original title.

Most obviously these changes meant that the media could no longer portray Christmas supplies restricted to interstate beer as the most heinous imposition. International labels began to line the racks in bottle shops and eventually the tap-handles and barrels in bars. The Christmas strike, when confined as it typically had been, to the one local brewing firm, lost any potency. It survived instead as a reassuring and politically useful device through which the media turned attention away from the globalisation of the brewing industry, and towards recalcitrant unionists. Any strategy to transfer public disdain from the brewer to the worker seems a considered response to the public suspicions of the big brewers, as they grew even bigger. As Driscoll's beer history noted:

> Ever since they began, breweries have been the business that everyone loves to hate. Drinkers blame them for crook beer or for monopolistic price fixing while publicans from time to time have complained bitterly about the tied house system or their business relationships with them.

Union picket outside CUB in Carlton, 1986 (United Workers Union)

What better folk devil to replace the brewer than the anti-Christmas, Marx-inspired union leader, and his killjoy followers? In reality, the strikes themselves made little dint in beer consumption in any case, as Victorian Year-Book figures for the war and immediate post-war years made clear. Rather than the Christmas strike threatening alcohol consumption, in following decades, a gradual turning away from beer to mixed drinks and especially wine, registered in ABS statistics and challenged brewers. Brewers hoped in vain as it turned out, that by investing in publicity campaigns with saturation television advertising and when that was restricted, sponsorship for sporting events (most memorably a Fosterised Melbourne Cup and Foster's AFL/VFL Grand Final), could stave off decline.

To this end, even sympathy or at least curiosity, about beer boycotts and strikes was inevitably framed around the 'working man', the tough toilers on docks and in mines whose beer was actually an aid to productivity and who should be able to enjoy drinking on holidays like Christmas. Unfortunately for advertisers, whose imagined consumers were drinkers in British pubs or American bars, their archetypes composed a declining proportion of the Australian population as a whole and more significantly of those who drank alcohol. Clearly, these symbolic and masculinist figures, even if played with enthusiasm by famous comedians in advertisements, were losing cultural authority. As they did, the once-prized sinecures for the semi-skilled, on the bottling line at a major brewery, no longer counted for much. The male redoubt of the public bar changed, and at a rapid rate after loosened licensing hours. In due course the pub itself, if it survived at all, became a different, less masculinist and far less proletarian place, one in which mass-market brands faced challenges from wine, cocktails and craft beer.

CUB picketers in Melbourne stand in front of a mural by Van Thanh Rudd, 2016 (Rudd)

The later 20th century's increasingly hysterical, if occasionally nostalgic responses to brewery strikers had grown in parallel to the globalising corporate structure of the 'beverage' rather than brewing industry; the change in recreational life from a male-dominated pub to a late night drinking venue for men and women; and a more varied alcohol diet, away from beer to wine, and mixed drinks, as ABS figures make clear. Beer remained in the first instance an emblematic commodity through which workers could respond to increased prices and the power of the brewers by way of participation in, or sympathy for strikes. At the same time, beer symbolised an apolitical popular commonality, potentially undermined by radical unionists. In any case, by the end of the twentieth century, globalised beverage conglomerates had just about transformed the entire Australian brewing industry, and were typically untroubled by beer shortages. Their customers were more likely to see Christmas as a time for prosecco, cocktails, or perhaps a craft beer, rather than any mass-produced beer product. We would thus not find explanations for the annual and ritualised Christmas beer strike in the actions of unions. Rather, from about the 1940s through to 1990s, this recurrent trope, of the Christmas strike, reflected the flexible consumption intrinsic to neoliberalism, and the restructure of class and gender relations produced through that ideology.

Brewers and Strikers in the New Century

The Christmas Beer Strike then has had a history as unsettled as December beer supplies themselves. Arousing localised fears after World War One, workers occasionally and creatively supported boycotts with strikes. After the interwar Depression, when alcohol consumption plunged in any case, workers may have threatened strikes but generally found a way to get beer flowing before Christmas. Strikes where they did occur, were generally short-lived and localised, and in fact remained more often than not, proposals rather than actual conflicts. If the spectre of a beerless Christmas routinely haunted Australia after 1940, this threat stemmed in the first instance from state-imposed shortages rather than from strike action. After 1950, panics over Christmas Beer Strikes were conjured up by media rather than through union action. As a result, the Christmas beer strike had little to do with the actual availability of beer, and depended rather more on the role of the media, and the workplace changes demanded by monopolistic employers. Threatened droughts typecast union leaders as killjoys, while propping up the deflating image of the male worker as parochial, and unadventurous, unthinkingly encouraging unsafe work routines, and readily manipulated by communists and their ilk. Such an image could easily be employed to justify intrusive workplace surveillance, and transnational control of a localised industry.

As masculine drinking routines have disintegrated, the beer strike has lost much of its potency. So brewery disputes in the 21st century have taken on a different character, for which Christmas is irrelevant. An uneasy, even volatile integration of brewing into beverage production has only intensified issues of workplace surveillance, sub-contracting and wage stagnation. In response strikes are generally longer-lasting rather than seasonal. For example, the 180-day stoppage at Carlton and United in 2016 (brought to an end two weeks before Christmas). As *The Age*'s reporting pointed out, crises in union membership, as employers tried to reconstruct employees as subcontractors, drove conflict. Such protracted strikes point to far more fundamental threats than any dread for a dry Christmas Day.

CHAPTER 18
PUB BOYCOTTS, LOYALISM, AND UNIONS IN QUEENSLAND
Iain McIntyre

During the late 1910s workers across Queensland regularly called pub boycotts over female hotel workers' wages and conditions, as well as issues such as the cost of accommodation and beer. Charleville, Cloncurry, Mount Mulligan, Mount Morgan, Wolfram Camp, Maryborough, Emerald, Gordonvale, Mosman, Rockhampton, Irvinebank, Brisbane, Normanton, Riverstone, Kuridala, Maryborough and Richmond all experienced beer strikes, the majority of which were successful.

These disputes occurred in the context of the broader social upheaval that had arisen during World War One. Out of this emerged a wave of industrial and political disputes involving fierce tussles between militants and moderates in the labour movement. This period also saw activists attacked by right-wing nationalists, fired up by xenophobic, pro-war and anti-socialist ideology.

In November 1919 the majority of the local mill's workforce struck in Prosperine after the owner refused to dismiss five men who had broken a hotel boycott. This came after physical assaults on picket lines, at which shots had been fired, and was followed by a 400 strong meeting of right-wingers. Summing up loyalist sentiment the local magistrate, in sentencing a picket to two months in jail declared, 'It was time the town was cleared of such dregs of humanity which appeared to come like a wave ... by every train from all parts of the Earth, preaching sabotage and direct revolution, endeavouring to damage the district and paralyse industry.'

Such calls for action were inspired by the severe beating and deportation of activists, including Australian Workers Union and Queensland Railway Union organisers, in Hughenden over a series of days in late October 1918. During the purge one hotel employee witnessed dozens of boycotters being 'kicked nearly to death' as loyalists 'drunk with grog supplied by the squatters and publicans...hunted in packs of 20 to 30 from house to house.'

These assaults occurred in the early stages of what would become a 19 month boycott over the refusal of local hotels to backpay female bar staff part of their overtime earnings. The violence followed unsubstantiated media

The Great Westernv Hotel, which was subject to the boycott in Hughenden (Flinders Shire Historical Collection)

reports of 'agitators' and 'extremists' attacking soldiers who had attempted to patronise banned hotels. The most fevered included claims of uniforms being torn off backs and military badges being trampled in the dust and spat upon by female strikers.

Despite the evictions being framed as the spontaneous response of rank and file soldiers subjected to intolerable abuse, military intelligence reports from the time, later uncovered by historian Raymond Evans, show that they resulted from an anti-union pact. As alleged by victims at the time, this involved right-wing officers joining together with station owners, hoteliers and other local business-people to bring returned and serving soldiers into the area.

A town meeting came on the heels of the bashings and deportations. Drawing on grotesque distortions of leftist militancy the town's mayor declared an end to the beer strike and pledged to 'exterminate the hotbed of IWWism from our midst.' In doing so he advocated the removal of ALP members from the town council, as well as the formation of a Vigilance Committee.

The beer strike was far from over, however. Boycott organisers quickly returned and regrouped. The executive of the Townsville Industrial Council unanimously passed a resolution on 22 October placing bans on the handling of 'any beer consigned to Hughenden.' Two exceptions were made, one regarding the state-owned railway refreshment rooms and the other the Hughenden Hotel, which had acceded to bar staff demands. Industrial action broadened after warehouse owners in Townsville sacked 60 carters for refusing to handle goods. Following intervention from the state ALP government, which included closing all of Hughenden's pubs for five days, transport bans were lifted.

Despite industrial courts ruling against hoteliers, the dispute dragged on. Rowdy meetings, numbering up to 450 people, resumed in the streets. Much of the focus shifted to action by shearers, railway workers and others who firmed up the boycott by isolating defaulters. This was generally accomplished by forcing employers to remove them or by forming work gangs made up solely of abstainers. Station cooks played their part by refusing to provide food to those who had patronised black banned hotels when in town. Through such sustained economic and industrial pressure the campaign was finally won in July 1920.

A police inspector and others posing outside the black banned Central Hotel in Hughenden, 1919 (Flinders Shire Historical Collection)

CHAPTER 19
CECILIA SHELLEY: FEMINIST, ACTIVIST, TRAILBLAZER
Daniel A. Elias

Cecilia Shelley struck fear into the hearts of the men at the Trades Hall of Western Australia, in what was then a male-dominated labour movement. Her charismatic and tough presence gained her the moniker 'Tigress of Trades Hall'. Her significance to history is that she was the first woman to become a paid Trade Union secretary in Australia. From her humble beginnings in the Western Australian goldfields, she led the life of a feminist trailblazer, identifying at a young age the importance of collective direct action for mutual gain. Organising a successful strike in 1919, she made her mark at Trades Hall with her notably militant approach and would subsequently lead her union in several other disputes. Her reputation earned her scorn from conservative elements of society and praise from others, particularly women. Her egalitarian disposition drew her to the works of Marx and Lenin, equally she was drawn to the Western Australian Labor Party (ALP). Her advocacy for women, and women's issues, prefigured the onset of second wave feminism in Australia marking her as a woman ahead of her time. So, who was this radical organiser, Cecilia Moore Shelley?

Cecilia was born on 3 January 1893 and was the sixth child of an Irish family of nine. Like many families during the late 19th century, the Shelleys moved where the winds of economic opportunity led them. Born in Adelaide, South Australia, her family moved to Esperance, Western Australia, when she was about three or four. Like thousands of others during the Western Australian goldrush, her father sought fortune in the goldfields to the north in Kalgoorlie. She and her family followed, making their home in Boulder where they would stay for many years. Her formal education was short, she attended a Catholic school and left at around the age of thirteen or fourteen. Shelley did not receive further education, which was customary of young women during that era. She was expected

Cecilia Shelley (State Library of WA)

to join the workforce, and at a young age she did. Despite her education, Cecilia left school with a firm grasp on arithmetic, reading, and writing, the last of which was not her strong suit. As a result, there are scattered personal written records of her time as a union leader. Her formative education would be the practical skills and experiences of everyday life, especially those experiences that only women would know of. Her nature having never dissipated with age, she later educated herself further on political philosophy in radical reading groups, familiarising herself with the writings of Marx and Lenin.

Her family's working-class background made them sympathetic to the labour movement. Her father was a labour activist in his early years, while her brothers volunteered their time for the ALP – bringing Cecilia with them. While in her late teens, with no formal skills, Cecilia moved to Perth looking for work. Since there was very little manufacturing in Western Australia it was common for 'unskilled' women to work in the service industry where they did 'women's work': cleaning, cooking, and serving. In a pivotal conversation with her father, Cecilia and her sister were complaining about their working conditions, when he remarked, 'Why don't you get yourselves a union...'. And so they did.

Shelley had a handful of significant experiences informing her worldview as she joined the workforce and the labour movement, from her first experience of direct action to major turning points in world history. The split of the ALP over the World War One conscription debates troubled her. She was surprised how little opposition there was in the Western Australian constituency to the pro-conscription position. At a Perth Town Hall public meeting, attendees rose to welcome Prime Minister Billy Hughes whom the pro-conscription campaign invited. In protest, Cecilia proudly remained seated. She was angry at the federal government for sending so many boys to be killed on the slopes of Gallipoli or at the barbed-wired fields of the western front. On the eastern front, revolution broke out. The 1917 October Revolution in Russia captured Cecilia's imagination. She recalled in her oral memoirs that she, 'was walking on air... I attended meetings on the Esplanade and even collected money for the Russian people.' The revolution demonstrated to her that the labour movement had real potential to enact positive change, a lesson she took to her union organising.

Cecilia also learnt through personal experiences early in her working life. As a waitress she began work at 7:45 am and finished at midnight. Lunch was provided but she had to forgo eating breakfast to pay rent. She could not afford both meals, as she recalls, 'We were starved.' One day her co-worker, Lil, was

Kalgoorlie's York and Oriental Hotels, circa 1910s
(National Library of Australia)

fed up with being starved, and asked Cecilia if she would join her in a work stoppage for a cup of tea at 11 am. Together they took direct action and had some tea and bread when the clock struck on the hour. They were afraid but they were successful. From then on they were allowed a short tea break every shift. This illustrated the effectiveness of direct action but also demonstrated the importance of having a rapport with co-workers. Much of her success was found in her ability to inspire other women to take industrial action.

Shelley's trade union was the Hotel, Club, Caterers, Tearoom and Restaurant Employees' Union (HCCTREU). At her first few union branch meetings she made an immediate impression. In one anecdote the union secretary George Dixon dismissed the grievances of a group of women, arguing men's grievances ought to be addressed first. Cecilia, recognising that a large portion of the membership base were women, argued against Dixon's dismissive tone. In doing so she won the respect and loyalty of many of the women union members. Dixon was a dull functionary stuck in the past, when men made up a majority of the HCCTREU membership base. World War One changed the workplace, and made women play a more prominent economic and social role in Australia. Cecilia understood this, Dixon did not. With the rapport and loyalty of the union's women, she immediately made use of their numerical advantage. In 1919 she was elected to be a union organiser and Cecilia wasted no time getting to work. Her friend and advisor, Alex McCallum, ALP Secretary, recommended that if she wanted to get outcomes she should, 'Keep away from the Arbitration Court.' She obliged. An early scheme of hers was to inform the hotel employers that she was going to withdraw her members if they did not accept a new wage agreement. The threat seemed to work at first, but the hoteliers were speaking out of both sides of their mouths. They accepted a new award rate replacing the agreement of 1916, but never planned to implement it.

The game was on: McCallum backed Cecilia by releasing a story in *The West Australian* newspaper calling on the hoteliers to, 'sign the agreement or be blacklisted.' The following day a list of the hotels which signed the agreement was published in the same paper, giving HCCTREU members a guide on whether or not they should go to work. Cecilia capitalised on her rapport with the members, calling a strike by going door to door of each hotel. 'Out!' she called, 'All out!', with many women following her.

After the war Western Australia was experiencing significant industrial unrest, with strikes at the Kalgoorlie goldfields and on the Fremantle wharves. The workers at Kalgoorlie could not come to an agreement with their employers and went on strike multiple times, and there was an all-out riot at the Fremantle wharves, ending with the martyrdom of a worker. Not so coincidentally, the threat to blacklist hoteliers happened at the first anniversary of the wharves erupting. Perhaps because of such unrest, and fear of further rioting, Cecilia's strike action came to a rapid conclusion only hours into its commencement. *The West Australian* called it the 'shortest strike in the record of the State...' with the hoteliers

A police officer guards a barbed wire barricade across Howard Street, Perth during a trade union demonstration over conditions at the Esplanade Hotel, 1921 (State Library of WA)

quickly capitulating. They agreed to sign the new award agreement increasing wages and improving conditions.

The award she helped win did not cover Kalgoorlie and its surrounds. The union was confident in her success, so Cecilia was sent by them to her home ground in the goldfields. Her skill as an organiser was endorsed by the ALP's state executive, who agreed to pay for her journey to Kalgoorlie and half of her expenses. Still working under the auspices of Dixon, Cecilia did not take direct strike action in the goldfields. Undeterred, she used her autodidactic skills to study the award agreements from different states across Australia, grasping the finer details to prepare the case in Kalgoorlie. Shelley used her charisma to her advantage, organising women to testify before the arbitration court too. The unified experience of underpay and victimisation the women attested to led to the union's application for a wage increase to be approved. Following her success, she returned to Perth and replaced Dixon as secretary of the HCCTREU. Her election to the role made her the first paid woman to lead a trade union in Australia, making her mark on the movement the moment she took over.

There were two significant industrial disputes in the 1920s, both of which resulted in strikes. The decade saw a marked hostility from employers towards the HCCTREU, and so the Union responded in kind. The adoption of militant tactics defined Cecilia's early approach to industrial disputes. She learnt from her lesson as an organiser in 1919 and was not afraid to use direct action. Upon becoming secretary in November 1920, she issued a pre-Christmas threat to employers demanding an increase in wages similar to the award rate she had bargained for in Kalgoorlie. The hoteliers were still bitter about the increase of 1919, and refused the wage increase. With a confrontation brewing, the employers pre-emptively locked-out workers to stop them from going on strike. They were better prepared this time around. The union was unable to cause a disruption to business and so agreed to negotiate. Cecilia's experience at the arbitration court in Kalgoorlie proved useful, and she again employed her experience before the private arbitrator, Magistrate Canning. In the negotiations, she skilfully advocated for women in the workforce utilising her own experience and others to make her argument. Combined with her knowledge of other award agreements from across the country, she countered the employers' arguments with devastating precision. Canning was convinced there needed to be change to better protect women at the workplace, and an agreement was reached in early 1921. In what became known as the Canning Agreement conditions were improved, holidays and a reasonable spread of shifts were gained, and wages were increased anywhere from 10 per cent to 28 per cent. Aged just 27 years old, it was another feather in the cap of Cecilia Shelley.

The Canning Agreement led to the first confrontation in March 1921, where a waitress at the Perth Esplanade Hotel, collecting union dues, was sacked. Concerned that employers would begin to dismiss all unionised staff after such a victory for the Union, Cecilia decided that the dismissal would not go unopposed. She insisted the worker be reinstated, and the employers refused. A walk out was called, and the strike was on. The dispute lasted nearly half a year, 22 weeks, with the Employers' Federation lobbying the State Government for Cecilia to receive a summons as they believed it was, 'time this union secretary was forced to learn her duty to the public.' Yet there were no grounds for her arrest, so the strike continued with Cecilia a free woman. But on 8 July the employers were about to get their wish, with a drama playing out with typical defiance from Cecilia. A report in the *South Western Times*, 'Unionist Secretary Fined: Miss Cecilia Shelley', stated that Cecilia was arrested and charged with 'disorderly conduct' for participating at a picket line. A witness reported that a Constable Robinson accused Cecilia of breaking past the picket line. The Constable called out, 'Look here Miss Shelley, keep away from this place.' She persisted and strode forward towards the hotel responding to the Constable with cheek, saying, 'I will do what I dash well please. You can go to hell backwards for all I care.' The Constable's threats were not empty. She was promptly arrested. As she was cuffed, she exclaimed, 'I will make you suffer for putting your greasy hands on me, you dirty rotten mongrel.' The witness report is unverifiable, nonetheless it marks an escalation in the dispute. Cecilia was arrested and faced Judge W.A.G. Walter, R.M., before the City Courts, pleading not guilty. The ruling was the minor charge of disorderly conduct that meant Cecilia received a slap on the wrist and a minor fine, and it was not long before she was back out on the streets organising.

A dark dimension to this dispute was the issue of preferential European labour. The White Australia Policy was still in place, and it was stipulated in the Canning Agreement that preference would be given to, 'members of the white races.' However during the strike the Esplanade Hotel employed Chinese workers to break it. This caused an uproar within the labour movement, with thousands of protestors descending upon the Esplanade green to show their solidarity with the HCCTREU members. The crescendo to the dispute was reflective of three major issues which were consuming Western Australia society at large. The first was what had initially animated the dispute, the denied reinstatement of a victimised woman at her workplace which essentially proved the point of the Canning Agreement – that women needed better protections at the workplace. Secondly, the precarious nature of the workforce during the 1920s was a powder keg ready to explode, with race relations aggravating an already tense environment. And finally, that class distinctions still meant something in the early 20th century, with the bulk of the protestors coming from a working-class background.

Previous years saw a steady rise in unemployment, fluctuating between 5.2 per cent to 8.5 per cent. When thousands came out to attend rallies, conservative elements of society recoiled. They were alarmed that there was a mass of working class interest coalescing behind the dispute. In anticipation of a repeat of the rioting at the Fremantle wharves, the police sent an armed and mounted contingent to face-off the protestors. A partisan police Commissioner issued the order that the police were to, 'safeguard the rights of "property".' Under the polemical editorial supervision of John Curtin, the *Westralian Worker* added, 'A number of firms are refusing to supply the Esplanade lazarette [supply stores]'. Acting in solidarity with the HCCTREU other unionised workers began to deny foodstuffs and liquor to the hotel. Despite the escalating tension, no violence broke out and the standoff continued. Yet the dispute would soon be unravelled.

From the onset of the dispute the ALP Disputes Committee considered the industrial action an 'impetuous' move by a newly elected woman secretary and dismissed it accordingly. Perhaps they took this position because Cecilia did not consult them before acting, but she did not have to. Or equally they were afraid of the optics of a prolonged strike, having lost the last state election in the same month the strike began. Nonetheless, the unsteady relationship between trade unions and the ALP began to rear its ugly head once more at Trades Hall. The solidarity actioned by the brewery workers was vetoed by the Labor Council, the combined executive committee of trade unionist and ALP members at Trades Hall. The Council directed the brewery workers to continue supplying beer to the Esplanade Hotel. This severely undermined the HCCTREU industrial action, effectively kneecapping the strike. Four months into the dispute, after Cecilia's arrest, and upon the rapid escalation of the strike the Disputes Committee and Mr. H. Millington, ALP Secretary, decided to increase their involvement in the affair and overrule Cecilia's authority at Trades Hall. They put 'pressure' on the Esplanade Hotel to settle the dispute. Cecilia recognised the threat that the Disputes Committee involvement posed. It would give rise to the perception that the union capitulated. This was dangerous, because it would weaken the union's capacity to recruit members thereby reducing their bargaining power and ability to enforce the Canning Agreement. In the end Shelley's anxieties came to pass.

The strike ultimately failed, and the workers involved were not re-employed by the hotel. The failure was not from a lack of effort from Cecilia. Nor was it also from a lack of solidarity from the community at large, which at one point saw a remarkable 7000 protestors attend a rally where Curtin spoke. It was, rather, the intransigence of the hoteliers that meant the negotiations to settle the dispute became protracted, and the union did not have the funds to support the striking workers for much longer. The Trades Hall Labor Council abandoned Cecilia and the HCCTREU members, and folded to the Esplanade Hotel. The following election for secretary of the union saw Cecilia step aside from the role, and the radical George Ryce take over. His personal philosophy made him one of the founding members of the Perth branch of the Communist Party of Australia. He was of a similar temperament to Cecilia, and the two became close friends. It is unclear whether they were romantically together, but it is clear they had a deeply personal relationship. Their professional partnership significantly impacted Cecilia's outlook, with Ryce introducing her to radical reading groups. It is here that she learnt Marxist theory, which placed her on the far left of the ALP and resulted in her expulsion from the party in 1925. She did, however, remain with the HCCTREU as an organiser where

she focused on building membership: nearly doubling the size of the union in 1922 from its position in 1919.

The industrial unrest which ensued in the post-war era was followed with an economic recession in Western Australia. Wages and conditions stagnated until the second major confrontation Cecilia was a leader in took place in January 1925. The HCCTREU requested to renegotiate the award agreement with the United Licensed Victuallers (ULV), hotelier's association, and catering employers. Their central claims were to improve regulations around working hours and a general wage increase. The first claim was to reduce the maximum working hours to 44 hours per week, in line with the Factories and Shops Act of 1920. Unsurprisingly, these demands were met with hostility from employers who claimed they were 'totally unreasonable'. Strike action was again necessary and this time around the union was not to be outmanoeuvred. Trades Hall had to be involved for the industrial action that Cecilia and Ryce had planned. The ALP Disputes Committee, now led by the sympathetic P.J. Mooney, joined in the fray.

Their approach was innovative and effective. Work stoppages were called in intervals by different sections of the workplace. Mooney coordinated and organised the support from other trade unions with the Brewery Workers Union and the Barmaids' and Barmen's Union joining the industrial action. The cross-union cooperation allowed for rolling work stoppages that meant employers could not close their doors because alternating sections of the workplace were still operational. They were technically not on strike but effectively they were causing a significant disruption to their employers. At a monthly meeting of employers, the ULV suggested that 'perhaps the payment of a few shillings would get the association out of trouble.' However, no agreement was reached at the meeting regarding the number of workplace hours. The resolution reached by the employers was that they agreed to the wage increase but disagreed with the reduction of work hours. They wanted to maintain the 48 hours per week for hospitality staff. It was recognised in the meeting that the hotel association was under considerable duress, and that they believed it was time for them to go on the offensive. The conservative media concurred, revealing the misogynistic views society still held about women and in particular targeting Cecilia's involvement.

Unsettling headlines for any modern reader, unsurprising headlines for a reader in the 1920s stated the striking women were, 'Amazons on the Warpath', or the 'Amazon at the Doorway'. They added that women were behaving in an 'unfeminine' manner, using 'uncouth language'. The papers reported that it was 'Shelley's Army' causing the problem. The employers were convinced that the unions did not represent the rank and file of the workforce. They were in for a rude surprise. 900 workers convened at Trades Hall for a meeting regarding the employers' response to the work stoppages. With so many workers at the meeting, an opportunity was recognised to gain more momentum behind their cause. The meeting was adjourned, and some hundred workers slipped out to rally more to join the meeting. It

Katherine Susanah Pritchard, circa late 1920s
(State Library of NSW)

PJ Mooney, 1927 (State Library of WA)

was a move straight out of Cecilia's playbook in the strike of 1919: striking workers were going from bars, to tearooms, to hotels urging workers to 'down tools'. Numbers swelled at the reconvening of the meeting at Trades Hall, this time attended by 1,450 workers.

The dispute under the combined leadership of Shelley, Ryce, and the Disputes Committee was effective. They suggested, once more, the need for a private arbitrator to settle the dispute. The employers agreed, and negotiations began. When the clause preferencing the employment of unionised workers was rejected, the stoppages evolved to a prolonged strike – it seemed that militancy was to be the order of the day. Although it was a polarising dispute, amid some strikers receiving threats of violence with a proprietor pulling out a gun among gathered protestors, the employers sealed their fate by denying improved working conditions. Once again employers were blacklisted if they did not agree to the new award agreement, and businesses were picketed. An impasse was reached, and Cecilia's old mentor and friend McCallum had to mediate a resolution. Now a Western Australian parliamentarian, McCallum's intervention ended the dispute.

The agreement hinted at the future direction of the women's movement and was where Cecilia's attention would turn to next. The new award did not retain the preference clause, but it was ultimately a win for the trade unions involved; granting them a 44-hour work week, with 4 hours overtime pay and a wage increase. The introduction of penalty rates and the five-day work week began to meet the needs of women and domestic life. However, the direct industrial action Cecilia took in 1925 would be the last time she used such militant tactics. Her dexterity as an advocate for the lived experience of women at the workplace would be used at the arbitration court in the future. She was re-elected secretary upon the death of Ryce, who passed away in 1929, and would serve the union and the labour movement for another 42 years.

When Ryce died her labour militancy diminished, yet she did not receive the moniker 'Tigress of Trades Hall' for nothing. In the years following the Great Depression she relentlessly advocated for women's rights and their welfare, recognising that market logic did not meet the needs of social life. She had never forgotten what drove her to become a labour organiser: the mistreatment and exploitation of women in the service industry. Cecilia and famous radical writer Katharine Susannah Prichard created the Unemployed Girls and Womens' Defence Committee. Established in July 1932, it was set up to act as a watchdog of the private employment registry industry. She helped establish food-drives, and assisted people in finding shelter at the height of the Depression.

Shelley's energy was also put into the international peace movement. She was struck by the futility of World War One, where she saw droves of young men leave never to return, amongst whom was her teenage sweetheart, Allen. By the time it was becoming clear that another major global conflict was on the horizon, she and others established the Western Australian Movement Against War and Fascism. The Movement held rallies, where on 1 August 1934, Cecilia was the keynote speaker at the Rechabite Hall. An extension of her two passions resulted in her helping to establish the first Western Australian International Women's Day which was held on 13 March 1936. Hosted at Arundle Hall, Perth, Cecilia was able to express her vision for a better world for women, from economic concerns to social issues. Held annually, every International Women's Day discussed different themes bringing together various feminist interest groups, helping to elevate women's rights into the political sphere and propelling the movement forward. She extended her time and energy beyond the labour movement to the fundamental belief that the world could be a better place. Cecilia Shelley is a significant and understudied figure in Australian history deserving of more time and research by contemporary historians.

CHAPTER 20
COMMUNIST JOCKA BURNS AND GRAPE PICKING
Alex Ettling and Iain McIntyre

In 1926, the young worker Jocka Burns took off from Melbourne with swag in tow. Aged 16 he remained 'on the track' for the next 12 years as an itinerant bushworker, including spells picking grapes for winemakers. Such people played a vital role in the rural economy, carrying out harvesting and other seasonal labour as required. As with hoboes in the US, their lifestyle was both romanticised and demonised. They were fiercely exploited, working long hours for little pay and living in destitute conditions. This locked them into poverty which, when combined with social ostracism and police harassment, kept them homeless and on the move in search of further work.

Rural workers in Australia have always been subject to abuse and exploitation. As in other industries the profits generated from producing grapes, hops, wheat, sugar and other raw materials for alcohol have relied on generations of cheap labour.

The sourcing of such labour has been internal and external. Convict labour initially dominated but following the end of transportation in the mid-nineteenth century the proportion of agricultural work being done by people hailing from other vulnerable groups increased. First Nations community members were, and well into the twentieth century would continue to be, either employed under slavery-like conditions on farms and stations or engaged in exploited but paid seasonal work.

During the nineteenth century South Sea Islanders were regularly deceived, kidnapped, and forced into working on sugar plantations. They were subject to racist and repressive laws and contracts which made it illegal to organise in the workplace or take part in various community activities, including drinking alcohol.

From the latter part of the nineteenth century onwards unions excluded a range of workers deemed to be 'non-white'. Beholden to colonial ideology, they sought to remedy the undercutting of wages and conditions by demanding that victims of the hyper-exploitation be removed from workplaces and the country. As a result rural workers from South Sea Islander, Chinese and other backgrounds joined those from Indigenous communities in having to largely fight alone. Unsurprisingly this weakened the working class as a whole and contributed to ongoing poverty and exploitation.

Following the introduction of the White Australia Policy, immigration restrictions and deportations led the sugar industry and others to draw on new sources of labour and expand some older ones. This included workers, such as those from Italy and Greece, whose categorisation as 'white' varied over time, and who had to initially campaign to be admitted into rural unions. Their primary allies in doing so were fellow members and supporters drawn from and influenced by organisations such as the Industrial Workers of the World and the Communist Party of Australia (CPA).

Burns came to join the ranks of the latter. He already had experience of labour militancy, having organised a strike on a station while working as a rouseabout, but in 1930 he became a communist, and would remain one until his death in 2002. Like many low-paid workers he could not always afford to pay for travel and often jumped freight trains. He first met a member of the CPA, known as 'Apples', after being arrested enroute to Mount Isa. A key argument that brought him around to the revolutionary cause, as recalled in an oral history with Wendy Lowenstein, was 'that you've got a Labor government in NSW... and what are we doing? We're in and out of jail all the time, cadging food and getting fingerprinted.'

Burns went on to become a member of the Young Communist League, and took part in many political activities across Australia's east coast. When in work he recruited people to unions and the CPA's Militant Minority Movement. When out of it he took part in unemployed struggles over work-for-the-dole schemes and other forms of inadequate and exploitative welfare. Anti-eviction activity and jousting with members of the fascist New Guard movement was accompanied by street speaking and selling the *Workers Voice* and other party publications. All of which led to 28 arrests and numerous periods in jail.

A typical working year would see Burns travel up and down the east coast working and organising in canneries and sheep stations before engaging in 'snatching' and carting plums, cherries and grapes. A ruthless contractor in Rutherglen dominated hiring for the latter. In the vineyards Burns found conditions that numbered amongst the worst, telling Lowenstein, 'There were no amenities and no facilities on the job whatsoever ... sometimes you camp where they just chuck the horse out of the stable.' There were no showers either. Lowenstein asked about toilets. 'No no, you go down to the vines', replied Burns.

Although the efforts of Burns, and those that followed him into union organising, have at times improved conditions, wage theft, exploitation and abuse remain widespread in contemporary horticulture. Then, as now, there is a dirty story of social relations behind the fine wines that are so often traded as a luxury good.

Workers in the Best's Vineyard, Victoria, circa 1900 (Victoria Collections)

CHAPTER 21
THE MATTEOTTI CLUB
Iain McIntyre

Made up of anti-fascist exiles and others opposed to Mussolini's regime, the Matteotti Club was formed in Melbourne in 1927. It was named after Italian socialist, Giacomo Matteotti, who was kidnapped and murdered by blackshirts near Rome in 1924. This followed a speech he had given in parliament against electoral fraud.

The club actively worked to oppose fascism in Italy and Australia. Founded by anarchists, the Matteotti Club brought together people from a range of political persuasions, including communists, republicans, socialists, and others. At its peak it had a membership of 500-700 subscribers. It published and distributed literature, and raised money to support political prisoners at home as well as Italians involved in strikes and other political activities across Australia. In addition to building and maintaining a network of exiles it lobbied the federal government over racist and anti-leftist immigration policies and drew union attention to the Italian consul's role in coercing recently arrived migrants into strike-breaking activities.

Central to the group's activities was its clubhouse. This was initially located in Spring Street but, owing to its popularity, moved to the Horticultural Hall opposite Trades Hall at 31 Victoria St, Carlton in 1928. This provided a space for Italian people to gather at a time when they faced much bigotry and discrimination. Beyond providing a radical library and a meeting space for campaigns, the venue included several rooms, among them a ballroom capable of fitting over 500 people. Social events, including card games, parties, meals, bocce matches, and drinking sessions were a regular part of the club's activities.

Held up to three nights a week, the club's dances were particularly popular. One event held in April 1931 saw Peter Baffigo break the world record for marathon dancing by remaining continuously in motion for 204 hours and 20 minutes.

Facilities were also made available to radicals outside of the Italian community, hosting for instance the first conference of the CPA's union oriented Militant Minority Movement in 1930. Members also organised annual bilingual commemorations for the club's namesake, which were attended by a wide cross-section of Melbourne's labour movement.

The Matteotti Club also served as an organising point for the physical confrontation of fascists. This included the disruption of a filmed speech by Mussolini during Melbourne's first screening of a 'talking picture' in 1929.

Anti-fascists enjoy a night out at the Matteotti Club
(United Workers Union)

In another incident that year club members busted up a gathering of black shirts held at Melbourne's Temperance Hall to celebrate the anniversary of Mussolini's March on Rome. For their part members of the Melbourne Fascist Club, one of a number of chapters auspiced by the Italian consulate, regularly smashed the Horticultural Hall's windows.

Consular officials, informers and agents from the Italian government kept a close eye on club activities with one report stating, 'They have rented a hall in which they gather and, along with women of ill repute, dance on Sundays and abuse alcoholic substances.' At this time General William Blamey, leader of the shadowy far-right paramilitary group the League of National Security, was serving as Chief Commissioner of Victorian Police. With protesters and street speakers regularly bashed and arrested in Melbourne, it did not take much for consular officials to convince local authorities to take action against Italian leftists. Raids of the club were carried out and Italian anti-fascist publications suppressed and censored.

Other forms of harassment, such as arrests of patrons upon leaving the club were also employed. Many of these involved 'catch all' type charges, such as when Betty Wong Ying was taken into custody in Victoria Street for 'Offensive Behaviour'. This consisted merely of 'throwing her arms about, and calling out in a loud voice, "I'll drink what I like, and dance with whom I like".' During a similar case, involving a charge of 'Indecent Language' against a man who had been heading home after a game of cards, a magistrate called for the club to be put 'under strict supervision', if not 'closed altogether'.

The club weathered such vicissitudes before collapsing at the close of 1933. This came about in part due to economic difficulties imposed by the Great Depression, as many members had left Melbourne for work elsewhere and few remaining could still afford their fees. It also stemmed from bitter personal disputes and political differences regarding how best to continue anti-fascist resistance in Australia and abroad.

Members of the Matteotti Club outside the venue's original location in Spring Street, Melbourne, 1927 (Italian Historical Society)

CHAPTER 22
'WHAT SHOULD WE DO...': MARITIME WORKERS AND DRINKING
Alex Ettling

In the maritime industry in Australia, both the seagoing and land-based sectors have been major sites of working class struggle and mobilisation. It was an industry too where alcohol and hotels were significant cultural presences. This was particularly the case in the early times of sail and steam, but continued well into the twentieth century as the industry variously modernised.

Seafaring was a lonely, insular life and therefore the escapism of intoxicants could hold a particularly strong appeal. A lot of seafarers found themselves isolated when on leave or between jobs. Pubs provided an ideal spot to find companionship and relief from loneliness, including accessible sexual partners. Indeed, some seafarers made favourite pubs regular if not lifelong

Wharfies drinking at New Hunter River Hotel, 1972 (*Tribune*/Search Foundation, State Library of NSW)

accommodation. The Mansions Hotel in Sydney's Kings Cross was such a place and some seafarers called it home.

Before coming to an end in the 1940s, the despised and corrupt 'bull system' operated in the Australian stevedoring industry.. This system gave employment agents the freedom to pick and choose workers for available jobs. Pubs were handy places to learn of job opportunities coming up and alcohol could sometimes help secure work. For example, waterfront worker Jack Ryan reveals in Elizabeth Knight's documentary film *Wharfies: A History of the Waterside Worker's Federation*, how the provision of significant quantities of beer to agents could enhance future job selection prospects. With the alcohol described as being brought *up from below* deck, it is apparent that managers were compelling desperate workers to do the dirty work of stealing on their behalf. This relationship pattern would continue, exposed sensationally during the 1982 Costigan Royal Commission with the revelations of bottom-of-the-harbour tax evasion schemes.

Before the unionised 'gang rotary system' was won, replacing the 'bull system', stevedoring work provided little in the way of job security or protection for workers; conditions during shifts of 12 to 24 hours were quite literally back breaking.

Damaged dock workers with no access to workers compensation took solace in drink. They had companions at the bar in unemployed workers who felt the stress of not knowing when the next pay would come in. They were often joined by seafarers escaping a strained or non-existent home life, not helped by long absences out at sea.

Alcohol use was regularly weaponised by shipowners against workers and their unions, but little responsibility was taken by management to improve underlying issues. As recorded in *The Seaman's Union of Australia 1872-1972: A History* by Brian Fitzpatrick and Rowan Cahill, a claim was made by shipowners during World War Two that in one port, 29 consecutive ships had been held up due to seamen being drunk. The notoriously anti-union *Daily Telegraph* made claims in the 1950s that wharfies were 'drunk, lazy and strike-prone.' This slander provided the impetus for a piece of contemporary agitprop theatre written by Lionel Parker as a riposte, as detailed in Lisa Milner's edited anthology *The New Theatre*.

Whilst pubs provided a means of assuaging physical pain and mental sorrow, they, as in other communities, were also accessible sites

Wharfies in Hobart having a pint, 1910 (Libraries Tasmania)

Bar workers at the waterfront pub the Hero of Waterloo, 1951 (*Pix*)

for convivial and industrial congregation. It is therefore unsurprising that the history of workers' collective activity crosses over into pub life. For example historian Diane Kirkby in her study *Voices from the Ships: Australia's Seafarers and their Union* describes how it was not uncommon for Seamen's Union meetings, right up until the union become part of the Maritime Union of Australia in 1993, to adjourn to local pubs where officials learned more about what members thought and felt about issues than they were prepared to say at larger formal meetings.

Research by Michael Quinlan in *The Origins of Worker Mobilisation: Australia 1788-1850*, shows how seafarers – merchant mariners, sealers, whalers – in Australian waters and ports were particularly industrially active, demonstrating a collective impulse. They mobilised in ship-based ways and between ships. Onshore they tried to build welfare and friendly societies.

Pubs often featured in these early mobilisations, being traditional refuges ashore, handy to waterfronts, accommodations for many, and offering cheap or free meeting spaces. Quinlan notes that these included 'well-known meeting places like the Orient, Hero of Waterloo and Whaler's Arms hotels in the Rocks, Sydney.' Quinlan's research shows that between 1790 and 1850, seafarers in Australian waters and ports chalked up close to 800 informal industrial actions before the formal existence and legality of trade unions. These workers took part in strikes and mass absconding (desertion), gathered petitions, and organised court actions seeking redress of grievances.

In 1872, seamen in multiple Australian ports established union organisations, and pubs again featured organisationally as meeting places. Between 2-7 August 1872, Sydney seamen created a union; between 9 August and 25 September 1872, Newcastle seamen created a union; on 21 September 1872, Melbourne seamen created a union; and between 23 and 25 September, Port Adelaide seamen created a union. The evidential paper trail at present is fragmentary and inconclusive. What seems to be the case is that the Sydney and Melbourne seamen's outfits had strength and longevity and that they provided the muscle that was to become the Federated Seamen's Union of Australasia in 1890 (later renamed the Seamen's Union of Australia - SUA). It was the Melbourne organisation that had the nous and leadership to foster inter-colonial worker unity and bring the two main outfits together.

The formation of unions covering various maritime occupations was no doubt a concern to management in the shipping industry, but on at least one occasion, in 1912, it was seen as an opportunity for a different kind of business owner. Publican John Ryan purchased a hotel on the waterfront in Maryborough, Queensland, an establishment what is today known as the Criterion Hotel. Ryan cannily donated the land adjacent to his pub to enable the construction in 1918 of the still extant, timber structured Waterside Workers' Hall. Some operations at the port required prospective employees to meet in open sheds at the docks. Others such as the local timber firms, Hyne and Sons and Wilson Hart, were willing to use the enclosed and more comfortable worker's hall

Wharfies appreciate a better ambiance inside the Harbour View Hotel, Sydney, 1952 *(Daily Telegraph)*

as a pick-up centre. In such situations Ryan's business likely found extra clientele while wharfies waited for jobs.

In the 1950s, with militancy at a peak and standards aboard ships and on docks much improved, workers had greater ability and confidence to push for better conditions elsewhere too. Wharfies at Sydney's Harbour View Hotel made a demand for flowers in a pub that was otherwise dingy and utilitarian. As uncovered by historian Mick Roberts, the Sydney *Daily Telegraph* in 1952 reported, 'Dreamy-eyed with ecstasy, wharfie Gus Girdler, of Stanmore, savours the delicate fragrance of a daffodil in the "Blue Room" of the Harbour View Hotel.' Although the tone of the article was mocking, the issue reinforced the sentiment that blue collar workers should enjoy the good life as much as anyone else.

During the post-war period much industrial negotiation took place in waterfront pubs. Negotiators could match each other eyeball to eyeball, threat for threat if necessary, until understandings were reached and deals struck. Prior to the Prices and Income Accord being introduced by the federal ALP in 1983, with the subsequent dismantling of the arbitration and conciliation apparatus, such contestation was a recognised part of the industrial relations process. This was also a time before the ubiquity of Human Relations managers, when Australian shipowners and sizable Australian flagged fleets still existed. As a result local employers used industrial negotiators with significant maritime work experience and careers. Waterfront pubs were in a sense neutral and mutually familiar territories, and places where the unfamiliar faces of spies and journalists stood out, readily identified as outsiders, 'new faces on the block'. In this era, the apparatus of the spy: cameras and recording equipment, tended to be cumbersome. Which is why former prominent SUA member and communist Fred Wells, later *Bulletin* and *Sydney Morning Herald* industrial roundsman, was such a bonus as an inside informer for ASIO regarding the Left, ALP, and trade unions.

The issue of alcohol consumption in the maritime industry has long been sensitive. There is an argument that workers are entitled to leisure time and should not be subjected to moralism, or criticism disproportionate to any other section of society and their drinking. However, when alcohol consumption intersects with work safety it becomes more than a personal issue. This is what happened in the SUA post-1945 as the union gained the right to have beer on ships, and as drugs joined alcohol as a concern. The union had tried to deal with membership alcohol problems in-house and personally with advice and referrals but as historian Diane Kirkby details, by the late 1980s the matter had become one needing more robust intervention and an industry approach was sought involving the union, employers and the government.

The culture of care evident within the maritime industry was also extended to other oppressed workers and social groups. Sometimes this was focused on the industrial issues of others. An example is when waterside workers took solidarity action in support of wage claims by hospitality workers at one of their favoured drinking locations, the Spot

Wharfies drink at New Hunter River Hotel, 1972 (*Tribune*/Search Foundation, State Library of NSW)

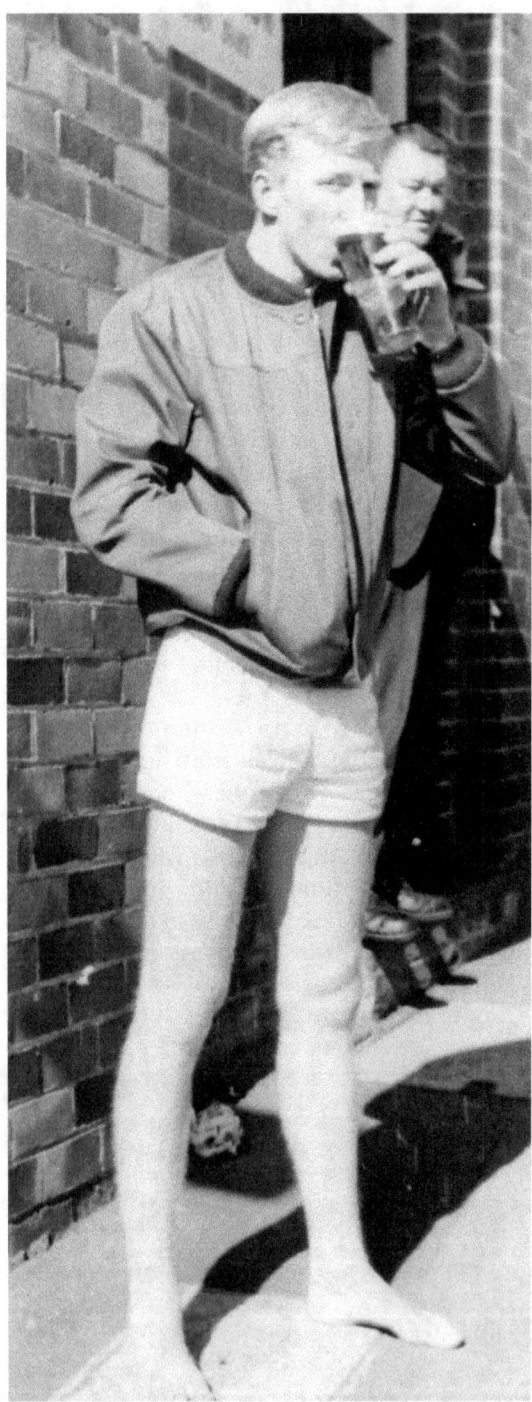

Wharf worker in his recreation time, 1970s (Waterside Workers Federation of Australia, Noel Butlin Archives/ Australian National University)

Cafe in Wollongong during 1941. As detailed by union leader Ted Roach in his biography, 'We put the tar brush on it, and picketed the place.' The militancy of their union was respected and gave them the power to decisively impact the outcome of disputes, not just for themselves but others, in this case a numerically-small female dominated workplace. As Roach explained, '[the police] didn't "pinch" me, they knew there might be a ship stoppage if they did. I knew that and they knew it too.' The dispute ended quickly and in addition to the pay rise, a sizeable amount of back pay was secured for the striking hospitality workers.

Solidarity actions extended beyond Australian shores, with actions that defied the racism coming from the top of Australian society. As has been expressed by militant seafarers, most people think of the sea as dividing the countries of the world, whereas maritime workers see the ocean uniting people across borders. During the 1960s, in an iconic moment of anti-war union action, members of the Seaman's Union of Australia refused to crew a number of ships taking material to South Vietnam. Amongst supplies on the banned ship the *Boonaroo* was beer for the military.

In an earlier era, when the Japanese empire invaded China and slaughtered millions of Chinese civilians, waterside workers in Port Kembla had taken similar action. In 1937 unionists provided sanctuary to the Chinese crew of the *SS Silkworth* after they walked off the vessel in protest at Japan's action. Dockworkers also refused to load strategic cargoes bound for Japan, putting forth the demand 'no war on the Chinese.' They did so, conscious that the conservative federal government and shipping industry would punish them and their community financially. In response to the unionists' refusal to load the *Nellore* until its owners agreed not to take supplies to Japan, the ship's Chinese crew took up a collection. They handed over the money to the Australian wharfies, saying that they wished to 'shout drinks'. The money was gladly accepted, but instead distributed to strikers for financial relief. Or so it was reported in the papers. The union was conscious that their opponents would attempt to undermine the integrity of the solidarity action by smearing workers as slothful boozers.

The ongoing dispute over banning supplies came to largely focus on the *SS Dalfram*. During negotiations Roach advised union reps to refuse offers of alcohol from their opponents and only drink Pilato (small bottles of orange and lemon juice). On one occasion a 'beano' (a party) in the local Agricultural Hall was put on for the reps in the dispute, and unionist Rae Elliott recalls, 'There was food laid on, white table cloths and bottles of whiskey, open, on the tables' – the unionists were prepared and only drank Pilato.

During the 1998 waterfront dispute, when stevedore company Patricks sacked dock workers en masse, there were indications of how the culture of pubs and drinking continued to be used as a sign of support for unionism, as well as its opposite. The oral history collection *In and Out of Port: Voices from the Port of Melbourne* notes that, 'Paul and Val McGahan, the publicans from the Hibernian Hotel, brought food for the picketers every day the strike was on.' There was also a cynical eye directed towards ALP figures who brought beer down to the picket, which strikers were trying to keep dry.

In the aftermath of the lock out, it was made clear to those that had undermined the picket and union that they were no longer welcome in the community. One observer said, 'Some of these rattlesnakes, when recognised, have already been refused service in restaurants and pubs in Williamstown and surrounding areas.' Just as in earlier periods there were clear consequences for those who had put their self-interest before the collective wellbeing of the maritime community.

Boonaroo Protest, 1966 (*Tribune*/Search Foundation, State Library of NSW)

CHAPTER 23
'VALOUR AMONG THE VATS': 1937 CASTLEMAINE BREWERY DISPUTE
Carol Corless

In 1937 the workers at Castlemaine Brewery in Milton, Brisbane, undertook the first stay-in strike in Queensland. This was one of many strikes of this type that were enacted around the country to achieve changes in working conditions. The workers were seeking a 40-hour week and a pay rise. They turned their backs on arbitration, which was the preferred method of the Australian Council of Trade Unions (ACTU), the Queensland government, other individual unions, and the ALP. At the end of the 30 day strike, at least 80 workers, including some from the second Brisbane brewery, were left without a job due to actions of the employers.

The stay-in or sit-down strike had been an IWW tactic in industrial disputes in the early 20th century but a worldwide wave of stay-in strikes had originated in France in May 1936. This method of striking spread to Belgium and was used in the United States at the end of 1936 and early 1937. Australian workers began using the tactic in February 1937 with the first stay-in strike conducted at the North Wallarah mine situated just north of Swansea, New South Wales. As reported in the *Daily Mercury* (Mackay) this strike lasted 38 hours and the wives of the miners were credited with settling the strike. The striking miners' wives and women friends had prepared provisions for the men and they drove to the mine with the supplies. They were prevented from handing them over by a police cordon. Approximately 250 people, mostly women and children, marched to the home of the mine business manager. After a conference, the business manager accepted a compromise on behalf of the mine owners.

15 September 1937 was the beginning of the stay-in strike at the Castlemaine Brewery. The workers' representatives approached management about a pay increase and a reduction in hours to a 40-hour week on 10 September. The representatives were two of the workers at the factory, one of whom was the President of the Queensland Branch of the Federated Liquor Trades Union (FLTUQ). They requested an immediate weekly wage of £5 for union members, with an extra 5 shillings for cold cellar hands and a 40-hour week,

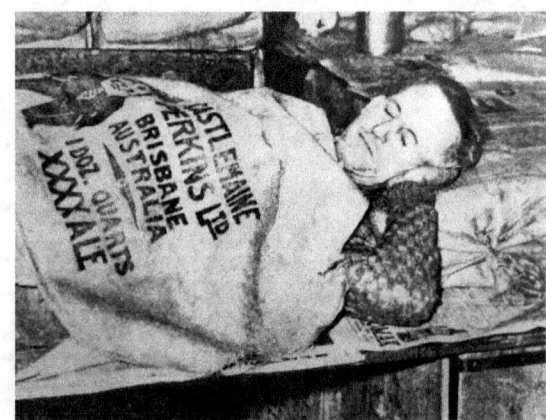

Strikers inside the Castlemaine Brewery site, 16 September 1937 (*Telegraph*)

with a limit on overtime to four extra hours per week. The Castlemaine-Perkins Brewery employer representatives said that as this issue affected the other brewery in Brisbane (The Queensland Brewery, based in Fortitude Valley) the demands would need to be referred to the Brisbane Brewers Association (BBA). The response, given on 15 September, was that if the employee representatives applied to the Industrial Court for the pay increase then the BBA would not oppose the pay claim but they would oppose the reduction in hours. According to the *Courier Mail*, the response from the workers' representatives was that they were happy to take the pay increase but would be ceasing work 'until the 40-hour week was granted.'

In an unpublished manuscript written by one of the 1937 strikers, Jimmy Hayes recalls that:

> On September 15th 1937 at Castlemaine Brewery at 10.30 a.m. a 'Stay in' Strike was declared, on the grounds of altering the working hours from 44 to 40 hours a week with 8/- rise in wages, bringing it up to £5.0.0, with £5.5.0 for cold cellar work, and a limit of 4 hours a week overtime. All the men from each department gathered together in the Bottle Department, where we stayed, much to the annoyance of the management of the Brewery.

The men settled into the stay-in strike by setting up improvised beds out of bales of straw and bags of bottles.

Brisbane newspapers *Courier Mail* and *Telegraph* reported that the BBA decided immediately to apply for the deregistration of the FLTUQ, and the Association's spokesman, Colonel F. A. Hughes, stated that they believed that the strike was illegal. The secretary of the FLTUQ, Mr D. Skehan, defended the strike. Skehan stated that the strike was legal under the Arbitration Act as a vote had been taken by brewery employees on the 40-hour week and that the Castlemaine Brewery members by a large majority had agreed to cease work for the cause. Mr Skehan was questioned on the situation at the Queensland Brewery, and stated that they were not involved. The members at that brewery were not on strike and as far as he knew 'they were working as usual.'

The BBA escalated the conflict by deciding not to make deliveries to hotels from either brewery during the dispute. At the time hotels were tied to particular brands of beer and were mostly owned by the individual brewing companies which meant that many hotels in Brisbane were not serving beer.

The press reported daily on the dispute with the reports filtering through to the regional newspapers. An article in the *Courier Mail* went into the ins and outs of the strike, suggesting that it was farcical and that the men were playing a 'childish game of "valour among the vats"...' As recalled by Jimmy Hayes in his unpublished manuscript:

> Right from the start we were invaded by Press reporters, and pictures were taken, and published in the front pages of the daily papers. The Japan Chinese war, was forgotten for the time being, as the people of Brisbane were concerned only in the Beer Strike, and how long the beer would last in the Hotels.

The newspapers also interviewed the wives and girlfriends of the strikers. The focus of these interviews were on how they were coping with the men not at home. The story in the *Telegraph* ranged from the women happy about the men not being at home as they didn't have to prepare meals to wondering 'how much money do we get tomorrow.' Jim Hayes, lead striker, sent a reporter out to his home at West End to speak to his wife about what she thought of the dispute. The *Telegraph* reported that:

> Mrs. Hayes, busy washing her husband's shirts, ready to be taken out to the scene of action – or is it 'in action' – gazed in astonishment as a Press reporter and photographer walked up her front stairs,

and drying her hands on her apron said, 'Heavens above; what a job Jimmie's given you. I don't know anything about it. Haven't time to worry much. Yes, come in, of course. Haven't had time to do much to the house this morning; it's washing day'. 'No 40 hours a week for you, Mrs. Hayes?' Mrs. Hayes indicated her scorn and derision. 'But the men – they work hard out there. They deserve their 40 hours.' Strikers' wives are loyal.

Some of the wives, children and girlfriends were reported as missing their men, the reporter going as far as to say that the headline should be 'Sit down strikes ensure domestic bliss.'

When the men went on strike, it was reported in the *Telegraph*, that there was £35,000 of beer left in vats that needed to be processed or it would have to be dumped. The head brewer, Mr. A. K. Hall, believed that it was a more important story that six men had managed to save this product 'than that the strikers had spent a comfortable night.' It was reported that four brewers and two foremen worked to move beer in various stages of fermentation around the plant to storage. All equipment had to be left clean and the six men worked 16 to 18 hour days to ensure that this happened. The head brewer also stated that there were hogsheads in storage that needed to be seen to. He pointed out that this work was normally done by 40 men.

Meanwhile the men involved in the dispute had spent a comfortable night in their surroundings. Foodstuffs, tobacco and cigarettes were amongst the items donated to assist the men in their stay-in strike. It was reported in the *Telegraph* that Mr J. Hayes had stated amongst the group of strikers on 16 September, 'We are quite comfortable and will stay for six months if necessary. If the breweries can last seven days then we can go for 70 days.'

On the second day of the strike the *Courier Mail* stated that there had been a donation of a special food item along with an entertainment source. A hessian bag of oysters was to be shucked for dinner. A radio was donated with the licence transferred into the name of Jimmy Hayes with the address being the Milton brewery so that it complied with the regulations of the Postmaster-General's Department. In the unpublished manuscript, Jimmy Hayes recalls that:

> In the room where we were staying was 3000 dozen bottles of beer, which were not touched by anyone, it was declared 'taboo' by all. There was also two Customs officers in the room day & Night, as the beer was under Government Bond, and was being watched by the officers.

The officers were there to ensure no beer left the premises without payment of the customs duty. Meals for the men was a hot topic in the newspapers as it was reported nearly every day what they were eating, and photographs appeared of the preparation of the meals. Jimmy Hayes recalls that:

> We soon had two copper boilers at work, in a Galley which was erected nearby; and two of the men who had been cooks before they had worked at the Brewery, soon had hot meals ready for us, and the old call of 'Come and get it' was heard at meal times,

Occupiers give up alcohol for milk, 16 September 1937 (*Telegraph*)

and the men who were always orderly waited in a long 'queue' with plates & cups in their hands, waiting for their hot meal.

The *Telegraph* reporter wrote that he was greeted with the sight of a new galley, erected overnight, when he visited on the Saturday. He noted that the chefs were garbed in white aprons and chef's hats and that nearby men were shelling peas. Close to them were donations from the city barrowmen of a bag of potatoes, a case of apples, a case of pears, and carrots and turnips. The previous afternoon the men had been visited by their wives and girlfriends. They had been treated to a reverse of normal roles where the men waited on them with afternoon tea and dainties.

By Friday 17 September reports of the hotels in the city having run out of draught beer were the news of the day in the *Telegraph*, in conjunction with stories of the strike. In the *Cairns Post* it was reported that bottled beer was being used, not being sold as full bottles but rather rationed out in short sixpenny glasses. The secretary of the Licenced Victuallers' Association, C. M. Jenkinson was quoted as saying that most supplies would run out by Monday morning. It was reported in the *Truth* that one hotel enterprisingly had decided to bring in draught beer from a Toowoomba hotel via a car. The licensee of the Grosvenor Hotel in George Street was told swiftly by the FLTUQ secretary that if the beer was sold then the hotel would be declared black and all bar attendants would be withdrawn. The beer was pulled from sale.

It was reported in the *Northern Miner* that the men were tired of the strike. Hayes interviewed every striker and stated that to a man they were willing to stay out until the 40 hour week was won. A letter to the editor published in the *Courier Mail* that said that the wives of the strikers had met and were urging the men to go back to work for the pay rise and to achieve the 40-hour week via political means, was also denied by Mr Skehan. In his unpublished manuscript, Jimmy Hayes recalled that:

Rumers [sic] kept coming in about us being tired of the strike, and we were ready to go back to work, these tales used to make us very hostile, and they were denied in the next days Press. On one occasion one of the daily papers published a false statement about us on the front page, and we therefore declared that paper 'Black', and advised other unions to do so.

The paper that was declared black was the *Courier Mail* as detailed in a report on the strike written by Michael Patrick Ryan.

It was reported in the *Courier Mail* that the employers' application to the Queensland Arbitration Commission to deregister the FLTUQ and cancel the Brewery Employees Award – Brisbane and Toowoomba – was heard on 20 September.

The Court was comprised of Messrs T. A. Ferry and W. J. Riordan. Riordan believed that the best way to advance workers' interests was through arbitration rather than direct action. The employers were represented by Colonel F. A. Hughes, secretary of both the BBA and Castlemaine Perkins. As a part of the employers' case he cited an earlier meeting in November 1936 where the response of the BBA to the union demand for a 40-hour week had been that the union should make an approach to the Industrial Court to apply for a variation

Occupiers vote to continue their strike (*Telegraph*)

of the Award. It was alleged by the BBA that at the time of this discussion the secretary of the union said, 'We are not going near the Court: when we are ready we will take 40 hours.' It was reported in the *Morning Bulletin* that the employers argued that no ballot had been undertaken for the strike.

In the same newspaper it was reported that the FLTUQ was represented by Mr D. J Skehan, who outlined various issues that had led to the men deciding to strike. Mr Skehan outlined that the dispute was only with Castlemaine Perkins but the affidavit mentioned the Queensland Brewery. He said that the other brewery could continue to supply their product as the brewery had never been part of the negotiations for the 40-hour week. Mr Skehan also vehemently denied ever making the statement about taking the 40-hour week and that the earlier meeting had been complicated by a separate, long term dispute with the employers about illegal hotel trading hours.

The Industrial Court questioned why the union had not notified the Industrial Registrar of the strike, (as required under the Industrial Conciliation and Arbitration Act 1932), until 17 September, two days after the strike began. Also, why the ballot paper had asked for a simple yes or no to a long list of demands including 'observance of legal trading hours, a 40-hour week, a minimum wage of £5, overtime limited to four hours per week.' One of the arguments that Skehan used was that as the employers had broken the law with regards to opening times of hotels then it should not be a problem that the strikers had done so. He was quoted as saying 'what was sauce for the goose was sauce for the gander.'

The Industrial Court ruled that the award be cancelled, and that the preference clause be removed from all awards that the FLTUQ was party to. This ruling was to take effect on 22 September at 9am if the men had not returned to work.

At the time of the dispute the FLTUQ was awaiting approval for affiliation to the Brisbane Trades and Labour Council (TLC). This was already jeopardised by FLTUQ members support for the Industrial Labour political party, with most TLC unions, and the TLC, backing the ALP. The Industrial Labour Party had been formed in 1917 with the stated aim of establishing a true industrial democracy, as reported in the *Queensland Times*.

Reported in the *Telegraph*, the Amalgamated Road Transport Workers Union (ARTWU) made representations to the TLC due to 18 of its members, employed in delivering by the breweries, being left without work, five of whom were directly employed and laid off. It was noted in the *Courier Mail* that many TLC affiliated unions were unhappy as they supported arbitration in practice and principle and the first they had heard about this strike was when it was already underway. The TLC was asked by its affiliates to appeal the decision of the Industrial Court; if the strikers were evicted the employers could use non-union labour, plus widespread strike action in support for the evicted strikers might not be controlled by the unions.

The men did not return to work on 22 September. Although the Industrial Court ruling, published in *The Queensland Industrial Gazette*, stopped short of deregistering the union, it removed the clause that gave preference of employment to members of the

Strikers catch up with family members during the occupation (*Telegraph*)

union. The preference clause was important to the union as it favoured members of the FLTUQ in hiring with employers respondent to the awards. The preference clause was removed from seven awards covering breweries, malthouses, bars, aerated water factories, and wine and spirits stores in Brisbane and the South east division.

It was reported in the *Telegraph* that on 22 September, at 9:06 am the head brewer Mr A. K. Hall had entered the bottling room where the men were and asked if they were going to return to work. He was answered by Mr Hayes with a 'no' on behalf of the men and a 'that is right' by Mr Martin Anderson. Mr Hall returned in the afternoon and asked again if anyone was going to return to work. This time he urged them to return under police protection. The men heckled him but one striker requested to be escorted out by police. As he left he said, 'Cut out the heroics, men. Who is game to follow me?' Most of the strikers turned their backs on him. Mr Hall proceeded to interview each man but only the one decided to leave. Mr Hayes said that the employee who left was only a recent employee.

The *Courier Mail* reported that the same day a vote was taken at the TLC in support of the striking workers. Affiliated unions decided to support them financially and actively. A further motion resolved that the 'Government be asked not to allow the police to be used against the stay-in strikers at the brewery.'

As reported in the *Daily Mercury* (Mackay), on 23 September, the employees at the Bulimba Brewery (Queensland Brewery), many of whom were Coopers Union members, were paid off. The carters, coopers and tradesmen of Castlemaine Brewery were paid off on the 24th. It was reported that rumours were rife that the men were to be evicted.

Colonel Hughes approached the Commissioner of Police on 23 September for assistance in removing the strikers from the Brewery premises at Milton. Hughes originally had verbally approached the Commissioner but then followed up in writing to request a police presence at the eviction. Hughes cited Section 277 of the Criminal Code, saying that the strikers were trespassers. Hughes wanted a police presence as he believed that the men would resist their removal. A copy of this letter is held in the Qld State Archives Police Correspondence file with other material relevant to this strike. Jimmy recalls in his manuscript that:

> Everything ran smoothly until Friday 24th when at 5.30 a.m. we were suddenly awakened by someone crying 'Right-oh' boys the Police are here, and so they were, 180 of them and the Heads of the Firm. We stood on our beds half asleep and watched the police walking around waking the chaps up. Some were very indignant at being awakened, but were very surprised when they saw all the police in the room. We were told that we were trespassing and that we should go out quietly, which we did, after collecting our goods: And so we were evicted.

The men left almost immediately with their goods and chattels. It was reported that Inspector Toohill, in charge of the police at the eviction, offered the use of a truck for the men to remove their items to their homes but that this was refused. Although there was resistance from the police to photographers taking images of the eviction, photographs appeared in several newspapers with one of all the evicted strikers as a group run in the *Telegraph*. The paper reported that 120 policemen were involved in the eviction. The policemen arrived in a fleet of police cars with headlights extinguished and entered the buildings just before dawn. It was reported in the *Courier Mail* that in Parliament the Premier, Mr Forgan Smith, was asked if the government had taken the initiative to evict the strikers and he stated that it was the employers who had requested the police to assist.

The strikers on leaving the premises held a meeting to decide on their next steps. Local homeowners offered their land as a temporary camp for the goods and chattels on the footpaths. Later in the day the strikers erected a tent as shelter for the duration of the strike. The employers, as reported in the *Telegraph*, stated that they had not considered free labour and that the striking men could return to work on the same conditions as previous. In the unpublished manuscript Jimmy Hayes recalls that:

> This day became known as 'Black Friday' but to me it was 'Busy Friday'. It was the Greatest day of the Strike. We crossed the road to a near by house, under which we had breakfast, we then had a meeting to decide what we would do and we then agreed to hire a Marquee tent, and erect it in Mr Raines Paddock. We approached Mr Raine who kindly allowed us to put up our tent on his ground, much to the chagrin of our enemy, 'The Brewery Heads'. It hurt them very much to see the way we 'dug in'.

Reported in the *Courier Mail* was that the marquee was erected on a vacant allotment in Drane Street to the rear of the brewery. The cook's galley was relocated to the marquee by the men lifting and carrying it to the new headquarters. Once the men were in their new home they took a vote to continue the strike. At the same time, they decided to strengthen the picket of the brewery. Local householders offered the use of their baths to the men. That night the picket was strong at the front and back of the brewery and police guards occupied strategic points.

After these developments in the dispute, the workers being paid off at both breweries and the eviction, the TLC Disputes Committee met urgently to discuss the issue. All unions that had members on strike were represented and the conduct of the dispute was placed in the hands of the committee. Previously the strike committee of the FLTUQ was responsible for the handling of the strike.

The official report from the Disputes Committee, which was detailed in the *Courier Mail*, was that the Secretary of the TLC, Mr H. J. Harvey, was to seek a conference with the BBA with an intention to resolve the dispute. Harvey was to be the official spokesman for the committee and all reports of the proceedings of the Disputes Committee were to come from him. It was stated by Harvey that, 'The unions are solidly behind the men involved and it is intended to take all action necessary and possible to obtain a satisfactory settlement.' There was an appeal to other unions for financial assistance for the men who had been thrown out of work.

A conference between the TLC and the BBA was held on 28 September and according to the *Courier Mail* ended in a deadlock as neither party was willing to concede their position. On the same day an article was printed in the editorial column of (the ALP supporting and AWU affiliated newspaper) *The Worker* that said the actions of the FLTUQ in trying to achieve the 40-hour week through direct action were stupid. It suggested that the FLTUQ should have used arbitration and that the leaders of the strike had sabotaged themselves. It cited the case that the FLTUQ had run to get the 40-hour week for bar attendants where the Industrial Court had said that they would be willing to look at granting the 40-hour week

Pickets outside the brewery, September 24 1937
(*Telegraph*)

if the employer could afford it and if it would create employment. At the time, the Industrial Court when ruling on the basic wage and standard hours had to consider the economic impact on industry and the community.

It was reported in the *Northern Miner* that the AWU consequently applied to the Industrial Court for a 40-hour week in the Northern Australian Breweries Award on 1 October. The union argued that the employers could afford it and presented the balance sheet from 1936 as evidence. The employer representative, Mr J. Holiday, appearing for the North Queensland Employers' Association, did not deny prosperity but argued that the court should not rule for individual employers. He argued that the union should be asking for the 40-hour week for the whole industry rather than one individual brewery. It was noted in the *Telegraph* that the Industrial Court on 5 October granted the 40-hour week to the employees of the Cairns Brewery without loss of pay. There was still some cloud over whether the reduction in the working week would bring about an increase in employment. As part of the decision it was stated, 'that it will award a forty hour week where the employers can afford it and more employment will result.'

In the *Telegraph* it was reported that on 7 October the Coopers Union filed an injunction against Queensland Brewery in the Industrial Court. The injunction alleged that the brewery had breached the Industrial Conciliation and Arbitration Act by paying off its employees in Fortitude Valley and therefore locking out members of the Coopers Union. The Coopers Union had informed the TLC of this action earlier that day. The TLC subsequently voted unanimously to black out the lighted advertising on the roof of the Trades Hall Building that advertised Bulimba Beer; though this was not carried out for contractual reasons.

On the afternoon of 7 October, the BBA advertised for labour at the Bulimba Brewery, the Valley and Castlemaine Brewery, Milton.

Applications for employment were invited from former employees and unionists on Saturday morning. The terms of employment were the same as prior to the dispute, a 44-hour week and the existing weekly wage. The Disputes Committee met, and unions were advised to not let any unemployed members apply for the offered positions. According to the *Morning Bulletin* the strikers had met and none would apply for roles until the requested terms were offered by the company. Jimmy Hayes recalls in his manuscript that:

> Then on the 6th of October the Brewers called for free Labour, and during the next few days we had chaps coming to us, who wanted to know, how to get work in the Brewery, we told them they would be 'scabbing' but they said that they did not mind. We got quite used to the chaps and on Saturday morning, the 9th we went up to the front of the Brewery and saw about 800 chaps lined up, and passing into the Office to get their name down. The scabs stood on one side of the road, and we stood on the other side with about 700 men who were in sympathy with us, we had papers with 40 hour week, on them, and as the trams came along we pointed to the scabs, for the benefit of the tram passengers.

Pickets take down details of cars entering and leaving the brewery, October 11 1937 (*Telegraph*)

The employers believed that they would get sufficient labour to be able to begin production the following week. The FLTUQ members at the Bulimba Brewery all reapplied for their jobs as they were not originally part of the dispute. None of the strikers in the camp applied for their jobs at Castlemaine Brewery. There were a few who had left in previous days who did apply. As reported in the Sunday Mail, the ARTWU instructed the carters to attend the breweries the following day to start deliveries.

The *Telegraph* reported that on October 11 the reemployed FLTUQ members at Queensland Brewery were instructed to work with volunteer men and show them the job. Only half of the original employees had been employed and union men asked the head brewer to employ the other union men. When told that the head brewer was not going to reemploy the old hands the men refused to work with the volunteers and left the premises. In the *Morning Bulletin* it was reported that deliveries were made from the two breweries but in the case of the Castlemaine Brewery the carters were not asked to commence work. Publicans made their own arrangements with many picking their supplies up in private cars. In the *Telegraph* it was also stated that the coopers had not turned up for work on the first day of the return to work. The employers said that it did not make a difference at this stage.

The members of the Federated Engine Drivers and Firemen's Association (FEDFA) at both breweries voted in a ballot, 21 to one, that they would not join the strike. They had not stopped work during the dispute and had kept the refrigeration equipment going. This ballot was in response to a Disputes Committee decision the previous day that all unions should involve themselves in the strike.

It was soon reported in the *Courier Mail* that the strike was collapsing. Some of the strikers at the Bulimba Brewery decided to return to work. They had been picketing the brewery but by the Wednesday were reapplying for their jobs. Picketing at both breweries had stopped by the Wednesday night. There was consideration given to calling out the bar attendants by the executive of the FLTUQ. This was a task given to the executive by the TLC Disputes Committee after some straight talking at the meeting earlier in the day. It was pointed out at the Disputes Committee that while the beer was declared 'black' at the brewery due to volunteer labour being used, that members of the FLTUQ were still serving the 'black' beer in the hotels. The executive refused to make the decision and handed the matter back to the Disputes Committee. The Coopers Union, who were on strike, met at Trades Hall to discuss the decision that had been made by their executive to join. The Disputes Committee asked the executive of the FEDFA to reconsider the decision to not strike.

The *Telegraph* reported that at a meeting of the strikers from both breweries at Trades Hall on 14 October the strike was formally declared off. It was then decided that they would reapply for their jobs as a group. The FLTUQ members attributed some blame to the Disputes Committee in so much as the committee had tried to put the onus back on the FLTUQ to call

Barmaids pouring drinks as draught beer becomes available again, October 13 1937 (*Telegraph*)

out the bar attendants in the preceding days of the dispute. The strikers' camp was broken up after the men had one last meal together.

An analysis of the strike was written by one of the participants, Michael Patrick Ryan, described in police correspondence as one of the leaders of the Communist Party in the state. The analysis was only issued to Communist Party members and contacts but the police obtained a copy. The report details the strike and what Ryan believes went wrong with it. In the report the author outlines the lessons he believed could be learnt from the struggle in ten points. These included:

1. That Sectional Strikes can be won in exceptional circumstances only, and in this case the circumstances were not sufficiently studied...

4. That no struggle can be won on tactics, that have no relations with mass action...

7. There cannot be too much propaganda put out to the public and the workers in particular, acquainting them of the issues involved and what is being done, linked up the issues with the grievances of the masses generally...

Ryan's report on the strike included an analysis of what he considered treacherous behaviour of the other unions involved: FEDFA and the Coopers Union. He apportioned blame to the belief that the employers would not band together and cited 'an underestimation of the degree to which the Capitalists are united as a class against the workers...'

This dispute lasted a total of 30 days from the beginning to the end. It is difficult to attribute blame for the outcome to any one source and while they did not achieve the goal they desired, there are some valuable lessons that can be taken from this strike. While this dispute left many of the strikers still out of work at the end of the strike, they showed courage in the face of opposition from the employers, the government and from some other unions. These men never wavered from the ideal of the 40-hour week and displayed incredible valour among the vats.

CHAPTER 24
THE BATTLE OF AUSTRALIAN MODERNISM
Alex Ettling

There was a stimulating period in the early 20th century when modernism seemed to hold within it the promise of human progress. Or this was the theory – and there was no shortage of it, around the development of art. For some, the debate over modernism was a crucial battleground. At stake was pursuit of the most advanced expression of how we see the world: what it reveals to us, and how it might inspire change.

For left-wing radicals in art, it was a battle for humanism and progress in an industrialising capitalism that had been grey and cruel, where commodification was absorbing everything.

Australia was late to the party in the international story of art modernism, separated by a vast ocean that delayed the arrival (and potential influence) of a number of art movements. But in the years around World War Two, there was a furious contestation over modernist art in Australia between different political and artistic groupings, with pubs and social spaces providing a key venue of debate.

Modernism in Australia

The advancement of modernism in art was, for some intellectuals, absolutely crucial to 20th century progress. This could mean a more sophisticated form of capitalism, or shockingly for some, the total upending of this economic system and the installation of communism. The potential threat of modernism had high ranking opponents readily presenting. In 1937, future conservative prime minister Robert Menzies asserted: 'great art speaks a language which every intelligent person can understand. The people who call themselves modernists today speak a different language.' The establishment was firming up on culture and Menzies had endorsed the new peak body, the Australian Academy of Art, which was tasked with being the intermediary to dole out rewards for artists that played the game. This was not so different to how things already operated. A number of the non-conformists from the 1890s had adapted to conservative tastes and were now in a position of controlling the galleries. They had been actively excluding modernism for years, judging it as both primitive and decadent, indicative of Europe's moral decay. The new peak body of artists was intended to self-regulate – both in form and content – pushing radicalism *out* of the art scene.

Art students at the National Gallery School, 1940

A battleground with the political right around art had formed, but it was a complicated terrain for the modernist revolutionaries. The Soviet bureaucrats of culture had also recently rejected modernism, making collaboration between different schools of leftism a difficult prospect. There was also a cohort of cosmopolitan capitalists, notably including media baron Keith Murdoch, who wanted to stay in touch with international cultural trends and so embraced modern art aesthetics – as long as it did not stray into any messaging that pressed for economic redistribution. But the layer of new art radicals, who embraced anti-capitalist politics and wove it into their enthusiasm for modernism, was not so easily pushed aside. Nor were they easily assimilated into the eccentric wing of capitalist-friendly modernism. As historian Tony Moore writes, the self-styled revolutionaries of modern art were keen to distinguish themselves from the effete 'bohemians' that preceded them and quite often sold out: 'not for Max Harris the smokos and wine and cheese clubs of the older generation.' Of course, most of these radical artists engaged in very similar social activities ... but this time with a streak of red.

For a time, the Australian modernist movement was not just led by communists, but fought over by factions of different *sorts* of communists. The commitments of some of these modernists were likely to extend into difficult areas for a Stalinist party to accept – questions around individualism, collectivism and authority. The Communist Party of Australia (CPA) was uncomfortable with the relationship of individual dissent with communal action. Where did creative freedom fit into this?

For a time this tension was left unsettled and what helped the flourishing of collaboration between the modernists and Communists was probably just the lack of attention the party leadership gave to art. To the extent that there was an awareness of what the arty types were doing it was curious endeavours like the sectioning off of the creatives into their own branch of the party in 1938 – the Artists Branch.

But these periods of disinterest in cultural activity were also punctuated with high-level interventions from local leaders and decrees from Moscow. Notably an anti-modernist framework that suited Russian ruling class interests and seemed to extinguish the cultures of dissent, therefore starving oxygen from the dying embers of the Bolshevik tradition. In Australia, analysis of the internal counter-revolution in Russia was shaky and only present at the furthest margins, the beleaguered Trotskyist movement, with little influence in Australian politics. So there was an open hose for Stalinist cultural terms like Zhadanovism

Nancy Wills and Geoff Wills, 1956

A gathering of modernist artists including Albert Tucker and Adrian Lawlor, early 1940s (State Library of Victoria)

and socialist realism to be clumsily sprayed on to existing creative practices. This did shape the art of some Communists to a limited extent. But for a period in the late 1930s and early 40s, it could be said the screws were rather loose. There was the party-sanctioned Communist view on art, and then the reality of what was going on as led by creatives animated by their own interest in what they considered communist ideas.

One reason why so much looseness was evident and accepted was that artists within the CPA were working out their positions at a time when the party was going through a particularly volatile period, with a quick succession of about-faces. The party's trenchant opposition to fascism was followed by the Hitler-Stalin pact. There was a firm anti-war position, and then full support given to World War Two. The United Front concept was expanded to now be a *Popular* Front, which welcomed collaboration with the bourgeoisie. Not everyone could follow these twists and turns.

The party was declared illegal for a short period during the war, but then after being made legal again, thereafter pursued enthusiastic collaboration with the state. The period of illegality opened up a contradictory space, and possibly was of positive benefit to dissident creatives within the party. They were now encouraged to participate in the not banned mainstream organisations, and were also more able to argue their positions free from the censure of party overseers.

But achieving any kind of consistent 'left position' on art proved challenging. Within the spectrum of modern art there could be an array of progressive intentions: unprejudiced scientific rationality, raising awareness of suffering, extending humanism, deepening sympathy with particular groups, and expanding utopian social horizons. The potential was obvious to social reformers. But really, there was no tidy left-right divide presenting itself, and co-existence between different factions became increasingly untenable.

Tony Moore points to a 'factionalised group lifestyle in Melbourne centred around studio apartments, cafes, galleries, libraries, Leonardo's bookshop and the Swanston Family Hotel.' It was in the environments where drinking took place that the opposing factions most vigorously sparred.

The Mitre Tavern

One venue which played host to many crucial encounters and debates was the Mitre Tavern. Since its founding in 1868, it had long been a favoured drinking hole for artists and eccentrics, including bohemian poet of the 8 Hours movement Marcus Clarke and the visual chronicler of early Victorian working life ST Gill. The tavern is located in central Melbourne, and still functions today. An impressive list of former habitués have leaned an elbow on their bar, including Arthur Boyd, Peter Herbst, Max Nicholson, and Tim Burstall. The Communist playwright and arts organiser Nancy Wills (née Macmillan) recalls that lefty enfant terrible Brian Fitzpatrick would drop into The Mitre from time to time and add 'salt and pepper' to the already highly spiced conversations about art, politics and economics.

Communist artist Noel Counihan, a significant protagonist in debates around social progress and art, also drank at The Mitre and was open to sparring in the pubs. Alister Kershaw jests in his memoir that Counihan only held back from calling him a fascist in one of their parleys because of a heavy-built, literary-minded military barfly Kershaw had befriended earlier in the drinking session. Kershaw offers a puffed up recollection of his various stand-offs with his red rivals in his memoir: 'they would glower at us from as far away as they could get. It was worth going to The Mitre just for that.' This particular pub seemed to be an especially fractious meeting point for the frenemies within the Melbourne intellectual underground. But it was also where soul mates were found.

Mitre Tavern, Melbourne, 1930 (State Library of Victoria)

At The Mitre in 1946, Nancy McMillan met Geoff Wills, a tall, blond curly-headed young man who, until he had decided to become a seafarer, was on the path to becoming an accountant. He dropped out of these studies and dedicated himself to life on the water. As well as working in commercial shipping, for recreation, he achieved a long-lasting Sydney-to-Hobart record on the yacht *White Wings*. Wills had joined the Communist Party in The Mitre Tavern, recruited by Bob Priestly, who was a lecturer at Melbourne University. When Wills revealed this to Wendy Lowenstein in an oral history, Lowenstein's response was: 'A lot of people did, I think', exclaiming, 'It was a great meeting place for Communists!' And so it was in such an environment where Bill Cook, Secretary of the Rationalists, adopted the role of cupid when he introduced Geoff to Nancy with the simple words: 'You two should know each other. You're both reds.'

On Tuesdays and Thursdays, between 4.30 pm and 6 pm, a segment of the Melbourne creative scene crowded into a particular space at The Mitre Tavern known as Justus Jorgensen's Brown Room. The architect and famed builder of the Knox House, Alistair Knox, explained in his memoir:

> Jorgie had for many years enjoyed the privilege of a private room at the tavern for those two evenings each week when he taught at his nearby studio. It became the nexus of artistic bohemian Melbourne. Beer was a shilling a glass. Trays full of glasses would be purchased at the bar and carried, through the jostling mob, to the private room to be consumed in somewhat more orderly surroundings. Jorgie always occupied a brown leather armchair in the corner, receiving and acknowledging greetings from all who were permitted entry, which depended on their knowing him or some of his pupils.

In Melbourne, the organisation of social life was for so long shaped by the six o'clock swill and the developed patterns of travelling from place to place when last drinks were called. At The Mitre, 'an aggressive electric bell' would signal the end, whereby most of the drinkers in the Brown Room would proceed to the Latin Club where wine could be consumed with meals until 8pm. Knox observed that 'the rapid beer session, followed by half a dozen speedy glasses of claret, left the face flushed and the heart palpitating as at the conclusion of a race. The new age was noted much more for energy than for grace in its social activities.'

Another segment of the Melbourne art scene also claimed The Mitre, the group around leading protagonists of modernism: John Reed, Sidney Nolan and Max Harris. Harris and Reed had established a publishing venture, and one of their first commissions was to publish a book of poems by Alister Kershaw. It indicated that there was space for non-Communists in their cultural revolution, such was their faith in the power of cultural interventions in society. Harris paid Kershaw with a cheque and helpfully informed him it could be cashed over the bar at The Mitre. They proceeded to drink it all away in celebration, and so it was a particularly successful day for Harris.

Around their art and publishing activity, Reed also worked on youth leader Malcolm Good's electoral campaign for the CPA. Harris was collaborating with party leader Jack Blake, and published his views on art in the modernist journal *Angry Penguins*. Like their journal collaborator, the painter Albert Tucker, their engagement with the Communist movement did not last beyond the tumultuous period of the war, and eventually the Marxism that animated their cultural activism fell away. But for a brief period, it is intriguing that the debates around modern art seemed at their most potent between protagonists who were, in various ways, all associated with the Communist movement. Notably this included Noel Counihan, who most consistently channelled the interests of the Party, although not fully subscribing to socialist realism. Within shared spaces such as The Mitre Tavern and the Swanston Family Hotel they would discuss and debate, and such encounters in no small way defined this period of Australian art history.

Alcohol, Politics, and the Formation of the Contemporary Art Society

A comprehensive narrative of the heady days of radical modernism is beyond the scope of this chapter, but we shall look at some more of the significant players, and a number of important early events. These contributed to forming an institutional alternative, rival poles of attraction to the status quo as embodied by the Australian Academy of Art. Relevant to our interests, the presence of alcohol is very much evident, as is the elevated importance of pubs, house parties and other meeting points between artists and communists.

For many modernist artists there was a strong interest in recording the reality of human, social and interior psychological experience – especially in relation to social crisis. It was easily applicable to a socialist mindset, the anxiety around dispossession and trauma that was so often within people who had lived through the Great Depression and were now entering a new war. Images of urban apocalypse, insanity and moral decay were strong in the work of both Albert Tucker and Arthur Boyd, two leading modernists shaped by Communist ideas. As historian David Carter writes:

> Tucker's war-time Melbourne is a hell-on-earth, full of the grotesque and the fallen ... Far from the official images of the noble AIF, Tucker gives us drunken, grotesque diggers brawling and vomiting in the streets. He uses the Victory Girls to personify moral degeneracy: leering school girl prostitutes waiting on street corners wearing miniskirts made out of American flags.

Tucker's Melbourne paintings were rich in symbolism for a city he felt was hurtling into the abyss. Tucker was a CPA member and leading cultural voice. As we will explore later in more depth, he was someone who found the party's shift in support of the war intolerable. His slant on the depravity of this epoch also bears the hallmarks of the CPA's moralism around drink and sexuality. Ultimately, Tucker did not last as a Communist artist.

Painter James Gleeson pursued the political aspects of surrealism which tended towards an exploration of interiority. This art movement was only briefly pursued by CPA artists. Sadly, famed art historian Bernard Smith destroyed most of his own surrealist work after shifting away from it. There were firm messages from Soviet cultural bureaucrats that surrealism was not the path to follow, too associated with Trotskyism was one problem, and so many Communist sympathisers embraced figurative social realism, which was something of a pathway out of high modernism. Gleeson recounted:

> For a while, especially during the war years, I did think of Surrealism as a revolutionary weapon. I accepted Breton's contention that by utilising the subconscious one could arrive at a condition that held the rational mind in balance and perhaps prevent such disasters as war, indifference or fanaticism.

In Melbourne, surrealist activity crystallised around the *Angry Penguins* journal – which we will come to shortly – and also the Contemporary Art Society (CAS). This period of modernism, when the Communists were driving the interest in Australian surrealism, has a claim to being its most vital era.

In the same year as the CPA Artists Branch was formed in 1938, the CAS was formed to push the cause of modern art, with the debates in the next few years significantly impactful on the shaping of the Australian art scene. The subsequent battle within the CAS, for leadership of this new institution of Australian art, had material significance for left-wing modernist artists, and beyond. For one thing, it was almost impossible for non-established artists to exhibit independently and gain enough public attention to sustain a career. The CAS appeared to be the only vehicle that had the power to promote the values of this new art. The CPA was strategising to set up unions for commercial artists, while vying for leadership of the peak bodies in fine art like the CAS. Their intervention into the 'mainstream' CAS was consistent with the broad approach of the CPA during the Popular Front era. To what ends, was a key debate between the different hues of communist red.

It was a tumultuous period in Australian art history, with significant figures arguing for their theoretical positions as much as wielding paint brushes. In Tim Burstall's diaries he recounts an argument with George Bell, an early Australian modernist and founder of the CAS, that took place in the Swanston Family Hotel. As Burstall recounts, a lubricated chat over the response to Noel Counihan's latest artworks spilled over into a full blown discussion about the purpose of art.

The CAS, in its vital early period, was under the leadership of radical modernists, with Albert Tucker on the committee and John Reed a secretary for a period. Along with the communist sympathies of these figures, you also had the presence of a leading CPA figure (and printmaker) in Malcolm Good, another CAS council member. For a period, the debates between the different radical tendencies could be said to be productive. The CAS was welcoming of argument, proactive in pushing a vision of art. It hosted lectures and welcomed critics of the CAS, such as Vic O'Connor, to present their views. This was its heyday, when it was at the centre of the discourse, hosting epochal art events, but also organising more targeted political interventions such as the Anti-Fascist Exhibition on 8 December 1942. The battle against reaction in culture was conjoined to the battle against fascism and

Young Communist students at The University of Melbourne were regulars at jazz events, pictured here l-r, Ian Turner, Amirah Gust and Stephen Murray-Smith, 1947 (Search Foundation)

Germany, and this held things together to a point. It also raised the stakes and possibly hastened fragmentation. We can only guess the role of alcohol in the recurrent debates that ensued inside the pubs and cafes.

The divisions within the left inside the CAS progressively sharpened. There was debate about how to represent the human condition in creative works. Debates about exploring 'ways of seeing' with the use of abstraction. There was the psychological explorations of surrealism, and then the elevation of emotional responses to the unjust world through social realism. Ailsa O'Connor was a CPA member, and a CAS member, and summarised the ideological differences between the group around John Reed, which she argued stressed private and personal trauma, as distinct from the social realist group, which emphasised communal agony. These competing approaches were significant enough, but also in the background was the Communist Party, and their designs on the art scene.

The debate came to a head with a dispute in 1943, which was essentially going to determine what sort of restrictions the CAS would begin implementing, and who was going to be in control. Attitudes to the war had in the preceding period made things more complicated and tense. With the USSR now with the Allies, the CPA was in full support of the Australian war effort. The CPA artists participated in the exhibition 'Australia at War', whereas the Angry Penguins boycotted it. Along the way, with their various jags, the Communists picked up artists who were attracted to their positions. Going back to 1935, the party initially pushed for the unity of all working class organisations against fascism. As mentioned earlier, the concept was then adjusted to include sections of the capitalist class who were supposedly 'democratic' – a 'Popular Front'. A tactical alliance among all groups who opposed the common enemy. These were not just temporary alliances though, the party began to sacrifice some basic socialist principles. The popular front was in effect the subordination of the working class to the liberal bourgeoisie, and so with this broad openness it can be seen why the CPA was perhaps more open to participating in ambiguous institutions like the CAS, along with their collaborations in the military and wartime labour boards.

This was quite the departure from an earlier period when the Movement Against War and Fascism was able to build an 'International Peace Campaign' which held a congress of 4000 in Melbourne in 1937. In this period, there was also a high profile protest against Count von Luckner, a Nazi visiting Melbourne in 1938. During these years when fascists were on the ascendancy, the party press described them as 'degenerates' who were 'loaded with beer'. The *Workers Weekly* on 10 February 1933 reported on a police force which protected them and was 'using girls just out of school as agents and sending these girls into sly grog shops and houses of ill fame to obtain evidence.'

With such a vigorous denunciation, the movement was deeply traumatised by the news of the 1939 Hitler-Stalin Pact. Respectable allies turned away from the CPA and their working class supporters were bewildered. Things turned around in 1942, when the USSR, under attack by the Nazis, joined as an ally against Germany, and the CPA was returned to a legal status.

If the party was losing the support of some intractably anti-war artists, it was gaining others who were either more patriotic or felt a responsibility to join a military intervention against the Nazis. The CAS's 1942 Anti-Fascism Exhibition – not *anti-war* it should be noted – should be viewed in this context. The party was also now much more acceptable in mainstream society, to the extent that Joseph Stalin was put on the cover of *Women's Weekly*. Despite some unease about the various flips in position on the Nazis and the war, broadly speaking the art scene was relatively open to associating with the CPA. It was the discomfort with the CPA's cultural policy, however, which finally broke the collaboration apart.

Angry Penguins

The leading antagonists of the CPA within the left were the modernists that came to be labelled 'Angry Penguins', via their association with the journal. The publication was initiated by Max Harris and others in Adelaide in 1940, before being published by Harris and John Reed in Melbourne from 1943. The title Angry Penguins belies the alcohol-infused passions that were an undercurrent running through the scene, derived from the Max Harris poem 'Mithridatum of Despair' which featured a line: 'as drunks, the angry penguins of the night.' *Angry Penguins* was a sensation and, along with *Art in Australia*, was the most important cultural magazine of the early 1940s. This was a unique period in the art discourse when overtures were being made to the far left rather than the centre left, as indicated by John Reed's desire for *Angry Penguins* to be re-named '*Comrade*'.

By 1943 the Angry Penguins group had drifted away from their sympathies towards the CPA and firmed up its own faction. Only CAS artists, and those supported by John and Sunday Reed, would be promoted. As discussed, *Angry Penguins* cohered the surrealist activity of the arts scene and the other creative expressions disregarded by the Communists and social realist painters. But it would not be accurate to describe the Angry Penguins as the side to represent freedom or an equal platform for all, given their own exclusions. For the Reeds, it helped that they were wealthy and had the means to launch projects, as well as to absorb favoured artists into their orbit through the lure of financial support – a key example being Sidney Nolan.

Not all of the key protagonists in Australian modernism were going to be drawn into formal spaces of debate. For someone like Sidney Nolan, this is where the impact of participating in left-wing social life around venues like Swanston Family Hotel was particularly influential. Nancy Underhill, biographer of Nolan, concludes that 'put simply Nolan was not a joiner and certainly not a willing committee man.' It is apparent that Nolan was an anti-capitalist though, and certainly a leading figure in the development of Australian modernism. He was also a participant in the Anti-Fascist Exhibition in 1942. He was kept in the loop with the CAS activity by correspondence, and is significant in the sense that he was the most sensational of the modernists and his artwork was to be found in CAS exhibitions. As Underhill explains it, when it came to discussion at the Swanston Family Hotel, 'Marx and Engels' *Communist Manifesto*, Engels' *Anti-Duhring*, plus works by Rabelais and Zola were deemed worthy texts for argument, not the likes of romantic escapism by Rimbaud, Rilke or William Black.' Whatever conclusions

Angry Penguins journal 1945

Nolan took from this pub talk, as Underhill contends, the 'sparring sharpened both sides'. Nolan's art was not agitational, but also not entirely aloof from politics. His social critique was sufficiently opaque to not impede his eventual status as the most recognisable, and in the final accounting most well-loved, of the Australian modernists.

The Australia Hotel

On 28 October 1941 the CAS held an exhibition that is now considered 'a landmark in Australian art.' Art historian Richard Haese describes the show as 'a massive assault on all assumptions about art in Australia.' The National Gallery of Victoria refused to host the exhibition, which was instead mounted inside the Australia Hotel. Built on the former site of Café Australia in 1939 and located in central Collins Street, this was one of the premiere meeting places of the day among the cosmopolitan. Twelve stories high, the hotel combined 94 rooms with bars, dining and function areas, cinemas and a shopping arcade. Robert Menzies was a regular patron and the Packer family kept a suite there for decades. A residence for US military officers during the war, two of its stories were used as General MacArthur's headquarters for a period.

The 1941 exhibition, simply titled 'Contemporary Art Society', featured works from leading figures Sidney Nolan, Albert Tucker and John Perceval. As well as Danila Vassilieff's Fitzroy street scenes, surrealist paintings by James Gleeson, an anti-war painting by James Cant, the Yosl Bergner paintings 'Refugees' and 'Pie Eaters' made their first exposure to a large audience. Also displayed were two paintings by Noel Counihan, significantly his first exhibited artworks in this medium.

Contestation could be seen in the varied approach to modern art on the canvases, but the intensity of debate around art was also evident at the launch. CAS members were going through the crowd gathering signatures on a petition to protest the failure of the NGV to represent the contemporary movement in art. J.S. McDonald, Director of the NGV, had described the modernist art movement as 'the exalting of the discordant and ugly!' It was clear that the conservative layer controlling the art institutions was stifling the potential for modernist artists to bring their art to audiences, as well as the possibility for them to earn a living off it. At the exhibition launch, the petition was seized by two disgruntled opponents: military officers. Military personnel were residing in the Australia Hotel during the war. The two defenders of art conservatism ran to the toilets and attempted to flush the insubordinate petition away. Melbourne newspaper *Truth* reported that John Reed called for 'six moderately sober volunteers to rescue it from these uniformed representatives of the establishment.' *Truth* painted their own evocative picture of the launch:

> The show on Tuesday brought together the strangest combination seen in Melbourne for a long time ... Long haired intellectuals,

The Hotel Australia, on Collins Street in Melbourne, changed its name to the Australia Hotel following renovations in a modernist style (State Library of Victoria)

swing fiends, hot mommas and truckin' jazz boys rubbed shoulders on friendly terms. While swingsters hollered 'Go to town' and jittered in the aisles, the intelligentsia learnedly discussed differences between rhythm of hot jazz and pigment of Picasso ... Jitterbugs shimmied to a weird new brand of swing music and lank-haired collarless 'modernists' argued about what-have-you...

The exhibition was a formative event for then Communist, and future leading New Left thinker, Ian Turner. It was his first exposure to jazz but also an example of a vibrant meeting of politics and art. In 'My Long March' Turner retrospectively made the case:

> I felt then as I still believe that there is no barrier, indeed that there is a necessary communion, between what is innovatory and exciting in arts and in politics. Both offer new ways of seeing the world, new ways of living: the individualism and anarchism of radical art are needed to temper the collectivism and authoritarianism of radical politics.

The experience of Turner, and the journey he went on, was no doubt the sort of impact the political radicals in the CAS were hoping for.

The story of how this venue for the exhibition was chosen is intriguing. With the conservatives withholding the NGV from the modernists, and few alternatives for such a large scale survey, the CAS organisers would have to get creative. The Australia Hotel on Collins Street was deemed a suitable makeshift art gallery. In its newly renovated form it was also, appropriately, an architectural incursion of modernism into the city. Haese's view on the exhibition was that: 'Its dramatic character, both in quality and quantity, was enhanced by the nature of the venue and the events which surrounded its presentation.'

It is not clear exactly how the CAS secured the venue. One account is that the idea was sold to the hotel management 'which agreed to provide the space on the promise that the exhibition would draw not only large art crowds, but thirsty ones.' Joy Hester, a founding member of the CAS, and newly married to Tucker, was also a barmaid at the Australia Hotel, and the drinking environment was the subject of several of her artworks.

Lilian Macmillan, the mother of Communist arts figure Nancy Wills, held a significant role in the operations of the Australia Hotel. She had the job of recruiting during the Depression years, and one of her new hires was Audrey Blake, who was then only 16 but would become a significant Communist leader (and partner of Jack Blake, who was to varying degrees friendly with Reed and Harris). In her memoir

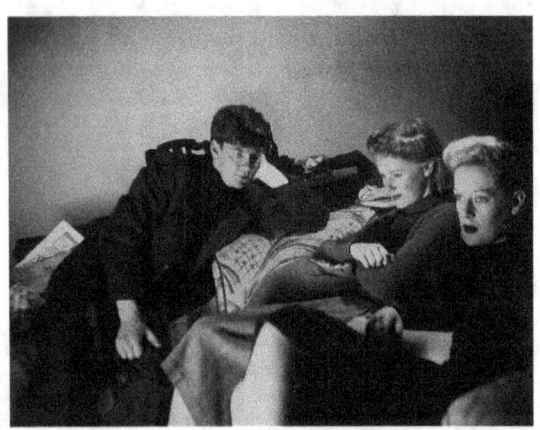

Arthur Boyd, Yvonne Lennie and Joy Hester (Albert Tucker, State Library of Victoria)

A convivial gathering at Heide, including Sidney Nolan, Sunday Reed, John Sinclair and John Reed, 1946 (Albert Tucker, State Library of Victoria)

Shades of Red, Wills describes how after her mother quit working at the hotel, 'it wasn't long before they were employing one man and two women to do the job she'd been doing single-handed.' With such an expansive role, it seems quite possible that the fellow traveller may have played a decisive role in facilitating this epoch-making event in Australian art. The account in *Shades of Red* of Macmillan's experience at the hotel deepens the story as, 'it was that pub, and that particular big boss, that made her a communist.' Two years after the CAS exhibition, after 16 years of working there:

> She couldn't stand it any longer. She fronted the boss and gave him two weeks notice. He tried to find out why, tried to talk her out of it, offered her more money, much more money – this last only confirmed Lilian in her determination … 'Liberation Day' finally came, and she walked down those steps for the last time, feeling just great. And who should she bump into but Audrey Blake. Audrey was one of the girls she'd put on from one of those ads. She was only 16 when she got the job, a little political firebrand – Lilian had liked her right away.

Lilian and Audrey went for a drink, and at this moment she was convinced by Blake to transfer her skills from running the bar in the Australia Hotel into taking up the role of operations in the CPA's Melbourne party office. It was 1943 and Blake's pitch was recounted in *Shades of Red*:

> We're legal again, but we've been so long in the shadows, it's going to be very hard; you could set up the Party office, get the business part of *The Guardian* going again, and see that the suburban bookshops get off to a good start. Oh, do come with us Miss Mac., there are a thousand things that need to be done, and you could do them so well.

And so the curious relationship between the Australia Hotel and Communism ran deep.

Conclusion

The debate over modernism and the political possibilities of art became increasingly polarised through the 1940s. To unsympathetic observers, it could be reduced to authoritarian Communism versus a wishy-washy liberal anarchism. Whichever side an artist fell on, the other side appeared to be particularly uncomfortable to work with.

For the Stalinists, there was no appeal in the idea of pursuing creative freedom alongside commitment to the revolutionary party. The atmosphere of cultural pluralism was being briskly wound back. Also, the disciplinary strands of their approach to democratic centralism could more easily be operationalised when the party was made legal in 1942.

On the other side, Angry Penguin Max Harris's yearning for a society substantially transformed by radical culture within liberal capitalism did not eventuate.

The cosily productive period of CAS activity was a brief few years. It was followed by a period of disputes that lasted between 1943-46, after which the discourse ran out of steam, with the eventual demise of the Melbourne CAS in 1947. The culture war was spent with the conservatives still in power. With peace in Europe, it was now that many artists could pursue their long delayed wanderlust out of Melbourne. It had been a brief period when art was politically charged with grand possibilities, something none of the protagonists would ever again experience in the world of art.

CHAPTER 25

GOLD DIGGINGS AND COMPANY TOWNS: FROM THE BUCKLAND RACE RIOT TO THE ROSTREVOR HOPS FARM

Alex Ettling and Iain McIntyre

It was a white Californian who struck gold in Buckland Creek in 1855. One lesson from this history is that it is prudent to keep such things to oneself. Unfortunately for the American, 'one of his mates, whose tongue was loosened by the free liquor provided by the storekeepers of those days, gave the show away.' There was an immediate rush into the area and within six months 6000 diggers were on the ground. The town experienced its first dramatic population degrowth, not long after when 'colonial fever' decimated the population. After this typhoid outbreak Buckland lost its golden reputation and was now known as 'The Valley of the Shadow of Death' – shunned by miners. In 1857,
Chinese migrants decided to make another go of it.

As was common in the gold rush, these new mining towns attracted a diversity of immigrants from around the world. Tensions between different groups started to build, which is not unusual in areas of scarcity and competition. In the context of a settler colony steeped in British imperial ideology, the conflicts became heavily racialised.

In a retrospective article published by *The Argus* in 1932, the story told was that gold had been discovered in Buckland after a particularly strenuous effort. As this had involved a white miner, the area was considered by some racists to be 'a white man's field'. Resentment against Chinese diggers had been cultivated through accusations that they moved in only after the challenges of the gold discovery process had been completed.

Unrest built up to 4 July 1857. White American miners were celebrating their nation's Independence Day and liquor was flowing freely. In the morning, a meeting of whites at the Buckland Junction Hotel decided that if the government would not remove Chinese miners then they would take matters into their own hands. Later in the day, no doubt after a hefty drinking session, things became more heated as a result of another gathering held at Tanswell's Hotel. Outside the hotel, a

Contemporaneous illustration of Chinese workers on the road to a gold diggings (Palmer), 1875
(Australasian Sketcher)

group of approximately 40 agitated men armed themselves with picks, axe handles and pieces of wood. This became Australia's first anti-Chinese race riot and resulted in white miners driving an estimated 2500 Chinese people out of the valley.

In a procession the group headed to the camp on Louden's Flat and it was here that the first attacks occurred. Several Chinese stores and 20 or so tents were quickly torn down and set fire to. At the Maguire's Flat settlement the mob set alight a tent with four Chinese people inside. Along with expulsion, there were personal thefts, lootings and bashings. Terrified people running away from their attackers fell into potholes and some stumbled in the river, where a number drowned. One Chinese man was found lying near a fire in the bush with his foot burnt off. There were reports of some people who were caught up in the river crossing, also being rescued by the rearguard of pogromists, suggesting a spectrum of violent intentions amongst the racists.

On the day there were also whites who showed sympathy and solidarity. This included Frank Scott, the publican of Scott's Hotel. An account published in *The Argus* on 14 July 1957 stated, '[He] was threatened to have his house burnt down because he gave shelter to a few married [Chinese people] for the night.' One Chinese man had tried to find protection by hiding in a hole but had the earth fall in on top of him. Having found the trapped man, Scott helped free him and gave him food. Advised to go home by Scott, the terrified man instead ran away.

The official tally of carnage was three deaths, and the destruction of 750 tents, 30 Chinese stores, and the Chinese joss house of religious worship. Twelve men were charged over the events: three were found guilty of unlawful assembly and one of riot. In the ensuing enquiry, Chinese people were denigrated as 'deceitful' and their evidence dismissed. A Chinese resident of Buckland, Lip Tip, gave eyewitness to the burning of the tents. His evidence was countered with racist logic: 'We can't tell Chinese people apart, so how can you tell any white people apart?'

A white woman, Elizabeth A-Leen, who was married to a Chinese man, also gave testimony. Her detailed account included a situation where rioters had approached her for liquor. She handed over half a bottle of pale brandy. A-Leen witnessed an accused man, Taylor, lighting matches to set fire to a tent. After making these statements, she was accused of betraying her race, and her reputation was called into question with the theft of property insinuated into a suggestion of A-Leen's

A set of signatures from an 1857 petition to the Victorian Legislative Assembly which called for an end to racist taxes (Public Records Office of Victoria)

drunkenness. One accusation was that she was 'in such a state of intoxication as to render her evidence inadmissible.' The seizure of alcohol and the staging of attacks from pubs suggests that throughout the day's events alcohol was a significant factor.

The day after the riot, an Anti-Chinese League had formed and met at Tanswell's Hotel. When the twelve ringleaders of the Buckland Riot faced trial, this group raised funds for their defence. A man referred to only as 'Mr Scott' assumed the role of vice-president of the new league. This was a common surname, but if it was the same person as Frank Scott, the aforementioned publican who was sympathetic to the plight of the Chinese community during the riot, then it suggests a quick about-face. Possibly a cold business decision with a view to attracting patronage to his pub given the town's demographics had dramatically changed in the last 24 hours. There is also the possibility that some whites supported expulsion but were disapproving of violent methods, especially after witnessing the reality of a vicious pogrom. Thus, the formation of a formal organisation may have been a means towards encouraging a more ordered approach to racism.

There appears to have been little regret from many white miners in the aftermath of the riot, with one report of the events at Tanswell's: 'The dancing was kept up from 8 pm until midnight.' A rousing welcome awaited the acquitted rioters in Buckland. Celebrations began at the Hit or Miss Hotel. The men were marched up the valley, stopping at different pubs along the way, until they reached the Britannia Hotel.

Across the diggings, there was no uniform hostility to the Chinese population. As historian Liam Ward has explained, 'While the inherently competitive nature of life on the goldfields did spur conflict, on numerous occasions diggers of "non-white" backgrounds, including Bengalis, Maoris and African-Americans, participated and even led mass protests that unified people across racial lines.' George Thomson's paper *The Diggers Advocate* stridently argued that Chinese people were welcome and for hostility to be directed instead at the 'race of capitalists' which was 'invading' the goldfields. Most famously events at the Eureka Stockade included people from a range of ethnic and cultural backgrounds.

William 'Billy' Thomas Panlook 1957, (Jeff Carter Archive/National Library of Australia)

Racist sentiments circulated throughout society but were certainly stoked from above. Significantly there were politicians and business leaders with a material interest in scapegoating Chinese people. They passed laws and regulations aimed at driving the Chinese community out of Victoria entirely. One of the most notorious laws enacted during the era of the Buckland Riot was a racially specific entry tax into Victoria. This resulted in some Chinese migrants being dropped off their passageway in South Australia only to walk the 400 km to get to the Victorian goldfields.

The Chinese community resisted this and further racist taxes through protests and non-compliance. Decrying the 'insults and oppressions from the ignorant, the cruel, and the malicious', petitioners, including supporters of European descent, called for equality under law as well as an inquiry into racist stereotypes and allegations.

After some taxes were rendered unfeasible through widespread non-payment and the exploitation of loopholes, authorities introduced a new set accompanied by increased penalties, including prison. These were met with civil disobedience and boycotts of racist businesses, as well as protest meetings and public demonstrations in various towns. One rally in Castlemaine, numbering 3000, featured a speech declaring, 'We have feelings like other men, we want to be brothers with the Englishmen – why not let it be so?' Mass tax refusal by tens of thousands, which saw many fined and jailed, piled on costs and pressure to the point where authorities eventually annulled the laws. Racism, of the legislative and public kind, would continue to be stoked however, eventuating in the exclusionary White Australia Policy of 1901.

After the Buckland Riot, the entire Chinese population left the diggings. When authorities promised to protect any Chinese miners who returned, few trusted them. Those that did faced ongoing persecution.

One who attempted to return was a man named Panlook. He had recently renovated his general store, which had been torched in the riot. He went back to Buckland but it was never the same. Panlook's great-granddaughter Carol Moore speaking on ABC Radio National recounted, 'My mother told me the family story was that her grandfather, Panlook, had died of a broken heart because of what happened in the Buckland.' The family shortly thereafter moved to the neighbouring Ovens Valley.

A common solution to persecution in mining districts was for Chinese migrants to shift into industries without the same level of economic competition and racial targeting by whites. Most did so as workers, some as employers. Small scale agriculture was one way to generate an income, allowing people to live the life they wished to lead, and to avoid at least some harassment and discrimination. Panlook's family made a transition from the general store to market gardening

Miner photographed in the 1860s (State Library of Queensland)

and eventually into larger scale agriculture. Originally they cultivated tobacco in Victoria until devastating frosts and unreliable prices saw them make the shift into hops farming. Led by Panlook's son William and his brother Ernest, Rostrevor Hop Gardens was established in Eurobin in 1890.

Hops farms are spectacular sights. The towers of vines are something out of the Southern gothic imagination. When in bloom the green-yellow flower clusters are harvested and they become the ingredient that makes the bittering and flavouring agent for beer. The nature of such a seasonal product makes sourcing labour a challenge, and there is always the pressure to expand to achieve more favourable economies of scale.

William Panlook placed an advertisement in *The Argus* newspaper each year for casual workers in the lead up to harvest time. The business was a major undertaking and toward the end of summer, Rostrevor Hop Gardens would welcome nearly a thousand pickers, creating a 'make-shift town' for the duration of the harvest.

The company made a much greater effort than most to provide employees with facilities. It also put a lot of time and energy into publicising its work. As such, it is notable to examine the sort of 'company town' that the business sought to create in the hops industry. Insights can be gained from business histories by descendants of William Panlook, company-sponsored photos, and newspaper reports.

Photos published in newspapers in 1926, 1937 and 1941 provide insights into how the firm wished to represent itself. The images include workers in their white uniforms, alternately enjoying each other's company or otherwise joyfully working the farm. Sometimes they wear veils to keep the flies out of their face as they pick hops. Photos of smiling workers having tea parties suggest a quaint and leisurely work experience.

There is more than a small possibility these photos were highly staged. Photo collages of the work experience were published in mainstream publications. There were no depictions of work specific ailments, such as 'hops rash' or bad backs, commonly experienced on such farms. It was seemingly a campaign to encourage workers to travel to Eurobin to take up this line of work.

It is of course possible that the Panlook Family were genuinely proud of the workplace culture they had established, so distinct from the misery of the goldfields and a step up from conditions on other farms. According to *The Herald* in 1937: 'We are very proud of our people, Mr Panlook said. They are an excellent type. The work is not hard and they all enjoy themselves.'

Other newspaper reports, in the years on either side of this quote, and during the time of the publication of photos from the farm, indicate that workers perhaps did not share the same rosy view of the job as their boss. A series of incidents provide us with snapshots of

Full page spread about the Rostrevor Hops Farm, 1941 (*The Weekly Times*, National Library of Australia)

Weighing the hops, Rostrevor, 1957 (Jeff Carter Archive/National Library of Australia)

workers' resistance. A pay dispute at the farm in 1924 involved a strike followed by a test case which was heard in the Myrtleford Police Court. With the enterprise under the management of a Mr Campbell 500 of the workers went on strike in 1936.

In 1938, the farm's workers held another strike and were able to successfully raise their wages. *The Argus* reported on 25 February 1938: 'Hop-pickers at Eurobin went on strike today for a higher rate of pay. After a long discussion with the managing director an increase of 2d. a measure was granted.' A strike does not necessarily indicate misery, although it does represent conflict, and there were reports of management refusing pay claims within the process of the dispute. This was one of a number of farms the AWU was organising within the hops industry, including placing people with agitational placards at farm gates.

Nearly a decade later it appears that antagonism remained between farmers, managers and their workforces, to the point where hops picker strikes were once again held in Tasmania and Victoria. In the case of the Rostrevor Hops Garden *The Herald* on 26 February 1947 reported: 'Hop pickers at Eurobin are on strike. More than 300 from Panlook's garden, who met at the hall on the grounds on Sunday night, decided to strike until they received 15 [shillings] a 100 [pounds] – an advance of 4 [shillings].' Newspaper reports also included details of police observing the dispute.

The attitudes of strikers, and the sense of community amongst hops pickers, are difficult to gauge as there are no historical testimonies from workers themselves. Certainly, there are no images of strikers in the photo montages. In a historical piece written for the Australian Broadcasting Commission by Miyuki Jokiranta, the amenities were described as including 'rudimentary huts for the pickers to sleep in as well as community kitchens, a school, a police station, and a great hall for entertainment and dancing.' Workers gathering together created their own culture to make the day go by, and made entertainment in the evenings for recreation. Such activity was readily promoted by the farm management.

The presence of a school within the company town sounds generous and forward thinking. Less so when put in the context that Rostrevor Hops Gardens, as with farms owned by farmers from European and other backgrounds, used child labour. The presence of a police station inside any workplace is concerning and raises the question of whose behaviour was being policed. Perhaps a watchful eye on workers agitating around better pay and conditions? There was certainly police intimidation during the 1947 wages dispute.

While elements of living conditions on the Rostrevor Hops Farm were better than those in other parts of the industry, where people generally slept outdoors or in tents, the story of this period suggests the limitations of paternalistic business models. The Panlooks' employment practices formed a common response at this stage in the development of capitalism. Many major companies, most famously Ford, projected an approach to production that offered better conditions than competitors: childcare facilities, changerooms with showers, worker sports, etc. These encouraged higher productivity and employee retention but the companies involved were often also fiercely anti-union and intent on maintaining a price for labour power that was highly profitable.

Looking from a contemporary historical vantage point, we might ask if Rostrevor Hops Gardens could have done better than 'rudimentary huts' for its workers? Workplace conditions which might have seemed generous for the time now appear to be a minimum standard, clean lunch rooms and accommodation out of the rain for instance. Any form of generosity from management was welcome, but would not remove the inherent exploitation of the social relationship.

Today, Rostrevor Hop Gardens is owned by Hop Products Australia (HPA). In a more sophisticated era of craft beers it supplies key products for the Australian alcohol industry. Hops varieties used in craft brews such as Galaxy, Topaz, Vic Secret and Ella are all supplied by this historic hops farm which has expanded to be the largest in the southern hemisphere. Today, seasonal farm labour is to an extent sourced from backpacker tourists on working holiday visas, but also from workers from the Asia-Pacific region on temporary work visas. The industry enforces low wages by Australian standards, but taking the journey to the Australian regions promises a more hopeful economic situation for some than that which could be obtained in their home country. These conditions reflect those that inspired Panlook to migrate from China in the 1800s.

If the Chinese population was not driven off the Buckland goldfields it is quite probable that the Panlook Family would have flourished in their new home, servicing the mining community with their general store. Deplorable historical events, ones driven by the logic of racist colonial ideology and competitive capitalism, meant they instead ended up being key figures in the history of Australian beer.

CHAPTER 26
FOLK, JAZZ AND BOOZE: MORAL PANICS FROM 1940s–1970s
Alex Ettling

Graeme Bell's jazz band at The Uptown Club, 1940s

Alongside new directions in visual arts and literature during the 1940s, Melbourne's non-conformist arts scene expressed an enthusiasm for 'hot' or traditional jazz. It was a style that combined an emphasis on both improvisation and authenticity, and bohemian Communists embraced it with gusto.

The launch of the 1941 Contemporary Art Society exhibition at the Hotel Australia included musical performances by Graeme Bell's Jazz Gang, Donald Banks, and Ron Howells. The inclusion of live jazz and boogie astride avant-garde visual works directly laid down a challenge to Melbourne's conservative art establishment. Earlier in the year National Gallery director J.S. MacDonald, had exclaimed that 'Decadence in art [is] a product of a generation revelling in jazz, jitterbugging... committed to ungainly attitudes [and] the exalting of the discordant and ugly.' In response to such blinkered views, networks formed which would sustain an important intersection of political radicals and culturally adventurous people. Graeme Bell wrote:

> We jazz musicians and the contemporary artists discovered that we were in the same camp. To be modern or anti-conservative during the prevailing climate was to be anti-fascist and therefore left-wing. If anything was anti-conservative in the early 40s it was jazz. It was a matter of record that the conservative forces in the arts were linked to right-wing politics... leading writers like Max Harris saw jazz as part of the total art phenomenon...

The traditional jazz style promoted rolling improvisation by soloists, which Bell saw as democratic, free and interactive – and an art experience in opposition to commercialised music.

Bell was spending a lot of time in pubs, often drinking at the Fawkner Hotel in Toorak Road. The Graeme Bell Jazz Gang also had a residency at the Swing Inn coffee house on Flinders Street, above Young and Jackson's Hotel. A scene of drinking and entertainment in private houses was nurtured by the restrictive licensing laws which made it an offence to drink alcohol in or within 100 metres of a premises where there was dancing. Bell's new South Yarra apartment attracted a modernist clique where artists, musicians, racing drivers, sportsmen, writers and African-American servicemen would participate in Saturday afternoon drinking and jazz jam sessions. As music historian Craig Horne writes:

> It was all about trying to escape the general gloom of the war years... guests found release letting the Bells' music dump them like a wild wave... Drinkin' at the flat was *de rigeur* with the hip bohemian crowd and everyone who was anyone was there.

The bohemian scene around John Reed converged at the flat. It was where Sidney Nolan sumptuously painted a series of nudes by just dipping his finger in a jar of red pigment.

Jazz symbolised freedom among dissenters, so it makes sense that all sides of the debates around modernism amongst communists liked it and backed it in a big way. In 1944, Harry Stein, a member of the CPA's Eureka Youth League and a jazz drummer, started up the Eureka Hot Jazz Society. This provided a regular gig for Graeme Bell's band, and two years later, when the Uptown Club was established he was a main attraction. This new venue was located in the Eureka Youth League building, which had a previous life as the Temperance Building.

The attitudes of the Temperance Union were no longer relevant to the space but the licensing laws and police surveillance they had given life to very much were. Soft drinks

Roger Bell, Dizzy Gillespie and Graeme Bell, 1948

were sold in the foyer, along with cups of coffee and tea. Horne writes that 'there was grog smuggled in via medicine bottles and the odd Dexedrine tablet to speed things up a bit.' Historian Bill Liddy recalls that people could smoke inside the EYL Hall, but if they wanted to consume alcohol they would have to go into the back lane where people would make do drinking warm longnecks because there was no cooling.

By 1946 the genre was increasing in popularity with Bell hosting a weekly radio show on 3UZ entitled *Come In On The Beat*. In the same year Harry Stein organized the first national jazz convention, which met in the Eureka Hall for five days of discussion, listening, and jam sessions that went long into the night. Papers were given at the conference and a souvenir program published in the *Angry Penguins* journal. In his introduction, Bell thanked those concerned for 'sticking their necks out in the early forties.' Bill Miller presented material under the heading 'Origins of Jazz', featuring field recordings of Alan Lomax and including blues, African-American lullabies and chain gang work songs. In Harry Stein's memoir he reminisces:

> As I recall those delirious days in North Melbourne... I can once again, feel the unspeakable excitement in the discovery that out there, in other parts of Australia, were young blokes on the same wavelength... there will never be anything like the 1946 Convention where we walked on air in a state of euphoria for five days.

By 1953, communist party theorist Paul Mortier was urging young people 'to turn their backs on the eroticism, escapism and subjectivism of Jazz.' In its place, he advocated what he saw as a more authentically working class genre: folk music.

Flyer for jazz event at the Eureka Youth Club, in the former Temperance Hall, North Melbourne, 1946

The modernist *Angry Penguins* journal promoted the jazz convention at Eureka Hall, 1946 (National Library of Australia)

The Communist Party went on to play a leading role in the revival of Australian folk. The Eureka Youth League did not entirely ditch its connection to jazz and gave young people an exposure to political music from both genres during the 1950s and 1960s. This included musicians and enthusiasts Peter Dickie, Ken Mansell, Lyell Sayer, Mick Counihan, Bill Berry, Jeannie Lewis, Chris Kempster and Shayna Bracegirdle (Karlin).

In late 1963 trombonist Frank Traynor opened his eponymous Folk & Jazz Club. Commonly referred to as Traynor's, it became a Melbourne icon. Like the Melbourne Jazz Club, which he had established in 1958, it was revolutionary and played a key role in the folk revival in Australia (while at the same time keeping jazz music alive after the boom had collapsed).

Melbourne's leading role in the Australian 50s and 60s folk boom is accepted, but the popularity of this coffee lounge era was built on a foundation of things like the New Theatre's *Reedy River*, a musical about the 1891 shearer's strike. The fieldwork of party members and fellow-travellers to the CPA, such as Edgar Waters and John Manifold, also played a role; as did the formation of an infrastructure of scholarly Folklore Societies, Bush Music Clubs, and Wattle Records.

Folklore historian Wendy Lowenstein argued that in the 1950s and beyond, a number of Communists opted not to leave the organisation, but 'merely removed themselves from the party and became obsessed with folk.' Jim Buchanan, a party member, and also the business manager of the folk publication *Tradition*, took the CPA lead into folk seriously and committed himself to mastering the lagerphone. Lowenstein observed his sincerity: 'He was fighting for socialism by singing "The Old Bush Hut" and playing the lagerphone.' When disabused of the notion that this would bring socialism nearer, Buchanan became so upset he left the Party.

With these connections to left-leaning and leftist institutions, it was predictable that Traynor's would be subjected to claims that it was a Communist haven. Despite this, the ABC profiled the club positively on a current affairs TV show. The segment included Brian Mooney's Carlton loft which 'provided a bohemian touch.' Mary Traynor remembers that Mooney's attempts to tidy the loft could not prevent the cameraman from lingering on rows of empty bottles neatly lined up against the wall.

Traynor's itself was nominally alcohol-free, a dimly candle-lit coffee lounge with barrels for tables and canvas fold-up stools for seating. Student activist Doug Kirsner recalls the flagons of claret that regularly made it in. There was another drink which was provided only to performers, served in a mug to look like coffee and aptly named 'Black Death'. One participant in the scene recalls, 'My job was to keep serving [performers] Black Death, a mixture of claret and coke that became more coke and less claret as the hours went on.' The lounge was never going to be a lucrative operation, as people smuggled in booze and penniless friends of the artists sat all night over one or two cups of coffee.

Folk musicians, 1967 (Wendy Lowenstein Collection)

Historian Malcolm J Turnbull argues that during this era 'everybody associated folk music with drinking' and that the male folk-singer (in particular, the male *traditional* singer) faced considerable pressure to live up to the 'mighty drinker' stereotype. Audience members who enjoyed sitting around the bar with a charismatic larger-than-life performer, imbibing his songs and stories along with the ale, usually failed to realise that the singer probably went through the same well-oiled social ritual night after night. As a result Turnbull claims, 'There was no way [such a singer] could not become a drunk.'

Traynor's performers would often hang out at local pubs between sets, and it was not uncommon for some of them to be 'rather too primed' by the last bracket of the evening. Booze subsequently became a non-detachable adjunct to performance with the move to pub based clubs, and Turnbull identifies a high incidence of problem drinking or alcoholism among performers in the 1960s and 70s.

The shift into pub folk clubs was generally considered a vastly inferior alternative. Listening to music often became subordinate to socialising. Inevitably, performers found themselves competing to be heard over patrons who had become loud and obnoxious after a few drinks. Amplification became more of a necessity, which in turn favoured semi-electric bands and multi-member acoustic ensembles. Fast-paced jigs that attracted good-time audiences tended to dominate, and the more contemplative storytelling around left-wing songs got less of a hearing.

Shirley Andrews playing the lagerphone, 1967
(Wendy Lowenstein Collection)

Wendy Lowenstein and Geoff Wills 1967
(Wendy Lowenstein Collection)

Australian Tradition cover featuring Geoff Wills, 1968
(Wendy Lowenstein Collection)

Political performers like Glen Tomasetti soon vowed 'never again' to pub shows. Peter Laycock was knocked out one night at the St Andrews Hotel by a drunk who had taken exception to something he sang. The pub environment was also off-putting for the patrons who had become accustomed to the relative sobriety of places like Traynor's. Another issue was that strong demarcations within the Melbourne folk pub scene formed with one pub being belligerently Irish, another just as determinedly Scots-English. With all these complications, it is not surprising that some people tried to establish a scene in their houses, just as the jazz scene had under different circumstances.

Nancy Wills and Geoff Wills joined the Communist Party in Melbourne but built a vibrant workers art scene after moving to Brisbane. This was based in no small part on the intersection of folk and alcohol. Events were hosted at their home at 229 Whites Road in Lota, where guests were greeted with a 'bamboo', a home-made bamboo mug full of home brew. As well as folk music, they put on educational arts talks on subjects such as writers Jack London and William Morris, and musical instrument making. They also set up a collective that hosted events and published books such as Bill Sutton's *The Champion Sticker Licker*. Writing at the time, Nancy Wills enthused:

> The monthly meetings in our garden are often hilarious, helped somewhat by the bottles of home-brew, rosé and Pernod that clutter the table. We get through the agenda and we nearly always have a barbecue afterwards. It's not a meeting we miss if we have any chance.

One aspect giving rise to the success of the events was likely the free beer on offer, a result of Geoff Wills' homebrew operation. The historian Michael O'Loghlin argues that 'inexpensive home brewing on a large scale was an important part of Geoff's philosophy: it was the only way he could afford to extend appropriate hospitality to the large number of guests who appeared there.' Being a seafarer, his approach was to bottle the beer before a trip away. It took a week to ferment, so by the time he arrived back home, he had fresh stocks to offer those that attended their gatherings.

Demonstrating the place of home brew in the folk scene, music luminary Don Henderson wrote 'Five Pence A Bottle' in 1963:

> Oh, the first lot they made was a bit of a risk,
> for you sometimes got poisoned before you got... full;
> but the brew has improved by making some tests
> on daredevil friends and unwitting guests.
>
> *Chorus*
>
> Oh, it's five pence a bottle and that is the rub.
> That's less than we pay for a glass in the pub.
> Each sip I take fills me with wrath.
> Who gets the cream while I get the froth?
> With more dedication than Madame Curie,

Don Henderson, 1967 (Wendy Lowenstein Collection)

with care that would shame to Resch's Brewery,
they made a good drop. Oh, yes it's a beauty,
at five pence a bottle and no excise duty.

Homebrew was not legal before 1972 when the Whitlam Government's Attorney General Lionel Murphy struck out the prohibition. When interviewed by Wendy Lowenstein, Wills lamented his experience in 1968, as before the liberation, 'I was prosecuted and they even took my bloody fermenters.'

The close relationship between the folk musicians and Communists likely spurred on more political songs about workers' experiences. It also encouraged musicians to engage in active strike support, such as during the famous dispute at Mt Isa in 1964-65 when Don Henderson and Geoff Wills visited the town to play for the strikers. They performed a number of specially written songs including 'Isa', 'Who Put the W in AWU', and 'Talking Mt Isa', before being run out of town by the police.

This cosy relationship did not go unnoticed. As historian Thomas Vuleta has detailed, in July 1964 the University of Queensland Folk Club and Coolibah Folk Lounge caught the attention of Catholic far-right organisation the National Civic Council. This led to a *Sunday Truth* report about a crusade against the 'ghastly Communist plot to indoctrinate Australian youth' via the introduction of folk singing into suburban homes.

There were continued efforts to bring folk music venues above ground, but the opposition of the church to Sunday dancing in these venues persisted. In October 1963, after a challenge by several music venues to Brisbane's restrictive Sunday trading hours was unsuccessful, a protest was organised

Port Phillip Folk Festival, including Ken Mansell and Karl Armstrong, 1967 (Wendy Lowenstein Collection)

by the Brisbane branch of the Eureka Youth League. Three hundred mostly teenage protestors met outside 'teenage nite club' TC's, a location chosen for its association with folk music, but also other music scenes like rock'n'roll. The protest moved in groups of 12 to circumvent the ban on street marching, and during this event a new dance emerged: the 'sit-down stomp'.

The intimidation of the local folk music scene continued, and in fact any youth venues that were not associated with the church, or had the slightest implication of leftism were under suspicion. In 1966, *The Truth* reported on a police raid on De Brazil's coffee lounge, a venue for jazz and folk, where detectives uncovered 'one bottle of rum, four bottles of beer, a flask of whiskey and an empty half-gallon spirit keg.' De Brazil's manager Les Williams did not deny the incriminating evidence unearthed by detectives but denied his club's involvement in underage drinking, arguing his cafe 'did their best' to minimise the practice.

The newspaper concluded 'there can be no doubt that long-haired weirdos and their gaudy girl friends are drinking – some openly and defiantly; others secretly – in some of the city's coffee lounges.' Their reporter observed 'bottles of wine on tables occupied by pimply faced kids', while 'four mysterious drug pedlars' moved amongst the tables offering 'kick-up tablets'. Fiery claims to stoke a moral panic, not the first and not the last.

The Danny Spooner Group, part of the 1960s era folk revival (Wendy Lowenstein Collection)

CHAPTER 27

BEFORE, AFTER AND DURING WORK: ALCOHOL AND THE DEVELOPMENT OF NOEL COUNIHAN AS AN ARTIST

Alex Ettling

Noel Counihan (1919-1986) was not like the other young artists of his time; he had the restless energy of a radical bohemian, and his eyes open to proletarian experience.

At the beginning of the 1930s, aged 16, he was spending hours working with charcoal, doing academic tonal drawing under Charles Wheeler at the National Gallery of Victoria. But he grew tired of formal training, as he recounted to Barbara Blackman: 'I was getting bored and I was turning up after having had a few beers and making a nuisance of myself.'

Noel Counihan in the Herald building, 1937

On another occasion, speaking to Mark Cranfield, Counihan was explicit about why he drank:

> One of the roles of alcohol was to provide a defensive skin with which I could operate and that's common. ...More confident, less inhibited and I really didn't give a stuff for a lot of the people who were totally opposed to me. I mean soberly or with the help of alcohol.

Counihan's attendance at life drawing classes enabled him to make the social contacts required for an entry into the boozy world of the Melbourne underground. He maintained that a number of artists from the advertising agencies, 'Used to come along to refresh their souls, to cleanse their souls in many ways at a life class, you know. To get away from the cliches of advertising art.' One such person was Jimmy Hannan, who drew advertisements for Carlton and United Brewery: 'He used to draw the brewery horses. They were very elaborate pen and sometimes scraper-board drawings. And they looked very bold on the newspaper page. And I met him at Oscar Binder's life class.'

Illustrators such as Hannan demonstrated that there was a living to be made in art, and Counihan followed this path, at one stage providing illustrations for Richmond Brewery pilsner. Perhaps more significantly, through the life drawing classes Counihan also met Nutter Buzzacott and Roy Dalgarno, two Communist artists who were making a go of it in both the commercial and fine art spheres. 'We were very close friends and heavy drinkers', as Counihan assessed of their relationship.

In the early 1930s, the Buzzacott-Dalgarno studio on the second floor of the St James Building became a favoured centre for after-pub parties by lithographers, advertising artists and their romantic partners. It was close to bohemian haunts, the Wattle Cafe and Mitre Tavern, but just as much revelry happened inside the studio itself.

Counihan was still sixteen when he joined the Buzzacott-Dalgarno studio and began absorbing the culture around him. He recounts that Josl Bergner 'came to Buz's studio and we'd light a fire in the fireplace. Lunches were rather convivial and pleasant. You'd get a bottle of beer or two.'

It is clear that Counihan's early interactions with the Communist artists were heavily mediated by alcohol and the joyous social settings of bohemian pubs and studios. Descriptions of studio parties include an account of one reveller who 'when full of beer would talk from the side of his mouth and recite endless verse of "The Ballad of the Piddling Pup".' Others would also contribute drinking songs. Bill Hunter brought to the studio a china chamber-pot decorated with erotica. Holding it high, filled with beer, he pronounced it the chalice of bohemia. And on special occasions the cranium of the studio skull was filled for communal ritual drinking.

Women were present at these 'beer parties', as partners but also artists and CPA members. Adrienne Parkes, who would soon collaborate with Counihan and the Workers Art Collective on large illustrated banners for May Day, was a participant. At a young age, Counihan met figures like Sam White (whose appearance was said to resemble Mayakovsky), Cyril Pearl and Alwyn Lee, as well as other leftist writers associated with the avant-garde magazine *Stream*. Launched in July 1931 by Pearl, Lee, and Bertram Higgins, the magazine, and carousing, also brought Counihan in contact with long time bohemian radical and on/off CPA member Guido Baracchi. *Stream* balanced its sympathy for high modernism with a general commitment to radical politics.

Noel Counihan's Free Speech cage, 1933 *(The Sun)*

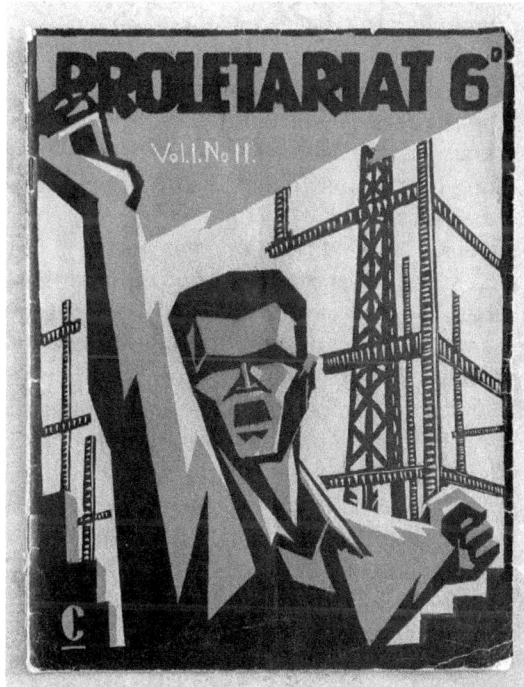

Noel Counihan cover of *Proletariat* (Melbourne University Labor Club publication), 1932

In its final edition, a symposium on Australian writing was advertised under a title that seems to sum up the predicament for many aesthetes in Melbourne's radical community: 'Paris or Moscow?'

Counihan was initially exposed to sly-grog establishments through a friendship with the Communist Gordon King (later a leading maritime unionist, see elsewhere in this book). Jack Maughan, a poet who worked on the waterfront, also introduced Counihan to important left-wing artistic influences like George Grosz and Otto Dix, and the illustrator Hugo Gellert's work in *New Masses*.

Counihan's ideas were not fully formed on arrival, and much of his political development took place over conversation in the art studio, helped along by visitors who were prepared to debate with the cherubic upstart. He later reflected that, 'This intellectual drubbing was exactly what I was in need of.' A representative example involves the cape and beret wearing leftist Sammy Samson, who arrived at the studio with beer in brown paper bags, along with a drunk Brian Fitzpatrick who was in a celebratory mood after getting his poems to the printers. An account of the revelry sets out that Fitzpatrick 'gave him an Irish toast, a sláinte, burst out singing "The Wearing of the Green", tossed back a couple of glasses. Then he walked with mincing majesty towards the camp stretcher and pitched onto it face first, his hat rolling across the floor.' With Fitzpatrick passed out, Samson and Counihan began to talk about political events in Europe and the rise of Italian fascism. Counihan knew little and his proffered opinions were met by Samson exclaiming, 'What utter bloody rubbish, where the hell did you pick up that load of crap?'

It was the first of many spirited debates Counihan had with interlocutors helped along by alcohol. Counihan later recalled an evening over the oyster shells at the Swanston Family Hotel where he and Judah Waten engaged in a debate with Esmonde Higgins over a key theoretical distinction between Stalin and Trotsky.

Higgins had been one of the best-informed among the local party theoreticians and after a bruising exit from the party at the hands of the local Stalinists, was drawn towards Trotsky's theory of permanent revolution. The conviviality of the setting was of no help to Higgins in breaking Counihan and Waten from their loyalty to Stalin's rival theory of 'socialism in one country', however.

Counihan discovered modernism and Marxism simultaneously in 1931. Within the same year he co-founded the Workers Art Club with Jack Maughan and Nutter Buzzacott, as well as the Young Communist League. Well before his emergence as a painter in the 1940s Counihan was a participant in setting up radical institutions at the intersections of the anti-establishment art scene and the Communist movement. Perhaps of equal significance to some of these small artistic ventures was the social scenes he nurtured. These included the raucous share house that formed at 112 Hotham Street, East Melbourne, that came to take the name 'The House of Culture and Rest'.

A significant event for Counihan, and one that rivalled the fame of his art, was his role in the fight for free speech that came to the forefront during the rise of radical unemployed organisations and direct action based anti-eviction campaigns. In May 1933 Counihan was

The Cough... Stone Dust, 1947 (Noel Counihan, Estate of Mrs P Counihan)

arrested for addressing crowds from within a locked cage mounted on a cart at a popular speaking pitch located at the corner of Phoenix Street and Sydney Road. Police tried, and failed, to smash their way into the enclosure before the artist eventually surrendered.

The embarrassment this created helped a long running campaign bring an end to police repression of street speeches in Brunswick, and the event would be memorialised via a monument in 1994. It also meant that the young artist ended up in Pentridge prison, where he experienced the state's *way of seeing* via repression of communication and a panopticon of surveillance. Within prison, he experienced certain comforts. Future liquor union secretary Jim Munro, along with other unemployed activists, was also locked up, and these older activists provided political nurturing. At times singing of 'The Internationale' could be heard around the prison. When Counihan was released, he celebrated with his fellow radical bohemians Judah Waten and Bill Dolphin at the Saracens Head pub.

Counihan made his living through commercial art, including cartooning for mainstream media publications such as the *Sun News Pictorial*. A more satisfying job would likely have been his illustrations for Communist author Alan Marshall's fiction. Counihan's partner Zélie Pimlott, a CPA member who was trying to break into journalism, managed to sell articles to the major newspapers. Counihan illustrated one of her first published articles, on the history of beer, which was published in *The Sun* in 1937. The compelling offer of an illustrated piece was perhaps enough for the publishers to overlook the political background of the contributors. That's if their employers knew, as both Pimlott and Counihan chose to work under pseudonyms.

Strontium 90, 1959 (Noel Counihan, Estate of Mrs P Counihan)

Election material for Communist Party candidate Max Ogden, 1973 (Noel Counihan, Estate of Mrs P Counihan)

When not drawing, Counihan spent much of his time drinking and yarning in pubs frequented by pressmen, which was considered an essential part of the game. He pronounced:

> I've been drunk for up to six or seven days ... Part of the way of life of a milieu. Part of a freelance newspaper artist's life. Part of an artist's life in general, per se. And partly because it freed me from inhibition. I think that's probably, basically the most common reason why.

This lifestyle was hard to sustain and he later stated that, 'I was spending too much in Melbourne. What I earnt I was tending to spend on grog'.

After Judah Waten was expelled from the CPA in 1934, Counihan had joined him on something of a working pilgrimage through the eastern inland regions of Australia. They sought out the pubs that journalists frequented, sometimes with help from supportive Communist artists with connections like George Finey. They would negotiate to get a line of credit from the hotel and then pay back the cost of lodging and drinking via cartoons and commissions that Waten would act as an agent for. This was not always a smooth process, as caricature by its nature shifted the masks people wore in public life and provided a glimpse of what was concealed – often to the dissatisfaction of the poser.

A later example from 1938 proves the point. Counihan spent time in Broken Hill at the invitation of the Broken Hill Technical College Museum and Art Gallery, where he produced work for an exhibition of industrial scenes, sketches of miners and mine management, as well as other notable figures in town. The boss of one of the mines sat for Counihan, and after seeing the result told him that he would not have sat for him if he'd known he was such a *rank amateur*. Later, Counihan 'enjoyed tearing up the drawing in the presence of some drinking pals in the Social Democratic Club who shared his dislike of (the boss).' Cartooning was one of Counihan's greatest contributions to the Australian left, but his skills in this form, as with all satire, ruffled a few feathers.

A crucial turning point for Counihan was in late 1940 when he contracted tuberculosis and found himself confined to a sanatorium until Easter the following year. Significantly, it prevented him from serving in combat during the war. But it also allowed him the time to consider his future interventions in Australia's cultural scene. The illness also precipitated the adoption of an ascetic lifestyle, an unexpected intervention that likely saved him from an early death due to alcoholism. As Counihan recalled, the doctor at the sanatorium said:

> "I see from the nicotine on your hands that you're a heavy smoker. You won't be able to smoke here so you might as well cut it out now". I said "ah". He said "Do you drink?". I said "Yes". He said, "Well you won't be able to drink here so you may as well cut it out now".

With fewer recreational distractions, Counihan had time for sober reflection, and a key decision was to transition his creative practice to painting.

The artworks that followed Counihan's period of 'drying out' in the sanatorium came to assure his vaulted place in the popular narrative of Australian art history. From the 1940s he became associated with 'social and critical realism' and 'expressive social realism', as he would term it. Perhaps the most important works were paintings done to support militant workers, such as those in the Wonthaggi coal mines, where he went underground in 1944. Other than providing sympathetic depictions his presence created political ripples as the threat of industrial action was required to overcome resistance from the mine manager to allowing a communist artist on site. One of the paintings produced during this period went on to win first prize in 1945's highly regarded Australia at War exhibition, which was hosted at the National Gallery of Victoria.

Counihan made several overseas trips. During one in 1940 he was deported from New Zealand for engaging in political activity. To raise funds for the trip Counihan did an illustration of his regular drinking buddies who joined him at the Swanston Family Hotel, a group referred to as 'The Troops'. He sold prints of the illustration to these boon companions, who were generally more financially secure.

After the period of jousting with the Angry Penguins group over the future of the Contemporary Art Society, Counihan joined the post-war exodus to Europe where he attended the World Congress of Peace Partisans. By the late 1940s, after being welcomed back into the fold after a brief expulsion (for endorsing a cross-class wartime unity government, possibly a logical conclusion drawn from the Popular Front position), Counihan was regarded once again as a reliable CPA representative.

Funds were raised by party members, aided by Communist union official George Seelaf who helped with the sale of the artist's prints. During the congress he made the acquaintance of major figures and persuaded a number of them, including Pablo Picasso and Pablo Neruda, to lend their support and signatures to a message calling on Australian intellectuals and artists to support the event and its goals. Likely stolen by authorities, the letter never arrived.

During the 1940s and 1950s Counihan came to see himself as the main Australian painter concerned with the depiction of Australia's people at work, whether men or women. He also painted workers at play, with one of his more notable series of paintings being pub scenes of drinkers, rendered in his expressive social realist style. These drinking scenes were derived 'largely from memory', of gatherings in the Swanston Family Hotel and other pubs. One of these pieces, 'After Work' won the John McCaughey Prize in 1958 for a painting 'of an Australian subject or way of life'. For Counihan himself, drinking remained a part of his life. At times he drank due to depression, but intoxication also continued to bring inspiration. These were themes that were reflected in his sympathetic depictions of workers existing in capitalism.

Counihan's drinking in the latter part of his career was no longer a concern to the party. The CPA had relaxed their attitudes on alcohol, but additionally they now viewed him as an asset. He was one of their celebrity members, with an assured position at the top echelons of Australian art.

Counihan remained an artist and Communist up until his death in 1986.

Pub Talk, 1962 (Noel Caounihan, Estate of Mrs P Counihan)

CHAPTER 28

'THE INNS ARE OUT': THE PUB, THE PEOPLE AND THE POST-WAR NEW ORDER

Tanja Luckins

In 1945, on Melbourne radio station 3KZ's *Labor Hour*, journalist E. J. Trait urged his listeners to think about the pub in Australia's post-war social order. He acknowledged that housing, hospitals and employment were all important concerns of the post-war reconstruction programme but suggested that the pub should be included in new order planning. During World War Two, government regulations and wartime circumstances had put drinking conditions, trading hours (especially early or 6 pm closing) and brewers' cavalier control of pubs under the spotlight. According to Trait, Australians should not think of the pub as a 'glaring gin palace or a stuffy beer bar,' a place devoid of cheer and entertainment. The 'inns are out' but they should not be. He posed the question: what kind of pub should there be in post-war society? Trait's solution? The people should shape the pub of the future. How this could be achieved in the face of powerful brewers, politicians and the temperance movement was the subject of lively discussion in the war and immediate post-war years.

World War Two: The Drink Question

Alcohol was the subject of both federal government regulation and moral concern during the war. In *The Government and the People 1942–1945* (1952), official war historian Paul Hasluck explains that the federal government, led by Labor Prime Minister John Curtin, implemented strict alcohol controls in order to reduce consumption and to conserve grain stocks for the war economy. Fearing for its security after the Japanese bombed Pearl Harbor in December 1941 and Darwin in February 1942, Australia strengthened its war effort. In March 1942, the government reduced alcohol output by a third and limited hotel hours to seven per day. Under a quota system, preference was given to army canteens over public supply – like alcohol consumed in pubs. At the Premiers Conference in August, Curtin persuaded the states to restrict hotel trading hours by another hour a day, ban women from public bars in hotels and prohibit drinking in parks and public places. During the war, all

Petty's Hotel in York Street, Sydney, 1941
(State Library of NSW)

states except Tasmania and Queensland had early (6 pm) closing, and cities and metropolitan areas adopted alcohol restrictions.

Despite the decrease in public supply, demand for alcohol remained high. In order to cope with shortages, people switched from draught beer to cheap spirits and home brew – coppers were known to be given over to home-brewing. Bottled beer often found its way onto the black market. The *Royal Commission to Inquire into Certain Allegations in Respect of the Administration of the Licensing Act* (1942) heard from Constable Henry O'Hehir, who had been with the Victorian Licensing Branch since 1926, that sly-grog prosecutions had increased during the war. To make matters worse, pubs often ran dry and had to close. Many thought it unfair that war workers, who were more likely to drink beer in a pub than wine and spirits in a private club or at home, should face the brunt of shortages. Despite this, pubs were a focal point for large numbers of soldiers, war workers and civilians who drank, dined and socialised in them, resulting in increased crowding in the early evening. This was especially noticeable in the south-eastern states, where most of Australia's wartime production was located.

While it was recognised that the war created unusual conditions, many believed that sobriety was preferable to excessive and illicit drinking in a time of national emergency. This echoed the arguments of World War One when a broad temperance mood and wartime patriotism and austerity prompted most state governments to implement a 6 pm closing time of hotel bars. In 1942, staunch Methodist and tireless temperance advocate, Reverend Irving Benson, used his weekly column in the Melbourne *Herald* to express his concern about wartime 'beer swilling and the swinish aftermaths of it that are to be seen any day or night.' He advocated that manpower used in beer manufacture was better used in national service, equating moral fibre with national efficiency. Reverend Harold Hackworthy, chair of the United Churches Social Reform Board

US and Australian servicemen drink at a cricket ground during WWII (State Library of Victoria)

in South Australia, blamed mixed drinking in hotel lounges for young women's moral lapses. A disturbing increase of venereal disease in young women was quoted as evidence of this immorality. For many women, though, the war provided new social and economic opportunities. One of them was the tens of thousands of well-paid and glamorous American GIs, who arrived in droves from 1942, when the US Army established its regional Pacific base in Australia. American servicemen preferred the lounge bar in hotels, which allowed them to mix with women, who were only banned from public bars. This glamour was tarnished when it was revealed that the 'Brownout Strangler', American serviceman Eddie Leonski, who murdered three women in Melbourne in 1942, had been drinking with one of his victims at the Astoria Hotel in the city.

What was the reaction of the pub-going public to the wartime conditions? Male war workers believed they had a right to a drink at the end of the day, but with so many working shifts, the actual end of the working day was a point of contention. The fact that a businessman in a suit could get to a hotel before closing time was highlighted, but a worker in overalls could not. In November 1942, in Lithgow, New South Wales, 3000 munition workers demonstrated outside the city's six hotels when police closed the public bars at 6 pm. Hotel keepers claimed that police granted them a 'courtesy privilege' to serve alcohol between 7 and 8 pm, when the workers finished their shifts. 'They work hard from 7 am to 7 pm', the licensee of the Grand Central Hotel, Mr H. Sampson, remarked, 'surely they are entitled to a drink when they knock off.'

War workers also resented higher excise duties imposed on alcohol, realising that any increase would be passed onto the consumer. In 1942, the federal government hiked the excise duty on beer from 3 shillings a gallon to 4s 7d. Following instructions from the Licensed Victuallers' Association [ULVA] and the Minister for Trade and Customs (Senator Keane), hotels in New South Wales stopped serving schooners before 4 pm, forcing drinkers to purchase smaller and more expensive middy glasses. This upset pub patrons. In 1943, there were numerous union-led boycotts of pubs, especially in industrial areas, which refused to sell schooners throughout the day. Here, though, the 'schooner question' was not resolved in the workers' favour, who reluctantly accepted that their demands were not a vital part of the war effort.

While some considered it an insult to insinuate that the worker was only waiting to down their tools and rush to the nearest bar for a beer, the working man's link with the pub was well-known. From the early-modern period onwards, across Europe and north America, workers and peasants frequented drinking establishments in their leisure hours. In *Conditions of the Working Class in England* (1845) Friedrich Engels argued that industrialisation and the terrible living conditions in industrial cities had led to workers' reliance on liquor and the pub as their sole source of pleasure. Social surveys from the twentieth century, like the *New Survey of London Life and Leisure* (1935) and Mass Observation's *The Pub and the People* (1943) emphasised the importance of the British public-house as a working-class social institution, where patrons spend much of their leisure. This is not to say that all war-workers and soldiers went to the pub, took a drink or felt at ease with the masculinity of the public bar. Furthermore, alcohol was not just consumed to slake a thirst, it could be used as a psychological and emotional prop for war stress.

The pub-going public, on the other hand, was not exclusively male. As Clare Wright shows, working-class women would sip shandy, wine, port and sherry, and 'do the beans' (shell peas and beans) in the ladies lounge/parlour before going home in the afternoon to prepare dinner, care for children and so on. During the war, women were shift workers in the munitions factories, many socialised in the pub after

CHAPTER 28 'THE INNS ARE OUT': THE PUB, THE PEOPLE AND THE POST-WAR NEW ORDER | 178

Herbert McClintock illustration, 'Sane Liquor Control Could Make Drinking A Pleasure', 7 August 1945 (*Tribune*/Search Foundation, State Library of NSW)

The Tribune had no doubt that brewers were the real 'swillers', reluctant to address licensing law reform because it would diminish their profits, 21 February 1947 *(Tribune*/Search Foundation, State Library of NSW)

work. These women objected to being told it was 'cheap' to frequent hotels. One Tasmanian, whose husband was away on military service, said she was doing full-time war work and used what little leisure time she had to socialise with her friends in the hotel lounge. Mass Observation identified a similar wartime pattern in England, where established leisure networks were disrupted, and middle-class and young women discovered the pub as a place to socialise.

The pub was not the only source of leisure for the worker in Australia – mechanics institutes, church groups and sporting clubs were also important – but it catered for a wide range of needs: convivial company, local news, recreation activities, warmth, food, cold beer on tap (very few Australians had refrigerators in their homes), and quality beer, unlike that obtained on the black market. Moreover, as very few working-class homes, flats and boarding houses had the space to accommodate a group of people, where else could they meet? How many could afford to dine in the hotel lounge, which was permitted to trade until 8 pm? This made the public bar's closure so soon after the end of the working day a harsh reduction of the worker's leisure time. Drinking with one eye on the clock, in unpleasant conditions, annoyed people. The *Truth* newspaper, a ready supporter of the blue-collar male, argued that 'the average man doesn't want to swill at the pig trough', he wants to 'exercise his right to drink in an ordinary pub in ordinary licensed hours.' A *Sydney Morning Herald* journalist explained the impact of World War Two: before the War there was the 'six o'clock rush' when men rushed from work for 'purposeful and dour drinking', but the War brought about 'trough drinking' caused by a war mentality and beer rationing. From this collective conversation a new term – 'six o'clock swill' – emerged to describe male drinking practices in the public bar before closing time. But this was not all public bars. The 'swill' was more evident in metropolitan hotels than country pubs. For country folk, the pub had a different tempo, one attuned to the needs of both men and women – for example, farmers, stock and station agents, and women on market days – making the swill less apparent.

Saner Liquor Laws

With its vivid image of hungry pigs at feeding time, 'six o'clock swill' signified uncivilised drinking behaviour. Was swill drinking indicative of a piggish society? The answer was that sane and rational drinking should represent human reason rather than the instinctive swilling of animals. This was the theme of social-realist artist Herbert McClintock's illustration titled 'Sane Liquor Control Could Make Drinking A Pleasure', published in the Communist *Tribune* in 1945. McClintock contrasts the swill conditions of a public bar with the 'decent' surroundings of a post-war hotel. Some of the porcine patrons, including servicemen, jostle at a serving counter covered with watery froth. They contrast sharply with the relaxed expressions of men and women seated at tables dining, conversing, listening to music. Blunt perhaps, but McClintock was convinced that 'saner' licensing law would lead to changes in social habits.

It was no accident that calls for liquor reform became louder when the Allied victory was certain, and Australians could contemplate a peacetime society. Liquor reform was a popular topic in newspapers, magazines, hotel trade journals and on the radio. *The Nation's Forum of the Air*, a popular programme of the Australian Broadcasting Commission (ABC), visited it several times. 'Alcohol and the Citizen – Should the Present Controls be Relaxed?' was the title of one 1944 debate. This debate concluded with one of the speakers suggesting that the 'digger' should speak for himself. And he did. Returning diggers and war-workers demanded better citizenship conditions in exchange for their service to the country. Not only were houses and jobs important, but so was the freedom to have a drink in a pub when they wanted to. Stated one, 'the hotel hours as they stand in most Australian states are an insult to the free life we proudly boast.' The restriction on liberty was at odds with life in a democracy, wrote South Australian John Anthony in 1945, the law as it stands 'breeds an unhealthy furtiveness in taking into dark places something that should be as free and open as our blue and sunny skies.' Corporal Arthur Barron said he was not a drinker but asked why 'the average man' was not entitled to his relaxation in congenial surroundings. Norman Willoughby, of St Kilda, Melbourne, who served in both world wars, said the returned serviceman should 'have the right to have his drink if he wants it.' Willoughby was reminded of World War One when the digger returned from active service to find their previously enjoyed leisure and recreation in the pub had been taken away. Back then, soldiers were annoyed that the temperance movement had imposed their morals on a section of the public. Did the blind legislate opening hours for the cinema? By and large, arguments about the drinker's rights during World War Two were made by those who had served overseas and experienced English pubs and drinking practices in continental Europe and the United States. One returned airman claimed that evening opening of hotels and late licensed eating establishments seemed to work in Europe and North America. Why not here, he asked?

Responses to this question did not necessarily draw on the well-rehearsed argument of the moral dangers posed by alcohol itself. According to Victorian Premier Albert Dunstan, there was a 'new order' aiming at gaiety and pleasure instead of dealing with the big task of reconstruction and rehabilitation of the fighting services. The younger generation also questioned the need to reform licensing laws. In September 1945, just after the war in the Pacific ended, university graduate Linda Rivers wrote to the Melbourne *Herald* claiming that young people fought for a better world, and needed houses, hospitals, schools and public amenities. Reforming licensing law was a superficial 'bread and circuses' distraction from the real, material issues that faced Australians. Then again, William Ferguson, president of the Aborigines Progressive Association, pointed out that the problem for Aboriginal people was not one of drinking in swill conditions before 6 pm but the right to drink in hotels at all. Aboriginal people fought side by side with their white brothers and sisters, he said, but were denied basic citizenship rights in Australia.

Herbert McClintock also claimed that licensing laws and wartime National Security Regulations benefitted two key groups: first, brewers, whose monopoly of beer sold in tied houses (pubs which only sell beer from a particular brewery) was the cheapest method of distribution, and second, black market profiteers who sold bottled beer at inflated prices after hours, forcing men to crowd in the pub before closing time just to get a drink. Was this fair on the pub patron? The *Australian Worker* thought not. The immediate concern, it editorialised in 1945:

> Faced as we are with huge post-war difficulties and problems, is a constructive reform of our existing licensing laws, with full and complete cooperation of the Commonwealth and the States to clean up the trade in its every aspect, and to make decent and comfortable provision for the needs of the people in our hotels and restaurants as they may be required.

The federal-state relationship was a thorny issue. While the nation was the wartime priority, it was hoped that when the National Security Regulations restricting alcohol production were lifted in 1946, reform would follow. However, the federal government insisted that licensing law was a state matter, it was up to the premiers of the states to legislate post-war reform. Wary of the powerful temperance lobby and the brewers, the Labor premier of New South Wales William McKell held a referendum in 1947 to give the people a say over hotel hours. By this time beer rationing had been lifted (although shortages continued for several years) and Queensland and Western Australia had removed wartime restrictions. South Australia, Victoria and New South Wales also lifted wartime restrictions but did not abolish early closing. While the temperance movement, predictably, supported early closing in the New South Wales referendum, many returned servicemen (and the Returned Services League) strongly pushed for 10 pm closing. Country folk argued that early closing was unsuited to rural labour patterns during harvest time when farmers followed nature's organic clock and worked until 8 or 9 pm. Police also favoured late closing, believing it would result in far less drunkenness and crime, especially sly grogging. The trade unions were divided. The Liquor Trades Employees Union endorsed early closing, while the Liquor Trades Council and the Hotel, Club and Restaurant Employees Union, led by the formidable Flo Davis, advocated 10 pm closing. Davis struck a deal with the ULVA to ensure her many female members (barmaids, cooks and domestic staff) would receive penalty rates. Alice Jackson, editor of the *Australian Women's Weekly*, surprised many with her support for late closing. If the post-war hotel was 'less of a pig swill', women might want to accompany their husbands to the local in the evening. Why could not 'every normal citizen' drink in 'civilised standards', she pleaded?

Calls for new closing hours did not capture the imagination of the wider voting public. Was the focus on liberties and citizenship a little too abstract? The over-whelming majority voted to retain early closing. The 'no' campaign, led by the temperance movement, ran an effective message aimed at women, family and the home. While most country areas voted for late closing, the only metropolitan electorates to vote in favour of 10 pm closing were those in the inner-city, including the cosmopolitan area of Kings Cross where there were many flats, cafes, restaurants and residential hotels. Analysts concluded that voters believed late closing would simply move the 6 pm 'swill' to a later hour and allow the continuation of the pernicious tied house system. As the *Australian Worker* observed, the war may have impelled

Mixed drinking, waiters and colourful umbrellas at the Petersham Inn, Sydney, 1948 (Ivan Ive, State Library of NSW)

Enjoying a drink behind the bar in the mixed lounge at the Petersham Inn, 1951 (Noel Butlin Archives/Australian National University)

swill conditions, but the hotel and liquor trades' contemptuous disregard for the needs of the people brought public anger to a head. Would longer trading hours necessarily improve conditions inside pubs?

'A solid crack at the booze combine'

The Department of Post-War Reconstruction was established in 1942 with the goal of realising hopes and dreams for a post-war new order. In *Australia's Boldest Experiment: War and reconstruction in the 1940s*, Stuart Macintyre writes that its fundamental objectives were housing, health and employment, as well as the repatriation of servicemen and women. It was a root and branch rethinking of the federal government's role in the planning of the nation. Hotel reform was not on the agenda. Economist H.C. 'Nugget' Coombs, Director-General of the Department of Post-War Reconstruction, was adamant that building materials be directed to housing rather than pubs. Even so, the hotel trade embraced the idealism for post-war reconstruction. The state-based licensed victuallers' associations established post-war planning committees, whose aim was to investigate particular amenity concerns: whether or not a bar or lounge would be more popular; the role of food and accommodation; and what provisions should be made available to women and tourists. During the war pubs had physically deteriorated due to increased patronage and publicans were unable to keep up maintenance due to a shortage of materials. Furthermore, many older pubs still lacked basic utilities like hot and cold running water and proper sanitation, especially in country areas. Many did not have adequate toilet facilities for women, even for the ladies lounge, itself invariably an uninspiring spartan room (Flo Davis insisted that hotels needed to modernise and appeal to women). Bedrooms were typically a jug and water basin set-up. The anticipation was that post-war prosperity would encourage tourists, not only from overseas but Australian day trippers and holidaymakers who would expect improved standards.

Historian Diane Kirkby explains that a 'new era' in hotel architecture aimed to open up the pub: larger windows would make dark bars lighter and airier, particularly on the ground floor, while larger rooms with tables and chairs would reduce 'perpendicular' drinking and allow dining and consumption of a wider range of beverages like wine and coffee. The Licensed Freeholders Association of Victoria, which published annual illustrated booklets on hotel improvement and rebuilding, agreed that hotels needed to modernise. Its 1947 publication featured photographs of interiors, comparing English, American and Australian hotels. To the Licensed Freeholders, who preferred American modernity to English nostalgia, the message was obvious: Australian hotels (it didn't use the more plebian 'pub') should be more than just a bar and had to provide a variety of comfortable and stylish revenue producing spaces to cater

Brisbane bar, 1940s (State Library of Queensland)

for the post-war patron. Boosterism aside, the association believed that improved lounges and dining amenities would help to remove the pub's 'slop shop' reputation and give freehold owners an advantage over brewery-run pubs. While the hotel industry embraced American modernity, pubgoers wondered if a pub should be more than just style and service. Why could not the charm of the traditional English pub, where one could play darts and cards and engage in leisurely conversation with mine host, be recreated in Australia? Alice Jackson, for one, envisioned the local as an English pub, a place where women and men could enjoy a 'homely, genial gathering.'

The continental beer garden was a popular idea. Was not Australia's climate ideal for outdoor drinking and dining? Beer gardens were common in the tropical north and in country pubs. In the southern capitals, the idea was enthusiastically taken up. Sydney already had quite a few, almost all in freehold hotels, like the Petersham Inn. In 1948, the Fern Tree Gully Hotel, in Victoria's Dandenong Ranges, run by two returned servicemen, added multi-coloured umbrellas and brightly painted tables and chairs to give its beer garden a 'continental atmosphere'. The following year Melbourne's first suburban beer garden opened at the Terminus Hotel, Brighton Beach. Was the continental beer garden only a passing fancy? Perhaps. Would it help to relieve the desperate crowding in inner-urban pubs? Most likely not. However, many hoped that beer gardens might change people's drinking habits – men and women dining together at tables would help to reduce swill drinking and drunkenness. Composer Alfred Hill regarded beer gardens as an opportunity to introduce culture to the masses. He recalled fondly beer gardens in Leipzig, where he studied music. Orchestras could play while providing employment for returned soldiers. In its annual report of 1948, the New South Wales Licensing Board recommended more inside lounges and outdoor beer gardens to meet the growing public demand for

The Hotel Renmark, 1945 (State Library of SA)

'away from the bar' drinking. By this time, the New South Wales Liquor Act (1946) had been passed, introducing club licences and allowing restaurants to serve alcohol with food. This meant that the pub lost its monopoly to sell alcohol with meals, and it had to find new ways to attract the dining patron. Even the brewers acknowledged the public mood. In the wake of the 1947 referendum, the major New South Wales brewery, Tooth and Co announced that beer gardens and outdoor lounges 'designed in the continental style' would be 'a major feature of Tooth's post-war reconstruction policy', to be carried out as soon as the housing shortage was overcome.

Some feared that the influence of impure 'foreign' social practices would tarnish the Australian pub's British heritage. Temperance advocates were alarmed even more by the suggestion that drinking and dining could be shifted from the pub to the pavement, another disturbing continental concept. In 1948, the *Argus* newspaper columnist Oriel reflected,

> In Melbourne soon there grew a passion
> To drink in Continental fashion
> Upon the pavement, chairs and tables,
> And bottles with distinguished labels.
> Beneath the awnings there we sat,
> For civilised quiet sips, and chat,
> On fine and sunny Melbourne days,
> To watch the world go by, and laze
> On balmy starlit summer nights,
> We linger there in softer lights,
> With everything from beer to brandy,
> And friendly waiters always handy.
> Apology! I'm ill-advised
> To dream that we are civilised –
> The verse above is just a crime,
> For six o'clock is closing time!

Oriel knew that those who dared to dream faced powerful foes. Despite their ideological differences, the temperance movement and brewers both knew that they had the politicians' ears. Brewers also contributed to the government's excise coffers and were well-known for their donations to political parties. According to the left-wing press, the problem was the beer barons who slugged the workers, not the drinking habits of pub patrons. Could brewers be trusted to spend their wartime profits on improving hotels? One answer was that there could be no improvement in amenities until the running of pubs was separated from the brewery monopoly. But how could the power of the brewers be broken? Pub patrons, their patience and tolerance tested, used the boycott weapon, as they had during the war. In 1946, the *Sydney Morning Herald* reported that in the past few months over a dozen hotels in the Sydney metropolitan area were 'black' banned for not selling bottled beer, serving middies instead of (larger) schooners, and serving (more expensive) beer in lounges when it was off in the public bar. A few of the boycotts had union backing but most were organised by disgruntled patrons. Locals picketed the South Hurstville Hotel for eight days, protesting against trading hours and the lack of bottled beer for take-away purchase.

Many on the political Left advocated the nationalisation of the liquor industry. However, Ben Chifley (prime minister after Curtin's death in 1945) resisted calls from the rank and file of the Labor Party to nationalise the breweries, stating in parliament that liquor was not an essential commodity. The Newcastle Ironworkers' Union proposed that if Labor's nationalisation plank was no longer viable then licensed workers clubs would be a means of 'having a solid crack at the booze combine.' Controlling the supply of beer would do away with unseemly drinking and unite the workers more in political and social activities. Responding to the Ironworkers, fellow Novacastrian R.A. Martin pointed out that the Scottish coal mining towns of Fife and Lanark had successfully adopted Sweden's Gothenburg System, the aim of which was to regulate alcohol consumption. Miners bought shares in a pub and ploughed the profits back into community amenities like libraries, parks, sports grounds and creches. These pubs were known as 'Goths' in Scotland, 'community hotels' in Australia. The best-known in Australia were in the fruit growing Riverland region on the Murray River in South Australia. Renmark Hotel was the first, in 1897, established to combat the sly-grog trade along the Murray. Due to their location in small country towns and utilisation of the collective ideals of the region's fruit grower's cooperatives, over time these community hotels became an effective way of keeping brewers at arm's length while capturing the tourist trade.

As publicity officer with the Department of Post-War Reconstruction, Lloyd Ross toured Australia explaining federal government post-war plans. He visited the Riverland region several times and was impressed with their community hotels. Recognising that hotel and liquor reform were not a formal part of the nation's reconstruction program, Ross nonetheless suggested that community hotels were an important opportunity for citizens to contribute to local affairs. Privately-owned breweries supplied alcohol ('nectar for community gods') while the 'little man' resisted the brewery monopoly, remote bureaucracy, unsympathetic churches and conservative municipal councillors. Community hotels also benefited the 'little woman'. Women had long worked in the pub as publicans, barmaids, cooks and domestic staff, and during the war they had claimed new social spaces in the pub. Now the war was over, women wanted change. Liquor reform, argued Rose Quinton, president of the women's auxiliary of the Queensland Trades and Labour Council, was an essential part of post-war reconstruction and should be addressed by citizens as a body, not merely as individuals. For this reason she supported community hotels since they were more than just bars and offered a range of amenities and community outcomes that benefited women.

In New South Wales, community hotels were a widely discussed option to solve the tied house problem and give people control of their local pub. However, it proved difficult to put the idea into practice. Newcastle tried and failed. In 1954, after several years of toing-and-froing, the Newcastle Council voted down a proposal for the council to run a community hotel in the city centre. The aldermen cited their lack of experience in the liquor trade as a reason for their decision. This echoed the ULVA's (self-interested) arguments against community hotels, namely that only a real publican could run a pub, not an inexperienced committee. Both the aldermen and the ULVA might have added that the 1946 New South Wales Liquor Act empowered municipal bodies to establish community hotels only if they could buy an existing license or obtain a new license by proving that no existing license was available for 'purchase on reasonable terms.' This protected the brewers. How could a local council compete with a wealthy brewery to buy a pub?

....

When British economist and architect of Britain's post-war social welfare state William Beveridge and his wife Janet visited Australia in 1948, they were disappointed that cities were 'empty' places after 6 pm. In their lively account of this trip, *Antipodes Notebook* (1949), they lamented that Melbourne and Sydney were not 'thronged with carefree people enjoying their legitimate pleasure.' Like the Beveridges, the Australian pub-going public made it abundantly clear that they wanted the post-war pub to be a place for legitimate pleasure in the evening, a place with congenial surroundings for men and women. Planning for Australia's post-war social order was an opportunity for people to articulate their visions for the pub. As E.J. Trait commented, there was much talk about the socialisation of industry and the people's right to freedom, but not enough about the role of the people in planning the pub of the future.

CHAPTER 29

FOR ABORIGINAL HUMANITY: THE SOCIAL JUSTICE AGENDA OF THE WOMAN'S CHRISTIAN TEMPERANCE UNION IN AUSTRALIA

Alison Holland

Doris Blackburn in her office with her secretary, 1940
(National Library of Australia)

The Woman's Christian Temperance Union is an international movement which has played a key role in shaping feminist activism historically. While focussed on the prohibition of alcohol it was among the first feminist organisations to apply principles of Christian service to diverse social questions. Initiated in the late nineteenth century American West by missionary women, its message of temperance, women's suffrage and peace rapidly spread from America to many sites around the globe, being taken up enthusiastically in settler societies such as Australia.

In the record of Australian feminist history, the WCTU stands out for its long-term wide-ranging reform agenda. Notably, it was the first feminist organisation to tackle the question of race or 'colour prejudice' as they framed it. It played a key role in articulating and advancing a social justice agenda for Aboriginal Australians, including collaboration with Aboriginal people. It was the first feminist organisation to explicitly articulate a feminist anti-racism in Australia, adopting a civil rights agenda in the mid 1930s which led to its split from the national feminist movement.

In this chapter I demonstrate how the issue of Aboriginal drinking rights and, in particular, the WCTU's defence of such demonstrates how a commitment to social justice ultimately saw them relinquish the centrality of their anti-alcohol message (including within Aboriginal communities) for the primacy of what they articulated as Aboriginal human rights.

Defending Aboriginal Rights

As a feminist group the WCTU came to the 'Aboriginal question' in the mid 1930s in the context of an increased authoritarian Aboriginal policy agenda, which saw lengthy and complex extensions to already prohibitive restrictions on Aboriginal lives under state-based protection laws. The interwar period was notable for a volatile political landscape around Aboriginal affairs, generated by a burgeoning humanitarian movement which contested the administration and proposed arguments for Aboriginal advancement.

One of the key sources of contestation had been feminist intervention around the position and fate of Aboriginal women and girls. Despite the attempts of leading activist, Mary Montgomerie Bennett, to get the support of the broader national feminist movement – the Australian Federation of Women Voters (AFWV) – to prevent what she termed the victimisation of Aboriginal women, she ultimately parted company with them when they endorsed the state's determination to biologically absorb Aborigines into the white majority and, in 1936, refused to endorse the principle of equal citizenship for Aboriginal people.

She turned to her friends in the WCTU, which was more democratic in membership. Just as the AFWV rejected the principle of equal Aboriginal citizenship, the WCTU endorsed it and from this moment in 1936 remained deeply engaged in the cause of Aboriginal rights and justice. In particular, through the important middle years of the twentieth century, the Aborigines Department of the national WCTU was led by prominent post-war Aboriginal rights activists, Phyllis Duguid and Doris Blackburn. Duguid was the wife of leading humanitarian, medical doctor, Charles Duguid. Together they had become deeply involved in Aboriginal affairs via the key humanitarian lobby group in South Australia, the Aborigines' Protection League. By the late 1930s they were promoting a different solution to the Aboriginal question and were critical of government policy. Blackburn was an active member of the WCTU, as well as a peace and Labor activist and civil libertarian. As a short-term Federal Labor minister she was one of the few parliamentary voices protesting the British testing of atomic weapons across Central Australia in 1946.

It was at this time, too, that a human rights movement for Aborigines emerged on the national scene, partly stimulated by atomic testing as well as the simultaneous strike of Aboriginal workers in the Pilbara demanding better wages, conditions and an end to their legal restrictions. At the national and state levels, the WCTU had strong representation in the activist response to both events. Notably, the leading figure involved in the Pilbara strikes, white unionist and supporter of the Aboriginal workers, Don McLeod, subsequently wished he'd marshalled their support more fully, as the workers became the subject of surveillance and widespread hostility into the 1950s.

The Aboriginal workers' strike did fuel demands for better living and working conditions and wages for Aboriginal people at the post-war women's charter conferences. It was at these conferences in the 1940s that the WCTU took a lead on resolutions relating to 'Aborigines and Coloured People'. The inclusion of these resolutions was novel in terms of feminist commitment to racial justice. Never before had such an extensive feminist reform program been developed around Aboriginal rights and conditions. This focus was illustrative of the conscious shift to a political agenda by the Charters' founder, Jessie Street, as well as the huge number of labour, union and communist female delegates at the conferences.

The resolutions were shaped by the Atlantic Charter which Phyllis Duguid canvassed at the 1943 conference, noting how its principles of self-determination, self-government and trusteeship should guide Australian policy. A key reform was full property rights in land and resources, full payment of wages to Aboriginal workers and cultivation of Aboriginal racial pride. By 1946 the resolutions had expanded to a recognition that Aboriginal people were part of the world's colonised people whose rights and independence as national minorities must be recognised. These resolutions demonstrated the influence of peace and labour activism within charter ranks and to the WCTU leadership on Aboriginal reform.

Members of the WCTU continued to play a vital role in the post-war rights movement, drawing inspiration from the UN Charter of Human Rights to articulate a race-blind theory of Aboriginal advancement. It was at the Charter conferences that they urged women to use their influence to eliminate colour prejudice from the social life of the nation. They also demonstrated such in their praxis, long having gone to and worked with Aboriginal communities, initially in a Christian charitable and temperance mode and, after the war, in working with Aboriginal people to defend their rights to land, community and political collaboration, in the struggle for equality and citizenship. Indeed, the first national lobby group, the Federal Council for Aboriginal Advancement (FCAA) was initiated in Willard Hall, WCTU headquarters in Adelaide, and largely made possible by key WCTU women in each of the states.

The Victorian Aboriginal Advancement League, for example, was initiated by Doris Blackburn. After the Labor party's Federal defeat in 1949 she became deeply involved in the inter-racial campaigns for Aboriginal rights that characterised the Victorian movement. Blackburn collaborated via the League, the WCTU and the Women's International League for Peace and Freedom, all of which worked closely with Aboriginal activists whose lives had been shaped by cycles of poverty and exclusion induced by expulsion and closure of their reserve lands, loss and dispersal of communities under protection legislation, and constant state interference and surveillance of their lives. This period was notable for some close connections being formed between white and Aboriginal women as Aboriginal women began to participate in organisations like the WCTU and in political demonstrations such as International Women's Day.

Despite a state-centric approach the Aboriginal rights movement was shaped within a wider national rights-based agenda. A major spur for the establishment of the Victorian Aboriginal Advancement League, for example, was the national coverage given to the Warburton crisis in 1956/57. This was occasioned by the exposure of malnourished, diseased and poverty-stricken communities expelled from the Central Aboriginal reserve as a result of atomic testing and living vulnerable lives in and around the Warburton ranges in the north-west. Concern was sparked in Victoria after Aboriginal leader, Doug Nicholls, returned from an investigatory trip to the region with film footage confirming the community's plight.

These moments around the peripheries of the nation catalysed local movements as they exposed reverberations in local examples and contexts and demonstrated the vulnerability

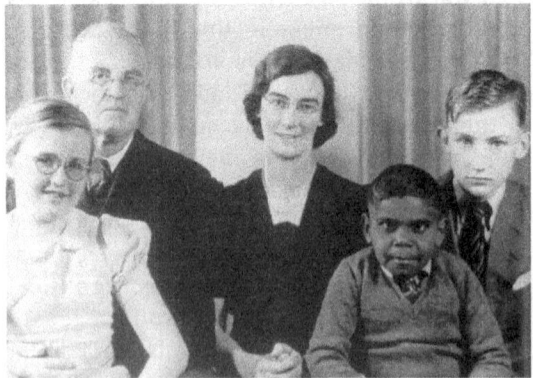

Phyllis and Charles Duguid with their family, circa 1944
(National Library of Australia)

and lack of basic rights of Aboriginal people in the nation. The state-based advancement leagues in South Australia and Victoria became the engine rooms of a rights-based agenda and demands for reform, particularly around equal citizenship, the right to vote, to an education, to wages and to better living conditions. The women of the WCTU were often at the helm of these activities and, in a real sense, in collaboration with Aboriginal leaders, they drove the rights agenda in the critical period between 1940-1960.

Defending Aboriginals' Right to Drink

A commitment to civil rights for First Nations people saw the WCTU marshal its significant fund-raising and public education abilities for the cause. In the late 1940s and 1950s they put their efforts into working with Aboriginal communities to fundraise for the establishment of hostels where Aboriginal people could stay when they came to the city for work. These developments spoke to the WCTU's concern with post-war assimilation policy. Working closely with Aboriginal communities it became obvious how circumscribed Aboriginal lives were under assimilation. While it promised citizenship and inclusion for all, it was in fact based on deep exclusion and segregation. It was also premised on proximity to whiteness.

Under the terms of various protection and Aboriginal welfare laws, a condition of Aboriginal citizenship was the abrogation of one's Aboriginality. Individuals applied for exemption (in the form of a pass) from the confines of the legislation but they had to enter white society and effectively leave their Aboriginal kin behind and live the same as the white majority. The WCTU were early critics of this system. With others they articulated notions of Aboriginal minority rights and promoted integration as an alternative to assimilation on the basis that it was not premised on denial of Aboriginality. In Blackburn's terms, for example, hostels for Aboriginal people could provide a means by which Aboriginal people could move into and share in the benefits of white society, while staying grounded within their own. She said:

> Here was a home made ready for the Aboriginal girls coming to the city for employment. Comfort and security under the care of a matron of their own race could make the first steps in integration easier.

When reformers queried the discriminatory nature of legislation targeting Aboriginal people, governments responded that they were about greater protections for them. As with all other Australians, Aboriginal people became Australian citizens under the terms of the 1948 *Nationality and Citizenship Act*. Governments justified their discriminatory treatment of Aboriginal citizens on the basis that they were under 'special laws' for care and assistance until they were ready to take up full citizenship.

The clash between the aims of the reformers and the assimilationist commitment of post-war Governments was most graphically demonstrated in relation to Aboriginal access to liquor. Aboriginal people were prohibited from drinking alcohol or frequenting licensed premises by the Aboriginal Act or Ordinance. In theory, those who encouraged or engaged in illicit supply with Aboriginal people were also

Pastor Doug Nicholls, 1950 (State Library of NSW)

breaching the law, although administrators spoke of the difficulty of policing this offence, while reformers complained of a transparent and unpoliced trade which worked in the suppliers' favour. Emphasising the discriminatory nature of Northern Territory law, the Duguids asked why Aboriginal people were frequently penalised for drinking alcohol when they saw so many white men doing the same within the law. As Phyllis Duguid explained, it was only by gaining exemption from the Aboriginal Ordinance, and thus the status of citizen, that Aboriginal people could legally obtain and consume liquor. Accordingly, there was a widespread view amongst both Black and white that Aboriginal citizenship was equated with Aboriginal drinking rights. This created anxiety amongst white Territorians, rural folk and some missionaries about the granting of citizen rights to First Nations people, and in the 1950s and 1960s much public debate on this matter ensued.

It also created something of a dilemma for temperance activists whose *raison dêtre* was prohibition, but who were also advocates of the abolition of discriminatory laws. In the course of the 1950s they called for the repeal of all such laws and urged that all forms of racial discrimination be made a punishable offence. They argued that citizenship should be the immediate birthright of all but nomadic Aboriginal people. Yet reformers were well aware of the historic effect of the introduction of white man's alcohol on Aboriginal communities. While campaigning for Aboriginal citizenship in the 1950s, Union members were simultaneously concerned about the legalisation of the sale and manufacture of alcohol in the mandated territories of Papua and New Guinea. According to some of the more progressive thinkers in the Union, the solution in this case was not prohibition, but alcohol education.

As far back as the 1890s, fledgling temperance societies had earmarked Aboriginal stations and reserves as areas in need of evangelising. They'd sent missionaries to preach the 'dangers of alcoholic beverages'. In some cases they had provided temperance lessons and demonstrations and obtained some 'pledged abstainers'. By the 1940s, all State Unions pooled resources to establish a special fund which was to be dedicated to Aboriginal alcohol education, particularly of young Aboriginal people, through their Loyal Temperance Legion (LTL) departments. The Unions also slowly began to recruit Aboriginal women members who worked with them to stem the growing tide of alcoholism in their communities. According to missionary and temperance worker Violet Turner, it was in the late 1950s that such evangelism became more dedicated and organised. Reporting on the work of the South Australian branch, she noted speakers travelling into other states to 'spread the word'.

Under the superintendence of Phyllis Duguid, the Union focussed attention on educating Aboriginal children, groups of whom were able to participate in the annual LTL camps with white children via the Unions' Aboriginal Fund. At these camps Aboriginal children were taught principles of abstinence and Christian citizenship with non-Aboriginal children, via study, games and prayer. By 1956 the Union reported the formation of an independent, all-'native' Union at Nepabunna consisting of seventeen members with an LTL of thirty members. Two years later, it reported an LTL group at Oodnadatta. Beyond that, at state and national level, Unions were urged to increase their efforts to make available to Aboriginal people simple and effective alcohol education.

This increased commitment in the late 1950s was directly related to the case of Albert Namatjira, noted Aboriginal water-colourist from the Lutheran Hermannsburg mission in Central Australia. Namatjira's was one of those peripheral moments that powerfully shaped the rights agenda in the 1950s and 60s. Having risen to fame on the basis of his artwork on Central Australian themes, particularly amongst the middle-classes of the southern cities, he became the administration's poster-boy of assimilation. As a 'full descent' Aboriginal man, the government's conferral of citizenship on him in 1957 was a means of demonstrating their universalist and equalitarian claims to citizenship for all in the post-war world. In a highly political act, the Federal government was showing that conferral of citizenship was not about colour or caste, rather it was about readiness for living in white society. The fact that he was a 'full descent' man was important as there had long been a concern amongst activists, including Aboriginal activists, that assimilation rested on eliminating Aboriginality altogether and that it was premised on driving a wedge between those of 'full' and 'mixed' descent.

Like all others, in accepting citizenship, Namatjira was required to disassociate himself from his Aboriginal friends and family. The swiftness of the government's reaction when it was discovered that he had shared alcohol with a family member demonstrates just how rigid this notion of inclusion was. Within a year of the conferral of citizenship on him he was charged under the *Northern Territory Welfare Ordinance* for supplying liquor to an 'unexempted' man, his brother, near Hermannsburg Mission. When Namatjira declared his intention to appeal his conviction and sentence, humanitarians in the south rallied to his cause. For them, it exposed the problematic nature of Aboriginal assimilation and the unreasonable and discriminatory cost it imposed on Aboriginal lives. So well-known had he become that his pending imprisonment was considered a national disgrace. Members of Melbourne's peace, Aboriginal rights and civil libertarian community were particularly vocal.

Being in the centre of this community Doris Blackburn and her colleagues in the Advancement League decided to support Namatjira, setting up a defence fund and providing legal counsel. Constitutional lawyer, friend of Blackburn's and member of the Australian Council for Civil Liberties, Mr M.J. Ashkanasy, appeared on Namatjira's behalf in the Northern Territory Supreme Court, declaring the Northern Territory Ordinance invalid and appealing against the harshness of the sentence. In dismissing his claims, Justice Kriewaldt referred to the serious social consequences of Aboriginal people consuming alcohol and reduced the sentence from six months hard labour to three months imprisonment. Namatjira's subsequent appeal to the High Court, which was financially and morally supported by the Victorian Advancement League, was also lost when the Court confirmed Kriewaldt's earlier findings. While Namatjira served his time at the Papunya Native Reserve in Aranda territory, the League condemned the Northern Territory administration, claiming that it had consigned Northern Territory 'full descent Aborigines' to years of discrimination, exploitation and degradation.

Rights Rather than Prohibition

Equal citizenship rights for Aboriginal people was the first working principle of the FCAA, a resolution that was endorsed at the National Convention of the WCTU in 1958 and, in fact, had been endorsed by the group as early as

Albert Namatjira and Hermannsburg Mission community members, 1956 (Library and Archives NT)

1936. At the second annual conference of the FCAA, at WCTU headquarters in Melbourne, Doris Blackburn presided as Federal President and a large Victorian delegation comprised a number of women's organisations and other key humanitarian organisations. As well as resolutions regarding education, social services, wages, housing, health care, and land, it resolved to support the Victorian League in its defence of Namatjira. It recommended that 'the hazards of liquor must not be used as a hindrance to granting citizenship rights, but that all Governments should direct their activities to controlling the alcohol rather than the Aborigines.'

Doris Blackburn subsequently channelled her efforts on this question towards educating temperance workers about the need to focus on Aboriginal adults. This was to counteract a pro-prohibition stance taken by many of her temperance colleagues. As national superintendent in the 1950s Phyllis Duguid had occasionally suggested that Unions needed to make stronger efforts against colour prejudice. As superintendent of this department in the early 1960s, Blackburn wrote of constant reports from country colleagues describing the hopelessness of their work amongst Aboriginal communities with frequent complaints of children stealing, and parents being 'impossible', 'lazy' and 'good for nothing'.

Many temperance workers shared the popular critique of Aboriginal citizenship, believing that it would merely give Aborigines the right 'to go to hotels to drink'. Aboriginal rights activists pointed out that liquor knew no colour bar and that Aboriginal drunkenness was a symptom of a greater ill. Blackburn argued that the discriminatory clauses in the liquor laws pointed to the Aboriginal person as inferior, which exacerbated their feelings of resentment and drove them to drink. Indeed, that the denial of drinking rights actually increased Aboriginal peoples' desire for such and led to a defiant style of alcohol use has subsequently been confirmed by historians of race relations and anthropologists.

To combat the prevalent racism surrounding this question, Blackburn emphasised the importance of education. She argued that it was important to understand the essential differences between 'ourselves' and Aboriginal people, and to get a proper perspective of their past and present conditions. She pointed out that many adult Aboriginal people had been denied education or training and therefore stood ill-equipped 'between one life system and another, confused and too often degraded.' She argued that dispossession and detribalisation, caused by white settlement, conferred a special responsibility on white people to assist in reinstating Aboriginal dignity and self-respect, 'as a right, not as a charity, not as his superior.'

Blackburn believed that before any reform could begin Aboriginal people needed to be educated, just as the working-class had been at the beginning of the temperance movement in nineteenth century Britain. She argued that whereas education had been used historically to raise the standard of living in every progressive society, it had been denied to Aboriginal people. She further suggested that the argument about Aboriginal people needing special protection was actually an excuse for defining them as primitive children, sanctioning making them 'wards of the state' and surrounding them with restraints and prohibitions, such that 'though an adult he is no longer a free man':

> Legislation became a sort of benevolent despotism, a form of patronage by one group or persons 'telling the lower orders how it is good for them to live'. Temperance legislation has historically been of this kind but it seems reasonable in this more enlightened age to provide education and opportunity for acceptance of responsibility to a people who are free.

This link between issues of class and race had underpinned leftist thinking and demands on the rights and status of Aboriginal people. But it also underpinned the commitment to advancement. According to Blackburn and the other women reformers leading the advancement call, Aboriginal people were capable of achieving everything that non-Aboriginal people could, if they were treated on terms of equality and given the same opportunities to 'advance'. For Blackburn, as for Phyllis Duguid, temperance education was a way of facilitating this and at the same time promoting inter-racial fellowship. Their flexibility on the question of Aboriginal liquor consumption demonstrated the pre-eminence of equal citizenship and anti-colour bar sentiment in their notions of Aboriginal advancement and human rights.

Conclusion

The WCTU's motto for 'God, Home and Humanity' is a succinct statement of the sequence of concern and commitment in WCTU public engagement. Not meant as a hierarchy it is nonetheless the case that the humanity they referred to only included Aboriginal people, properly, from the 1930s when their conscience was awoken on the topic of colour prejudice. It is the case that they had been interacting with and performing their characteristic Christian service in and around Aboriginal communities from 1900 and their commitment to racial equality was foreshadowed in a commitment to social justice generally. By the 1940s discrimination based on colour was added to an anti-discrimination agenda in relation to sex, class and creed. In the annals of Australian feminist history they stand out for a commitment to racial equality. This was greatly facilitated by the more democratic nature of their membership but it was also conditioned by their Christian humanism which was itself facilitated by developments around human rights in the mid twentieth century. As Phyllis Duguid maintained in 1952, the elimination of colour prejudice should be the special preserve of every Christian woman. Their defence of Aboriginal rights to drink alcohol like all other adult citizens demonstrates just how critical a conception of Aboriginal humanity was to their sense of equality and citizenship. It demonstrates their capacity for flexibility when it came to advancing rights over prohibition.

Historians of decolonisation in Australia have noted how challenging it was for Indigenous Australians who were outnumbered by the white settler majority when the movement gathered momentum in the 1950s. Yet, although not mentioned here, Aboriginal people had fought a long campaign by then for civil rights, justice and freedom. The work of groups like the WCTU, across the critical years of the 1940s and 1950s, should not be underestimated in this context. They not only brought significant organisational skills and infrastructure to the cause, they formed networks and collaborated with Aboriginal people caught in increasingly draconian, apartheid-like laws under assimilation regimes. Their anti-racist praxis in the Australian context was, in many ways, ahead of its time but it demonstrated the power of human rights to expand and advance Aboriginal claims to rights and justice, including to group identity and belonging.

CHAPTER 30
DRINK DEEP: THE LONG LIFE OF JACK CLANCY
Alex Ettling

'Done all the bad things in life', the *Horsham Times* reported Jack Clancy saying on his 100th birthday celebrations in 1954. Clancy, a Mallee wheat farmer for most of his years, had not been cowed by any moralising from wowsers during his lifetime: 'I smoke and drink and have done all the things I should not have – including betting.'

At age 100, aside from one time he was hospitalised after falling down a well, Clancy was now receiving hospital care for only the second time in his life. It was not his natural state of being to be sick, and so he was caught sneaking out fellow patients from his ward at the Warracknabeal District Hospital to go on a pub crawl.

Clancy seems to have been open to bending an elbow at opportune moments. Including when he drank with Ned Kelly.

The town of Jerilderie in the Ned Kelly story is most often raised in connection to the Jerilderie Letter, the closest thing to a political statement made by Ned Kelly. It was an excoriating account of injustices from the ruling elite against poor working class people like his family. But for Clancy, Jerilderie was also the location of an encounter he would tell stories about for the rest of his life.

The *Melbourne Weekly Times* reported on 26 May 1954 Clancy's account of his interaction with the Kelly Gang:

> I can remember the time I was at Jerilderie and Ned stuck up a bank there. I was shearing sheep and had come into town for some beer. Ned Kelly stood in the middle of the street and made a man chop down the telegraph pole with an axe. Then Ned said he didn't want to make trouble, and was going to have a beer with us. We went with him.

There's no record of the conversation topics between the bushranger and the young shearer. If Ned Kelly had life advice for him it's been lost. But in 1954, on the occasion of Jack Clancy reaching a century, he was asked about the secret to his longevity: 'Drink deep, smoke like billy-oh, work as hard as you have to, and hate the Tories good and proper.'

CHAPTER 30 DRINK DEEP: THE LONG LIFE OF JACK CLANCY | 196

Jack Clancy in hospital, 1954 *(Sydney Daily Telegraph)*

The burnt remains of the hotel where the final confrontation between Ned Kelly and the Victorian Police took place. A sign still stands: 'The Glenrowan Inn, Ann Jones, best accommodation', 1880 (State Library of Victoria)

CHAPTER 31
A COLD WAR SHIRTFRONTING
Rowan Cahill

During the height of the Cold War militant Australian trade unions, particularly the maritime unions, became creative regarding the protection and deployment of their funds. It was such creativity that frustrated and angered punitive legislators. Conservative and Labor governments alike, at State and at Commonwealth levels, variously sought to isolate unions from their funds in times of industrial conflict. A range of legal measures were used, everything from hindering the collection of monies from trade union members to freezing trade union funds. Simply, without funds a trade union organisation finds it difficult to operate.

Use of the notorious Transport Workers Act during the 1920s against the powerful Waterside Workers Federation (WWF) effectively created rival unionised and non-unionised workforces in a number of key Australian ports. The creation of significant preferential scab labour forces in the ports where it was enacted, white-anted union funding by destroying the traditional membership base. The Act almost destroyed the WWF.

The Chifley Labor government froze trade union funds and jailed union leaders during the 1949 Coal Strike. Anticipating the freeze, the WWF withdrew £6000 from its funds. This was hidden on a need-to-know basis under the home of a friendly café owner, prior to its transfer to the striking miners. At one stage during a police raid on the union's Sydney offices in search of 'illegal' donations, a quick thinking female member of the office staff with a background in lefty amateur theatre, secreted incriminating money in her underwear. Gender stereotyping and charm took care of the rest.

In 1951 Australian trade unions contributed some £50 000 to striking workers in New Zealand during their 151 days long wharf strike. With punitive anti-union legislation in place, it was a clandestine operation, the Seamen's Union of Australia (SUA) assisting the transfer of funds across the Tasman via members crewing the trans-Tasman motor vessel *Wanganella*.

During World War Two the SUA helped Indian, Chinese, and Indonesian merchant mariners, marooned in Australia and working out of Australian ports, to organise their own trade unions. Post-war, in solidarity with Indonesian nationalists, the SUA was part of the long-running campaign by Australian unions that successfully hampered the return of the Netherlands East Indies government, the Dutch administration having decamped to

Eliot V. Elliott (Sydney Trades Hall Collection)

Australia when Japan invaded the Dutch colony. Solidarity and fraternal actions like these strained union finances, and the SUA sought a financial base that did not take resources away from bread-and-butter trade union matters.

In 1951, the SUA set up its Peace and Progress Fund to bankroll and support progressive cultural, political, and industrial campaigns and initiatives. A pay levy was struck, but organised right-wing Grouper-led opposition within the union stymied this in the Arbitration Court, and the fund came to rely on voluntary contributions. However, the money-making capacities of picnics, raffles and goodwill donations are limited. Effective solidarity initiatives are expensive.

Enter 'indemnity payments'. As modern technology kicked in post-1945 and antiquated Australian flagged shipping was modernised, there was the threat and the reality of job losses. As old ships were sold off the coast to overseas interests, and new ones came on to the coast, some shipping interests were determined not to engage Australian crews on delivery and maiden voyages. Further, by 1956 it was apparent that the number of jobs in the maritime industry was decreasing due to modernisation.

Spearheaded by the SUA, the maritime unions resolved to make the shipping industry pay for cost cutting initiatives and for job losses. To wit, cough up large swags of cash or face the consequences. Not a piss and wind threat in the highly unionised maritime industry where shore-based and sea-going unions had long traditions of solidarity. In one early case, a ship being sold off overseas was held in port by bans for two years.

The money extracted via indemnities was substantial. Between 1956 and 1958, for example, after payments were distributed to ships' crews affected by modernisation, the SUA banked £38 585 tax free into its Peace and Progress Fund, and into another discretionary Emergency Fund. A considerable fortune in its day, and today once dollar conversion and inflation are factored in.

The scheme operated behind closed doors, but in 1957 came under close and hostile scrutiny via anti-communist political journalist Alan Reid in the *Daily Telegraph*; in Federal Parliament via Senator Frank McManus of the anti-communist Democratic Labor Party (DLP); and by the anti-communist organ of the National Civic Council, *News Weekly*.

It all came unstuck in Sydney on Friday night, 7 February 1958. It had been a dirty weather day in the city, with enough rain to make Noah blanch. In the CBD, Hyde Park was awash; parts of the underground rail system were flooded; shoppers waded in water over their ankles; cars and trams created 'bow waves'. Around 5pm, SUA leader Eliot V. Elliott took an envelope containing £1125 from his office, his union's share from the sale of a vessel being sold off the Australian coast. It should have been banked earlier, but urgent industrial matters had intervened. Saturday banking was still operating, and the union's safe had once been gelignited. So Elliott put the envelope down his shirt front, a precautionary measure amongst old waterfront hands to safeguard against pickpockets, and with a colleague went into the early night.

Eliot V. Elliott, at right, 1960s (Sydney Trades Hall Collection)

Elliott was a communist militant, variously feared and respected depending on your politics and encounters. Ruggedly handsome, always neatly dressed with collar and tie, he had a groomed upswept mass of hair, and a full moustache. Charismatic, astute, forthright, he was one of the communists who came to national power in Australia during World War Two in the essential strategic industries. Under his leadership, the SUA, shattered by a crippling strike in 1935, had become a powerful and largely unified industrial organisation. By birth a New Zealander, he had gone to sea as a teenager, working as a fireman in the stokehold, breeding ground for many a militant. He had come onto the Australian coast in 1922.

The two men ended up with fellow seafarers in the Lord Nelson Hotel in the Rocks, then after a meal, at the Commercial Hotel on the corner of George Street North and Essex Street. Pubs were part of the SUA culture, safe places for socialising, for yarning freely about life, politics and industrial matters, and for many seafarers they provided affordable accommodations. In the nineteenth century when Australian seafarers were developing the port-based organisations that merged in 1872 to form the SUA, pubs were de facto union meeting rooms. But tonight there was no safety.

When Elliott and a colleague were leaving the Commercial, they were confronted by members of the 21 Squad, a notorious police 'flying squad' (terminated in 1981), well known for throwing its weight around and cutting legal corners. Arrested for being drunk, they were carted off to Central Police Station. During the 1950s, police harassment of SUA members across Australia was common, to the extent the *Seamen's Journal* cynically reckoned being bashed by police should be regarded as an industrial risk warranting financial compensation.

Elliott and his colleague were detained as long as possible, even though bail money was quickly arranged by WWF leader Jim Healy. Meanwhile police leaked news of their bust to Alan Reid at the *Daily Telegraph*, who arranged for a photographer to be present when Elliott was released. The resulting ambush photograph, subsequently given prominence by Reid, showed dishevelled Elliott threateningly pointing his index finger at the photographer: 'Ah, the Press', he reportedly said, 'I ought to smash your camera.'

Nationally, the arrest and the wad of money were given press prominence, some of the reporting hostile with implications of union corruption. In 1963, Reid would mastermind another photographic ambush. The resulting

Commercial Hotel, 1960 (Noel Butlin Archives/Australian National University)

Eliot V. Elliott, second from left (Sydney Trades Hall Collection)

notorious 'Faceless Men' photos with their sinister implications would help keep the ALP out of Federal government until 1972.

For those who have come in late, the 'Faceless Men' photos were published in the *Daily Telegraph* and serially trotted out thereafter by anti-ALP propagandists. The noir paparazzi-style shots showed ALP Federal parliamentary leader Arthur Calwell and deputy Gough Whitlam standing in the March darkness of late-night Canberra outside the Hotel Kingston waiting for the results of a crucial vote by the party's 36-strong Federal Conference meeting inside. In the hands of Reid and hostile conservatives the photos were used to depict the parliamentary ALP as the creature and puppet of a cabal of 'virtually unknown men' – unelected, and unaccountable.

Following news of Elliott's arrest and the ambush photo, there was some membership disquiet about his sobriety at the time of his arrest, and the cash he was carrying. Eventually, however, all branches of the union forwarded expressions of confidence in him and his integrity.

In politics, the photo gave parliamentary enemies of the SUA the traction they needed and later that year a Senate Select Committee investigation into indemnity payments commenced. Boycotted by the ALP, it comprised anti-communists drawn from the Liberal and Country Parties, and the DLP. Particular attention focused on Elliott's arrest and the money in his possession.

By September the show was over, and in its Report the Committee reckoned the indemnity payment system contravened Sections of the Crimes Act as it involved 'conspiracy, extortion, and intimidation'. The Report invited the anti-communist Menzies government to take action accordingly. But that never happened. Meanwhile, in accordance with an earlier inquiry by the Australian Council of Trade Unions, the indemnity system had been ended by the maritime unions.

The dramatic photograph of the threatening Elliott was redolent of the famous British World War One recruiting poster featuring Lord Kitchener. It went on to decorate mess rooms of many union ships, captioned 'Have You Paid Your Union Dues'.

The ALP faceless men scandal originated from a photo in the Kingston Hotel, 1964

CHAPTER 32
GEORGE SEELAF: A POLITICAL LIFE AROUND BOOZE
Alex Ettling

George Seelaf with beer in hand, 1970s (Seelaf Collection)

I'd read quite a bit, and had satisfied myself that the capitalist system was a system of exploitation, and there was no future in it for the workers. While there was private control of industry, well, then the worker would never get a fair go. And there was a need to change it to an alternative system and the only alternative system was socialism. I was convinced of that not emotionally but morally, and I haven't changed my mind.

This was George Seelaf speaking to filmmaker John Hughes in 1985, laying out the philosophy that had guided him for fifty years, just a few short years before his death.

After struggling through the 1930s Depression, Seelaf's first consistent job was in the meatworks. This work was not for the faint hearted but securing any job was cause for celebration. Tasks included such things as cleaning out the 'save alls' where the fat used to settle – skimming it off and delivering it for dry rendering. Seelaf's role was known colloquially as a 'sparrow starver', collecting up the detritus of animal carcasses around the site. The advantage of such a position was that it took him all around the Footscray grounds, opening up conversations with workers across the many different departments of the Angliss meatworks. Along the way, Seelaf realised he had skills in communicating and organising.

Soon he became a union organiser, pushing for better pay and conditions. Then, in 1940, he joined the Communist Party to pursue a more thorough, systemic solution to inequality. He was elected as the secretary of the Australasian Meat Industry Employees' Union, Victorian and Tasmanian branch in 1947, leading the butchers all the way into the 1970s.

Seelaf was more than just about getting pay rises. His pioneering activities in an industry where heavy drinking was a cultural norm offers insights into the relationship between work and alcohol.

At Angliss, the pubs that the meatworkers drank at included the Pioneer and the Braybrook. Some workers would even squeeze through a hole in the fence at lunch time for a cheeky few at the nearby Richmond Hotel. Seelaf explained to historian Ken Mansell how drinking was so routine that it was integrated into workplace organising.

> We used to have 5 o'clock meetings in Footscray... we'd buy a few bottles of beer and sit down and instead of going to the pub we'd have a few drinks and talk about what was going on at the works and how we're going to do things, running campaigns and initiating campaigns and doing all sorts of things like that.

Butchers union organiser Jack O'Toole discerned an exhausted workforce, tired from strenuous repetitive labour and eager to dull their aches. A significant number of (mostly male) workers had broken relationships at home, and found little comfort in the family environment. The high occurrence of alcoholism was readily observable to Seelaf and so he explored different approaches to the issue throughout his leadership. In the sixties, the butchers union was the leader in research into industrial health, through their Trade Union Clinic and Research Centre. They partnered with organisations such as the Buoyancy Foundation to research alcohol addiction in workplace settings. The union had founded the clinic as part of their commitment to occupational health and safety, but also as an intervention into the grossly unequal pre-Medicare health system. They offered the broader working class population access to basic healthcare which was often out of reach, and sought out treatments for the problems of those within their community when the establishment showed little interest.

Seelaf addressed the issue of alcoholism without moralism, and in his own circles demonstrated a care towards those who struggled with the condition. One such person was his long-standing office assistant Olive

George Seelaf (left), 1934 (Seelaf Collection)

Frost, who O'Toole discerned may have been dismissed in a less sympathetic workplace, but was essentially on a sinecure. Seelaf's successor as butchers union secretary, Wally Curran, was also known as a leading figure in craft and ceramics in Australia. This somewhat peculiar convergence emerged out of Curran's own alcoholism and Seelaf's pragmatic approach towards helping him. Curran explained:

> Pottery relates to me physically, I can thump 30 pounds of clay rather than thumping a meatworks boss. I suppose it's one way of getting tension out, rather than getting drunk. But he [Seelaf] encouraged me to do that. I used to go at night-time. I did adult education classes for 2 years, and I was lucky I had a very good tutor. But that encouragement was there.

Seelaf also enjoyed a beer, and saw the pub as a place to experience joy and connect with people. He presented an optimistic and warm persona in the pub environment. Women's organiser and unionist Carol Willis recalls, 'I was always pleased when George came in because he always had something good to say, and was jolly. They could get pretty intense in there.' Willis was referring to the politicised atmosphere inside the pubs across the road from Trades Hall on Lygon Street.

Seelaf took the approach of generally avoiding confrontation. He oriented himself towards getting something useful out of interactions in these environments – even if they were with drinking companions not politically aligned to him. He was known as a good conversationalist, aside from one topic which he abhorred, which was horse racing. Indeed, for many years he organised events for workers at Footscray Park on Melbourne Cup Day to offer an alternative.

Seelaf regularly participated in political events that had alcohol integrated into them. He helped hold fundraisers for the Trade Union Clinic where they offered the wholesome staples of food and raffles, as well as bringing in kegs of beer for those that wished to buy alcoholic beverages. Seelaf was involved in so many diverse activities, he was continually raising money through various schemes, shuffling funds every which way, in an effort to help start-up community initiatives find success.

Seelaf was particularly driven to improve access to culture for workers, whilst also facilitating these same people to express themselves through their own art. Like most working class youth, he had no option to continue school past age 14, and initially very few pathways to further his education or develop creative interests. For most ordinary people, the base recreation and culture was to be found in the pub, and often focused towards gambling. Seelaf wanted *more* for working class people, and at the very least, access to the same enriching arts experiences that the wealthy had.

Seelaf was not fussy about which artforms. In the early 1950s he played a key role in the research, manufacture and distribution of *Power Without Glory*, the sensational novel by Frank Hardy. This detailed the rise from poverty of a corrupt politician named 'John West', a thinly veiled cover for real life businessman and ALP powerbroker John Wren. Much of the information was sourced within the pub environment, as Seelaf explained:

> (Hardy) used to use me as a stooge, going round interviewing people, and drinking beer with people in clubs, which wasn't a bad sort of pastime anyhow, and getting information. And I used to act the innocent, and Hardy used to keep it all stored in his nut. He couldn't take notes of anything of course, and then he'd go off and rush off and take notes later.

After the controversial novel was effectively banned, Seelaf took responsibility for coordinating the underground manufacture of the book. Workers all over Melbourne sewed pages together around their kitchen tables, to meet the insatiable demand for workers literature. When Hardy was taken to court over the book's content, he and Seelaf met every day at the Holyford Pub to talk through trial strategy and figure out how they would get the money together to pay the QC (who would not appear unless he had the cash in advance). Seelaf would visit wharfies pubs on the waterfront, passing a hat around to raise funds for the legal defence.

Seelaf never wrote a novel or painted himself, but through his extensive organising efforts was acknowledged as one of the most significant figures in the history of Australian art. So much so that the Australia Council commissioned a documentary in 1985, *Is It Working?*, to explore Seelaf's unique form of cultural practice. Amongst other curiosities, the film featured Frank Hardy telling his side of the story inside the Carlton countercultural drinking hole, Stewart's Hotel.

Seelaf's interest in finding ways for artists to collaborate with unions, and bringing creativity into workplaces, was foundational to the

George Seelaf, 1970s (Seelaf Collection)

ethos of the community arts model. In several instances, the relationships that led to activities were developed over a beer in the pubs on Lygon Street. Seelaf was a supporter of some of Australia's leading artistic figures from the 1940s into the 1980s. Artist Rick Amor recounts that:

> In about 1979, George and I were in the John Curtin Hotel having a drink at lunchtime, and he said sort of jokingly, let's apply to the Australia Council for a grant for an artist-in-residence at Trades Hall ... thinking it would never happen. And they gave us the grant! So that's why I was the first artist-in-residence, up in the tower.

Seelaf wanted to support artists who were sympathetic to the workers movement to help them pursue artistic excellence, but he also wanted to find ways to bring art to the workers who did not yet have the confidence to engage in art. As Amor explains, 'George had me going out to factories at lunch time and doing portraits ... It was George's idea to connect with the workers.' Amor found the portraiture task tough going, and so it was an idea that came and went. Union organiser Ian Jones also recalls Seelaf approaching workers in pubs in Footscray, such as the Guiding Star, in an attempt to stimulate their interest in arts programs. These were workers who had never had such opportunities before, had never even considered doing art, and Jones recalls a certain embarrassment in response to Seelaf's overtures.

Seelaf was inclined to stop in at the Barkly Hotel in Footscray, a pub where he knew journalists for the local newspaper liked to drink. As well as for his own enjoyment, this provided opportunities to promote the various projects that needed publicity.

One of the most ambitious endures to this day. Seelaf was a founder of the Footscray Community Arts Centre in 1974, a pioneering cultural organisation in Melbourne's working class western suburbs. Possibly with prior experiences in mind, he attempted a different approach to overcome the obstacles of imposter

The John Curtin Hotel across the road from the Trades Hall, where politics continued outside of the meeting rooms. A number of Seelaf's initiatives were developed in this pub, 1970s (Carla Rizio Collection)

syndrome that some working class people had. Robert Hughes, the centre's first long term director explains:

> The main thing we did in the first few years… was to use the arts as pretexts to have parties. Someone yesterday said the arts are communication and I agree. We *communicated ourselves* into some of the most epic hangovers I can remember. It was beaut. It was about people having a good time. Whether that was in an art class or theatre group, or had to do with the 10 oz glasses of wine we used to sell for 20 cents, was pretty irrelevant to me.

Seelaf accepted that people drank alcohol, *he* liked a drink himself. Moralising about harms or promoting abstinence was not his approach.

Seelaf looked for opportunities within the everyday lives of people, as a feature of his political practice. He knew that pubs, although fraught environments, offered some potential for organising based on the fact that they were where many workers gathered. Seelaf used these low key environments to explore the potential for people to get involved in his initiatives, but he was also keen to see people get out of the pub and try other things. A praxis of initiating relationships within pubs was just one of the ways the wily communist agitated for people to make their lives better and to improve the world.

Frank Hardy met with George Seelaf in various pubs during the production of *Power Without Glory*, collating material for the book and organising Hardy's legal defence, 1950s *(The Age)*

CHAPTER 33
CRITICAL DRINKING WITH THE SYDNEY PUSH
Wendy Bacon

In November 1966, I completed my exams at Melbourne University, turned twenty and caught a plane to Sydney to live with my boyfriend, a young town planner.

We lived in Balmain where we shared a house with Bill Lindbergh, a silver-haired man with twinkling eyes who had been connected to Sydney's bohemia since the late 1940s. At this time, he worked from an old stable in Glebe where he cast elaborate lamp bases, which earned him a living although they were not to his own taste. Bill was part of the Sydney Push, not that I knew that back then, or even that there was a Push.

It was through Bill that I started drinking at the Forth and Clyde Hotel, a hotel in Balmain near the shipbuilding yard Morts Dock, which was already closed.

With wide verandas and three-sided bar, this was the first pub where I became a regular. On Saturdays, we headed for the Forth and Clyde. Here I met a wide range of people including the radical historian Terry Irving who has written about the Forth and Clyde in this book. There were academics, architects, students, journalists, writers, teachers, librarians, wharfies and tradesmen. We drank middies and schooners of old and new beer. By the end of the afternoon, the place was packed with people, some sitting outside in the gutters, ready to move on to a party.

The Forth and Clyde drinkers included Labor Party members, communists, anarchists and others like me who generally rejected conservatism and mainstream respectability. Two big topics of the time were the Vietnam War and capital punishment.

Ronald Ryan was hanged at Pentridge prison on 7 February 1967. We were invited to a huge wake in the rambling garden of a house in Balmain owned by Kep Enderby who went on to be Attorney General in the Whitlam Labor government. I remember a sombre mood but can't remember if Ryan was about to be hanged or had been already. The party was

Wendy Bacon after being released from jail, 1972 (*Tribune/*Search Foundation, State Library of NSW)

thrown by Liz Fell, a tutor at Sydney University, and Roelof Smilde, both members of the Sydney Push. I'm not sure I met either of them that night, but I began to sense that here was an exciting crowd that I might join but wasn't sure how that could happen.

The group that I got to know best at the Forth and Clyde were the Filmniks who were devoted to promoting film culture. They included Mike Thornhill, Ken Quinnell, Edna Wilson and John Flaus, an anarchist who often wore no shoes and was passionate about B-grade movies. They were talking and writing about film and a few years later would all become active participants in the rebirth of the Australian film industry.

There was a literary group that included Frank Moorhouse (also one of the Filmniks). He was having trouble getting his short stories published due to the prevailing self-censorship among Australian publishers.

All these people were part of the Push. So by spring 1967, without even knowing it, I had fallen into the Sydney Push. By then I was also drinking at the Newcastle in The Rocks, the oldest area of colonial Sydney. There, on Friday nights and most other weekdays, you'd be sure to find someone you knew to talk to, as well as a host of potential friends and parties to finish off the evening.

The Push was a social milieu involving hundreds of people. In international terms, it could be described as bohemian but its unique characteristics came from a smaller group within it called the Sydney Libertarians.

It was at the Newcastle that I met the Sydney Libertarians. They introduced me to an intellectual framework that fundamentally influenced my life, including my politics. That involved reading but also a lot of talking, much of which took place in pubs and one or two cafes over the next few years.

They called it 'critical drinking', a wordplay on critical thinking: drinking with lots of talking – discussing ideas and chatting over projects and events. This chapter focuses on the critical drinkers who gathered in Sydney pubs over nearly three decades from the late 1940s to the end of the 1970s. These social spaces were shaped by a crowd who pushed through conventional boundaries of class, gender, sexuality, ethnicity and age. The milieu was generally anti-authoritarian and egalitarian but was shaped over time by changes in the urban fabric of Sydney and the broader politics beyond.

I will return to the Newcastle Hotel. But to discover why critical drinking and the Sydney Push were influential, we need to go on a pub crawl back to the aftermath of the Second World War in two locations – a corner of the quadrangle at Sydney University and a block in the heart of the Sydney CBD between Martin Place, King and Phillip streets. Here you would find the Lincoln Café in tiny Rowe Street and the Tudor Hotel on Phillip Street. Today a small historical brass strip on a pavement overshadowed by high-rise buildings is the only trace of the critical drinkers who for a time made this locality their own.

So who were these drinkers and where did they come from?

Newcastle Hotel, George St, 1957 (Cecil Lynch, State Library of NSW)

A key figure in Sydney's intellectual life in the 20th century was Scottish realist John Anderson, Professor of Philosophy at Sydney University from 1927 to 1958. Without him, the critical drinkers would not have existed.

Those who adopted Anderson's views were called Andersonians. Anderson was president of the Freethought Society, which promoted critiques of moralism and religion and was opposed to censorship.

His politics were a moving feast. Originally a communist, by the start of the Cold War he had become virulently anti-communist. This did not sit well with the generation of students who flooded into Sydney University after the Second World War. They included mature-age returned servicemen, some of whom had been radicalised by soldiers who were communists; working class students getting access to the university through the Commonwealth Financial Assistance Scheme that was introduced to boost university numbers; middle class students, some of whom had experienced childhood deprivation during the Great Depression and Second World War; and the children of European refugees who fled Europe before the war.

Lincoln Coffee Lounge & Cafe, Rowe Street, early 1950s (Brian Bird, State Library of NSW)

One such student was Grahame Harrison. He left a first-hand account of the events that led to a split with the Freethought Society in his memoir *Night Train to Granada*.

Harrison's father was a railway worker. His teachers at Newcastle Boys High included respected communist Bill Gollan, who organised debates after school with teachers linked to the anti-communist movement Catholic Action. Other teachers included an Andersonian who brought a banned copy of James Joyce's *Ulysses* to class.

When he left school in 1945, Harrison couldn't wait to get to Sydney University where he imagined a life of freedom awaited. Instead, he found conditions for students whose families lived outside Sydney were tough. Rented rooms were tiny and landlords imposed onerous restrictions. Work was hard to find and he couldn't always get enough to eat.

Harrison soon made friends with a group of students who gathered in the university quadrangle near the Philosophy Department. Some were studying philosophy under Anderson. Others, like him, studied philosophy in their own time. Among Harrison's friends were Darcy Waters, who had grown up with his widowed mother in Casino after his railway fettler father died in the 1930s, and George Munster, the son of a Jewish Czech industrialist and Catholic Austrian mother, who migrated in 1939. (Later Munster became editor of independent publications *Nation* and *Nation Review*, and was a pioneer in Australian investigative journalism).

Harrison and his friends were influenced by anarcho-syndicalist critiques of Stalinism, having read every book available on the Spanish Civil War including George Orwell's *Homage to Catalonia*. He attributed anarchism as well as Andersonianism to 'making us what we were.'

They joined with other radicals to protest against Labor Prime Minister Ben Chifley's decision to use troops to break the 1949 miners' strike. They were dismayed when Anderson supported Chifley's actions.

The Menzies Liberal government was elected in 1949. In 1950, Bob Menzies proposed a referendum to ban the Communist Party of Australia. The Freethought Society radicals wanted to host a speaker for the No case against the ban. Anderson refused to allow it.

When there was talk of conscription being introduced during the Korean War, Anderson's critics formed an anti-conscription committee. Anderson accused those involved of 'proletarian mythologising'. He scornfully called his critics the Paddington Push. The word 'push' was derived from the description of 19th century larrikin gangs as 'pushes'.

Today a wealthy suburb, Paddington was then known for sly grog and poor housing. The Paddington Push name only lasted briefly and it was some of this group that started the Sydney Libertarians. These developments led to a move downtown. From this time onwards critical drinkers could always be found in one or two hotels in the inner city where the drinkers came from a wider range of occupations, ages and educational backgrounds than those in university pubs. The broader group, of which the Libertarians were a part, became the Sydney Push.

Libertarian meetings still took place in the Philosophy Department after which academics and students would adjourn to the Forest Lodge or another university pub. There were also meetings in the Ironworkers' Hall near the Newcastle Hotel, Liberty Hall nearer Central Station and later in a building in Darlinghurst owned by Greek anarchist and newspaper publisher Nestor Grivas. The topics of early papers are a signpost to Libertarians' interests. There was one by June Wilson, who argued that no fundamental social change could happen without a change in sexual relations, and others on anarchism and the Industrial Workers of the World. The latter were known as the Wobblies; they promoted the idea of One Big Union and 'building the new society in the shell of the old.'

The first downtown venue, the Lincoln, was not a pub, but a dimly lit cafe in Rowe Street, which was already a hangout for artists, writers, musicians and sci-fi fans, some of whom became part of the Push. On the walls were paintings by modernist John Olsen and the bohemian Rosaleen Norton, who was branded a witch by a hostile media after her paintings were banned at the University of Melbourne in 1949.

In the afternoons, the Lincoln was abuzz with people arriving from classes or jobs. These early critical drinkers rejected stifling restrictions on sex and social behaviour and censorship. They included Lillian Roxon, who left Brisbane State High School in 1948. She wanted to be a journalist but when this proved hard, she enrolled in philosophy and contributed to the student newspaper *Honi Soit*. She moved to New York in the late 1950s and became a famous rock journalist, but remained a Push member until she died in 1973. She was friends with Maggie Elliot (later Fink), an art student who lived with the bohemian poet Harry Hooton and later became a successful filmmaker. There was also Jewish Hungarian immigrant George Molnar on his way to becoming a philosophy lecturer, the poet Lex Banning, and Roelof Smilde who, rejecting the

John Maze and Jan Evans at the Tudor Hotel, 1950s
(Willie Russell)

ideas of his puritan Dutch father, transformed rapidly from captain of North Sydney Boys High to university dropout and Libertarian.

In 1952, new owners took over the Lincoln and wanted more upmarket customers. The crowd moved to the nearby Tudor Hotel, which became the first Push pub. Like the Lincoln, the Tudor was already a popular venue, partly because the Journalists' Club and barristers' chambers were nearby. But it now needed to meet the Push requirements of being open to women on the same basis as men. Push drinkers were also unwilling to pay different prices for drinks in different parts of a pub. These battles were won.

In the early 1950s, many people didn't have home phones. So, each afternoon, they'd head to the Tudor to catch up on and debate the latest news, get word about where the weekly card game would be held and tips for casual jobs such as working on trams, in factories, on the wharves and even fighting a plague of Argentine ants. If you left Sydney, the Tudor was where you tracked down your friends on your return. Until 1955, closing time was 6 o'clock. Even when hours were extended to 10 pm, pubs shut for an hour until 7 pm, which meant people had dinner nearby at one of a handful of cheap Italian and Greek restaurants before heading back to the pub.

In his memoir *Appo*, Richard Appleton describes how he briefly joined the Communist Party but finding that too authoritarian, joined the Push. A poet and teacher who later edited the *Australian Encyclopaedia*, he describes how, in 1953, he and other Tudor drinkers, including artist John Olsen, joined students in storming the NSW Art Gallery to protest against the Archibald Prize for portraiture being awarded to the conservative William Dargie rather than the modernist William Dobell. According to newspaper reports, they carried posters proclaiming, 'Death to the Art Gallery Trustees' and 'Away with Victorianism'.

Another Tudor regular was David Perry, who grew up in an overcrowded home on Sydney's North Shore. He left school and became a newspaper illustrator. On completion of compulsory National Service, he dreamed of becoming an artist. In search of friends with similar interests, he found the Tudor. In his 2014 memoir he wrote: 'This was more like it...the atmosphere was hugely inclusive.' He quickly made friends among the crowd who were:

> Drinking beer, talking loudly...The most immediately striking thing about the people was that men and women shared the same space (virtually unheard of in Australian pubs then and indeed until many years later), and that men and women shared the same language, an earthy, vulgar and very direct language that called a fuck a fuck. The talk was about books, movies and politics without the preciousness and sheer bullshit that usually attended

Poet Lex Banning in the Assembly Hotel, 1950s
(Willie Russell)

these things (and sadly still does). Authority figures from the police to the Queen and all between, were regarded with contempt.

In the early 1950s, less than 4 per cent of young people enrolled in university and only one in five of these were women. Women who enrolled in university were often reminded that along with a degree, they should find a good husband. There were far fewer than 4 per cent of women in the Science faculty which is where critical drinker Marion Manton enrolled. The few female students were showered with sexist comments by male students as they entered the lecture rooms. After class, Manton gravitated to the philosophy students and soon embraced Sydney Libertarianism and the wider Push. She recalls:

> Going to a civilised pub like the upstairs bar at the Tudor was a new and exciting experience for me. I'd seen the tiled walls of other pubs as the doors opened and shut and a roar of loud male voices could be heard and then after 6 pm the men would pour out onto the street raving and shouting and staggering about. Scary to be nearby. So the contrast at the Tudor was wonderful. Real conversation was possible. If drunk, there was no problem of violence.

Development of Libertarian Ideas

The core ideas of Sydney Libertarianism developed during these years with philosopher Jim Baker contributing the most. A star Andersonian student, he studied at Oxford University in the late 1940s, returning to Sydney as a lecturer in 1951. He too broke with Anderson and later wrote of his approach at that time: '"Exposing illusions" became almost entirely exposing the illusions of Communism, and he seemed more and more to find Communism almost everywhere.'

Baker wrote up his ideas in essays which became key readings for younger Push members and which in 1968 turned me into a Sydney Libertarian. Baker rejected the idea of a simplistic line from Andersonianism to Sydney Libertarianism. While the Andersonian realist approach to philosophy and critical inquiry remained strong, Libertarians were also interested in the operation of power elites and the way in which ideologies mask the special interests of groups that promote them. They agreed with ideas associated with revolutionary anarchism but rejected utopian ideals. They described themselves as 'pessimistic anarchists' and were influenced by the idea of 'permanent protest' promoted by the New York-based intellectual Max Nomad, originally a Ukrainian anarchist.

The Libertarian approach to sexuality was influenced by Wilhelm Reich, who was a Marxist and a Freudian. He believed political and sexual repression were inextricably linked, so that plans for fundamental change must involve both. It was not so much that Sydney Libertarians didn't recognise jealousy but that they thought you should suppress it. Their promotion of non-monogamy – popularly called free love – attracted the most public attention, but became less remarkable in the 1970s.

In 2009, Sydney Libertarian Roelof Smilde, then in his eighties, told journalist Robert Milliken that 'here was a way of interpreting the society that I was in.' Few Push members

Archibald Prize protest, 1953 (Laurie Shea)

subscribed to the full set of Libertarian ideas but they were attracted to the irreverent anti-authoritarianism and fun that swirled around the group.

The Push Finds Its Own Pub

In 1957, the Tudor closed to make way for development. A move to the nearby Assembly Hotel in Hunter Street failed because of tensions because the incumbent clientele were not keen on the unconventional Push crowd.

It was time for the Push to find its own pub. George Molnar went on a scouting mission. Eventually, he and other Push members interviewed the publican of the Royal George Hotel in what was then the seedy end of King Street near the busy Darling Harbour docks. The carrot was a regular income stream so long as basic requirements were guaranteed. These were that women should be on an equal footing with men and people should be able to move around the pub with drinks purchased at a single price. Marion Manton remembers going with Molnar to check it out. She gave it her seal of approval and so the George was born as a venue. It was the most successful Push pub and the highpoint of critical drinking. Those of us who came after the George felt we had never truly experienced the Push.

By the late 1950s, the Cold War was entering its second decade and the Menzies government was entrenched. Some critical drinkers headed overseas, including Lillian Roxon who by then was a full-time reporter. In New York, she produced her groundbreaking *Encyclopedia of Rock*. Manton won a scholarship to study her doctorate at Columbia University. But there was also a steady stream of new recruits. Barcan in his history of radical student politics at Sydney University describes a shift in the political atmosphere towards a 'more liberal

George Molnar and André Frankovits in The Royal George, 1960s (Doug Nicholson)

Lyn Gain, 1960s (Doug Nicholson)

humanist spirit' and a move away from left-wing Stalinism, especially after the Soviet Union invaded Hungary in 1956.

This was a time of growth for the Libertarians and the broader Push. New students enrolling in 1957 were introduced to the Libertarians in the Orientation handbook as a 'protesting minority, promoting freedom and opposing authoritarian organisation and mentalities.' Students who were part of the student newspaper *Honi Soit*, the Sydney University Dramatic Society or the crowd that still gathered in the quad near the Philosophy Department were likely to find themselves invited to the George.

Brenda Linn and Jane Gardiner (then Iliff and later Matheson) were students at this time and remember the sense of agency they experienced in going to a pub where they could not just drink as equals but where their contributions to discussions were taken seriously, and virginity was seen as something to be lost rather than prized. The wider society still judged women who drank in pubs, let alone fucked without being married, to be immoral. But secure in a thriving subculture, most Push women were enjoying themselves too much to be worried about external disapproval.

There was enough space at the George for different groups to find their own scene. There was a main bar which led to a back room where the Libertarians tended to gather. Here, Robert Hughes who was then a student painted a mural of Push characters (he later became an internationally famous art critic). In the basement, there was folk singing and blues. Gardiner remembers long Saturday afternoons with lunch from a nearby fish and chip shop (pubs did not serve food until later). Well known singers, Marion and Don Henderson, Welshman Declan Affley, Brian Mooney and Jeannie Lewis sang at the George. Another folk singer – Johnny Earls – sang revolutionary Cuban songs. When Earls was arrested for not paying a train fare, a pub collection was taken up to get him out of Long Bay prison. Earls later moved to Peru where he became Professor of Anthropology and helped develop a dictionary of the native Quechua language.

Judy Perry, Doug Nicholson and Ken Buckley (foreground) in The Royal George, 1963 (Michael Baldwin)

Anti-voting street poster, 1961

The George had another smaller bar where what was known as the Baby or Bayview Push drank; here there was more dancing and less talking. This was a younger crowd including some who had grown up on the Northern beaches. On one occasion a man dancing on a table jumped through an open window onto the street.

There were a number of gay men in the Baby Push. Male homosexuality was illegal and while there was always a gay scene in Sydney, there were also 'poofter bashings' and police harassment. Earlier in the 1950s, the entire NSW Police Vice Squad had conducted campaigns to eliminate any place in Sydney frequented by gay men, who were also subject to beatings and demands for payment. One gay man, now in his early eighties, who drank at the George with his boyfriend, remembers the atmosphere as homophobic, although not as much as in other pubs. They preferred the back bar at the Rex Hotel in Kings Cross, which was an established bar for gay men. Arrangements between corrupt police and licensees meant that drinkers there were relatively safe from harassment.

Feminist Germaine Greer moved from Melbourne to briefly join the Push. She told author Anne Coombs that the sharp-edged, logical and straightforward talk that she experienced when critical drinking at the George had a lifelong influence on her. She gave a paper on Libertarianism and sex and sang at an anti-censorship event at Sydney University. She then headed to London where she became involved in London *Oz*, European paper *Suck*, and published her landmark feminist book *The Female Eunuch* in 1970.

Others went straight from school to the George. Push member and teacher at North Sydney Boys High School Neil Hope (nicknamed Sope) brought his students Ian Bedford, Ross Poole and John Roberts, all of whom later became academics, to the pub. Sope, who was a close friend of Lillian Roxon, himself left Sydney soon afterwards to set up an English language school in Italy.

Andre Frankovits attended Homebush Boys High School and did one year of medicine in 1958 before dropping out, studying philosophy and becoming one of the core group of Sydney Libertarians who produced the *Broadsheet*, an irregular roneoed foolscap publication. Another who joined at this time was Sydney university student Richard Brennan. He initially went to the George intending to gather material

Cam Perry (with pipe), Inge Riebe (back) and Lyn Gain (foreground) in The Royal George, early 1960s (Doug Nicholson)

Annual Balmain Pub Crawl organised by Frank Moorhouse, including Elaine Walls, Irene Walls and Danny Ralston, 1970s (Rob Walls)

for a film script by quietly listening to the pub talk. He quickly found himself absorbed into the Push.

Lyn Gain describes in her memoir *Witch Girl* how she left her selective high school at sixteen, preferring to work, and was taken by a friend to the George:

> It was full of people talking, from immature discussions about the meaning of life to sophisticated arguments about philosophy, society, politics, art and literature. The conversation was non-stop but so was the folk-singing, partying and forming and reforming sexual liaisons. I had never seen such fun or imagined such a good game. I rushed right in and never really left.

Some women found the atmosphere overwhelming, or came under pressure from family or friends to stay away. We will never know how many people tested the George and disappeared. The big age difference between younger members of the Push and older men, and academics mixing with students would today be regarded as fraught with potential for sexual exploitation. In the 1970s, Push women critiqued the sexism and informal hierarchies in the Push, but this was later.

There was always talk about card games and the races, but this only involved a few. To find out what else critical drinkers were discussing, we can delve into Sydney Libertarian *Broadsheets*, books and memoirs about the Push, especially filmmaker Albie Thom's well-documented *My Generation* and the Push Canon, a record of books and films that were Push favourites, compiled by Marion Manton and Brenda Linn.

In the late 1950s, the Libertarian *Broadsheet* published articles about the civil rights battles in the United States and the limitations of student representative politics. There were reports of how union leaders and the arbitration system were suppressing rank-and-file workers, and theoretical articles analysing various strands of anarchism.

Doug Nicholson, who was one of the original sci-fi fans at the Tudor hotel, remained a driving influence behind the Push's interest in dystopian and science fiction. Contemporary American novels such as Ray Bradbury's *Fahrenheit 451* (1952) and Anthony Burgess's *Clockwork Orange* (1962) which critiqued political authoritarianism, censorship and thought control, appealed to the Push. American novelist John Dos Passos' trilogy *U.S.A.*, which mixed factual reporting and fiction, was essential reading. At the time he wrote *U.S.A.*, Dos Passos was a left-winger and sympathetic to the Wobblies.

Anything to do with how to avoid getting pregnant was of interest. While abortion was criminalised, women could still get pregnancies terminated if they had the name of one of the few doctors who provided the service, and had more cash available than did most young women of the time. When Push women needed abortions, the hat was passed around the Pub or they relied on a lucky day at the races.

Protest against the jailing of Bacon and Cox, 1972 (*Tribune*/Search Foundation, State Library of NSW)

A Sydney Libertarian *Broadsheet* in 1961 announced the first sales of the contraceptive pill in England and its importation into Australia for clinical trials. While the Pill opened up choices for my generation, the early formulations had uncomfortable side effects which were also discussed.

There were other subjects that were not much discussed until later when Push feminists broke through the silence. These included the vaginal orgasm, the idea of which some Push men embraced, though some women admitted later they had faked orgasms.

Another topic discussed in the George was activism – or rather what sort of activism, since giving papers and publishing were regarded as a form of activism. But there were some among the Push who were more attracted to direct action than others.

For example, Smilde and Frankovits recruited David Perry to design a poster proclaiming: 'Vote Informal - whoever you vote for a politician always gets in.' They pasted hundreds of them on poles and walls around the city before several elections including the Federal election in 1961.

Frank Moorhouse wrote a *Broadsheet* article arguing that Libertarians should make efforts to persuade others to support their ideas. The next issue carried an article by Charlie Brown which mockingly rejected Moorehouse's proposal ending with, 'I don't intend to take time off my drinking, talking and fornicating in order to get myself abused in order to make someone else's world safe for them.' Charlie Brown was an art teacher at the exclusive private boys' school Cranbrook, an occasional drinker at the George and friend of London *Oz* editor Richard Neville.

This *Broadsheet* dispute led to a seminar (with drinks) in the George attended by 100 people. Moorhouse, Brown and Sydney Libertarian and anthropologist Les Hiatt debated the issues. Moorhouse later told Anne Coombs that he felt his case was vindicated by the growth of activism in the 1970s.

While these debates were happening in the Push, the times were indeed becoming more activist and the stifling cultural restraints of the 1950s were breaking apart. Albie Thoms provides an illustration of how this played out. In his orientation week in 1959, he attended a meeting where he heard, for the first time, women, as well as men, talking openly about sex. He soon discovered that these students met in the quadrangle near the Philosophy Department. Warned against being infected by their views on free love, he was attracted rather than deterred. He was soon taken to the George by fellow student Ian MacDougall. McDougall was a non-aligned socialist rather than a Libertarian but was drawn to the folk scene at the George.

In these early years, Thoms found the cacophony of talk and music at the George exhilarating. He especially enjoyed the folk singing. He wrote that it 'paved the way for young musicians to give expression to the Youth revolt.'

While drinking at the George, Thoms became friends with some of his university tutors including Cam Perry and Terry McMullen, who orally passed on the basics of Libertarianism and Push history. There was an egalitarian atmosphere that would not be possible today when friendly relations with

Darcy Waters and Ian Milliss (Ian Milliss Collection)

academics are not encouraged. It was also through the Push that Thoms met David Perry, who had not been to university. They became major collaborators in Theatre of the Absurd and experimental films. Among those they worked with there were Push friends including Terry McMullen, Sue Howe, David Ferraro, Richard Brennan and Aggy Reed as well as others who were not in the Push. Thoms tells the story of his involvement in the Push in his book *My Generation*, while also noting the other political movements that were simultaneously influencing him: the development of the New Left and the rise of the anti-Vietnam War, anti-conscription and Aboriginal rights movements.

In March 1960, South African police killed 69 unarmed protesters and injured hundreds more in the Sharpeville massacre. Thoms, McDougall, Molnar, Paddy McGuiness and hundreds of others marched to Martin Place where they were confronted by gangs of plain-clothes police. Thoms was stomped on by the police. It was a terrifying experience but he took on board the advice of Aboriginal activists, who drew the students' attention to the daily abuse of their community and Australia's own apartheid system.

The NSW police have a long history of violence and corruption, so it is relevant to consider how much attention police – or 'wallopers' as the Push called them – paid to such a hotspot of anti-authoritarianism as the George. Working class pubs attracted far more police attention than middle class venues, and the George crowd may have had some protection by having academics among them. Certainly, nothing happened that compared to the brutal daily policing of the First Nations community in Redfern. But this doesn't mean the police were absent. A *Sydney Morning Herald* article later referred to a university student who visited the George, only to be arrested and carted away in a paddy wagon when he left. The coppers warned him of the moral risk of being led astray by Push women, a warning that only made him keener to get back to the pub.

Ken Buckley was a British economist who was a lecturer at Sydney University in the 1950s. While never a Libertarian, he drank with the Push. He records in his autobiography *Buckleys!*, an occasion when police advanced on three drinkers and without explaining why, arrested one of them, a teacher. Buckley followed the paddy wagon and later laid a complaint. He was invited to attend a meeting with police the following day. When he arrived, he found the arrested man there with his lawyer. An agreement had been made that the young man would not be charged as a teacher, which would have led to him being sacked, but as a labourer, on condition that Buckley dropped his complaint. Doug Nicholson remembers another occasion when Germaine Greer talked herself out of arrest by two police who had roughly pushed their way into the bar.

The end of the Push's time at the Royal George was triggered by the mysterious deaths of Gilbert Bogle and Margaret Chandler on the banks of the Lane Cove River on New Year's Eve 1963. Ken Buckley, who now rented Kep Enderby's house in Balmain, held a New Year's Eve party attended by Push members. Margaret's husband Geoffrey Chandler, who had nothing to do with his wife's death, went home with a young Push woman Pam Logan. He then returned to his own home to be told his wife had been found dead. The Push connection led the media to link its free love philosophy, the partner swapping in which the Chandlers were involved and the unsolved deaths. Intense media harassment led to Logan fleeing Sydney and Chandler and his Push friends being forced to drink in a secure room in the George. More outsiders were also visiting the hotel hoping for an easy fuck. In his memoir, Richard Appleton recalls one Saturday afternoon, when he and some friends were drinking in the back room, when three men surrounded their table and accused them of 'looking at them and laughing ... They picked up drinks and poured them over us.' Appleton attempted to stand up and one of the men smashed him in the face.

A month after the deaths of Margaret Chandler and Gilbert Bogle, in February 1963, another unwelcome event occurred at the home of Andre Frankovits, Bonnie McDougall and Jane Gardiner. A quiet party of about 20 people including Jim Baker, ABC journalist Jack Gulley, Ken Buckley, doctor Ross Byrne and others was underway when three police entered the flat overlooking William Street in Kings Cross. One of them abused the people at the party, accusing them of being 'nothing but a group of homosexuals.' They kicked open the door of the room where George Molnar and a woman friend had been fucking. Another followed a terrified Jane Gardiner into her bedroom where he asked her what a nice girl like her was doing hanging out with such degenerates. Asked to identify themselves, one of them said he was Inspector Thomas.

After they left, Buckley, Frankovits, Gulley and Molnar went to Central Police Station to complain. Thomas turned out not to exist. The man who used that name was the notoriously corrupt Inspector Giles who ran sex worker rackets in Darlinghurst. An internal investigation found that the police did not exceed their duty. This and police harassment of the Redfern Aboriginal community were two specific examples that Buckley gave in a paper to the Freethought Society at Sydney University and later published in the *Broadsheet* where he announced the formation of the NSW Council for Civil Liberties. Now 60 years old, the Council continues to play an important role in tackling abuse of police power.

In the end, the Royal George publican himself pulled the plug by selling the hotel and moving elsewhere. It was time to find another pub. This time, it was Frankovits who found the United States Hotel further along Sussex Street. Since demolished, it was a big barn-like tiled pub that stood on the corner of Druitt Street. According to those who were there, Richard Brennan could be relied upon to separate any drinkers who looked like starting a fight. Brennan later organised a co-operative film project shot in a single day of the Vietnam Moratorium in 1970 and became a successful filmmaker. The United States only lasted a couple of years as the favoured pub and by the end of 1965, the Push moved onto the Criterion, also in Sussex Street, then to the Vanity Fair and Lismore hotels and finally back to the Criterion in the mid-1970s.

The downtown drinking scene was gradually losing its excitement. This was partly because as gentrification extended in Balmain and Paddington, the local pub scenes there grew. After the Forth and Clyde closed in 1972, the London Hotel became a popular Push pub, and Moorhouse and friends initiated an annual Balmain pub crawl that visited 27 pubs. The literary crowd had grown and Moorhouse, Michael Wilding and poet John Tranter organised well-attended poetry readings at which some other Push people also performed.

In Paddington, the Windsor Castle was a major focus. The crowd here, who were sometimes called the Paddington Push, included artists and would-be artists. Many of the George's Baby Push drinkers moved across to the Windsor Castle. The drinkers tended to be less overtly political and more stylish and interested in marijuana, LSD and the latest trends in youth fashion. Thoms lived nearby and wrote that by the late 1960s he found the

Anti-censorship protest in nuns' habits with slogans, 1969

scene more stimulating than the inner-city Push scene that now seemed a bit boring, dominated by talk of punting on the races.

But through the years one city pub, whose bohemian roots went back to the 1930s, remained very lively. This was the Newcastle – always a popular drinking spot, especially on Friday nights. Publican Jim Buckley allowed young artists to display their paintings, including nudes, on the pub walls. As a new member, I felt connected to a wider world. I remember friends pointing out two old men sitting in a corner who had fought in the Spanish Civil War. Push members who had moved overseas would drop in when in Sydney. Most had become involved with broader radical politics. One of these was Michael Taussig, who had studied medicine at Sydney University before becoming a Marxist anthropologist and ethnographer in South America and later a professor at Columbia University.

Throughout 1968, there was talk of uprisings in the United States, Prague and Paris. Paddy McGuiness, who drank at the Newcastle, was the first person I met who had actually witnessed what we saw as a near revolution in Paris. (He later became a right-wing journalist.) I had been drawn to the anti-authoritarian, Marxist-influenced Libertarian theories including the notion of permanent protest, but the times felt more optimistic. There was increasing interest on the Left in what some called anarcho-Marxism. In 1969, Jim Baker, Liz Fell and I all gave papers in a series on the connections between Anarchism and Marxism held at the Third World Bookshop, then owned by the Trotskyist Bob Gould. After the papers, we adjourned to the left-wing Sussex Hotel.

Younger people drawn into the Push saw themselves as part of the broader New Left. These included Bill Gollan's daughter Kathy Gollan and Gillian Leahy, both of whom were involved in anti-Vietnam protests while still at school.

By then, I was a close friend of Liz Fell, who was teaching in the new UNSW department of sociology. Another friend was fellow student and Push member Rick Mohr, who was involved in the anarchist group that held talks at Nestor Grivas's meeting place. Our interest in Sydney Libertarianism and anarchism merged with our study of power elites, early Marxism and the connection between the personal and the political. In 1969, along with two other radical students, Val Hodgson and Allan Rees, I took on the editorship of the student newspaper *Tharunka*, which had been involved in censorshipstudent newspaper *Tharunka*, which had been involved in censorship battles earlier in the 1960s. This led to an intense campaign against the NSW censorship laws that ended up with us facing obscenity charges. We then moved to producing underground newspapers *Thorunka* and *Thor*. While the story of that campaign is a longer one, it is important in this context to understand that scores of Push people were involved in the production, writing,

George Molnar and Roelof Smilde opposing the Victoria Street evictions, 1974

distribution and defence of *Thorunka*. Frank Moorhouse used the publications as an outlet to publish suppressed literary works, including his own. Younger people like designer and cartoonist Jenny Coopes, Val Hodgson and novelist Inez Baranay were part of the Push crowd at this time. We pushed through sexual taboos by publishing frank discussions of masturbation, menstruation and orgasms.

We still drank at the Newcastle and in Push pubs in Balmain and Paddington. But we had less time for critical drinking because we were covering costs by distributing hundreds of copies of *Tharunka* in suburban pubs, which were still mostly filled with men. I was arrested in the Manly Hotel with Push member John Cox and together we faced trial. Push friends including Germaine Greer gave evidence in our defence. There were protests when we were briefly sent to prison on remand for sentence on convictions against which we appealed and were acquitted. Andre Frankovits was arrested protesting near the court.

In October 1972, the Newcastle also fell foul of developers. The Sydney Cove Redevelopment Authority had plans for a high-rise hotel so publican Jim Buckley called on the NSW Builders Labourers' Federation. The BLF had been promoting the idea that workers should have a say in what they built, including by supporting communities who wanted to preserve housing and their local pubs. NSW BLF secretary Jack Mundey made a passionate speech at the Newcastle farewell party promising that the union would place a ban on the site and save the pub. It was one of the first of what were soon known as Green Bans. Unfortunately, Buckley's licence was transferred to the Sydney Cove Redevelopment Authority which shut the hotel in May 1973. It was later demolished.

We had already been distributing *Tharunkas* on BLF work sites and reporting on militant union actions. But then another connection sprang up which drew the Push closer to the BLF. In 1973, Arthur King and hundreds of fellow residents living in low-cost housing in Victoria Street, Kings Cross faced eviction by developer Frank Theeman. King invited fellow Push people living nearby including me, Darcy Waters and Sue Varga to assist. The NSW BLF placed a Green Ban on the street. Then in March, King was kidnapped and held for several days by thugs employed by organised crime bosses. A wave of fear rippled through the Push. When he was released, King contacted his friend Andre Frankovits, who later explained that King was leaving the street and quitting the campaign. A group of Push people including Liz Fell, Darcy Waters, Roelof Smilde, Susan Varga, John Cox, Peter Wright and myself remained and supported squatting in eight huge terraces. Others who became involved, including activist artist Ian Milliss and gay anarchist Sasha Soldatov, became connected to the Push at this time. When we were evicted in early 1974, several Push people including George Molnar joined us in the squats overnight and were arrested. The heritage facade of Victoria Street was eventually saved but its low-cost housing was lost to gentrification.

Arthur King's withdrawal was understandable. He later became an anti-corruption campaigner who worked for the independent MP John Hatton. He went public with his story after newspaper publisher Juanita Nielsen was murdered as a result of her involvement in the campaign to save the street in 1975.

These events led to a fracturing of the Push scene. Those who were not involved in the Green Bans became more focused on Balmain where the literary and film scene flourished. Those of us involved in Green Bans struggles began drinking in the union pub, the Sussex Hotel and then the Criterion, which since 1975 had become the last of the Push city pubs. For a while, Jim Baker lived in a room in the pub. These pubs, both also now demolished, stood opposite each other at the intersection of Sussex and Liverpool streets.

The Criterion morphed into a big left-wing pub. Some of us moved between both pubs. In the Sussex, you could find publican Stella

Moresso who supported the builders' labourers including women organisers who were among her regulars. By then the NSW BLF had been crushed by the union's Federal branch and the Master Builders' Association. On any Friday night in the late 1970s, the Criterion crowd spilled out onto the pavement. Here in the crush you would find Push people like Liz Fell, who was involved in the Prisoners' Action Group, introducing ex-prisoners who had become activists to the crowd. But as well as Push people, there were members of the Communist Party and Labor Party and a wide range of left-wing unionists. There were socialist feminists, anarcho-feminists, radical feminists and members of the reformist Women's Electoral Lobby. There were left-wing journalists from the *Tribune* and mainstream reporters. There were Labor lawyers, more progressive lawyers and students who were intent on revolutionising legal practice through community legal centres. Even progressive magistrate Kevin Anderson was drawn to the Push crowd.

By the early eighties, this scene, too, had faded. While the Push remained important to those whose lives it had shaped, it stopped attracting new people. Of those who remained, some supported the ALP while others supported independent parties or the Greens. Very few moved to the right. Some remained steadfastly sceptical of involvement in parliamentary politics and were lifelong non-voters. Push people continued to put their ideas into practice through their relationships and work. To name just some of hundreds: Andre Frankovits became an Amnesty and Human Rights campaigner; Jane Gardiner took over the publishing of Australian *Rolling Stone* and was a journalist for many years with John Fairfax and Sons (now Nine); Lyn Gain became the chief executive of the NSW Council for Social Services; and Liz Fell was a prominent feminist and founder of the ABC feminist collective that ran the *Coming Out Show* on ABC radio. Brenda Linn, who was a librarian, has organised the digitisation of the Sydney Libertarian publications for the National Library. Until last year, she, Marion Manton and others organised talks in Glebe for what they called the Sydney Realists, adjourning afterwards to the Toxteth Hotel to continue critical drinking.

Many of the Push have passed on to what we call 'the other bar' and the pubs that provided physical spaces for their critical drinking have been swept away, apart from the Royal George – which became the Slip Inn. Today's inner-city hotels are filled with sports screens, poker machines and oyster bars.

The Sydney Push was born during the rise of vehement anti-communism in the post war period and was shaped by the radical left currents of the sixties and seventies. Today, as right-wing populism sweeps the world, the influence of disinformation and propaganda demonstrates that a continual critique of social illusions is as relevant as ever. Governments and powerful interests continue to ignore the threat of climate change threatening the lives of billions. In this situation, the Sydney Libertarian anti-utopian ideas of permanent protest and civil disobedience remain inspiring and essential.

Liz Fell (Sue Willis)

CHAPTER 34
THE 1962 VICTORIAN BEER BAN
Iain McIntyre

On Friday 8 December 1962, the Victorian Trades Hall Council's Disputes Committee placed a complete ban on the export of beer from Victoria. This led to an immediate shortage in NSW towns bordering the state and left more than 10 000 cartons of beer sitting on docks and in warehouses. The action not only provided crucial support for brewery workers in their fight for improved wages but also marked a new step in the long running fight against the federal government's anti-union 'penal powers'.

Originally introduced by the ALP in 1949 to break that year's coal strike, anti-union legislation was deepened by the conservative Menzies government during the 1950s. Australia's arbitration courts had long been responsible for setting standards in various industries and regularly intervened in industrial disputes. Post-war penal powers expanded their ability to effectively ban strikes through the levying of huge fines on unions, officials, and individual members. It also enabled them to jail union representatives.

Although the penal powers had a chilling effect on most union leaderships, militants challenged their use, albeit at a major cost to their finances. One dispute that illustrated how the powers could be confronted arose in 1962 when the Council of Brewery Unions in Victoria took on both Carlton United Breweries (CUB) and the Arbitration Commission.

Having recently taken over one of its few remaining competitors, the Richmond Brewery, CUB dominated the Victorian industry. Combined with increased automation, which enabled the company to slash its workforce while doubling production, this had increased its profits by around 25 per cent in the previous financial year. Demanding a greater share for employees, the Council of Brewery Unions put in an ambit claim in February 1962 which included an extra two pounds a week in wages, an added week's leave per year, and the introduction of the 35 hour working week.

This was immediately rejected by the company. Their refusal to negotiate, and a demand that employees work up to 30 hours overtime a week in the run up to Christmas, led to the holding of a stop work meeting of 1500 workers in May. CUB turned to the Arbitration Commission, which prohibited the unions involved from undertaking any form of industrial action. The workers met this with a ban on working more than 8 hours' overtime. When the commission fined the union £200 plus costs, they stopped work to march on the court.

A series of further stop works and fines followed. Concerned at developments, the federal executive of the Liquor Trades Union (LTU) attempted to force its state branch to end the dispute. This was strongly rejected, both by the dispute's steering committee, led by Victorian LTU official and CPA member Jim Munro, and the union's membership. Instead bans were soon expanded to include night-time shifts, and a voluntary levy set up to cover rapidly escalating fines. For its part CUB ran full page newspaper advertisements attacking the unions while cutting off free beer for employees and applying to remove Christmas bonuses from their awards.

The deadlock was eventually broken via a further expansion of bans to cover weekend work, as well as by the December intercession of transport workers, which brought the number of unions involved to 20. With shortages mounting, the brewery unions put the onus back on CUB, claiming that thanks to the export bans there was now plenty of beer available for Victorian consumers.

The widening of the dispute eventually brought the company to heel and, with assistance from the Arbitration Court, it cut a deal just before Christmas which provided brewery workers with a major increase in pay and improved overtime. The company also withdrew contempt of court proceedings against the unions. The fines remained in place however, and the need to confront penal powers would continue until a general strike in 1969, over the jailing of tramway's union leader Clarrie O'Shea, rendered them unenforceable.

Communist Party of Australia anti penal-powers pamphlet, 1958
(Reason In Revolt)

CHAPTER 35

EDUCATION IN REVERSE? THE DRINKING CULTURE OF BRISBANE'S STUDENT RADICALS

Alex Ettling

In 1962, the young activist Humphrey McQueen began studying at the University of Queensland (UQ). McQueen, later to become a prominent Australian historian, was keen to explore the possibilities of campus politics. He recounts:

> There was a Labor Club at the university, and you had to have seven people to get registered. We could get five. Two people from the Conservative Club agreed to sign on as Labor Club members because part of the deal was that you then got the equivalent of a flagon of sherry. So they agreed – if they could come and drink the sherry. So that's the state that university politics was in.

McQueen concluded there was no point pushing labour politics, and so shifted to pressing the boundaries of humanist liberalism: 'I thought if we had a Free Thought Society, we could have religion, sex and politics.' This milieu was associated with three notorious events which tested morality and social norms. As a provocation towards sexual liberation McQueen advocated during one meeting that every suburban house should include a masturbatorium. For this he received a suspension. Another member, Ingrid Palmer ingested a contraceptive pill live on stage – 'a *live sex act*' jokes McQueen. And Merle Thornton, a member of the Free Thought Society, most famously chained herself to the front bar of The Regatta Hotel in 1965 to protest women's exclusion from the public bar.

The first half of the sixties was characterised by these embryonic campaigns around issues of civil rights and free speech, as well as the peace movement, and anti-racism. Brisbane's student politics developed towards a distinctive New Left thinking – emphasising participatory democracy. After the federal government's decision in 1964 to conscript unwilling citizens for the battlefield, campus politics shifted into a new phase with the explosion in growth of the anti-Vietnam War movement.

A significant moment came in 1966 when student Brian Laver stood up on a table in the university refectory and voiced his opposition to the war. This disobedient act did not meet immediate acclaim from the student body, and

Humphrey McQueen speaking at a rally in Centenary Park organised by the Vietnam Action Committee in 1966 (Frank Neilsen, Radical Times Archive)

the young man was pelted with apples and oranges. Undeterred, regular speak-outs by a small number of activists at UQ attracted a growing minority of students interested in taking action against the war. Student activist Michael O'Neill, quoted in 'Remembering the University of Queensland Forum', claimed that 'crossing that space, the ant-line of students heading for hamburgers and coffee was detained, half-unwilling ... Munching students digested ideas rawer and more exciting than those they were fed in the lecture halls.' Anyone could get up and test their rhetorical skills on this unofficial political stage. Student Jack Thompson, before he found fame as an actor, was one such speaker who assayed 'our location on the bottom of a pond being pissed on by capital.' The Forum at UQ was a sober, politicised space where minority positions could be intellectually appraised. It was a key innovation in campus life that facilitated the Brisbane radicalisation.

The Brisbane Left's orientation towards political meetings on university grounds, and social gatherings *with a twist of politics*, was a logical path for subversive expression in this troubled city. Heavy legal restrictions on street protest made it difficult to do in Brisbane what regularly took place in other cities. The anti-democratic laws had been introduced by the Labor Government in an earlier era to stifle their rivals on the left, the Communists. Now they were being found quite useful by Queensland's right-wing coalition government who were in the middle of an unbroken hold on power that extended from 1957 to 1989.

For the Left, a novel solution to the problem of not being able to freely march on the streets emerged from Humphrey McQueen's job as a bartender at The Jubilee Hotel the previous summer. In 1966, he conceived of an anti-war demonstration with a starting point at his former workplace. He knew the pub, close to the CBD, featured a large car park, something not uncommon in an era when drink driving was more socially acceptable. Anti-war protesters could meet in the pub's car park, march through the city, and finish at ANZAC square. Radical activist and co-founder of radio station Triple Zed, Jim Beatson, took inspiration from this spirit of activist innovation:

> Humphrey was imaginative. He said it was ridiculous we were forever getting arrested in large numbers by police. He got a group of people – there had to be one leader for every five people, so five people could sit in a car. So he gave probably about 50 drivers a little slip of paper, and it just said 'meet at', and it was actually a pub in The Valley. So all the cars arrived there, all at the same time. All parked their cars, all leapt out of the car, and we marched on the road. And we did it so quickly that it was all done and dusted before the police even arrived.

In fact, when police arrived they refused to believe the march had even taken place. McQueen reflected on this event, critically:

> I learnt an important political lesson out of that. While a degree of organisational secrecy can be important, what is really important is mass work. No one knew it had happened! We'd put all this effort into organising something and it may as well not have ever taken place.

The action was, however, an early instance of trade unions and students collaborating – an important strategic goal for many in the movement. Ample parking was crucial for a protest action reliant on passenger vehicles, but a pub was also chosen in part because it was well known to both demographics they were hoping would participate. Culturally, both workers *and* students liked a drink.

Little encouragement was needed for young scholars to put down the books and head to the pub. Although the drinking age was 21 in Queensland there was an active drinking culture amongst university students. Academic and campus radical Dan O'Neill reflected, 'it was sort of taken for granted that people drank a fair bit, y'know. I just remember endless parties with rock music in the background or Bob Dylan or whatever, and that was just sort of part of the movement.'

Student activist John Stanwell's impressions of the drinking culture of his youth include details that 'people drank beer out of long necks and drank flagon wine. If you wanted to get shit faced you'd drink Brandivino. Double fortified, like a port with extra brandy in it. It was a high octane student drink.'

Student activist Anne Richards, financially struggling as she had been kicked out of home due to her political activism, became equipped with a knowledge of the budget options: 'You could get a glass flagon of wine for $2 or something. It was really bad, shitty wine.' Finances were a consideration for many students in the expanded post-war higher education boom. 'If I bought one drink, I could make it last all night, particularly a brandy', affirmed Richards.

Tastes were also evolving. McQueen grimaces at the memory of left political gatherings where older comrades would drink room temperature sauternes in the tropical heat. In the sixties, student activist Margaret Bailey drank Bundaberg rum, ice and lemon. Dan O'Neill remembers 'drinking endless rum and cokes all through that period.' By 1974, an edition of student union newspaper *Semper Floreat* featured a cover promoting four topics: US Bases, Premier Joh Bjelke-Petersen, Japanese Students and, simply, 'wine'. The inclusion of the latter was a reflection of young people embracing new drinking trends, and a sentiment of accepting the culture of immigrants.

In John Stanwell's view UQ, and in particular its student union, played a larger role than any other Australian university in the broader cultural life of its host city. Like at other universities, the UQ Student Union hosted a concert venue and also ran a student newspaper. Less commonly, it also operated an avant-garde cinema, an exploratory live-theatre venue, an art space and a radio station, making it an integrated part of Brisbane intellectual life. There were ample opportunities for drinking adjacent to many of these cultural activities. But it could also be posited that they provided entertainment for those that did not want to engage in drinking culture.

John Stanwell (Daryl Jones)

Professorial room protest, including Dan O'Neill, Brian Laver and Graham Jones, 1969 (University of Queensland Archive, Radical Times Archive)

There *was* a formal space for drinking on campus. Dan O'Neill, as a member of staff, was granted access (which he rarely used). However, the restrictions were not rigidly enforced: 'There was a University of Queensland Club or something of that nature where you could get a beer, and there was a staff club that students weren't supposed to go to but students *did* go to, and you could get grog there.' The presence of alcohol was integrated throughout university life in a way that seemed unremarkable, as it was so commonplace everywhere else. Students however were generally taking their drinking elsewhere on university grounds. John Stanwell contends that the worst drinking culture on campus was associated with the largely right-wing, engineering students. Similarly, the 'Law Society Smoko' was an 'appalling piss-up, no redeeming features, just alcohol. They made money to put on more piss ups.' Events such as these would occur on campus in hired spaces.

The Red Room, underneath the refectory student complex, was one such space that was repurposed for the mixed use of students. It was described as an empty concrete shell with a table and few chairs, 'functional for non-fussy students.' It was also not monitored, which was useful in various ways. Students could do anything in there from screen printing posters for protests to social drinking. As Richards attests, 'If you had an afternoon's drinking session after a demo, you'd end up in the Red Room' – invariably sharing bad wine.

In Brisbane, a curious phenomena was that many key figures in the student movement were culturally minded, but did not drink heavily, if at all. Jim Beatson claims:

> Most of the leaders of the radical movement at UQ were non-smokers, non-drinkers and saw their devotion to the radical movement as more important. But of course that all changed by 1970. Everybody is drinking and smoking. Probably the big push came after the 1967 demo.

This iconic protest – The Big March – marked the explosive radicalisation of the movement, which we will come to shortly. For Beatson, a non-drinker, it was not difficult to recognise and accept that alcohol was a means that his collaborators in the left used to relax:

> People went from having a beer or two on Friday night, or 4 pm. By the early 1970s people were in pretty large numbers at The RE [Royal Exchange]. But I think it was more socialising and trying to get a fuck, was what was going on. A lot of sexism. There was a huge amount of sexual liberation going on – so called. And really people went from either being indifferent to drink, or a small social drinker, to taking on marijuana and LSD – with a vengeance.

Advertisement for The Royal Exchange Hotel in student magazine *Time Off*, February 1979 (University of Queensland Student Union)

As an underlying presence in the radical movement, as throughout broader society, drinking was rarely commented on. There were a number of socially oriented events that were linked with a subversive purpose, typically for fundraising or the discussion of an activist project. One novel phenomena was 'False Registration Form Parties', or more jovially expressed, a 'Fill Out A Falsie' party. John Stanwell hosted a number of these events at his home:

> You could go to the post office and pick up a stack of forms. We'd basically invite people to come round in the afternoon mostly, occasionally at night, and people would bring a bit of booze, and it would be a sort of quiet party. And we'd get phone books from other cities, and we'd basically fill out hundreds of false national service registration forms, at each of the two intakes a year. I think we did it three times, and then it became impossible to get numbers of forms. It was fun – and it was destructive.

All strategies that might slow down the bureaucratic war machine were considered fair game. Anne Richards also participated in this low-key act of subversion, turning up to Stanwell's house on Ascot Terrace with 'plonk, pens and a phonebook.' She later acclaimed the events as 'stress release, protest and party all in one!'

For the young men that were called up by the military, and then elected to become draft resisters, The RE was a place to find support, both material and emotional. Its association with the left was also known to the authorities. One particular occasion when Special Branch entered the beer garden of The RE in search of draft resisters is told evocatively in the Anne Richards memoir *A Book of Doors*:

> The couple of activists on the run were quickly shuffled to the back, into the darkest corners of the garden. It was intuitive, big yawns went with large coats lifting arms up to cover the gaps in the crowd, hiding shifting shadows along the side trellis, down the pub's hallway, out over the kegs, low creeping behind the cars, quick knee lift. Up over the high wooded fence onto the littered banks beside the railway tracks. Sensing that the search was useless, the plain-clothed cops were checking IDs and ages, gruffly dismissing statements of citizen's rights and chucking out the too young. The legal drinking age was 21 and half the pub was underage. Gin miraculously became lemon and ice, an inverted Jesus miracle. Older guys sat happily in front of four glasses of beer as the crowd thinned. We sat back hoping the smoke laden air didn't lead to body searches.

Draft resister Steve Gray, interviewed by author and journalist Andrew Stafford, claimed that 'during my time as a draft resister, there was enormous support, in unexpected places ... One afternoon I was in The RE and they said "There were federal police asking questions about you".' Gray had been living at The RE, but the punters at the bar didn't snitch. The pub had a reputation more broadly as a place where anyone in need could potentially connect themselves up with support. Stanwell asserts, 'If you were at uni you could just lob into The RE and you'd have a bed for the night. If you were broke, you'd have enough money to get by. It was a really good scene then.' The hat was passed around the pub to raise money to bail people out, or for activities supporting the First Nations community. Richards agrees, it was 'a normal

Royal Exchange Hotel beer garden (Radical Times Archive)

part of the process. Everyone supported each other, it was good.'

Anne Richards also recalled, 'The RE was the main pub for the radicals...The Regatta was more for the engineering and right-wing students. But occasionally we'd dare to break into the confines of the Regatta if we wanted to have a more intense dialogue with some nasties.' The origins of this reactionary association was the Great Public Schools regatta. After the end of the elite rowing competition people would drink in the grand old pub, with its laced verandahs. When Richards was kicked out of home for her political activity, she chose to not steal from The RE but from the bottle shop at the Regatta Hotel.

The RE was half a kilometre away from The Regatta, also in Toowong, but closer to the university at St Lucia. Significantly for the students, as Anne Richards claims, 'The RE let you drink no matter age you were.' She describes the social and political atmosphere of The RE in her memoir:

> Picking up the pamphlets announcing the next demo, as well as gossip about the next street performance, party or farm happening, we cast a collective vote to go to all of it. We moved through the crowd, then settled around a couple of jugs of beer, relaxing in the buzz, a bit buzzed out already. Sitting in the mellow night, I watched the crowd, catching the flair of a skirt, the jangle of bells on scarves or ankles.

The pub was not a location for formal political meetings but, as the gathering point for left-wing students, it inevitably became the site of political discussion (typically of varying quality). Richards recounts a drinker holding court in the beer garden, expounding:

> A philosophy of the body's fluid functions as the golden drop was downed, circulating messages of encouragement through its vast internal systems. It was an eloquent exposition of the Australian collective conscience, a tribute to the amber god.

For all the political contributions social drinking culture offered, it also caused some to get waylaid, quite literally. In considering the iconic street march that took place on 9 September 1967, Brian Laver assessed, 'I think a couple of hundred left at the Regatta, they couldn't take the distance.' This thirst could potentially have been a life altering decision as what is now referred to as The Big March is commonly considered *the* transformative event of the Brisbane radicalisation. Dan O'Neill surmised, 'After that big march, all bets were off. There was the opportunity to talk about any issue.'

By the end of 1966 the student left had become committed to protesting for civil liberties as a natural outgrowth of the anti-war movement. With the Traffic Act being used to suppress marches, defiance of it, and heavy police responses, were hardening experiences

Regatta Hotel, 1967 (Alexander Henry Love, State Library of Queensland)

Royal Exchange Hotel (Radical Times Archive)

for many young activists. There was a new confidence to assert politics that broke from what was previously considered acceptable. The desire to highlight personal freedoms and new ways of living was integrated into political events. Dan O'Neill, in an oral history with activist Di Zetlin for the State Library of Queensland, appraised:

> A period that went on for about three years, in which you had this feeling that people had been suddenly revealed to one another in a fresh way. As if a hard skin had been taken off you and you felt that the world could be a wonderful place in which you could learn about what it was to live more openly, and more communally.

Issues such as censorship and laws around drugs and alcohol were raised with provocative displays at the gatherings on campus – as noted, a much more secure and protected space than anywhere else in the state. On 16 July 1969, an *Erotica* happening took place on campus, billed as an attempt to scandalise and provoke conservative society. There were 'obscene' plays, and the demonstrative sale of alcohol to all students *except* those over 21. There was public pot smoking and the conservative Vice Chancellor Hartley Teakle was provocatively handed 'a marijuana cigarette' (although sadly for him it did not actually contain the substance).

There was a strong social component to Brisbane's student radicalisation, but it also produced a high standard of theoretical

Triple Zed journalist Barry Weston at the Royal Exchange Hotel beer garden, 1976 (Radical Times Archive)

Dan O'Neill (foreground) and Cam Cunningham, 1969 (University of Queensland Archive, Fryer Library)

contributions. A legacy of the particular New Left expression at UQ was the publication of *Up The Right Channels*. This was a unique effort at laying down theories of education under capitalism, a '230 foolscap page printed book with a hideous but unmistakable purple cover.' The project was coordinated by an editorial collective, and involved over 100 people in its development, exploring ways to reform the University to make it an institution of critical thinking rather than a 'tool of industry and commerce.' Dan O'Neill lived close to campus at 22 Schonell Drive, St Lucia and hosted many small gatherings and a number of parties over the period of 1969-70. These were a useful, if not formally strategised, part of bringing people together on a challenging collective project.

O'Neill was a working academic, and one of the most prominent figures in radical politics, but remarkably at one stage also committed time to tutoring a high school student. This teenager was Margaret Bailey, who had been expelled from the entire school system in Queensland due to her activism. In the battle over standards and morality in this era, Bailey had objected to the discipline meted out to a fellow student for wearing a miniskirt. Already known for distributing subversive Students In Dissent literature on school grounds, Bailey's insubordination was made an example of. She subsequently made headlines around the country after chaining herself to the government education building, an echo of Bognor and Thornton's protest at The Regatta Hotel a few years earlier. Described

Brian Laver, with sign, demonstrating at a May Day march, 1971 (Grahame Garner, Fryer Library)

as a 'star' of the Brisbane radical scene, and in O'Neill's words 'a symbol of the movement', this elevated profile made her a target for character assassination. Bailey describes a traumatic incident:

> I went to a party one night – there was going to be a whole lot of young high school students. Students In Dissent were having a party and somebody offered me a drink, and I didn't want it because I thought I really needed to keep my wits about me at the moment. And I'd had a warning from George Negus. He used to be a teacher in Brisbane before he became a journalist. George was very sympathetic. He warned me that they might try and do something to discredit me.
>
> At this party I went to, I dunno, I just thought it was some deadshit bloke, he was trying to force me to have this drink. It was vodka that I didn't drink anyway. He was insisting that I have it. My sister took it from him and she drank it, and all of a sudden she was freaking out. There was something in the drink. About five minutes after she took that drink, we were calming her down, and the cops started to arrive. And that was really nasty. We got her home to her flat. We thought the cops had turned up to the party for some reason, but when I got to her flat as soon as we got her inside and calmed down, all of a sudden the flat was just full of coppers, and I mean full of coppers.
>
> She went ballistic because she saw coppers and she thought they were trying to hurt me, so she physically attacked them. And they physically restrained her. They called an ambulance because she was kind of freaking out from the drugs, and freaking out from the behaviour, and they took her to the hospital. And they took me to the watch house. On the way to the watch house a copper said to me, 'You know your sister is going to die and it's going to be your fault. You have involved your sister in this disreputable behaviour, and she may not pull through.'
>
> It took me about two minutes to realise it, but they'd pulled all the political posters off the wall of my sister's flat and put them up in this copper's office that they'd held me in. That was a particularly nasty incident. And George thought that was deliberate.

Bailey was not to be intimidated and continued with her political activity. This included touring building sites with the support of Aboriginal unionist Bob Anderson from the Building Workers Industrial Union (BWIU) to discuss the political persecution.

There were a number of similar examples of links being made between workers and students. Students participated in a picket of postal workers, a tram workers strike, and the epochal 1969 general strike against the anti-union penal powers. Trades Hall, under the leadership of Communist Alex McDonald, had hired student activist Brian Laver as a research officer and agreed to make the building available for what their new hire described as a 'revolutionary speakeasy...but without the alcohol.' This became the pioneering multi-media political and cultural youth venue, FOCO [further discussed elsewhere in this book].

The period of tentative collaboration between the trade union bureaucracy and radical students came to an end after events at the 1969 May Day rally. Labor leader Gough Whitlam was accosted by students bearing radical flags, a source of embarrassment for conservative officials. The left-wing of the union movement, however, delighted in the militancy of the students, and invited them to 'The Wharfies Club'. Anne Richards recalls:

> We went down to this wonderful bar down on the wharf, which had a beautiful big window, and old time dancing, and all the wharfies would dance with their wives to this music. We had an absolutely fantastic afternoon there. Through that we met some of them and were invited to their homes. It was good like that. They were much more social and accepting of people

being disruptive, and being young and stupid as we were. So there were some lovely friendships that came out of that one.'

John Stanwell was another student who went to the Wharfies Club after the May Day events: 'The lefties would go over to the Communists or the Wharfies Club, and student troublemakers were welcome at both, and we'd go over there and sing the Red Flag, and drink lots of grog, tell tall tales.'

The radicalisation in Brisbane was particularly noteworthy for its interplay of ideological formations, pulling in strands from liberalism, anarchism and Marxism. Historian Judy McVey argues the radicalism took a shift from the 'liberal humanist moralism of the American civil rights movement' to revolutionary Marxism. Gramscian ideas about building a counter-hegemony in a worker-student alliance became a goal that different forces could temporarily unite around. However, as the beliefs of the young radicals matured and hardened, it became clear that political sensibilities were pulling in different directions. Leading activist Mitch Thompson explains some of their strategy: 'There were subcultural spaces set up to attract people. And then there were spaces that were radicalised, such as the gathering areas at the university.' The two approaches were intended to synthesise, but this soon fell out of favour. Thompson acknowledges, 'SDA (Society for Democratic Action) parties involved a lot of alcohol (mainly beer) and drugs.' It was not the imbibing that was the problem however, it was the blurring of politics and partying together that was considered problematic. SDA had once gone so far as to contemplate setting up a late night cafe, but there was now a vocal opposition raising objections around social and cultural approaches to building the left. Alan Anderson, a founder of FOCO from the Communist Party, wrote in a retrospective article in *Tribune* how, 'The student left developed a theory that FOCO was not aiding the revolutionary movement ... suggest[ing] it was channelling potential revolutionary people into non-revolutionary activity.' Criticisms of FOCO had already emerged, but the most reviled event for those who held this perspective was one that occurred on campus: Peoples Park.

The People's Park concept attempted to bring more bohemian, culturally inclined 'hippies' together with radicalised students. It was seen as an 'experiment in a new culture, a new way of living', a 'festival of life in contrast to the living death in the classroom' as well as the bloody events occurring in Indochina, South Africa and the United States. A leaflet advertising the event stated 'a people's flea market ... will be operating and there will be a people's coffee, music and relaxation centre running non-stop.' Unofficially, there was also the presence of alcohol, Richards confirms.

In a retrospective essay in *Semper Floreat* in 1970, the People's Park was denounced as a 'sick kind of political sideshow', which 'only served to disturb those serious-minded ... groups who did hope to hold valuable discussions on the Moratorium issues.' The most biting charge was that the event resembled 'a continuation of the Commem program.' Commem was the university's sanctioned week of rowdy student activity, often involving pranks with a light overtone of mocking conservative society. By the early sixties people had tired of it, considering it middle class and pretentious. Even amongst countercultural activists, People's Park, and a second iteration held in late 1970, was identified as coinciding with an 'anti-political' turn in the movement towards a more lifestylist direction.

As the radical wave dissipated, students moved onto spaces that were not neatly categorised as left or right. Harnessing energies to rebuild momentum became a growing concern. The forces who were less inclined towards building a revolutionary organisation were generally attracted to arts and media activities, which were to varying degrees political and anti-system. Nimbin, and its place in radical lifestylism, emerged in this period. The role of the Australian Union of Students in organising the Aquarius Festival that established the modern permutation of Nimbin, changing the demographics and culture of parts of Northern NSW, is sometimes overlooked. The event included 'de-schooling, a learning exchange', as a consciously different model to 'the Leninist party approach'. Whilst there were undoubtedly stereotypical hippy activities, and these caught the eyes of the media, there was also a continuation of a form of lifestylism that most students were used to and comfortable with: drinking. John Stanwell reveals, 'there was plenty of alcohol at Nimbin.' Anne Richards drank at The Freemasons Hotel on the town's main drag and recalls it as a fond meeting point for different worlds: 'We all drank with the locals and it was great fun.' In Jon Piccini's 'Building Their Own Scene To Do Their Own Thing' he documents that the countercultural activists in the HARPO group ended up spending a lot of time in this pub.

An episode of the ABC's youth television show *GTK* that aired on 22 May 1973, reported on the Aquarius Festival and included a segment about The Freemasons Hotel, with the reporter questioning locals on their feelings towards the young students who had made a new home out of their town. One local was enthusiastic and responded: 'Really great. Beautiful people', and with a twinkle in his eye added, 'I'm people – I'm one of the beautiful people too.' Another local drinker beamed, 'The kids up here, we'd like to keep them, because they're so nice.' Some did stay, and created communes and a counter-cultural

Aquarius Festival attendees outside the Freemason Hotel in Nimbin, 1973 (Harry Watson Smith)

ethos that continues in small pockets today, but not without first working through friction with some of the less welcoming locals. Others were happy to drive back to Brisbane and return to anti-capitalist politics. However most were taking a journey towards leaving activism behind them and integrating back into mainstream society. The rise of countercultural lifestylism as exemplified by the Aquarius Festival, and the collapse of street protest, is recognised widely as representing something of an end for a wave of student radicalisation.

The election of the Whitlam ALP Government, and the ending of conscription among other significant reforms, had diffused youthful radical energies. The three national Moratorium marches held in 1970 and 1971 had been some of the last big events in this period of radicalisation, with chants that included 'One two three four / We don't want your fucking war!' and the more whimsical 'Draft Beer, Not Boys'. In popular memory, it is these anti-war events that define the long sixties. However, it is often overlooked that Brisbane in some ways led Australia with the radicalisation that kicked off in 1967. And as we've surveyed, this event had its own precursors that built up the activists who seized upon that opportunity.

The array of activities carried out during this radical period has fundamentally shaped Brisbane to this day. It is also apparent that organisational tactics can be fruitful – or decaying – depending on how they fit in with the upturn or downturn in political struggle. This is perhaps epitomised by a story UQ student activist and historian Ian Curr tells of a party on campus held after the election of Whitlam. Ostensibly it was to celebrate the achievements of anti-war campaigners and what this might mean for Vietnam's National Liberation Front and communism going forward. No one turned up.

People would, however, turn up once more to challenge the right-wing rule in Queensland. In large numbers they hit the streets over civil liberties in the late 70s, in something of a unique Indian summer of rebellion that shone only on Brisbane's radical movement. Had all this social glue played a part in the endurance of a low-bubbling activist-sensibility in the city, just waiting for another moment, or was it simply that Joh's increasingly odious rule prompted a quite separate and distinct fightback? Whichever the case, in 1977, and for several years after, students would again be a key force in taking on the conservative government. And the left would flourish both politically and culturally.

No doubt with quantities of Bundaberg and XXXX drunk along the way, and hopefully less room-temperature sauternes.

Featured in the Queensland University Revue *Life wasn't meant to be...*, 1977 (Bruce Dickson and Max Hughes, Radical Times Archive)

CHAPTER 36
COLOUR BAR – THE FREEDOM RIDE AND THE WALGETT RSL
Lisa Milner

Jenny Bush performs at Paddington Town Hall at a Student Action for Aborigines event, 10 February 1965 (*Tribune*/Search Foundation, State Library of NSW)

Whilst many Aboriginal Australians have served in wars, beginning from 1914, the systemic and blatant marginalisation that was a feature of Australia showed its ugly face in the ex-service organisations that were supposed to support these Australians. At the end of World War One, the main organisation was the Returned Sailors and Soldiers Imperial League of Australia, whose name was changed in 1965 to the Returned Services League of Australia (RSL); and whilst it did have some Aboriginal members, there are many stories of exclusion.

After the end of World War Two, when that organisation became licensed for the service of alcohol, things got much worse. Whilst they were tolerated in many RSL clubs on Anzac Day, Aboriginal people were denied entry on every other day of the year, almost always were not allowed membership of their local RSL club, and were refused service of alcohol there.

There was no uniform pattern of this type of discrimination. Reg Saunders, who was an Aboriginal veteran of World War Two and the Korean War, had been elected President of the St Marys RSL in 1962. But that was in Sydney, where more enlightened values were in evidence. Out in rural and regional areas, life was very different. The horrendous racism of country RSL clubs affected Aboriginal people on top of the blatant prejudice in so many other parts of their lives – with many town facilities such as pubs, schools, theatres, and swimming pools being closed to them. In NSW this was particularly prevalent in the north and western areas.

In Walgett, for instance, the RSL simply banned Aboriginal people from being members. There was no logical reason why they shouldn't have been. In 1964 a NSW Labor Council investigation into the treatment of Aboriginal people at Walgett found that RSL officials denied that this was racial discrimination and said that they were only following past practices.

The following year, action came to the Walgett RSL Club. A landmark civil rights protest adopted from the American Freedom Rides of 1961 and adapted to the Australian situation was the 1965 Student Action for Aborigines Survey and Demonstration Bus Tour, or, as it became known, the Freedom Ride. Undertaken by a group of around 30 students, mainly from the University of Sydney, the aim of the ride was non-violent direct action in a dozen NSW towns where racial discrimination was evident. Amongst the group were Charles Perkins, Anne Curthoys, Bill Ford, Darce Cassidy and Aiden Foy.

In the towns, including Moree, Bowraville, Lismore and Walgett, the students talked with local Aboriginal people, surveyed their living conditions, and challenged segregated facilities in a number of ways. Like many towns in rural NSW in those years, segregation was practiced in Walgett – at the pub, the café, the school, the swimming pool, and even the graveyard. Walgett was a particularly horrendous place for Aboriginal people to try to attain civil rights. Aboriginal women could not try on dresses at the Walgett frock shop; its proprietor believed that white women would not touch any clothing they had worn. The cinema was segregated, and Aboriginal patrons had to sit downstairs. Considered by some to be the most significant act in Aboriginal-European relations in the twentieth century, the Freedom Ride 'marked the beginning of substantial European awareness of the problems of Aboriginal people.'

Whilst the RSL had allowed local Aboriginal men in their audiences when they came back from World War Two, for one day, the next day all were banned for good. This practice was unchanged for decades. When the Freedom Riders arrived at Walgett, they found out from talks with the RSL Manager and vice-president that Aboriginal men, ex-servicemen, were not allowed to become members. They decided to picket the RSL. In an interview, Charles Perkins said:

> Well as everybody knows in Walgett and all the Aboriginal people do know, and I think most people throughout New South Wales know, the Walgett RSL does discriminate against Aboriginal people on the basis of colour alone, that's the criteria used, and we just want to show them we object to this on principle, we don't think this is a good thing, and we're doing it in a very passive way.

Charles Perkins interviewing community members near Walgett, 1965 (*Tribune*/Search Foundation, State Library of NSW)

Protesters painting placards for the protest at the Walgett RSL, 1965 (*Tribune*/Search Foundation, State Library of NSW)

One of the Freedom Riders, Ann Curthoys, wrote in her diary:

> About 12.00 we began to demonstrate outside the RSL. We just stood in a long line outside the RSL holding placards like 'Acceptance Not Segregation', 'End Colour Bar', 'Bullets did not Discriminate', 'Walgett – Australia's Disgrace', 'Why Whites Only', 'Educate the Whites', and so on.

Another banner read, 'Good enough for Tobruk – why not Walgett RSL?'

The students soon attracted a small crowd, both white and Aboriginal locals, that eventually grew to about 400 people, coming out in the hot February weather. It was the first time anyone in Walgett had seen a protest with banners. Curthoys wrote, 'the speeches turned into a public street debate… Darce recorded one man saying: "I reckon if I'm good enough to fight for the country here, save other people's lives, why shouldn't I walk in there?"' Freedom Rider Aiden Foy remembered:

> I think the locals were just absolutely shocked. They were stunned. There was no opposition really. There wasn't the sort of scene that occurred later. After we'd been there for a little while, the employees of the RSL came out and offered us soft drinks, which of course we all refused to take. There were some speeches made. Charlie made a speech, I'm sure Harty Hall made a speech and George Rose made a speech, I'm fairly sure, just talking about the segregation of the Club.

Some of the townspeople just looked on, while others began arguing with the students. Curthoys recalls that 'the levels of hostility [were] high.' Cassidy remembers that one of the locals jeered at the protestors, 'Look at 'em. The brains of Australia. You could buy 'em down the Sydney market at two bob a head.'

The *Tribune* wrote that 'in the beginning, the white people in the crowd were laughing, but they then joined in a long mass discussion on discrimination, with many Aborigines also taking part. Many people in the crowd seemed concerned that Walgett might become known as a racist town.' Perkins said:

> All the members of the RSL had to pass right past us and they read the banners. They either laughed at us or spat at us or on the banners. Some of them got banners and tore them up. Some of the local smarties wanted to bash a few of us up. They said, "You're stirring up trouble. The dirty niggers don't deserve any better and they are happy how they are."

The students picketed the RSL until almost 7 pm. After protests from the leader of the Anglican church where they had planned to stay, they left town late that night, to cheers from local well-wishers; Perkins shouted, 'Give our regards to the RSL.' But the hostility of white racist locals spilled out of the town centre, and a mob of them followed the bus. About three miles out of town, they attacked. Bill Ford, who was driving the bus, said:

> Three times this Dodge truck tried to run us off the road. The third time I swerved, I had to run over the bank, otherwise collide severely with the truck. As it is, he slightly damaged us, the bus rolled terrifically as we went over the bank.

Cassidy remembered that:

> Food and suitcases were thrown all over the bus. When the bus came to rest, we could see that we were surrounded, four or five sets of headlights pointing at the bus from all directions. It seemed that we were trapped, alone with four or five carloads of hoodlums on a country road. But there were thirty of us on the bus and it looked like the numbers were just about even.

The students walked back to Walgett to report the attack to police. This was the event that catapulted the Walgett protest to national media attention, and it was front-page news for a couple of weeks. Charles Perkins said that 'the incident outside the RSL club, that was the most dramatic part of everything. A lot of things fell in place after that. We knew what we had to do. It set the pattern, the template.'

One young Aboriginal man watching on at the RSL club that day, Bob Morgan, knew things 'weren't right' in Walgett, but he found it hard to put into words. Listening to Perkins and the other students, though, made a deep impression on him; 'I'll never forget how he made me feel'. Morgan soon left Walgett for a brighter future, and is now well known internationally as a highly respected and acknowledged Aboriginal educator and researcher.

Things change slowly in rural Australia; it was not until 1971 that any Aboriginal people were admitted as members of the Walgett RSL. This was one outcome of national pressure generally, as well as from individuals such as Reg Saunders, who was now acting as the liaison officer for the newly formed Council for Aboriginal Affairs.

Other regional RSL clubs were slower to change, however. In 1974 when they were law students, John Austin and Michael Dodson took a fact-finding trip to a number of NSW regional towns. At Brewarrina, they found that:

> The people said that there were no black members of the local RSL, this was generally the norm for all towns visited. Racism in the Brewarrina RSL was so blatant that the local employment officer who was married to a Murri was refused membership even though he had been a member of the armed forces. This is another instance where there ought to be a legal remedy available, because country RSLs exist as 'dens of racism'.

And as recently as 1991, Aboriginal filmmaker and actor Essie Coffey was denied membership of that club. It seems that the 'dens of racism' are slow to change.

Students outside the Walgett RSL, 15th February 1965 (Pat Healy)

CHAPTER 37
BALMAIN AND THE POLITICS OF DRAUGHT
Terry Irving

The Forth and Clyde Hotel, 1970 (Noel Butlin Archives Centre, Australian National University)

The Dry Dock Hotel, 1970 (Noel Butlin Archives Centre, Australian National University)

In the 1960s and 70s I watched two drinking cultures slide past each other in the pubs of Sydney's Balmain. Heading out to the western suburbs was Balmain's proletarian drinking culture, the product of a hundred years of working class industrial and political life; coming in was the culture of the 'political drinkers', as Frank Moorhouse called them, the young bohemian radicals who were the trend-setters of a new class of white-collar, highly-educated workers, workers. Arriving in the mid-sixties I was one of the 'political drinkers', although coming from a communist family I was more radical than bohemian.

The Balmain I discovered while walking its crooked streets confirmed my radicalism: an imposing 'working men's institute' in the main street where local union branches met; the national headquarters of the Ship Painters and Dockers union in a side street; a huge co-operative store – no longer trading, alas; a local community hospital with strong trade union representation on its board; and a plaque commemorating the foundation of the Labor Party at the back of a pub called the Unity Hall. And I discovered the pubs: small, intimate, a coal fire in the grate in winter; no pokies, no beer gardens. They seemed to be on every corner. In fact, historians have documented the existence of 55 pubs on the Balmain/Rozelle peninsular. Some of them didn't last long, but in 1970 there were 28 that I might have visited. I can claim to have had a drink in ten of them over the 17 years I lived in Balmain, but most consistently I drank at the Forth and Clyde.

The Forth and Clyde is now on the State Heritage Inventory because of its 'historic, aesthetic and social significance.' From the outside it's handsome: a two-storey sandstone building, on a corner, with a long return verandah on the second level sheltering the pavements below. On sunny afternoons we drank on the pavement; in the evenings we packed the only bar, a large square room. There were few stools or benches, so most drinkers spread around the four-sided bar. Even with the fire lit in winter, in truth it was a cheerless, spartan space, and its urinal was repulsive, but as newcomers to the suburb we happily embraced it as our first 'local'. The publican, Tom Martin and his wife Patti, welcomed us, and before long we were invited to stay after closing time, warily watching the licensing police drinking with Tom on the opposite side of the bar.

The pub's historic significance was due to its address, on a corner at the end of Mort Street opposite Mort's Dock and Engineering Works. The first dry dock in Australia, Mort's Dock opened in 1855. The Forth and Clyde served its first patrons two years later. When the dock closed in 1958, the pub was in trouble but the arrival of 'political drinkers' from the new working class kept its doors open for a few more years. We were a mixed bunch: artists, academics, students, businessmen with unconventional hankerings, blow-ins from interstate (Phillip Richardson – now dead from Covid – flew down from Brisbane university every few weeks) and assorted riff-raff. We rubbed shoulders with a few polite bikies, some tolerant locals, and the SP bookie. As we drank, we looked across the road at the derelict buildings of the dock secured behind cyclone wire fencing. From old-timers in the pub, we learnt of its importance in Balmain's working-class politics.

Balmain's history of militancy was built by general labourers as well as skilled tradesmen, for the engineering shops needed ironworkers and the docks needed labourers to dock, chip and paint the ships. The NSW ironworkers formed a union in the 1860s, but it was Balmain parochialism that led to the colony's first union of dockworkers, the Balmain Labourers Union in the 1880s. For the first 30 years the union met in various pubs, and then in the Workingmen's Institute, where it played a major role in setting up a Balmain Trades and Labour Council. In time the Balmain Labourers Union became the Ship Painters and Dockers Union whose members took the decision to form the Balmain Labor Electoral League in 1891. Later, syndicalists, communists and Trotskyists would also find recruits in its ranks.

By the Second World War, the shipbuilding industry in Balmain and nearby Cockatoo Island was Australia's largest, employing 8000 metal workers. The work was dangerous, the hours long (average weekly hours worked in the boiler shop at Mort's were 60), and the labourers' meanly housed, as landlords had provided the cheapest possible dwellings

Caricature of Nick Origlass, 1945 *(Smith's Weekly)*

to satisfy the employers' demands for a locally residing workforce. According to Hall Greenland, 'Balmain was classic Marxist proletarian country.'

The strength of parochial loyalty in Balmain's working-class politics was again in evidence during the Second World War. From 1942, the Communist Party leadership in the Federated Ironworkers Union was vigorously supporting the speed-up measures of the employers and the state, a union policy arising as much from the Communists' desire to assist the Soviet Union – at this stage an ally in the anti-Fascist war – as from Australian patriotism. In Mort's Dock, the shop committees resisted the speed-up – and the Communist leaders of the union countered by interfering in the internal affairs of the branch. In 1945, led by Nick Origlass, a rank-and-file worker and Trotskyist, 3000 Mort's Dock ironworkers went out on strike against both the union and the employers. The strike, which lasted for six weeks, was a success, and it was the beginning of the end for the Communist leadership of the national union, brought down two years later by its authoritarian methods and blindness to workers' needs.

The extent of Origlass's understanding of workers' needs extended to what they drank. During the campaign to assert the right of Balmain's workers to run their own lives – at work and in the community – he and his supporters established the Balmain Workers Social Club, a place for organising and socialising. During the war beer was in short supply, so the club took up the issue. In its newsletter, Origlass wrote: 'Beer is a beverage that has established itself as a necessity for a majority of workers in the Australian climate ...'. But the beer dearth continued. After the war, an attempt was made by the peak body representing workers' clubs to persuade unions to brew their own beer, but the brewery they established at Brookvale failed after about five years because it was unable to provide the clubs with a regular supply.

After the war, individual Communists on the shopfloor at Mort's regained support, and I have some tangible proof of this. By the mid-sixties the security of the derelict buildings of the dock had been well and truly breached. At the Forth and Clyde several objects scavenged from the site were passed around, including a circular cast-iron plate. About 20 centimetres in diameter, with a ring on the back so that it could hang on a wall, decorated on its concave front with an elaborate coat of arms, it was clearly a presentation plate. Around the perimeter were words in German that I could not translate, except for a person's name, 'Karl Liebknecht'. I knew enough German history to know who he was. One of the founders of the Communist Party of Germany, Liebknecht was shot by the Freikorps in 1919. In full, the translated inscription reads: 'Presented by the state-owned heavy machinery factory, "Karl Liebknecht".' But how did it end up at Mort's Dock? I surmise that it was brought back by a member of a metal trades union delegation to Europe that had, under Communist Party pressure, visited East Germany. My later research revealed that the coat of arms was

'Karl Liebknecht' cast-iron presentation plate from Mort's Dock (Terry Irving)

that of Magdeburg, a town in Saxony where Liebknecht was born, and that there was indeed a heavy machinery factory named after him in the town. I also discovered that there were prominent Balmain locals in an East German Friendship Society. So, the plate was a gesture of friendship between workers divided by Cold War politics.

Soon after I arrived in Balmain, the President of the United States came to Sydney. In my circle of political drinkers, opposition to the war in Vietnam was the issue that defined our radicalism. We were organisationally unattached, although some of us had previous experience of revolutionary politics. Of course, we were alive to the currents of cultural rebellion among young people – we were 'folkies' and 'peaceniks' – but our sympathy for the resistance of the Vietnamese people and the defiance of Australia's draft resisters made us potential activists. The visit of Lyndon Baines Johnson on 22 October 1966 made the potential actual. At first the conversations in the Forth and Clyde expressed our amusement at the sycophantic behaviour of the organisers of the 'official' public welcome planned for Johnson as he drove through the city. Gradually, as we heard the rumours that the anti-war organisations would be on the streets to protest, we began to discuss how we might indicate our opposition. Where would we meet? Would we make signs? It was decided. On the day, in small groups of friends, we made our way into the city, booed and held up our signs as LBJ's 'bubble-top' car swept past, joining thousands of other protesters. The

Anti-war protesters disrupt US President Lyndon Baines Johnson's motorcade in Sydney, 1966 (*Tribune*/Search Foundation, State Library of NSW)

police waded into us. Next day the capitalist newspapers carried 'LBJ Souvenir' supplements, but it was the dramatic photographs of the 'ugly demonstrations' that caught the eye. In the *Sunday Mirror*'s souvenir, the caption below a full page photo of some protesters read: '"Stop the War" the banners implored – but it was almost as if the war had come to Oxford St., as rioters surged forward against police barricades waving banners and fighting and abusing police.' Momentarily, the Forth and Clyde had become an informal site of political mobilisation.

In 1972, the brewery that owned the Forth and Clyde transferred its licence to Chullora, a commercial and industrial area where no-one lived. In Balmain, the 'political drinkers' migrated to other pubs: the London, the Unity Hall, the Royal Oak, or the Dry Dock where Tom and Patti Martin took over as publicans. But the old style of bohemian classlessness was retreating. Friendships were fracturing while new faces appeared, looking to be assimilated. Pub life changed. Drinkers wore 'smart casual' on Saturdays; there was jazz at the Unity and there were steaks to barbeque at the Royal Oak. Gentrification was overtaking 'le ghetto Balmain'.

However, Balmain's parochial tradition of militancy kept on kicking. In the late fifties, Nick Origlass and his Trotskyist comrade Issy Wyner, an official of the Ship Painters and Dockers Union, stacked the local branch of the Labor party with left-wing unionists. At the same time the new middle class gentrifiers were becoming alarmed at State government plans to turn the suburb into Sydney's main site for container wharves and chemical tanks. To form an alliance between these apparently disparate groups, Origlass and Wyner proposed a political program that combined environmental politics with radical ideas about democracy. The middle class New Left theorists called it participatory democracy, but the idea of rank-and-file control had been a staple of radical working-class politics for a century. It was a brilliant and pioneering program, that foreshadowed the Green Bans. It was only possible because Origlass and Wyner had renounced 'substitutionist politics', the temptation often found in revolutionary organisations to demand that the masses march without question behind their banners. Balmain's left-wing workers and New Left professionals, from their respective bases in Balmain Labor and the Balmain Society, went on to conquer the Balmain ward in the sixties and then the entire municipality of Leichhardt for a new style of urban politics, including a radical model of council governance, the 'open council'. Representing the Balmain ward, Nick Origlass was mayor of Leichhardt in 1971-3 and again in 1987-88; Issy Wyner was mayor in 1989-90. By this time the NSW Greens had been formed, partly as a result of Nick and Issy's contribution to environmental urban politics.

The middle-classing of Balmain's pubs has also continued. Today, on my count, there are just 12 pubs left, most of them with beer gardens, some with 'hatted' restaurants. Wherever the 'political drinkers' of today are, they are not in Balmain.

Author Terry Irving, 1968 (Terry Irving Collection)

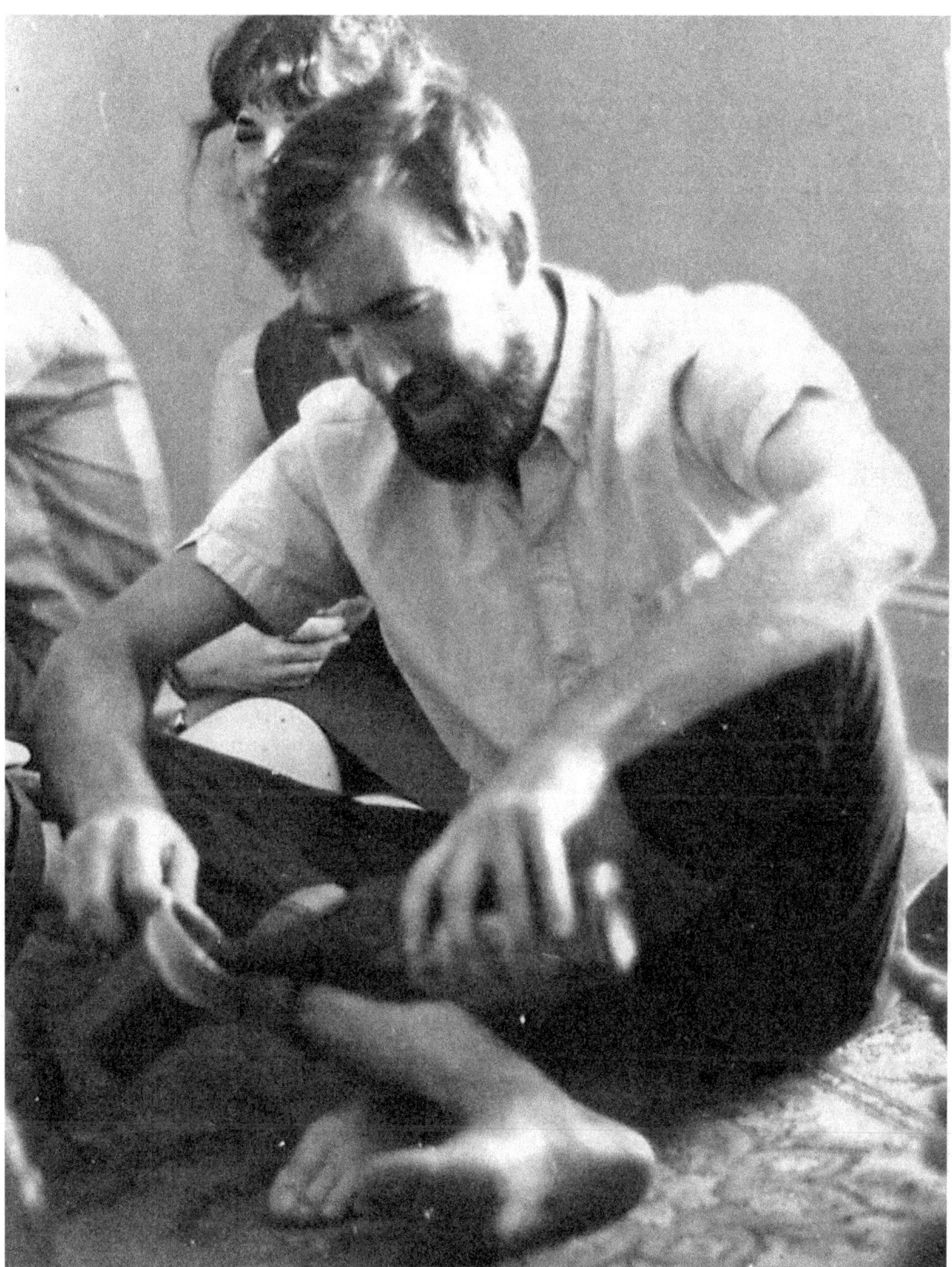
Author Terry Irving pours beer into a mug at the Sydney Free University, 1967 (Terry Irving Collection)

CHAPTER 38
JEAN YOUNG, KATH WILLIAMS AND THE FIGHT FOR EQUAL PAY
Iain McIntyre

Bar maid working at Scott's Hotel in Melbourne, 1940s
(National Library of Australia)

In April 1941 20 unionists at the Hotel Alexandra walked off the job after their employer J. Richardson refused to address a lack of facilities for women staff to rest, bathe and change. Waitresses, who were required to wear uniforms, had long been forced to change into them in a hallway outside a men's toilet. In demanding improvements, the workers carried out the first official hotel strike in Victoria.

After a fortnight the dispute escalated and the Liquor Trades Union (LTU) threatened to pull out the Alexandra's other 70 staff. Pressure was further ratcheted up after stink bombs were set off in the hotel's bars and dining room. The day after these sent patrons running, management relented and agreed to put in the necessary facilities. Subsequent refusals to re-employ strikers led to a boycott of a number of hotels, wine saloons, caterers, and bottle shops owned by the Richardson family.

Central to the campaign's success were the efforts of LTU organizer Jean Young, who was no stranger to militant or ground-breaking activity. According to an account of her life written by union historian Alleyn Best, she emigrated from Scotland in 1927 under a migrant scheme that required her to work for two years as a domestic servant. Following that she was employed at the Esplanade Hotel. Involvement in supporting the bitter timber workers strike of 1929 led to her being threatened with deportation.

Young subsequently joined the CPA and sold its *Working Woman* newspaper on the streets, outside factories, and by going door to door. As an activist within the Unemployed Workers

Movement's Womens Committee she spoke at numerous meetings and rallies during the 1930s. She also helped organise Melbourne's first International Women's Day rally in 1931 and worked as a paid CPA functionary for a time. Her connections with the party, combined with employment as a bar attendant in the Victoria Palace and Australia hotels, led her to join a rank and file reform team within the LTU. This union covered a number of fields related to hospitality work and alcohol production, and Young became its first elected female organiser in 1938.

Empowered by the union's newly elected left-wing leadership, Young played a key role in recruiting members and organising amongst long neglected restaurant, café and boarding house workers. In this she was assisted by other women unionists, including her former co-worker at the Australia Hotel, Lorrie Shore, and Susan McComb, who in 1937 became the first woman elected to the LTU's management committee. Employer resistance to the unionisation of canteens within department stores was broken and gains at the likes of Myer generalized to other eateries.

Such success enabled Young to overcome internal union resistance to her organising in pubs, which the leadership had previously not considered 'suitable places for a woman to enter.' Long running temperance activism had curtailed the number of women employed as bar staff in Victorian pubs, but some still remained. In *Barmaids: A History of Women's Work in Pubs* historian Diane Kirkby states that 'between 1902 and 1908 all the Australian states introduced legislation limiting or restricting employment, and by 1916 two states and New Zealand had succeeded in passing prohibitory laws.' Ranked among the latter, Victoria dictated in 1916 that only those women already working in the industry could continue to do

Rank and file LTU activist Lorrie Shore (United Workers Union)

LTU organiser Jean Young (United Workers Union)

so. This was not as strict as in South Australia, where women were banned altogether, but attrition saw numbers drop steadily over the following decades.

In addition to clearing obstacles to her own work, Young persuaded the union to reduce union fees for female employees in 1940, on the basis that they were paid roughly 40% less than men. She also convinced the LTU to adopt a 'militant and progressive policy for equal pay for the sexes.'

This was the context in which the 1941 Hotel Alexandra strike took place. Such effective militancy could lead to obstacles. Young's role in firstly recruiting workers at the hotel, and then organizing the strike, reportedly led the Victorian Minister for Labour to prevent her renomination to the state's Hotel and Restaurant Board.

The recruitment and conscription of men to fight in World War Two opened new employment opportunities for women to work in pubs, as well as to be paid equally. Faced with major labour shortages Licensed Victualler Associations (LVAs) in South Australia and Victoria lobbied governments to change the rules regarding female eligibility. The LTU agreed to support this but only if the LVAs also guaranteed to pay women the same as men. Its position was undoubtedly influenced by Young and other women's activism, but also reflected a desire to preserve male wage rates.

Western Australia was the only state at this time in which all bar attendants were paid equally. Seemingly progressive on the surface, its introduction in 1911 was guided by other motivations. Kirkby observes that the 'award

Bar attendants working at the Hotel London in Elizabeth Street, Melbourne, 1953 (Laurie Richards Studio, State Library of Victoria)

specifically stated that it was an undesirable occupation for women and that they had been granted equal pay in the hope they would be forced out of the industry.'

Despite this precedent it took decades, and the exigencies of war, to achieve equal pay elsewhere. Following some stalling, and a failed attempt to keep wages down via the arbitration courts, employers in Victoria and South Australia agreed to concede equal pay as well as shorter working hours. With wartime regulations giving the federal government the power to overrule state governments, SA opted not to challenge the lifting of the ban. It did succeed however in limiting the age of female bar staff to over 30. Under pressure from the Anti-Liquor Alliance the Victorian government delayed change for a time before eventually settling on a hiring age of 35.

Lacking the leverage of unions in South Australia and Victoria, workers in states which had never placed strict restrictions on women's bar work were unable to achieve wage justice at this time but did improve pay differentials. Most other alcohol related jobs similarly saw inequality continue, although women in Victorian distilleries did win equal pay in 1944.

Achieving wage equality for bar staff in Victoria took more than a year of negotiations. While Young got to witness this victory in 1943, she did not play a direct role in its conclusion. Burnt out from decades of activism, her health declined and she resigned from the union in mid-1942. She continued her involvement in the CPA but core activism on the question of women's working rights fell to others.

Among these was Kath Williams, another communist, who was elected as a full time LTU organiser in 1948. In *Kath William: The Unions and the Fight for Equal Pay* biographer Zelda D'Aprano describes the conditions and nature of William's work:

> [She] commenced work on a very low salary. She was expected to 'bring in her own wages', which meant walking from one hotel to another, going from restaurant to restaurant and also being responsible for canteens. Her job entailed recruiting staff into the union, collecting dues, listening to the members and taking up the issues which concerned them. She was on her feet all day and constantly dealing with difficult employers reluctant to negotiate or agree to a settlement of disputes.

Williams focused on organising the most exploited workers within the industries the LTU covered. She set up the first meeting of café and restaurant workers since Young had retired and helped lift recruitment from 50 new members a month to 500 a month by 1949. To maintain membership in a high turnover industry she also established a strong system of shop stewards.

Her appointment came at a time when the equality of pay mandated by wartime regulations was being steadily wound back across Australia. As D'Aprano argues:

> It was taken for granted that pay justice for women was a burden on the economy; thus women were condemned to go on being financially dependent on men and to subsidising the economy both by their cheap labour in the workforce and by running their homes for their men in the workforce.

Pushing back against prevailing trends, the LTU put a claim before the Federal Arbitration Court calling for conditions to be maintained in SA and Victoria and equal pay to be introduced elsewhere. According to Best, when the commission instead moved in 1949 to wind women's wages back to 75 per cent of male bar attendants' it inexplicably left Victoria out. This was welcomed by workers in that state but opposed by local temperance advocates, who wanted women to be phased out of pubs once more via the re-introduction of former restrictions. Licensees were happy to keep employing women but wanted low-wage parity with their interstate peers.

An attempt by publicans to overturn the decision in the courts was met by a determined campaign. When an appeal reached the

Arbitration Court in December 1949 a stop work action involving 400 women, roughly 80 per cent of the state's female bar staff, was held. The action drew support from the Seamen's Union, whose secretary Bill Bird stated his members were angry at the prospect of 'hard working women' losing their jobs and pay. Maritime unions promised to put a ban on malt supplies should dismissals occur while the LTU itself warned of major disruption in the industry. By the next year the commission's original decision was upheld and agreement reached between unions and employers to protect equal pay and women's access to bar work in Victoria.

D'Aprano argues that Williams was deeply influenced by her close contact with arbitration courts and wage boards during this period. Off the back of major reversals for most women she saw that making the principle of wage justice a national standard would require 'massive support from the ACTU, professional associations, all Trade Union Labor Councils, the trade unions and the support of women all over Australia.'

This would clearly be a long-term undertaking and became one that Williams committed herself to within and beyond the LTU. Her efforts in building support across various industries led to her being elected organising secretary of the Victorian Trades Hall Council's Equal Pay committee upon its formation in 1955. Along with other female unionists, and progressives in organisations such as the Union of Australian Women, she took part in numerous Victorian and national campaigns and events over the next twelve years. While change was often incremental these activities kept the issue of discrimination in the public spotlight via rallies, petitions, leaflets, reports, conferences, debates, deputations, appearances before industrial boards, and other means.

Aged 72, Williams retired from her LTU organiser role in 1967. In the context of rising industrial militancy and changing social mores, her work, and that of a multitude of others, began to finally breakthrough in the years that followed closely after. Nationally LTU members had long kept the issue of wage justice alive in her sector. Following stop-work meetings and a coordinated July 1967 hotel strike in four states, the federal Arbitration Commission included equal pay for female bar staff in the January 1968 Hotel Award.

In the same year the ACTU and the meatworkers union lead by George Seelaf (see elsewhere in this book), began pursuing what Williams and others had long advocated, an equal pay case before the federal Arbitration Commission to cover all women in the country. The court ruled in favour of 'equal pay for equal work' in 1969 but this was strictly defined and only covered the minority of women whose roles matched their male counterparts' in every way. Further campaigning in workplaces, courts, and the streets was required for the commission to adopt the principle of 'equal pay for work of equal value' in 1972. Since then workers and unions have had to continually fight for this to be applied correctly as well as to achieve wage justice through the lifting of pay and conditions in heavily feminised industries.

LTU organiser Kath Williams, 1960s (United Workers Union)

CHAPTER 39
COUNTERCULTURE CARLTON AND THE PUBS
Alex Ettling

The wild and the whimsy of counterculture Carlton has been shaped by some cold economic facts. It's the rise and fall (and repeat) of the economy – and its real estate market – that has greatly influenced who lived in the suburb and what went on behind the shopfronts. An upmarket area on the edge of the Melbourne CBD, it lost its bourgeois lustre after the economic crash of the late 19th century. With money leaching out of the suburb, it accepted a variety of subcultures, all in search of cheap rent and like-minded community.

A centre of Jewish life, and then home to the migrant wave from Italy with their late-night espresso culture, Lygon Street has adapted to each group that moved into the neighbourhood. The youthful carousing of students from adjacent Melbourne University, has also played a role in Carlton becoming one of the centres of intellectual and cultural life in Melbourne.

Young scholars would spill out from the university campus to the surrounding pubs. From the post-war period onwards, Jimmy Watson's Wine Bar was perhaps the most enduring drinking establishment for those seeking culture and conversation. Some major intellectual innovations occurred in the nearby pubs instead of the desks on campus. Australia's first satellite, 'Australis', was designed on the back of a beer coaster at Naughton's in nearby Parkville. This pub was the drinking hole of the university philosophers – and the Rationalists, the most powerful club at the university with a membership that spanned from the far right to the far left.

In the cramped back bar at The Mayfair, the right-wing DLP Club and the left-wing Labour Club could interact. The ALP Club also met at The Mayfair, and at another stage the (entirely different) Labour Club made its haunt the University Hotel. Former student Bill Garner asserts, 'The pubs had been sites where one's views could be challenged and where one might even change one's mind. They were not places of comforting agreement. You had to be on your mettle.' However, Garner claims that it was the Vietnam War that led to a polarisation of positions, so much so that the open pub debate that had previously crossed political lines disappeared forever. He states, 'From about 1968 the left only talked to the left and the right only talked to the right.'

There were obstacles to women participating fully in this pub culture. In 1964, the editor of *Farrago*, John Helmer, escorted his then girlfriend Kerry Dwyer, into the public bar at The Mayfair as a protest against male exclusiveness. Brian Boyd, later to be secretary of the Victorian Trades Hall Council, recounts an experience a few years later of challenging the same men's-only space at The Albion. With 10 other students, both men and women, they initiated a confrontation:

> They wouldn't serve us. The locals wanted to have a blue with us about having the beer cut off. We were pretty tough in those days. I don't think the locals wanted to take us on. We waited out the publican for about a half and hour, and eventually we got a

deal to get all the women one beer each and then we'd go. Just to prove our point.

The Carlton pubs could be diverse places, and increasingly so in the 1970s. They were a venue to rub shoulders with celebrity footballers, at a time when the clubs had a major presence in their suburbs. Historian Stuart Macintyre observed that 'Carlton players were known to frequent the pub in Royal Parade, Naughtons, opposite the university, in a backbar where members of the Labor Club used to hang out (and with an eye out for discovery by Barassi).' Some footballers adopted the left politics of the times, such as Geoff Pryor and Ted Hopkins. Activist Garrie Hutchinson regularly interacted with the maverick Carlton player Brent Crosswell at Stewart's Hotel. 'Tiger' Crosswell, then at the pinnacle of his playing career, was sufficiently integrated into the Carlton counterculture to umpire a charity football game organised by a bar worker at The Albion. The notice in underground newspaper *The Digger* read:

> Ladies and gentlemen, boys and girls, babies and bottletops, desperados and drunks your friendly Albion Hotel barman, Peter Roussos is organising an all-day, all-in football match with food, booze and entertainment at the Donnybrook Mineral Springs Oval on Sunday June 24. For $2.00 – children free – you can play in a football game umpired by ace Carlton footballer, Brent Crosswell... Anybody can try for the team – 'boys and girls, we don't care if we've got 80 on the side' – fighting shoulder to shoulder with bartenders and patrons of the Albion, Lemon Tree and Clyde.

Bill Garner, Eric Beach, Danny Kramer, out the front of the Albion Hotel, 1981 (Ruth Maddison)

As the sixties counterculture developed, progressive students increasingly found themselves exiting the university grounds not towards the Parkville pubs, but in the other direction towards Lygon Street. The pubs of Carlton were many things, including an incubator of progressive arts in a period of great optimism towards social change. The origins of one of the most influential independent publishers of the era, Outback Press, were located in The Albion. Four young men drinking inside the pub agreed that there was a need, and concluded they were the ones could do it, launching the project in 1973.

Carlton is also remembered for its rich performing arts tradition, in part based on the history of Jewish theatre at the Kadima. The emergence of new ensembles in the 1960s and 70s were particularly influential on the future direction of Australian performing arts. The different scenes tended to congregate at different pubs. In actor Rod Moore's recollections, La Mama Theatre was connected to The Albion (being located directly opposite), and the Pram Factory milieu tended to gather at Stewart's. The Pram Factory itself, with its various tendencies and groupings, is an intriguing study in how intoxicating substances and meeting locations can influence organisational and artistic outcomes. Anyone was allowed to lay out their publicity material in the foyer of the Pram Factory, which meant that the full spectrum of left politics was on display for those who took an interest. Performer Mark Minchinton, writing for the Pram Factory's history website, summarised the situation:

Australian Performing Group reading of Bertolt Brecht's *The Mother*, 1975 (Bill Garner)

I begin to see there are factions, cannot yet make out the differences between them, but begin to get the basic ideas – Australian content: good; working class (of which I am an unaware member): good; Mao: good; Unions: good; CPA: problematic but basically good; beer: mostly good; dope: okay; smack & smackheads: boring but tolerated; coffee: to be drunk in vast quantities; Tiamo coffee shop: to be referred to as Tamani's (which I still do for nostalgic reasons and to signal that I know something most people don't). Stewart's pub is a meeting point for many. I don't like pubs or social drinking and hardly ever go. Homo-social, anglo-celtic, verbal jousting dominates.

Jack (Jean) Weiner recalled a vision of that time, with Australian Performing Group (APG) people: Wandering around Carlton more often than not garbed in overalls of various hues. The Pram Factory seemed to be like a beehive with workers in uniforms buzzing in and out of it at all times of day. Yet they didn't seem to pay much heed to the rest of the world; their world consisted of the Pram Factory, Stewart's Hotel and, of course, Tamani's.

The Pram Factory was a literally disused factory, with open industrial flooring which was repurposed into performance spaces, and a tower that became a notorious residential space. Author and performer Jon Hawkes explains, 'We never congregated in the tower itself, only small numbers around the kitchen table and that would only fit like four, so life took place either in Stewart's Hotel or Tamani's (now Tiamo) in Lygon Street.' Nevertheless, actor and writer Bill Garner also recalled that 'after the pub

Australian Performing Group factory show, 1970s (Ponch Hawkes)

closed they'd all come to the tower for a joint or another drink.'

At the end of the night, if not before, the frisson in the pubs could lead to sexual encounters. In this social environment, with the contraceptive pill now more accessible, there was a degree of sexual liberation unknown to the preceding generations. The Albion, which the arts scene began patronising in 1968, reached its liberatory peak between 1972–75. As Garner recalls:

> If people came there they knew what its reputation was. It was in fact our lounge room. There were no bands and you could talk and talking leads to sex. The Albion died with the Labor Government, it was a party which started in the Albion and it went on for three years.

The vibrancy of the scene, with its various expressions, meant it attracted all sorts. Lindzee Smith, described as something of an urban cowboy of the scene, offered his perspective to Sue Ingleton:

Australian Performing Group newsletter, 1976

It was a cultural kind of movement so with that you get the bad as well as the good and there were some bad bastards hanging around Fitzroy and Carlton in those days. The days of The Albion and that was also a tradition that had arisen at La Mama when you used to get drunks in the audience, breaking up the show and abusing you and stuff, so there was always that edgy feeling to it.

Within the performance scene there were those who were relatively abstemious, and others who were heavy drinkers. Bill Garner recalls Michael Byrnes who lived in the tower:

> If we thought we were drinkers we just didn't know what a real alcoholic was until we saw him. I never saw him taking any solid food. Alcohol, particularly sherry, must have a lot of food value in it. I've seen him choke over a thin chicken soup, he just couldn't take it, yet I've seen him take a full bottle of sherry before breakfast. He had no ability to look after himself at all.

The Pram Factory scene was, by contemporary standards, extraordinarily understanding of those that took intoxicating substances to excess or developed addictions. Lindzee Smith openly disclosed his heroin use and discussed the impact of needle drugs in the Pram Factory scene with Sue Ingleton:

> Junk is such an anti-social thing. It was the very anathema to what was going on at the PF which was supposed to be a social activity. And so because of the nature of intravenous drug abuse people had to sneak off to dark places to do it. It's not the sort of thing you do in a collective medium like smoking a joint or drinking alcohol.

Jon Hawkes, not a regular drinker, observed the need to follow the separate scenes into their different meeting spaces:

> out of necessity, though I was at times both a Stewart's and Tamani's person. There were some perceptions about the APG being about

different drug-based cultures which was true; there was a coffee and dope culture, there was drug culture, there was an alcohol culture and there were people who crossed those barriers.

Hawkes developed an opinion on which locales were the best to organise in, and favoured the restaurant:

> Tamani's was a much more congenial atmosphere to do deals in than the pub. At the back table you could seat fifteen people, whereas in the pub you'd spend most of your time looking over other people's shoulders and getting drunk. I'm not functional with alcohol. Couldn't handle it.

Sometimes being in the pub, and noticing who wasn't there, was an indication of shifting alliances. Rod Moore describes his experience where:

> There came a time when gradually the people who'd been there from the beginning Graeme [Blundell], Kerry [Dwyer], Garrie [Hutchinson], myself would be round at Stewart's pub or somewhere and we'd be wondering, 'Where is everybody?' and they'd all be round at the Hannan's [Lorna and Bill] and he'd be giving them meals. Max [Gillies] and all the other people were there and what he was doing was caucusing.

At a democratic election when positions were voted on, Moore and his friends found that they had lost their position of influence inside the APG. Moore possibly lacked the political experience to recognise a heightened contestation of ideas, and so 'After these elections, and Bill Hannan's coup, again we were at Stewart's and we said "What the fuck's happened here?"'

A fuller understanding of these different approaches and disputes within the Pram Factory can be pursued in the substantial writings and documentaries produced on the influential theatre. It is certainly notable that those involved were engaged in innovations in creative forms, as well as being responsive to the interests of working people and socialist ideas. Bill Garner, writing for *Arena* in 2017 states, 'The APG became a self-managed company controlled by "theatre workers". No bosses. Directors were chosen by the actors. It was a revolutionary moment in Australian theatre.' In various ensembles, they went into workplaces, and performed stories about working class experience.

The impact of this cohort on the Australian arts scene has been immense, staging provocative shows and developing boundary-pushing cultural forms. Alison Richards, speaking at Enter the New Wave in 2009, also claims that, 'there was a fundamental commitment to materialism, which moved against the uptake of metaphysics really. I remember Bill Garner giving us lectures on materialism – generally in the back bar or in the car on the way to somewhere else.' Jon Hawkes was also engaged with the politics of the labour movement, 'In the 70s, Lindzee and I called ourselves psychedelic Bolsheviks... we were influenced all that time by living with Eddy van Roosendael. He was a communist who despised every form of existing Communism.'

It was however a spectrum of influences and dissatisfactions that led people to pursue new forms of political and artistic expression within this Carlton scene. In doing so they were interrogating their own psychology and exploring alternative models for making a better world. In an intoxicating era of possibilities, conversation was imbued with vitality, whether it was lubricated or not.

CHAPTER 40
BLACK AND WHITE SOLIDARITY IN THE PUBS OF BRISBANE
Alex Ettling

Oodgeroo Noonuccal at Moongalba, Queensland, 1982 (Juno Gemes/Juno Gemes Collection)

Brisbane, 1960: the plan was to emulate the incendiary sit-in movement that had recently electrified the civil rights movement in the United States. Three protesters – Aboriginal activist Oodgeroo Noonuccal (then known as Kath Walker), and two young white radicals Humphrey McQueen and Bob Harney – dressed up in their best outfits and headed out to the poshest hotel in Brisbane. They entered the genteel lounge of The Carlton Hotel one afternoon when the lounge was full of respectable women attired in hats and gloves. Reflecting on the events 60 years later, McQueen outlined their plan: 'Go in and order a drink. They wouldn't serve us, and we'd go out and complain. The students would come back three days later and have a protest.'

However, the Brisbane franchise of the explosive anti-racism moment of Greensboro, North Carolina was not to be. As McQueen recounted, 'Well, we go in, we sit down, the waiter comes up and takes our order. And brings us a drink. That was the end of that.' So strong was the segregation in Brisbane that the dissonance of a smartly attired Aboriginal woman presenting herself to be served liquor – defying the legal prohibition – seems to have only prompted confusion. And fulfilment of the order.

The following year, an Indian member of a student cricket team was refused a drink at a pub after a match. Again, Humphrey McQueen was involved in the action as an organiser of a small demonstration that marched on the pub. He recounts:

When they get there the publican comes out and says 'I'm quite happy for him to drink here, but the law says we cannot serve Aboriginals, and my barmaids are not in a position, if there's 30 or 40 people in the bar all wanting a beer, to decide if they're Black, who is an Aboriginal and who isn't. So I'm more than happy – but you've got this other practicality of how the barmaid is supposed to operate in this situation.'

Such were the challenges of the officious implementation of racism in Australia's North.

These small actions, and attempts to grow solidarity against racist government policies, continued throughout the 1960s. In Queensland, one of the strongest organised forces against racism was the Communist Party of Australia (CPA). It included First Nations members such as Torres Strait Islander activist Eddie Mabo, and a number of white activists significantly committed to the cause such as Kathy Cochrane and Joyce Tattersell. The CPA also brought into its periphery high profile Aboriginal activists who were active in unions where the Communists were in the leadership, notably Bob Anderson of the Building Workers Industrial Union (BWIU).

As well as militant unions, the churches were another social force supporting Aboriginal struggles. Pastor Don Brady, who began as a lay pastor in 1964, was a figure of respectability who was also willing to organise with political radicals. The *Australian Dictionary of Biography* staes that he earned the nickname 'The Punching Parson' because of 'his ability to handle homeless inebriates frequenting Musgrave Park.' Through the efforts of such individuals, and a number of organisations with social weight behind them, there was sustained resistance throughout the sixties. However, there was yet to be a major breakthrough.

Builders Labourers' Federation float, May Day procession in Brisbane, 1967 (Grahame Garner, Fryer Library)

Pastor Don Brady and Oodgeroo Noonuccal in King George Square, Brisbane, 1970 (Grahame Garner, Fryer Library)

On campus, where there was a small opening for progressive organising, Student Action Against White Australia formed at the University of Queensland (UQ). In a challenging political climate they organised protests, such as demanding a halt to the deportation of Chinese national Willie Wong in 1962, after eight years of residence. These actions were modest in number and impact, but were successful in bringing new activists into the fold, who then had experience to draw on as the sixties upsurge unfolded. The era-defining campaign that was the furnace of the radicalisation was the Vietnam War. It featured a strong anti-racist theme, along with the opposition to militarism, conscription and imperialism.

In Black politics, a catalyst to radicalisation was the 1967 Referendum. When eulogising Oodgeroo Noonuccal in parliament in 1993, Liberal Party leader John Hewson, spoke of a curious interaction that took place on a Federal Council for the Advancement of Aborigines and Torres Strait Islanders (FCAATSI) delegation to Canberra in 1963:

> In a meeting with Prime Minister Menzies, Kath Walker, as she was then known, asked for and was offered a glass of sherry by Prime Minister Menzies. On receiving the glass, Kath Walker told the Prime Minister, 'Mr Prime Minister, it is only fair that I warn you that under the laws of Queensland you would be in the position of either getting two weeks in gaol or a fine of £50 for giving me this.'

Noonuccal had essentially done a re-run of the stunt from three years earlier in Brisbane. Civil rights leader Faith Bandler in *Turning The Tide: A Personal History of the Federal Council for the Advancement of Aborigines and Torres Strait Islanders*, later claimed this was 'the turning

Members of the Aldermaston Peace March in Brisbane wear slogans reading 'Make friends not foes in Asia', 1965 (Grahame Garner, Fryer Library)

point' in the campaign for constitutional change, a moment which prompted Menzies 'to give the situation of Aborigines more thought.' The 1967 referendum energised a broad layer of activists for Aboriginal rights and passed with large approval. But neither the changes in law, nor the symbolic victory, significantly improved the position of Aboriginal people in society.

The issue of the racial background of those in pro-Aboriginal organisations came to the fore, due to demands for 'Black control'. What followed was a series of splits and formations of new organisations. Some activists such as Noonuccal, who had previously been advocates of Black and white collaboration, were adopting new positions that varied from wariness to hostility. In an internal paper for FCAATSI titled 'Coalition of Black and White Australians – July 1969', Noonuccal was now expressing a scepticism of white activists and 'intellectuals such as students, who want to "come alive" through black organisations.' In this era, the Aboriginal community was a world away from the young white scholars at a sandstone university. Nevertheless, the prevailing youth dissatisfaction and rumblings of radical left politics had opened the minds of Brisbane's emerging dissidents to the oppressed living in their own city. Aboriginal activist Tiga Bayles stated in an interview with historian Andrew Stafford:

Celebrations after the passing of the referendum, including Faith Bandler, 1967

We used to have a lot of meetings at the university. That's one of the good things, one of the good memories about the universities, about those days was the uni students. They were so organised, they were so strong and well organised and supportive of the Indigenous struggle at that time. This is in the early '70s ... Knowing we could rely on some support from the university, access to resources and expertise out there as far as posters and banners and things like that.

Support for Aboriginal people was often expressed in donations for education initiatives, such as ABSCHOL, a funding and lobbying body run by the National Union of Australian University Students. Sometimes fundraising activities aimed at providing tertiary scholarships and resourcing campaigns were relatively straightforward, a pass-the-hat in the beer garden of The RE (Royal Exchange Hotel) to raise money. Organised collection drives would also be made in classrooms and lectures, such as in 1971 when the cause was to provide funding for the Brisbane Tribal Council, a more explicitly political formation that rivalled FCAATSI.

The Tribal Council was located in different areas, and for a period took residence upstairs above the 'Black discotheque', The Open Door, at 64 Turbot Street. This warehouse space, reinvented as a 'drop in' centre, had earlier functioned as a rock'n'roll music venue, before becoming the key social venue of the Brisbane Black Power scene. It provided the safety in numbers desired when socialising in a racist society. Even gatherings that were sympathetic to Aboriginal people could attract a backlash, as student activist Anne Richards experienced during a house party fundraiser for an Aboriginal school. Their event attracted the attention of 'hooligans who beat the shit out of us', including her brother who was knocked out.

In July 1971, the foundations of a firmer coalition between First Nations leaders and the young radical left were formed during actions opposing the Springboks tour. Premier Joh Bjelke-Petersen set a standard in Queensland by declaring a legal *state of emergency* to protect the orderly conduct of games played by the whites-only South African rugby team.

During the tour, it became clear that many Australians did not want to be associated with such brazen racist policies, and were willing to take action. While pitch invasions understandably captured the most public attention there were many other actions which repudiated any connection with South Africa's apartheid system. One of the largest wineries in South Australia's Barossa Valley refused to allow the Springboks to tour the facility while it was publicly open. Factory workers and drivers at Tooheys' Auburn bottling plant placed an indefinite black ban on the supply of liquor to the Bondi Motel where the Springboks were staying.

Anne Richards was active in organising events in Queensland and tried to encourage participation from Aboriginal people by distributing flyers in the South Brisbane pubs. She explains, 'I knew that was where the Aboriginal people hung out, and it was only the really run down pubs that would let them in. So, I thought that was where they should be given the message of what was happening.' As a white woman handing out flyers at a pub at 11am on a Saturday morning, she was met with some bemusement.

Events during a protest at the Springboks' accommodation on 22 July 1971 became a touchstone for Brisbane politics due to the police brutality. There were estimates of 300 demonstrators but 500 police. Future Queensland ALP premier Peter Beattie was among those arrested outside the Tower Mill Motel. Special Branch categorised their subject as 2E1528, E being the category for political activists. Other codes being used were A for communists and B for Jews.

If the greater numbers of police weren't sufficient intimidation, then there were the extreme threats of violence. Warwick Vere, interviewed by Stafford, contends, 'The police had turned up with dogs and they had been particularly blunt to some of the females there, saying, "Get out of the road or this dog will rip your cunt out, love."' Officers also gave warnings that people found demonstrating again would be shot.

These shocking events were a catalyst for political organisation that, in no small part due to the leadership of Black Power activists, directed a layer of the white left towards recognising police violence and increasing their focus on homegrown racism in Australia. Sam Watson,

150 protested at the Regatta and Adelaide Hotels in Brisbane, 1971 (Radical Times Archive)

4000 University of Queensland students and staff vote to strike, 1971 (Peter Gray, Radical Times Archive)

a young Aboriginal activist at the time, speaking alongside Denis Walker in a 'Retrospective Discussion' (2006) for the *Taking To The Streets* exhibition, explained that:

> During 1971, the same time we were running the Smash the Acts campaign, the white left across the east coast of Australia were building up for the Springboks tour in July 71. We went to meetings at Trades Hall and other places, job sites, to try and present the viewpoint that we support the struggle against apartheid. But right here in Queensland and across Australia, there are these protectionist acts that also operate in the same way that apartheid operates in South Africa.
>
> When the Springboks arrived in Brisbane, there was a way in which the Aboriginal political leadership and the white left could do business together. So, we were very closely involved in that entire Springboks struggle here in Brisbane. We were able to channel a lot of that energy after the Springboks went home. We were able to maintain that connection, and maintain the focus on racism here in Australia.

The day after the police brutality of the Tower Mill demonstration, 3000 students gathered at UQ and voted to take action. Watson asserts, 'We took the university out on strike for the duration of the tour, suspending lectures and tutorials so students could discuss and debate racism.' In the days ahead, discussion took place around Aboriginal people's experiences of racial discrimination, which included in the pubs.

On 27 July 1971, 150 people marched on the Adelaide Hotel to picket the pub for racial discrimination. Non-Indigenous protesters wore black-face, singing and dancing on the protest route. In student newspaper *Semper Floreat*, Roger Stuart claimed, 'The response to that demo was interesting. There was little of the traditional public hostility towards demonstrators, more bewilderment to amused curiosity.' There were no arrests apart from academic and activist Dan O'Neill, who was charged with disorderly conduct for drinking in black-face at the following stop on the march, The Regatta Hotel. This had famously been the site of an earlier stunt action against gender segregation in 1965.

For O'Neill, the performative concept was about representing the extreme racism that Black people experienced and 'dramatising that fact, rather than taking up some kind of complicated attitude, like a paternalistic attitude to Black people or a failure to respect them … Back in those days we would have thought of it under the broad umbrella of solidarity.' There is no record of any opposition to the use of black-face during the period. Regarding attitudes about black-face today, O'Neill reflects that 'suppose that someone had come up to me, like one of

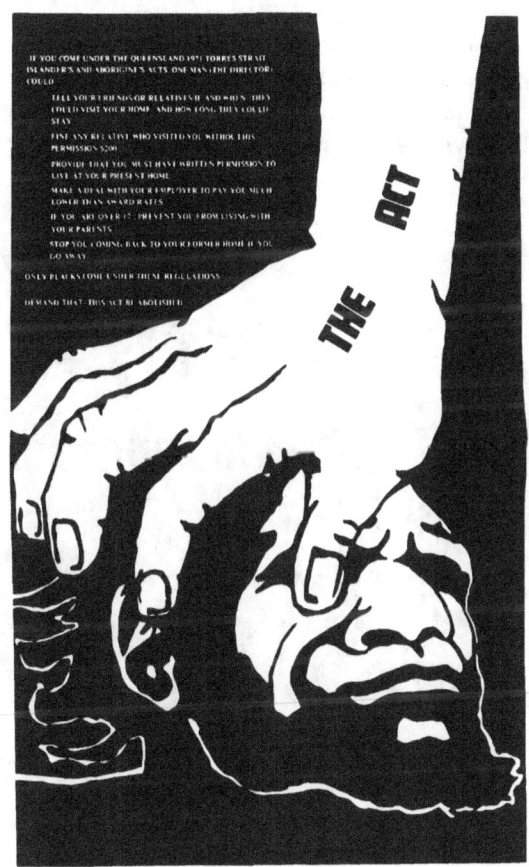

Smash the Act poster, 1971 (Radical Times Archive)

the Aboriginal activists and said "No, don't go with black-face, let me do it", I'm pretty sure I would have welcomed that.'

There were also social gatherings that came out of the university strike, including a Kup Marri held on a Saturday night. This was the first UQ campus social gathering between First Nations people and white students.

There was momentum off the back of these events, including further agitation against racist legislation known as 'the Acts'. These laws allowed the state to control the lives of Aboriginal people including who they could marry, where they could work and, if they received their wages, how they could spend their money. The first iteration, *The Aboriginals Protection and the Restriction of the Sale of Opium Act* had been passed in 1897 and included a clear focus on intoxication.

Sam Watson told *Green Left* about running a major campaign called Smash the Acts, which culminated in a demonstration on 23 November 1971, where he estimated 200 protesters met 300 police. Attention also continued to be paid to the issue of racism in pubs. As Watson explained in 2006:

> Ship Inn, Plough Inn, The Palace, Manhattan, Adelaide. Across the northside of course, you had The Grand that was down near the gardens. The Alliance that was near Spring Hill. And down the Valley you had The Wickham. These are the pubs the coppers would target, and they had these huge black mariah vans and they'd just jam the blacks in there like sardines ... Process at the watch house. Take the $2 bail off them.

Tiga Bayles speaking in 2002 recalled of this harassment in the pubs, 'My mother was locked up more than once, and she doesn't drink!'

Social work student Lindy Morrison, who would later play drums in The Go-Betweens, had been at the Tower Mill demonstration and was radicalised by the era. In her last year at university she took up a student placement working for ATSILS (Aboriginal and Torres

Smash the Acts march, 1971 (Radical Times Archive)

Strait Islander Legal Service) where she met Aboriginal activist Denis Walker and subsequently became his romantic partner. Walker was the son of Oodgeroo Noonuccal, and had been a seafarer for much of the sixties until he was forced to spend six weeks in Darwin's Fanny Bay Prison for assaulting a publican. The 6 February 1967 edition of the *Sunday Sun* quotes Walker: 'He tried to throw me out of his hotel and called me a black bastard ... It was a bad mistake – his bad mistake.'

Speaking to Stafford, Morrison recounted their experiences in the seventies:

> We couldn't get a drink in a bar, because Denis was Black ... Denis took me to places I had never seen, where not many white people would have had the kind of experiences that I had in the early 70s.

This included witnessing impoverished living conditions and participating in social gatherings which included drinking in open areas such as Musgrave Park. In Tracey Thorn's biography of Morrison, *My Rock 'n' Roll Friend*, Morrison recounts, 'There are Black pubs and white pubs, and I'm suddenly drinking in all the Black pubs. It's where I learn to play pool.' Thorn describes Morrison as 'doing social work over the pool tables, passing on valuable information about how to get the benefits they are entitled to, how to get kids back out of care, how to get a place to live.' At one particular pub, Morrison encountered drinkers who slept all together in the basement.

Similar to what was taking place in the United States and Sydney, Morrison also joined up with the local 'Pig Patrol'. This was established by the Brisbane Black Panthers and centrally organised out of Pastor Don Brady's church. At 10 pm they would go out and try to stop people getting arrested by police. The intention was to head off Aboriginal people from entering the legal system in the first instance – something which generally led to grim outcomes. Musician Brad Shepherd revealed to Andrew Stafford a horrific experience that he witnessed as a young punk, while in the lockup:

> I saw them pick this Black guy up and speared him into the corner [of the jail cell], knocked him unconscious. He was in the cell across from me and then they just dragged him out by his hair and just left this trail of gore along the floor of the South Brisbane watch house.

The sentencing of Aboriginal people was also discriminatory. Activist Neil Fraser had been killed by a drunk driver who ran a red light. Anne Richards was his partner and was infuriated that the driver was given a six-month suspended sentence when 'the two young Aboriginal boys who tried, unsuccessfully, to steal his motorbike a few months before were

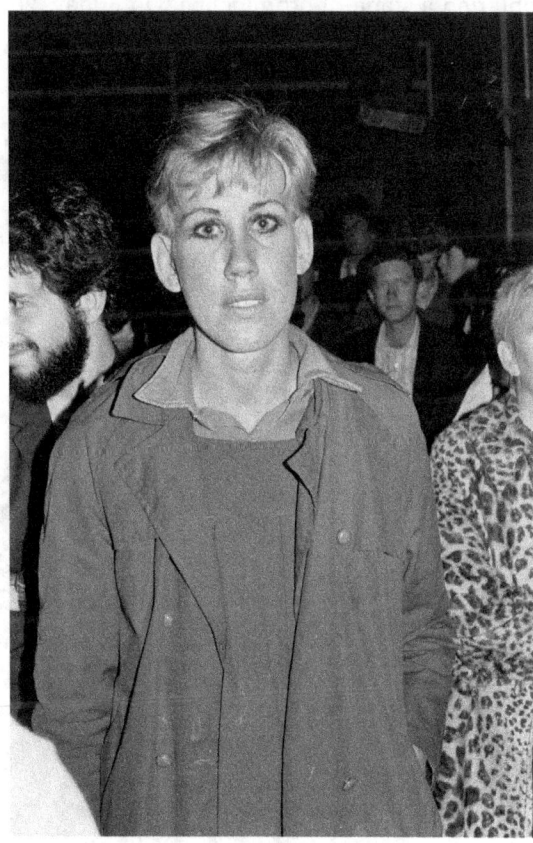

Lindy Morrison, 1970s (Paul O'Brien, State Library of Queensland)

given two years at Westbrook detention centre. I was angry, property over life.' It was in this context that activists like Denis Walker and Lindy Morrison would regularly attend the Magistrates Court and apply for bail for whoever had been arrested the night before (often outside the Black pubs) and invite them back to the ATSILS office for assistance.

The government had by this stage defunded the Brisbane Tribal Council, but the activists salvaged a gestetner out of it. On Friday and Saturday nights at The Open Door, as Watson attests, 'you'd get up to 300 or 400 young Blacks there. So we were able to pamphlet the disco, and let people know who we were and what we were doing.'

Just as the radicalisation of the *long sixties* was nearing its end, Aboriginal activism began entering a stage of prominence. On Friday, 28 January 1972, 350 white, predominantly student activists, and 50 Aboriginal activists, gathered for the Action Conference on Racism and Education, which would run for six days at UQ.

The lead up to the conference included some provocative flyers, written by white organisers. They were intended to motivate participation and engagement from white activists with morally charged rhetoric. The conference was attempting to balance a high-level discussion on oppression, particularly in the area of education policy, with discussion coalescing towards: 'action'.

A white American academic, Dr Neil Eddington, had been involved in civil rights activism in the US and was the opening speaker. Eddington made direct criticisms in his speech of Denis Walker who was in the audience. Walker interjected: 'You don't have the pigs on your back like we do. You can go into a hotel for a beer without being victimised.' In this era

Denis Walker, Smash the Acts protest, 1971 (Radical Times Archive)

it was not unusual that the civil right of access to drinking was presented as the foremost example of discrimination – it was relatable. Dan O'Neill, who was chairing the event, gave Walker his right of reply, whereupon he took the opportunity to announce the arrival of the Brisbane Black Panther Party. It was their first public appearance, and Walker recited to the audience the 'Black Panther Party Australia Platform and Program – January 1972' and 'Black Panther Party Australia Manifesto No. 1 28/1/72'.

In the following days heated debate took place over the connections between racism, gender and class, as well as what would constitute effective activism against racial discrimination. There was a sustained air of grievance, and it was apparent that the politics of solidarity was under severe strain. It was a distinctive event, because as historian Lewis d'Avigdor asserts in 'Black Power and White Solidarity': 'White activists were confronted by a formidable group of Black Power activists who were as critical of their white allies as they were of the white establishment'.

Gary Foley later revealed their intervention was a pre-arranged strategy, designed to 'test the mettle of their white allies'. It also related to their frustrations with the Australian Union of Students and ABSCHOL (led by white students), and the recent history of Aboriginal organisations that had resisted the leadership of the new layer of Black radicals, e.g. FCAATSI. As Foley explains in 'A reflection on the first thirty days of the Embassy':

> Black Power activists in Australia at times appeared to derive a perverse pleasure from subjecting earnest, small 'l' liberal white Australians to occasional brutal challenges… Black activists held some of the white political supporters in high regard, but out of fun were not about to let their white comrades know that. It was considered a better strategy to 'keep them on their toes'.

A vote was taken on the opening night that unanimously accepted the principle of Black leadership over the conference. In the original program, the final two days were set aside for discussion of Black and white alliances and joint action against racism. But the Conference did not run according to the advertised agenda. The trade union working group was one casualty, possibly a result of the prevailing antagonism towards people at the conference raising class based strategies of solidarity involving non-Aboriginal groups.

There was a sizeable depletion of attendance after the opening sessions. It was likely not the experience some attendees were hoping for. Walker was canvassing the possibility of violence: 'the spilling of blood', as one ASIO spy recorded it. Walker wanted to find a hardened group of supporters who would not be put off by such rhetoric. He was at this stage one of the most prominent radical activists in the country, someone who had put his body on the line fighting for Aboriginal rights. But aspects of his politics were difficult to reconcile for some of the left-wingers he was organising alongside. Walker opposed class struggle politics, and in the aforementioned interview in 2006 he explained his perspective as a concept of 'spiritual oneness'. He advocated that Black people 'get into a hunter gatherer mentality', arguing that 'the class and the material thing didn't work, we've got to go spiritual'. These politics lead him towards positions such as opposing the equal pay campaign of the Gurindji people.

However, with a considerable amount of moral authority behind him it was a combustible situation for those who wanted to challenge his positions. Walker himself was keenly aware that there were internal differences of perspective within the Aboriginal community, recounting in 2006 that others 'wanted to see us go down'. Within the radical milieu of Black activists there was not unqualified support for Walker, but publicly, there was little to reveal this.

Bruce McGuinness, a significant Black leader in Victoria, was at times at odds with Walker during this period. Despite sharing similar perspectives on some issues Gary Foley notes, in a 2021 article, that McGuinness, 'speaking in 1969 as Director of the Victorian AAL [Aborigines Advancement League], declared that Black Power "does not necessarily involve violence"'.

An ASIO report, if accurate, also indicates possible division on other issues. It includes a conversation from Robin Beadle about how McGuinness allegedly distributed marijuana to other Aboriginal people attending the conference at UQ. The report claimed that Denis Walker was furious and threatened to shoot McGuinness. The first two rules of the Brisbane Black Panther Party were clauses against drugs. For that matter, rule number three was: 'No party member can be DRUNK while doing daily party work' [their emphasis]. How much these rules were followed, and where the line between party work and socialising was drawn, is unclear. There were mobilisations at drinking venues, as we will get to, and there was also the open circulation of flyers at the conference informing people of a party at Peter Wertheim's house.

Brisbane Black Panther Party member Marlene Cummins, in the 2014 Rachel Perkins film *Black Panther Woman*, made a general case about the need to protect Walker and others who were under a large amount of pressure from the state and a hostile media. In relation to Walker, Cummins also claims:

> I do know that he had glassed a woman, smashed a bottle, struck her in the face, with a broken beer bottle. And I saw a side of Denis that I didn't particularly like, and that was enough to drive me away.

Walker in a statement at the conclusion of the film, disputed Cummins' version of events.

During the conference, however, there was strong public unity amongst Black participants. Merle Thornton was in attendance, a figure of prominence due to the previously mentioned 1965 action at The Regatta Hotel over discrimination against women in pubs. When Thornton brought her particular approach to feminist politics to the conference, and questioned the freedom of the Black women within their community, the ASIO spy recorded she was 'shouted down until she had to leave the stage', including by Black women in attendance.

Despite the conference sessions being 'gruelling', the gathering did manage to organise two protests. There is little recorded about these actions but they revolved around discrimination in pubs. This came out of an immediate reaction to repression, rather than a strategy to develop longer term anti-racist campaigns. As reported by the *Tribune*, Sam Watson was arrested at The Open Door the night before the conference. He was 'punched and beaten by police in the van. The next day he was admitted to hospital with severe abdominal pains'. Conference participants attended The Open Door that evening as a measure to prevent another unprovoked attack.

The next action organised through the conference occurred four days later at the Terminus Hotel in South Brisbane where, as *Tribune* reported, 'Blacks had been refused service in the hotel's lounge. The publican reluctantly served the protesters before closing down the lounge due to "lack of staff".'

The relatively small-scale actions at these bars, as the main outward activity coming out of such a significant gathering, likely reflects something of the broader political outcomes of the Anti-Racism Conference. Following its conclusion there was only limited agreement to be found on the politics that should direct multi-racial organising. Further complicating any firm conclusions about what this political moment did for local anti-racist organisational capacity was the emergence of the Aboriginal Tent Embassy in Canberra at the same time. It quickly attracted the interest and participation of many activists in Brisbane and became the focal point of Black politics nationally.

Despite the frustrations with students and the unions, it was also apparent that a key audience for Black radicals existed within this milieu. Walker and Sue Chilly visited Melbourne in March 1972 to continue agitating for the Black Panther program on campuses and elsewhere.

In Brisbane, in the immediate years following the Anti-Racism Conference, there were more fractures between Denis Walker (and his supporters) and other forces in the Brisbane left. This included disputes with the Self-Management Group. As documented by historian Tim Briedis, Walker allegedly cut the face of one of their members with a pair of scissors. Briedis argues that the discord with the SMG, then a leading force in the Brisbane far left, made initiatives such as the attempt to establish a 'Black Embassy' in King George Square difficult to sustain. The anti-racism actions for the rest of the decade were not on the scale as that which had occurred in 1971.

The Brisbane Tribal Council and Brisbane Black Panthers were organisations that inspired others through their defiance, and though they did not prove enduring, the political experiences of participants carried people forward in campaigns to come. The development of Aboriginal activist leaders, and the connections made in Brisbane in this earlier period, would come to the fore in 1982. With the protests against the Commonwealth Games, Brisbane hosted one of the high points of Aboriginal activism, and another example of the power of Black and white solidarity politics.

Sam Watson (left) argues with Liberal Senator Neville Bonner, 1972 (McGuinness Aboriginal Embassy Collection)

CHAPTER 41

'ALK!': PUBS, COMMUNITIES, AND A BROTHERHOOD IN ITS CUPS

David Nichols

This chapter reviews three lenses onto the changing nature of drinking culture – or, at very least, its representations and the aspirations of those who would alter it – in Australia at the time when the nation was dragged, only sometimes kicking and screaming, into the late 20th century. Most of this change took place in the 1960s and 70s, usually but not always under the influence of Labor governments at state or federal level. While these are mere slices – based variously on reportage, dramatization, and projection – we can see distinct changes in Australia's drinking culture that broaden the definitions of who can drink, why they drink and the additional options for creativity in the drinking realm. These examples, largely from Victoria with a cameo from South Australia, illustrate a rapid alteration in broad social attitudes between the 1960s and the 1980s between which the common conception of the pub morphed rapidly from a row of dead-eyed male imbibers numbing their normie pain to a cultural and entertainment achievement.

'That's right... off to the pub'

'If you find an Australian indoors,' wrote the British journalist Jonathan Aitken in his contribution to the beleaguered genre of books about Australia by foreigners, read in large number by Australians, 'it's fair bet that he will have a glass in his hand, as drinking is far and away the most popular national pastime and social activity.' Aitken's 1971 book, *Land of Fortune*, conflates drinking with sex as Australia's two most popular 'indoor sports', but drinking was in his eyes a predominately male pursuit and 'an integral part in the average Australian's working day.'

Notoriously, until the late 1960s in most states the pub was the habitat of addicts and predators. Some examples from late 1960s Australian television allow insight into the way the pub was seen in popular culture at the end of the 1960s, with the caveat that these should be taken alongside Graham Kennedy's observation – in his 1967 book celebrating Melbourne – that while throughout most of the 20th century to that time 'hotels were planned for hard, solid beer swilling', after the late 1950s' introduction of 'more sensible hours for drinking', 'eating and drinking habits have changed more than somewhat.'

Hey You was a 12-episode comedy series screened on Melbourne's ATV0 in 1967 and repeated as late as 1972. Local comedy was a rarity on Australian television in the 1960s with the towering exception of *My Name's McGooley, What's Yours*, and *Hey You*'s greatest legacy was, in hindsight, that it filled the gap for producer-director Godfrey Phillipp, scriptwriter John-Michael Howson and actors Ernie Bourne and Colin McEwan, between the children's hits all three had worked on: *The Magic Circle Club* and *Adventure Island*. Bourne and McEwan were the credited stars of *Hey You*, though Margaret Reid, as Mrs. McNugg, was the third key cast member. The show was set in a lowly boarding house which the opening credits seem to indicate was in St Vincents Place, South Melbourne: at the time, a grandiose nightmare slated for demolition, now of course highly valued, thoroughly gentrified property.

Alcohol is, if not the raison d'etre of the main characters' existence, at least one of its most ardently beloved components. Bourne, as the Terry-Thomasesque bounder Hugh T. Worthington, and McEwan, as the always-overalled 'Ocker' Ramsey, share a room in Mrs. Myrtle ('don't call me "madam"') McNugg's establishment, alongside a nervous spiritualist, Mrs. Farthington and an effete bohemian, Mr. Simpkins.

Worthington keeps his eye perpetually out for the opportunity to purloin Mrs. McNugg's genteel spirits; Worthington and Ramsey also, however, often frequent the local pub, where they interact with Jock, a temperamental Scot who rails against Worthington as a 'pom', and the unnamed barkeep. That pub scenes are short, almost palate cleansers, is made clear by a running gag in the show, in which the bartender ends up regarding unfinished beers left by characters in a hurry to advance that week's plot. Typically, he downs the leftovers himself, one of the few recurring elements of the show to bring forth broad laughter from the studio audience.

Mrs McNugg does not drink in a pub. She is however a frequent purchaser of sherry and brandy and her sister Ophelia, a perpetual hypochondriac, is similarly a constant imbiber in the household. In one scene Ocker, spying her pouring large glassfuls from a bottle on the shelf, yells a simple word at her across the sitting room: 'Alk!'. In the episode of *Hey You* entitled 'The Crisis', Ocker and McNugg

Homicide advertisement, 1964

Hey You advertisement, 1967

have an argument leading to his moving out; we are given a survey of his replacement premises. Despite the fact that Mrs. McNugg asks Worthington where Ocker is now living, and answers herself with the observation that the 'Public bar of the Queen's Arms is the only place he'd be happy', he in fact finds board in a dystopian rooming house where both his landlady (played by Roma Johnston) and his elderly, drunken male roommate (Don Battye) have amorous intentions towards him. In this instance, Worthington repairs the rift between Ocker and McNugg through machiavellian ministrations that see him tell each that the other needs them; the conversations with Ocker take place, naturally, at the pub. The Queen's Arms in *Hey You* is the place where plans are hatched and plotlines twisted; Ramsey and Worthington, unlike (for instance) the perpetually enraged Jock, are not alcoholics per se, although Worthington is unable to ever refuse a drink.

The frequent use of the pub in *Homicide* is strikingly similar, suggesting a common understanding of the working-class hotel in the 1960s. A much better remembered television program than the short-lived *Hey You*, *Homicide* was one of Australian television's first mainstream successes and a national institution by the time it ceased its 11-year run in 1975. Notoriously a show in which Melbournians in particular relished seeing their own city on the screen (those in other cities had to be content that it was, in any case, recognizably an Australian milieu) the program's mid-1960s production budgets ran to outside action – filmed without sound, which was later overdubbed, with varying degrees of effectiveness – and set-based exposition as small and cheap as possible. Yet the pub was, for *Homicide*, a useful and appropriate venue, particularly for drunken outbursts and angry confessional conversations between criminals, or when characters sought information. The episode 'Moment of Truth', which aired 29 November 1966, is set in an unnamed working class suburb, although as the central scene of the crime in this episode is the premises of Sentex, we might assume it is somewhere near High Street, Prahran. Dick Abbot (George Mallaby, in a guest role the year before he signed with the show to play 'Peter Barnes' for what was to become 265 episodes) is shot by a policeman while he is apparently fleeing a factory robbery. His parents, Bull Abbot (Vic Haggith) and 'Mrs Abbot' (Stella Lamond) argue over the pressure they have put on Dick. Bull has, apparently, been honest for some years but he is a lazy braggard, dependent on his son to plug the income gaps between his occasional employment. To end the argument, Bull grabs his coat and leaves the house. 'That's right,' sighs his wife to herself, 'off to the pub.'

The pub is quiet but simmering with tension. Bull encounters the men ('Slasher' Blake and Frank Duncan, played by Alan Walden and Paul Karo respectively) who he believes were also involved in the incident, and tells them that he'll break the neck of anyone who persuaded Dick to take part in the robbery.

There are three pub scenes in this episode, and each one propels the action rapidly, showing the pub as a place where crooks plot and crow. The second pub scene sees a man known only as Rogers, whose car was used in the robbery, demanding the return of his vehicle from Blake and Duncan; they abduct and beat him. Rogers, bloodied, returns once again to the pub where Bull encounters him partaking, dazed, of a restorative beer. The two men establish a quick working relationship whereby they pursue Blake and Duncan with pistols.

Five and a half years later, *Homicide* occupied – or created – a very different world. The episode 'Time to Kill', which aired in July 1972, contains frequent references to drinking and pubs and indeed the show begins with an incident in a pub, ostensibly in the leafy suburb of Eltham. Everything else, however, is different. The episode, written by Patrick Edgeworth, neatly approaches aspects of early 70s drinking culture in Australia, and the culture itself, from a host of angles.

'Time to Kill' concerns the death of a young man, Mike Moore (Stuart Faichney), who we first see picking a fight with an Aboriginal, Jack Lewis (Bob Maza), quietly sitting by himself. Moore blames Lewis for protests (presumably, something in the realm of anti-apartheid activism) at sporting events, although clearly the two men have never met. There is no actual fight, but Lewis is thrown out of the hotel by the barman, who chose not to observe the dynamics of the argument as shown to us, the viewers. When Moore is found murdered the next morning, Lewis is naturally amongst the suspects; 'Some abo got stroppy', Moore's remarkably effete hairdresser tells police. Vignettes of casual racism experienced by Lewis follow – the trope of the inability of Indigenous people to 'handle' alcohol is of course expressed, too – until he is cleared when detectives discover he has 17 cohabitants in his Fitzroy house who attest he was at home the night Moore was killed. 'Try not to lose your temper', he is advised at Russell Street, to which he replies, 'It's not easy'.

Suspicion for the murder then rests on the recently freed ex-con husband of a woman (Thelma Taylor, played by Kirsty Child) Moore had a relationship with. Jimmy (John Stanton) presents a different perspective on drinking culture. When he tells Thelma he is going to the pub he asks her if she wants 'a couple of cans brought back'; another time, when he announces he is again heading to the pub she replies 'I'll come with you, I could do with a break'. Although the pub scene at the beginning of the episode presents an all-male environment, it is clear that the phenomenon has come to pass of the young woman/wife whose desire to drink beer with her husband is neither stigmatised nor problematic: a far cry from Myrtle McNugg's respectably sly tipples. As it transpires, the murder was actually committed by Mike's friend David, tired of being taunted for his lack of success with women (if there is a subtext regarding the effeminate David's desire for Mike, it is probably in the eye of the beholder). David explains to the police that Mike was drunk – and that was the reason he was cruel.

Australian television of the 1960s–70s was not cinema verité, or even genuine reportage: the exigencies of economic production no doubt restricted options for subtlety at every step in the chain of creating tight, appealing drama. Yet beyond the fictionalised pub we can see some core truths of the presumed meaning of the pub as a working class retreat in Australia. Women with pretensions, like Myrtle McNugg and her sister Ophelia, drank at home, copiously if no-one was watching; their 'daughters' (so to speak), women like Thelma Taylor, can drink in a bar or at home with impunity. Men like Ocker, Jock, Hugh T. Worthington and the criminals of *Homicide* drank in public with other men, mechanistically serving a need for solitude rather than camaraderie, often arrayed along a bar as though at a urinal. The pub is rarely depicted as a happy place, more a numb limbo; of course such depictions must surely have been influenced by a popular cultural impulse to regard such places with wowserist disapproval. The possibilities of the pub environment as it came to be understood in the 1970s were so far removed from these depictions as to be another world.

Bob Maza speaks at the Aboriginal Tent Embassy, 1972
(*Tribune*/Search Foundation, State Library of NSW)

Social Centres in New Cities

Another world *did* emerge, in the early 1970s, under the influence of a host of interested parties at federal, state and neighbourhood levels. Whitlam hoped to redraw Australia socially and politically, and one method chosen gives us great insight into the expectations engendered by the Whitlam revolution. The DURD new cities program of 1973–5 was a key element of this change and proposed an initial tranche of five new cities in four states (Queensland refused to be involved; Tasmania was too small) to recalibrate regional voting patterns but also to relieve pressure on extant cities, particularly the inner city. Researching the way the new towns' designers visualised a new Australian way of life casts light on ideas of 1970s Australia and inhabitants' expectations of their society.

Since the late 19th century new cities were intended to espouse, and often prescribed, a particularly middle-class lifestyle. The garden city principles espoused by Ebenezer Howard intended to remake the urban world in entirety, not least by removing the landlord from the equation. For reasons unclear – but possibly related to the Quakerist backing for a number of early purpose-built settlements in Britain – a popular impression quickly developed that new town or garden city idealists aspired to discourage, perhaps prohibit, alcohol consumption. There was, it appears, a fear of similar prohibition when the Labour party set up a new town program in the immediate post-war period in Britain. Thus the running joke in the 1947 British propaganda film *Charley in New Town* in which a sot, on being asked to assist in the planning of the ideal town, places four pubs at the four corners of an intersection and his house in the middle of the crossing. 'Oh no you don't!' a woman's voice is heard; the narrator laughs and assures the drunk there will be plenty of pubs for him in the new town.

Australia had been a forerunner in the creation of new cities, be they agricultural centres like Mildura, a technologically innovative settlement of the 1890s, or Canberra, a political centre of the 1920s. Both of these, incidentally, resisted the introduction of licensed premises for considerable periods. Elizabeth, in South Australia, was the closest of the Australian new cities to the British model, established in the 1950s on a Wakefieldian principle in which middle-class residents would mentor the lower classes and induct them into the new lifestyle. In the early 1970s, a proposal for a second new town – initially known as 'Murray New Town' then Monarto – came into being under the Dunstan regime. Of the Whitlam-era developments, the unrealised Monarto was the most innovative and aspirational. While Dunstan was originally sceptical about the value of a

Monarto Act, 1973 (State Library of NSW)

second 'new city' for South Australia, he became a major supporter of the project in the scant few years it seemed to be a serious proposition. As part of his swathe of reforms delivered to South Australia in the 1960s and 70s, Dunstan committed himself to 'improved and more civilised drinking provisions', writing in his memoir *Felicia* that 'it was essential to give people better access to social drinking conditions in clubs and societies.'

The two incarnations of Monarto – the first plan by Dunstan's school friend Boris Kazanski, the second by the internationally renowned architect John Andrews – sought to interpret the vision Dunstan and his acolytes had for the new (South) Australia. Dunstan said Monarto would 'probably be unlike any other city in Australia in its design:'

> [A] new vision of the Australian city – one that takes the best of what we have in social planning and family convenience, and gives it a new refreshed and national place in the sun. … it will not seek to reproduce some kind of variation of some kind of ideal European living style… we can probably expect a shady, compact, walkable, easy-to-live-in city.

Planning for the city would, he added, have 'fewer legislative restrictions than exist in Adelaide and other major Australian cities' and would incorporate 'alternative life-styles, co-operatives, autonomous housing and rural villages.' The Kazanski design utilised 'a monorail local public transport system' to 'run through the development, linking "honky tonk" entertainment situated at the lake edge to a transport interchange … at the civic knoll.' The 'Honky Tonk' (also known as the 'Honky Tonky') was an undefined entertainment and exhibition precinct at the heart of the city. Kazanski declared that the '"Honky Tonky" entertainment clusters on the lake edge could include a variety of bright and lively fun uses.' In the main, these were unspecified, and it is possible that to the degree that the Monarto Development Commission considered the ways in which alcohol should or could be consumed it preferred a dispersed design. Certainly, it espoused a community-based ideal which drew implicitly from the spirit of post-war community programs such as that at Nuriootpa; the proud South Australian tradition of the Gothenburg-model community hotel; and the small neighbourhood centre hotels of Canberra:

> It is the Commission's intention to encourage the building of small neighbourhood 'pubs' where social drinking and conversation can be enjoyed in a homely and unhurried atmosphere. It is hoped that the 'human scale' of these mini-hotels will help towards a feeling of belonging and combat the suburban loneliness so apparent in today's larger centres.

Don Dunstan, wine in hand, on the cover of *Campaign* magazine, 1976 (Australian Queer Archives)

Rock In The Pubs advertisement, 1979

There is a sense, then, in which the Monarto planners strived to create a drinking environment which furthered social support and neighbourliness. This proposal, like many of the more enticing of Monarto's experiments, was more a 'vibe' than anything, notwithstanding that the MDC commissioned an extraordinarily large number of reports in preparation for its ideal new city.

Yet even as the Monarto plans were hatching, the reality of the pub experience was undergoing an extreme makeover in the extant major metropolitan centres: the pub would become a late 20th century locus not merely of new entertainment modes but new forms of cultural expression.

Pub Rock

Pub rock is not a genre, even if The Angels' 'Take a Long Line' instantly sprung into your head just then. The graduation of popular music into hotel environments – which often, at least in the imaginations of witnesses and creators, served as proving grounds – became de rigeur in the 1970s. The appropriation of hotels such as the Kingston, Richmond in the mid-to-late 70s by aspirational litterateurs Johnny Topper and Peter Lillie have become legendary elements in the story of Australian pop music: their bands the Leisuremasters, the Relaxed Mechanics and most prominently the Pelaco Brothers emerged from this crucible.

In the ten years between 1965 and 1975, consumption of live music at a 'local' level underwent a huge change. Broadly speaking folk coffee houses, which did not serve alcohol or feature amplified instruments, were a recognised phenomenon (to the degree that, like pubs, they were a frequent locational device in *Homicide*) between the early and late 1960s. They coexisted with both suburban dances in town halls or similar clubs and frequented by an all-ages audience, and 'discotheques' which, once again, did not allow sale or consumption of alcohol. Yet all were to be superseded after

1970 by pub rock: two or three electric rock bands on one night at a bar between 8pm–1am; alcohol served and clientele, officially, over 18.

Of course, people who attended suburban dances in the sixties and seventies will tell you that there was alcohol to be had – particularly if you smuggled it in, or perhaps swilled outside – but overall the phenomenon of rock music and drinking as a snug fit was not greatly understood or appreciated until the early 70s; at this time it went hand-in-hand with a liberalisation of the drinking laws which saw the legal limit for entry to licensed premises go down from 21 to 18. Bruce Howe remarks, in Victor Marshall's book recording the history of the South Australian group Fraternity, that in the early 1970s '[t]he pub scene in South Australia allowed eighteen-year-olds to go to a pub, open till midnight. You could put on a rock show and get sixteen-year olds who would pass for eighteen.' Along with other external factors the new development saw a greater disjunct between teenagers and young adults in terms of music consumption and creation: there were now 'heavy' and 'progressive' bands, and lighter, bubblegum bands. Progressive bands preferred not to play to drunk crowds; the (correct) assumption was not only that alcohol made people more violent, it also made them less intelligent.

TF Much Ballroom advertisement, 1970

Lou Williams of the Village Green Hotel claimed in 1971 to have started the pub rock scene a few years earlier. An article written by Peter Walsh in *Daily Planet* in September of that year quoted Williams saying that 'People come from everywhere' to get to the hotel; 'from every side of the city, from country areas, even from other states. They drive, they walk, they hitchhike.'

Walsh himself observed:

> A curious aspect of the 'Village Green' is that its character changes abruptly when the rock and roll groups have gone. If the bands are not there, neither are the beautiful people. In their place are to be found the usual beer-slurping, back-slapping young groovers; getting drunk in serene harmony with their elders. So don't linger after the band finishes its gig.

During this period, some performers like Russell Morris refused to play in hotels, 'which my manager can't understand 'cause that's where the bread is ... I want people to listen to what I'm doing, plus of course, I'm still trying to overcome my pop star image.' Peter Weir's 1972 film *Three Directions in Australian Pop Music* captures a show at Melbourne's T. F. Much Ballroom featuring Spectrum, Wendy Saddington and Captain Matchbox; much more of a 'head' experience, at least ostensibly, Weir not only captures a time and space but also overlays a subtle storyline, of an archaically-attired outsider who stumbles on the show hoping to make friends and finds himself ostracised by the 'in-crowd'. While Weir is not hereby making a direct comment on rock music in pubs – he's commenting on the elitism of art rock audiences generally – there is definitely no atmosphere of camaraderie evident in this display: the clientele are stony-faced and cross-legged.

By the 1980s groups like INXS were readily peddling the story that their hardiness as a band was founded in the mythic 'beer barns' of the Australian suburbs. Australian audiences, the story went, forced groups to trim the fat, limit experimentation, and serve punters succinctly. Yet groups like Do Re Mi – operating on their own terms – moved to Sydney from Melbourne in 1981 eager to avoid the standard circuits. 'There must be something in the air that make some people say: "G'day mate, givvus a Fozzie"', Helen Carter told *On the Street* magazine's Peter Holden in 1984. 'We want to avoid that kind of presentation – not because we are ashamed of Australia or we have the cultural cringe, it's just we don't talk or behave like drunken idiots.'

Famously, another group negotiated this entirely reasonable position to a new place soon after Carter's diatribe. What was most extraordinary was that Hunters and Collectors morphed from what Stuart Coupe described as 'an arty, idiosyncratic band who explored complex rhythms' and founder-member Greg Perano described (half-jokingly?) as 'Reggae funk fusion with rock roots and a tinge of New York underground in the guitars' to a hugely successful rock group with an underpinning in pub rock. Their second LP, *The Fireman's Curse*, was a dense artistic statement, ostensibly a 'fuck you' to their British label, Virgin. It does contain one song – 'Drinking Bomb' – which might point the way to their future ('Come with me now and we'll drink this dream away'). The group's music, beginning with their third album *The Jaws of Life* – ostensibly a concept album inspired at least in small part by truck driver Douglas Crabbe's drink-fuelled murder of five patrons at the Inland Hotel, Uluru in 1983 – changed considerably. Solid and dense, the songs were shorter, wordier and more pointedly concerned with heterosexual relationships from a male point of view. Seymour ascribes the change not to the departure of core members, or to the group's nominal 'failure' in the UK following *The Fireman's Curse*, but to his experience of seeing the seminal group X at the Manly Tavern. He writes in his memoir *Thirteen Tonne Theory*:

> About two hundred people turned up and watched X blow us away. It was humiliating. They were a three-piece rock band that played a kind of deep, grinding R&B, with a singer

who howled in agony and a bass player who slammed the beat into the floor. They were overwhelming, committed, passionate... we never came close to generating the same level of power. I never forgot. I raved about them.

The present author recalls strong resistance amongst the tastemaking cognoscenti (this is not sarcasm) of Melbourne when Hunters and Collectors firstly, refused to disintegrate in the face of 'failure' in Britain and secondly chose to refocus away from the inner city and toward a specialised – if broad and often free-spending – market, that of lonely and/or misunderstood men in pubs across the metropolises of the nation. That their base might, from a 21st century perspective, have the slight taint of the incel about it is not a critique of Hunters and Collectors. The group merely identified a cohort and a mindset, and there was more self-loathing than misogyny in their songs. In so doing they broke down barriers between band and audience, but also spoke to the drunken self-pity of the alcoholic male in a way few had achieved previously. This became their entrée to the mainstream – the 're-vamped/re-booted' group designated 'Mk 2' by member Jack Howard in his memoir *Small Moments of Glory* has now entered the echelons of 'classic rock', for better or worse. It was also the time at which the group produced its best work.

The Old Man's Pub

Morphologies do not come with clean breaks. However, a specific moment in time, which I would place at around 2005, can" provide an effective ending to this overview. At this time some friends were assisting in the operation of a renovated Brunswick hotel which offered not only live music every night but also dining on premises, in a room reminiscent of a 1960s café.

One major issue was the old customers, who continued to regard the gentrified hotel as theirs, and who sought to establish their ownership by bringing food from nearby takeaways into the front bar on a daily basis. I have often dwelt on a remembered scene of a young female employee snatching a kebab out of a middle-aged man's hands. Both were angry, but he and his cronies were laughing, too; he was with his men, and they had achieved, in essence, a victory in having upset a young woman.

This scene is merely a reflection on class conflict and associated misogyny but it does bring together the three slices of this chapter in one illustrative outcome. Whereas the hotel in question had long been of the variety depicted in the 1960s representations mentioned above, and had resisted (as had much of Brunswick) attempts to drag it into the idealistic, leisure-, family-, community-based ideal of, for instance, the 1970s new towns, a live-music-led gentrifying push was the final nail in the coffin of these particular men's watering hole. Putting aside what any particular pub should be, the changed nature of what it could or can be over half a century has been remarkable.

CHAPTER 42

ALCOHOL AND THE LAW: THE 1979 FRANKSTON RIOT AND OTHER STORIES

John Finlayson in conversation with Alex Ettling

John Finlayson has had a lifelong commitment to social justice. His activism began as an apprentice and member of the Young Christian Workers during the late 1950s and early 1960s, before he went on to work as a youth advocate. In this chapter he discusses the role of alcohol in fundraising for political causes, and associated hazards, as well as his role in the founding of the Fitzroy Legal Service. The recollections outlined in the following oral history also cover the provision of legal advice at the Rainbow Hotel, organising in pubs, and the events leading up to and following the 1979 Frankston Riot.

Unionism and Joining the Young Christian Workers

I hated school. I tried to fail every subject to let my old man know I didn't want to go back. It was so authoritarian. And it didn't hold my attention at all. I deliberately tried to fail Christian doctrine. No catholic would fail Christian doctrine, but this little fella (points at himself), he did everything possible. And they still passed me (laughs). I got out of school at Year 9 in 1958, and I became an apprentice moulder.

Sinclair and Duncan was the company, it had about 120 workers. It was working with liquid metal in a foundry where they have these big furnaces. Five tonnes of liquid metal, poured into castings.

It was covered by the Federated Moulders Union. If you've got really well organised trade unions, the workers will have some fundamental rights. The workplace had been on a successful strike, so I experienced all that. It wasn't just over wages, it was over occupational health and safety conditions. A foundry would probably be one of the worst places in Australia for OHS dangers. Your chances of death or serious injury are really high. Liquid metal. Have you ever seen liquid metal on skin? It melts it. It melts *you*. Once a ball of liquid metal bounced off me and went down my boot. I was off for three and a half months. It's very scary.

I was still in my fifth year of the apprenticeship during that strike. Apprentices weren't allowed to go on strike, it was a breach and you'd lose your apprenticeship agreement. I was allowed to attend union meetings, which I would.

After the strike I started to learn how to communicate with other tradies about injustices, because I didn't exactly know how to put forward what convinces people in meetings and stuff like that. I started to teach other young people, who were apprentices, how to stand up for our rights. Apprentices were fundamentally being abused, given all the shit jobs, told to get lunches, all this sort of crap. It wasn't learning the trade half the time, it was just being used up.

So we were starting to stand up for our rights. So my social justice activism started in the foundry.

On one occasion I was in the office of the managing director, Mr Sinclair, and I argued he should give his workers minority shares. It would be much more collective, and he'd get more money. He exploded, he told me I was a communist and wanted to know who'd been influencing me, 'Where did you get these ideas?! If I see you talking to any other worker about what you've been talking to me about I'll sack you on the spot. Get out of my office!' They were Young Christian Workers (YCW) ideas.

With the YCW, the emphasis was on the workers, and I was one. They would encourage you to be in a union, to stand up for other young workers. In 1966 I became a full time youth worker for the YCW.

I realised a lot of things in the late 60s. That's when a lot of YCWs and lots of Catholic Priests broke away and tossed it in. What happened was there was a bloke called Pope Paul XXIII, and he was a radical sort of pope. And he was into participation in decision making by the laity, that's the people not the bishops. He created what is called the second ecumenical council (Vatican II).

This guy was a pretty radical sort of fella, pretty progressive. It started to impact in the local areas right across Australia. But when the pope died his successor wound it all back. You could take the Pill, and now you couldn't, things like that.

The YCW was seen as a fairly progressive side of the Catholic church, and it was very strong. There were 40 000 or 50 000 members, that's a lot of young people. The young people were the decision makers in the local branches. You'd be encouraging young people to participate. It was about empowerment.

It was teaching young people to be decision makers in issues that impacted them. Then you'd apply the religious part: 'What would Christ do in a circumstance like this? How would he deal with this?' 'Christ in Action' so to speak. What would Christ do when he was confronted by a pack of arseholes, how would he handle it? You'd apply that to the practise of what you're doing in everyday life. And I became good at doing it, but I didn't know I was good at it until many years later.

There were two sides of the ALP then. The Democratic Labour Party was an [anti-communist] offshoot created by the Catholic Church. B.A. Santamaria was behind it all. I saw him as an extreme right-wing prick, I couldn't stand him or anything he stood for. So I suppose you could say I was more on the socialist side, although in the YCW circles you never talked about that. You never talked about it In political labels, you just talked about it in rights terms. Young workers rights, injustices in the workplace. Those were the words you would use.

I was an activist, and I went to protest marches. I was really heavily into the Vietnam stuff, and that was a major issue for the YCW. That was why there was a breakdown between the Catholic Church and the YCW. We were absolutely opposed to the draft, sending a young person aged 20 years, to send them off to fight.

Iron Moulders Society of Victoria banner, 1873
(Australasian Sketcher)

Draft Resistance, a Police Raid and the Fitzroy ALP

I was involved in the Draft Resistance Movement. It was 1972 or 73. There were three draft resisters who had been charged and put on bail, and so this woman had put up $2500 of her own money to get them out. It was a lot of money then, enough to put a deposit on a house.

She lost it because if you put up bail money and they abscond, you lose the money. So they put on a fundraising event because it was felt she shouldn't be the one to carry the responsibility, that the draft resistance movement should wear it.

I was the caretaker of this YCW building in Brighton. So they asked me if I would be prepared to allow it to be the place where they held the function. There were a lot of people that went, maybe 300. They had a band lined up. But the main thing was that they would make profit through the buying of the grog because they got most of the grog donated to them.

And we got busted.

The Draft Resistance Movement's headquarters were in Chapel Street Prahran. It was the DMZ bookshop, meaning demilitarised zone. They always seemed to wonder why the Commonwealth cops knew what they were doing in advance, and ASIO. We hated ASIO. I still don't like ASIO, they're arseholes.

Draft resistor Bob Scates, a member of the Socialist Left of the ALP with John Finlayson, in 1989 published an account of the movement called *Draftmen Go Free*. Scates is pictured on the cover holding a beer just after being released from Pentridge prison.

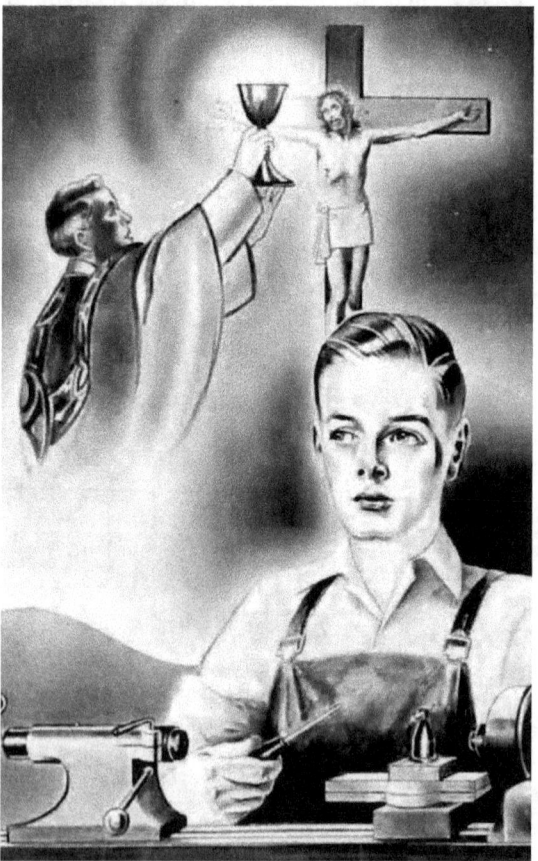

Illustration from *I Pledge Myself to Save Young Workers*, a Young Christian Workers pamphlet, early 1960s (Victorian Collections)

This was a period when beanbags were really in, they were really popular in the early 70s, and they had them at the DMZ bookshop where they'd have the meetings. One day they had a bean bag fight, and eventually one split open and this bug spilled out. Most of the bean bags had bugs in them. Commonwealth cops had planted all these bugs, no wonder they knew everything.

The cops came into the fundraising party and busted us. The feds couldn't bust us 'cos it's a state law. So the feds got the vice squad to bust us instead.

We had an 18er and 9er [beer kegs], all got confiscated. 12 dozen bottles of red, 12 dozen bottles of white. Flagons, not just bottles. They confiscated the lot, and I got charged with 'serving alcohol on a Sunday without a license.' I had to go to the Brighton Court, and that's when I got lined up with these barristers, Peter Farris and Remy van de Wiel. They ended up being the first lot of volunteer lawyers for the Fitzroy Legal Service.

The line of defence was 'he wasn't aware of what they were doing, he thought it was just to help young people', blah blah blah. And, 'he also believed there were five other functions going on in the area that were all serving alcohol on a Sunday.' They were footy clubs and sporting clubs. And that's what it was, the whole area, the whole of Victoria, serving alcohol on a Sunday without a license because everyone was doing fundraising functions.

At this stage I was also working as a youth worker for Fitzroy City Council. I remember the Fitzroy mayor came up to me one day, and he reminded me that he was aware that I could be in a bit of trouble for serving alcohol on a Sunday without a license. 'Mr Finlayson, if you go down on that you've lost your job.' He was the big boss, and he was going to sack me.

Fitzroy was the Labor Party branch I was involved in, and I was involved when it broke from the machine politics. A number of ex-YCWs joined the Socialist Left of the Labor Party. I used to have long sessions on Marxism and the understanding of Marxism, and the means of production and the relations of production which are relevant for workers.

The old guard of the Labor Party were very right-wing. They used the votes of dead people to maintain their power. They had all these people rising up out of the grave to vote for them. They were using the Fitzroy Community Youth Centre as a cover for a lot of the work they were doing. We were not supposed to know, 'you're just the youth worker, John.' I'm telling you the truth, it was amazing stuff.

So the only way we could ever break their stronghold open, was to chop out the vote area that was illegal, and that's what happened. We went to every house door to door in Fitzroy and

Fitzroy Legal Service did outreach at the Turana Youth Justice Centre, *Bits of My Life: A Turana Book* (Department of Health and Human Services, State Government of Victoria)

North Fitzroy to see which persons were alive and which persons weren't alive. It took two elections, but they eventually got routed.

Anyway, I wasn't found guilty of alcohol charges and the old guard Labor mayor couldn't sack me.

Youth Work and Legal Advice

I wasn't a lawyer. I was a youth worker and the coach of a footy team. And it was the footy team where the problems with the law arose. That's how I got involved in the law.

A couple of blokes knocked on my door and said 'we're from the YCW, and every Friday night we get a lot of young people together, we've got our own youth club rooms, would you like to come?' And I thought, 'oh why not? I think it might be a good way to reach young people, a good idea.' There was a whole range of different social issues where young people were fundamentally being marginalised by society. My brief was in experimenting in youth work. And what they meant by experimenting was carrying out new ways of dealing with young people and setting up alternative youth programs.

Really the sort of thing I was doing, formally it became called 'outreach youth work'. That means where the youth worker wasn't working within a youth centre, so much as they were working on the street, or wherever those young people were. You'd reach them and get to know them, find out about them and what they were interested in, what sort of things they'd like to get interested in.

The Young Christian Workers had footy, a big structure, a huge structure. Something like about 500 footy teams in Victoria. It was a really good recruiting ground for the VFL because it was under 19s. So I was the coach of the Fitzroy YCW team in 1972. This is the team that a year later joined with a Westgarth team to become the Fitzroy Stars after our team got kicked out of the league.

Our biggest problems was our spectators. And the rules in the YCW competition were that you were responsible for your spectators. But we couldn't control these spectators, and some of them had guns, and they'd shoot them in the air. I'd have to blast the shit out of them and say, 'if you do it again, get yourself another coach! I'm not going to put up with that shit.'

At the time lots of kids were getting in trouble with the cops for street offenses. A lot of street gangs then. Burglary, shoplifting, theft, assault, break and enter. Theft of motorcars was really big. They had a law then called 'illegal use' which was basically joyriding.

Young people, some of whom were in the football team, would say, 'Look I've just been charged by the cops, I don't know what to do.' They knew I was a youth worker as well as a coach, so they thought I might know. They needed legal assistance but didn't have any money. They were all under 18, so it was mainly children's court stuff. These kids were going before the courts and sticking their hands up for stuff they didn't do because they were so frightened, very much frightened by the cops in the cop shop. If you're belted into submission, you admit things you didn't do, because you

Fitzroy Legal Service produced books and pamphlets for the public, 1970s (John Corker)

don't want to be belted anymore. It's a very common practice, especially at places like Fitzroy cop shop.

So I was going to the children's court or the magistrates court to speak up for them.

Magistrates, they want some background about: why did this character break the law, what's behind it? They needed an advocate in court to go against the cop's testimony.

They were going to end up generally in Turana Youth Hostel (age 15-17) or Baltara (age 10-14). These were youth institutions. I was anti-institutions. All of them. Institutionalisation, that's something that really disturbs me.

So that was the story, and I thought, 'shit this is terrible.' That was the turning point for me.

You get a reputation without knowing you're getting a reputation. Often you'd get kids not going to jail but on a good behaviour bond or an adjourned sentence. Or instead of going to the youth institution they got two years probation. So that was happening by me going to the courts, and it got around. Other young people when they were in trouble, they'd say: 'go see the coach, he'll help you.'

I had so many young people that needed lawyers, and I had no lawyers, and I was desperate.

There's more to youth work than being a character witness. I was going to court three or four times a week. It takes time, you've got to go into the city, you've got to dress up in a bloody suit. You've got to do your research on the kid a bit. The amount of kids was just banking up.

The problem was legal aid didn't exist. There was a thing called the Victorian Legal Aid Committee but it was in high demand, with no response for 4 months, so useless. And if they were eligible, they had to pay it off like you pay off a TV set. I was swamped and I couldn't keep it up. So I held a public meeting. About 12 of those young people from my football team came to that meeting and spoke at the meeting saying that they wanted lawyers. That's how the Fitzroy Legal Service started in December 1972.

Fitzroy Legal Service, with John Finlayson second from right, 1970s (John Corker)

With our volunteers we were open six nights a week, from 5.30 pm to 11 pm. I was interviewed on the second day by Channel 9 and the ABC. It exploded. We were averaging between 100-150 people. The queue would go around the town hall and down the street, which goes to show you the unmet legal need in Australia.

We then started outreach law programs through the Fitzroy Legal Service. We would run legal education programs for young people, things about what to do if you were arrested, what were your rights when you are a tenant.

We'd do outreach law at the high rise flats. At the Turkish welfare centre in Brunswick during Saturday morning shopping. We did one in a pool room called Johnny's Green Room. I would be the non-lawyer and I'd have a lawyer with me. We'd go there at 10 o'clock and stay there until 1 am.

I had one in Turana – *inside* the institution. And I was teaching young people their rights, and of course the screws hated my guts.

There were seven of these outreach programs. I even had one in a pub. The pub was the Rainbow Hotel. I lived there for nine months at one stage when the cops were after me. It was a folky club, folk musicians used to go there, and I knew the publican really well who was an ex-priest. A bloke called Costigan. You know Frank Costigan, the 'bottom of the harbour' bloke [who led a royal commission into the Federated Ship Painters and Dockers Union and then organised crime and tax evasion]? This was his brother, Paul Costigan.

It was a lunchtime program. Pam O'Connor was a full-time lawyer with Fitzroy Legal Service. I would go there with her every Tuesday and Thursday, and she would have lunch there. And in that time, anyone at the bar, if they wanted to speak to a lawyer, she'd go upstairs into a room. It became well known that program.

So you're bringing the law to the people, you're not making the people go to the law.

We would have semi-meetings in pubs. You'd say, 'How bout we have a beer and work out something.' I did that for years. I used to hit the piss a lot. I was a heavy drinker, but not in the sense that I was drunk every day.

I had firsthand experience of the six o'clock swill. When I was a young worker, hotels closed at six o'clock. So young people would get bored shitless. What are they gonna do after six o'clock? Y'know they can't have a drink, or if they can they'd have to get access to the grog before it shut. It didn't give you much time if you were a worker. So that's why they called it the six o'clock swill. You had 15 minutes to knock down your drinks. If there's a team of four or five of you, you're sculling four or five drinks in 15 minutes. In that period if you were young then you wanted to show you could drink, to prove yourself. That was definitely part of the culture.

Drinking and the law are incredibly related, absolutely. Lawyers drink a lot, especially barristers. The drinking culture was sometimes inside the cop shop too. They'd be pissed and sometimes they'd be out of control.

The Frankston Riot

I'd been in Fitzroy for four years. There was a job going to be community centre director in the Pines Forest Community Centre, employed by the Frankston City Council. The bloke who talked me into it was Albert Van Moorst. He said it would do me good. 'Move on, don't stay in one place too long. Don't become institutionalised.' There's a really strong philosophy on this approach to life, particularly as you're working with the public. If you stay in one place too long you'll become entrenched and you won't be a change agent anymore for development. So his line would be, your body changes every day until you die, so you've got to be changing with it. Good line when you think about it. Great philosophy, if you can implement it. It's very easy not to implement it. The brain looks for alternatives not to work hard.

Pines Forest was a Ministry Housing Estate. Roughly 3800 houses, roughly 10 000 residents. 180 of those homes were navy homes, sailors employed in the navy, that's where they'd live because it was near Hastings. You've got two little roads on the side of this estate, that was the only access. On the back of that estate were two 18 hole private golf courses, and the other side of the estate were sand dunes. It was a classic ghetto. The State Government of Victoria created a ghetto, the people didn't create it.

The background to the 1979 Frankston riot was that six months before, a campaign had been developed to get young people off the streets. Downtown Frankston has heaps of shopping areas and young people would hit the piss. They might urinate in a doorway, or leave their bottles and empty cans and rubbish from hamburgers and whatever else they were doing. The shopkeepers were saying, 'You're the council, what the bloody hell are you doing about it?' The council started putting pressure on the cops. The more they were moving the kids on or charging them, the more the young people were starting to get really pissed off. So over this period of six months the relationship was getting really bad. Young people were coming to me with these ridiculous charges. And their complaints seemed to be pretty reasonable. You'd have write ups every week in the local newspaper about young people doing something bad.

The message being passed on by young people to the community was that they were very unhappy with life and they were pissed off. They were in this ghetto and treated like shit, and if you were from The Pines you were a 'Pines Boy', and you were a rat bastard and not worth looking at twice.

So this is developing, and it all exploded one Friday night. In a whole municipality of about 80 000 people, all they had was these four pubs, and three on one intersection. There was this disabled man, he was well-known and well-liked by the drinkers at the pubs. When he walked he walked like he was pissed, but he wasn't pissed. It was just part of his disability. He had a walking stick but he didn't like using it, particularly when he went to the pub as he wanted to be accepted. He felt like if he had this walking stick he was out of place. And they really liked this guy, he was a nice fella, he'd usually only have a couple of drinks and go home.

This particular night, he finished his drink, and he's walking down Davey Street, which is the main street of Frankston, and the cops spot him. They see he was staggering and think that he's pissed, so they pull him over and throw him in the back of the divvy van. There's 30-40 teenagers looking out the windows of the pub, and they can see what they're doing and they lose it. They all rush out of the pub and they're saying, 'Let him go, he's not drunk. Let him go, you're being really unfair.' So they tried to help, they tried to do the right thing, and the cops ignored them. Which cops do. They told them to shove off because you're distracting them from their duty, that's how they see it.

They shut the divvy van doors and drive him 200 metres down the road to where the cop shop is. They kids chased the van. The cops get the bloke out of the van in time before all these young people try to get into the doors of the cop shop. And this is amazing, it just explodes, because people from the other two pubs see

Three pubs were concentrated at this main junction in Frankston

what's happening down the road, and the word is getting around about what the cops are doing. Next minute they charge the cop shop and before you know it there's young people swarming around this cop shop.

They were up on the roof, ripping tiles off the roof. So the whole thing is out of hand. There was also a hall opposite the cop shop where there was an unlicensed discotheque happening, so no alcohol, and young people from there also joined in. It was classified as an 'affray'. An affray is like close to being a revolutionary situation. They read the Riot Act. The last time that ever happened in Victoria. They called cops from all over the eastern side of Melbourne.

The Fitzroy Legal Service began exposing corruption in the Victorian Police and was shortly after set on fire, 1980s (John Corker)

So they save their cop shop and get it under control, and after the dust settles they start charging people. There were 13 young people charged. Guess where 11 of those people were from? The Pines. So does that mean that the only people in that riot were Pines people? Not at all. They were just plucking people out of the crowd that they recognised, that's what they did.

You had people going down in the courts who shouldn't have been. One of those arrested, he was a 17 year old English boy on a holiday who had been at the discotheque and was watching but wasn't involved. He was sent to jail. It was terrible, it really damaged him long term.

They had to get an example. That was what they were into. It was like 'if none of you bastards go down, that will encourage them to do it again.'

I knew some of these young people. I found out the story the next day when I went into work. It didn't take long to be in touch with most things that happened on that night. I spoke to the publicans too. They thought the young people were badly done by. They didn't blame them for doing what they did. They didn't agree with what they did, y'know jumping on top of the cop shop, that was a bit too much for them. But they could understand why they did what they did.

The story needed to be told. Sonia Humphrey, a journalist from the ABC, she wanted to interview me live on *This Day Tonight* on the Monday. I got a call from my manager saying you're not allowed to go on television. I said, 'Why not?', and the answer was that the Chief Executive Officer of the Frankston City Council has demanded that you do not appear, and if you do appear you've lost your job. We found out the next day that the reason was because it would have uncovered that it was the Frankston Council that set up this campaign six months earlier. I really wanted to do it, I really wanted to expose the bastards. I wanted to stand up for young people that needed their side of the story to be told. They might have done all these naughty things along the way, urinating and all sorts of stupid things that young people do, and they might have swarmed the cop shop. But why did they swarm the cop shop? Why did they lose the plot? What caused that?

Six weeks later I was back working with the Fitzroy Legal Service because they'd asked me to apply for a job as the administrator. So I was back in Fitzroy after four years in Frankston. After I left the job I made a statement about what was happening in Frankston around the riot, and it was on the front page of the *Frankston Standard*. The police carried out a major investigation to figure out what to do if such a thing were ever to happen again. And out of that became the creation of community policing in Victoria. That was a consequence of the Frankston Riot.

The riot would never ever have happened, but for the six months build up of harassment. The young people were on edge, right across Frankston. In regards to going into pubs, or going anywhere in downtown Frankston, because the police would harass the shit out of you. Society itself has to take some blame. Young people are not the decision makers, we didn't give them that power. Decision making is an exercise in power. What those young people saw was an abuse of power, they saw cops abusing their power by treating that disabled person like that.

And some of those cops never forgave me. I've got a few enemies down that way, trying to stand up for young people.

Living at the Rainbow and Taking Up the Law

I continued to be part of a public campaign against police misconduct, not just in Frankston but also in places like Flemington and Northcote. The Fitzroy Legal Service was set on fire in 1981 because someone was trying to burn all the files – the complaints against the cops. I was picked up 31 times in a period of six weeks, in my car. And then I started to get death threats. I knew who the death threats were from but I couldn't do anything about it. It was a copper. Then I was told by some very senior lawyers not to live in the house where I was living in, because I was at risk.

So I went into hiding at the Rainbow Hotel in 1981. I was there for somewhere between six and nine months. It was fascinating living in a pub. That's when the folk music was still in full flight. Every Thursday night it was on, and sometimes those folkies would just come other nights and just play at the bar. And they were really good. I was a single guy then, and it was very distracting. It was an amazing place.

Over the years I was getting pressured by a lot of people to do law. So eventually in 1991 I started my law degree and it took me six years doing it part time. It was like getting out of jail when I'd finished it. Once you've done your law degree, and then you've done your article clerkship, you then have to be admitted to practice. You go before three judges. Every person who makes their application has to make a declaration of any misdemeanour. Even if you've been to court and found not guilty you still have to declare it. So I had to declare the 'serving alcohol on a Sunday without a license'. And I did that, but it wasn't enough for them. They wanted to interview me.

We sat down and they asked me a series of questions, not just on the 'serving alcohol on a Sunday without a license', but they wanted to ask me a lot of questions to do with the Fitzroy Legal Service. And the main question they had was 'Did you found the Fitzroy Legal Service?', and they all had these big smiles on their faces. Found out a couple of years later they were betting on it: everyone wants to say they're a founder of the Fitzroy Legal Service. They were having a bet on whether I'd say it!

CHAPTER 43

BLACK POWER AND ALCOHOL: AN ORAL HISTORY WITH GARY FOLEY

Gary Foley in conversation with Alex Ettling

Professor Gary Foley (b 1950), actor, activist and academic historian, was a key member of the Aboriginal Black Power movement. He has been at the centre of major political activities in Australia for more than 40 years. Foley was involved in the establishment of some of the first Aboriginal community-controlled organisations including Redfern's Aboriginal Legal Service, the Aboriginal Health Service in Melbourne, and the National Black Theatre. His acting career began with the revue *Basically Black* (1972), and he appeared in the seminal films *Backroads* (1976) and *Dogs in Space* (1986). Since 2008, he has been an academic at Victoria University.

Gary Foley: I've always blamed Billy Hunter for what I consider to be my alcoholic decade.

Here's how we did business in the old Black Power movement. I got a phone call one day in about 1974, and at that time I was living between Sydney and Melbourne, Redfern and Fitzroy. And I got this phone call, 'My name's Phillip Noyce', and I said 'yeah, so what.' 'I'm a film maker and I'd like to consult you about this script.' I said 'Yeah sure, come and see me in my office'. He said 'Where's your office?' In those days the way you tested out whitefellas who rung us up in Redfern and wanted to talk to us, was you made them come and visit you in Redfern which most whitefellas wouldn't do. They were too scared, it was a scary place, especially after dark. I said, 'Sure, come and visit me in my office. The Cricketers Arms Hotel, which is the next pub down from The Clifton.' Because I knew I was going to be there that night having a drink with Kevin Smith and some people.

So, to my surprise this guy turned up, and he walked in the door, I knew him straight away because he was 6'6 tall, built like a brick shithouse, and looked everything like a cop. So as soon as he walked in, everyone in the pub turned around and froze (laughs). And he was looking around, and then he spotted me, and he came racing over, he said 'Gary Foley?' I said 'Yes.' He said, 'I'm Phillip Noyce.' I said 'Quick, buy me a drink otherwise everybody here is gonna think you're a cop.' So, then he said have a look at this script, and I had a look at it and a week later I called him up and I said, 'The first thing you gotta do is throw out this dialogue because it doesn't ring true.' And then he turned around and said, 'I'd like you to play the lead role.' And I said, 'I'm not a fucking actor.' He said, 'I saw you in *Basically Black*.' I said, 'That was years ago, and I'm not an actor.' Then he told me what I might earn from playing this lead role, and I gotta say at the time it sounded like a hell of a lot of money. But as I discovered later in life, and at the end of making this film, it wasn't that much money at all.

I said I want to choose the person who plays the white redneck in this film. He said, 'Oh yeah, who?' I said, 'A bloke named Billy Hunter. He's a bloke who knows blackfellas, he's known in the communities where I suggest you make this film, and he knows the sort of person that this character is.' So Noyce said yes, and next thing we know we end up in this caravan park in North Bourke, and the next morning we're about to start filming *Backroads*, and we're sitting around this campfire, and I pull Billy aside and I said 'Hey Billy, can I talk to ya?', and he said 'Yeah', and I said 'Listen, I've told this Noyce character that I can act, and you and I both know that I can't act. What am I going to do tomorrow morning?' He said, 'Don't worry Foley, do what I do. Just watch what I do and do what I do.' I said, 'Oh yeah, okay.' We'll see how it goes.

The next morning, five o'clock in the morning we're set up to shoot the first scene in this film, and everything is set up, and suddenly Billy says, 'Right, that's it, we're not working', and Noyce, greenhorn director, this was his first feature film, gets flustered, he says, 'What do you mean?' And Hunter says, 'We're not working, sorry, we're downing tools, so to speak.' Noyce says, 'What's going on?', and Hunter said, "We're not starting work until you've got two slabs of VB here on set.' And Noyce says, 'Where the fuck am I gonna get two slabs of VB at five o'clock in the morning in Bourke?', and Hunter says, 'I don't care. It's not our problem.' About 20 minutes later Noyce comes roaring back with two slabs of VB, and Hunter said to Noyce, 'Right. Relax for 10 minutes.' And Noyce went away and Hunter said to me, 'Now, Foley. Here's your first acting lesson. Help me drink these.' And we drank a slab of VB, me and Hunter between us, and then Hunter said, 'Right Noyce, we're ready to work.' And from that moment on, if you look at that film, you'll see there's a lot of alcohol drunk. And every drop of alcohol that is drunk in that film is real alcohol.

Now 20 years later, Noyce had a biography written about him by some German academic. I read this biography, it's called *Backroads to Hollywood*. Anyway, in the first chapter it's about the making of *Backroads*. And Noyce claims to this German biographer, Noyce reckons because it was his first ever feature film he didn't realise that you use prop alcohol. The truth was he wasn't game to argue with Billy Hunter. But as I say to people, making Backroads was the last time I was sober for a decade.

....

Richard Lowenstein's film *Dogs In Space* is a key artefact of the Australian punk movement. Foley lived in the sharehouse that inspired the film, and performed in the movie. He was also invited by The Clash on their 1982 Australian tour to address their audience on Aboriginal political issues.

Gary Foley drinks cold tea as a prop to replace Southern Comfort in *Dogs in Space*, 1986 (Richard Lowenstein)

GF: When I was living in that fucking house in Richmond that was in *Dogs in Space*, I mean I was out of control then. And then when they made the film, 10 years later, that's when I wasn't drinking. So, I was playing myself as a drunk 10 years earlier but now I wasn't drinking, so when I was swigging that bottle of Southern Comfort, it had cold tea in it, and it tasted fucking awful (laughs).

I spent a good decade pretty much an alcoholic, I reckon. Drinking Southern Comfort, through the 70s into the 80s. At times I was drinking up to a bottle of spirits a day. And after I turned 40 I stopped drinking altogether for more than a decade. When I turned 40, I stopped and thought to myself, 'If I keep living how I been living for the last 20 years, I'll be dead before I'm 50.' So I stopped drinking for almost a decade. And these days I'll have two glasses of wine with mostly water, and usually I'll have a bottle of water and I just keep topping it up. I stopped drinking, I stopped smoking. I only lasted three years, and then I had a heart attack five years later and that stopped me again for a fucking long time. But then I started again, and had another heart attack, and I'm in the process of stopping again.

Alex Ettling: The town of Bourke in NSW is an iconic place: 'the back of Bourke' as they say. It's part of the story of one of Australia's most famous drinkers Henry Lawson, but it's also part of your story as well, isn't it?

GF: The guts of the Aboriginal Community back then lived on Bourke Reserve. After the 1967 referendum, the state government closed down the apartheid system, and abandoned the reserves. I went to Bourke to help them build an Aboriginal legal service there.

You can see what Bourke looked like back then in *Backroads*, that's filmed in the community. And the opening song in that film is a Dougie Young song 'Pass Him the Flagon Boys' and it's being sung in the film by a real life resident of Bourke Reserve. All the people in that film, and the conditions in that film of that community, that was Bourke Reserve, that was real people living in their real homes. I managed to talk them into letting us film in their midst.

Dougie Young was the Woody Guthrie of Black Australia. No history of Aboriginal country and western is complete without him. He's the seminal man. He lived in the fringe camps around Bourke and western New South Wales. He wrote songs about life in the fringe camps, on the run from the welfare authorities, and getting pinched all the time and locked up because he was a drunk.

Dougie Young, the poet of the fringe camps. In his song 'Victor Podham and His Rusty Hat' he talks about the three sharp turn which was a drink they had in the fringe camp. The hardcore drinkers like him, alcoholics, used to drink methylated spirits (goom). And back in those days methylated spirits used to come in a triangle bottle, and blackfellas being blackfellas to not let whitefellas know what they were talking about used to talk about hitting the three sharp turns which was a bottle of metho.

'Free to fight but not to drink', Bert Groves in the Australian Aboriginal League contingent of a May Day procession, 1947 (Australian War Memorial)

CHAPTER 43 BLACK POWER AND ALCOHOL: AN ORAL HISTORY WITH GARY FOLEY | 294

Clifton Hotel, 1973 (Syd Shelton)

Aboriginal people technically held access to most of the basic citizens rights in NSW, but being able to exercise those rights was another thing. In terms of legal discrimination, one of the last blatant race-based restrictions were laws concerning drinking. The origins of this control over Aboriginal people's alcohol consumption was shaped by the needs of pastoral industry in the 1860s, which had an interest in maintaining a sober Aboriginal population for use as a workforce in the rural economy.

Before March 1963, Aboriginal people in NSW needed a Certificate of Exemption to drink alcohol in public houses or in their own homes. Campaigning in 1962 focused on Section 9 of the Aborigines Protection Act, a cause of some unease amongst those wary of presenting alcohol as a primary issue in civil rights campaigns.

A range of methods were used to entrench discrimination against Aboriginal people. However, campaigning against them could be challenging because many were not explicitly race based. Even with the legalisation of drinking, the use of the Summary Offences Act allowed the police to continue to harass Aboriginal drinkers via the application of dubious minor offenses. There were arrests and imprisonment, and an unofficial curfew was enforced in Redfern. The piecemeal amendment of various restrictive laws coincided with the rapid growth of the Aboriginal community in Redfern and the beginnings of radicalisation.

GF: It was called the 'dog license' because under the old apartheid system in NSW, the only way you could be free from the conditions and application of the Aborigines Act would be to apply for an exemption. The exemption certificate was referred to by blackfellas as a dog license because people who applied for it were looked down upon. You had to prove you were an acceptable person to live within the white community, that's what the exemption was all about. So, it was an insulting thing, and the term dog license was applied in a negative way to the exemption itself and the people that applied for it. People like my father, and many who managed to evade the system, on a matter of principle refused to apply for a dog license. And I can understand those that did back in those days. In order to get a dog license you needed to establish that you were assimilatable, which was the objection that so many people had to it. And it was a hard thing to get anyway.

Once the old reserve system closed down, there was a mass exodus into Redfern. When I first moved to Sydney there were about 1500 Aboriginal people in Redfern, and within 3 years after the 1967 referendum, there was around 35 000. And the thing everyone had in common was poverty. It was an impoverished community but everybody seemed to be luxuriating in their freedom. Among those newfound freedoms was the ability to drink. A lot of people were unemployed and on the dole and getting by however they could, and alcohol for many fresh out of the system just dulled the pain.

But then the Black Power movement emerged out of these pubs, initially out of the Foundation for Aboriginal Affairs down in George St. And there was a pub just down the road from the Foundation where I had my first drink. In fact, three very strong, these days they're matriarchs, but back then they were these three women a bit older than me, and I was fresh from the bush in NSW, very naive, very wet behind the ears, very green. One of the first times I went to the Foundation of Aboriginal Affairs, someone got me to walk down the end of the street on George St to the Prince of Wales Hotel.

There's just a bunch of steps where the pub used to be. It's no longer there. I walked in there, 17 years old, I wasn't even old enough to be in there. I got grabbed by these three women from Cowra. Norma Ingram, and two of her sisters, Pamela and I think it was Millie. Pamela is dead now, but Millie and Norma are matriarchs in Sydney. They grabbed me and they said, 'Sit down, who are you?' They said 'Where are you from?' I said, 'I'm from Nambucca Heads', and Norma said to me, 'I'm married to Gary Williams.' I said, 'That's my cousin.' She said, 'I know, have a drink with us.' I said, 'Oh. I haven't any money', and she said, 'We'll shout.' And they put this glass of whisky in front of me, and they seemed to be drinking something similar or so I thought. And they said, 'Bottom's up.' They shouted me about four whiskeys, it did considerable damage to my ability to walk and other things that night, and they thought it was a great joke (laughs). I wasn't so certain.

AE: There must have been Aboriginal people around who were very anti-alcohol?
GF: They were definitely around. But as they say, 'ne'er the twain shall meet'. Most of the hardcore anti-alcohol mob would have been the Christian mob.

There's a Scottish comedian Kevin Bridges who talks how to handle old blokes in the pubs in Glasgow. Only difference between them and the older conservative generation of Aboriginal reformers is we're talking about drunks in a pub. There's always an old bloke in a bar who is sitting there mouthing off, and as Kevin Bridges says, the people in Glasgow deal with them in these tough pubs, they just sit there, listen to them for a minute. Put their hand on their shoulder and say, 'Have a good night brother', and move away. I mean, it's got to be said that there was a considerably greater Christian contingent in Fitzroy than there was in Redfern.

....

Pat Wedge was a Wiradjuri man, an actor who had appeared in the popular television show *Whiplash*. On 4 June 1963, he was killed by police at St Peters railway station. According to an account by Stephen Atkinson, the following day Ken Brindle, a labourer and an executive of the Aboriginal-Australian Fellowship, went to the Newtown police station to seek answers about what had happened. In the process, Brindle himself came under attack and was charged.

During Brindle's trial, police allege that he had been drunk. Rev. James Downing, a key witness who had inspected the lacerations inside Brindle's mouth immediately after the police assault, testified that there had been no smell of alcohol on his breath. He asserted that in all the years he had known Brindle, he had only once seen him have a drink, and this was for the benefit of television cameras following a successful action against a hotel that had previously refused to serve Aboriginal people.

GF: When I first met Paul Coe, and we started our political dialogue together, I asked him one day – cos I used to think to myself 'Gee, this fella's angry' (laughs) – this is what people used to reckon about me not long after. I worked up enough courage one day to say to him – I

Paul Coe, 1970 (*Tribune*/Search Foundation, State Library of NSW)

was only about 17 going on 18 – I said to him, 'Brother, what is it that kicked you off? What made you so angry to get into all this shit?' And he told me that his anger had been triggered by the police shooting of his cousin Pat Wedge at St Peters Station in 1963.

When that happened, Kenny Brindle went to Newtown Police Station and demanded answers from the cops. When I first moved to Redfern the King of Redfern was Kenny Brindle. He was a legend. He was self-educated, cunning, streetwise, he became a community political organiser. Brindle wanted details, he wanted to let the family know what had happened, and the coppers' response was to beat the shit out of him, arrest him, sling him in under these trumped up charges. As it happened, luck had it for Brindle that was exactly the same moment that a new organisation was being formed in NSW, the NSW Council for Civil Liberties. So, they took up his case. He pleaded not guilty, which in those days was unheard of anyway. And Brindle beat the cops, he won the case. Brindle became one of the key people for FCAATSI organising the 1967 referendum.

AE: Tell me about the role of the pubs in the community at this time?
GF: The only real points of social congregation that were available were at the local footy match on a Sunday, or more importantly any day of the week at the Empress Hotel or the Clifton Hotel. I mean, they were the pubs where the landlords realised they could make a lot of money out of a Black clientele, even though that would be a difficult clientele.

They were places of social congregation, and places where many of the meetings and gatherings of the emergent Black Power movement took place. The Empress was by far the rougher of the two places, it was a very tough pub. I mean, as I've said in other places, even coppers wouldn't go in there. They'd rely on having large numbers before entering the joint. It was a tough place. But if people there knew you, it was a safe place. As long as you didn't get into any fights, which depended on how much alcohol you consumed, a lot of the time it was dependent on that.

The Empress was different from The Clifton. The Clifton was probably more civilised if you like, in the sense that they had some pool tables in the front bar, and the dart bar. Mandatory pub stuff where you could go and just have a game of pool and a quiet drink with whoever turned up. And out the back was the sort of cabaret space where they had the band. Usually, Max Silver. They used to be called the Silver Lining, back in the late 60s. And in the 70s they became the band Black Lace, which is one of the legendary Aboriginal bands of all time. On a Thursday, Friday and Saturday night, there were these cabarets, just the band playing, dancing and drinking, and happiness, out the back of The Clifton.

....

The majority of charges laid against Aboriginal people were for being drunk or disorderly, vague offences open to police interpretation and victimisation. The 10 pm curfew enforced on Aboriginal residents in Redfern led to arbitrary arrests. The academic legal figure, Hal Wootten, observed that Aboriginal people walking quietly home just after 10 pm would be arrested and 'naturally such treatment often led to reaction by an indignant Aborigine which escalated both to additional charges of resisting arrest and assault [sic] police.'

In 1969, a counter-surveillance network developed to contest the legality of police tactics. The group wrote down police identification numbers and photographed incidents, passing the results onto the media. The attempt to gain acknowledgement of the problem from government failed, but the group attracted the support of non-Indigenous law students and legal practitioners, which along with the support of trade unionists, developed into a broader campaign for legal advice and legal aid.

In 1970, the Office of Aboriginal Affairs made funding available for a storefront legal service in Redfern. The establishment of this service fundamentally altered the dynamic with police who could no longer assume that Aboriginal people would plead guilty to whatever they were charged with.

GF: The Empress Hotel was central to the creation of the first Aboriginal Legal Service in Australia. Central in the sense that it was the provocation that we were experiencing daily and nightly at The Empress Hotel on the part of the police that prompted us to think about ways in which we might possibly counter what was going on. And we were aware, some of us, through the reading we'd been doing of things like Bobby Seale's *Seize The Time* and various other stuff that was coming out of America. We were aware that in Oakland, California there was a scenario that seemed very similar to what was happening to us in Redfern, in the way of police harassment, police intimidation tactics, beating people up and all this sort of shit. And so, we looked at what they had done in response, y'know among the many options we thought about, and eventually we thought the basic idea of what they were doing, what they called a pig patrol, this is the Black Panther Party, we thought that was a good idea. I mean, the idea of actually monitoring what the police were doing, so we could prove to outsiders what was actually going on. The way the coppers were staging nightly raids at The Empress and making indiscriminate arrests and sticking people in jail on trumped up charges and all this sort of shit.

One of the PhD students I'm supervising is doing a research project on the women of the Black Power movement, and I've been reading some of the interviews she's done and it's extraordinary reading interviews with these people I knew 50 years ago, talking about that. Because everybody is on the same page, our experiences as we recall them. Which is not always the case when you've got various people being interviewed about events of 50 years ago. But when it came to talking about our experience of the police harassment that went on, especially at the The Empress and The Clifton, and the manner of the underlying reasons of why we took the actions that we did in terms of deciding that police harassment was the number one issue that was confronting us, and then what we then set about to do to counter it.

It's interesting, when all of us are dead, these women and me, and the rest of us, people are going to see that what happened in Redfern in the late 60s and early 70s was a momentous change in Black Australia, and Australian history.

AE: John Newfong once referred to The Empress Hotel as 'the cabinet room of the Aboriginal Movement'. How many people were involved?

GF: I reckon you'd be lucky if there were 10 of us in the core group. Even in the Black Power movement as it emerged there was, in the inner circle there was ... in fact I threw them up on

Mum Shirl (Shirley Smith) speaking at Anti-Bicentennial March at La Perouse, Invasion Day 1988 (Juno Gemes/Juno Gemes Archive)

the screen at the 2022 Marxism Conference. That was the thing that ASIO was always trying to find out, who are the members of the inner circle?

AE: They just had to wait 50 years to find out.
GF: Well, all the Marxism Conference crew saw it before ASIO. Or probably at the same time I guess (laughs).

We all brought a variety of skills to the table. John Newfong was the media genius. Paul Coe was a smart, tactical, strategic thinker. Gary Williams was doing law at Sydney Uni. We all had a chip on our shoulder one way or the other. All of us were angry in our own ways about different things.

AE: Were there skirmishes with right-wingers in pubs?
GF: Mostly we didn't mix, but every now and then, if you weren't careful, going into certain pubs in Camperdown and Newtown and Glebe and places, you'd likely run into some of the mad Nazis. But when I think about it, all apart from The Skull, they were a pretty harmless or useless lot back then compared to some of the crew we have around today.

AE: Was there any sort of community of Aboriginal street drinkers in Sydney?
GF: Yeah, they used to call them the Goomies. Mum Shirl used to be the Mother Theresa for them. Mum Shirl was one of the Big Noises in Redfern at the time, the matriarch of Redfern. Fuck knows how she got it, but she had a badge that meant she could front up at any jail in NSW, flash this badge, and she was given the VIP treatment, and she could go and see any prisoner she liked at any time.

AE: What did this badge look like?
GF: It was the real thing, a NSW Department of Corrective Services badge, that she had badgered out of the authorities. She was a formidable woman, mate. Nobody argued with Mum Shirl. I mean I've seen big tough Redfern coppers get real meek in the presence of Mum Shirl. There wasn't a prison officer in the entire corrupt NSW corrective services system at the time who'd be game to stand up to her.

She was big and formidable and tough, swore like a trooper. But she was a devout Catholic and so she'd managed to whip into shape the local Catholic presbytery. The priest there was a bloke called Father Ted Kennedy who thought the sun shone out of Mum Shirl's arse. But Mum Shirl's deal was, 'Hey preacher, you've got an empty church here, there's an army of homeless drunken blackfellas laying about the street.' So she made him open up his presbytery, and all these homeless people dossed in there. And Mum Shirl would go around and hassle local grocery shops and things to get food and feed them and all that.

She was also Paul Coe's aunty. So, when we set up the legal service, once day [in 1971] Mum Shirl rings us up and summoned us young tough Black Power boys to a meeting. And when Mum Shirl summoned you, you didn't say no,

Black Ban on the Clifton Hotel after refusal to serve Aboriginal people, 1973 (Syd Shelton)

so we went along and she said to us, 'Listen you punks, there's enormous health problems in this community. Why can't we set up a medical clinic, similar to what you did there with your legal service?'

So we said, 'Alright, why don't we have a meeting'. And to this first meeting came this mad, mountain climbing, pipe smoking, communist, New Zealand eye doctor called Fred Hollows. And so Mum Shirl speaks up in this first meeting, and explains all the needs, and she said, 'We want to set up a shopfront clinic, like the legal service down the road.' So Fred Hollows and a couple of other people start to explain to Mum Shirl all 200 obstacles that would prevent such a thing from happening. Less than six weeks later we opened the doors to the first Aboriginal community controlled health clinic in Australia.

AE: It's been said before that the idea for the Aboriginal Tent Embassy came up in discussions in the pub, but it seems like there are a few different origin stories.

GF: There had been a range of ideas tossed around. Some argued that Jack Patten had floated an idea similar back in the 1940s, but y'know in Redfern since 1968, we watched very carefully the American Indian Movement occupation of Alcatraz. And at various times, including in the lead up to the embassy itself, which was more of a spontaneous thing, there'd been discussions. Someone suggested that we row out in the middle of the night in Sydney Harbour and take over Pinchgut Island, y'know Fort Denison. But even amongst all the big macho heroes of the Black Power boys, nobody was game to row a boat through shark infested Sydney Harbour in the middle of the night dodging ferries and things to take over Fort Denison.

But the basic notion of establishing something like that had been there. But on the night, I think those that were in Sydney, among the collective gathered, it was the collective that dispatched those blokes to Canberra. Half of us were in Brisbane that weekend because there was a big anti-racism conference being held by the Australian Union of Students and Denis Walker had put out the word saying come to Brisbane and let's take over this conference. I had been in Melbourne in the lead up to that weekend, and me and Bruce McGuinness and Marjorie Thorpe [Lidia Thorpe's mother] had drove from Melbourne to Brisbane. We were at that conference and we took over that weekend and had a bit of fun.

Some other important drinking places, ones that sustained the Aboriginal Tent Embassy, was the University Bar at the ANU. At the time the ANU was the only university in the country that had a bar on campus. And so, me and Bobby McLeod and John Newfong, and the crew from the embassy, used to drink there. And the pub straight down the road, The Albert Hotel. That was in walking distance from the embassy. And The Wello, The Wellington Hotel up towards Manuka. These were our drinking spots in 1972.

John Newfong, 1970 (*Tribune*/Search Foundation, State Library of NSW)

AE: There is sometimes an issue raised with drinking in political spaces like pickets and protest camps. Sometimes there's secret drinking which people turn a blind eye to. Did it go on?
GF: We had a no grog rule at the embassy. That's why we had these outside places where people would go if they wanted to have a drink, because it was better to have discipline, because we knew we were under the microscope constantly. We knew if the media wasn't watching from across the road, then ASIO was. It was better just to not have any drugs or grog at the embassy.

....

The National Black Theatre produced many memorable plays and screen productions in the early 1970s. Another important role it served was as a meeting place, in which actors, political activists, unionists and filmmakers could socialise and plan projects. It was observed in Kevin Cook and Heather Goodall's *Making Change Happen* that at this time there were few meeting places in Redfern other than pubs, so a relaxed and alcohol-free relaxed was welcome. Foley performed in the landmark revue *Basically Black*, directed by Bob Maza.

GF: Me and Gary Williams were also moving around then, in other circles. This is how come Billy Hunter was close mates with us. I knew people from the old Nimrod Theatre. Like Max Cullen, Chris Hayward, Billy Hunter, Dennis Miller, and some of these mad Sydney types. Compared to what was going on at the Pram Factory [in Melbourne], the Sydney underground acting scene were much more ocker macho Billy Hunter types. So, me and Gary Williams used to drink at The Beauchamp in Darlinghurst.

AE: Bob Maza was a significant figure in that scene. Was he ever at the pub with you?
GF: I don't think Maza was ever a big drinker. Or if he was, he didn't do it in pubs. I think he was more of a wine drinker (laughs).

AE: Can you tell me about how the liquor union worked with Aboriginal people to combat discrimination in the pubs?
GF: Les Collins is the father of Che Cockatoo-Collins, who used to play for Essendon. Les Collins, back in the day, was one of Dennis Walker's right-hand men in Dennis's Black Panther Party mob. Les had moved to Sydney from Brisbane to link up and become part of the Redfern crew that Paul Coe was running.

I can't remember how this came about, but Les must have had a bit of money. When I say a bit of money, I don't mean a lot of money, I mean enough to get this brand new, flash, flat. It was a two bedroom flat down in Glebe, just on Bridge Rd, looking down on Foley Park, just on the corner of Glebe Point Rd and Bridge Rd. And like blackfellas, we thought we were real uptown niggas living in this flash flat. It lasted as long as the first month's rent (laughs). And that was the end of Les Collins and me and the flat.

Not long after we first moved in, we were with Lester Bostock down at Central Railway, must have been down at the Foundation or somewhere. We went into the front bar of the Great Southern just to have a quick beer. We were going into a meeting or something. We walked in, and this barmaid came running across to us, and she said, 'We don't serve you black bastards in here. Fuck off.' And one of us, I can't remember, it probably wasn't me, one of us said to her, 'Excuse me, what did you say?' 'We don't serve black cunts in here, fuck off.'

So we walked out the front and we were a bit taken aback. Even for them days, that was a bit upfront. That was a bit more overt than we usually got. And so Lester said, 'What are we gonna do?' I said, 'I know what we're gonna do. Come with me.'

We went round the corner, it was only about four blocks from Trades Hall in Goulburn Street. We went into what was then the Liquor Trades Union and asked to see them. This organiser bloke came and had a yarn with us, and we told him what happened, and he said, 'I can't believe that this sort of thing goes on, not far from me.' We said, 'Alright mate, come with us and we'll show you.'

To our surprise he did come with us, and we walk into the bar and the same barmaid spotted us, came running over, 'I thought I told you black cunts, we don't serve you fucken bastards here.' And this Liquor Trades Union guy was shocked, and he said, 'Excuse me, what did you just say?!' And she said to him, 'If you're with those black cunts, you can fuck off too.' And he said, 'Right', and he was fucken livid, y'know he couldn't believe his ears.

So he said, 'Come with me', and we went back to the Liquor Trades Union, and they slapped – ironically – a black ban on the pub. No more grog deliveries until this ban was lifted and the barmaid apologised. Took three days. And three days later the publican was begging for mercy. And so we went back, me and Les and Lester. We ordered a beer, and the same barmaid came over and had to apologise with a red face and serve us. We took two sips out of our beers, and walked out and never went back. That was in the days before the amalgamation of unions into these super outfits. When you had decentralised unions you could talk to them about very specific problems that related to their particular field.

AE: The Sussex was a popular pub with lefties. Did you spend any time there?
GF: One of my great memories, I think it was The Sussex, the union pub down near the Communist Party of Australia offices. One of my fondest memories there is pouring a schooner of beer over the head of Paddy McGuinness, back in the days when he was a lefty, before he took a right-hand turn late in life. I can't even remember what the argument was about, but he was talking shit. And my only response was to pour a good glass of beer over him. And then in The Sussex, later in the piece, we used to hang out with Pringle and Mundey and Joey Owens, and that mob from the BLs in Sydney.

AE: Can you tell me about the BLF campaign to save The Newcastle from being demolished?
GF: The Newcastle is one of the places that I met Pringle and Mundey and Owens. They were among the crew that hung out there. I can remember going to The Newcastle in The Rocks about the time that The Push used to hang out there. What seemed to be The Push, Wendy Bacon and Paddy Dawson and all these mad bastards. It was a great pub to go on a Friday or Saturday night when they were there, because you could get pissed and they'd shout you a drink (laughs). So you'd get pissed while the pub was open and after the pub shut they had the best parties in Sydney, mate. That's where we smoked a lot of dope, met a lot of interesting people. It's one of those parties where I met Marius Webb who became a great mate, and still is 50 years later.

There was also the Sir John Young, I think that was later in the piece. That was a place to go to the back bar and I think it was a Friday night 'cos you could always be guaranteed to

John Austin, Gary Foley and Bruce McGuinness at the Glenrowan Hotel, 1972 (Gary Foley Archive)

end up at a party, and they were great parties. It was interesting discussions, and yarns, and shit talk, all sorts of things going on. Invariably interesting people.

AE: Aboriginal organising wasn't just in pubs, was it? Were there any houses that were important meeting places?
GF: The first one was Lyn Thompson's house on Burton Street in Darlinghurst. Lyn and Peter Thompson. Lyn Thompson was Billy Craigie's sister. They'd both been taken away when they were babies.

AE: Chicka Dixon's home in Surrey Hills was a meeting place too, wasn't it? Would people drink alcohol in these homes?
GF: Chicka was one of the world's most famous ex-alcoholics, I mean he could tell ya, and he would, frequently, if asked or not, tell you exactly how many days, years, minutes and almost seconds since his last drink. But if you had meetings at Chicka's place, there was always a bottle of beer in the fridge. He'd say, 'Do you want a beer?', and we'd say, 'No, you don't drink.' And he'd say, 'No, there's beer in that fridge for two reasons. Number one, for you fellas or anybody who comes to this house, you're welcome to have a drink, I don't, youse know that. Sweet whether you do or not.' And he says, 'The other reason I keep it in the fridge is because every now and then I talk to it.' I said. 'What do you mean?' He said, 'Well sometimes when I get the urge, y'know because you still get the urge fucken 40 years later, you still get the urge. I like to take it out of the fridge, look at it and talk to it. I like to say to it: 'You fucken thing you, you're not gonna get me!' And then he said, 'I put it back in the fridge.' Chicka was one of the greatest mates, he was a staunch trade unionist from the day he got off the grog.

The Great Southern Hotel refused to serve Aboriginal people. Following union action, Lester Bostock, Gary Foley and Les Collins receive their drink, early 1970s (Gary Foley Archive)

It was the politics of the union movement that made him what he was. Staunch wharfie until the day he died.

AE: How long did the Black Power movement hold together for?
GF: The inner core of the Black Power movement had essentially broken up in 1974, with this big argument. But by then I had more or less moved to Melbourne, and it was a crunch thing that happened in Sydney. Then Gary Williams moved to Alice Springs and I moved permanently down here.

AE: In that dispute did alcohol and the life around the pubs play any part?
GF: I think luckily for us, I think most of us on all sides of the fence were smart enough to not let alcohol be part of the then dispute or what's happened since. Those of us that are still alive moderated our alcohol intake, early enough... [Alcohol is] part of the freedom you found when you turned 18, and sorta, like most freedoms you overdo it at first.

AE: When Aboriginal people came to Melbourne, they would seek out places to find other Black people. There's the famous fig tree at the end of Gertrude Street, and Muhammed Ali went to the Builders Arms Hotel to find the Aboriginal people of Melbourne. As someone who was traveling around the country as an activist, what were the prominent meeting places in the 1970s?
GF: I knew where to find the sort of people I was interested in talking to. They were in the pubs. In Adelaide, Melbourne, Sydney, and to a certain extent in Brisbane. In Melbourne, 50 years ago it was the Builders [Arms Hotel]. And wherever you went back in those days. If I went to Brisbane, you knew that there were pubs down on the south side where the blackfellas hung out. In Adelaide it was The Carrington, and the pubs down at the port. The Carrington was the Adelaide equivalent of the Empress. Even Redgum wrote a song about it, 'Carrington Cabaret'. That was actually a fucking good song.

Gary Foley at Anti-Bicentennial March at La Perouse, Invasion Day 1988 (Juno Gemes/Juno Gemes Archive)

When I arrived in Adelaide to get involved in the politics there I was met at the airport by a very elderly Aboriginal woman, and she informed me that I would be staying at her place, which was not exactly what I was expecting when I left Sydney. Rather than hanging out with little old ladies drinking tea I was keen to get to the Carrington Hotel. But Gladys drove me straight to her place and immediately put the kettle on, and told me in no uncertain terms how much she disliked the way young people drank so much alcohol. In the end, we spent the night talking about the ideas and philosophies of the Black Power movement and she told me all these amazing stories of her experiences in political activism. The next morning, I came to the realisation that I had been subjected to some sort of test the night before, and I had passed. So I was able to connect with the Nunga community in Adelaide, and work alongside Aunty Glad, Vince Copley, Ruby Hammond and others. I did manage to spend a few nights at the Carrington though.

After one particular demonstration [in Adelaide] I found myself in an intense discussion with the artist Harold Thomas. We were both lamenting that the newly emerging Land Rights movement didn't have a symbol that both represented the struggle and might act as a unifying emblem. After a number of cans of VB and the consequent bravado that it brings, Harold and I decided that we would sit down and design one. Harold being the artist pulled out some pencils and a sketchbook and we began discussing a range of ideas. It was a great drinking session, and we emerged with the now familiar red, black and yellow design, along with an interpretation of what it meant.

AE: You moved to Melbourne around 1974. Can you tell me about your experience of pubs in that city?
GF: Over 50 years I've had a lot of drinking holes including the Clyde, Albion, pubs down on the southside in South Melbourne. Tankerville, before it was a pokies joint. The Night Cat. The Old Colonial down Brunswick Street. I used to drink at the Old Colonial when I was going to Melbourne Uni 20 years ago. But even around here The Albion was one of the great fucking pubs of Carlton. I got barred for life three times at the Albion. Back in those days it was a such a rough pub. You had this weird mixture of crims, students, people from The Pram Factory, Italians, all manner of nationalities, especially amongst the crims (laughs), a smattering of blackfellas. Me and Bruce McGuinness used to go there. I was better behaved at Stewarts. Then there was Percy's much later in life where I used to drink with a variety of people.

AE: You said that the Builders Arms was the main pub you'd go to find Aboriginal people in Melbourne. The whole of Gertrude Street was full of pubs, but the two most well-known

Billy Craigie, Kate George and Bruce McGuinness, Canberra, 1972 (Gary Foley Archive)

ones for the Aboriginal community were the Builders Arms and the Champion Hotel. What was different about The Champion?

GF: It was rougher and tougher. It was like the Empress was to the Clifton. The Builders was where the boxing people were, where the political people were, the health service, the co-op, the Fitzroy Stars. There wasn't any racism between people at the Builders Arms. You had a multitude of nationalities. Yugoslavs, blackfellas, and whitefellas, and drunks.

AE: Did you find that when you're in a pub and you're trying to get people to be politically involved, there can be frustration because people are there for drinking – they aren't interested in being politicised?

GF: It's also a way of reinforcing your own empathy with those that you see around you whose lives have been fucked. And you can see them drinking themselves to death in front of you, and you get angry about it. But before you get angry you've got empathy, and that's what helps to drive ya, y'know. It helps you be determined to create something better so people don't have to do this. They don't have to fuck themselves like that.

Karen Flick leads Land Rights March on NAIDOC Day, Gary Foley holding banner, 1981 (Juno Gemes/Juno Gemes Archive)

CHAPTER 44
'WE ARE GOING TO BLACKLIST THIS HOTEL': ALCOHOL AND THE ACTIVISM OF CHICKA DIXON

Alex Ettling

Chicka Dixon (1928-2010) grew up in Wallaga Lake Aboriginal mission. His first job at the age of 14 was in Port Kembla on the waterfront. Dixon was an alcoholic and talked openly about regretful actions he committed under the influence of alcohol. At the 2005 Jumbumma Annual Lecture he recounted his story: 'I got out of Long Bay Gaol on the 5th of April 1959, (and went) straight on the metho.' Not long after he made a proclamation: 'I'm not going to drink anymore', and threw the bottle of methylated spirits away.

> Four days later I was marching down George Street for justice for our people. Not power, power corrupts. I wanted justice for our people. Most Koories when they get sobriety, and incidentally I'm not holding an AA meeting, they either go to the lord or the AA. I went to the political struggle. Whenever I struggle for justice, I will never ever drink.

In 1963 he joined the Waterside Workers Union and the communist politics of this union shaped much of his approach to political struggle. Dixon was a co-founder in 1964 of the early Aboriginal political organisation the Foundation for Aboriginal Affairs. They held dances on Saturday nights and Sunday night concerts. As recorded on the *A History of Aboriginal Sydney* website, Dixon explained:

> What we needed was a place we could go socially and we picked the area in George Street purposely. I had a big sign put up at Central railway, "Aboriginals, visit your Foundation." If they need a little bit of help – they're coming in fly-blown – we give out food orders, a chit to get a three-course meal next door. Fellas coming out of jail. We had a hell of a lot of donations of clothes and that. People'd come and get a bit of beer. If you're talking about a typical day, there's no such thing. A lot of problems. Social problems.

Dixon hosted discussion nights at his home in Surrey Hills, mentoring a newer generation of activists, including Gary Foley, Michael Anderson, Paul Coe, John Newfong, Billy Craigie, and Tony Coorey. He was a prominent figure in the radical Aboriginal politics of the 60s and 70s, a key member of the Black Caucus that organised protests including the Aboriginal Tent Embassy.

Despite being an ex-drinker, Dixon organised against racial discrimination in the pubs, as recounted in *Black Viewpoints: The Aboriginal Experience*:

> I was in bed and three young Aborigines knocked on the door about 9 o'clock at night. They told me that a very dignified hotel down in George Street wouldn't serve Aborigines. I decided to go down and

find out. I took the blackest fella with me, walked in, and asked for a schooner of beer for my friend and schooner of lemonade for myself. The bartender said, 'I'm sorry... We won't serve Aborigines'. 'Well that's quite alright [Chicka replied], tomorrow evening I'll have 300 waterside workers up outside your joint here. Nobody is going to get in because we are going to blacklist this hotel. Then I'll go to the Trades and Labour Council and the Liquor Trades Union to pull the barmaids out'. Well, he did a complete [about] face. It's a remarkable thing, Blacks are welcome down there now!

In 1970, Dixon and others watched the activities of the police in Redfern for five weeks:

> What they used to do after 10 o'clock closing at The Big E, The Empress, they'd back up two big wagons, and as the Blacks were coming out of the pub they'd throw them straight in the wagon. They'd say things like 'Come on, you're drunk.' 'No, I'm not drunk.' 'Well, you're either drunk or goods in custody.' Drunk was a 10 shilling fine. Goods in custody was three months. So, they'd nod their head. This sort of rubbish is what was going on. That's why we decided to set up the legal service.

Chicka Dixon delivered a paper entitled 'Portrait of an Aboriginal Alcoholic' to the 1980 Pan-Pacific Conference on Drugs and Alcohol. This, and his general approach, was notable for the absence of moralism towards drinkers, despite the prominence he gave to his own struggle with alcoholism. Dixon was able to navigate the social hazards of alcohol but was tragically not able to escape the industrial crime that knowingly exposed him to hazardous materials. Speaking to the Maritime Union of Australia's journal in 2001, Dixon recalled the asbestos on the wharves: 'It would fly all over the place', he said. 'Heaps of it. My gang, we'd sit on the bags and eat our lunch. Bags and bags of asbestos. No one knew.' In 2010, Chicka Dixon died from lung disease.

Chicka Dixon and young Aboriginal people playing pool, 1967 (*Tribune*/Search Foundation, State Library of NSW)

Chicka Dixon watching Aboriginal bands play in Hyde Park, Sydney, 1980 (Juno Gemes/Juno Gemes Collection)

CHAPTER 45

'ROUGH AS GUTS': THE SUMMERHILL AND THE MAOISTS

Alex Ettling

Some pubs have bad reputations that overwhelm everything else. When the Summerhill Hotel was built in 1967 on the site of the old Preston Council gravel pits it was marketed as an upmarket, sophisticated alternative. Not even 20 years later it was branded 'rough as guts', notorious for illegal drug activity, with stories of violence and degrading behaviour attached to its decline.

The pub's name provided a variety of scathing pun nicknames: Scum-erhill, Summerhole, Slum-merhill. The northern suburbs it served were the territory of the Crevelli Street Boys, Sharpie gangs, and notorious Melbourne underworld figures the Kane Brothers and Peter McEvoy. Artist and academic Philip Brophy grew up in the area in the 1970s, and wrote of his experiences:

> As a teenager growing up in Reservoir in the 1970s, the closest thing to collaboration I was aware of was backing up your mates in a punch-up. Street violence was an accepted part of life in the northern suburbs. When the Keon Park sharps were hanging around Northland shopping centre on a Friday night, a blue with the West Heidelberg boys was on. A beer at the Croxton Park Hotel would more than likely end up with a visit from the Lebanese Tigers. I lived on the border of Reservoir (and that's 'rez-a-vor') and East Preston, just around the corner from the notorious Crevelli Street, a location into which one ventured cautiously and, advisedly, with at least two mates (it earned the moniker of 'Little Chicago' in the 1950s as a testament to its fearsome reputation).

Anecdotes of violent encounters at the Summerhill are present even in the innocuous aspects of pub activity. It was part of the pub rock circuit, providing joyful entertainment for many, but it was also where an audience member copped a beer glass in the throat during a Brian Cadd show. Other entertainers who performed at the venue were as diverse as Rodney Rude, Les Girls, Col Joye, and The Boys Next Door. Memorably, a heavily intoxicated Johnny O'Keefe performed at the Summerhill in his declining years, stumbling through his set before bringing the house down with the classic 'Shout!'. There was other entertainment, as Allan recollected in an online forum:

> A DJ or MC of sorts conducted a game of musical chairs. Only women were allowed to play. Instead of leaving the game when missing out on a chair, they had to remove an item of clothing. It was like strip poker. The one who was the first to end up stripping down won a lousy bottle of sparkling wine. So, this poor girl/woman removed her bra (much alcohol involved) and continued around the chairs to bawdy cheering from all the men. Anyway, the MC wouldn't give her the bottle of wine until she dropped her knickers as well.

With a rough clientele, it's unsurprising that the bouncers also held a reputation. Joey Quadara, before he was shot in the head in a gangland hit, was a Summerhill bouncer. A former worker behind the bar, Neil, recalls that before he worked at the pub he drank there at age 14, 'Joey Quadara used to hide me under the bar if the coppers ever came in.' Various wrestlers and boxers took jobs as security. The boxing champ Alec Marshall, and the brothers Statis and George Lamtzous worked there. Neil recalls George saying, 'If I hand you my watch and my false teeth, it's gonna be on so clear all the glasses and jugs.' Another online commentator, Paul, reflected: 'There's another aspect of Australian society that's all but disappeared; the public bar punch up: men beating the shit out of each other with chairs, glasses and possibly tables flying through the air.'

These and other comments on various local history Facebook groups, even if hyperbolic or jesting, offer an insight into the reputation of the Summerhill Hotel, and communal memory.

> **Sharon:** I worked in the kitchen for some work experience and the cook deep fried the sausage and then burnt it on the gas stove burner to look like it was grilled. Then he dropped the sausage on the floor and wiped it on his apron and put it on the plate. He said, 'You didn't see that, did you.'
>
> **Allan:** A bloke by the name of Black George used to pick up the emptys there in the early 70s. Drank anything that was left before returning glasses to the bar.

Summerhill Hotel, 1970 (Darebin Library)

> **Fliss:** I remember avoiding the blood on the floors from the fights as I left the disco. The good old days lol.
>
> **Stephen:** Wine tasting! lol some claret was spilt alright.
>
> **Ken:** I was literally thrown across that bloody car park by a bouncer at 16.
>
> **Mike:** Many a knuckle bumped there.
>
> **Steve:** Left in a divvy van after scrapping with the bouncers lol.
>
> **Russ:** Went there twice, got bashed 3 times.
>
> **Ron:** You'd see some bent and broken furniture in there... noses too!!
>
> **James:** Went there twice, second time to get my teeth.
>
> **Jane:** Some lovely people used to hang around there, car thieves.
>
> **Nick:** Heaps of good punch ups there. You walked out of Pentridge into the Summerhill or The Shamrock and Thistle to get your supplies.
>
> **John:** Shit hole
>
> **Lesley:** Shit hole
>
> **Phil:** Shit hole

The negative assessments are overwhelming. However, pubs by their very nature as a 'public house' welcome a varied clientele with their own experiences, shaped by the passage through different eras. A pub known for the grim aspects of human experience can also hold the story of its opposite. One person's 'shit hole' is for someone else the venue where they had their wedding reception or a 21st – the best times of their lives. As well as for sentimental events, the Summerhill is memorialised as a meeting place of sixties era student rebels in Melbourne's northern suburbs. So, the same pub that holds a reputation as a bloodhouse is also the place where the peace movement was cradled, with a jukebox playing Thunderclap Newman's revolutionary anthem 'Something in the Air'.

The story of the Summerhill, situated at the meeting point of Reservoir, Heidelberg West and Preston, is inextricably connected to its surrounds. In particular the arrival of the new university that emerged in 1967 out of a swampy valley just to its north. Writer and former student Don Watson poetically described it as a wilderness where 'friends went missing in ones and twos and sometimes larger numbers for whole days; lost between La Trobe and Northland, La Trobe and the Summerhill Hotel, La Trobe and Preston Cemetery, La Trobe and Larundel (the mental asylum).' As historian and former La Trobe student activist Barry York explained, writing in *Blast* in 1988:

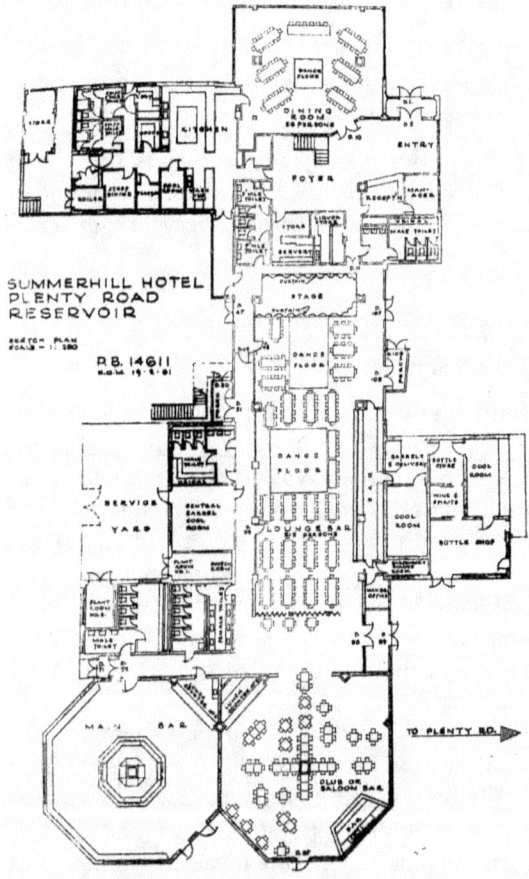

Floor plan of Summerhill Hotel (Public Records Office of Victoria)

The Summerhill Hotel symbolised much about post-war suburban Australia. It was gloriously spacious, served fast-food, was culturally male-dominated, heavily into laminex and coloured lights and was surrounded by vast asphalt carparks.

The Summerhill was the pub of La Trobe University, even though it was located at some distance from the isolated campus. It was a venue where students mixed with residents from the northern suburbs and workers from the surrounding light industrial belt. As York explains, 'Someone would just say, "Hey, let's meet up at the Summerhill tonight" and you might end up with a dozen fellow students at the table. On other occasions, we'd go there after a demo.' When bored at home, with nothing good on TV, York would make the 20 minute drive from his home to the Summerhill where there would likely be a table of student activists to join. Writing in *Blast*, he further explained how the different demographics of the pub interacted:

> 'They' drank in the public bar. 'We' gathered in the lounge where local schoolteachers also drank. The workers in the bar were quick, heavy drinkers caught in the boozers' zone between workplace and home. We were young radicals out to change society, caught in a limbo between reality and what we knew ought-to-be. The Summerhill provided long wide tables to rest our weary elbows, and golden amber to help the ideas flow ... Our chain of tables dominated the pub lounge, and our circle was alive with chatter and argument, and laughter and rage. We raged against the war in Vietnam and conscription but, more commonly, we raged against one another over the best ways to stop them. We ordered our beers in jugs, and our circle seemed an ever-expanding one.

Historian and former La Trobe student activist Fergus Robinson explains that there was social intermingling among the various groups on the left at the pub, unless there was an issue which had caused bitter division. On one occasion, in the early 70s, York witnessed a harrowing act of violence at the Summerhill involving two students. The aggressor was on the periphery of the campus activism scene and nearly killed someone:

> I heard glass break. When I looked back at the table, the young bloke was standing up from his chair, holding the side of his neck, and blood was spurting from his neck. I think everyone was in shock. He staggered through the tables, with blood spurting quite a distance from his neck, and it was clear he was heading for the front doors, presumably to get to hospital. As he exited the pub he was shouted at by a group of workers having a beer and a meal after work – upset he had spurted his blood on their table.

York also experienced a threat of violence after a discussion about politics in apartheid South Africa:

> As we exited the Summerhill, and walked around the corner of the pub, this bloke was waiting for me, with a very long sharp knife in his hand. He was furious, shaking with rage and yelling and swearing at me, insisting that there were more whites than Blacks in South Africa. He was ready to stab me but I talked him out of it. My friend and I then hurried to the car but it took me a few minutes before I could drive, as my legs were literally shaking too much.

These are extreme incidents. In broader society, there was some degree of enculturation to violence, everything from 70s-era VFA football to routine bashings from Sharpie gangs around train stations. This is an era when 'coward punches' were still 'king hits'. Despite the Summerhill being a site where such confrontations could happen, the pub remained a pole of attraction. It was after all also associated with the pleasures of good conversation, flirtation and beer.

Thursdays were always a popular day at the Summerhill. In the era of studentships and regular paydays the freshly moneyed La Trobe students and workers converged on the pub. In many ways, the lives of students and workers were growing closer together in the post-war era. As historian Jeff Sparrow writes in his essay 'Mao and Then: Thirty Years of Melbourne Radicalism', the need for a highly trained workforce in a complex economy led universities to evolve from institutions providing a liberal education for a small elite into modern degree factories. Larger sections of the workforce were serviced by universities, but there was a contradiction between *the idea* of the university and *the reality*. This, and other contributing factors led to campuses becoming breeding grounds of activism and the counterculture.

Young people were in large numbers inspired by radicalisation around the world. Students didn't just want to be a cog in the capitalist system, nor fodder for a war machine, and thus the campus became a hotbed of dissent. York remembers it as a time when the powerless were unafraid of challenging the powerful – including those administering the campus. La Trobe's Vice Chancellor 'ineffectually flip-flopped between headmasterly repression and tut-tutting tolerance' asserts Jeff Sparrow. As historian and former La Trobe student activist Mick Armstrong appraises, by 1970 La Trobe had taken over Monash's mantle as the radical Melbourne campus, a title it sustained for many years.

The social aspects of student rebellion were flourishing too. The Summerhill was the pub of the La Trobe University students, but there were other important gathering places: Glenn Caf on campus, and also the Student Union building (hosting only irregular events, it is notable for nurturing the street theatre tradition of the Maoist students). House parties were also prominent. The sixties radicalisation inspired a number of older academics on campus who were mixing with the students. York describes a tutor's party where everything was in abundant supply: flagon wine, flagon port, grog by the crateful, and the latest American music. In this intellectual party environment, 'music was an interlude between discussions of Marx and Marcuse.'

One of the radical academics on campus was Doug White, distinguished by a scar on his nose from having once been glassed in a pub. He would become a significant influence on the young Maoists in particular. As campus radicalisation further threatened the establishment, White found himself the target of state security forces. In January 1971, he arrived home to find photographic negatives strewn on the floor and books missing. Break-ins by the Operations (D) Branch of ASIO were routine, with signs left to make it look like an amateur burglary. In this case White noticed that bottles of beer had been stolen by the ASIO agents as well.

Campus radicalisation did not go unnoticed by the older generation of leaders in the labour movement. To offer them a sense of the youth rebellion, York invited two leaders of the Communist Party of Australia-Marxist Leninist (CPA-ML), Ted Hill and Ernie O'Sullivan, to join with his fellow student activists down at the pub and then on to a student party out in Eltham. The expedition had a political purpose as well, to make a good impression with the other La Trobe activists and gain legitimacy for the Maoists to lead the student movement. York recounted the events in an obituary of Ted Hill published in 1988:

> We decided to invite Ted Hill to the Summerhill Hotel because we wanted to prove to our fellow student rebels that the 'cold calculating communist' image was a creation of the capitalist press, and that Ted Hill was in fact on our side. ... The chain of tables grew and more beer was spilt as the doubters among us posed their questions to our leader; at times gently, at times hurling them. No matter how they were delivered, Ted responded with frankness, logic, and a unique brand of charm.

Ted Hill was accompanied by Ernie O'Sullivan, who would have been happier in the front bar. Ernie had been a prize-fighter in his younger days, and a former cab driver known for his contribution to the 1938 taxi strike where he went around with a plank of wood with a four-inch nail sticking out of it, puncturing the tyres of scabs. He said little, but even less escaped his eye. York explained:

> Ted and Ernie mingled as best they could, but there was a surreal quality to their presence. Ted Hill, with his thin rimmed spectacles and lawyer's suit and Ernie O'Sullivan with his cabbie's hat and crinkled overcoat had little in common with their hosts. We fashioned ourselves on cultural heroes like Che Guevara and Jimi Hendrix. We could identify with Ted because he believed in challenging the sacred cows of capitalist society, but I wonder to this day whether he could identify with us to any extent.

> Ted attended our pub night and party out of a sense of revolutionary duty. It was probably as onerous for him as doing a paste-up on a windy winters' night in Carlton was for us. Ted didn't smoke and never drank to excess. He believed that the fight to change society imposed a necessary discipline on the individual leaders of the struggle. ... To Ted, however, dialectical materialism dictated that knowledge came from experience, and he told me some days later that he had learnt from the Eltham experience.

> Strangely, that night had an important effect on the developing student movement at La Trobe University. We Maoists had won the night, and convinced everyone that Ted Hill was on the student rebels' side. We had neutralised his opponents within the movement, and even won some over to the fact that our leader was a good bloke. It was no longer possible for Anarchists and Trotskyists to promote the image of Ted as a cold calculating Stalinist, and

that was quite a victory in the struggle for political leadership of the movement.

York's assessment of the success of that evening reflects that Maoism was on the rise in Melbourne during the late 1960s. With an emphasis on militancy and third world liberation, Maoist rhetoric fitted the mood of urgency around the life-or-death issues of conscription and the Vietnam War. By 1970, the left was well-cohered at La Trobe and Labor Club membership increased to 150 – eight per cent of the student body. The emergence of a militant tendency accelerated the radicalisation of the university. The end goal of these radicals necessitated planning on how to confront the state apparatus. York argued:

> We understood the nature of the state, its violence, and prepared for revolution by training in rifle target practice at the Williamstown Rifle Range. CMF (army reserve) lads also trained there on Saturday mornings. We knew we wouldn't be using the rifles in the streets but wanted to be prepared.

Whilst increasing numbers of students were thinking about how to pull off a revolution in Australia, the immediate concern to most was the Vietnam War.

June 1970 saw the first occupation at La Trobe after seven students were suspended following a protest that forced military recruiters off campus. The political atmosphere was intensifying, with a group of La Trobe students who had been painting slogans on walls in the West Heidelberg area being confronted by security guards who fired shots at them. The most notorious event at La Trobe in this era was The Battle of Waterdale Road, a series of marches on 11, 16 and 23 September 1970 that remain significant in the history of struggle for free speech and the right to protest in Australia. The first of these peaceful marches was viciously suppressed by police, as was the second march in protest at the repression. A third attracted 800 people, including trade unionists, demonstrators marching in defiance along the street to the campus. Students who went to Northlands shopping centre to distribute leaflets and address shoppers on the upcoming Moratorium march were met with police violence, with two students clubbed unconscious. York writing for the Museum of Australian Democracy described how:

> The police laid into us, not just with batons but with fists and boots too ... in the media there were confronting pictures of a policeman swinging a female student by the hair. Inspector Platfuss was unrepentant and told a reporter, 'They got some baton today and they'll get a lot more in the future.'

Student activist Larry Abramson stated that as he was running away, the police aimed a gun at him and announced 'stop or I'll shoot', an alarming threat of force against non-violent student demonstrators.

Repression publication, 1970 (Museum of Australian Democracy)

Throughout these events, the Summerhill was a gathering point for the left. York describes the 'long extended tables of people who had been at that demonstration who gathered there and discussed what had happened and what should happen next'. They wanted a university extricated from any association with the war machine, and an education untied from the profit motives of industry. The student's model was direct action, and democratic structures of self-organisation. During the planning of the second Waterdale Road march York recalls that, 'One of the activists suggested that we make molotov cocktails and hide them in the bushes near the campus entrance. This bloke's idea was completely rejected and forever after he was regarded as a possible ASIO agent.'

Marxist politics dominated the students' thinking and so tactics of this sort were heavily frowned upon. Rather, the priority was building the connections between students and workers (with an emphasis on the tactical advantage of workers being able to freeze the flow of profits through strike action).

A local Heidelberg resident Noel Collingburn had been bashed to death in police custody a few weeks prior to the demonstrations, and so a chant during the marches was: 'Who killed Collingburn? Cops killed Collingburn.' This was an overture from the student movement to relate to the concerns of the working class in the area, the same impulse that led students to visit workplaces and shopping centres, and to embrace pubs. Filmmaker and student activist Rod Bishop described the transformative effect of these events, speaking at a 2017 panel talk, 'Film and student protest: Beginnings':

> We were marching back from Northland and had turned into Waterdale Road. ... The road is in a light industrial area with buildings on either side, a perfect place to trap and ambush the students, and that's what happened. We got the shit beaten out of us. What happened after that was a major change in student politics at La Trobe. The people who were anti-war and that's as far as their politics went, shifted considerably at that stage and moved very much in sympathy with the hard-core students. Not that everyone turned into a Maoist or a Marxist-Leninist, but it did become a much more politically conscious place and there was a gravitation towards what politics was about. It was like what Jean-Pierre Leaud talks about in Jean Eustache's *The Mother and the Whore* (1973), the moment when a crack in the consciousness opens up, meaning that in 1968 there was sort of a crack in the world consciousness in terms of politics. Well, that certainly was what happened at La Trobe.

The threat of violent treatment, and its implementation, had varied effects on the movement: it could attract numbers in defiance, as well as repel people in fear. It could traumatise people, but also, as student activist Brian Pola explains in his thesis *Perspectives on the Australian Radical Left Student Movement 1966-1975*, there was 'the "baton on the head become a radical" theory, where the more they pummel you, the more obvious it is that the police are the violent arm of the capitalist state.'

At La Trobe University, there was a close association with the war apparatus. Its chancellor, Sir Archibald Glenn, was the managing

Waterdale Road march, 1970 (Barry York Collection)

director of ICI, a manufacturer of munitions for the Vietnam War that also had arms factories in apartheid South Africa. Glenn symbolised the university's subservience to capitalism, imperialism and war. On 19 April 1971, more than 1000 students, roughly a third of the student population, voted unanimously for Glenn's resignation. The university administration responded with repression which resulted in the jailing of three La Trobe University students who entered campus grounds to carry out activism. In *The La Trobe Three, Fifty Years On,* York details how Vice Chancellor David Myers visited the students in Pentridge Prison, and:

> Wanted us to sign a statement repudiating violence on the campus. We were not prepared to do this either. Although the far right ironically described us as a pro-violence minority, we knew that the real pro-violence minority were those who relied on police violence and intimidation, not to mention those who sent troops to prop up a fascist regime in South Vietnam 'bomb back to the Stone Age' those who were fighting it. One of our legal advisors, communist lawyer Ted Hill, also visited us and advised us to sign the statement only on condition that Myers also sign the repudiation of violence on behalf of the Council.

The three students were released in August 1972. Freed prisoner Brian Pola was photographed celebrating with a beer. Barry York recalls that 'the media tried to set us up to have a stubbie in our hands for a photo on our release. We declined but Brian happened to have one.' Whether holding a beer was discrediting or made activists more relatable was a question for debate. Nevertheless these concerns came up in the context of broader debates around culture and morality in regards to Maoism, drinking and violence.

The reputation of La Trobe Maoists for violence was in part drawn from the actions of a second generation of campus activists who whilst employing violence to stifle Nazis on campus, were also accused by left rivals of using it to intimidate their small forces. There were also off-campus incidents, such as when Maoist student activist Ken White was convicted of involvement in a molotov cocktail and shot-gun attack on the Vietnam War connected Honeywell computer company, located in St Kilda. It was not a widely supported action. The Maoists' reputation was also not helped by media reporting about militant BLF secretary and CPA-ML member Norm Gallagher, which routinely painted him and his union' membership as thugs.

Broader factors also played a role, such as an identification with masculinist, 'ocker' cultural signifiers as Australian Maoists began to embrace elements of nationalism. Activities of Maoists overseas further shaped their image. These included reporting of grim political events in China surrounding the Cultural Revolution, as well as the armed struggle tactics of groups that perhaps tenuously aligned their projects to Maoism, such as the Red Brigades, the Red Army Faction, and The Weather Underground.

As can be seen from the various accounts discussed here, violence was present to a limited extent in campus politics, but also permeated all layers of Australian society. A proportional weighting of violent incidents, or

The La Trobe Three after release from prison, left-to-right: Fergus Robinson, Brian Pola and Barry York, 1972 (Barry York Collection)

perhaps worthy justifications, did not prevent the Maoists developing a reputation as 'dogmatic Stalinist thugs', which has persisted in the historiography of the Australian student movement. This is a cloud that hangs over the history of the La Trobe Maoists, despite the many aspects of their activity which were in opposition to military, state and other violence. Such reputational damage still grates on Barry York, who draws a distinction between the heyday of the Maoist scene of his time and the cohort that came after when the movement was entering a decline. Identifying causality between acceptance of violence at a cultural level, and then specific violent interpersonal acts, is a challenging task and certainly beyond our scope here. However, it is possible at the very least, to identify a hypocrisy when those complicit in large scale acts of state violence decry the relatively isolated violent acts involving activists.

Organisations which seek social transformation regularly face the question of how to evaluate the morality of oppressed groups that they either belong to or wish to work alongside. Dilemmas include how to relate to potentially problematic aspects of culture, such as drinking and fighting. One approach to working class culture has been to celebrate it as it is, and insert class consciousness where possible. A criticism is that this can devolve into uncritically promoting stereotypes, often focused on blue collar masculinist experience (which have been shaped by capitalism no less). Other working class cultures already marginalised by the status quo can be further sidelined, and there may not be enough space given for the emergence of new cultures.

In Australia, the Maoist attitude to working class culture during the 1970s tended to make a fetish of certain forms of Australiana. It was a process which ran in parallel to the left nationalism which flourished inside the CPA-ML. At its most basic it was an approach to gaining favour with an audience, in the process submerging the possibly alienating rhetoric of revolutionary politics. Since communism could seem like an overly utopian or intellectual argument, for some, better to demonstrate the need for revolution through the cut and thrust of everyday workplace and community politics. Maoists were determined to expand their influence, to eventually achieve a mass audience for their political ideas, so being culturally accepted – for instance, as workers who liked a drink – made sense.

An element of this approach involved defending the spaces where workers went for recreation. The Maoist led BLF placed bans on demolishing a series of pubs in 1973. *The Age* reported the union's position that, 'The Australian custom of a hard-working man enjoying his beer after eight hours of sweat deserves some protection.' Gallagher was quoted as saying, 'Our members don't wear suits to work. They come to do some hard yakka among the mud and sweat of a construction site and are finding in increasingly harder to get places to drink.' In *The Australian*, Gallagher added:

> We're opposed to developers knocking down these pubs and replacing them with modern taverns to which workers are not admitted in their work clothing. These

Political badge, 1970

people are just throwing a bit of carpet on the floor and putting up the price of beer four or five cents. We will not allow it.

There was also broad pressure on Maoist activists not to be read as 'students' when attempting to relate to a working class audience. This extended into time spent in social spaces, with Maoist student Fergus Robinson identifying that, 'There was an uneasy relationship with workers who attended the pub. Collectively students, particularly the counterculture Left, looked like freaks.' Activist Ken White gave an insight into attitudes amongst this political scene in an interview with historian Gordon McCaskie. Discussing his friendship with fellow student activist and future labour leader, Brian Boyd, he recounted:

> We got together because we both liked to drink, we were drinking comrades. We would get criticised for drinking too much but we thought our critics lived in an unreal world. We thought we still had contacts with ordinary people.

According to historian and former party member Rob Darby, the CPA-ML's 'youthful members were mostly ockers. They weren't into drugs. They were all mostly very straight.' In setting its cultural tone the organisation recruited few countercultural types, and dissuaded their members from engaging in the archetypal sixties alternative lifestyle. They were doing mass work and they were therefore *mainstream*, or at least they acted like it.

The strategic formulation in the CPA-ML towards this particular concept of 'mass work' was counterposed to 'left blocism': cliques of Maoists inwardly hanging out in their own groups. Darby, in a discussion with fellow La Trobe activist John Herouvim, observed:

> You had a lot of antagonism between people who thought what they should be doing was mass work, particularly ex-student factory workers who felt that it was legitimate political work for them to go to the pub with their workmates, and frowned severely on students who suggested they might do the same thing with their fellow students. And there was a lot of resentment and hostility between the two groups. There were those who emphasised just immersing yourself in the workplace and those who believed it was more important to get out and do things.

As the 1970s progressed and it became clear that a mass movement had not adopted the Maoist cause, Darby found wry amusement at the concept of 'left blocism', applying it to events like the social BBQs held by Norm Gallagher, which did not seem to be subject to the same critique.

Although the Maoists were concerned with relating to working class people in existing social spaces and on existing terms, there was

Norm Gallagher drinking with Percy Jones, football player and publican of The Dover, 1970s (Australian National University)

also genuine concern about the damage done through the use of illicit drugs and excessive consumption of alcohol. Both were considered a form of violence against the self. In their public discourse, Maoists took something of a public health stance on these matters, but when it came to internal issues, there was a strong emphasis on personal responsibility. The most significant test of how the CPA-ML responded was prompted by their leading member Norm Gallagher's slide into alcoholism. An article published in the March 1974 issue of the party's theoretical journal *The Australian Communist*, 'A Communist's Behaviour Must be Exemplary At All Times', stated:

> Ideally it would be desirable that the workers wage class struggle all the time. But again that is not real. The conditions of soul-destroying work require avenues of relaxation. One such relaxation is social drinking. But the bourgeoisie in Australia has developed a sort of cult of drinking. They use it in many ways. Amongst certain trade union leaders it is a part of life. They intrigue, gossip, backstab around the hotels near the trade union headquarters. Again in the history of revisionism this characterised the lives of revisionist 'leaders'. What is wrong with excessive drinking? It diverts the working class, it muddles the working class leader who must recognise that at any moment he may be called upon to participate in a critical decision, it destroys the health of the victim. Therefore, in the waging of the class war we do take a stand against excessive drinking and we think the workers themselves are conscious of this problem, they demand (in various ways such as lack of respect for excessive drinkers) leaders who conduct themselves as servants of the people.

Norm Gallagher and friends at The Dover, 1970s (Australian National University)

The article includes passages that were clearly relatable to Gallagher, who regularly drank at The Dover and The Lygon/John Curtin Hotel opposite Trades Hall. In the same month the article was published an ASIO spy report noted that the drinking habits of Gallagher were of concern to the Central Committee. Based on an informer, the report stated, 'It had been decided that he should be given a chance to rehabilitate himself and that this would be done in China where he was going for a trip.' Gallagher was accompanied by Party Chairman Ted Hill and it appears that the treatment was to some degree successful. Gallagher did not stop drinking, but seems to have successfully set limits on his consumption.

The CPA-ML took a much less equivocal stance on illicit drugs. A key text outlining its position, entitled 'Goddam The Pusherman! Oppose The "Drug Culture"!', was written by Barry York and published in October 1972. In the pamphlet York identified that the organisation viewed illicit drug use as something that dissipated the energies of the left. Key arguments, which could have been seen as equally applicable to alcohol, included that: 'People often use drugs due to the feelings of alienation and frustration imposed upon them by capitalism.' However, 'a revolutionary is someone who strives to "never gloss over reality", and investigates concrete reality.' For York, drugs were encouraged by the elite because they would: 'pacify militancy, divert rebellion and preserve the capitalist class dictatorship', or in short 'Give the kids drugs – they'll keep them quiet.' Assessing his, and the party's position during this period, York says:

> We certainly enjoyed a beer. Some more than others. At least one of the old Maoists became an alcoholic. We believed, in theory, that we shouldn't drink to excess but I know we sometimes were drunk – including yours truly. We drew a distinction between moderate use of alcohol and moderate use of marijuana because of the latter's association with the wider drug culture.

Certainly a number of prominent young Maoists drank little or not at all. How much of that was due to personal preference or political commitment is not certain. York is well aware that laying down lines on such matters did not always equate to successfully changing behaviour:

> Life can be funny. Fergus and I, I reckon, were the only 'Maoists' at La Trobe not to smoke marijuana. Many years later, old Maoist comrades would tell me of the fun they had at parties when they'd get stoned. I never knew at the time!

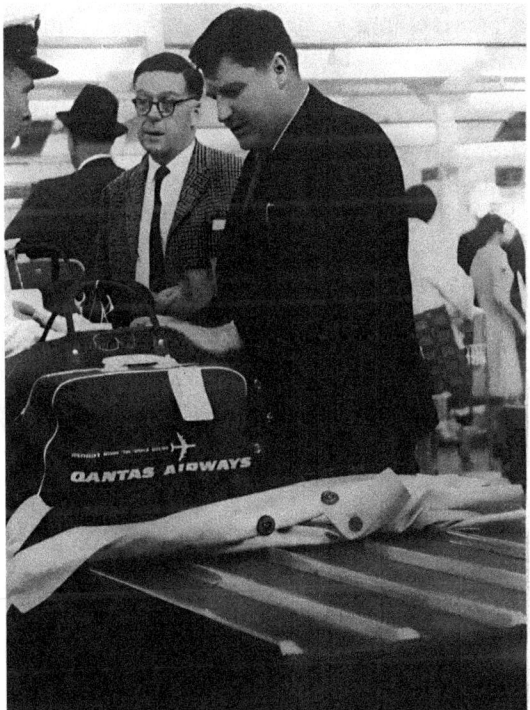

ASIO surveillance photo of Ted Hill and Norm Gallagher at the airport, 1960s (National Archives of Australia)

CHAPTER 46

LIBERATING THE LOCAL: WOMEN DEMAND ACCESS TO THE PUBLIC BAR

Diane Kirkby

In a small country town in Victoria in the winter of 1972 two Aboriginal women went from pub to pub asking to be served. Each time they were turned away, without being given an explanation. The Melbourne press reported they charged the publicans with racial discrimination. They were joining a long list of women who had taken it upon themselves to challenge the pub's discriminatory treatment.

Long celebrated as reflecting the nation's egalitarianism, largely because class differences were obscured, the public bar of Australian hotels was in fact a men's-only space. Its exclusively masculine beer-drinking culture was neither benign nor accidental. Class differences were maintained by charging higher prices in the saloon bar; gender differences were maintained by having separate spaces within the pub and confining women's access to the lounges. Men could drink with women in the mixed lounges, or with men, in the men-only public bar. Women could drink either in the mixed lounges or in the women's only Ladies Lounge. They also paid higher prices. In this period of the White Australian immigration policy, monoculturalism and homogeneity were taken for granted. A combination of law, custom, and most importantly business incentives ensured women, Aboriginal people, Asian and wine-drinking southern Europeans were excluded from the public bar culture and its associations with national values and the national drink. Segregated drinking spaces encouraged men to drink more, in competition with their peers, or in large groups where individuals took turns in 'shouting' for the group. Many pubs were owned by the breweries who promoted their own product, and stood to gain from the higher beer consumption. Proprietors and licensees enforced the rules for their own financial advantage as pubs had a legal monopoly on liquor trading, even as their customers' preferences moved towards more cosmopolitan customs and they broadened their alcoholic tastes.

This culture was at its height in the 1950s-60s, a period when it was also coming under challenge. Women saw connections between their freedom to move and drink in public and their inequality as workers. From the 1940s women journalists began to point to the impact and meaning of this segregated public drinking. Writers like Dymphna Cusack, who published a best-selling memoir of a barmaid in 1953, drew national and international attention to the degrading conditions of pub work under this artificially constructed drinking culture. For the women working behind the bar, or the working women wanting to drink at the bar, policing the boundaries between 'respectable' and 'disreputable' was no longer to be women's responsibility. Travellers and immigrants who had experience of other cultures saw the excessive drinking as adolescent, and restricted hours in pubs and the lack of licensed restaurants as circumscribed and unsophisticated. Law

CHAPTER 46 LIBERATING THE LOCAL: WOMEN DEMAND ACCESS TO THE PUBLIC BAR

Gender desegregation protest at the Petersham Inn's public bar, October 1970 (*Tribune*/Search Foundation, State Library of NSW)

reformers wanted to break that power of the breweries to control the liquor industry. It was time to overturn what Justice Maxwell, the 1954 NSW Royal Commissioner, described as 'the unedifying spectacle' of women being made to sit outside the pub, waiting for their husbands to finish drinking with their mates.

Extended hours of trading was the first step in breaking open the culture. This began with new legislation in NSW in 1955 and a decade later had spread to other states (Victoria and South Australia). The immediate impact on the public bar was to move much trade from city hotels – where patrons congregated in the hour between finishing work and 6 pm closing – to the suburbs where people could now drink at their leisure, with their family members, until 10 pm. The morning after the first night of late opening, on February 2nd 1955, the *Sydney Morning Herald* carried the headline 'Suburbs Crowded for "10 pm" But Quiet in City Hotels.' Most photos included women drinking in lounges and beer gardens, in couples and mixed groups or simply in the company of another woman.

The scene in the public bar of one pub, in the well-heeled waterside suburb of Mosman, was described as being 'typical of those in suburbs throughout the metropolitan area, And it does not look much different from any city hotel between 5 and 6 pm when 6 o'clock closing was in force.' It was crowded, and all the drinkers

The mixed lounge at the Petersham Inn, 1951 (Noel Butlin Archives Centre, Australian National University)

were men. It seemed the hotel business and its customs would survive the new longer hours. Seeing women drinking, especially in saloon bars, nevertheless became more usual. City workers, business, clerical and professional women, met together in small groups, suburban housewives could continue their custom of meeting at their local.

Further steps were needed to give women legal access to the public bar space. That had to be demanded by women themselves. There were other imperatives driving change. Research on the dangers of drunkenness and driving led to drink-driving laws and concentrated attention on the greater drunkenness caused by early closing. As various state governments modernised their licensing laws, women activists took action to give visibility to their demands.

In the 1960s, as the post-war baby boomers came of age, and more women entered the workforce, they became more forthright and persistent in demanding their right to be served equally with men, in the public bar. This often focussed on the local suburban pubs where workers would congregate or local activities were organised. Much depended on the licensee. A group of Brisbane women wanting to attend an art exhibition in a private bar of a hotel were turned away by the proprietor who thought it might be an offence under the state legislation for them even to enter the bar. Merely being in

Women in garb during a protest at the Petersham Inn, November 1970 (*Tribune*/Search Foundation, State Library of NSW)

the bar was not an offence, but the Licensing Commissioner explained that it had not been considered necessary to spell this out because if they were not being supplied with liquor, the legislators had not imagined any other reason for them to be there.

Queensland had not had 6 pm closing but it did have strict laws about women being served with liquor. Women were not barred from drinking in public or saloon bars but it was illegal for someone else – bar staff or patrons – to supply them. One brave lone figure, Marjorie Stapleton took it upon herself to exploit the loophole in the law which allowed women to drink alcohol in the bar provided they brought it in themselves. In her case the proprietor welcomed her presence, cheerily opening her bottle and proclaiming his support. Some customers quickly left the bar, but a larger group stayed to drink with her. Stapleton had chosen the saloon bar for her protest and the customers there agreed that women would be welcome in saloon bars provided one other bar was kept only for men. That culture was hard to break down.

The incident that is best remembered occurred at Brisbane's Regatta Hotel in 1965 when Queensland was revising its liquor act to allow more liberal drinking and dining rules. A large deputation of women had called on the Minister to allow women to drink in public bars but he refused their request. So Rosalie Bognor and Merle Thornton conceived another plan. They entered the public bar of the Regatta and ordered a soft drink. They were refused service and someone (probably the licensee) promptly called the police. They then chained themselves to the foot rail while their husbands handed out pamphlets in support of the cause. The men in the bar expressed their admiration for the women's action, several bought them a beer, and the police merely took down their names and cautioned them before withdrawing. Only the licensee was opposed. They repeated the action a week later, joined by another eight women and this time visiting three hotels, where the male customers cheered them on and the police refused to come when called. They had succeeded in demonstrating customer support for women's right to drink in public bars, a fact which had been substantiated in a NSW survey conducted in 1957. Only 23 per cent of those surveyed preferred to drink in male company only, and only 11 per cent preferred the public bar, the majority of them were over 60 years old.

In receiving support from patrons, and being successful in their goals of exposing the injustice of the laws, these actions were building momentum. Nevertheless, publicans still routinely refused women entry into the public bar. More concerted action and larger, more organised protests followed the emergence of the Women's Liberation Movement. Their strategy targeted local suburban pubs which maintained segregated spaces, charging them with discrimination. One group of Women's Liberation campaigners chose the public bar of the Petersham Inn during 1970. On various occasions they tried to order drinks, gave out leaflets and petitions, carried placards, and according to a report in the *Tribune*, 'dressed as men, with wildly curling pencilled moustaches.'

In cities across the country similar women's liberation groups took orchestrated action as part of a larger strategy of demanding their rights and removing discrimination. Being refused service was like 'a barb in the delicate buttock' of feminists. Another Sydney group visited several pubs in the beachfront suburb of Manly, where they engaged in a spirited protest. They chanted and banged on the bar, making a general din and refusing to be moved on by sitting on the floor, as they demanded a drink and fielded heated interjections from the customers. Four of this group got themselves arrested.

An even more violent protest took place in Melbourne. A large group of up to 40 women didn't try to persuade the customers with reasoned arguments and pamphlets when they were refused service in the public bar of a North Carlton hotel. Instead they linked arms and blockaded the bar to other customers. A fight broke out in which one woman was injured badly enough to be carried outside. The rest of the group then sat in a circle on the floor, and sang songs about liberation. The mainstream press (the *Sun*, 29 April 1974) reported the fracas, and that the police removed the protestors bodily, dragging them out by their legs, and charging twelve of them with offensive behaviour. The women's liberation newsletter, *Vashti's Voice* emphasised the men's violence towards them, 'abusing us, assaulting us, calling us moles, pushing us, pinching breasts, knocking one girl to the floor and kicking her in the stomach, breaking a billiard cue over another girl's head.' The police too got rough, 'scenes of incredible brute force followed' as the women, singing, dancing and laughing, 'bunched together and held on grimly to each other and the bar' refusing to move or be moved. Women were grabbed by the hair, legs, breasts, neck and clothes, thrown out of the bar and headlong into the police vans. One young woman 'was pushed over a car bonnet and beaten around the head.' Despite this, the women surged back in, 'angry and determined to reassert their rights.' This was a strategic campaign and one of several actions taken over a three month period 'by women no longer content to sit down and merely talk of their oppression.'

Their campaign was effective. Anti-discrimination legislation began to be introduced by state governments from the mid-1970s which made it more difficult for licensees to refuse them service. Other imperatives assisted the change. Pubs were transformed by new licensing laws which ended the hotel dining room's monopoly by extending the right to serve alcohol with meals to restaurants. Wine became more popular, and dining out more frequent with the impact of non-Anglo immigration on the choice of venues. Women were in the forefront of this trend. The 'perpendicular' drinking customs of the public bar which had separated drinking from eating and men from women declined further in popularity. Meanwhile, further legislation extended the retail outlets such as supermarkets in which alcohol could be bought, enabling men's beer drinking to continue at sporting events and be promoted in advertising as masculine, national cultural identity.

CHAPTER 47
A SUNKEN SHIP AND ITS SUNKEN BEER: THE TRAGEDY OF THE BLYTHE STAR

Alex Ettling

Mick Doleman was an 18 year old deck boy, the youngest of the 10-man crew aboard the *Blythe Star*. He had started work in seafaring two years earlier and 'loved going to sea.' The *Blythe Star* was a 146-tonne vessel, loaded with a cargo of superphosphate fertiliser and a ton of beer in kegs. The ship was likely overloaded, and it is reported that it was at a list, that is, not sitting straight in the water. Nevertheless, at 6:30 pm on 12 October 1973 the ship departed from Hobart bound for King Island, with the end goal being to satisfy some thirsty mouths (and a need for fertiliser).

Approximately 14 hours into the journey, after Doleman had finished his nightshift, he was thrown from his bunk. Water was gushing in at an alarming rate. The vessel had taken a starboard list before correcting itself. But this offered only the briefest moment of relief for the crew, as Doleman submits, 'it took a further list, which was a death roll. It just went over.' The ship sank off South West Cape with little time for the crew to do anything but save their lives. 'It is probably the most scariest thing to experience, standing on what is left of your world, surrounded by ocean', says Doleman. They were now floating on a liferaft 10 km out to sea.

The captain had not sent a distress signal before leaving the ship, and the ship's course had not been communicated to authorities. Those searching for the *Blythe Star* could not even be sure on which side of Tasmania the ship had sunk.

Over eight days the men drifted with the current, 400 km up and down the Tasmanian coast. They endured fierce seas and swells that drew them crashing towards jagged cliff faces. At other times they were perilously close to being blown out into the ocean towards Antarctica. Doleman recounts:

> The weather was absolutely appalling. We'd have enormous waves bursting through the canopy, so we had to get the water out. We were wet the whole time ... waiting for that raft to fall apart in these huge waves and for all of us just to disappear into the ocean, into the abyss. And that is a fear that you had in the darkness.

Blythe Star at the quayside (O'May Collection, Maritime Museum of Tasmania)

They survived on glucose powder and just 50 millilitres of tinned water a day. 'It was extremely cold and no sign of any land. Not even any birds, and if you can't see any birds at sea you're a fair way from land', Doleman explains. The animal life they did see only added to their anxieties. 'A shark came swimming past, it was a pretty big shark with its dorsal out. That was a worry'.

The first death occurred in the first few days on the liferaft. They initially kept the body on board, but eventually were forced to give John Sloan a sea burial. Survival led to practicalities. 'I was still in a pair of jocks and freezing so I took his socks and I was pretty sure that, although I didn't know John that well, he would have been more than happy for me to take those socks.'

As the days passed, and fatigue set in, a collective delirium overcame the group. Reflecting the centrality of alcohol to the trade's working culture there was a curious event, as Doleman recalls:

> For whatever reason, we thought we had visitors on-board the raft, so we knocked off whatever cans of water we had left, thinking they were alcohol or beer or whatever the case may be. We were all having the same experience. And I remember waking up, or coming to, might be the point ... I said, 'What have we done?'

With some rare good fortune, the tide brought them close to a shoreline and they made landfall in a cove with a freshwater stream. The crew's ordeal was not yet over. They had made it to land, but in one of the most remote and inhospitable parts of Tasmania. 'Funny part was, after we got ashore we all jumped out thinking we'll be able to run up the beach and just lay down and congratulate each other and everything,' seaman Malcolm McCarroll told the ABC in 1973. 'But you can't walk. It's as if you've been drinking all day, as if you're as full as a boot.'

Tragically, two more workers died on the beach of this isolated cove, succumbing to hypothermia and exhaustion. Determined to find a path to rescue via land, the rubber liferaft was cut up and used for make-shift shoes, hats and lap-laps. A three-party team entered the dense bush, making slow progress through high cliffs and dense bushland for one and a half

Mick Doleman (State Library of Victoria)

days. Eventually they came across a logging track and were discovered by a passing truck driver.

A contemporary journalist in Tasmania for TVT-6, Trevor Sutton, covered the event and was highly critical of the efforts to search for the *Blythe Star*. 'No urgency all, none, it was just a ship had gone missing and the government I think felt it would turn up soon, it had probably broken down. The search was botched right the way through,' Sutton told the Channel 7 *Sunday Night* program. Doleman also questioned the adequacy of the rescue operation: 'We weren't rescued – we had to rescue ourselves'.

In the aftermath there was plenty of criticism to go around for how such an event had occurred, a tragedy that cost the lives of three workers: Ken Jones, John Sloane and John Eagles. The captain had made a series of errors and not offered the leadership required. This was instead ably supplied by seaman Ken Jones. The judge also criticised the Transport Commission for its laissez-faire attitude to running a shipping operation. Historian Michael Stoddart has described the situation as 'a litany of indifference, failure and neglect displayed by those who had a duty of care for *Blythe Star* and its crew.' As with most industrial accidents, there were few consequences for the business owners. Trevor Sutton's view was, 'I can't really understand how no one was really held responsible at the end of the day. The marine court of inquiry into the disaster slapped a few wrists. The rest of it was forgotten about.' The inquiry did however lead to several safety reforms, such as an Emergency Position Indicating Radio Beacon [EPIRB] being installed on ships. The tragedy was also the catalyst for the AusRep system that ensures vessels regularly report their routes to authorities. Requirements that all liferafts be fitted with radio beacons were also introduced.

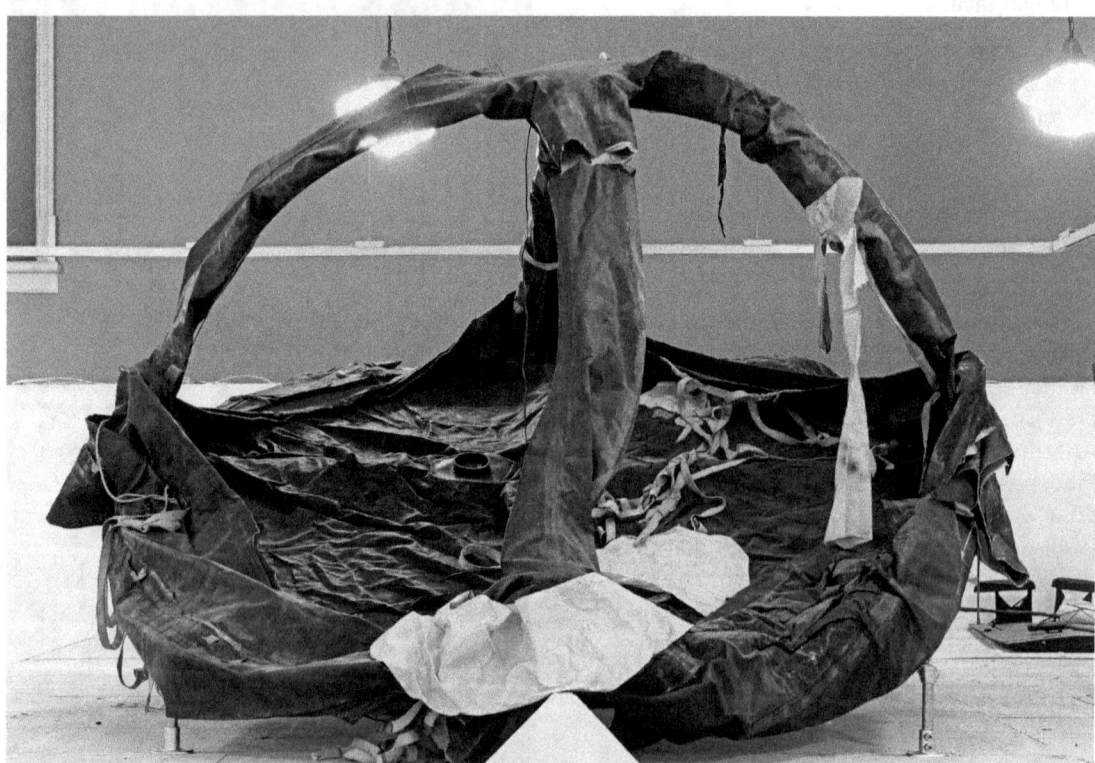

Liferaft used by the crew of the Blythe Star (Barry Champion, Maritime Museum of Tasmania)

CHAPTER 47 A SUNKEN SHIP AND ITS SUNKEN BEER: THE TRAGEDY OF THE BLYTHE STAR

The trauma of the *Blythe Star* disaster would inspire Mick Doleman to become a determined advocate for seafarers through maritime unions over a period of 40 years. As an official, he dedicated his career to improving marine safety. Speaking at the 2015 ACTU Congress before his retirement, Doleman stated, 'I don't think you can have a better life, in my view, than representing working men and women of this country, and the globe. United we stand, united we win'. At a casual gathering in 2016, Doleman was presented with a retirement gift: an engraved beer mug as an appreciation for his service in the union.

Doleman's journey began with something ordinary that became extraordinary: workers transporting goods from here to there, as part of the network of logistics that makes our modern world.

In this case, getting some kegs of beer from Hobart to King Island.

Life ring from the Blythe Star (Barry Champion, Maritime Museum of Tasmania)

Union official Mick Doleman receives an engraved beer stein as a retirement gift (Maritime Union of Australia)

CHAPTER 48
WHITLAM AND THE GURINDJI LAND RIGHTS CEREMONY
Alex Ettling

After a seven year strike for wages and land rights the Gurindji people won a landmark victory in 1973 against multinational corporation Vestey Brothers. Having petitioned the government and travelled the country, drumming up support from unionists and others, a section of their country was taken back after the meat-packing company's lease from the federal government ran out.

The photos of then Australian Prime Minister Gough Whitlam symbolically pouring sand into the palm of Gurindji elder Vincent Lingiari have become some of the most iconic images in Australian political history. There is another photo, also rich in symbolism, that is less known. In white culture, celebration is often accompanied by champagne. The travelling party to Daguragu brought a bottle with them. Whitlam offered the first drink to Lingiari, who had sworn off alcohol the year before but obligingly took a sip. Whitlam followed. The photographers were off the mark in capturing these symbolic moments. They requested a repeat performance of the sand being poured in Lingiari's hand. They had also missed the shared drinking and so they asked Whitlam to re-stage the pose of swigging champagne. It is clear there was a genuine intention of social exchange and a wish for this moment to represent a meaningful restoration of Aboriginal sovereignty. However, the presence of alcohol, and a somewhat bourgeois drink as champagne, brought with it other connotations.

After Lingiari took a swig, according to Charlie Ward's account, *A Handful of Sand: The Gurindji Struggle, After the Walk-off*, he sought Whitlam's help in preventing the negative effects of alcohol in the community. Lingiari made a speech to those gathered, and a party followed: dancing, food and drink. The elders in Daguragu were aware of the whites' culture of marking occasions with alcohol and so waived the ban on grog for the day. However, alcohol was in short supply. Partygoers soon learned though that saying, 'One for Mrs Whitlam, please' was the guarantee for procuring a cold beer. After it was all over, and the government VIPs had departed in their plane, the elders were reportedly 'disgusted' by the empty beer cans left behind.

There was some degree of naivety amongst the visitors regarding how celebratory alcohol would be seen by those in the Gurindji community. They were grappling with its presence as another European incursion on their way of life and had taken a decision to ban alcohol from their community. There are two ways of reading the situation. First, as an attempt at a more meaningful and genuine exchange by including two approaches to symbolic goodwill, side-by-side on equal terms. The other reading is that it is a reflection of the upper-hand of the Australian state, and a colonial arrogance, in foisting their means of celebration onto this community (and more egregious when the Gurindji were the wronged party in the dispute).

Certainly, the title deeds of the property were the most prized thing being handed over, and the Gurindji knew that this was what they really needed. The crisp white pages were enthusiastically passed around at the ceremony and came out impressioned with red dirt from many hands. They wished to behold the symbolic artifact that sealed their ownership in the eyes of the Australian state. It was a moment of victory for this community and First Nations people around Australia, gaining some control back after the colonial dispossession, but only one chapter in an ongoing struggle.

Vincent Lingiari looks on as Prime Minister Gough Whitlam swigs champagne after the symbolic handback of the Gurindji people's land, 1975 (Rob Wesley-Smith)

Vincent Lingiari reciprocates the celebration of drinking champagne, 1975 (Rob Wesley-Smith)

CHAPTER 49

FAREWELL FROTHIES? GLOBAL HEATING AND DISAPPEARING KELP

Alex Ettling

View from the forest floor of a remnant giant kelp forest in southern Tasmania, 2021 (Scott Ling)

Achieving the perfect froth on a pint of beer often comes down to the expertise of the pourer. More scientifically it accrues from the presence of a compound called alginate.

An operation to supply this product to the beer industry was established in Tasmania in 1963. Marrickville Holdings, a margarine maker, established a subsidiary Alginates Australia and commenced factory manufacture of this new product that same year. Within ten years the industry was dead.

What attracted the firm to Tasmania was the spectacular giant kelp forests that thrived in the sub-Antarctic waters. For workers in the town of Triabunna where commercial operations were based it was a welcome source of employment opportunities.

Puck Vaughan, a former worker at Alginates Australia described the process in a report by Zoe Kean for *ABC Science*. Barges sought out the offshore forests of Macrocystis pyrifera cutting it down like grass 'about two foot under the water.' The haul, 'a coupla hundred tonnes at a time' was brought in, chopped up and spun round. The resulting alginate was then extracted, squeezed, dried and packed.

The factory became well established, operating 24 hours a day and employing local people, until the kelp mysteriously began to die. Harvests reduced and a rot began to plague the beautiful strands of swaying forests. 95 per cent of the giant kelp forests along Tasmania's east coast were lost within just a few decades.

Not unexpectedly, some locals attributed the catastrophe to the mass harvesting of the forests by Alginates Australia. Whatever the culpability, the firm did not stick around to help solve the problem. Vaughan asserts, they 'just walked out the gate and wrote her off.'

With this extractive industry no longer operating, the reason for the failure of the kelp forests to regenerate is largely due to a broader environmental problem. Macrocystis forests on the east coast of Tasmania are uniquely placed to be an early victim of climate change. Temperatures in the area are rising at nearly four times the global average. The East Australian Current which sweeps water down to Tasmania is now warmer and poorer in nutrients. Macrocystis forests have become Australia's first federally listed endangered marine community type. With the loss of the forests, goes the entire ecosystem that depended on it.

Around the world, climate change is having an impact on the production of alcohol in different ways. Hops require a frosty winter and then specific warm weather conditions to flourish, an obvious agricultural product at risk. Australia's intense fires, and other weather and plague events, damage grain and fruit production. Linda Johnson-Bell, founder of the Wine and Climate Change Institute, warns that the wine growing map is being redrawn due to erratic weather events. Mitigation efforts include spraying grapes with a form of sunscreen and increased irrigation, including with treated wastewater, but these are considered temporary solutions. One study showed that if temperatures rise by 2° Celsius, wine-growing regions could shrink by as much as 56 per cent.

The damage caused by unsustainable production has devastating consequences for native habitats, but also for the locals who wanted long-lasting industries to build their communities around.

It's too late for the swaying and dancing underwater forests that Puck Vaughan remembers: 'If on a calm day you listened over the boat, you could hear it all clicking with life. It was beautiful.'

Alginates Australia's kelp processing factory near Triabunna, 1960s (Tasmanian Archives)

CHAPTER 50

'WE FOUND OUR OWN WAY': TALKING WITH GAY LIBERATION ACTIVISTS

Bruce Carter

Gay Liberation activist John Lee, Sydney, 1972 (David McDiarmid papers, State Library of NSW)

I came-out as a radical socialist at 14 and a poofter at 15. I found my queer self across the following decade through a meld of political activism and social recreation in the commercial queer spaces that inhabited Sydney's Darlinghurst and its other inner-ring suburbs in the 1980s and 90s.

As a young, white, cis-gay man, with some but not a lot of money in my pocket, I could walk from my cheap share-housing to a raft of pubs, discos, cafes or sex clubs, and find real-time queer company, *any* night of the week. Shift working as a student nurse on an apprentice income wasn't a hindrance to finding gay company and queer intimacy. This social scene in the 80s and early to mid-90s, pre-Internet, was a mightily different ecosystem to the one my queer activist elders knew in the 1970s, or of course, the virtual worlds and metaverses accessible to anyone, anywhere, today. Although, how much were 70s activists a part of the commercial gay venues where camps, gays, and poofters congregated? After all, wasn't 'out of the bars and onto the streets!' a rallying cry that echoed from North America?

Listening to a zoom presentation by long-time activist John Witte in 2022 I learnt of an oral history interview undertaken in the 1990s by historian Robert French with gay liberationist and academic John Lee. Chewing-over the heady and hopeful days of gay liberation's activist agenda in 1970s Australia, Lee said he felt he and his fellow gay lib activists *didn't have any idea or appreciation of, the everyday reality (of gay life). How difficult it was for so many people to live their lives at all. We had an extremely elitist approach to ordinary people who we saw as bar queens ... we saw ourselves as a kind of vanguard – we'd come out, they hadn't ... This was some kind of a moral failing on their part.*

Hearing this motivated me to revisit work I had undertaken in the 1990s for an undergraduate course on doing oral history, where I interviewed gay men about 1980s Sydney. I dug out and dusted off cassette tapes to take a listen after two decades. I also drew on a small number of interviews undertaken by Sydney's Pride History Group some years back. Mostly, I started talking to friends and acquaintances, my dear queer elders whose activism had smoothed the path for later generations like mine to declare who we were with less despair and often much greater life options than many queers had known before.

These activist elders were to varying degrees participants in the Sydney social scene, at the commercial bars that operated on the margins – sites like those once found in North American cities which writer Jeremy Atherton Lin suggested were best described as 'clandestine hideaways'. Venues whose owners, some activists would occasionally tell us in denunciatory tones, survived because they had worked hand-in-glove with organised crime syndicates. An operation I shall refer to as The Syndicate in this chapter was run by Abe Saffron. It controlled drugs, sex work, pornography, and illegal – after hours – drinking venues. During the 1960s and 1970s it had working relations with police, churches, some right-wing unions, and members of the Liberal and Labor parties in NSW. I had heard over the years tales of how 'hush money' passed to the forces of law and order assured the doors of bars and clubs stayed open late at night despite restrictive decency and liquor laws.

This chapter is an attempt to distil attitudes towards the commercial scene as some activists remember it, to scratch the surface a little to see what my queer activist elders feel now about their attitudes then. I use oral history here as it offers the greatest opportunity for an understanding of this recent past as remembered by those who lived it. In general, I have threaded quotes from oral history sources within the text, *in italic*. They are not separated from the narrative by quotation marks or indentation. I see this work as a conversation, and oral history is a co-created source, 'an exchange of gazes' as oral historian Alessandro Portelli has described it. In using italics threaded into the body of the text, I am acknowledging this dialogic process that, unlike a typed or handwritten manuscript, is a dynamic process of speaking and listening.

Terry: A whole lot of ice in the drinks!

Terry grew up in south-eastern Sydney and entered university in 1972 studying social work. For Terry an abiding memory is visiting Enzo's, one of Sydney's few gay bars in the early 1970s, for the first time. Terry had come out in 1971 and Enzo's was a small 'wine bar' in Oxford Street, opposite Paddington Town Hall, with a primarily well-to-do, older clientele. Straight-up, he was advised to familiarise himself with the most discreet exit that could get him out of the venue, fast. Raids by NSW police were commonplace. *They'd say when you go to a new bar, always check how you'd get out, work out a way to leave, if the police come, or there's a fire, make sure you know how to make an escape, that was advice I got when I was young. In those days my experience was people would look after you, if you were the 'new boy or girl' on the block, they'd sort of take you under their wing.*

Over-priced, watered-down drinks were the accepted standard, bar owners flagrantly operating with the knowledge that the city's queers were in no position to challenge them. Prices were higher in the nightclubs with drag shows after the pubs closed at 10pm. Terry recalls favourite drinks on a night out in the early 70s were a 'Dry & Dry' – dry vermouth mixed with dry ginger ale or *if I was particularly poor or it was cold, a Stone's Ginger Wine. I remember Chez Ivy's and the drinks! They were always half-full of ice; Zula, a tough German lesbian used to work there, and she put a whole lot of ice in the drinks, that's one way they got-away with not putting as much booze in!*

Bars and pubs catering especially to the port city's queer communities first appeared in the 1960s. Prior to this, homosexuals had gathered at bars that would tolerate them, where the back bar of a hotel, for example, may have been unofficially designated 'camp'. Outside certain bars at seemingly 'straight' pubs, people socialised at house parties and parties organised by social groups held in such venues as local community halls. One men's social group became famous for its popular parties held on long weekends in the Blue Mountains, two hours out of Sydney. Ken Johnson recalled in a 1980 interview with Garry Wotherspoon being *18 or 19 and climbing over the back fence and down the lantana after a raid by police of a party held in Bondi at the flat of a jolly group of queens who lived opposite the beach. The local cops using 'noise' as their basis to stop anyone having fun. Noise, queens, poofters, bingo!*

Social groups such as the Chameleons, Boomerangs and the Pollynesians held dances and shows in council halls, charity fundraisers such as large annual 'coming out balls', organised by telephone and mail. The Boomerangs formed after police moved the 'beat' or men's cruising area in Boomerang Street East Sydney to Darlinghurst Road. Boomerang Street sits in front of St Mary's Catholic Cathedral and from 1940 to 1970, Cardinal 'Stella' Gilroy, it has been said, maintained an intimate knowledge of what was happening at night between men in Boomerang Street. These social groups and their parties are a story for another time; it is safe to say, however, that queer social life in Sydney until the mid-1970s was kept on the downlow.

Chez Ivy's bar, Bondi Junction, 1966. Ivy Richter, the bar operator is seated at the bar, second from the left (Ivy Richter Collection)

The commercial scene was vastly different in ambience from the bring-your-own-grog Gay Liberation dances Terry and others organised – activist movement fundraisers held at municipal council halls or on university campuses. At these parties Terry says he felt a sense of safety he didn't feel at the bars as he was partying with fellow travellers, on common ground, joined together for a cause that ran deeper than just out and out fun. They would drink a little (Riesling or Moselle wine, beer or sweet cider) or smoke some pot: *we'd go to the Arts factory in Surry Hills and score a matchbox of weed*. Still, Terry enjoyed the possibilities of the commercial bars, such as Enzo's and Sydney's first pub to 'go gay', the Cricketers Arms in Surry Hills. Targeting a gay clientele in 1972 this pub was described by gay newspaper *The Star* as 'leading the way to the eventual development of lower Oxford Street as the centre of Sydney's night life'.

On the commercial scene Terry found a generous mix of people from across the city, allowing him to mingle with queers whose disposable income was greater than his tight student budget. It wasn't uncommon for their social and political outlook to contrast, either. *I went out to enjoy places and the company of other queens, but some, some people that I knew from Gay Lib, they just wouldn't do that* he reflects, recalling both the suspicion with which Gay Lib activists viewed 'bar queens' – a term often used disparagingly – and the reservations held by some of those who drank and socialised at the gay bars toward gay activists. *People used to speak about bar queens in a negative way, but I never saw it like that.*

Terry Batterham in black 'Poofta' t-shirt. Gay Liberation contingent, May Day march, 1974 (Anne Roberts, *Tribune*/Search Foundation, State Library of NSW)

Gay Liberation: action to change

In his 1999 book, *A Sydney Gaze: The Making of Gay Liberation*, activist Craig Johnston spelled-out the underpinning beliefs of gay liberationists noting that:

> Gay liberation ideology agreed with radical feminism that the personal was political, agreed with Black nationalism that the oppressed should be proud of who they were, and located particular aspects of the dominant bourgeois ideology as its enemy – insisting on some form of political commitment and action to change the structures which permitted and reproduced that ideology.

Today, Terry acknowledges some gay liberation activists viewed themselves as freer of the heteropatriarchal oppression they argued weighed-down life for bar queens. The spaciousness of many activists' lives – doing political work and studying at university, undertaking little or no paid work – played a part in this thinking, beyond the liberationist ideology they were committed to. *They were all students, at uni, so most people weren't working in jobs where you'd be exposed to all sorts of attitudes, and there was this, well, mostly we were young, and people would say 'we're not like those queens, we are different'.* The dominant attitude, Terry tells me, was that activist young gays were trailblazers out to change the world. 'Bar queens' – viewed by activists as closeted, cowed and apolitical – needed to be educated and 'raised' to the same political awareness as activists.

Handing-out gay liberation flyers at a bar Terry recalls being confronted by a lack of interest, with some people making it very clear they were feeling satisfied with life as they lived it. *We always asked whoever was working at the bars if we could hand stuff out, it might have been for a rally, discussion group meeting, gay lib party or whatever and sometimes they'd let us, other times we were told no. I remember some people would just turn their back on you, and one evening a queen leaned-in and said to me, 'We are just fine, don't stir it up, we don't need your liberation, go home'.*

In a piece in *William and John*, Australia's first glossy monthly magazine targeted at the surfacing gay men's 'market' in 1972, out counter-culturist and gay liberationist Jim Anderson's attitude to bar goers sounds pious and condescending when read today:

> ... they bop about in their own little groups. They are the people who form an oppressed class. They ape straight society and its values – the accepted standards of masculinity and femininity ... they accept their own oppression. It's really pathetic. These people only function behind the closed doors of a party, a bar, a dance or a pub. They've got to get out of these inhibitions and get themselves together as a conscious homosexual member of society.

In suggesting they were ignorant of their own oppression Anderson's critique of bar queens aligns with Terry's memories. Activists such as Anderson were frustrated at bar queens seeking temporary release from lives lived in the closet by partying at fire-trap bars operated by hungry gay capitalists and their criminal associates.

Barry: *we found our own way*

Barry came out to himself when he discovered Sydney's thriving men's beat scene in the late 1960s. By 1971 he was a member of Campaign Against Moral Persecution (CAMP). Started by Sydney friends and neighbours Christabel Poll and John Ware, this was Australia's first major lesbian and gay rights organisation. The group campaigned for social and legal rights and drew considerable media coverage. In 1971 they began publishing *CAMP Ink*, Australia's first community-based gay news magazine.

Barry soon found the more radical, social transformation politics of gay liberation that he discovered at uni spoke to him with greater force than the reformist agenda of CAMP. When I met him recently in a Surry Hills pub, I read Anderson's article out loud and he chuckled knowingly. *Many of the gay activists that I knew in the early 70s really did look down their noses at the general gay scene. Now, I may be being judgemental here, but I really think many guys in the movement were more... asexual ... their politics was so strong they didn't want to sully their image, like taint it with actual sex!*

He continued *...a conversation I remember like yesterday, I had a car, and with R, B and C went out to Balmoral Beach on a Sunday for a swim and of course I couldn't resist telling them 'here is a beat', and 'there's another one up on the hill there' and then coming back in the car I was like 'hey, last night I went to...' and C says to me 'Barry I don't think we want to hear about your sexual activities' and I recall I said 'sometimes C I think you resent my sexuality' and R from the back seat said 'you mean sensuality' and I said 'no, I know exactly what I mean, my sexuality'.*

For Barry, who grew up in working class Bankstown, drinking out in the bars cost money he often didn't have, so it was not something he did regularly, unlike gay beats which were everywhere in Sydney – at parks, beaches, railway stations. He was also not keen on the drag performance scene and found it hard to understand, admitting that his exposure to feminist politics through gay liberation distanced him from drag culture.

Of meeting men at beats, he said *I loved doing beats, never knowing how many men I would meet, or where – this was a culture we developed ourselves. The normal things like courting and dating and having dinner and so on weren't available to us as social possibilities, I couldn't afford it, and so we found our own way. A way of finding people in maybe a secret location, it had dangers of course.* That his enthusiasm for beats and the potential they offered to meet all types of men was frowned-on by Barry's fellow gay liberation housemates is something that is not lost on him still, 50 years later: *they were so removed from the universe of gay men I was discovering on the beats, the one's we were, we believed, fighting for.*

Ken: *the dominant bars had this sort of upper-class mobility aspect*

Ken became involved in gay liberation as a high school student, attending Sydney's 1973 Gay Pride Week demonstrations with fellow students and teachers from Epping Boys High School. The nationally co-ordinated week was the first time the concept of 'gay pride' was promoted in Australia. Ken's involvement in the events of 1973 was the start of a lifetime commitment to social change activism, and following school he got active in Sydney Uni gay liberation.

Like Barry, Ken recalls the dominant social scene for gay men at this time being class laden. To succeed within it you had to possess a certain degree of cultural capital. *I think the social scene and the commercial scene were, well, the dominant bars had this sort of upper-class mobility aspect, young gay people would adopt a whole lot of affectations, you'd adopt a sort of role, in femme, effete, middle or upper class type culture. They'd expect you to know who Maria Callas was, about opera and fine arts. I saw it as upward mobility, in terms of needing to know about formal culture and what you drank, what you wore, how to shop, all that sort of stuff.*

Garry: *I had my feet in both scenes*

Not all activists felt awkward about the scene, however. Garry loved the music and the ambience that he found at the bars. He shakes his head when I mention NSW Premier Askin and life in 1960s and 70s New South Wales under his command. *The very corrupt police were very willing to turn a blind eye to these basically illegal clubs for a price, and the gay world was* starting to happen. At the same time there was censorship of literature, the police were heavy, Australia was oppressive, young guys were being drafted to Vietnam, it really is no wonder that by the early '70s you've got Germaine Greer's Female Eunuch and Dennis Altman's Homosexual Oppression and Liberation coming out. Many of us, look, we wanted something else by the 70s!

Like Terry, Garry straddled both gay left activism and recreation at the bars, *I had my feet in both scenes* he tells me. For the women he knew in Gay Liberation life took a different shape. I catch-up with Penny who tells me bars came later for her. Steaming pots of tea, not alcohol, were the drink of choice in her early activist years.

Penny: *our little bubble of lesbian feminism*

Penny moved from Newcastle to Sydney in the early 1970s. She had seen a lesbian friend sent to a psychiatrist in her hometown. *I needed to get away, explore my sexuality which was going to be hard [in Newcastle] so I moved to Sydney and into a socialist household in Ross Street, Glebe. I was involved in the women's movement which led me to the lesbian movement, the radical feminist lesbian movement which I was more intellectually attuned to, and my first campaign as a feminist was to repeal the abortion laws. I was very young, still a teenager, and I realise now mixing with very sophisticated thinkers, feminists, lesbians.*

Penny lived for some time in Crystal Street, Petersham, which she remembers as a *famous lesbian feminist household prolific in fun, and prolific in questioning our values as lesbians and feminists. Every day was fun at Crystal Street, households were your family ... there were always women visiting, drinking cups of tea around the kitchen table, it was a very fertile time for the evolution of my identity and political thought.*

Women talked politics all the time at Crystal Street: *any cat and dog fight for women or for the gay movement we would be in it, and it was the most fun I've ever had I think because of the camaraderie – the people I was with were clever, and witty with it. We did everything together, we spraypainted together, we'd say 'all the lesbians on the bus please stand-up', we'd stand up and get off, then get on the next bus and do it all over again, stuff like that you know, fun!*

Other women found each other at dances and the small number of 'camp bars' that existed. Historian Rebecca Jennings's research on the post-WWII social scene for lesbians in Sydney notes that across the space of thirty years opportunities for lesbians to socialise broadened greatly. Some shared social space with camp men at the bars; one woman Jennings interviewed described the scene at the Park Inn bar in the late 1960s as 'full of lesbians from wall to carpet to wall you know? And drag queens'.

It wasn't until the 1970s that lesbian-specific meeting places emerged. Bars such as Ruby Red's, the back bar of the Cricketers Arms in Surry Hills, the Sussex Hotel beside Darling Harbour's dockyards, and later Playground in Surry Hills catered exclusively to women.

An energetic women's scene developed around the Rose of Australia Hotel in CBD-fringe Chippendale, where bands such as Lavender Blue, Sheela, Clitoris, Hen's Teeth and the Stray Dogs played. Penny spent nights there, recalling: *I'd go and watch bands at The Rose, that was sort of Friday night, Saturday night. I'd go down there like everyone else have a few drinks or whatever, pick up girls or not, the vibe was women, drinking, listening to music, dancing. I was around that scene, but there was too a lot of parties that were often fundraisers and, mostly we socialised, as the Left generally did, at parties – house parties and parties in halls to raise money for...whatever cause was of concern. I am not a big drinker at the best of times, I'd take two cans of VB with me to a party and that'd be it for me.*

Diane: *Bar dykes dressed more neatly*

Diane had arrived in Sydney from Melbourne in 1973, one of many lesbians and gay men who migrated to live an activist life in Australia's largest city. She had met people from Sydney at women's events and remembers her arrival was *interesting, meeting new women mainly, we were all politically active. I remember going to the Cricketer's Arms but like, we'd be wearing overalls, you know, the gear we wore at the time, overalls, and boots from the disposal shop. Bar dykes dressed more neatly and some were disdainful of our badges and t-shirts with bold slogans. We, really, just didn't fit with the bar dykes and bar queens, we were political, we were out, we wanted everyone to come out, publicly. Sitting here today, I think we were somewhat naïve to the dangers in coming out that could be very real for some people.*

Diane's reflections align with work by historian Sophie Robinson who noted in 2016 that lesbians who were feminist activists and those who socialised at the bars were 'two utterly different crowds – one an overtly ideological and political identity, and the other a non-political sexual identity that largely socialised in bars and clubs with gay men'.

Ken and John: *suddenly, it seemed, there were gay venues all over*

My interest piqued, I dig-out cassette tapes and listen to interviews with Ken and John that I did almost 20 years ago. Recalling debates in the movement in the 70s and 80s Ken remembered *sections of the Left in the 70s were very moralistic. Some were preoccupied with their horror at drag, the objectification of bodies, lots of suspicion of what was seen as 'role playing' in some same sex relationships, like the whole butch/femme thing that you might see at women's bars.*

John arrived in Sydney from northern NSW to start a degree in Fine Arts in 1971, an experience he says was *pretty horrific but also exciting. I turned up dressed like I was going to high school in Mullumbimby!* He recalls the bar Chez Ivy's and its small stage in the shopfront window where he watched off the-wall, in-your-face drag performance group the Synthetics. *I had done almost three years of fine arts by that stage, so I appreciated their outrageousness and got their aesthetic sense and queer sensibility.* Mostly though, John's encounters with other queers and alcohol happened in straight pubs, where drinking was cheaper. The beer-garden of the Forest Lodge Hotel was a regular hangout after weekly gay liberation meetings on Glebe Point Road. By 1975 gay liberation in Sydney had run short of steam like many other social movements, coinciding with the defeat of the Whitlam Labor government, while the commercial bar scene was growing.

'A funny thing happened on the way to the 1980s Oppression > Discrimination Liberation > Rights Movement > Community'

John recalls *by '78 gay liberation ideas were well and truly dying, by '79 they were dead, and people were on the reform track, people were always coming to conferences with a law reform agenda, there were clashes between liberationists and reformists, different expectations. I was still a liberationist but was involved in a gay trade unionist group that was purely reform, so getting support for gays on the job, rights and recognition in the workplace became my focus after the demise of gay liberation.*

In March 1978 Ken and fellow activist Anne Talve were asked by activists in San Francisco for solidarity actions on 24 June, at the same time as the annual Gay Freedom Day parades, on the anniversary of New York's 1969 Stonewall rebellion. Ken convened a coalition of groups that came to take the name Gay Solidarity Group. Initially the plan was for a downtown morning march, but some suggested a late-night street party – a festive celebration, or 'mardi gras', in Oxford Street. The idea was to try and engage punters flocking to the emerging gay nightlife scene.

With a permit, the parade left Taylor Square late at night, and many people joined in from Oxford Street, but the police became hostile, halting the celebration at the city end of Oxford Street. Revellers turned into marchers and the police initiated a brutal riot. 53 arrests ensued and savage physical attacks were meted-out by NSW Police. The community consolidated in anger and action in ways never before seen.

While The Syndicate had run gay bars in Sydney since the mid-1960s, this expanded after the Wran Labor government threatened their operation of illegal casinos in 1976. Saffron's group transformed these premises into new venues targeting gay men, resulting in a rapid expansion of gay options in Darlinghurst. In a move that came as a surprise to many activists, Lorraine Campbell-Craig, hôtesse-en-chef at Capriccios – a drag club established by The Syndicate-aligned Dawn O'Donnell in 1969 – and Trixie Lamont, drag compere and performer at Patchs, a popular disco bar run by The Syndicate – made announcements about the arrests and asked bar goers to open their wallets towards bail money.

Jeffrey: Last night a DJ saved my life

Jeffrey had been involved in gay liberation events since the early 70s. In a 2012 Pride History Group Sydney interview he recalled: *we had been in the Vietnam moratoriums, going*

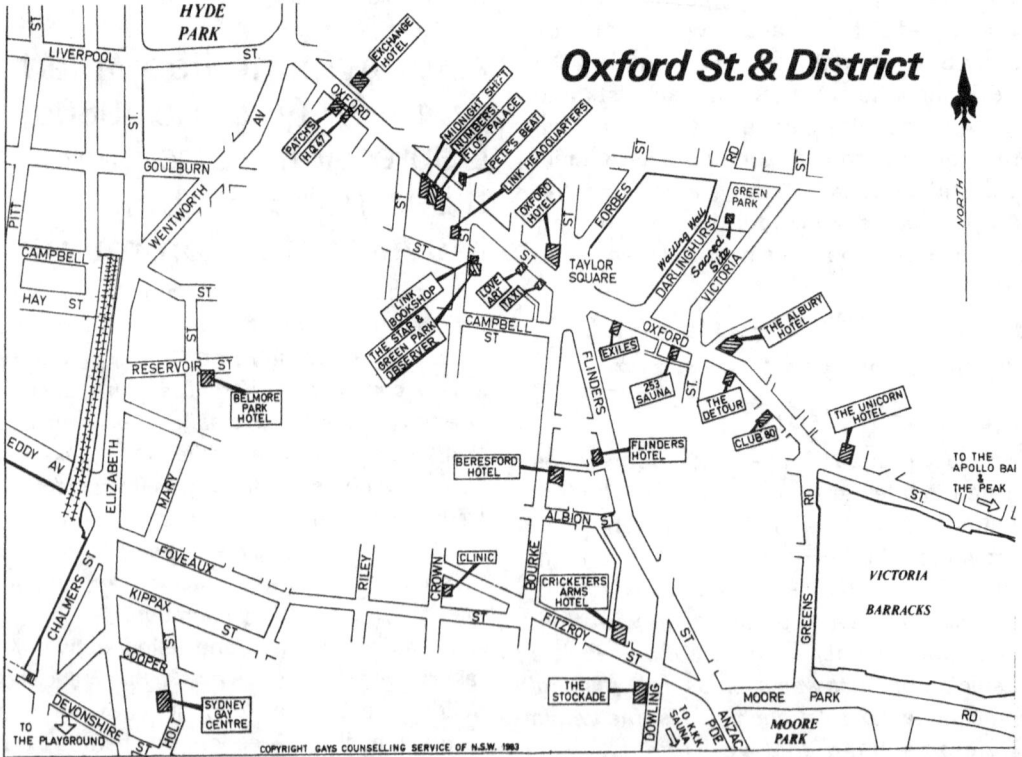

Map of gay and lesbian venues, Darlinghurst, Sydney, 1983. (Sydney Gay Guide, Gays Counselling Service NSW, State Library of NSW)

to a demo was not new to anyone, we'd been marching up and down George Street for years! It became 'let's do it for ourselves!'.

By 1976 he was increasingly attracted to the release the dance floor offered, recalling *we just wanted to go out, party-party, but we'd be aware when there was a demonstration on, and we'd go to marches ... we felt different – Oxford Street was becoming the centre of our world.* He remembered this unforeseen gesture of solidarity in 1978 – passing the hat around at Cappricio's and Patchs as *...the most astonishing thing.* He recalls that at the time a club such as Capriccios was to most young and politically-conscious gay men a site *almost alien, you couldn't get into Capriccio's dressed the way you were dressed on any normal occasion – you weren't allowed in in runners and jeans – so the fact that those people actually did that I thought was an extremely important thing, and I believe, an interesting little turning point.*

In the following two months marches demanding all charges be dropped saw a further 125 people arrested. Protesters gave new life to the old chants, 'Out of the bars and onto the streets!' and 'Stop Police Attacks on Gays, Women and Blacks'. Jeffrey had attended the night march on 24 June and escaped being arrested. But on the daytime march on 15 July, he was grabbed by police and charged.

The first Mardi Gras crisis in the black of night on 24 June 1978, launched gay rights, civil liberties, and police powers as central public policy issues in Australia. The success of the second Mardi Gras in June 1979 set up a new trajectory of engagement between activists and the burgeoning community, with militancy and visibility accelerating change. In 1979, most of the charges from the 1978 arrests were dropped, Jeffrey's one of them. Yet sex between consenting males was still against the law.

The increasing number of gay men coming-out and moving into the inner-east of the city saw new drinking venues open which were not controlled by The Syndicate. Referred to as 'independently operated', Darlinghurst pubs such as the Beresford and Unicorn Hotels and the men's club Midnight Shift (originally named 85) opened and operated in upfront defiance of The Syndicate. These developed rapidly in the late 1970s, establishing the city as a centre of gay capitalist culture.

Writing in gay men's monthly *Campaign*, Sasha Soldatow chastised gay movement activists for what he saw as rolling into bed with beady-eyed capitalists keen to get their paws on the lucre offered by the bars, discos and clubs targeted at the gay community. He lambasted what he viewed as an 'unholy alliance between a newly-emergent strengthened class of businesspeople – the gay capitalist, and the so-called gay activist'.

The evolution of *The Star* – a newspaper targeted specifically at out gay men was central to the developments Soldatow and some other activists found distasteful. Established by North American Michael Glynn in July 1979, *The Star* heavily promoted the gay commercial scene, spruiking 'think gay, buy gay'. Glynn needed advertising revenue for his new paper and was originally aligned with The Syndicate operated bars who opposed the second Mardi Gras in 1979. Later, he promoted the 'independent' businesses while endorsing a style of identification and dress for gay men that was straight out of San Francisco and New York.

Robert: *when I blacked-out the lights people screamed*

Robert arrived in Sydney from Forbes in rural NSW and found himself working at Patchs in 1980, an Oxford Street disco bar operated by The Syndicate which became hugely popular.

He recalls a regular daytime task: *we'd sit down in the locked-up booze room and we'd get all the good spirit bottles, Johnnie Walker, Stollies, the high-end brands, we'd then fill-up the bottles with cheap stuff so it was half-half and it would be charged as top shelf* (laughs). *They tried to do it with Southern Comfort, but* it went all milky so I'd always tell people, if you like to drink Bourbon, you're safe, that was the one the owner couldn't touch!

Overhearing a conversation one morning stopped him in his tracks and left him in no doubt as to who he was working for. *I walked into the office and heard one of the owners saying 'such and such is going to end up in the bottom of the harbour'. I gulped, turned around and walked straight out, knowing I'd just heard something I wasn't meant to.*

Hanging out at the club with his friend Stephen who was DJ'ing there, Robert began playing with the lighting rig *...the owner realised more people drank if there was lighting 'cos it got everyone excited – people, like, screamed! 'cos I started doing black-outs and white-outs and you know, no one was doing that anywhere else at the time* [at gay venues] *and I noticed when I blacked-out the lights people screamed, hands would fly up in the air. I thought 'wowee, this is something wonderful'. Before the Midnight Shift opened, everyone used to come down, after the Shift opened, none of them came down. The Shift changed Patchs for good.*

Glynn's *The Star* newspaper was fundamental to changes in image and dress style being adopted by gay men, supporting the independently operated bars that were opening that catered to the 'gay clone'. Dress historian Shaun Cole observed that the gay male clone represented the hypermasculine characteristics of 'toughness, virility, aggression, strength, potency. There was a real attempt to dissociate from the ridiculed effeminate ... and to become a "real man", or at the very least to look like a "real man".'

The 'clone' sporting short hair, a moustache or beard and wearing tight t shirts or a flannelette shirt (in a softer version, a Lacoste polo shirt), Levi's 501 jeans and leather work boots became the dress style many men moving to the ghetto adopted. The central partying spot for clones was The Midnight Shift bar, advertised as a 'man's disco'.

While Robert expressed his belief that The Midnight Shift permanently altered the scene at Patchs, what The Midnight Shift represented – the emergence and adoption by many gay men of the idealised hyper-masculine clone 'look' – is arguably what shifted the vibe at venues on Darlinghurst's 'Golden Mile'. Gary Bennett, writing in Australia's *Gay Information* commented in 1981 that:

'Only We Can Do It' poster, putting the gay male clone as activist front and centre in the call to mobilise community to a decriminalisation march and rally, 1982 (Lex Watson papers, State Library of NSW)

> The 'clone' phenomenon has created what has been referred to as a 'new masculinity' amongst homosexual men. The dominant stereotype of the feminised man (that is, the 'queen') is still very prevalent but it is no longer sufficient. The 'macho-clone' has had a very real impact on the male homosexual category. The male homosexual is no longer necessarily the 'genteel' man.

For Ken, clone was problematic ...*the thinking by its supporters was that being clone was somehow democratic. Very fast there's this new constituency of masculine homosexuals in the bars, that's a particular moment, and for me there is an element of it all that is misogynistic, like if you're wearing a flowery shirt, you're probably going to be thrown down the stairs of the Shift. Suddenly people valued masculinity – they had been struggling against masculinity and suddenly you were supposed to value it and act-it-out. We went very quickly from 'men need to learn to cry and do work on getting in touch with our femininity' to being told its time we embraced our masculinity. For a time, drag performers were unwelcome in most gay bars.*

Activist Craig Johnston claimed the gay male 'clone' enabled any man to be out and proudly gay, unlike fashion-conscious camp culture which he saw as less accessible due, partly, to economics. Johnston argued:

> The macho gay clone would not have been possible without gay liberation as he shares its ideology. He rejects the traditional stereotype of a male homosexual, yet his masculinity is not absolute; he is self-consciously gay and not at all ashamed; he flaunts his sexuality through the very clothes he wears; above all, he is public.

A New Gay Dawning

Diane noticed that the women's scene was changing, and she recalls meeting more women in the bars receptive to politics, while she herself was more comfortable socialising in the bars. *In late 1978, '79 and '80 I was living in Darlinghurst, and I used to go to Ruby's, and it was a much more melded kind of scene. There were a lot of women who went there that I knew who didn't have an aversion to politics, unlike a lot of the older bar dykes who seemed anti-political to me. They felt threatened, I think. We drank a lot then and looking back I think that was a result of the stress after the first Mardi Gras. It was a whole lifestyle of work, meetings, out afterwards for drinks at Ruby's at least four nights a week.*

Penny also recalls going out to the bars in the early '80s – something foreign to her during the gay liberation years. *I went to the bars as a place*

"Those two champions of the mystique of the heterosexual male, brewers Tooth & Company and Toohey's Ltd, have been thrust into the frontline of gay entrepreneuring" - 'Macho Chic at the Pub', Philip McCarthy, *National Times*, 14–20 September, 1980

Patchs, 'Sydney's Hottest Gay Disco', Ruby Red's, 'where Sydney girl's meet', gay community media advertisement, 1980

to meet people and I remember taking a woman home and she said 'why do you think you're gay, what happened to you?' and I said 'just lucky'. If you don't have a political framework to put your sexuality then I think a lot of those women thought there was something wrong with them.

The years immediately prior to law reform were eventful. The resolve of the community was growing and people's expectations of equality in law and an end to police harassment continued to build. Serving as its co-convenor for many years, Barry recalls the strategy of the Gay Rights Lobby at the time: *We had the support of the people in the bars plus, there'd been a transition from mafia – or Syndicate – owned places to the gay-owned places. So you had the owners of the Shift 100% on and the owners of the cafes like the popular café Green Park Diner, they supported all the demos. There was a support and awareness that hadn't been there in 1978 and most definitely not in 1973!*

Yet relations with the forces of law and order had not sweetened. Antipathy from police remained a constant into the 1980s. Police harassment was not uncommon and was set amidst a generalised climate of fear with men being bashed – sometimes to death – at beats across Sydney. This was commonplace with a 2022 state parliamentary committee of inquiry into hate crimes against gay and transgender people hearing that on average 20 gay men were attacked each day in NSW between 1970 and 2010.

Reporting on the harassment of two men on Oxford Street in 1982, Michael Glynn wrote in *The Star*, 'Over the last year we have received numerous reports from gay women and men about the attitudes and actions of certain members of the police force. The situation is abhorrent ... all of us everywhere should be filled with anger and outrage'.

In 1983 police raided Club 80, a popular men's sex club, not once, but three times. 200 men were arrested on dubious charges. From the bars to the cafes to the streets the anger in the city's queer communities was palpable and once again people mobilised to demand an end to police harassment, the dropping of all charges against those arrested and, most crucially, for reform of the law which still criminalised sex between consenting males.

Bar owners working with The Syndicate were none too amused, recognising that law reform posed a threat to their established modus operandi. Michael Glynn revealed in an interview in 2006 that he had come under considerable pressure from bar owners aligned with The Syndicate to go silent in his newspaper on law reform. *Dawn and Roger sat me down and said 'we don't like this law reform business. We want you to stop it' and threatened me with their advertising ... They did pull out their advertising. It was a struggle.*

Finally, in 1984, after a sustained campaign, sex between consenting males was decriminalised in NSW, albeit with an age of consent of 18 as opposed to 16 for heterosexuals. It would not be until 2003 that the NSW government equalised legal standards.

Looking Back

Returning to where we started, with activist John Lee's assertion that gay liberationists in the 1970s didn't understand 'bar queens', how do my activist elder associates feel about Lee's statement today?

Ken says he'd still agree with John Lee's assessment, stressing *I think there was a snootiness from gay liberationists, like 'we know what's right for you', there was a hostility between gay lib and bar queens but also between gay lib and members of CAMP, let's be honest. In the early 70s nearly all the bars were for the middle classes really, the Rex in Kings Cross was an exception. Mostly, you needed a good income to drink at the early bars. For younger people, your lived experience of going into social groups or the bars was difficult in terms of how people from very well-heeled backgrounds would treat you, not to mention how they would react to your politics!*

Garry and Terry – who had managed to enjoy the early 70s bar scene and keep politically active – concur with Lee's assertion also. Garry tells me: *I can understand why a lot of the bar queens didn't want to stir up trouble, they could quietly go to the bars or steams [bath houses]. Police might turn up, but mostly it worked, many people on each side regarded the other as less than necessary at the time. One side saw them stirring up trouble, the activists saw bar queens as get off your bums and do something because your life can be very different!*

Terry adds: *I think that some of the people I was mixing with (in gay liberation) saw themselves as superior to the average bar queen, yes, sometimes I thought they didn't even engage in sex, it was just like they knew what their orientation was.*

Penny is upfront in calling-out the lack of understanding of activists towards those not politically engaged back then. *Yes, we did go into the bars as feminist-gay liberationist-evangelists 'have you heard the word about feminism, do you know about gay liberation?' Thinking about it now, it was madness, but I think we had a hunger to not be in that scene, where you saw people dressed like men, butch/femme, we wanted something more.*

We were quite up-ourselves because we felt we had insights that these people who were drinking a lot and blaming themselves for their sexual identity didn't. But in reality, all, most, gay people of that time have had to deal with guilt about their sexuality. Ultimately, I think it was about class. We were a middle-class lot mostly, and the women drinking at the bars in later years, like at The Rose or Ruby's, were not necessarily.

John concurs, saying Lee's observation was 100% correct, *people really thought they knew better, had received the word and collectively, us activists, we were 'better', but did I feel better? I don't think so. I think gay liberation did me no harm, it was good for me, but I never pushed it on people, I never suggested going on demonstrations to my other friends who weren't politically active. When I went to work in the real-world at the parcels office at Central Railway I met all sorts – co-workers from the Middle East, men who had sex with other men, and some bar queens, and I liked them. There was a working-class identification with them, we were organising through the union for the greater good. I respected them and their situation.*

Diane admits there was a lack of understanding of people's lives, *but I wouldn't say we were elitist. There was a divide between the early 70s activists and the bar dykes, but really, after the first Mardi Gras in '78, because there were so many people who came out that night, people became activists by just walking out of the bars to see what was happening and then feeling so angry they got involved when they perhaps wouldn't have if it hadn't been so awful and violent. 'Out of the bars and onto the streets' was taken straight from US activists, but it was very applicable to our struggles.*

For my generation who came out after the first Mardi Gras – yet before law reform – the queer bar and social scene in Sydney we got to know, and helped grow, was in many ways a transforming entity.

We celebrated at parties and parades overflowing with colour and creativity. We disowned stigma, demonstrating on the streets for access to HIV treatments, and celebrated the lives of our loved ones gone too soon during the 1980s and 90s AIDS crisis. We did this with, and through, our queer elders, those who had come before us. In the 1970s they had occupied two frontlines of resistance, both exposed and vulnerable: one on the streets working for change and the other in the bars constructing new queer social spaces. These memories of struggles past, personal and political, can open-up intergenerational understanding, and offer a living resource for queer activists mobilising today.

CHAPTER 51
FOLK, POLITICS AND THE LAW AT THE RAINBOW HOTEL
Alex Ettling

Originally established in 1869, Fitzroy's Rainbow Hotel has been a key music venue for decades. In this interview publican **Paul Costigan** recalls the hotel's intersection with folk, politics and the law in the late 1970s and early 1980s.

Alex Ettling: How did the Rainbow become a mainstay of the folk scene?
Paul Costigan: What happened was that the folk scene at the famous Carlton pub, the Dan O'Connell, it seemed to have gotten a bit cliquey. A number of the folkies felt they weren't getting a chance to perform. We'd had a singer Jean perform on Tuesdays, folky jazzy type stuff. Fitzroy is a small place, so somehow or other word had got to the disenchanted people at the Dan O'Connell, and they came to me and said, 'How would you feel about some of us coming and having a sing on a Thursday night?' We were pretty desperate. I tried not to say 'Please! Please!' Instead I said, 'Yeah that sounds alright.' We became very friendly with them. And that's how it grew from there, and the pub became relatively successful.

When we'd taken over the pub we realised that [the previous owner-publican] had been trading illegally on Sundays, and that was his busiest day. When we found out we refused to do it, and refused to pay the local cops to do it.

AE: Did the cops make it clear that they would turn a blind eye if you paid them off?
PC: In a funny way, yes. One night, Patty and I were cleaning, after 10 o'clock, because it was 10 o'clock closing. I had a big ashtray that I was taking outside. There was a knock on the pub front door, and I answered the door with a big bloody ashtray in my hand. There were two cops there and they said, 'Oh, are you closed?', and I said, 'Yes, it's the law to close at 10 pm and have everyone out by quarter past.' And they said 'Oh, well where's Frank?' And I said, 'Frank has established a lease, and I'm Paul and that's Patty, and we've taken over the lease.' 'Oh, oh. Well, um, ahh, um, well umm Frank, well actually Frank owes us a barrel of beer. For the children's Christmas party' (laughs). Having been involved in parents gatherings at primary schools, it's only recently that alcohol has been

Rainbow Hotel, Fitzroy

frowned upon. I think I said, 'Well okay, can you come back during the week when we're open and we'll fill up the barrel.' An 18er by the way. And that was the last I heard of them. Until they tried to do me over and book me.

AE: What's that story?
PC: There was a demonstration against Malcolm Fraser up in North Fitzroy. I'm not quite sure what it was about. I knew at the time, and we had signs up in the Rainbow Hotel encouraging people to go. But we were going to the country, it was a Sunday afternoon. We almost by accident realised that we were driving right past where the demonstration was. So we parked the car and jumped out, and joined it. And I witnessed the police using their horses to physically bust, or you might say molest, the peaceful demonstrators. And it was really quite frightening, they had the horses doing that tap dance that horses can do. So, on the Monday I wrote to the, I can't remember, *The Sun* or *The Age* or whatever, deploring the use of police violence at what would have been a peaceful demonstration.

Thursday night was the big folk night. We used to get [extended] licenses for someone's birthday, because I found a loophole that you could get a license to up to 2 o'clock in the morning and you didn't have to serve food. So the folkies drew up a list of people with birthdays, and we went merrily on our way. The Rainbow only had one women's toilet. The law in those days was that it was considered that 25 women could use one toilet, and women would probably be half the numbers. So we were limited to 50 people.

The police raided us on the Thursday, three days after I had criticised them and Fraser. They didn't actually count anyone, but they ended

Anti-Fraser protest in Melbourne, featuring Liquor Union banner, 1980 (*Tribune*/Search Foundation, State Library of NSW)

up charging me with various things, including having more people than was allowed. So I had to front the Fitzroy Court in front of a magistrate who regularly had lunch in The Rainbow Hotel. He never came after that (laughs). I always say, why tell the truth in the court, when if you tell lies you will get away with it (laughs).

I got bad advice from the barrister. I queried that there were more than 50 people. That night we had two folk bands playing, each had about 6 or 7 people. They weren't being paid, and nor were they paying for their drinks. It was a deal we did in those days with the folkies. So I thought I'd be on the safe side and I said there were 55 people present on the premises, but at any one time, 7 were playing in the band, and the other 7 were resting and getting free drinks. So it ended up that I had 47 people, I claimed. And the bloody magistrate ruled that whether they were paying for their drinks or not, they were on the premises. So it turned out I had 55 people on the premises.

I got given a 12 month good behaviour bond and had to pay $75 to the poor box, which I did as soon as I was dismissed. I went back to the Rainbow Hotel. We were in the same street. And there was a friend of mine there who was on the pension and pretty poor. I sent her straight up to the courthouse, and she spun a tale and got the $75 and came back and drank it at my pub (laughs). And I survived the good behaviour bond. It's the only time I've ever been charged with anything. But that was a classic example of what the police did.

There was another time when they tried to do me over about these birthday loopholes. First of all, the police got up in the licensing court and said, 'Is it not true that you serve lesbians and homosexuals in your hotel?' And I saw the magistrate looked shocked. I turned to him and said, 'Your honour, I am not in the habit of enquiring into the sexual preferences of my customers.' And he said, 'Rightly so'. And he turned to the copper and said, 'How dare you ask a question like that?'

But then he went on and he asked my witness whether he was going to a birthday party on Thursday and what was his name. And it was something like "Allan". 'Well, what's his second name?' And he said 'I don't know'. 'And you mean to say you're a good friend [and you don't know his second name]?' 'I've been playing in the same band as him for the last five years and I still don't know his second name.' Which was very true, it was all first names. And often people became 'Paul from', so I was 'Paul from The Rainbow', and there was a guy who was living with us who was 'Tom from', and you'd line up the second name with what they did. So it was 'Bill the Lawyer', or 'Jack the footballer'. It was too hard to remember all the second names. In the end we didn't get fined.

Folk musicians at anti-Fraser protest in Melbourne, 1980 (Search/State Library of NSW)

CHAPTER 52
THE WOOLSHED KISS-IN
Graham Willett

The door of the Woolshed Bar, Hotel Australia, closing night 29 September 1979 (Ivan Polson for *Klick! Magazine*, Australian Queer Archives)

Kissing – it's not just for fun! In late 1979, 100 women and men gathered outside the Woolshed Bar downstairs at the Hotel Australia on Collins Street, Melbourne, a long established watering hole of kamp people. The crowd was engaging in a little public pashing. Police, gathered other side of the road, watched this 'kiss-in' impassively. This event is odder than it might seem. Not only was there public pashing – it was politically motivated!

The Hotel Australia had been a gathering place for kamp men at least as far back as the 1930s. As it was built and rebuilt, decorated and redecorated over the years, the homosexual crowd ('kamp' in the language of the time) stayed loyal. In its final incarnation, the hotel had two bars – one upstairs on the first floor, one in the basement. Upstairs, the bar was a rather sedate affair, for men in suits and ties, discreetly imbibing an afterwork drink with friends; kamp, but not obviously so. Downstairs was a different story entirely. Its unofficial name, the Snakepit, gave a clue. 'Rough trade' gathered there – working class men, sailors in port, crims recently released from prison. And flocking to them, their admirers, men willing to pay for a few drinks and a meal in return for sexual favours.

The barmaids are remembered fondly. But the owner of the hotel was not keen on this clientele, changing the downstairs décor to discourage the riff raff. At one point he installed hay bales and other paraphernalia to create a woolshed theme – and was aghast to find that this masculine vibe did not scare off the kamps at all.

Finally, he decided to close it down. Fans of the Woolshed gathered for one last hurrah, becoming increasingly raucous, souveniring bits of the décor. The cops were called but weren't really in a position to do much about this. Until, that is, two patrons, Terry Stokes and Darren Turner, were leaving. They stopped at the top of the stairs, and kissed good night – a very passionate kiss, with much tongue, lasting 15 seconds according to a cop nearby, who promptly arrested them for offensive behaviour. They were charged, brought to court, convicted and fined.

In the days that followed, word spread. A couple of women – their names lost to history – were so outraged that they organised a protest, the kiss-in.

So far, so fun. But up at Melbourne University, things were turning ugly. Terry Stokes was a student resident of Graduate House. His conviction and his crime came to the attention of the authorities, and he was expelled from the college. A storm of protest erupted – academic staff objected; students occupied Graduate House for four hours; letters fired off to the Vice Chancellor led him to announce that the university did not condone any form of discrimination. Strikingly, a Liquor Trades' Union meeting of the cafeteria workers passed a motion deploring the eviction and warned that, if Stokes was not allowed to return to the college, further stop works would be held and other unions contacted. This was an early example of unionists acting against anti-gay discrimination.

In the end a compromise saw Terry being offered back his room at the college. He declined to accept, but the point had been made. With university authorities, students and staff and local trade unionists raising their voices, a new world in which gay people could be accepted for who they were was on its way.

Kiss-in protest at Hotel Australia, 1979 (James Spence, Australian Queer Archives)

CHAPTER 53

'DRINK AND GO TO WORK': THE SAINTS AND THE BRISBANE PUNKS

Alex Ettling

Chris Bailey, singer of Brisbane band The Saints, was asked shortly before his death what gave him the courage to not conform. He told interviewer Kirsten Knauth, 'I could say Bundaberg rum, but that would not be true. Injustice. My parents.'

Bailey's family were Irish immigrants to Brisbane, his father particularly engaged in the politics of Irish independence. His sisters were described as 'all fierce women' by music writer and family friend Clinton Walker, 'they were always talking about politics, about culture.' When Bailey was 12 years old he participated in a protest with his sister Margaret, during which she chained herself to the government building of the education department. Margaret had been expelled from every school in Queensland in a dispute that had exploded over the freedom to wear a miniskirt. This spirit of defiance was formative for the singer, whose buzzsaw rock'n'roll band came to be described as one of the pioneering acts of the punk era.

The political context around the band represented both the upturn and downturn of Brisbane radical politics. Bass player with The Saints, Ivor Hay:

> We used to sing 'The Internationale' at parties. I don't know if we were revolutionaries, but we had that sense that something was happening. [With the band] we were doing something that we thought was going to change something. Chris was particularly good at pushing things, at being anti-everything.

In its early years the band was assisted in a small way by Margaret's membership of the Communist Party of Australia (CPA) and her connections to radical politics. The Saints' guitarist Ed Kuepper assays the support from the CPA as being that they 'got to rehearse there a couple of times for free and got to use the stencil printer to do some handbills for one of our shows.' Chris Bailey recalls:

> We did do several shows for the Communist Party of Brisbane, because we used to actually rehearse in the ground floor of

The Saints play at Club 76, 4 Petrie Terrace Brisbane, 1976 (Jennifer Fay Gow)

their building and they used to let us have it for nothing, and I thought that was very comradely of them. And the first ever show I remember, I don't think it was a fundraiser, I think it was just a dance and we were the dance band of the evening. And we were very cute, I think I even wore a tie.

Margaret herself recounts:

I spent a lot of time with them when they were practising, when they were playing, even organising gigs for them – in a place like Brisbane which was very hard to do. Just ringing up halls, seeing if they could play, that sort of thing. I organised a couple of gigs for them at the university, at the Communist Party, just providing places for them to play.

Chris Bailey, interviewed by writer Andrew Stafford, speaks of a broad interaction with the social spaces of the left:

The Waterside Workers were great, I loved going to their dos. The Communist Party was pretty good to us as kids, they were very indulgent, they let us have their space to rehearse in and all of that. That's because Margaret knew them all. We certainly weren't a Party band, but because we were somewhat left, there was some kind of sympathy there. The older generation that Margaret was in just thought we were young scumbags who were after their women.

In an interview on the *Workers Power* radio show on 4ZZZ, Virginia Clarke recalled 'carousing at the CPA HQ with chicken sandwiches and lots of beer.' Working class institutions in Brisbane also supported the arts activity of the youth, especially when family members were active in the movement. Clinton Walker told Stafford:

I sort of remember them playing the famous show at Trades Hall in Brisbane, you know, up near the doctor's [area at Wickham Terrace] as I recall, and it was sort of like the lunch room, or something, you know, it had wood polished floors, it was kind of a big room, but there was no one there, you know, as I say, us mob were there, there was Margaret and Mary Lou and some of those kind of people, and my sisters maybe – various people. We were like little brothers and little sisters, you know.

The mob were a crew who knew members of the band, mostly kids from the working class suburb of Inala. It was an area of Brisbane with few things to occupy bored youth, and a suburb targeted by police. Inala was also described as a font of political activism, a hotbed even, penetrating into high schools. Chris attended Corinda State High School briefly in 1972, Ivor was

Poster advertising a show by The Saints at Sherwood RSL Hall, 1975 (Radical Times Archive)

already a student, and Ed attended in 1972/73. Both Ed Kuepper and Chris Bailey had previously attended Oxley High School where they met in the detention room, punished, according to Kuepper, 'because we had long hair and we were wearing political badges.' They got chatting about music and other shared interests. In an interview with Andrew Stafford the guitarist argued:

> There was an environment at the school that was fairly hostile to student dissent – students having any sort of political expression, at Oxley High School anyway. It was a totally reactionary, right-wing group of teachers that we had at Oxley High School, to the point that you wouldn't be allowed into classes if you had a Moratorium badge or a Women's Lib badge. And that was the sort of stuff I was starting to become involved in.

Bailey was committed to politics in his early years and adopted the same markers of youth political rebellion as Kuepper:

> Yeah, I believed in the possibility of revolution ... We were a bunch of kids from the wrong side of the tracks who weren't part of the big white shoe Queensland real estate dream. I think it's fair to say, generationally, it was certainly fashionable to be a little bit politicised. I would like to think in retrospect that it was a bit more heartfelt for us on account of we were actually working class. We were trying to cause revolution through music.

In speaking to Stafford, Kuepper emphasised:

> There were other things that linked people together in those days. Politics was an important area. Australia was still involved in the Vietnam War, so moratorium marches were a big thing and you'd meet people – they became big social events as well as being expressions of political consciousness.

Kuepper, Bailey and Hay all took part in the Moratorium marches. Kuepper also attended an anti-Springbok demonstration at Albert Park. At a certain point after being 'fairly politicised', Bailey withdrew from regular activism, but recognised its importance to his development: 'It was of great benefit if you could be on the dregs of all this stuff.'

For Kuepper, there was a distinction between the performers associated with the New York punk scene and their situation. 'The Saints were a working class band', he asserted. At age 15

CPA Rooms had been hosting events for many years, 1960s (Communist Party of Australia Collection, Fryer Library)

The Saints at 4 Petrie Terrace Brisbane, 1976 (Jennifer Fay Gow)

Bailey was working in an abattoir, and he also held a job on the Queensland Railways. These experiences were in areas which did not feature an activist union culture. As a young worker, he was inspired by the collective sentiments of the workplace – skiving and drinking after a hard day's work. He also leaned into a certain amount of cynicism towards other segments in society that were organising, specifically students, who were dismissed by some as middle class.

In the flat period of political struggle in Brisbane circa 1972–76, the window for Bailey to deepen his political activity was not as open as it had been just a short time earlier, nor a short time after with the revival of confrontational street protest in the city which started in 1977. The band had left the city to embark on a career as professional musicians. The conditions of frustrated rebellion in the mid 1970s were however ideal for developing the sort of band The Saints became: boisterous and anti-establishment – an alienated person's drinking band.

The Saints formed at the end of 1973. In an interview with John Willsteed, Hays recalled that the members would go to the Oxley Hotel overlooking Ipswich Road on Thursday nights, and 'just sit up there having beers, we wouldn't have been much more than 17 or 18 at that time. Chatting about all sorts of stuff.' There were political discussions and philosophical debates, and also chats about comics. In *Eccentric Voices: A Scrapbook of Brisbane Cultural History, 1965-1995* Hay remembered the mid-1970s as a time when:

> No-one went out much in Brisbane, because there wasn't anywhere to go to. Connectivity was a problem. Finding other people of a like mind. You'd have the pubs, and that's where you met a lot of people, but there were no venues to go to.

Inspiration came as an unlikely by-product of the Vietnam War. Bailey explains: 'Brisbane at the time was a popular place for US soldiers serving in Vietnam to go for a bit of R&R. They used to bring these amazing records with them.'

The band members spent their time developing their skills. Despite the aesthetic of indifference, as Bailey told Kirsten Knauth, 'We were disciplined, we rehearsed every week. All we did was music.' Some degree of work ethic was expected, which led to the dismissal of drummer Jeffrey Wegener. Kuepper explains, 'He just wasn't turning up, and when he did he was pissed. And for all the reputation that The Saints had, we still had to try to get certain things happening.'

The musical aesthetic was in part influenced by their technical limitations, what they termed 'primitive amplification'. As Bailey surmises, 'Rock and roll and amplification in the wrong place.' Observing their visual aesthetic, musician Mark C. Halstead in an interview with Stafford recalled, 'A British journo described them as having the dress sense of dead winos once. Chris with his op-shop suit and bottle of rum in his hand.' The alcohol soaked aesthetic was complementary to the songs of alienation. Lyrically, the themes were contemplative in the philosophical sense, delivered in a dissonant rock'n'roll form.

A compelling tension existed between these aspects of the band, and their musical form with its assertive hallmarks of R&B, soul and punk. As Ed Kuepper explained in the *Stranded* documentary, 'It wasn't supposed to be a fist in the air call to arms or anything, it was more of a reflection, recollection.'

The issue of class was embedded into these concerns. Bailey, specifically, had an eye to looking beyond some of the most surface cultural interpretations of class, to one which was more about the haves and have nots – who flexes control in society and who has autonomy in their job. No doubt these views were formed by his own work experience, his family's class position, and growing up in a working class suburb. Speaking to Knauth, Bailey explained:

> It was very obvious to me as a youth that Australia, despite the accent, was in fact a class society, and there was barriers, and it wasn't "We're all in it together mate",

there was a class structure in Australia. It was a bit more insidious because of the whole ANZAC notion of everyone is equal.

When asked on ABC Radio about the meaning behind their most famous song, '(I'm) Stranded', Bailey replied, 'It's pretty obvious, it is a song about alienation.' The single of this track was independently released in 1976, and instantly made an impression both locally and overseas. It pre-dated the first UK punk single, The Damned's 'New Rose', by several months, and the records of The Sex Pistols. Upon Chris Bailey's death in 2022, the headline in the *New York Times* summed him up as a 'Snarling Frontman Who Introduced Australia to Punk Rock' – it could possibly have been expanded to 'the world.' Chris Bailey, speaking to *MOJO* magazine in 2001, described the recording of the song, 'It was our first adventure in a recording studio. I recall it all felt rather natural. Drink and go to work.' It holds its place as an iconic song in the rock music canon, whether categorised as 'punk' which the band rejected, or 'gutsy realism'.

Equally influential was the reputation of The Saints as a live act in Australia. In Brisbane however a continual issue was the lack of opportunities to play. Until the late 1970s, when Triple Zed fostered a live music circuit, the venues for The Saints style of music were invariably one-off events. For a period there was the phenomena of pool parties, whose popularity was no doubt influenced by Brisbane's humidity. Ithaca Pool proved a popular venue, especially in summer, when patrons could dive in and cool off. Centenary Pool was another venue, notable for an early show by The Go-Betweens when a gig attendee did a naked bomb off the high diving board and split his anus requiring stitches. This was not the only OHS concern during the pool party phase.

The Saints played several shows on UQ campus, including a pool party for the local community radio station. Triple Zed identity Steve Gray, speaking to Stafford, noted the contrarian nature of Chris Bailey:

> We had a fundraiser down at the university pool, and we had set up some speakers and we were playing Triple Zed. So he made a point of being an arsehole and actually coming around and turning it on to the most poppy of the commercial radio stations, and would do so repeatedly.

This was harmless rascal behaviour. John Stanwell recounts a more serious issue that revealed itself during the event:

> The Saints were intentionally difficult, that was part of their schtick, and their crowd was worse. And that got worse as it went on, other bands were more notorious. We did one thing at the pool, it seemed like a good idea at the time. Again we're talking Brisbane. Outdoors. Two problems we discovered, and fortunately we were able to police, you don't think about it, but if a glass gets thrown in the pool they have to drain the pool, and that puts your hire through the roof. So we ended up not taking that risk again. We didn't go back.

> The main problem was that it was even closer to the river than the student union building, and so the wealthy people in the riverfront houses on the other side of the river went ballistic and rang the police all night. And this was at just normal rock volume.

The band's reputation for unpredictable behaviour made them an exciting prospect for audiences, but generally less so for those responsible for those doing the hosting. Clinton Walker recalled a time The Saints played on campus where:

> They were told to stop, so they sort of did – but what Chris Bailey did was, he took the money that they'd taken at the door in a hat and threw it out into the crowd. Which again, was only us, so we'd given the money to them anyway!

Robert Forster from The Go-Betweens was inspired by seeing The Saints play at UQ. When speaking to Virginia Clarke and asked to describe the overwhelming visual memory of his early impressionable years on campus he said, 'There were posters for everything, Marxism, feminism, socialism, gay rallies, you name it, any iteration of politics.'

For some young people, the subversive mix of underground music and radical politics was an expected part of campus culture. For others, there was novelty in entering the space of an elite, sandstone university to see such a band. The Saints played a fundraiser for East Timor at the Relaxation Block at UQ where Margaret Bailey explains:

> The people that came were bikies, people from The RE [Royal Exchange hotel], teenage plumbers and sparkie apprentices and things like that, all our mates from Corinda and Inala. So it was an interesting time, because I think of it as bringing the working class into uni. Even though I was there as a student, I didn't feel like I belonged and that was a similar thing for a lot of my friends from working class suburbs.

With limited options, and a string of hosts who were not keen to repeat the experience, The Saints were compelled to create their own venue. 'Club 76' was an unregulated space, situated in a sharehouse first occupied by another of Chris Bailey's sisters, before both Chris and Ivor Hay moved in. It was a modest tin and timber building at the busy intersection of Petrie Terrace and Milton Road. The band started playing shows that were barely distinguishable from house parties. Although

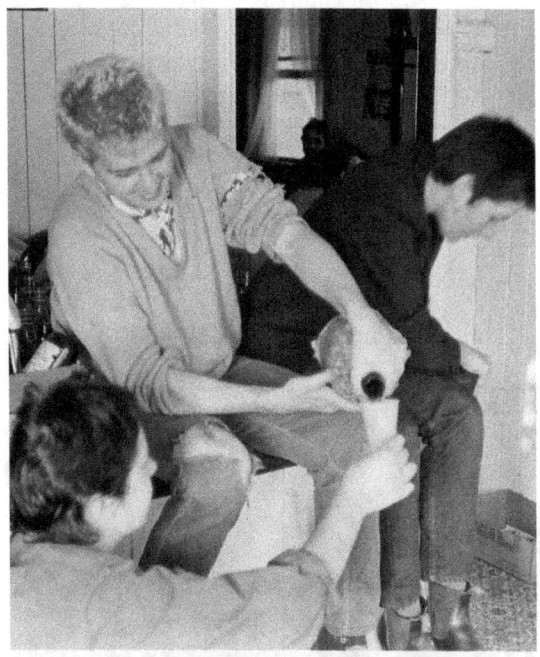

Members of the alternative music scene drinking in a Brisbane house, 1970s (Paul O'Brien, State Library of Queensland)

there was a rock band performing, the noise of the main road seems to have offered some protection. The presence of a police station directly across the road strangely does not seem to have led to immediate intervention.

Ed Kuepper explained to Stafford, 'It started off with maybe a dozen people coming along and ended up with literally a full house in a fairly short period of time.' There was no admission or sale of drinks. As Bailey told *Foster Child* fanzine, 'We just thought of the kind of revolutionary radical notion of being a highly politicised young rock band and we played for the people for nothing.' He also explained to Kirsten Knauth:

> There wasn't a stage. Everyone was on the same level. Except it felt quite professional, and we did sets, and everyone would drink and chat. And then the band would play and people would go bonkers.

These were usually affairs that involved heavy drinking. Bailey assesses that, 'depending on the amount of alcoholic intake, the response was ecstatic! Euphoric, almost.' The singer was fond of the comment from Dick Pike, a friend of Ivor Hay's, who surmised that, 'He thought that The Saints were the best band to listen to when you were smashed, and to this day I still think that's a hell of a compliment.'

The entertainment that the band offered, and the environment it was in, seemed to encourage a particular exuberance. Ed Kuepper asserted:

> The band was pretty wild and the people who were into it were pretty crazy, and the band in those days definitely inspired

Ed Wreckage (left) and Warren Lamond (right) of The Leftovers (*The Brisbane Devotee*)

a sort of total throwing off of any inhibitions – people danced wilder, and we had a pretty drunken crowd all of the time, too.

In November 1976, *Rock Australia Magazine* journalist Andrew McMillan ventured to Club 76, where he found 'a couple of hundred kids packed into every room of the house, tugging on cigarettes and bottles of beer and wine and whisky and dancing.' Clinton Walker observed a crowd spilling out of the venue in between sets 'waving Fourex longnecks and generally seeming to threaten the traffic whizzing by only inches away.' At a certain point, a window at the front of the house was broken, and so a piece of plywood replaced it, upon which was scrawled 'Club 76'. Andrew Kidd Fraser and John Willsteed, writing in *Eccentric Voices* assert:

> It was a very public statement. It was a party house, lotsa drinks and drugs, and when The Saints started thrashing out their earthy rock 'n' soul there was always a slightly menacing air both inside and out on the footpath: drunks waving around long-necks of beer, abusing passers-by, and threatening traffic and customers at the nearby greasy-spoon café, the Windmill.

In Bailey's estimation, the 'police and the government felt very threatened by that sort of punk thing that was around', and so it was not a surprise that this semi-public venue was shut down after a brief but memorable existence. As Kuepper explained to Stafford, it was more than police intimidation that lead to the demise of Club 76, 'I think the health department came around, the fire brigade or somebody closed us down, because for starters we didn't have a licence, secondly there weren't adequate fire exits and toilets, that sort of thing.'

By necessity the band continued to source venues in creative ways. They hired RSL Halls, suburban halls, church halls, 'twenty bucks a night-type thing', explains Kuepper. Margaret Bailey, who helped organise a couple of shows, asserts:

> The gigs that The Saints did, the important thing was getting a hall, getting somewhere to play. Having alcohol was never part of the equation, people just brought their own alcohol. Those gigs were never fundraisers as such. It was just getting somewhere where you were allowed to play.

Willsteed similarly contends:

> It was really important for us as young people to have a space where we could play and when I say play I don't just mean play music but really have a playtime because being out on the street was so horrible and suburbia was so foul and debilitating so we needed to create fun for ourselves.

Speaking to Andrew Stafford, musician Mark C. Halstead, who had also been a young member of the Self-Management Group, recalled:

> The way we'd do things, like hire halls, and somehow wrangle booze licences or dodgy sly grog – it was quite amazing, there really was community stuff going on, without the warm inner glow or any hippie aspects of it, that's for sure. It was of necessity, and that was good. I think it may have been a little exciting, because we were all young and doing something we weren't supposed to be doing. And yeah, the us-and-them thing.

There were one-off gigs to support causes such as Gay Solidarity, Control and the Caxton Street Legal Centre but Brisbane's repressive atmosphere meant that contention emerged in other ways as well. Margaret Bailey asserts, 'The cops to some extent politicised music. They always turned up, whenever The Saints had a gig, whether it was a hall or a private party, the cops always turned up.' Lindy Morrison, an activist and member of The Go-Betweens, observed in the 1988 documentary *Brisbane Bands* that:

> The police were just going crazy at that time. They just didn't want groups of people anywhere – groups of young people that were rebellious. All that was tied in at the same

time, the music explosion happened at exactly the same time that they said we couldn't demonstrate. It was a highly charged political situation in Queensland in the late 70s.

Ed Wreckage (Dziduch) from The Leftovers experienced a particularly disastrous gig at Hamilton Hall. Interviewed for the State Library of Queensland, he explained that police would arrive due to noise complaints and underage drinking. He also claimed that the police threw bottles at windows, leaving him to pay the council for the damage. Wreckage was a sheet metal worker, making steel drums, and would strike them during work as a method to write percussion lines for The Leftovers. The pay was not high though, and it took him five years to pay the bill for the damage to the hall.

Wreckage identified that The Leftovers had a gay following, which meant their crowd was targeted twice over. The band charged a $2 entry price for their shows. Often this was then used to pay the $4 fines that many of their audience received for being 'drunk and disorderly'. Wreckage, speaking to Stafford, explained:

> Right from the very first gig [late 1978], outside the pub at Shorncliffe. It was at Sandgate Town Hall, about 20 people turned up, and within about 10 minutes a dozen cop cars came and dragged everybody off, taking them away for liquor ordinances or some crap. Because you weren't allowed to drink at this particular suburban hall, so that was enough to lock people up. There was no licensing, anyone with a jacket could walk in with a bottle of booze. We didn't really care … we didn't believe there was any real need for any form of security.

Great Western Brain Robbery at Colossus Hall 1979, and advertising new singles for Razar and The Leftovers (John Willsteed music poster archive/State Library of Queensland)

Control Benefit at CPA Rooms, 1982 (Loveday, John Willsteed music poster archive/State Library of Queensland)

Despite his moniker Wreckage did not accept that his band was oriented around destruction, but observed that a change in culture occurred around 1979, possibly influenced by reporting from the punk scene in the UK. At this time, people in stereotypical punk outfits came to shows and smashed things up, a favourite being to knock the sinks off the walls inside the toilet areas. Triple Zed identity John Stanwell argued, 'We had a fairly anti-social element in our audience, watching too many idiot punks on TV. It was a disaster waiting to happen and eventually it did happen.'

The underground music scene was a space for a variety of ethics, and the punk subculture offered variations in approach. The Brisbane scene absorbed transnational influences, largely from the UK and America. The punk scene and political activism were for a time largely entwined in bands' names, such as Gerry Mander and the Boundaries. This referenced the way that the conservative state government was holding onto power in an undemocratic way by weighting the votes of their rural constituency higher than those from the city. The band RAZAR wrote one of the iconic songs of the Brisbane punk era, 'Task Force', about the repressive role of the police. Band member Marty Burke explained to Stafford, 'There was a political bent to our music but that was unavoidable because of what was going on at the time.'

For other people in the scene, an affirmative view towards left politics was less integrated into their music, and expressed more in an appreciation for how political groups supported the underground. Tex Perkins, who first played in Tex Deadly and The Dum Dums, and was later known for The Beasts of Bourbon and The Cruel Sea, was a young Brisbane punk who came onto the scene in the early 80s. He spoke about his experiences to Andrew Stafford:

> The thing is with really fucked places ... people tend to make their own fun ... Situations like Brisbane in the late 70s, early 80s, there'd be a lot of in-house sort of stuff. The pub scene wasn't anywhere [near to Sydney]. There used to be a venue, a communist hall, on the top of Brunswick Street and St Paul's Terrace, somewhere up there at the top of the Valley ... We loved the commies. There was a gig there ... I was a punter, and I'd taken some sort of inebriant and I was particularly out of it, as they say. And I made a complete buffoon of myself, falling over, knocking over stairs. I actually fell down this very large, long staircase. Broke windows ... just in this completely abandoned kind of way. And a month later I was at a nightclub and these two guys came up to me and said 'Aren't you that guy who was causing havoc at the communist hall?' And I went, 'Er, yeah.' 'You want to form a band with us?'

The CPA made another significant contribution to the local music scene when it sold its headquarters to Triple Zed at a below market rate, thus allowing the community radio station to establish itself with some degree of security. As discussed elsewhere in this book, Triple Zed was a significant presence in the Brisbane music scene.

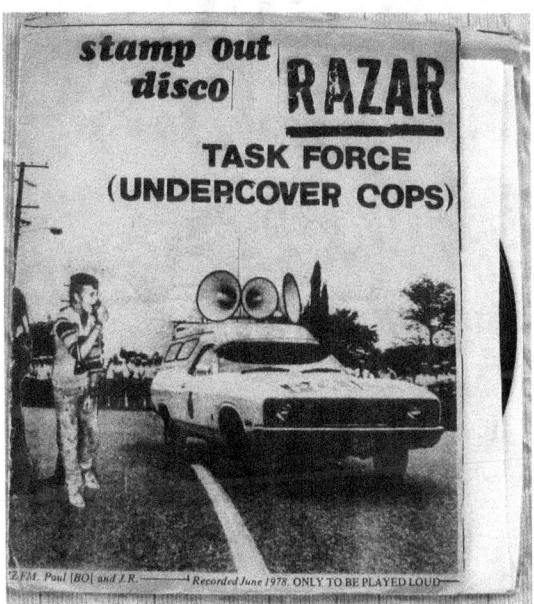

Razar's single Task Force addressed Queensland Police harassment (Radical Times Archive)

The story of how music, intoxicants and politics interrelate is a rich narrative, and one that is not exclusive to this period of Brisbane. It is possible to discern three strong themes in the underground music of this era: agitational political messaging, contemplative social realism, and affirmations of life at the margins. This included the ways in which those in the scene used liquor, drugs and cigarettes, as well as found love and connection.

Perhaps the most iconic song of the era that fits into the latter category was The Leftovers' 'Cigarettes and Alcohol'. Ed Wreckage comments on his lifestyle at this time, 'If you weren't drunk at 10 o'clock in the morning, life wasn't worth living. ... some of us took that to extremes, and they're not here today unfortunately.' The Leftovers, and many of the people affiliated to the band, gained a notorious reputation. Wreckage explains, 'a lot of our songs were relevant to drug culture. (Heroin) was what destroyed the band, we couldn't trust each other.'

A wave of heroin entered Brisbane in the late 1970s. The underground scene was soon awash with people needing money for drugs, on occasion leading to some particularly objectionable behaviour, such as thefts from Triple Zed. As Wreckage notes, use was so widespread that at one point The Leftovers' heroin addicted management would steal the takings before the band members could spend it themselves on the drug. Cycles of trauma and self-medication were observable to all within the fledgling scene.

Illicit drugs such as marijuana and heroin were tied to the legal drug of alcohol through the marketplace where they were often obtained, The RE. Andrew Kidd Fraser and John Willsteed detail the scenario in *Eccentric Voices*:

> Suddenly, in 1977, marijuana supplies began to dry up. While some pot smokers took the DIY ethic to heart and grew their own, most supplies were scored at the pub from someone relatively anonymous but with a shady background. 'Whatever you want, I can get it for you,' said one pusher ... But in the second half of 1977, suddenly, these figures would start pressing heroin. The regular connection in the beer garden of The RE would explain that there was no marijuana around but there was some good heroin. All this made for a more explosive scene.

A particularly tragic case is Johnny Burnaway (John Gorman), member of The Leftovers and other bands from the era. He lived, more or less, on a diet of Vegemite sandwiches, beer and shots of heroin. This is not to obscure the contribution he made to the underground music scene, particularly his innovative approach to guitar tuning. There were stories of Burnaway and his partner spiking people's drinks in order to steal their money for drugs. On the last day of Johnny's life, 5 July 1988, he drank excessive

Rock Against Petersen, 1983 (Lachlan Hurse, John Willsteed music poster archive/State Library of Queensland)

amounts of bourbon, and police found a silver packet of tranquilisers next to his body. His life was so absorbed in the culture of imbibing, that at his funeral, whilst some tossed into his grave cigarettes, one is reported, in Joe Gorman's 'Looking for Johnny Burnaway', to have thrown in coins and offered sympathetically, 'Get yourself a drink, John.'

Some left-wing activists found that the nihilistic basis of the punk ethos made it challenging to collaborate on projects around social change. The ornery nature of some punk era musicians, such as The Saints, contributed to this. The suite of gestures associated with the 'anti-everything' pose were only one expression of punk. Nevertheless, they were in contradiction to very defined positions on social transformation, commitment to institutions of the labour movement such as unions, and left-wing values of community before individualism.

Minority instances of destructive behaviour at punk events were believed by some amongst the left to have undermined the late 70s 'right to march' campaigns. But one socialist group did make a particular effort to relate to punks, the International Socialists (IS). Historian and activist Ian Curr argued that punks were often anti-police but not really political in a deeper sense. The emphasis placed by the IS on recruiting punks was a mistake, he argued, as they swelled a membership base that was not wholly convinced by socialist politics. This meant that if they didn't develop quickly the organisation would not be able to sustain itself in the long term. IS member Ian Rintoul, described as 'a working class lad from Ipswich', was said to rail against the punks and hippies associated with his group, who in his dismissive assessment 'slept on water beds'.

Despite cultural and political differences, for many the politics of solidarity remained the order of the day within the left, reaching out between different groups, and recognising common oppressors. In Brisbane, it was relatively easy to identify at least one shared enemy: the right-wing Premier Joh Bjelke-Petersen. In general, there was a large flourishing of cultural activity in resistance to his government. In practice, amidst contradictions, there was a sustained crossover between the punk sensibility and left sensibilities all through the 1970s and beyond.

A night out at The Nash, 1984 (Mark Chandler)

CHAPTER 54
THE STAR HOTEL
Graham Willett

While 'pub rock' has been a big thing in Australian life, there aren't a lot of pubs actually celebrated in song. 'The Pub with No Beer' springs to mind. But *the* song is Cold Chisel's 'Star Hotel', written and performed after one of the biggest riots in Australian history.

The Star Hotel had been operating in one form or another since the mid-nineteenth century but by the 1960s it was well-established in Newcastle working class nightlife. As described in *Radical Newcastle*, it offered a 'heady mix of pot, booze, jobless youth, bikies, live music, uninhibited women dancing on the bar and yet-to-be-legalised gay pride.'

It was open to working class youth, old blokes who saw it as their local, and the best live bands that the city could provide (of which there were lots). Women were welcome in all

Patrons at the Star Hotel, Newcastle, 1979 (Bernadette Smith)

parts of the pub, then still a bit of a rarity. And from about 1969 it was the premier gay pub in the city. Not the only one, but certainly the most popular, with drag acts in the middle bar.

These distinct crowds each had their own space – the old men in the front bar, the bands and their fans at the back and, in the middle bar, drag queens, all dolled up and singing (or perhaps lip-syncing) their hearts out: 'very active, very cruisy', reported *Campaign*, the national gay newspaper, in July 1977. There was plenty of movement between the different spaces – the front bar was less crowded and easier to buy drinks at; everybody loved the drag shows (many of the best performers went on to bigger things) and hundreds would swarm in to watch and maybe to hang around after to see what might eventuate. You didn't have to be straight to appreciate the hypermasculinity of many of the rock bands. You didn't have to be gay to love the drags.

In January 1979 the owner of the Star suddenly decided to rid his pub of the poofters and, as reported in the April 1979 *Gay Solidarity Newsletter*, put ads in the local newspaper to make sure everyone got the message: 'The Star Goes "Straight"; No more "puffs" at the Star; No more "Camping" in our new Guitar Bar... SO, GO STRAIGHT TO THE STAR.' It turned out he had already been sacking gay staff. With the drag queens gone, and the openly gay ambience of the middle bar gone with them, there was not much to attract the gay crowd. Gays from Sydney and Newcastle demonstrated outside the pub on 3 February, and there was a complaint to the Advertising Standards Council (ASC). Both fell on deaf ears. In the case of the ASC, because it was still perfectly legal to discriminate against homosexuals. The *Newcastle Herald* explained that it had published the ad only because its staff did not know what 'puffs' and 'camping' and 'straight' meant!

In any case, the Star Hotel was not long for this world. The owners decided to close it down. Thousands gathered on 19 September for the last night, spilling out into the streets. Whatever the exact origins, it was pretty clear that police heavy handedness, both inside the back bar and out in the streets, played a part in sparking the riot that followed. Rocks and cans flew through the air, a police car and a paddy wagon (abandoned by frightened cops) were overturned and set alight, people arrested were freed by the crowd. Forty-eight were charged with 185 offences but a surge of support from the citizens of Newcastle, including the Mayor and staff of the Trades Hall Council, kept the penalties to a minimum.

Like most riots, this one left little behind. But Cold Chisel's 'Star Hotel' and its official video, with its news footage and shots of the audience the Chisels were performing to, are a reminder of the passion and the fury that lay often just under the apparent calm of everyday life.

'No more puffs at the Star', advertisement in the *Newcastle Morning Herald*, 1979 (Australian Queer Archives)

CHAPTER 55

TRIPLE ZED'S JOINT EFFORTS: BEER, BANDS, AND BREAKING THE NEWS

Alex Ettling

It was a 'silly, undoubtedly drunken or stoned-influenced rave about a pirate radio' station between friends that set into motion the founding of one of the world's great pioneers of community radio, Triple Zed (4ZZZ). Established in 1975, the initiative came about partly in response to a conundrum for Brisbane's New Left. Worthy political ideas were being offered to the public in high quality, off-set printed publications that were creatively expressed and well-designed. However, this cohort of radicals did not have the numbers, nor implantation in social institutions (e.g. workplaces) to *effectively spread the word*. All too often these cool looking publications languished in bundles in peoples cars. It turned out, it was more enjoyable to make them than to sell them.

Coming up with the Idea

John Stanwell was one of the founders of 4ZZZ, and it was he who had the inebriated conversation with fellow activist Alan Knight about British pirate radio, leading to 'this fantasy about doing one in Brisbane.' Another founder Jim Beatson had spent a period of time in London in the late 1960s and, having seen the flourishing pirate radio scene first hand, was taken with the potential for building a 'mass minority audience' through the airwaves. Such an enterprise was daring, and in Beatson's conception would require some uncomfortable relationships to pull off. Running a community radio station would be expensive, but moving beyond the limitations of the underground would justify such compromises:

> You're not talking about a megaphone; you're not talking about a worthy thing in someone's [car] boot that's not being distributed. You're actually talking about using the tools of the state, of the mainstream, with full knowledge that that was going to lead to compromises...We made a bloody alliance with the heart of capitalism: that could see we had something to offer.

The alliance Beatson was referring to specifically involved the music industry, in all its aspects: record companies, hi-fi manufacturers, venues, promoters. There was little alternative for a start-up radio station trying to build off the back of youth culture. Although the station would be run on a not-for-profit basis and be volunteer driven, there were still significant costs to cover.

Fundraising

In the preceding era, substantial funds for the radical left's media initiatives, such as an offset printing press and the purchase of the Red and Black Bookshop, had come from the canny stock market trading of mining shares by activist Mitch Thompson. By the mid 1970s, when Triple Zed was being schemed up, Thompson had become bankrupt from an investment gone sour. There was a significant amount of in-kind support from the University of Queensland Student Union, but with no more white knights on the scene, raising funds would involve grunt work.

A variety of approaches were welcomed, some of them quaint. There were yearly sales of 'Triple Zed Red', first organised by John Stanwell with cleanskin bottles of cabernet-shiraz. The bottles featured a distinctive label illustrated by regular Triple Zed artist Matt Mawson, who, while deriding the contents of the bottles as '30 per cent bio-toxic sediment', approved of the good cause. Stanwell explains his approach to fundraising:

> It's like the school fete, when people come you want to give them the maximum number of opportunities to spend money. So on the first anniversary of Triple Zed I organised a low-cost catered dinner at one of the ethnic clubs, Greek I think it was. You paid a price and you got a light meal, and there was a pay bar. Probably raffles and things like that. It was a fundraiser.
>
> We asked friends who were running restaurants, and they put us onto a winery. They just supplied a cleanskin wine and we bottled it. Some of us drank red wine. The thing about beer in Brisbane is that's what you drank because you're in the tropics. In those days it wasn't that common for people to drink red wine, but people were starting. The rhyming Triple Zed Red, just sort of ran off the tongue, and seemed like a good thing. We sold out, and did it again next year and sold out again.

But these were small earners. The majority of revenue for the station was raised through events. The most significant of which were the Joint Efforts, which offered a slate of

A selection of the founding staff and volunteers of Triple Zed, 1975 (Gordon Curtis, Radical Times Archive)

entertainment, making money off ticket sales and alcohol sales. Beatson explains:

> The way you made a lot of money was to serve beer. People drank a lot of alcohol because it was the social thing to do, getting slightly pissed and rocking on to the music. It was really important to us that we made an awful lot of money to pay for our considerable costs.

Triple Zed Red, a recurring fundraising initiative (Matt Mawson)

A Political Culture of Arts Events

There was already a tradition of music events within the left and radical youth culture, and views had been formed regarding the principles involved. Stanwell was the key figure behind the Joint Efforts and brought with him a significant amount of experience running arts events. In his view, by the mid 70s there was a rejection of commodified countercultural music festivals:

> It was all about big egos, with big amplifiers on a big stage, playing to a passive audience. There was a bit of dancing. But basically it was a one-way festival. By this time we'd had enough of the music industry. Rock festivals had been killed by the entrepreneur.

Stanwell had variously been a participant, organiser, and lead coordinator of some of the iconic countercultural events and groups of this period: FOCO, HARPO (How About Resisting Powerful Organisations) and the 1973 Aquarius festival. He had learnt to value leaving some things unstructured as well as the importance of genuine community involvement.

FOCO existed across 1968-69, and was located in the Brisbane Trades Hall building, 'a multifaceted extravaganza incorporating music, poetry, political discussion, film, literature and theatrical performances.' Less favourably, it was described as 'Australia's most evil and repugnant nightspot' by federal politician Don Cameron. The club's resident DJ 'doubled as a lecturer on pop music's relationship with modern art and culture.' There was politics – but there was also dancing. Anti-establishment messages were diffused through arts and culture. On one occasion, the rock band Coloured Balls, headed up by former Purple Hearts singer Mick Hadley, led a chorus in response to a police raid on the venue: 'We'll sing you a song and it won't take long, all coppers are bastards.' The participation of bands with street cred was aided by the involvement of activist Larry Zetlin, who had connections from working as the Brisbane correspondent for *Go-Set* magazine. The success of the bands at FOCO, in an unconventional setting for gigs, was strong evidence that people would come out to see subcultural rock music events in Brisbane.

FOCO was a unique collaboration between the youth based in the Communist Party, labour movement activists, and young radicals around the newly formed SDA (Students/Society for Democratic Action). In an interview with writer Andrew Stafford, Brian Laver argued it was a strategy 'to institutionalise our movement in culture and entertainment.'

As a membership-based event held on the third floor of Trades Hall, FOCO has been described by Laver as akin to a 'revolutionary speakeasy', only without alcohol. The event was held on Sundays, with largely underage attendees. A range of interviewees have expressed no recollection of alcohol being present at FOCO, certainly it was not sold. The experience of FOCO would inspire the Joint Efforts to come because it was on the edge of the avant-garde but also popular, consciously steeped in radical politics but in a way that didn't seem to turn anyone off. Imagine what could be done if you added booze and actually tried to make money!

Activist and Triple Zed identity Steve Gray, interviewed by Stafford, claimed 'FOCO didn't last a long time, but it had a big impact on the way people saw politics. They saw politics as a cultural package.' The performance art group HARPO offered something of a continuation of the spirit of FOCO, including an event, 'Harpo's Nite Out', that featured a combination of political theatre and live music. HARPO activists were elected to the arts activities positions in The University of Queensland Student Union, and subsequently helped organise the 1973

FOCO events featured spoken presentations, including Brian Laver reporting on the radical scene in Europe, *FOCO Newsletter*, 1968

Triple Zed staff: Steve Gray, Jim Beatson and John Stanwell (Radical Times Archive)

Aquarius festival. Some members, including John Stanwell, later became involved in the creation of 4ZZZ.

Fundraising with the Joint Efforts

The first Joint Efforts took place only a few months after the station went to air, over two successive nights during Orientation Week in February 1976 at the UQ Union Relaxation Block. Amongst the live performers were Carol Lloyd, formerly of Rainroad Gin, country rock band Whyte Lightning, and local 60s-influenced punks The Survivors. Stanwell asserts that the Joint Efforts 'drew on the best elements of HARPO and FOCO', but 'the most important thing was that we made a lot of money. It was unashamedly money making. And that meant selling a lot of alcohol.' At the same time he contends:

> It wasn't just alcohol, it was a combination of alcohol and contemporary rock music, and we turned that into a way to make sufficient money to run a variety of radical and alternative enterprises. And so it was a vehicle. The star was the music. If we just had this thing with cheap beer, we wouldn't have people coming, it was because of the bands, that's why people came. The alcohol was a vehicle to make the event feel successful, but of course 'maximise the spend' as the economists would say.

The student union had a liquor license as part of their own catering deal. In turn Stanwell was able to negotiate good terms because of the events' scale, in which the student union were effectively suppliers. He explains, 'We had a cold room full of kegs, if we had a particularly good night or bad night it didn't matter. They just supplied us as we needed it. They would close a bar if a keg ran out and you weren't going to sell another whole keg.' Operating the bar to maximise sales, while dealing with crowds, was its own skill. Beatson claims:

> All Zed staff were masters at taking the money and delivering the alcohol at record speeds. So even though there were thousands there you didn't have to queue up for hours, you were served fast. The station staff used to call the rapidly served queues 'The Lager Monster' because after an hour or so the volume of drinking dramatically increased to match the speed of the music and the excitement of the event.

Stanwell argues, 'If you go to a bar that is run to make money for someone, the workers are just drones so they work at an average pace, whereas we were fanatics working for Triple Zed so we needed to make the money as quickly as we could.' An advantage of enterprises that are fundraisers is that labour can be sourced from enthusiastic volunteers and the Joint Efforts

Joint Effort Three, 1981 (Damien Ledwich, State Library of Queensland)

involved an army of them. Up to 50 people a shift, with two shifts per event. Stanwell says a 'huge camaraderie' existed, and 'volunteers would get a hamburger ticket and two beer tickets – and that was their pay!' Gray speaking to Andrew Stafford, noted:

> One of the ironies of the whole thing is that as a young student it was always a sport to gatecrash things, and all of a sudden *we* were the landlords, as it were, repelling boarders! So there was a role reversal and there was a fair amount of moral turpitude, I found, because all of a sudden I was the one who was kicking people out, making sure entrances were staffed and banning people who were totally off the wall, or the bloke found stealing beer one night for instance.

Stanwell asserts that as a community initiative the events saw few incidences of trouble: 'The crowd was totally supportive of us. There was never any issue where the crowd would side with the trouble maker, it didn't happen. So even though we served an awful lot of alcohol it wasn't a problem – it was part of the context.' He also noted the advantage of operating at a university, with its 'upper middle class protection, that all campuses enjoy – a level of "turn a blind eye" to modest bad behaviour.'

Triple Zed announcer Michael Finucan cleaning the station toilets (Radical Times Archive)

Band Nights

The radio station built a roster of regular performers from the local music scene, and expanded into hosting international acts. There were now frequent Joint Effort events at the university refectory, as well as a growing pub circuit fostered by Triple Zed's activities.

Stanwell was wary of moving off campus because of the loss of the aforementioned 'upper middle class protection.' There were obvious advantages in growing in scale, and taking in more revenue, but predictable issues soon arrived. Volunteers were crucial, but an insufficient number of paid staff made planning more complex events a difficult proposition. This led to the beginning of outsourcing: food, alcohol and security. Hired bouncers were the source of complaints, referred to by Triple Zed identity Michael Finucan as 'gorillas in red shirts.' However, others considered it reasonable that the job be given to professionals rather than having volunteers responsible for de-escalating potentially violent altercations. Similarly, volunteers could offer useful help with cleaning up the surface messes, but it was also deemed necessary to pay for professional services.

The Queen's Hotel, at the intersection of Creek and Charlotte Streets in the central area of Brisbane, was perhaps the most significant venue that the radio station developed external to UQ. The use of the pub corresponded with new leadership in the Triple Zed promotions unit as Peter Williamson and David Darling headed up the expansion in the scale of operations. The first event was held there on 28 May 1978 with a crowd of 800 packing into the pub on a Wednesday night.

The Queens Hotel, late 1970s (Paul O'Brien, State Library of Queensland)

As historian Thomas Vuleta argues in 'Ups and Downs: Music Venues and Popular Music in Brisbane 1959 - 1989', although the Queen's Hotel was privately owned, Triple Zed played an active role in its rejuvenation, making them effectively a partner. The station paid for sound proofing in the beer garden (well remembered for its fake palm trees). In exchange, Triple Zed was given 'carte blanche' with curation. In line with standard commercial practice the venue took the bar revenue and, as promoter, the radio station kept the door sales. For some the way the events were being run was at odds with the station's original values. Vuleta details how Finucan emphasised the then existing gap in expectations between student radicals at the station and the Queen's management, as Joint Effort became *joint venture*:

> We work there in conjunction with the management of the hotel. They are not young, they are business people, not rock'n'roll fans looking for fun...They want a good, stable, well controlled predictable environment to calculate their profit margins in. They want everything that rock'n'roll should not be – i.e. safe, inoffensive, stable etc ... So the Queens is always going to be a compromise between their practical constraints and our ideals.

Nevertheless, the pub became a key venue identified with Triple Zed and helped cement its association with the punk subculture. Assistance from Triple Zed was also critical in the development of the large scale national touring circuit that came to include Brisbane. However, political hostility towards the radio station also placed the venture at risk. Darling argues, 'the government did everything to close it down.' In 1979, the Queens Hotel had its temporary entertainment licence revoked. Noise complaints came in from the other side of the river. Despite efforts by the hotel to address the concerns, the Licensing Commission rejected any compromise and the hotel shut down.

Ongoing Government Hostility

Briefly time jumping in this narrative, the Joint Efforts hosted at Cloudland in 1979 enjoyed similar popularity, but the station's use of this venue was also halted by licensing authorities. To some degree it was Brisbane's humidity that was to blame. After bands would end their set, the lubricated crowd would pour out of the steamy band rooms for respite in the fresh air. This was nothing new, the venue had been packing in crowds for decades. Neither was the harassment of lively gig goers. After all this was the city which had employed a dedicated 'Bodgie Squad' of police to crack down on rock'n'roll back in the 1950s.

Writer and Triple Zed station coordinator Anne Jones was in attendance at the Joint Effort at Cloudland that led to the cancelled liquor license. She explained to Andrew Stafford:

> Cloudland was a big beautiful place, and everyone rushed out and just was hanging around. And because it was suburban there was quite a lot of noise. And the other thing, the legend has it, but I didn't see it, people were fucking in the front yards of people's houses! All this meant, and in fact it wasn't the cops, it was liquor licensing, they pulled our liquor license. And the next week, we had a gig one week later, which was The Members, they were a British punk band. But we had to run that as a gig that was dry, they wouldn't let us have [alcohol] ... we couldn't continue to run it because really, people weren't going to come without the booze. So that was really the end of it.

The venue was pulled down in 1982 to make way for apartments. The belief that Triple Zed's association with Cloudland led to its demise, first as an operating venue and then as an existing building, only furthered deep resentment from the arts community towards the government.

The Commerce of the Punk Scene

Returning this narrative to the beginning of the punk scene, Triple Zed, although in some aspects resistant, had nevertheless come on board to seed this vibrant new arts scene. With the punk movement and live music scene booming, there were a number of venue options during the late 1970s. Many received harassment from various arms of the state. Punk gigs were hosted at the Baroona Hall (which had a long and distinguished history as a site of left-wing activity), Colossus Hall, Atcherley Hotel, New York Hotel, Exchange Hotel/279 Club, Silver Dollar disco and The Curry Shop. Brett Myers, guitarist in The End and later Died Pretty, told Andrew Stafford that some of the larger venues used by the punk bands were economically focused on the equation of 'crowds-income-beer sales', but that the Curry Shop 'didn't give a fuck, it was whether they liked the music or not.'

Even within a subcultural movement that was antagonistic to being absorbed into 'the system' alcohol sales and commercial considerations played a role in shaping the music. Triple Zed tried to encourage innovation and introduce new blood by pairing larger bands with smaller acts. Inevitably a more avant-garde scene developed at venues where less pressure to secure alcohol-based revenue existed, whether for virtuous Triple Zed fundraising or private interests.

At the end of 1979, Darling and Williamson broke with Triple Zed to form their own promotions company under the name 'The Piranha Brothers'. In discussing the radio station and its relationship to venues the duo had wondered, 'Why doesn't the radio station run a pub?' This would have represented a major step up in the station's business dealings and the proposition was unlikely to gain traction. Darling and Williamson instead pursued their entrepreneurial vision outside of Triple Zed. This decision was perceived by some to be channelling the revenue keeping the station afloat into their own pockets. Another accusation was that the industry knowledge and contracts gleaned from Triple Zed allowed the now private promoters to book major bands, who may otherwise have been drawn into promoting the Triple Zed ethos.

Whether the funding opportunities of an increasingly commercialised alternative music segment would have otherwise stayed with the radio station is uncertain. It was a unique arrangement and quite different to the economic functioning of most other music scenes. The scale of business was perhaps beyond what a community radio station could sustain. Nevertheless the sense that the scene was being commodified for private gain clearly rankled. Darling was aware of the negativity towards them: 'We were traitors because we were leaving the group at the station...There was a bit of falling out there but there was a lot of support too.'

Triple Zed publication *Radio Times*, 1976 (Matt Mawson)

Pub dancing, late 1970s (Paul O'Brien, State Library of Queensland)

Expansion of the Market

The Piranha Brothers sensed an opportunity to tap into a moribund market: the red light district in Fortitude Valley. Taking live music further into the clubs and restaurants of Brisbane was not without trepidation. Many young people avoided The Valley, in part due to the horrifying events at the Whiskey Au Go Go in 1973. Fifteen people had been murdered when underworld figures, rumoured to be associated with corrupt police, firebombed the bar.

Local promoter John Reid believed that after the bombing, and subsequent curiosity regarding who was responsible, Fortitude Valley club owners were reluctant to welcome a new cohort. Many believed it would 'only bring trouble on them.' Although some entrepreneurs were not making the profits they could, the clubs remained geared towards an older audience, the stereotypical salesmen-on-a-night-out looking for strippers and gambling. The government turned a blind eye to such activity, part of doing business amongst the white-shoe brigade. The police ran protection rackets, in the process becoming further enmeshed in organised crime.

The rise of a new night-time economy involving young people and their music nevertheless took root, and in doing so quickly posed a threat to existing business arrangements. The liquor licensing authority turned their attention to these new music venues and a campaign of harassment towards the young people attending ensued.

As well as serving the interests of those that officially and unofficially paid them, Queensland police at this time had a culture all of their own. Reid, in an interview with Andrew Stafford, stated that the licensing squad officers and Special Branch detectives would 'come up to your door stinking of grog', seeking free drinks for themselves. 'The police can get away with anything, as long as it seems that the young aren't running wild.'

Officers were known to use entrapment, but undercover detectives famously made themselves easy to spot. Sporting unfashionable Hawaiian shirts and police-issue haircuts they would menacingly approach a patron asking where they could 'score some pot'. Reid was amused by the ineptitude: 'It was hard to keep a straight face but I did, pointing (one) off to the bikies and telling him the code was "The moon rides high tonight".'

Reid was an entrepreneurial figure in the underground music scene (who in fact did sell marijuana on the side). He was keen to get Darling and Williamson into promoting shows in Fortitude Valley, claiming to Stafford that he did it 'so Triple Zed would get behind it and advertise the Valley, I thought I'd get some sort of spin-off from that. That's the first time that those kind of cult bands started playing in the Valley.'

In April 1980, the Silver Dollar opened as a live music venue, arranged via a deal made with Fortitude Valley night-club impresario Ron Cantarella. The Silver Dollar became known as a punk venue with lax standards and a loose approach to order, in all manner of ways. There was no running sheet to schedule the bands, no green room for the performers, and punters were known to jump the bar and serve themselves because the service was so poor. In another context these conditions would not have been tolerated, however, in the punk era the chaotic nature of the venue was embraced (or perhaps simply accepted).

Reid was particularly keen to reinvigorate another venue in The Valley on Ann Street named Pinocchio's. As Vuleta outlines, for a short time, patrons at Pinocchio's could 'listen to some of Brisbane's most interesting experimental rock in an authentically humid' venue. Along with a congealing bowl of spaghetti bolognese to satisfy cabaret licensing regulations. Reid also opened Romeo's on the same street, which was still operating as a strip club while entertaining punk bands – it was also a popular venue for Aboriginal people.

Musician and historian John Willsteed, interviewed in *The Guardian* in 2014, made the case that the club was owned by the 'famous hoodlums' the Bellinos and that the underworld operators 'put on punk bands because they couldn't give a shit.' It was an arrangement of mutual benefit and Willsteed asserts: 'The good thing about the Valley was that it was where the more marginalised would hang – punky kids, blackfellas, gay people. The night-time places were much more blended – it took the 80s to separate them out.'

The provision of a place for minorities to socialise was always subject to the whims of bar owners. In the end a disagreement between the Bellinos and Reid saw the arrangement at Pinocchio's end, but it had already been struggling as a commercial endeavour. Reid asserts: 'You couldn't get them to come into Pinocchio's. That was more what they considered the seedy sort of end [of the area]. You know, this is going to turn into another Whiskey Au Go Go.'

Debating the Role of Triple Zed

In the midst of this, according to an interview by Stafford with activist and Triple Zed journalist Jon Baird, 'the venue situation started to get squeezed and it had a direct relation on [our] ability to make money.' A financial shortfall not only threatened the overall survival of the radio station, but also how much resources could be put into initiatives such as the well-respected Triple Zed news room. New ways to keep funds coming in would have to be found.

Whilst encouragement of the local music scene and bringing people together at events was a mission for Triple Zed, there were also the original intentions of the station – consciousness raising and political mobilisation. Such goals did not always mesh together comfortably. Since the creation of the station there was an imperative to expand its reach beyond the radius afforded by the antenna at the UQ campus. They had the equipment but needed a higher power FM broadcasting licence. This required approval from the state and therefore a controversial policy was introduced which involved tempering support for certain left campaigns, justified as a temporary measure.

In 1977, both the MegaHerz show and the Civil Liberties Coordinating Committee show were taken off air. Activist and historian Ian Curr was involved in the latter and was critical of what the radio station had evolved into: 'Zed was run by a social clique that was neither left wing nor amenable to political organisation. To them we were engaging in boring loud hailer journalism.' The general line of criticism directed towards the station from the progressive side was that it was fostering a 'social left', with political engagement and encouragement towards activism losing out.

This is not to say that the station was not engaging in political reporting. Triple Zed had led the on-the-ground coverage of the demolition of the historic Bellevue Hotel in 1979, and earlier the raid at Cedar Bay in 1976 (where notoriously, police stopped in their chopper to pick up a six-pack of beer, after terrorising a commune of hippies at their beach home). Rather, the debates within the station were often about the overall direction of political culture and finding ways to raise the profile of activism within it.

The 'cultural drift' which the station was charged with, inevitably included the apolitical socialising associated with much pub culture, and the at times atomised activity of music listening – both of which the station was thoroughly embedded in. The intention from critics was not to condemn these aspects of the station, but to re-assert the goal of building an activist culture.

Triple Zed News Room

During the early 1980s, Triple Zed's commitment to campaigning journalism received a boost, particularly when the station became more confident in asserting its political identity.

A crowd watches the demolition of the Bellevue Hotel, 1979 (Ross Gwyther)

Despite potentially bringing in more pressure towards the station, there were advantages. Beatson believes, 'The station had its largest audience when it was at its most confident politically, and certainly that period of the early 80s, where it would take very strong stands on things.'

One of the areas Triple Zed reported on was the state's involvement in unlawful aspects of the night-time economy. Beatson asserts, 'we got to know all of the stories of how corrupt the Fortitude Valley branch of the police force was.' There had also been consistent reporting on the activities of the notorious Task Force going back to the 1970s. The conservative *Courier Mail* would report the state's interpretation of riotous events, the squad busting up punk shows of Brisbane band RAZAR for instance. Triple Zed took it upon itself to do more rigorous investigation regarding what had gone on.

The journalists at Triple Zed became steeled towards the corrupt activities of the state, and several ended up becoming high profile investigative journalists after leaving the training ground of the station's news room. Triple Zed journalist Shaun Hoyt played a role in the iconic *Four Corners* television program 'The Moonlight State' that aired in May 1987. It is generally considered a catalyst in bringing down the repressive government of long serving Premier Joh Bjelke-Petersen. ABC journalist Chris Masters employed Hoyt as a researcher, and Beatson argues that the program was 'largely the product of all of the work that Triple Zed had been doing over the years.'

The crucial evidence revealed in the program was the link between Geraldo Bellino and Vittorio Conte, and former Licensing Branch officer Jack 'The Bagman' Herbert. Monthly bribes to police were referred to as 'The Joke', a corrupt arrangement which greased the wheels of illegal activity in Fortitude Valley. Within days the ABC's report prompted the announcement of the Fitzgerald Inquiry, which ultimately led to the jailing of a number of powerful Brisbane figures, including the police commissioner and Bellino. The Premier, long the bête noire and persecutor of the left, narrowly avoided jail but ended his career in ignominy and disgrace. Although this did not lead to deep rooted and long term structural change, it substantially rattled Queensland's ruling class and increased police accountability for a period. In doing so it had a major effect on Brisbane's social fabric.

The contribution of Triple Zed alumni to toppling the regime is a point of pride for those connected to the station, then and now. Triple Zed continues to broadcast 24/7 in Brisbane, hosting a range of radical programs dedicated to challenging the status quo.

CHAPTER 56

'A PUB OF OUR OWN!': THE KINGSTON HOTEL, MELBOURNE'S WOMEN'S PUB

Janey Stone

The traditional image of pubs in Australia is a place for men to swill alcohol. But in the 1980s a new pub for women was set up more as a multi-purpose social space. The alcohol itself was relatively unimportant.

Film maker, teacher and women's liberation activist Pat Longmore ran the Kingston Hotel in Highett Street Richmond (an inner Melbourne suburb) between 1980 and 1986. Because of the licensing laws, the public bar had to be open to men as well as women, but there was also a bistro. Pat felt that it was important to have an eating place in conjunction with the bar; she wanted to help establish something other than yet another women's bar.

Sheril Berkovitch, in her obituary for Pat, who died in 1992, commented on how well known Pat was:

> I'd probably be correct in assuming that hardly a dyke in Melbourne hasn't heard of Pat, either from her early days in the women's liberation movement and lesbian groups, through the film world ... [and] through the many innovative and creative events she organised.

I also knew Pat through women's liberation. But why did she turn her energy to opening a pub at that time?

Pat had emigrated from the US not long after the 1956 Olympics.

In America at the time I decided to leave there was still the residue of McCarthyism and nothing was being done or was going to be done about the disenfranchised in society. In Miami there was still a six o'clock curfew for blacks.

In Australia Pat threw herself into what she was passionate about: doing things to benefit women. And when it came to the Kingston her aim was to create a safe, welcoming space for women. It wasn't a place just for lesbians or a 'raging bar', but a 'social ground for all women to relax in each other's company.'

> A lot of people laughed at running a pub as a safe place for women, but those same people who laughed at me were the first to go broke. It was a period of large social changes – there was the introduction of .05 and they couldn't even get good crowds into football stadiums.

Although it was open to all women, there was a strong lesbian presence. All the bar staff were lesbian. 'Bar dykes held the pool room downstairs.' Pat thought it was probably the only pub in Victoria where lesbians could know they were not seen and treated by male staff as freaks. The regulars at the Kingston came because it was unlike lesbian cruising bars: 'There was no screening at the door or hungry hands ready to grab whatever bit of flesh available.'

CHAPTER 56 'A PUB OF OUR OWN!': THE KINGSTON HOTEL, MELBOURNE'S WOMEN'S PUB

The Kingston Hotel proudly presents Women's Wednesdays, 55 Highett St, West Richmond, c.1980s (Australian Queer Archives)

There are many stories about how warm and friendly the environment was. Even wrong numbers on the phone got a friendly 'darling'.

The local men who had previously frequented the public bar continued to do so after the takeover. Although they may have been a bit bemused, it appears they accepted 'the very obvious changes in management and clientele without comment, and certainly without animosity.'

This did not stop one John Somerville Smith writing an abusive and threatening letter to the local newspaper *The Tiger Rag*.

Under the header 'Richmond becomes "lesbians" capital', John expressed his astonishment at the number of lesbians in Melbourne. 'Why they pick on Richmond as their headquarters, will never be known' he cried. But the harmless if perplexed tone turned quickly into something much nastier.

> I still think they should all be fenced off from areas where there are little kids, and with a big, barbed wire fence. Preferably with high voltage power on the Homo's and Leso's side of the fence [spelling in the original].

No wonder people felt the need for a safe place in the 1980s.

And Pat worked 20 hour days to achieve this. The pub was a popular place. It was a hive of activity with fundraisers, pool competitions, book launches, concerts and many other events. Sue Jackson still remembers the 'fun times' at the Kingston when the New Zealand folk singing and comedy duo The Topp Twins performed.

But probably most important is the simple fact that it was a safe place just to socialise. As Pat said:

> By the end of my time there it was like a big club. Everyone would hug everyone and you wouldn't know who was with who. A lot of men came for the safety too.

No title (Two women embracing, 'Glad to be gay'), 1973 (Ponch Hawkes)

So why did this big club come to an end? It's not clear but probably Pat had had enough of her 20 hour days and by the late 1980s she was moving into organising film festivals and other activities. Sheril Berkowitch notes that she hated collectives, so would not have been one to share the management of the pub with others.

But there are other more political considerations. In 1980 when the pub opened, Malcolm Fraser was still the prime minister. Difficult as things were under Fraser, there was still a considerable degree of social conflict – many people, no doubt including most of the pub's clientele, had maintained their rage.

But by 1988 things were very different. There had already been years of the Accord under the Hawke government. Social movements were seriously dampened and the mood was much flatter. Those struggles that did occur were largely defensive.

Women's liberation as a movement was on the decline and activity moved away from protests and campaigns and more into welfare projects in partnership with government. The gay liberation movement also was changing. The movement peaked in 1978 with the riot at the Sydney Mardi Gras. From 1980 there was a change in focus from being a movement for liberation to 'community' activities – working within the system rather than challenging it.

The establishment of the Kingston sits squarely within this transition. With political activism on the downturn in 1980, but attitudes to gay people still threatening (as we can see in the *Tiger Rag* letter), the creation of a safe place to socialise seemed like a worthwhile goal. But by the late 1980s a new crisis – the HIV/AIDS epidemic – led to the need for a new type of organising. Although the illness itself struck men, lesbians were a major force in the response. In fact it was young lesbian Alison Thorne who made the critical call for action. Sitting back and socialising no longer seemed so attractive – and no place was now safe.

Nonetheless the Kingston remains as a strong memory for many people.

The Topp Twins performed at The Kingston Hotel, 1980s
(New Zealand Ministry for Culture and Heritage)

CHAPTER 57

THE OXFORD HOTEL 'RIOT', WOLLONGONG, 1981

Nick Southall

For my former partner and I the evening of New Year's Eve 1981 began, as did most evenings, with a session at our flat. A group of our friends sat around the lounge room smoking cones, catching-up on news and making plans for the night ahead. Fresh out of the parental home, I lived with my girlfriend in a small flat conveniently located at the top of Crown Street, the main street of Wollongong, just above the city centre. When our friends were on their way into town, they could be fairly certain that if they called into our place there would be a session going on, sometimes with the whole lounge room ringed by people, and bongs moving around the circle in both directions. Punks, mods, trendies, yobbos, bikies, and those not so easily labelled, could all be found sharing space and 'substance abuse'. If you lived at home with your oldies and wanted to get stoned before a night out, were on acid, or abusing prescription drugs, or just looking for interesting and eclectic company, engaging conversations, and the chance to hear some of the latest alternative music, our place offered a warm welcome.

On New Year's Eve 1981, one of those who called-in on us was a young man named 'Stephen'. Only staying briefly, he headed off into town to meet some of his mates. Eventually, we all ambled down Crown Street to the Oxford Hotel. The Oxford, or 'The Pox', as we called it, was the underage pub, where kids could go and get drunk without being hassled about their age. It was also a place where drugs were easily accessible, it had an outlaw culture, and at times they'd be alternative bands performing.

Many of those at 'The Pox' that night were on acid. The potency of this batch was indicated by a group of local bikies, possibly the source of that night's 'trips', who were huddled together in the centre of the pub, clearly 'off their faces' and feeling unusually vulnerable.

The Oxford had a licence to stay open till 3 am and as midnight approached many of the patrons spilled-out onto Crown Street to celebrate the New Year. Shortly after, they were joined by many others coming from nearby local venues, forced out by the more general 12 o'clock closing time. Soon, any cars attempting to drive along the main street were being slowed, rocked to-and-fro, and occasionally kicked or hit. As the crowd grew, it took over the whole street. With Crown Street now a New Year's Eve party venue in full swing, a young man in the middle of the crowd decided to sit crossed legged on the road. A short time later, a car attempted to push through the sea of bodies, initially bobbing from side-to-side and then being more aggressively rocked. The driver, feeling in danger, revved his engine and lurched forward, parting the crowd before him. Carving through the melee, his car struck the young man sitting on the road. The car hurtled on, as the young bloke on the road began having convulsions, violently thrashing about, while the crowd re-took the street around him.

Most of those on the street were very pissed and, unable to see the young man's plight amongst the wild commotion, continued their revelry and street occupation. However, someone called an ambulance. Soon it arrived at the top of the block with its lights flashing.

Attempting to get to the accident site, it encountered an unmoving wall of excited people. Unable and unwilling to enter the fray without some protection, the ambos were quickly joined by a couple of police paddy wagons.

By now the crowd numbered in the hundreds and the sight of the approaching police was met with jeers, taunts, and a couple of beer cans thrown in their direction. Rapidly there were more cop cars and paddy wagons on the scene. Determined to advance, the cops inched forward, as the crowd grew and consolidated. While the ambos managed to reach the injured man, there was no avoiding a confrontation between the massing force of police and the increasingly agitated crowd. A sense of expectation grew amongst most of those present, as the face-off intensified.

Wollongong Out of Workers dance poster, 1985 (Michael Callaghan)

This was a scene reminiscent of, and popularised by, the Star Hotel riot in Newcastle, which had erupted two years earlier. The Star Hotel riot occurred on the night of that pub's closure and involved around 4000 people who fought the police for two hours. Newcastle was in many ways a mirror image of Wollongong, a coal and steel town on the New South Wales coast not far from Sydney. In both cities, youth unemployment was growing rapidly, along with resultant desperation and anger.

During the late 1970s and through the 1980s, the Wollongong region felt the impact of major economic restructuring, technological change, deregulation and privatisation. Over the next decade, the city's working class was decomposed through changes in work and workplaces, mass sackings, unemployment, poverty and social crisis. At the start of the 1980s, unemployment in the area was around 10 percent of the workforce. 25 000 people worked for BHP Steel and thousands more worked in the local coal mines. The mass sackings of the 1980s would see the closure of three quarters of the mines and the steelworks' workforce reduced to about 5000. The early eighties also saw the reorganisation and closure of half a dozen local clothing factories. By 1983, there were more than 19 000 people registered as unemployed and the local Commonwealth Employment Service listed only 108 job vacancies. Yet, this was only part of the picture, as these figures didn't include 'the hidden unemployed'. Counting these people would take the number of unemployed people in Wollongong during this period to over 30 000 out of a total population of around 200 000. Young people were the most likely to be jobless and poor.

Already, by New Year's Eve 1981, thousands of local youth were unable to find work. That year BHP had stopped employing ironworkers and it soon became clear that thousands of workers would be losing their jobs, as the company began mass sackings. The steelworks had provided most of the city's jobs for the previous 40 years. While working there, or going into the pits, was not an attractive prospect, for many young people these industries had been reliable employers when nothing better was available. When 300 final year apprentices were told that, despite their four years of training, they wouldn't be employed by the company, it was clear the dole queue was now the most likely destination for this 'no future' generation. In the poorer suburbs of Wollongong, the youth unemployment rate would soon rise to one in every two.

The young people of Wollongong who had missed TV news, or documentary footage, of the Star Hotel riot, were likely to be familiar with Cold Chisel's immortalisation of the confrontation in their song 'Star Hotel', released in 1981, and had probably seen the song's film clip on TV featuring scenes of that night's clashes, including the torching of a police car and paddy wagon. The song's lyrics were:

> All last night we were learning
> Drank our cheques by the bar
> Somewhere bridges were burning
> As the walls came down at the Star
> Squad cars fanned the insanity
> Newsman fought through the crowd
> Spent last night under custody
> And the sun found me on the road

> At the Star Hotel
> They better listen cause we're ringin' a bell
> Ain't no deals, we got nothing to sell
> Just a taste of things to come, at the Star Hotel

> Those in charge are getting crazier
> Job queues grow through the land
> An uncontrolled youth in Asia
> Gonna make those fools understand

According to local media reports, at its height the crowd outside the Oxford Hotel on New Year's Eve 1981 numbered 1500. As this was occurring just around the corner from the city's main police station, and now involved many cops, one of the local police commanders was soon on the scene overseeing operations. He was, no doubt, determined to avoid any replay of the events in Newcastle. Taking charge of his troops, he waved-in the assembled paddy wagons and began advising and organising his men. As he did, a chant of 'Pigs! Pigs! Pigs!' grew into a crescendo. We all knew it was about to get ugly.

As the crowd's chanting, taunting, pushing and shoving grew in intensity, and those at the front became more brazen in their confrontation with the 'boys in blue', one of the cops pulled out his pistol and aimed it at the crowd. Holding the gun at arm's length, he slowly walked across the road in front of the line of police, pointing his revolver at the heads of those in the front

The Oxford Hotel, 1980s (City of Wollongong)

Young and Pissed Off (YAPO) graffiti on the Wollongong Department of Social Security Office, 1980s (Southall)

lines of the disobedient mob. While his gun held the crowd at bay, the snatch squads began lunging into the throng. Under direction from their boss, small groups of cops targeted the biggest, angriest, and most defiant.

Known local 'toughs' and 'trouble-makers' were amongst those snatched. They were quickly bundled into the waiting paddy wagons. But the cops didn't just throw them in and shut the door. During the Star Hotel riot, many people had escaped and were rescued from the paddy wagons. The Wollongong police weren't going to let this happen. As they threw those arrested into the wagons, a few cops got in behind them. It soon became clear that those unfortunate enough to find themselves inside these mobile metal cells were being beaten with fists and weapons. Most of the prisoners offered little resistance, but some, including a young man with a reputation for being 'Wollongong's hardest', refused to be cowed, resulting in more police joining in to subdue him.

The people arrested were eventually ferried away to the Wollongong police station. Yet, if you were amongst those who the police thought hadn't been punished enough for that night's or past 'offences', it was to be a long night. There was to be no replay of the Star Hotel riot outside the Oxford and the police eventually managed to clear the road, close the pub, and herd everyone in different directions, until the centre of town was deserted.

We made our way back up Crown Street and returned to our flat. A little while later 'Stephen' was at the door; he had come straight from Wollongong Hospital, a few yards up the road, and his head was terribly swollen and bandaged. He'd been outside the Oxford at midnight, was

Wollongong to Sydney Right to Work march, 1982 (*Tribune*/Search Foundation, State Library of NSW)

grabbed by the cops, and had been bludgeoned with a large police torch. To make matters worse he was still tripping on acid.

Two days later, the *Illawarra Mercury* ran a story headlined '30 New Year's "revellers" arrested'. In the accompanying article the paper reported that those detained were charged with resisting arrest, assaulting police and malicious injury. The article also quoted the Oxford's publican who said she 'was pleased there were no fights inside the hotel.' Not surprisingly, there was no mention of the police violence or the injuries of those arrested. Nor was there any coverage of reports that one of those taken into custody, and later transported to Wollongong Hospital by the police, had their fingers deliberately broken in the emergency waiting room, after loudly complaining about being bashed by the cops. Soon afterwards, a New South Wales Nurse's Association meeting at Wollongong Hospital resolved not to accept police violence, to question any police account of incidents they were involved in, and to report any suspicious incidents to the South Coast Labour Council.

Later that year, Wollongong would be hit even harder by the deepening economic, jobs and poverty crises. In response, the city was rocked by a powerful collective fightback organised by local employed and unemployed workers that would play a significant part in bringing down the Fraser Coalition government and the election of the Hawke Labor Government on a platform of 'Jobs, Jobs, Jobs'. The first indication of what this platform really meant for Wollongong came via the implementation of the 1983 Steel Industry Plan. Here the Government accepted BHP's long-term strategy, by supporting the provision of

Wollongong Out of Workers protest, 1984 (*Tribune*/Search Foundation, State Library of NSW)

hundreds of millions of taxpayers' dollars to the company, which was then invested in job-displacing technology. The Steel Industry Plan was rejected by local workers and their unions. But as the steelworks' general manager, John Clark, pointed out at the time 'there is nothing like the contemplation of the hangman in the morning, to get people to cooperate.' While some would learn to cooperate with BHP's plans, many of Wollongong's unemployed instead became their own executioners, driven to suicide by the despair of joblessness.

Meanwhile, the main regional 'jobs plan' implemented by the Hawke government was the Community Employment Program (CEP). This 'short-term work experience scheme' was supposed to 'create additional employment opportunities for unemployed people through the funding of labour-intensive projects of social and economic benefit to the community.' Eight hundred jobs were created in Wollongong during the first twelve months of the program. The average length of the jobs was 26 weeks. No CEP jobs were permanent, unionised, or led to full-time work. In many cases welfare and charity organisations, under increasing strain and facing shortfalls in government funding, took on CEP workers. These workers would then be sacked and were often replaced by other CEP workers. Over time, more and more of the CEP funding went to 'private projects' and a wider range of work experience, training, and work-for-the-dole schemes were deployed.

In order for places like Wollongong to expand their economic base, 'the market' demanded increased labour 'flexibility', the cutting of labour costs, more profits, increased management power and an undermining of the power of labour. To grease the wheels of the 'new economy', people socialised in a region dominated by relatively stable unionised work, advanced wages and conditions, and class consciousness, would have to be re-trained and re-educated. As mass unemployment and social breakdown grew, employers and governments created new ways of managing employed and unemployed workers, often with the cooperation of concerned labour and community organisations. These new forms of labour were specifically focused on social containment and control via the various training, retraining and temporary employment schemes. These training and education programs not only prepared workers for transformed ways of working but often operated as short term casual non-unionised workplaces themselves. The legacy of mass participation in these schemes has been the creation of a more flexible and mobile workforce conditioned to expect short-term or casual jobs, with poor conditions and low pay.

Today, unemployment in Wollongong is still higher than the national average, and in the less affluent suburbs around one in every two young people are out of work (when 'hidden unemployment' is included). The average income of Wollongong workers is now significantly less than the NSW average and the lack of local jobs sees 25 percent of the workforce commute to Sydney each day for work. Many of Wollongong's unemployed remain economically and socially marginalised, condemned to a life of poverty and insecurity, consigned to the worst public housing estates or homelessness, and subjected to Centrelink, employment agency, and police harassment.

CHAPTER 58

A PUB AT THE END OF THE WORLD: MAKING SOMETHING MEANINGFUL IN TASMANIA'S WILD WEST

Alex Ettling

In 1911, Thomas Connolly, dressed in his navy blue serge suit and cap, exited the Rosebery Hotel and took his first steps heading out into the remote rainforest of Tasmania. He was a publican, not a miner, but Connolly was hiking out to Bam Bluff in pursuit of greater fortunes. His Rosebery Hotel had been established to service the miners and prospectors of the region. Now a fully-fledged town was growing up around it. As a barkeep with his ears open he was becoming aware of the potential for riches from up out of the ground. In the end it was the discovery of metals, not in the ground, but contained in a watch and a small knife, that helped identify the anonymous bones that were found several months after Connolly failed to arrive at his destination.

The area around Rosebery is known as the Tarkinya. It is prized for its 3000 year old Huon pines, stands of leatherwood, myrtle beech, blackwood, southern sassafras and messmate stringybark. It is the mosses that account for the verdant splendour that wraps this ancient Gondwanan rainforest. The only thing that obscures this stunning sight is the heavy fog that settles over it. It was on such a day when Connolly lost sight of the path. Cold, wet and miserable, after exhaling his final breath, the bacteria and lichen hastily dealt with anything left on the bones that the scavengers left behind. The 'wild west' was untroubled by the ambitions of Thomas Connolly and his attempt to extract the minerals within, but the clash with modernity had only just begun.

Agnes Connolly, now without a male earner, followed the path of many early colonial widows – she became a single woman running a pub. There was still a demand for what the Rosebery Hotel offered, with others willing to take the same risk as her late husband. For decades, would-be mining magnates were aware of the minerals locked inside the west coast. Tom McDonald had found zinc-lead ore body at Rosebery in 1893. However, the challenges in retrieving these commodities and then getting them to market were considerable. Mountains, rivers and dense vegetation were barriers, roads were unreliable, and coming by ship meant dealing with the gale swept coastline.

There were no local investors with sufficient capital or will to invest in a train line. The dilemma of aligning with investors from the outside was that the spoils would largely go elsewhere: to the big city of Hobart, or across the Tasman Sea, or possibly even further overseas. So, for decades the west coast of Tasmania slept with its bounty undisturbed, as capitalism continued its rapid expansion across the globe.

When a railway line finally arrived in the region, the west coast extractive industries boomed. Mining progressed at speed, and profits roared in. Rosebery, the town at the bottom of the world, literally the last postcode in Australia: 7470, became a flourishing community.

Agnes Connolly spent many years in Rosebery, and when she announced she was moving to another town, she was gifted a tortoiseshell toilet seat. It is not clear whether the gesture of appreciation was for her early contributions via the pub, or her financial support for the medical co-op. Town folklore holds that in the early days of settlement money was raised to build a hospital, but at the final moment the funds were diverted towards building a hotel. It is an apocryphal tale, but the persistence of it is indicative that there are two pressing needs in a remote mining town like Rosebery. There is an element of care in both – hospital treatment for illness and injury, and the emotional solace afforded by a rich social life. In Rosebery, alcohol was a balm tasked with doing a lot.

Miners' work is physical, skilled and dangerous. The ways that one can die in this industry are numerous – machinery malfunctions, poisonings, crushings and drownings. There is the threat of repetitive stress injuries – ailments like 'white finger' from holding the growling heavy drills that cut off blood circulation. These industrial machines have evocative names – pumas and panthers – which are possibly less exhilarating once a finger has been amputated. The miners of western Tasmania spent much of their working lives in steamy tunnels, coated in black dust, with the persistent risk of serious harm. The safety record of the EZ mining company in Rosebery was poor. The medical union was created in the absence of proper state healthcare. But what was available was minimal. Adequate medical help was sometimes only accessible if a mishap was timed with the train timetable, or fortuitously coincided with the schedule of the travelling doctor. Working life does not conform to such good order, so there were grim accounts where the prolonged wait for treatment involved days of agony.

Most people who chose to live in this part of the world did not expect things to be easy. But it was clear that the workers had it much worse off than the people at the top of the company hierarchy, and conditions in the town were visibly class divided. The mines manager lived in what was dubbed 'the White House', a part of town that was neatly manicured, where the leisure activities were associated with the golf course and tennis courts. The workers had housing provided for them by the company too,

The Rosebery Hotel, Tasmania, 1923

Aerial photo of Rosebery (Tasmania Archives)

a way of attracting new workers into the mines. The most basic accommodation was the 'single man's quarters'.

Mine worker Andrew 'Ian' Jamieson, known more commonly as Jammo, started work in the mines in 1984 and lived in this accommodation, 'There were a few suicides in the single man's quarters over the years. It wasn't very pleasant. There were no amenities.' The company boasted of its suite of workers' welfare services and the attractive lifestyle on offer, but this was limited to things like having *two* pool tables in the mess hall. It could only be appealing when compared to the generally woeful standards for workers in the region.

There was little obscuring the social divisions in Rosebery, included the drinking culture. The town for many years had a 'top pub' and a 'bottom pub'. They were marked as such by their geographical placement, but this also had deeper meaning. The Top Pub, which was formerly The Plandome, was where the upper hierarchy of the mining company drank in the lounge. The pub even had a top hat painted on the exterior. Jammo explains, 'a lot of people kept away from The Top Pub because the managers were there. You couldn't really talk union much without them getting to hear about it. So it was down in The Bottom Pub that a lot of the unionists drank.'

Mixing in pubs was possibly a liability for both sides within the town's antagonistic workplace relationship. An industrial officer for the mining company, known as The Lip, was known to spill sensitive information, like redundancies, after consuming a few beers.

The Bottom Pub was what The Rosebery Hotel of the Connolly's came to be known as. It was associated with the blue collar workers of the community. The Top Pub was solid brick and reflected the confidence of the town, whereas The Bottom Pub, constructed in the early settlement period in 1898, was made of softer materials – oregon, cedar, King Billy pine – a legacy of the town's looming threat of impermanence. The interior of the hotel was considered by most to be basic. Different eras were marked by additions like the clawfoot bath in the residential area, and later on, brown vinyl booths.

Rosebery mine, development end (State Library of Victoria)

Rosebery mine worker and socialist militant Jammo, 1970s (Jeff Richards)

Drinking and pub life was central in this town. As Jammo explains, 'It was very easy just to go to the pubs and have a few beers and really get to know people.' Drinkers recall joy filled evenings dancing on tables, along with classic tales of drunken misadventure, such as the time a reveller thought he could jump over the veranda of The Bottom Pub. Although he managed the feat, he lost much skin in the process.

Other recollections shared in the 'West Coasters, Who Remembers When' Facebook group include Kym Rubens meeting champion Aboriginal boxer Lionel Rose, who signed a beer coaster for her. Dean Hampton writes, 'I'll never forget the 30 pear [sic] of underwear hanging off the main bar roof after Mad Monday with the Hawks.' More romantically, Sue Hopner shared her most important memory, 'Hubby and I met there on a blind date over 40 years ago, we'll never forget it.' Christine Underhayes surmised, 'It was a lovely old hotel, it wouldn't matter what time of the day you would walk into the hotel there was someone in there to chat to and one would stay longer and drink more.'

Other memories of the hotel include celebrating sporting premierships of both men's and women's team sport. A fond recollection was shared by one person of their dad giving them their first beer, age 13. There were also lingering memories of food and drink: steak with Diane sauce, raspberry spiders on lunch breaks from school.

The pub created a shared bond, but it also represented something of a limitation. Jammo states, 'There was nothing else to do in town. There was only two TV channels, WIN TV and the ABC. You'd never watch TV, you'd just go down to the pub.' There were also negative aspects to the dominant pub culture. The community spirit in Rosebery, which could be described as 'tribal' in a positive way, could also be more derisively seen as cliquish. The popularity of pub life led to something of a monoculture, which could be problematic in developing a healthy diversity in the community, whatever the leisure activity may be. Jammo asserts:

> There was no social life there other than the pubs, and if you didn't like that culture, you were ostracised, not deliberately, but you

T-shirt of a drinking club at the Bottom Pub (Brendan Bennett)

The Top Pub, Rosebery (Tasmania Archives)

weren't part of the community and you were always considered an outsider, and eventually you'd end up drifting away and go elsewhere.

There were a number of alcoholics in the mines, and so attempting a lifestyle change away from drinking was a challenge. There were also fights inside The Bottom Pub, not always but enough for it to develop a reputation. A number of workers in the town, as a commitment to their union values, sought ways of strengthening ties in the community without alcohol involved. One event during the 1980s was a 'bake-off' using the new model Weber BBQ's that had exploded in popularity. Many people in town had recently bought one. Jammo explains, 'We organised the Zeehan Senior Citizens to come to a special event where they had to judge who of the dozen or so cooks on their Webers provided the best meal'.

Developing alternatives was always going to be an uphill battle as activities that did not include alcohol found a way of becoming adjunct activities to pub life. Sport was the main recreation and routinely finished with drinking. If there was enough booze consumed you might return to another sport: the game of 'fiery footy'. In the words of one participant, it required 'soaking a toilet roll in kero or petrol and then lighting it and playing football with it.' A game intended never to be played sober: 'just add alcohol and a few bad ideas and there you have it.' The hijinks of fiery footy included women as players which was in its favour for fielding a team.

The most prominent recreational activity in town was of course standard footy, a sport generally only suitable for fit young-ish men. Playing Australian Rules football was probably as hazardous as fiery footy, especially on the west coast of Tasmania with its notorious ovals. Queenstown is well known for its silica, gravel oval but Rosebery has perhaps the second most infamous football oval in the region. It has the luxury of grass – until it gets wet and then just turns into a bog (and it is *always* wet). The oval was placed on top of an old sewerage works, therefore it was accepted that falling in this mud with any sort of open wound would likely result in something worse than a gravel rash.

Although only played by one segment of the population, football culture drew in people across the community as spectators and club volunteers. Following the fortunes of the town's team created a sense of belonging. Even older, unfit, out-of-form players like Jammo would be roped in for a season, before enduring a second enforced retirement through injury. Jammo states, 'Football was part of the glue that held the community together, and that was particularly so in Western Tasmania. People would go to the football then to the pubs afterwards.' Drinks in the club house also added funds to the club.

In Rosebery, the club's facilities were available for activists and unionists, suggesting something of the balance of forces in the community. Jammo explains there were:

> No problems using the club rooms for political activity. I think one of the things was they had a bar at the back which they could get a bit of profit from people after the meeting. My first time at a stop work meeting, that was held at the footy club rooms. If it was a quick stop work meeting, or a shift meeting that we wanted to hold off site, we'd use the footy club rooms.

Workplace bulletins were not considered as necessary in a town such as this. As Jammo notes, 'If word had to be passed on, it wasn't hard to do it in the pubs.' The managers of the pubs were always onside with the unions. Jammo contends:

> Even in The Top Pub they wouldn't cross the unions because the publican knew it wasn't good for him. The unions had a lot of social power if you like. We could always hit the pub owner up for a couple of hundred dollars, and they'd gladly contribute because he didn't want to get a reputation of being against the union because no one would drink there.

Jammo reveals the unique political dynamics of these social spaces in Rosebery:

> We never had any union meetings in The Bottom Pub, there was a lot of union talk in the Bottom Pub, but no meetings. All the campaigning and strategising, a lot of that was done in the pub over a beer. Talking to people and getting their ideas. And they'd come up to you, 'what about this and what about that.' We did have formal executive meetings, but these were really a rubber stamp. More of the in-depth stuff was always done at the pub, over a beer or two. If anyone wanted to come into town, political figures or union figures, if they wanted to meet people, they'd always go to The Bottom Pub. Michael Fielder who was leader of the Labor Party at that time came to The Bottom Pub trying to get me to sweet talk to everyone else. [Future state Premier] Jim Bacon came to The Bottom Pub as well.

The gravitation of such prominent ALP figures to this one pub in a small isolated town is an indication that for a period, particularly in the 1980s, community engagement and union participation was especially strong in Rosebery. Jammo asserts that:

> Whatever was needed, the townspeople would rally around the union at that stage. These were also years when our little Rosebery executive, bold as brass, decided to fix up every issue and problem on the entire mine site and town.

Beyond community issues workers won a reduction in the working hours, giving everyone an extra day off every month. They were also successful in fending off management initiatives to introduce unfair pay arrangements that would have divided the workforce. Rosebery is also notable for the way in which it repelled the negative influence of 'sell-out' AWU officials and ALP politicians. Jammo contends that these forces:

Jammo speaks to workers from the EZ mine, 1980s (Butch Johnson)

Had no power there, and gave way to the combined union committee. We said we'd pay our dues to the AWU but we had nothing to do with them. You don't have a right to come in over our heads and talk to the boss. We made sure the bosses only talked to us. It meant nothing if they wanted to collaborate with the AWU officials in Hobart.

When it came to implementing decisions it was the combined union committee, with the support of the rank and file workers, that held power. An indication of the remarkable strength of the workers was that after one notorious betrayal from union officials, discussions at the pub included the idea to paint a line on the road leading into Rosebery so that no AWU official could step foot in town without prior permission.

Every so often, the ALP would make an overture to bring the staunch unionists back into the fold. Future Labor Premier Paul Lennon on one occasion flew a private jet to the west coast to meet with prominent union activist Joe Pringle to wine and dine him. Lennon was disappointed to see that Pringle had brought along a companion: his socialist comrade, Jammo. As Jammo recounts, 'Joe was his affable self and for hours asked questions about the ALP structures, what he was expected to do with the branch, and seemed to be enjoying himself. I finally twigged.' The evening was an exquisite exercise in trolling, extracting jug after jug of beer, further reeling Lennon in. Lennon said, 'Well Joe, I've been here for several hours and paid for you and your mate's meals and drinks – what do you think about the Labor Party?' The answer was always going to be: 'No'.

The stirrings of a long series of attacks on workers by management had begun in the early part of the 1970s. The workers for a heroically lengthy period fought them off until their defeat in the early 1990s. To begin with, the EZ mining company took the offensive, installing a new management team from South Africa. In *Radical Tasmania: The Selected Histories*, historian Robert Hodder explains that the new boss George Mackay came with experience, he had been smashing organisations of Black miners using the racist laws of the South African apartheid regime. Mine loco-driver Reg 'Trout' Bracken observed of the new regime, 'They want you to work like they made the Blacks do over there – no chat back, do as you're told and we'll feed you.'

Rosebery locals were well aware of the importance of the mine to the regional economy. The mining company had done effective PR work, financially supporting many of the social activities in town, so some had to adjust to holding a less rosy view of Rosebery's main employer. 'I was brought up that the company were angels', the disgruntled Trout added, 'Not any more though.'

Although Rosebery had built up a strong union presence, this could not provide inoculation from threats like global economic crises, technological advances, and trade wars. From the mid-1970s, volatile world zinc prices took a series of hammerings. Management were out to make workers pay the price of the economic downturn by cutting the workforce, driving down wages, and eroding conditions. Resource companies were always inclined to chase lower prices and faster rates of profits elsewhere. Rosebery, a small town in an

Rosebery workers picket EZ work site in Hobart, 1983 (Renfrey Clarke Collection)

isolated area, with one major employer, was particularly vulnerable to the economic forces that dominated it. Employers used peoples' anxiety over losing their livelihoods to their advantage in negotiations, as well as in their union busting efforts.

On a number of occasions the workers and residents in Rosebery were able to organise collectively to push back against decisions that came from on high. In 1983, Rosebery miners were drawn into a large confrontation with management. This dispute is particularly interesting because it also illuminates how drinking was enmeshed in the culture of the workforce. An account of the strike is covered in activist and historian Renfrey Clarke's *The Picket*, the source of the details that follow.

This particular strike necessitated the Rosebery unionists to picket not their own workplace, but another site owned by the company in Hobart. Jammo explains that, 'There's no need for a picket in [Rosebery]. If you walked out, no one would dare go anywhere near the mine.' However, the company began developing alternative sites as a tactic to break the strong unions of the Tasmanian west. There was a committed core of Rosebery workers and union leaders who got the picket at the EZ Risdon site going. But they needed more people to have any hope of success. Getting workers to make the long drive from Rosebery to Hobart in one of the coldest winters in memory was a feat in itself. The culture of the workers came along with them. One car load had the misfortune to hit a cow on route and with nothing else to do until they were retrieved they got fantastically drunk.

As is usual in picket line situations, people demonstrate their individual talents. With the flourishing of collective organising you see the kernel of how people could potentially run broader affairs themselves. Often the most capable leaders were made marshals, tasked with organising their comrades into formation when there were stirrings that the picket might be confronted. But also crucial in holding it all together was the role of the charming larrikin, important in keeping spirits up as the strike endured. In this particular dispute the role of glue-guy was played by the aforementioned Trout Bracken. His alcoholism was commonly known, but for this role it was little impediment.

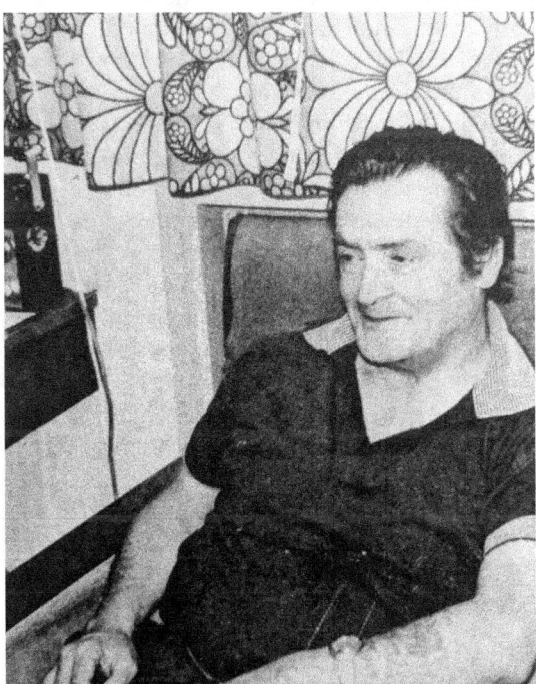

Trout Bracken, 1983 (Renfrey Clarke Collection)

EZ workers picket line, 1983 (Renfrey Clarke Collection)

In the early period of the picket there was a strong presence of alcohol. Stoppy's Waterfront Inn was just down the road. The publican immediately warmed to the strikers, even bringing in their favoured beer, Boags. Strikers quipped of the fortune he made off the unexpected arrival of this heavy drinking west coast clientele. In return he supplied the workers with Stoppy's branded hats and shirts. It is a shame they were not scarves and beanies as it was bitterly cold on the picket line, and some effort was needed to keep spirits up. Union leader Jimmy Gilleece recounted that, 'If morale was down they'd bring in cartons of beer, help them get a bellyfull of piss in them.' A supporter of the workers, Marjorie Luck, would bring round tea as well, in an effort to ease the drinking. On other occasions when confrontations on the picket looked imminent, Luck warily collected up the empty bottles as a precaution.

Picket line activity could be entertaining, but also tiring. It was difficult to sleep in the camp-style conditions. Strikers ending their picket shift would come back with a carton of beer to unwind, inevitably disturbing the peace. It did not help that the bell ringer to the sleeping quarters, designed to loudly clang and announce a presence, was made out of beer cans and beer bottles.

There was, however, a degree of discipline imposed with the drinking. It is recorded that 'the magical piss-up' that some people imagined was not evident. Trout explained that if anyone was too drunk the punishment was a 'double header', two shifts in row after sobering up.

Alcohol became politicised during the strike. *The Picket* includes an account of a visit from ALP politician Terry Aulich who arrived at the picket with pizza and bottles of beer. Aulich's gifts were treated with suspicion. The fact that no ALP reps ever came again seemed to confirm that the gift of alcohol was a mischievous attempt to damage the reputation of the workers.

Amongst concerted attempts by enemies to undermine the picket was the circulation of a rumour that the men were having, euphemistically, 'a great time'. The implication was that it was all sex and booze. Rather than a hive of sexual escapades, the picket camp in fact featured a masturbatorium, a room with a TV and porn videos.

In an attempt to secure the reputation of the striking workers, a restriction was placed on women being on the picket line late in the evening. A statement to counter the innuendo was also made by Marjorie Luck, published in the strike bulletin that circulated in Rosebery. The porn went, and the strikers instigated a ban on alcohol on the picket line.

The ban was generally adhered to. However, after a shift on the picket, the workers were free to engage in their accustomed approach to leisure, which was well lubricated.

The dispute ended in a celebrated victory for the workers. However, fatigue was blamed for one unfortunate error in the final negotiation, where a demand of the electricians (concerning not having to work alone underground or in isolated areas) had been accidentally bargained away as they were going through the extensive and complex paperwork in the early hours of the morning. The question of tiredness in such a long and grinding dispute is difficult to parse. Fatigue in part caused by drinking when they went through the details in paperwork? Fatigue from the muddle-headed exhaustion of being away from home for an extended period of time? It is possible to take the conclusion that more attention to rest in the way they were used to (i.e. drinking) could have helped, as much as drawing a conclusion that total abstinence may have prevented mistakes.

A few years later, still in the volatile 1980s, a political battle had to be won over workers compensation. This time, members of the Rosebery community made the long drive to Hobart and came dressed in their mining gear. They filled the public gallery of parliament, and glowered down at the besuited politicians intent on stripping the workers of their accident safety net. Jammo recounts:

> When we won the workers compensation issue, Liberal Premier Robin Gray took it on himself to come up to Rosebery. There was a media contingent – it was all 'aren't I a great premier? I conceded to the miners, the miners love me', and so on. So he ended up in The Bottom Pub in front of all the cameras, talking about what a great guy he is. He tried to bring me into it, saying 'I suppose all you and your mining mates will be voting for me in the election?' In front of the media I really deflated his balloon, I said 'There's no fucking way we're ever going to vote for you. We just fought you and won, and we'll do the same again next time.' He left with his tail between his legs.

If anyone had hopes that an end to conservative rule would lead to an improved position for the workers they were to be disappointed. The world's first Labor-Green Government was installed in Tasmania in 1989, and soon embarked on an austerity programme to pay back public debt to the banks. Cuts to education, health and transport followed. In Rosebery, the proposed hospital closure became the prominent issue that drew in the whole town. Jammo explains:

> We kept pointing out, every year Rosebery would be locked in for a week because of snow. What are you going to do? They replied, 'Oh, we'll get a helicopter in.' In snowstorms? I don't think that's possible. There is a need for a hospital here.

> When they made the announcement of the closure of the hospital there was a very serious accident underground and a mate of mine was lucky to survive. These big electrical cables, it whiplashed on one level, took his legs out, it crushed him. He was in a really bad way. And people were absolutely furious because he could have lost his life if the hospital wasn't there. He wouldn't have made it to Burnie or Queenstown. So, people understood what the hospital meant.

A demonstration of 2000 people from Tasmania's west marched in Hobart and a 'miner's claim' was theatrically pegged on the steps of Parliament. A caravan was parked next to it for a week, registering a protest against the regressive policies of both the ALP and the Greens. They won, and not only was the old hospital saved, a new one was built as well.

One of the other demands at the demonstrations in Hobart was to also save the Rosebery Hotel, which was beginning to founder. It was recognition of a broader problem – the pub's decline was emblematic of what was happening to the town as a whole.

In the 1980s, mining accounted for approximately 40 per cent of Tasmania's wealth. When the global economic recession of 1991 made its impact on the extractive industries in Tasmania's west, a series of attacks finally broke the strength of the union. One hundred miners were sacked effective immediately, with leading militants such as Jammo and Pringle targeted. All the mines on the west coast were in the crosshairs. With the left-wing union leadership now on the dole queue the forces of the right-wing AWU filled the vacuum. These officials played on the insecurity, as well as the inexperience of sections of the local community, to solidify their position. There was some resistance to the attacks, but it was not enough. It represented a historic defeat for union power in Tasmania's west coast mining communities, which they are yet to rebuild from.

The mining company itself had gone through a series of ownership changes, but these did not seem to make a significant difference to the situation for workers and the Rosebery community. Mining continued, unlike in other parts of the west, but it was clear that the town had experienced a peak and was now managing a rapid decline.

New economic sectors were floated like tourism. A great asset of Tasmania's west coast is its natural beauty. In the 1980s and beyond, there was increasing attention on environmental issues in Tasmania (most famously the proposed Franklin Dam). The impacts of industrial pollution had long been evident in Rosebery and the various limitations of extractive industries were now a well-known existential threat to communities in regional Tasmania. However for many, it seemed like there were few options. A difficult dynamic was created where mining workers and environmentalists were increasingly counterposed.

There were weak promises from mining companies to steward the environment in a more considered way. The industrial strength to compel the company to act on their promises had been lost, however. There were socialist miners like Jammo, who were pushing for both sustainability and a better deal for workers, but they were in the minority, and eventually pushed out of the industry.

In response Jammo and others focused their attention on trying to raise the political confidence of locals in other ways. Hodder asserts that 'people remember socialists like Jammo and Julia Perkins not just for blue collar unionism, but also for encouraging this working class community to develop

EZ mine workers, Jammo (left), 1980s (Butch Johnson)

their voice.' In 1997, along with miner Paul O'Brien, the *Rosebery Miners, Axemen, Bush and Blarney Festival* was established. Jammo explains:

> Paul and I were inspired by the many hidden cultural talents of working class families – musicians, storytellers, poets, actors and artists. I also took a cue from an old anarchist slogan, 'Remember kids, when you are smashing the state keep a smile on your lips and a song in your heart.'

Musicians across Tasmania continue to make the yearly convergence on Rosebery to join with the locals in a slate of activities, in pubs and the other gathering points in town, sharing their interests and encouraging support for community activities.

In 1998, Julia Perkins from Rosebery and Jenny Shaw from Zeehan, initiated a theatre project, where they worked within the community to write, produce, organise and perform a working class play based on a poem by a local writer. The poem's author Marie Pitt was a committed socialist and working class activist from an earlier generation, one of the first non-Aboriginal women to live in the area. The poem entitled 'The Keening', although published in 1911, continued to inspire with its enduring theme: profit gouging mining bosses.

Over 100 people were actively involved in staging and performing the theatrical production. Those acting in the play included miners and other workers, their partners and children. The chosen location for the first performance was The Bottom Pub. Jammo's first reaction was, 'It was a logistical nightmare because of the layout of the pub. Most of action had to take place in amongst where people were drinking', but he also concluded that this became a strength as it 'made them all feel part of it.' During the play, there was the call for an all-out strike, much to the delight of the audience.

Even though it was a historical story, for Jammo, 'It was our way of getting back at the current treatment of miners by the present owners of the mine, given the smashing of militant unionism a few years before. People were still smarting from the retrenchments.' The play didn't shift the situation in any direct way, but Jammo contends that 'it made people say, "yeah we know who the bastards are". It was an assertion of who we are.' This act of commemoration was something that workers could do at a particular low point in the struggle, and they did it where people were, in the pub.

The story of depressed mining towns in the neoliberal era is common around the world and people might assume the trend for west coast mining towns is only downward. However, with the global economy grappling with the looming climate catastrophe, there has been an unforeseen change in the narrative. There is a glimmer of a new mining boom in Tasmania around a commodity that is of particular importance to energy storage and the transition to a carbon neutral society: rare earth elements (REEs).

The prospect of returning to a time when mining communities in Tasmania were flourishing has been unexpected. However, unlike during the early 20th century mining boom, there are a number of questions being raised regarding how such an extractive industry might be organised, how toxic by-products will be dealt with, and who will benefit?

The recurring theme of problems in Rosebery has been that ultimately workers are subject to chaotic economic forces outside their control, be it global mineral prices, high level imperialist manoeuvres, the competition between firms operating within market capitalism, the level of investment the state is willing to put into urban development, the price of labour, the availability of trained workers, etc. An examination of the history of Rosebery suggests that the level of investment in the community, the degree of control over affairs in the town, and more generally the quality of life, was not determined by the nationality of the firm or their sense of generosity. It was the strength of organised labour in conjunction with profit rates that allowed the workers to extract more from the mine owners.

If there happens to be a reversal of fortunes for Tasmania's west, there will sadly be no revival for Rosebery's iconic Bottom Pub. The pub burned down on 29 June 1999. The fire itself, fed by the all timber structure, was ferocious. The 'West Coasters, Who Remembers When' Facebook group includes accounts of the sad last moments of its existence. Greg Blake observed, 'Beer ran down the gutter as the kegs exploded, there was a weird bluey green flame coming from the bar area, we were thinking it was all the spirits going up.' As the pub burned, its history and secrets were revealed. Kim Murrell Shepherd witnessed the fire, 'I remember watching it burn down, doors coming alive that we didn't know were there, they had been covered over with tin.'

The pub had been struggling for years, going through cycles of different management. In the opinions of some, it was no longer an inviting place to be and many had already chosen to drink elsewhere. Nevertheless, losing such an iconic establishment was a bitter blow for a town already experiencing decline.

It is not the services provided by the hotel that people long for, as these are still serviced by The Top Pub and other venues in town. The legendary ghosts that lived upstairs at The Bottom Pub have had to find new haunts in what sadly occupies the site now: a car park, public toilet and caravan waste transfer station. Joey Rubens shared, 'I still have an unopened bottle of Bundy black', one of the few objects salvaged by firefighters that night. You don't keep a bottle of Bundaberg Black unopened for decades unless it symbolises something more meaningful than just the alcohol within.

CHAPTER 59

CONFRONTATIONAL TEMPERANCE ACTIVISM AMONG INDIGENOUS WOMEN

Maggie Brady

In a recent book, American political scientist Mark Lawrence Schrad has boldly reclaimed alcohol prohibition and its advocates from the largely dismissive and sometimes flippant treatment they have been given by many historians and sociologists of alcohol. Prohibitionists were said to be 'moralising' individuals with puritanical proclivities, they were conservatives promoting illiberal ideas. On the contrary, Schrad argues, these people were radical, pushing against the status quo, and prohibition was the most popular, influential, and longest-lived international social reform movement in the history of the world. Campaigners were linked by a robust, transnational network in their battle against what was then commonly called the 'liquor traffic' – and the *traffic* is what it was all about.

Temperance activism was usually not aimed at the individual drinker, but at the excesses and predations of big business. Those who campaigned against the trade in, and promotion of, alcohol were not (as John Stuart Mill argued) the enemies of individual liberty, but defenders against predatory capitalism. In the process of this rousing analysis, Schrad reinstates the figure of anti-saloon campaigner Carrie Nation, famous for her dramatic and assiduous use of rocks and later a hatchet, on the saloon bars of 19th century America. She wittily referred to her saloon and barrel-smashing activities as 'hatchetations'. Rather than condemning the drunkard, she focused her activities on the sellers of alcohol, reportedly greeting bartenders with a 'Good morning, destroyer of men's souls!' Her activities were determinedly focused on defending the integrity and safety of the home. But despite leading hundreds of women to oppose saloons, inspiring them to fight for their civic rights, and establishing perhaps the first ever women's and children's shelter for those escaping violence in the home, she has been scorned as 'demented', 'hysterical', 'odd' and a bigot, and her eccentricities deliberately exaggerated.

Reading Schrad's book, I was reminded that a focus on the 'liquor traffic' – rather than railing against the hapless drunk – is the common thread linking much of the grassroots community-based action engaged in by Indigenous Australians in their struggle to deal with alcohol-related troubles. They too have tended to direct their attention to the businesses selling alcohol, rather than the consumers of it, and this has been the case since the first organised Aboriginal opposition to a liquor licence, in 1970, on the Gove peninsula, NT. Since then Aboriginal people in several regions of the country have organised themselves to resist the incursions of liquor sellers, or to contain the activities of those already established. Some of these Indigenous actions have been spontaneous demonstrative uprisings (including one instance of bar-smashing reminiscent of Carrie Nation herself), while others engaged with the regulatory frameworks available to them under state and territory laws to lodge formal objections. I discuss some instances of these strategies below under the headings 'Taking direct action' and 'Taking on the licensing system'. In a few cases however, to deal with a troublesome outlet an Aboriginal community association has decided to buy it themselves.

Buying the Hotel

Since the mid-1970s a handful of Indigenous entities have purchased hotels, usually in remote or rural regions, prompted by differing local circumstances, the motivations of their protagonists, and experiences of discriminatory treatment. Other reasons for hotel purchases included the sudden availability on the market of a local hotel, the desire to create an economic base and to 'keep the money in the community', commercial joint ventures with entrepreneurs, and the need to deal with alcohol-related harms by exerting local control over sales. It's important to remember the unconscionable selling practices engaged in by hotels that were largely taken for granted in the Northern Territory and across much of remote Australia. Many pubs routinely excluded Aboriginal people from the main bars (ostensibly because of dress requirements); there were 24-hour licences; and large quantities of cheap fortified wine were happily sold to Aboriginal people (usually from the back door) irrespective of the consequences. Australia has no 'dram shop' laws like the US, in which a business can be held liable for selling alcohol to an intoxicated person who later causes death or injury to a third party. Even in the 1990s, the normal practices of Central Australian hotels included happy 'hours' that lasted longer than two hours; 'buy one get one free' drinks; pay a set fee and consume as much as you can; and organised drinking competitions and discounts.

Three examples illustrate Aboriginal attempts to rein in bad practice by purchasing the pub. The first was the Finke Hotel, NT, where, once race-based alcohol restrictions had been lifted in the mid-1960s, Aboriginal people had started to drink heavily like the local pastoralists and there were frequent brawls and injuries. Two local elders from Finke complained to

Carrie Nation, 1900s

Northern Territory politician Bernie Kilgariff that the man at the Finke Hotel was 'a bad bugger – he is killing our people'. As the hotel was up for sale, they wanted to buy it and bring it under Aboriginal control. In 1975 Kilgariff helped wrangle funds from various Aboriginal affairs grants and the Aputula Social Club bought the hotel. The new Aboriginal owners immediately banned off-premises sales. With the re-routing of the Ghan railway line in 1980 the population declined, the hotel manager deliberately let stocks run down and eventually the hotel closed: its building was renovated and became the Finke Shire office.

The second example is that of the Transcontinental Hotel in Oodnadatta, S.A. It sold 'flagons for breakfast' as elder Maude Tongerie recalled, and there were constant alcohol related injuries and trauma. Like Finke, Oodnadatta was an outback railway town with some employment for Aboriginal people until the early 1980s when the new rail line bypassed the town and people became unemployed. In this case, resistance to the selling practices of the Transcontinental Hotel cohered around a respected Aboriginal couple the Tongeries, welfare workers with temperance leanings; Maude was a non-drinker associated with the Woman's Christian Temperance Union and George was an ex-serviceman and JP. Under their leadership and with the support of other senior community members, funding from the Aboriginal Development Commission and a personal connection with Charles Perkins, in 1986 the Dunjiba Community Council bought the hotel and the general store. The first act of the new Aboriginal owners was to dig a pit, line up all the flagons of port – known as 'red ned' – and invite 'the boys' to get their rifles and shoot the flagons into the pit. It was a spectacular and symbolic statement of their resolve to change the pattern of drinking. Dunjiba imposed restrictions on daily purchases and allowed wine and spirits only in the dining room.

In the third example, it was a history of discrimination that undoubtedly influenced the decision by the Aboriginal Development Commission (ADC), under the chairmanship of Charles Perkins, to acquire the Oasis Hotel in Walgett, NSW in the early 1980s. Twenty years earlier Perkins had led the Sydney University student Freedom Riders through NSW, and they had demonstrated in Walgett, drawing attention to the discriminatory treatment of Aboriginal people there who had been excluded from both the Oasis Hotel and the Walgett RSL. When in 1983 the ADC bought the Oasis and then leased it to an Aboriginal community company, Gamilarai Ltd., not only were they hoping to create employment and advance social and economic development, but the purchase also provided symbolic justice for past slights. Unhappily, the Oasis purchase in the end was not a success, but that is another story.

Taking Direct Action

An accumulation of traumatic alcohol-related events such as violence, homicides and car accidents has been the catalyst for grassroots action by segments of the population in several remote Aboriginal communities. When pushed beyond their limits of tolerance, people have taken matters into their own hands, and in doing so have challenged many deeply embedded social and cultural norms as well as risked a backlash from drinkers.

Beginning in the late 1980s there was a series of community mobilisations in response to such crises, primarily led by Aboriginal women, that involved public demonstrations outside liquor outlets, pickets at licensed roadhouses, speech making, and marches through the streets of remote towns. Most of these women were themselves abstainers, lifelong non-drinkers, and they often pursued a hard line on availability, arguing for total bans on sales and questioning the validity of attempts to inculcate moderate or 'social' drinking among their fellows. In other words, they echoed the sentiments of the earlier cohort of temperance campaigners who supported prohibition in the late 19th and early 20th centuries.

Probably the earliest of the Indigenous uprisings (and the spark that ignited them) took place in 1988 in the ex-Catholic mission of Wadeye (then known as Port Keats), southwest of Darwin. And in a remarkable echo of Carrie Nation's saloon-smashing 'hatchetations', it involved the destruction of the community's licensed club by women (and men) wielding axes and other weapons – all in the name of protecting women and children. These actions were even more remarkable because they took place in a social and cultural context in which community members normally have limited powers of persuasion over the behaviour of their fellow residents, and in which there is a strong ethic of non-interference in, and tolerance for, other peoples' activities and freedoms.

In an attempt to provide a safe drinking environment and inculcate moderate consumption, a licensed club – the Murrinh Patha Social Club – had been established in the late 1970s with the help of several of the Catholic clergy at Wadeye. Eventually housed in a recreation hall surrounded by grass and with an outdoor stage for music events, the club became the focal point of most social interaction in the town. It was financially viable to begin with and it contributed to the community both socially and financially, selling limited allocations of beer in cans (rules established by the Aboriginal governing board), with its profits devoted to community needs. But over a ten year period, with a turnover of managers, deteriorating rationing regimes and local board members who were all devoted drinkers, the club became more of a liability. In the club itself limits on purchases were flagrantly breached, people gambled with their beer tokens, and the board members and employees were the beneficiaries of special perks. Meanwhile there had been a population explosion in the community and the ratio of young to old people increased dramatically, leading to a weakening of customary means of social control and the emergence of rival youth gangs, who fought one another.

Growing social unrest, family violence and other crimes, the breaking of the church windows, and a fatal stabbing eventually provoked the non-drinkers (who were members of a sobriety group composed of women and some men) to take action against the club. One day they met to plan an invasion of the club. After assembling at the entrance to the club, a senior man wearing a red loincloth, body paint, holding a woomera and a shovel-nosed spear, and calling out in language, led members of the sobriety group and a contingent of female health workers into action, wielding small axes or hatchets and star pickets. They broke down the gate and, telling others to stand back ('We won't hurt you!'), proceeded to smash up everything inside the club. Men, women and children broke open the cartons of beer and smashed their contents. The unprecedented attack on the club (and by implication a challenge to the 'right' to drink there) was legitimised culturally by the seniority of the main protagonist, but also derived from the reasoning behind it. This man, deliberately clad in traditional dress, was reportedly very angry, angry at the violence, angry that women were frightened of their husbands and that everyone

Statue of the Virgin Mary at Wadeye (Brady)

was sick and tired of trouble from grog. The club-wreckers believed they were justified in their actions because of their concern for the welfare of women and children. The target was the club premises and the beer, not individuals, and despite the sensational and misleading headlines that followed in the Territory press, it had been a well-orchestrated action. A remarkable feature of the event was that several of the leaders gave themselves up to the police afterwards and, as one eyewitness said later, no person was hurt. Two of the club wreckers were subsequently charged with criminal damage and illegal entry; the case was heard in Darwin in October 1989. The magistrate accepted that despite being guilty, their motives were honourable and ordered that no convictions be recorded and the men were released.

It seemed that a tipping point had been reached, as previously the community had *tolerated* high levels of disruption, sleeplessness and violence and responded only with indirect and non-confrontational means. Several days after the attack on the club ten Aboriginal women, all health workers at the Wadeye clinic, wrote and signed a letter to the Liquor Commission in Darwin to justify and declare the reasons for their actions:

> Childrens [sic.] get sick from hunger because of the father and some mothers are spending money on grog ... If the club reopens again we'll do the same thing again, smash up everything and that's our promise. Because of the grog our people are getting sicker and sicker, high blood pressure, diabetes and liver damage.

News of the incident spread rapidly, and the Wadeye action seems to have emboldened women in several other communities. At Nguiu on Bathurst Island (a related Catholic community), women in the Mother's Club began to agitate about drunken behaviour and threatened to close down the community's drinking club as well. Further south, Pitjantjatjara women in northern SA had heard about what had taken place at Wadeye and were inspired by the active role taken by the female health workers. In July 1990 they began a ten year campaign against the sales of takeaway alcohol from a licensed roadhouse at Curtin Springs, sales that were causing injuries and accidents in the surrounding communities on the Pitjantjatjara Lands. Over 100 women from the NPY Women's Council started the campaign with a march along the highway to Curtin Springs, gave speeches at the roadhouse, and delivered a letter demanding restrictions on takeaway sales to community members. The owner claimed he would be accused of racial discrimination if he did so. The issue was later sorted out by the Race Discrimination Commissioner.

This march was followed by a series of demonstrations against outlets in Alice Springs, such as a group of Aboriginal women and children from Hermannsburg who in March 1993 travelled in to complain about the granting of a licence to a particular delicatessen. A much larger, and highly publicised 'walk against grog' also took place through the streets of Alice Springs, with Aboriginal women wearing full ceremonial regalia, painted up, bare-breasted. Men followed, clapping boomerangs. This march was not targeted at specific outlets, but it appeared to be a public statement of social

Central Australian Aboriginal Alcohol Programs Unit group painting in Alice Springs (Brady)

disapprobation about alcohol and the troubles it caused. In 2006 women from the NPY Women's Council walked through the streets of Coober Pedy with colourful hand-painted banners demanding the closure of bottle shops and an end to violence against women. These actions can be seen as part of a long tradition of strategising by the broader, international temperance movement that involved reclaiming the streets, using performance, dress and music, and openly demonstrating a rejection of alcohol.

Taking on the Licensing System

Like the people of Wadeye, at the other end of the country the people of Yalata in South Australia had long been tolerant of some community members' antisocial behaviour while intoxicated. By an unhappy accident of history (more of this later), the mission had been established close to the Eyre Highway running across the Nullarbor. This meant that once the highway was re-routed and sealed, the Lutheran mission of Yalata – otherwise very remote – found itself only 47 kms away from a licensed roadhouse: Nundroo. Once, Nundroo had been little more than a ramshackle store (whose manager treated Yalata people with contempt), but gained its liquor licence unopposed in 1976. Apart from a few local farmers and travellers crossing the Nullabor, Nundroo's customer base was primarily Aboriginal men from Yalata, to whom the licensee sold cheap port (fortified wine) in two litre glass flagons. In 1976 it was reported to the federal Standing Committee on Aboriginal Affairs, that Nundroo sold 170 flagons of port in one day. The police later negotiated an agreement with the licensee to stop him selling flagons, so people purchased cartons of 12 x 750ml bottles of port instead. These sales became the underlying cause of high rates of alcohol-related mortality and morbidity and to widespread distress, violence and sleeplessness in and around Yalata. Thirty percent of deaths there between 1972 and 1982 were alcohol-related. Only a year after its licensing, a drinker's camp grew up near the roadhouse, and there were increasing incidents involving pedestrian deaths, killed by semi-trailers on the highway. Some of these people had blood alcohol concentrations of between 0.300 and 0.400 indicating that they had been sold – and had consumed – life-threatening quantities of alcohol. Clearly something had to be done, and in order to avoid the perception of racial discrimination, the initiative had to come from the Aboriginal community itself.

In the early 1980s there was increasing talk about the land rights movement underway among their northern kin on the Pitjantjatjara Lands, their own options for land rights, and several families left Yalata to return to the desert to the north, near Maralinga, and set up an embryonic outstation. There, they were alcohol-free, and in 1984 the Maralinga Tjarutja Land Rights Act was passed securing their freehold title to the 'Maralinga Lands'. These were all promising developments. Back at Yalata a newly invigorated community council decided to take some action about the destructive drinking. They had already asked for a police station; now they asked for an amendment to the Lands Trust Act to make it subject to the Public Intoxication Act, meaning that the police could apprehend people and vehicles and confiscate liquor. In 1985 there was even talk of objecting to the renewal of Nundroo's licence, but this did not eventuate.

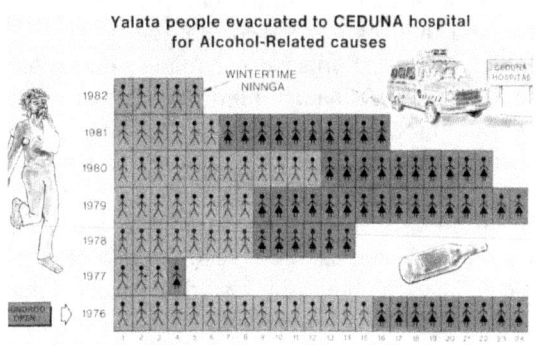

A poster to show the impact of the availability of takeaway alcohol (The Western Desert Project, Flinders University)

A year later a new South Australian liquor licensing commissioner approached Yalata council (after discussions with Aboriginal Affairs and the police) to see if the community would back a plan to ban sales of takeaway alcohol from the three nearest Eyre Highway road-houses including Nundroo. He would support it if this was what they wanted: and yes, the community did want this ban. Within weeks of these discussions, the licensee of the Nundroo roadhouse started a petition against the move. The petition, displayed for the public to sign, claimed that the Yalata Aboriginal Council's planned restriction of licences was going to 'discriminate' against landholders, residents and take away the 'rights and privileges' of the travelling public. The Ceduna district council (200 kms away) also opposed the plan, concerned (as it had been in the past) about the 'drift' of Aboriginal people into town if they could not buy takeaways elsewhere. As well as these obstructions, the bureaucratic processes and the many different players involved in the plan began to slow things down, and eventually after a year of inaction the community council got cold feet and decided not to proceed. Up until then, and like the people at Wadeye, the non-drinkers at Yalata had created their own avoidance techniques that did not challenge the drinkers themselves. When drunken visitors were expected, women would pack up their blankets and head further into the bush for the night rather than confront them directly. People doused their campfires so they were hard to find in the dark. Some women made excuses for their violent husbands: 'he doesn't know what he's doing' as one woman said. Undoubtedly there had been some dissension at home about the proposal to ban the takeaways: obtaining unanimity is virtually impossible when it comes to decisions about restricting access to alcohol, so freighted with historical associations with prohibition, citizenship, paternalism and discrimination. As well as the representatives of the liquor industry, some community members had vested interests in maintaining the status quo. The alcohol-related deaths continued.

In 1990, those Yalata people concerned about drinking tried again, this time demanding a complete ban on possession, consumption or supply of liquor on the Yalata land – to be applicable to all residents of Yalata including non-Indigenous staff such as teachers, nurses and tradesmen. At the time, regulations such as these were being implemented in numerous other Aboriginal communities, on the Pitjantjatjara lands, and in the Northern Territory. The amendment to their Lands Trust was passed, and Yalata became nominally 'dry'. The council tried to negotiate informally with the Nundroo licensee to stop on- and off-premises sales of port; he refused, and they approached the Liquor Commissioner again, reinstating the idea of the takeaway ban. Months passed with no progress, until a final, precipitating tragedy occurred.

On Good Friday, 1991, there was a car accident in which a young intoxicated Yalata man drove onto the Eyre Highway into the path of a semi-trailer. Five Yalata people were killed, and the community was traumatised. Within two weeks the council wrote to the Liquor Commissioner inviting him to visit to discuss restrictions on takeaway sales once more. Meanwhile, the community health service asked a social scientist (myself) to compile a report giving the statistics on alcohol-related deaths, injuries and illness to back up their case. On his arrival at Yalata in July 1991 the Commissioner was taken first to the women's centre where all the senior women and female council members gathered. They described their constant worry about the effects of alcohol on their community, particularly the children; they said there were no old people left because of alcohol. The women took an unequivocal stance, demanding a ban on takeaway sales and they wanted Yalata people banned from the bar as well. The subsequent council meeting endorsed their views, the

'Shut the bottle shops'. Women from the NPY Women's Council march through Coober Pedy, 2006 (Courtesy of the NPY Women's Council)

Liquor Commissioner decided to proceed and another round of complex negotiations followed. As before, the delay enabled the licensees to become organised; they created more petitions, announced they would all oppose the suggested conditions, and convened meetings with local farmers. This time though, one of the Yalata women circulated a letter as well.

> Will the government take notice of those people signing names? Or are they going to listen to the people who have been arguing for that strong law for a long long time? ... It's for a lot of the kids. How many times you see tjitji [children] wandering around here; no mai [food], no camp, no tucker. In many areas people have strong laws. Why can't Yalata stand up with those strong laws? Which bloke would stand up for Yalata and say 'we need kapi wiya'? [no grog].

Fitzroy Crossing sign listing restrictions introduced in 2007 following campaigning by local women (Brady)

Eight months after the Easter deaths, a Licensing Court hearing finally took place in Adelaide, and a large contingent of Yalata people, both community and council members, made the 1000 km road trip to attend. The licensees had hired lawyers to object to the restrictions, and Yalata briefed their own lawyer, but the Judge of the Licensing Court was under no obligation to hear from them and heard instead from the Liquor Licensing Commissioner on their behalf. In fact, the court took no verbal evidence from Yalata people, which was deeply disappointing. All these obscure difficulties contributed to the stress and bewilderment of the community members who had travelled so far. Finally though, the Judge announced his decision – to amend the licences to ban the sale of full strength alcohol for off premises sales to 'residents of, or travellers to or from', Yalata community and the Maralinga Lands. This wording, created first for use on the Pitjantjatjara lands, avoids any challenges to liquor restrictions on the grounds of racial discrimination. The ban was applied to three licensed roadhouses including Nundroo. Inexplicably, the Judge's ruling exempted low-alcohol beer (which had not been discussed previously), allowing it to be sold. Yalata was unimpressed with this, believing that 'their footsteps' would still lead drinkers to Nundroo.

It was a hugely important win for the community for a number of reasons. First, as mentioned, taking such decisive action to restrain the activities of others in the community was unusual, and in many respects culturally inappropriate in a society which considers drinking to be someone's 'own business'. As the anthropologist David McKnight explained, the prevailing feeling in many communities is that if someone wants to get drunk, they have the right to do so, and no one can stop them. The frequent hesitation and indecisiveness on the part of the community council over what should have been a relatively smooth process to give instructions to restrain highly damaging sales of alcohol reveal something of the underlying social conflicts. It took a major crisis in the form of the accident that took the lives of so many people to precipitate the council into decisive action: it shielded them, providing a legitimate reason to curtail certain freedoms.

Second, the South Australian liquor regulatory regime current at the time represented a gross power imbalance that inhibited the community from having a direct voice to the court. The Aboriginal community representatives were disadvantaged by having to rely on the Liquor Commissioner who had standing in the court to put forward their case to the Judge. In addition, the licensees, as profit-making enterprises had the resources to fund their own lawyers to represent them, while Yalata was dependent on a sympathetic Aboriginal and Torres Strait Islander Commission staff member and local NGOs (such as the Aboriginal Legal Rights Movement and the health service) to provide funds and logistical backup for the compilation of background material to support the case. It is the case that in Australia members of the public affected by liquor licensing matters have only variable rights to present their objections or their community impact statements to licensing courts or commissions, as these regulations differ between the states and territories.

The third and final reason why this success was particularly significant for Yalata was because this group of Aboriginal people has had a traumatic and dislocated background. The 'community' is made up of the descendants of tradition-oriented groups from the Great Victoria Desert, whose land includes what came to be known as Maralinga, used for nuclear (and other) tests, alongside other locations, by the British between 1956 and 1963. In effect, Yalata was a displaced person's settlement. The people had been uprooted from their previous location, Ooldea Mission, on the edge of their traditional homelands in the desert, and later they were blocked from entry to those lands for safety reasons during and after the testing program. It was a distressing history made even more traumatic by people's anxiety and bewilderment following the atomic tests themselves, the contamination of the land, animals and waterholes, the numerous incursions by outsiders, formal enquiries, a Royal Commission, scientific studies, and the confused messages in the years that followed. When Yalata people finally managed to successfully influence the Judge of the Licensing Court to prevent the sale of the most damaging form of alcohol from three public outlets, it represented a profound victory.

As I have discussed here, these Indigenous campaigners against grog (the club-smashers, the marchers, picketers, the lobbyists and petitioners) were not conservative, moralising kill-joys trying to deprive others of their 'right' to drink. On the contrary, they fearlessly confronted the licensees of liquor businesses, the roadhouses, corner shops and hotels they believed were profiting from damaging and unethical sales practices, businesses that usually refused to negotiate or to deplete their profit margins by reducing sales of certain types of liquor. As Schrad pointed out, the historic temperance movement was about opposing exploitation and profit.

Like the members of the temperance alliances of the last century, these Aboriginal activists espoused a form of confrontational temperance – at times quite militant – while defending their position as protectors of the family and the future generations. The speeches of Aboriginal women as they processed to roadhouses or gathered outside the council offices of rural towns, or wrecked the community's drinking club, told of their roles as carers and supporters of the family, and as health workers concerned about malnourished kids. Although no-one could legitimately criticise them for such reasoning, their actions and statements could be seen to implicitly criticise and shame drinkers, thus risking their ire and retribution. It was, and continues to be, a delicate balance.

CHAPTER 60

THE CHANGING FACE OF ALCOHOL CONSUMPTION & CULTURE FROM THE 1970s

Alex Ettling

The late 1960s and early 1970s were a period of major transformation in Australian society. Alongside the tumult in the global political economy, locally, there was a shift in focus to the service economy. The rise of economic 'rationalism' in the 1980s brought with it a range of new government policies and approaches. Australian society was re-shaping, and so came new patterns in alcohol consumption. Although Australian drinking culture had never been purely the domain of stereotypical working class ockers, a move away from beer and pubs as central elements of consumption was afoot. This chapter focuses on developments in Victoria and South Australia, demonstrating that by the twenty first century much had changed in terms of what was imbibed and where, along with the activities and meanings that accompanied it. At the same time certain themes, particularly workplace exploitation and concerns with drinking behaviour, endured.

The Rise of Wine

The early days of Australia's wine revolution in the 1970s were not glamourous, much to the consternation of government officials invested in the success of the industry. Drunk working class baby boomer revellers at the Rutherglen Wine Festival ended up in lines of hospital beds in 1972, waiting to have their stomachs pumped. Even more seriously, there were eight car crashes and four road fatalities on surrounding highways during the festival. Was Australia ready for this?

Rutherglen is situated on the Murray River in Victoria, but the beginnings of this new alcohol culture were being even more enthusiastically promoted further downstream in South Australia. The state was by no means a historic haven for cafe society. As recently as 1960 police had raided a wine-tasting event during the first Adelaide Festival of Arts. The South Australian premier Don Dunstan reminisced that, 'In 1950 licensed restaurants could serve liquor 'til 9, but at that time your glass was whisked from the

Watching sport and drinking beer, late 1960s (Jacinta Elliott Collection)

table whether you had finished your meal or not.' Restaurants were known to post lookouts or provide large vases on the table so that patrons could dump their wine into them should there be a visit from licencing inspectors. There was a popular saying: 'I went to South Australia... and it was closed.'

Broad economic shifts provided the incentive for change. Dunstan, in a 1996 interview with Susan Mitchell, argued he was, 'convinced that in a State whose manufacturing base is narrow, a thriving tourism industry can provide employment even in tough economic times "because you can't have a computer make a bed or prepare a meal."' Dunstan had taken note of other cultures on his visits abroad. His 1969 trip to Europe, in particular Rome, was an inspiration for his Mediterranean vision for Adelaide. He was also enamoured with Lee Kuan Yew's economic development in Singapore, where the state had taken a large role in establishing a tourism sector by funding big attractive ventures. Thus, in early 1971 the premier unveiled what the journalist George Negus referred to as a 'claret-driven plan for the city of churches.'

Dunstan is a curious figure in Australian political history. Most superficially he is known as the premier who wore pink shorts to parliament, and introduced Australia's first nude beach. He was something of an aesthete and epicurean, taking inspiration from the 19th century socialist William Morris who in Dunstan's estimations was 'a discerning food-lover and devoted to keeping a good cellar.' But Dunstan was no socialist. His political philosophy had little to do with organised labour and orientated itself towards the concept of 'active elites'. His rise to power was as an outspoken and articulate anti-communist, one of a cohort of urbane centre-right ALP figures that came from middle-class backgrounds. When in power the role of this new breed of Labor leader was to tame the socialist left of the party, and steward the de-industrialisation of the economy, with efforts to cultivate various service industries in its place.

Dunstan fitted into a particular conjuncture when there was a pursuit for modernisation and cosmopolitan sophistication amongst a layer of conservatives. Alongside dour Methodist and Lutheran culture, there was a segment of South Australian society yearning to keep apace with international sensibilities. With the guarantee

A pub getting a makeover on Gertrude Street, Fitzroy, late 1970s (John Corker)

of the ALP base behind him Dunstan was able to become a trailblazing bon vivant, the likes of which Australia had never seen.

As a vent for the alienation and exhaustion of proletarian experience, alcohol consumption – *bread and circuses* – has generally been accepted to some extent by ruling class figures as an effective part of managing society. How refined and ordered it is, that's another question. The events at the Rutherglen Wine Festival in Victoria, where 'over-drinking ended in tragedy and with it the festival', were an indication to some that a process of education and enculturation was needed for people to adjust to a new drinking culture. The Communist Party's newspaper *Tribune* took an interest in the fallout from raucous behaviour at these winery events, commenting in 1972:

> At the Rutherglen wine festival about 150 people were arrested on various charges. Victorian Chief Secretary Mr. Hamer said that a 'few larrikins and no-hopers' would not be allowed to ruin an enterprising festival. Remember that for the next youth pop festival. Incidentally, just imagine the row if a festival was named in honour of any other drug besides alcohol.

Graham Pont, who attended the early Rutherglen Wine Festivals responded to the carnage: 'You just can't drink that quantity – stomach pumps, murder, it's too strong, so that's the whole problem there. The whole problem involved with wine is management.'

By the time of the festivals, drinking habits were already changing, with beer consumption falling and wine increasing in popularity. In 1971, sales of dry table-wine exceeded the sweeter, fortified variety for the first time. On average, Australians drank 0.9 litres of non-fortified wine in 1956, which rose to 18.7 litres in 1986. The spike in wine consumption was in part due to increased drinking by women and more

BBQ at the BLF Banana Alley picket, 1986 (Liz Ross Collection)

alcohol consumption taking place in integrated social settings where family members participated. Homes could now keep a new Australian invention – a cask of wine – in the kitchen. The esky and drive-in bottle shops helped take drinking and socialising out of the pub. The suburban landscape also became dotted with free barbeques which became drinking venues in their own right. Beer remained popular, but maybe it was now more convenient just to *bring a bottle of wine*?

Consumption was also helped along by favourable changes to the taxation of wine in the early 1970s. Soon new vineyards and wineries were springing up in regional locations. Dunstan gave them a hand in South Australia by adding a licensing provision for tourist targeted museums and art galleries in wine growing areas.

The undertone of this shift in drinking and dining habits was in part a pursuit of middle-class aspirations. But Australians had always been willing to explore options for alcohol and food. The development of the hospitality industry had for decades been stifled by various protection rackets and racist laws that kept Australian culture Anglo, provincial and inward. When the state began removing such impediments it found a population enthusiastic to embrace new cultures.

Dunstan's health led to his resignation from office in 1979, but after a few years of convalescence he took up an opportunity to continue his interests in the tourism and culinary spheres. To the consternation of some South Australians, he switched his allegiance to Victoria.

Dunstan took the role of Director of Tourism for Victoria in October 1982, as well as positions with the Victorian Tourism Commission and Victorian Economic Development Corporation. Premier John Cain made the appointments, having won power in 1982 after 27 years of ALP opposition. In developing the arts industry, the new government continued the direction of its Liberal predecessors, but placed a greater emphasis on major tourism events. In this era

Advertisement in *Women's Weekly* for Porphyry Pearl, a light sparkling wine marketed by Lindemans, 1970.

there were developments with Moomba, the Greek Festival, Melbourne International Comedy Festival, Spoleto (now Melbourne International Arts Festival), and the Australian Open, amongst others. To help foodie tourism, a wine and food guide was promoted with television advertisements featuring Don Dunstan himself at the behest of the advertising agency.

It was not all smooth sailing for Victorian Labor. Part of their policy agenda was to tame successful unions that had won big wage increases in the boom period of the 1970s. The Builders Labourers Federation (BLF) was squarely in their sights, and the aspirations of the government's tourism initiatives were at times caught up in the decade long jousting. As part of a running battle with the Cain Government the besieged BLF were subjected to royal commissions, deregistration and the arrest of their officials. In 1986, a major confrontation took place at the Banana Alley Vaults site in Melbourne's CBD. This was a $4.5 million state-funded refurbishment of the vaults under the railway line, in a project aimed at promoting Victorian tourism, the drawcard of which was to be 'Wine Victoria'.

After months the union dispute concluded, but the optimistic vision for a new wine promotional body did not come to fruition as it closed after less than two years. Plans for a private company to take over the project, in conjunction with a 'Festival Market Place' proposal for the whole site, also collapsed. It was a vogue period for Labor propping up big business, and the failure of the initiative led to questions being asked in parliament.

Licensing Reform

Although this venture failed, the government did succeed in addressing one of the longest sore points in Victorian public policy, the state's highly restrictive system of liquor licensing. Victoria's laws had long been contested with prohibition referendums in 1920, 1930, and 1938. Prohibition was not achieved but early closing at 6 pm was, bringing with it the 'six o'clock swill'. An attempt to rescind this in the mid-1950s failed, to the embarrassment of many when international attention was focused on Melbourne during the 1956 Olympics.

Eventually, a Liquor Royal Commission was appointed in 1965 and used as an instrument to extend opening hours the following year. The legal structures of drinking remained a tangle of rules and regulations that included 29 license categories and a further 36 permit categories. Applying for a licence required fronting to a quasi-judicial body that could deny permission if it did not approve of the carpet, the wine list, or the position of the toilets. In one case during the 1960s, the licensing court spent a whole day debating whether a pizza constituted a bona-fide meal. In another, they denied a licence to Don Thompson, the Communist-affiliated former leader of the Building Trades Federation, citing concern for his mental health. Writing in *Meanjin* historian Michael Harden asserts:

> The powerful local chapter of the Australian Hotels Association, out to protect its interests and investments, had an unofficial policy that if a permit for a restaurant license was lodged in a particular area then all the hoteliers in that area were expected to lodge an objection. Mostly they were successful.

In 1984, the Cain Government announced a review of the Liquor Control Act 1968 under the leadership of economist John Nieuwenhuysen. Of the 184 recommendations in his report, the government accepted 167, so in 1988 Victoria's licensing laws went from being the most restrictive in the country to the most deregulated. The Liquor Trade Union opposed the Nieuwenhuysen reforms, largely because it would lead to workers having to submit to unappealing working hours with a detriment to their personal lives. This was a negative consequence to an intervention in drinking culture that most people otherwise accepted as being long overdue.

The reforms introduced six licence types. They also enabled the possibility for restaurants to sell alcohol without meals. Hotels no longer had to provide both food and accommodation. The cost of liquor licences was reduced and conditions were relaxed, encouraging European-style small bars rather than the 'vertical drinking' spaces of the large 'beer barns'.

Culture within Alcohol Venues

Changes in liquor licensing were partially influenced by concerns over drinking behaviour. They also represented an intervention into economic planning and urban renewal. Reforming governments in this era had a preference for well mannered wine festivals and non-confrontational art forms. However, this has only ever been one aspect of entertainment associated with drinking venues.

Governments continued to distance themselves from what they saw as unsavoury mores and events related to booze and underground cultures. In 1986 Dunstan was forced to resign his positions in the Victorian government after becoming embroiled in a media-driven scandal. This followed the surfacing of a photograph of him with activist Fabian Lo Schiavo, who was in character as a member of the gay political performance group the Sisters of Perpetual Indulgence. Today, ALP politicians regularly vamp to have photos with drag queens at queer events, such is the evolution and sanitisation of cultural forms.

With each reconfiguration of liquor licensing and pub culture came shifts in the entertainment and music scenes that have either conformed to (or occasionally rejected) the system. Perhaps the most impactful change for some was when the big sporting stadiums began to transition away from BYO. But in this chapter, the impact on music will occupy most of our concern because of its association with a defiant youth culture and collective acts of non-conformity.

The perception of the subversive nature of rock'n'roll (in the broadest sense) was not confirmed by any revolutionary deeds, however there were a number of social impacts.

In the era of six o'clock closing most youth-oriented live rock and pop music venues offered alcohol free events. Gigs in hotels took a few years to catch on, but the eventual result was the development of pub rock and large beer barn venues such as the Croxton Park Hotel in Thornbury, the Pier Hotel in Frankston, and the Village Green in Mulgrave.

The big suburban beer barns, often built around the boundary of a dry zone, could cater to after work drinks, sports clubs, family activities, and so bands were not always needed. Venues such as the aforementioned pubs, as well as the Southside Six, Burvale and Matthew Flinders, did however use bands to draw an audience.

Punk Gunk poster, Melbourne, 1977 (Phillip Brophy)

From the early 1970s onwards large gatherings were entertained by incendiary live acts like AC/DC and Billy Thorpe and the Aztecs, later to be joined by the likes of Midnight Oil and popular acts like The Reels which brought in electro components. It is notable that the Adelaide pub rock scene was also a by-product of similar liquor law changes in South Australia. Some of the era-defining bands associated with this development include Cold Chisel, The Angels, No Fixed Address and Redgum.

Sociologist Vivien Johnson made the case that this flourishing of live music transformed the pub into a mixed gender environment, although still weighted towards male participation. There was, however, a sentiment offered from some that live shows saw a diminution in cultural innovation as they became an environment where bands were booked based on how much cash their audiences spent at the bar. Music industry figure Bruce Milne, who was closely associated with the early punk scene, offered the view that, 'in general, it meant that the bands that catered (or pandered) to a drinking crowd got the work.'

This may have been the case with larger venues but deindustrialisation and urban decline also created new opportunities. With a population shift to the suburbs, and fewer workers around to frequent inner city pubs, a number of desperate publicans opened their doors to non-traditional forms of entertainment. Melbourne's 'Little Band' scene of the late 1970s and early 1980s was one of many assisted by failing pubs that welcomed punk and art rock to fill the void.

Despite the need for business some venue owners, due to moral reasons, found they could not stomach punk bands. Difficult conditions led to some people supplementing, and in some cases, abandoning the formal venue option of pubs by playing in unregulated spaces. The Punk Gunk show was to be held at a church hall in 1977, and when this was cancelled bands

Primitive Calculators play at the Crystal Ballroom 1979 (Clinton Walker Collection)

responded by playing on the street. DIY events in houses and halls became an unsupervised playground for groups and individuals pursuing alternative lifestyle choices. In some cases, such as the Little Bands scene, there was a flattening of hierarchy between audience and performer. A sense that anyone could do it, and a justification to rebel against an out of touch system. It was certainly not intended to contribute to the mainstream music industry, with a loose rule of the scene being that you could not have more than three songs, and could not play more than twice. The dynamic was at some level politicising, even if much of the content of the music was apolitical.

Some, such as the 'heavily Marxist and nihilist' Primitive Calculators, did use DIY venues and dying pubs to explore politics. Speaking to Jeremy Story Carter on ABC Radio National, band member Stuart Grant argued in 2017 that:

> We had nowhere to go, we were unemployed, we were really negative, we hated the world. We were part of the same critique the hippies had made of wanting to refuse capitalist society, but we hated hippies. We'd seen that they'd failed, and we thought they were just lightweight. The sense that the revolutions of the 1960s had failed led to this incredible nihilism...

While some alternative musicians crashed and burned, or joined the rest of their generation in the suburbs, the opening of space via deindustrialisation continued to play host to new cultural forms. Another expression of this dynamic came with the rise of rave culture in the late 1980s. In Melbourne, the story of this emerging subculture intersected briefly with that of the socialist movement. The Resistance Centre, located in a large warehouse space at 14 Anthony Street in the Melbourne CBD, housed the Socialist Workers Party (renamed the Democratic Socialist Party in 1991) and its youth group Resistance. Other than holding party fundraising events, it was also hired out to others. On 27 July 1991 it was the venue for Quadrant, one of the first raves in Melbourne. The event was quickly shut down by police for liquor licence violations. As one of the night's DJs, Richie McNeill (or DJ Richie Rich) described it:

> There were communist flags hanging and the venue was illegally selling alcohol. The cops came and shut it down and [one of the organisers] Mark was locked in the toilet. They were trying to pin him for organising it and for dealing drugs and he wasn't, but he was locked in the toilet for half an hour and [another organiser] Emmy was banging on the door trying to get him out. I was dealing with the police with [fellow DJ] Ollie Olsen. They wanted to arrest us because we were playing this music.

The Little Bands poster, Champion Hotel, Fitzroy 1979

When hosting events, the Resistance Centre would often serve alcohol, but used raffle tickets as a system of currency in an attempt to get around the licensing laws, or at least present a slightly less brazen target for police harassment. As activist Nick Everett recounts, 'It

 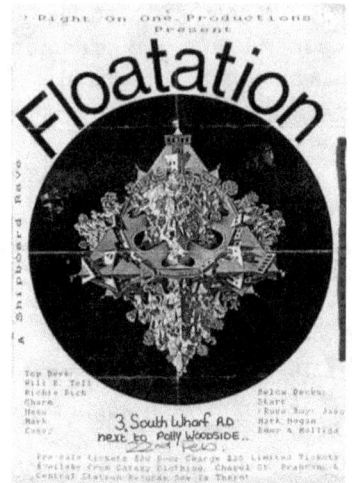 

Early rave flyers: Quadrant (design Nichi Hardcore), Floatation and Whirl-E-Gig. These events took place in former industrial spaces (Emmy Boudry Collection)

Quadrant dance party, 1991 (Emmy Boudry)

was common for us to sell alcohol unlicensed back then, that was our principle means of fundraising.' These events had long gone unharassed, possibly because of their relatively small size or because they attracted less noise complaints compared to a rave. The Resistance warehouse was later demolished to make way for a residential tower, emblematic of a trend that would only accelerate with gentrification. For their part rave organisers would move their events to new locations, including the Banana Alley Vaults.

The State's Entertainment: Fancy Art and Casinos

Underground and cottage industry cultural production contributed to Melbourne building a reputation for cultural vibrancy. This pulled in talent from around the country and helped foment a healthy alternative that ultimately contributed to the mainstream. For successful small scale arts activities that were not predicated on some kind of illegal activity (such as raves, unlicensed alcohol sales, and drug use), it made sense to move into regulated spaces once these became affordable.

The main game for government reforms has been to activate middle class economic activity around middle-of-the-road entertainment (big arts festivals, mainstream sports). The other focus has been on what could be gained by bringing in high-rollers and overseas capital, particularly entrepreneurs from east Asia. Offering a cosmopolitan tourism experience was a component of this, with gastronomy and the more elite end of liquor consumption. However, the prized reform was to introduce gambling.

During the early 1990s the ALP, under the leadership of Joan Kirner, approved the introduction of both poker machines and a casino. The succeeding Kennett Government was able to take this mandate and steer both reforms to their most business-friendly ends. It is worth noting that government reviews into gambling had been explicit that they would be of great benefit to money laundering, and so it has proven. The unregulated economy was also given a big boost in its operations, much of which was the growing market in party drugs. It is worth recalling that the same forces that jousted with the BLF at the Banana Alley picket, who dragged the union through the courts for supposedly violent tactics, also created an apparatus to enable the flourishing of organised crime and an increase in public violence.

The Kennett Government soon came up with a favoured way of dealing with fallout from the latter. Architect and urban designer Craig Allchin detailed this in *Broadsheet* in an article 'How Melbourne Found Its Laneways':

> The casino's owners didn't want to take the risk of operating under a single liquor license, which could have been revoked if there was an incident of bad behaviour. They wanted to spread the risk.

In 1994 the Kennett Government made amendments to the Liquor Control Act, in the form of a General Licence Class B to suit the needs of the casino. Allchin explained that, 'The unintentional result of the reform, however, was that it allowed lots of other small bars to set up all over the city.' Thus, another welcome development in Melbourne's culture – that of the laneways culture – was also an outcome of dubious government decisions.

Urban renewal: Small Bars and Laneways

The recession of the early 1990s had led to vast amounts of vacant commercial space in the Melbourne CBD. The state government and the City of Melbourne set a policy target of activating more shopfront spaces, creating a situation of cheaper rents. The plan of the city laid out in 1837 included service laneways, and so the activation of such real estate provided a space for activity that avoided main street rents.

Before the aforementioned casino inspired reforms in 1994, to serve drinks a bar also had to serve food. Now smaller establishments could avoid that, and with cheaper licenses and rent, there were more opportunities for new bars to open with a degree of experimentation. This was accompanied by an important shift in population flows that saw more people back in the city – service industry workers, residents, students and international tourists.

There was a desire for urban renewal, but the expression of how this was to take place was not uniformly shared. Small bars soon became a serious rival to the pub monopoly, and a threat to the brewers who relied on tying up pub taps to keep out smaller brewers. The 'artisanal' side of alcohol manufacturing benefited, as did the wine industry. A casualty of the shift was the BYO restaurant, which had been a crucial part of the transition away from pubs and beer. There was no campaign to support these venues, like there may have been in the heyday of temperance.

An expansion of upscale restaurants and wine bars appealed to most conservatives in the top end of town. This did come, but so did a more gritty and aesthetically adventurous sensibility that was pursued by the intellectual middle class. This favoured gastronomy but was also receptive to associations with provocative cultural expressions and hospitality. An example is the food and drink venue MoVida, located in Hosier Lane, that proudly emphasises their position in a 'graffiti-scrawled' laneway. This laneway is now acknowledged as a site of international art significance but graffiti in the city was, and is still, often suppressed. Describing contemporary mores Michael Harden argues:

> Graffiti-laden laneways full of fashionably dressed urbanites flitting into obscure venues behind hidden doors seem to be as ubiquitous a feature in Victoria's tourism campaigns as the sight of ecstatic footy crowds or trams sandwiched between Federation Square and Flinders Street station. But while members of the government might like what they see, they seem to lack understanding of how such a scene came to be or how to keep it functional.

Melbourne tourism has benefited from a cultural sector, often informed by progressive sentiments. The marketers selling the city know what they want to emphasise even if this does not correspond with the values coming out of parliament.

Whilst the Melbourne economy is still powered by traditional sections of capital such as agriculture, mining, and some remaining manufacturing, there has been a greater development of sectors like education, tourism and hospitality. There has been little problem in accepting the contradiction of an economy helped along by gritty urban culture, and persistent moral panics about music subcultures and graffiti. The solution seems to have been to cultivate a commodified, sanitised version of all these cultural forms. Thus musical groups like Primitive Calculators, or graffiti crews like 70K, pursuing irredeemably anti-commercial and politicised approaches to their artform in the new urban environment, have co-existed with 'artsy Melbourne' and its tourist-friendly commerciality, as exemplified by today's 'laneway' culture.

Exploitation in Small Bars

Small bars, while having much more favourable conditions to get off the ground, and thus include artists and others willing to try something different and cater to marginalised and niche consumers, exist in a context of capitalist competition. There have been grim assessments of working conditions within many of the city's trendy bars.

Hairy Little Sista is an informative case study. Located near the Melbourne Town Hall, for several years it was a popular late-night venue, including for creatives. The late-night drinking service was however, like many hospitality businesses, built on exploitation. In 2018 the Hospo Voice union campaign shared stories of several workers who were owed more than $3000 in unpaid wages, one of whom was subsequently fired for requesting their pay. Union leader Wil Stracke addressed one demo outside the venue pronouncing:

> Why are we here? We are here because we know that workers here are being paid $17 an hour cash in hand ... We know that some workers here are waiting weeks, in some cases months, to get paid. But we also know that workers are starting to stand up!

At a union protest action at the bar, demonstrators wrapped the premises in tape that read 'wage theft crime scene'. There were loud chants of: 'What's our protest? Stolen wages!' and 'Hey Hairy, listen up! Your workers are standing up!' The response of the employer was to increase the volume of Simple Minds on their sound system to drown out the protesters. In a coda to the story, Kristine Becker, owner of Hairy Little Sista, was subsequently ordered to pay $200 000 for playing music without paying for the licensing to do so.

The task of unionising hospitality workers in these enterprises has been challenging due to a combination of casual employment, precarity, high staff turnover, and the small numbers of employees involved. It has been the larger site of the casino, with its thousands of workers, serving alcohol but also performing a myriad of other roles, that has in more recent years offered more favourable conditions for union organising.

Struggling Music

The economics of the inner city based music industry has undergone a volatile shift in fortunes over the last 50 years. Few musicians have financially benefited from interest in live music, with most living in poverty or unable to make performing a full-time job. Although some promoters and venues have made major profits, smaller venues have often struggled due

Hospo Voice protest, late 2010s (United Workers Union)

to changes in rules regarding licensing, noise restrictions, and security.

Competition from poker machines has also affected profitability with the result that some owners have chosen to replace live music with gaming. Other venues have been demolished to make way for development while gentrification has more broadly driven up rents, affecting both licensees and gig goers. An element of artist-led gentrification may have contributed to making these areas more valuable, but it has been the broader global trend of state fostered urban renewal that has made city properties more profitable to redevelop than to keep as pubs.

In 2010 a popular campaign emerged out of broad public sentiment to protect the culture of live music in pubs. The catalyst for the protests was the closure of long running alternative music venue The Tote, which licensee Bruce Milne attributed to rising costs associated with new regulations. Many of the additional expenses hitting the venue at the time were related to changes in state mandated security requirements. The ramping up of these had followed an alarming increase in assaults on Melbourne city streets since 2000, and a subsequent moral panic promoted by the mainstream press. Again, the casino and large scale operations were given favourable treatment while venues with little or no history of attracting violence were caught up in an unsophisticated and highly expensive new licensing system.

A highly publicized and spontaneous protest of up to 5000 people took place outside The Tote shortly before its closure. An alliance was then made between sections of the music industry and the hotel industry. This culminated in the SLAM (Save Live Australian Music) rally outside Parliament House which attracted an estimated 20 000 protestors. The ALP government yielded to the protests, with some changes made in regulations for venues of this nature. Nevertheless, there has continued to be minimal support for this struggling sector of the culture industry, despite its oft-quoted major contribution to the local economy.

Conclusion

Throughout Australia's history there have been ongoing tensions and shifts regarding alcohol and the places where it is served, with the balance of state intervention and regulations creating cultural effects downstream. The influences on these changes have included broad cultural trends flowing in from overseas, but there have also been reactions to local concerns about public health and consumer discipline. Media sensationalism around violent acts has often catalysed the abrupt tightening of policies, but there have also been periods of liberalisation under economic pressures to support the night-time economy and tourism sectors.

A demonstrator takes aim at Crown Casino at the SLAM rally, 2010 (SLAM promotional material)

This has served as part of the context in which Australia's cultural forms have emerged. A recurring theme has been that government and business have routinely been inept in creating the ideal conditions for a sustainable and safe drinking environment capable of maintaining a vibrant cultural scene. Lacking access to cheap venue spaces, emerging and subversive subcultures have long been forced to either embrace unregulated spheres or find cracks within existing commercial spaces to operate in.

Following the Covid-19 pandemic the city entered another phase where, for some, there were increasingly attractive reasons to avoid the legal sphere of drinking venues. As a result familiar themes presented themselves. In 2022, *The Age* reported on a new version of an old scene unfolding out of difficult conditions:

Everyone is bonded by a sense of escape, a love of the music and a distaste for expensive alcohol. This rave goes all night and the sun breaks through the huge glass windows at dawn, illuminating a shaft of gleaming dust specks above the cigarette-littered ground. In the face of cramped, expensive and contrived events held in venues – and after a long, long lockdown – raves are making a comeback to rival the high of the '90s.

Melbourne's increasing geographical fragmentation presents challenges to the cohesion of emerging scenes, but history has shown that the will to party is strong, so new unexpected formations will always be just around the corner, if not so often at the old corner pub.

SLAM rally, 2010 (SLAM promotional material)

CHAPTER 61
FUNDING THE CAUSE: BENEFIT GIGS AT THE EMPRESS OF INDIA HOTEL

Iain McIntyre

As suburban pub rock began dying out in the late 1980s, live music in Melbourne became increasingly associated with a circuit of inner city pubs. Some of these had already played host to the more alternative and arty end of the scene for years. Throughout the 1990s hundreds of bands would grace the stages of venues such as the Tote, Evelyn and Prince of Wales, playing primarily original compositions in punk, folk, indie, rockabilly, hard rock, metal, noise and other styles, as well as combinations thereof. Like most of the acts they hosted, some of the venues were short lived. Others, such as Brunswick's Sarah Sands, Collingwood's The Club, Richmond's Great Britain, and Fitzroy's Punters Club, were bastions of live music but eventually closed down, or switched to servicing new markets, due to issues ranging from rising rents to poor management and declining profitability.

One of the longer running venues of the period was North Fitzroy's Empress of India. Located on the corner of Scotchmer and Nicholson Streets its profile built during the 1990s to the point where it was holding gigs most nights of the week. That perennial sign of late-stage gentrification, council crackdowns related to noise complaints from recently arrived neighbours, eventually narrowed the range of bands it could host. Citing family reasons, the licensees closed it as a music venue in 2013.

While other music oriented pubs held benefit gigs from time to time, the Empress generally had at least one every fortnight, and sometimes twice weekly during the early 1990s. Many were booked on Thursday nights by activists operating under the name of 'Blink.' As organiser Maureen Murphy recalled, 'Each week the "cause" was different and most bands played for free … Door takings went to the "cause" but maybe a little to the band to cover costs.'

With many activists fiscally challenged, benefit gigs were a key source of funding for grassroots and radical campaigns. Long time Friends of the Earth activist Anthony Amis remembered, 'We organised heaps of benefits at the Empress between 1992–97, that was how we funded our forest collective. Maybe 20 or so gigs. We'd make between $300 and $500 per night.'

With music a key part of many movements' identity these events not only raised money, but also built camaraderie and helped with outreach. Other than allowing them to show solidarity, they gave bands added exposure and some got their initial foot in the door with audiences, bookers and venues via them.

Groups and publications which benefited from shows at the Empress during the early 1990s included the Filipino International Society, Unemployed Workers Movement, International Socialist Organisation, Sea Shepherd, *Woozy*, the Wilderness Society, West Papuan activists,

CHAPTER 61 FUNDING THE CAUSE: BENEFIT GIGS AT THE EMPRESS OF INDIA HOTEL

Earth First!, Students Against Corruption, and *Green Left Weekly*. Campaigns that received support included one to defend protesters from charges arising from an Austudy demonstration and another to save the State Film Theatre. Some benefit gigs, featuring acts such as Tiddas and Nude Rain, were women's only events. Community radio station 3PBS regularly held fundraisers around town and a Christmas eve 'rent party' at the Empress featured the Guttersnipes, Throwaways, Mr Floppy and San Jose Cow Muzak. A number of gigs raised money for left-wing teams running in student elections. One show simply stated that its beneficiary was a 'Ministry of Housing Victim.'

Anarcho-folk punks Mutiny were a quintessential benefit band of the time, their politically charged lyrics resonating with many gig goers at fundraisers. They had their generosity repaid in 1992 after members of the band, and others, were evicted from a row of squats in Rae Street, just around the corner from the Empress. On the night Mutiny played a set while acoustic performances came from members of then Empress regulars Red Textas, Melt, Tlot Tlot, The Mavis's, Dangersharks, Nude Rain and the Mustard Seeds.

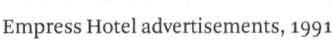

Empress Hotel advertisements, 1991

CHAPTER 62

THE SINGING SYRUP: MELBOURNE'S TRADES HALL GETS A BAR

Alex Ettling

How did a bar come to be inside Melbourne's Trades Hall, the grand 19th century Peoples Palace? When I interviewed the man who started it, **Paddy Garritty**, I asked him to explain:

AE: When you started Trades Hall Arts and Paddy's Bar in 1997 did you know how to run a bar?
PG: I didn't.

AE: What did you learn along the way?
PG: Fuck the theatre, the money's in the bar (laughs).

Along the way to becoming one of the legendary figures of the Australian art scene, Garritty found that if you could make enough money selling booze then you don't have to worry about making the art that accompanies it profitable – it only needs to be meaningful. The 'bar' in Trades Hall was initially little more than a trestle table and some beers inside an esky before it flourished into a full pub set-up and multi-room arts venue. The retail in liquor was a means to an end, what Garritty was passionate about was bringing people together to share the transformative power of art. For at its best, art could open up new worlds and go beyond a passive consumer entertainment experience to provide a renaissance for each individual. He knew, because it had happened to him.

In 1954, age 17, Garritty took to the seas for a life working on the ships: 'there was no TV but there was fucken good libraries, stacked by the Communists, over the porn books.' It was an unexpected introduction to literary culture in an environment conducive to heavy drinking. Although seafaring was an industry with an active union Garritty only became seriously active in politics towards the latter part of his 21 years at sea. This was when he had something of a revelation: 'I realised I had more to give to society. And I wanted to give, and I wanted to change. I didn't want to be a bloody ocker anymore.'

Garritty was interested in writing and had already started submitting pieces to union journals, which readily published them. In 1968 he studied professional writing at RMIT, which along the way exposed him to the rough and tumble of a certain kind of politics. RMIT was *not* one of the hotbeds of sixties student radicalism. The conservatives controlling the student union were less keen on protesting and more interested in discussing plans to start a pub. Garritty, no stranger to drinking, attended a committee meeting and asked a few pertinent questions: 'Who's going to be the licensee? And where's the money going?' He assessed that their motivation was: 'We'll get the bar going, and we'll get free beer!' He promptly figured them out, destroyed their arguments, and the project fell apart. 'They were right-wing little shits'. Thus, the first episode in the story of Paddy Garritty, politics and pubs is his stopping one. It was also significant in that he came to the conclusion that if you are going to have a bar, then it should have a purpose.

Garritty was no wowser, and when discussing this period he didn't obscure the facts: 'I was an alcoholic.' In 1972, he gave up drinking and entered a seven-year period of sobriety which coincided with an important transitional phase in his life. Garritty's partner and children were Aboriginal. During time spent at the Aboriginal Tent Embassy he met a group of musicians from Cherbourg Mission: Bobby McLeod, and Paul and Doug Meredith. They wanted to tour Melbourne and so Garritty found himself as a thoroughly immersed arts manager; sharing a house with the The Kooriers, and organising shows in workplaces during the day and pubs at night.

In the heady political days of 1973 Garritty described his role as something of a liaison between the Aboriginal movement and Melbourne Trades Hall. His work patterns as a seafarer were one-month-on one-month-off, so during shore leave he involved himself with union activities around Trades Hall. As a capable organiser with good people skills, he was soon doing events management for the ALP election campaign, coordinating performers for public meetings and workplaces.

Garritty's marriage had ended and so, in need of a new place to stay, Max Ogden, the Communist union organiser and recently appointed first Trades Hall Arts Officer, connected him with some friends who were also lefties interested in arts. One of these housemates, photographer Ponch Hawkes, took Garritty to a show at the Pram Factory where another housemate Robin Laurie was performing. The production was John Romeril's

Trades Hall Bar workers, early 2000s (Erina Watereuss)

The Golden Holden, based on a small book of economic statistics written for the Metal Workers Union. If the base material, written by Communist historians John Arrowsmith and George Zangalis, was somewhat dry, the theatrical interpretation was far from it:

> The third act was the one that always moved me. It was loosely based on an incident in 1972, when during a dispute at the Ford car plant in Broadmeadows, hundreds of striking migrant workers pushed the factory fence over. This dispute started over low pay and the monotonous, repetitive and dirty working conditions that migrant workers had to face in the vehicle industry.

Jon Hawkes had an important production role and explained, 'part of my job was to consume half a dozen tinnies before the "breakout" scene at which point they became missiles joining in the general mayhem.' On occasion Paddy was invited to help with this part of the performance. However, just being an audience member was enough to profoundly affect him:

> Even though I saw this show nine times, every night when those workers cracked up and started swinging the sledgehammers, I started crying. I may have been sitting in the audience but my heart was up on the stage and my spirit was with their angry souls.

Garritty was inspired to volunteer, and so he spent the next 10 weeks helping to build sets, painting, and unglamorous tasks like unclogging toilets, and all the other behind-the-scenes jobs that keep a theatre going. He also observed a new way of organising at the Pram Factory, based on themes of self-management and workers control.

Garritty's approach to politics was shaken as he exposed himself to the varied streams of the labour movement. A formative event was the sacking of the Whitlam Government, and his own role within the ALP in the tumultuous period after. At one demonstration he was stationed out the front of the elite Melbourne Club, as a precaution should protesters decide to angrily converge on this symbolic venue of ruling class soirees. The right-wing union officials and ALP leaders did not want the protest movement to spiral out of their control, and so the infamous instructions to the incensed crowd were to: 'cool it'. When demonstrators advanced on the Melbourne Club, Garritty told a lie to steer them away. The shame he felt afterwards was profound: 'That night I wrote several poems about my emotional feelings during this day. It should have been me who threw a

George Seelaf (left) and Paddy Garritty (right), 1980s, (Peter Haffenden, Melbourne's Living Museum of the West)

Trades Hall, Melbourne, 1908 (State Library of Victoria)

bottle through the window, but here I was being the good soldier obeying orders that I thought were wrong.'

Seven years later Garritty would make one of the most enduring memories many have of him, as a participant in the 1982 Melbourne Club sit-in, gleefully leaning out the high window with a champagne glass, toasting the crowd with revolutionary salutes. His experiences in the 1970s would develop him into a willing dissenter.

Although Garritty remained in the ALP, many of the important relationships that guided his approach to integrating arts and politics were with Communists. On a rainy day in 1973 he found himself at the John Curtin Hotel opposite Trades Hall with a number of unionists who all shared an interest in arts: George Seelaf, Max Ogden and Wally Curran. Garritty explains:

> That's when my relationship with George started. We used to go have a drink after meetings, and I'd be drinking my orange juice. You start to understand how things happen, and how the process is long and slow. Cos it took me 18 months to come to grips with this word 'culture'. George and Max are in the pub talking about culture, and I'm there getting educated.

Garritty observed the methods of Seelaf, who became his mentor. At its most basic, his approach was to use his institutional connections to look for openings, scrounge for money, and grasp people's enthusiasm with as much support as he could muster. Since the 1940s, Seelaf had been something of an unexpected leading figure in the arts, both within the union movement and the Communist Party. Having retired as secretary of the meatworkers union, he was now focused on arts and community organising, and building a case that unions should be integrating it into their activity. He initiated the arts officer positions at Trades Hall and later the ACTU, and was a founder of the Footscray Community Arts Centre. These were all precursors in developing the concepts that later came to be known as 'community arts' and 'Art and Working Life'. Through much of it, Garritty was gaining an apprenticeship at Seelaf's side.

Music became a prominent union-sponsored arts activity, with one of Seelaf's initiatives in the late 1970s being a series of folk nights every Friday at the John Curtin Hotel. Garritty helped out with duties on the door. These union organised gigs also helped make headway in the broader arts sector for union principles, such as the adoption of award rates of payment. In one instance, Seelaf encouraged a group of radical street poets to unionise, which they did at a meeting at Trades Hall. Thereafter the members of the Poets Union received award pay when performing at union events. Events were successful, but creating an arts scene out of nothing was inevitably a challenge. To ensure that artists were always paid properly Seelaf would pull money out of his own pocket if there was any shortfall from ticket sales.

In 1980–81, the pair established a regular monthly concert, hopping over from the pub to now be inside the council chambers at Trades Hall. Garritty came to stage manage these events:

> George didn't like to be out at night. So, George did all the organising and I would just run the shows. I'd be there to collect money at the door, organise the tea and biscuits, be the MC, etc. He'd put a couple of tables down, and put this big chipboard Gough Whitlam photo upside down [for a stage], so people didn't stand on Gough's face – and that was the concert hall. Up to 100-150 would come in to see the show. Charge them $3. George, he'd always have the biscuits and the cheeses, cups of tea. That was all for free.

Although performing arts had re-entered Trades Hall after a long absence there was certainly not going to be any alcohol served. Since its inception the institution had been shaped by temperance concerns. A member of the Drug and Alcohol Foundation, the right-wing secretary Ken Stone was particularly staunch in the politics around alcoholism. Industrial concerns about alcohol in the workplace would also be a central feature of Garritty's next major foray into union arts.

Between 1983–85, he worked at the Williamstown Naval Dockyard on various workplace arts initiatives, utilising a new Australia Council funding stream and growing support amongst left-wing unions. Garritty wrote up his experiences in a 1997 *Overland* essay 'Dockyard Daze: An Experiment With Art In Working Life in Williamstown Naval Dockyard 1983-85'. Alcohol was a problem in all sections of the yard:

> Up to six hundred workers went to the pubs outside the dockyard gates at lunchtime. White-collar workers drank in the saloon bars and blue-collar workers in the public bars. While workers faced the sack if they brought grog into the yard, senior management drank at the Naval Officers Club inside the dockyard.

The only recreation facility on site for the 2000 workers was a single dartboard in the lunchroom. Garritty organised lunchtime concerts, and other activities involving visual and performing arts, and opportunities for physical exercise. The formation of the Williamstown Dockyard Band was an initiative that had a deep impact on some workers. In an oral history with Wendy Lowenstein, Garritty told of a heartfelt exchange with a band member who told him:

> Paddy, you've been marvellous to us because I've stopped drinking. I used to go to the pub every lunch time, and then I'd go on the way home. My wife said I should come up and thank you for stopping me drinking.

Garritty was steadily accumulating experience that would inform how he later ran the Trades Hall Bar. This was not just gained from putting on shows and attending union committees, but crucially, from collaborating with diverse communities in the hot-house environment of left-wing politics. He spent a period in Tasmania organising with the Unemployed Workers Union, and unexpectedly further developed his business acumen when a fundraising initiative exploded in popularity: the sale of nuts and coffee.

After returning to Melbourne in the 1980s, he involved himself in various community arts organisations in the working class western suburbs, including the Footscray Community Arts Centre, West Theatre and Williamstown Summer Festival. He also produced five high production shows at the Melbourne Concert Hall for the Trade Union Labour Day Celebration Committee, pulling in assistance from comedy impresario John Pinder. They had already collaborated during the establishment of the iconic Last Laugh venue, where Garritty had installed the rigging and lights. He further expanded his abilities between 1985 and 1994 as a freelance theatre worker with Circus Oz, making good use of his seafaring skills tending the rigging of the circus big top. It was whilst touring with Circus Oz that Garritty observed how a number of heritage assembly halls had been converted into theatres for the Edinburgh Festival. Another seed was planted for Garritty's vision of Trades Hall.

The School of Design, Trades Hall, 1870 (Samuel Calvert, State Library of Victoria)

By the early 1990s the Trades Hall building was in a parlous state, and many unions had moved out into their own modern office spaces. There were less renters to pay for maintenance, and less activity drawing people into the building. Garritty simply described it as a 'morgue'. With the election of the Kennett Government in 1993, and the Howard Government in 1996, state support for workplace arts and union education disappeared. At one point the hostile Victorian Government even investigated ways of contesting the historic land title of Trades Hall in an attempt to destroy what is the oldest continuing union building in the world.

Unions were increasingly on the backfoot and directing their resources and organisational capacity towards campaigning against the Liberals. It was clear that new tenants needed to be found for Trades Hall. Starting in the early 1990s a number of left-wing cultural initiatives established themselves in the building, most notably a new iteration of the longstanding International Bookshop, the New International Bookshop. Garritty was given sanction to continue doing his arts projects inside the hall.

There was good reason to promote this cultural link given what Kennett was threatening with the land title. The building's association with creative practice went back to its 19th century origins, with the formal title being the Trades Hall and Literary Institute. Artisans were amongst those agitating for the construction of the hall, a resolution which was confirmed at a meeting of unionists in the Belvidere Hotel. The very location of this meeting reveals one of the motivations in constructing a dedicated trades hall in 1859. There was a divide in the labour movement around the question of alcohol, with some advocates of the hall doing so as a temperance measure to get union meetings out of pubs. In the building's early years, the caretaker's job description included a role to ensure no intoxicating liquors were on premises. The temperance voice was not strong enough to stop the construction of a pub across the road however. The division around alcohol was resolved in practise with the Lygon Hotel and Dover Hotel functioning as something of an annex to Trades Hall.

Among the pro-drinking forces of the union movement were the Painters and Paperhangers Society who in 1869 were successful in establishing an Artisans School of Design inside Trades Hall. Art students who trained inside the building include painters of the stature of Tom Roberts and Fredrick McCubbin.

The education of workers in creative fields continued as the building grew from its humble timber origins to the grand 'Palace of the Workers' that exists today. But as the Workingmen's College (today's RMIT) took over many of the educational and training functions, and right-wing leadership began looking at arts with suspicion, there was diminishing creative activity in the building.

Through the efforts of passionate individuals there were intermittent renewals in connections to arts. Seelaf was the leading figure in the post-war years, and coming on to the scene in the 1970s was artist Geoff Hogg, who established the Trades Hall Arts Studio in 1981. Hogg is notable for public art with a class consciousness, and for reviving the union banner making tradition. Acknowledging this legacy, one of Hogg's large banners was subsequently mounted behind the new bar in Trades Hall.

Garritty had the unfortunate distinction of being the final Trades Hall Arts Officer. Funding for the position had been lost, but he was motivated to keep things going. In 1996, Trades Hall Council had been persuaded to spend $90 000 to replaster and install stage lighting in the New Ballroom. It had once been the location for unionists' dances and was formerly the studios of radio station 3KZ.

Garritty now had some equipped venues to host arts events, but his greatest asset was his own enthusiasm and the goodwill he had fostered through his extensive networks. He set up an arts organisation separate from Trades Hall, called Union Promotions, to 'promote all aspects of trade union life.' Despite the formal separation from Trades Hall, Garritty asserts, 'in my mind, I worked for Trades Hall.' In small but significant ways there was ongoing support from the peak union body: 'I was given one day's pay a week because I had to shut up the building.' Perhaps more significantly a peppercorn rent agreement was put in place for Garritty to activate these arts spaces. Establishing a new cultural precinct in the upstairs of a historic building, on the edge of the city, was more than a full-time job.

The key turning point was when Garritty discovered the importance of alcohol in his plans. In 1997, comedy producer and founder of Token management Kevin Whyte, organised an event series called *The Kennett Lectures: Fiery Debate, Cogent Criticism and Gross Misinformation*. Whyte was a wunderkind of Australian comedy, having started producing shows when he was 14. He came from a left-wing Irish family, with Irish Republican Army sympathies, so it was not unexpected that he would be anti-Kennett.

As part of the Melbourne International Comedy Festival, Whyte organised a number of comedians, including Anthony Morgan, Wendy Harmer, Brad Oakes and Rod Quantock, to deliver a series of comedy lectures in the New Council Chambers, each Sunday at 5 pm. This was momentous for Rod Quantock: 'that's when I first started turning Kennett into comedy.' Later that year he continued the anti-Kennett polemicising with his one-man show *Sunrise Boulevard*. Quantock asserts, 'so many people were pissed off at Kennett. At some point I was getting 320 people a night, 5 nights a week, for weeks and weeks. It was incredible.' *Sunrise Boulevard* subsequently won a Green Room Award, making Quantock the first comedian to win the prestigious theatre award. He is, however, clear on his 'entertaining the troops'-style role as a political comedian: 'I don't in any way think I've changed the world one jot for the better, but I've cheered up some people who work really hard and who *have* changed the world.'

Quantock was pleased to see the success of his show help with the growth of Garritty's arts project, and more broadly the re-energising of Trades Hall. As he explains:

> What it did was it got unionists in, and it got all the standard, reasonable people in who hate right-wing governments. It was a great melting pot. When I was there, it was amazing how many people came into those shows and said, 'I always wondered what this building was', and they always came in through the Victoria Street entrance so they could see the old honour scrolls in the foyer, and go up the well-worn asphalt steps to the first floor where the bar was, and it was quite an education for people. The New International Bookshop stayed open until 10pm for it, so it had the effect of bringing the whole building to life.

Rod Quantock, 1970s (Rod Quantock Collection)

Garritty explains how Quantock's show was the catalyst for Union Promotions becoming a bar as well as an arts project:

> It was 3 o'clock in the afternoon and the show was to open at 7 pm. I said 'We need a bar.' So we got a couple of trestle tables, and I went down and got $800 of credit from a liquor store on Victoria Street near the market. Because $800 was a big order they delivered it. I got some ice. And I sold plenty of grog, so then I knew the money was in the bar. Went and paid them and they gave me more credit. And gradually the credit became an asset.

Quantock was supportive of the bar and its function in bringing people together during his shows:

> I always put an interval in my shows, so people could go to Paddy's Bar, and chat to one another. Paddy did a lot at the bar. The prices were really cheap, but the money he got off the bar he put back into developing the venue. The genius of what Paddy did was to open venues that were affordable. They were the cheapest venue in Melbourne, and they were in the centre of Melbourne, so they opened up your audience. When I was there early on, I think it was $150 a night to hire the council chambers, anywhere else that would hold 320 people would cost you $1500 a night. It would be better set out in terms of lighting and curtains and stuff, but nevertheless. Paddy ultimately put black velvet curtains in there which cost a fortune.

Garritty next took appropriate steps to firm his position. He licensed the five rooms he used as venues to ensure that no one else could move in on his turf, and in doing so created a multi-room licensed performance space around the hub of the bar, which was set up in the historic Old Ballroom. Built in 1884, with its kauri pine floor and union and social movement flags hanging from the rafters, it was a unique setting to attract people for a drink.

Garritty couldn't do all this alone. He was fortunate to find able collaborators in 'the two Jims': Jim Lawson and Jim Rimmer. Rimmer, who worked with Garritty between 1998 and 2004, explains how he got involved:

> It was about six months after Paddy had first started it. I was washing dishes, working as a care attendant. I was walking past the lower part of Lygon Street and I saw a big banner outside the building, something about the arts, a theatre show or something. So that sort of sucked me inside the building. I walked inside the Victoria Street entrance – and saw heritage. No one inside this cavernous building. I was just wandering around. I came by Paddy's office, it was him and another bloke called Jim (Lawson). I said, 'What's going on here, what are you blokes doing?' And he started talking to me about the theatre and the bars. I thought that sounded pretty cool, 'Do you need a hand?' Paddy is the sort of fella whose enthusiasm and authenticity brings you on board. We sat down and had a discussion about what I could bring to the table, which was graphic design and theatre, a bit of everything.

Rimmer describes the approach to business planning:

> There was a weird DIY energy that was happening in the arts sector at that time as well. Looking at it through the current paradigm it should have had a lot more stringency applied to business plans, procurement and all that sort of shit. But...*spit and handshake*. There was a vision and hope. There wasn't much planning behind it on the part of Trades Hall or Paddy. Fly by the seat of your pants sort of stuff. Exciting. Heaps exciting!

The trio took less pay for the first three or so years, working full-time hours for $100 a week. Rimmer was still working other jobs. They all knew that if they were going to make a go of the business then it needed more investment. Money was coming in and going out in a quick flow. There were other things that needed to be sorted out too, such as the name. The story of the name, or the lack of clarity over it, is explained by Rimmer:

> For a long time it had no name. People might have referred to it as 'Paddy's Bar', but it had no name. It was just the Trades Hall Bar. Paddy's initial business was called Union Promotions. I said straight up, 'This isn't a business name that gets much credit in the current environment'. So I prompted a moniker change toward Trades Hall Arts, which kind of explains more of what Paddy's bigger business entity was doing. And at the same time I suggested to him that we call the bar 'Bar UP', as a legacy of Union Promotions. It was upstairs, it was Union Promotions, and it kind of had a double entendre. But he didn't buy into that (laughs) and it kind of ended up being Paddy's Bar.

With a capable group of people to organise and run things, and firmer structures, the next step was to build the audience. As Rimmer explains:

> The Australian ethos of Friday afternoon drinks, knock off the work week. From our perspective it was a bit of a loss leader, I guess. The weekends were the biggest time for us. If we could start the weekends with an energetic venue then it kind of carried into the rest of the weekend's activities. We realised if we wanted to build patronage we needed to have more dependable hours. So then it moved to Thursdays, Fridays, Saturdays. And then we pretty much got to a point where it was Tuesday to Saturday, and then sometimes Sundays depending on what was programmed.

The orientation to transforming the venue into a regular bar, as much as a space to be hired was purposeful:

> It was also just a really, really good forum to bring together all those different networks. If they sat in their own cells and talked about their own shit, well and good. If they cross pollinated, that was great, that was ideal. The booze was cheap, but we didn't foster a kind of binge culture. Some people might have taken advantage of the low prices, and certainly the last 15-20 minutes of happy hour would be busier than normal. We were always conscious of keeping the bar prices not just competitive, but as accessible as possible. There were discounted prices for hirers, so if actors or theatre techs were working on a production they got discounted drinks during the period of the production because artists are some of the worst paid people in society.

Thought was also put into the schedule of events, with awareness of the importance of maximising bar sales. Start times were staggered, so with the intervals in shows and people meeting up pre-show and then chatting post-show with a drink, opportunities were maximised for people to swing by the bar. Rimmer details the method:

> During festivals, we'd have multiple performances running through those five rooms, from 7 pm at night to 1 o'clock in the morning. So we'd have 4000 plus seats going through the venue through the night. The bar itself had a capacity, it could probably safely deal with about 200 people. But in terms of the bar's ability to earn, it was about 120 people. Anything above 120 people in the bar – it had a good atmosphere and was good fun and stuff – but it just became too crowded for people to be able to get drinks so it would stop churning to a point that was financially optimum. Especially during the comedy festival when we had five rooms happening, that was a real caper. This is gruesome, gruesome capitalist talk!

Rooms within the labyrinthine Trades Hall had different dynamics, with some venues like the New Council Chambers and Old Council Chambers able to be entered bypassing the bar, a factor in programming. But as Rimmer explains, ultimately the success of the enterprise invariably had to work around Garritty's particularly generous approach to business:

> He ran a bunch of comedy shows and lost money, and so he thought he'd run a few more, and lost money. Cos he was giving people free beers, and slinging them free meals. Just cos he's a generous comrade.

The trio's ethics extended to hiring practices, where they prioritised giving jobs to artists and theatre technicians, notably those from Circus Oz, who during off-seasons would be without an income. This in itself was a significant contribution to the sustainability of the arts ecosystem. Unlike most other arts venues and bars, Paddy's Bar also served an array of social justice activities. Therefore, a flexible model was required when administering the space. Rimmer explains how they varied the price of room hire:

> We had a published price list. But y'know it was kind of measured on an ability to pay. Paddy's generosity versus outgoings I guess. And what it took to service hirers. So some rent was cheap as chips. If the Refugee Action Collective want to hold a meeting in a room with 8 people and a white board, it doesn't cost us, just let them do it for free.

On another occasion a clothing company wanted to use the bar space for a fashion shoot:

> Fuck me, charge them as much as we can squeeze out of them! So it was always a balance of who can pay what, and how they can supplement other activities that are contributing to a greater good.

This included hosting controversial arts activities that other producers and venues did not want to touch. Garritty's stated position was: 'any show that's not going to be put on for political reasons, I want!' This included the 1997 play *The Essentials*, which implicated a contemporary political leader in domestic violence, and had been jettisoned by The City of Port Phillip out of a wariness of legal action.

One of the most high profile theatrical performances launched inside Trades Hall was the Casey Bennetto musical *Keating The Opera*. There were other satires that did not have the same level of commercial success but nevertheless caused a sensation. In 2000, Lawrence Mooney and Damian Callinan's comedic nativity play *Midnight Mass* was picketed for days by religious groups, leading to front-page coverage in the *Herald Sun*. Trades Hall Arts hosted theatrical productions by Melbourne Workers Theatre, including the classic *Who's Afraid of the Working Class?* A memorable production in response to contemporary affairs was *The Torch* directed by Stephen Payne – a First Nations response to the Sydney Olympics.

There were earnest and deeply moving productions, such as *Kan Yama Kan* ('Once Upon a Time', in Arabic) which involved Islamic refugees talking to their experiences of home and migrating to Australia. There was a show about *Big Issue* street vendors, performed by the homeless vendors themselves, and based on the dreams and aspirations that ran through their minds between paper sales.

The Aboriginal music festival Songlines was annually one of the biggest events for the venue, and a highlight for Rimmer. He recalls a powerful moment in the bar space with Shane Howard performing an acoustic version of 'Solid Rock', with Crowded House's Paul Hester on drums, and two Aboriginal performers on clap sticks: 'Half the room were in tears, it was like one of the most moving things imaginable. Events like that, that just make me gooey.'

Other notable left-wing musicians who performed in the bar included Paul Kelly and Kev Carmody. However, its scope was broad, playing host to a variety of local and international bands in the indie scene who required an affordable, intimate venue.

The Hall also hosted a number of large festivals. It was the second biggest venue for the Melbourne Fringe Festival. It also hosted the Next Wave festival, and the Half Bent Jazz Festival, which was the fringe offering to the

Melbourne Jazz Festival. Write Out, initiated by Crusader Hillis, was a literary festival that existed within Midsumma, and this found a home in Trades Hall as well.

Possibly the most high profile ongoing association was with the Melbourne International Comedy Festival. It was clear to the Trades Hall Arts production team that there was potential for it to be a significant earner if they could bring production and programming in-house. With some wrangling they were able to do this and ended up becoming the second largest venue, and the largest independent presenter in the Comedy Festival. Although it led to an uneasy relationship with the festival organisers, the reasons for taking control were beyond financial. As Rimmer explains, it was:

> So we could have work that spoke more to the audience we were hoping to engage. Not necessarily around one-man shows, but also preferencing female performers. Having shows that were a lot more production focused, not necessarily production heavy, but something other than stand-up.

It therefore became known as a venue that took risks and developed artforms rather than just commercialising them. Highly regarded international comedians like Stewart Lee and Daniel Kitson could also be found in the bar, so even if bigger artists were not themselves performing inside Trades Hall, they were attracted to what it represented and helped nurture the scene.

Occasionally, Garritty and the Jims would get a huge break. It was a significant coup that Trades Hall was chosen to host one of the icons of the emerging anti-capitalist movement, as Rimmer explains: 'We had Naomi Klein when she launched *No Logo*. This is like really, really early stuff that was really galvanising the movement at the time.' There also existed a close relationship with The New International Bookshop, hosting literary events that were too big for its space. *Overland* magazine ran regular events there, as did the young writers magazine *Voiceworks*. Ian Syson's Vulgar Press hosted many book launches in the bar, and Melbourne University Press was a regular. At the ground floor of the literary production line, an RMIT writers group also regularly met there.

The bar also hosted occasions not connected to arts, including funerals for activists, which were given a powerful resonance inside the home of the workers movement. Private events were a money earner but could also be a risk, as Rimmer explains, 'nine times out of ten they were for people from the movement. Every now and then, they'd be a little bit more opportunistic.' One particular event stands out in Rimmer's mind, a 30th birthday party which was turfed out of the venue and almost lead to a brawl:

> The fella whose birthday it was, was standing at the end of the bar talking to his mates about how shit unions were, and I was like, 'What did you say?' And he started slagging off unions big time, and I was like: 'This party is over.' Turned the music off. 'You

Franklyn Ajaye, later of HBO TV series *Deadwood*, performs at the Melbourne Comedy Festival in Trades Hall, late 1990s

fuckers are gone.' It isn't just four walls and a ceiling. You're here because this place means something to you, or you're not.

The venue also hosted a number of famous political figures, including Xanana Gusmao. Rimmer recalls an occasion when Paul Keating and Bob Hawke were in the bar at the same time. Each had minders to ensure they came in via different entrances and did not have to come near each other. 'It was like alley cats. You could see them across the room bristle at each other'.

The Trades Hall Bar for much of its existence ran parallel to the rise of the global anti-capitalist movement of the late 1990s and early 2000s. Garritty himself was involved in campaigns, appearing in *The Age* on 15 October 2000 with a story of him running naked down Bourke Street, but for a placard highlighting Nike's exploitative manufacturing practices. This was during a time when there were regular protests outside the city Nike store, a symbolic target of the anti-corporate movement due to its involvement with sweatshops.

There was also a strong DIY media culture prevalent, in part as a response to the difficulty in getting decent reporting of protests from mainstream media. Rimmer highlights one particular event that was emblematic:

> Alex Kelly was quite prominent in those days. We held two *Media Circus* events. It was a coalescence of the DIY and media culture. It was more a *happening* than a conference. So a bunch of workshops, a bunch of presentations.

Another community media stalwart of the anti-capitalist era, *Indymedia*, had their offices not in Trades Hall but in Irene Warehouse, an anarchist and autonomist affiliated space in the northern suburbs. Rimmer asserts that this space, with its radical tenants and event space 'really superseded a lot of Trades Hall activity. Brunswick was kind of a yeast for those communities at the time.'

SKA TV were another outfit that used DIY media as an activist tool, and had become a tenant adjacent to Trades Hall Arts. On early weeknights the bar screened *SKA TV*'s weekly program on their big screens, with much reporting on refugee detention centres, a prominent issue for the left at this time. Videographer Anthony Snowden, who for many years has been a chronicler of Melbourne's activism, also screened protest footage at the bar, on one occasion attracting 200 people for an anniversary event of the iconic S11 protests against the World Economic Forum.

S11 was the key event of the anti-capitalist era in Australia, with three days of protests and blockades at Crown Casino in September 2000. Garritty had big screens installed at the bar so activists could return to Trades Hall after protests, unwind and discuss events, and watch mainstream TV coverage, as well as activist footage. Rod Quantock was at the S11 protest and detailed the police response in an interview on the ABC: 'I saw people who had broken vertebrae, broken sternum, broken arms, broken wrists, broken heads and all sorts of things. And I was disgusted, basically.'

Comrade Paddy's Bar promotional material

The Labor Premier Steve Bracks, who happened to be in the same Williamstown ALP branch as Garritty, described the protesters' behaviour as 'fascist' and 'un-Australian'. But it was Victoria Police who subsequently agreed to an out-of-court $700 000 settlement for 47 of the demonstrators they had injured. Rimmer explains how the bar was a central hub during these events:

> There were so many protesters that had come from out of town, that had no support network mechanisms available to them. The bar almost became like a triage space for people who had been beaten up by the cops. I know that really altered Paddy's perspective on that civil disobedience interaction. He was quite startled by it, as anyone with a heart would have been ... I remember taking a call from this bloke named Steve, asking to speak to Paddy, and I'm like 'Yeah sure, I'll get him, it will take a couple of minutes.' So I had to put the phone call on mute, wake up Paddy and transfer 'Steve' over to Paddy, and they started having this shouting match on the phone. Ultimately Paddy [shouted] 'Oh you're a cunt!' and slams down the receiver. I'm like 'Oh who's that?' And he's like, 'Steve Bracks'.

Garrity was successful in marshalling the votes for a no confidence motion against Bracks in their ALP branch. Given the state of internal ALP democracy it was perhaps of little consequence, but in the short term it ruffled feathers, making the mainstream media and embarrassing the Premier. Meanwhile Garritty was using all his avenues to draw attention to the injustices involved, including producing Quantock's next show. This focused on the S11 events and was controversially titled *Lest We Forget*. Rimmer explains, 'There were very, very few events during my years at Trades Hall that copped as much negative feedback. Just because of the ANZAC reference to "Lest We Forget".'

The S11 events, and Garritty's intransigent response within his own party, was the cause of a fracture in his relationship with some parts of the labour movement. In subsequent years there was a further erosion in his relationship with the leadership at Trades Hall. This finally

Paddy Garritty's farewell, 2007 (Peter Cahill)

culminated in the end of Garritty's tenure and the bar being taken over by new management in 2007. Rimmer, who left earlier in 2004 explains:

> There was a weird shift in circumstances happening between Paddy and Trades Hall, it was better to jump than get pushed. It just slowly became a lot harder to do what should have been pretty simple. It just felt like there was less support there.
>
> The transition plan wasn't successful. There were a few different iterations of trying to hand over the responsibility of the business, and looking at different structures of how it could be integrated or separated from Trades Hall. A lot of the success had been embedded in the personalities and that is never good for an enterprise – be it business or not-for-profit or whatever. You want the mission to rise above the people. I can see Paddy's perspective, I can see Trades Hall's perspective as well. Over the years they thought Paddy, the enterprise, had cost them more than it contributed. Cos it required cleaning, electricity late at night. It was very hard to measure those spill-over costs.

Although the parting involved some enmity, shortly before his death Garrity was welcomed back to Trades Hall for a tour of the recently restored event spaces. His contribution is now recognised with his name attached to an exhibition space, Paddy's Gallery. The broad appreciation for Garritty's efforts was evident after he passed away from Covid-19 in 2020. Charlie Sanders addressed these words to her departed comrade:

> Thank you for calling me 'comrade' so much that I felt normal calling other people 'comrade'. It's stuck, and every time I say it, I hear it in your voice. Thank you for making me feel like I mattered: to you, to the movement, to the world, and even to myself when I desperately, *desperately* needed it. You saved my life. You saved my sanity (it's all relative). You gave me love and purpose and a place to call 'home' (I still owe you about a billion dollars on my bar tab – I won't complain if you come back to collect, I swear!).

A measure of success for the bar was not only its artistic legacy, but the human connections that were formed. Rimmer shared a vision with Garritty, what he describes as 'progressive alliance building'. They were enthusiastic about the potential to bring various players into a space that could be collaborative and cross-pollinating.

Rimmer surmises, 'Art helps us explore and share who we are, and who we want to become. And people often want to do it with a drink in their hand.' At the end of his life, when I spoke to Garritty, he was intent on noting his forebears: 'It goes back to George Seelaf, in that bar. That would be the point.' There has been a connected string of labour activists with an interest in culture, Seelaf and those before him, and now Garritty and those that follow. The hope for many is that people will take inspiration from these sort of initiatives and find new ways to tell the stories of resistance, bringing people together.

Paddy Garritty, 2016 (Alan Attwood)

CHAPTER 63
STOPPING AIDEX '91
Iain McIntyre

In November 1991 Canberra's National Exhibition Centre (NATEX) hosted the Australia International Defence Exhibition (AIDEX). Located on the outskirts of the Australian capital this event brought together arms dealers and regimes from around the world. In response a campaign to 'Stop AIDEX' mobilised people involved in a myriad of political causes and countercultural scenes and gave them a clear, unifying goal, as well as the numbers and determination to meet it. For ten days the arms fair was blockaded by up to 2000 protesters using means ranging from road occupations and the picketing of entrances to setting barb-wired barricades alight. Although the conduct and effectiveness of different groups and tactics would be debated for years to come, the blockade was successful in majorly disrupting the event. No arms fair would be held on a similar scale in Australia for 30 years.

Although most of the action was focused on NATEX, other protest events were held around Canberra. Among these were two gigs held at pubs in the city. The blockade involved people spending whole days protesting in the hot sun, often on tarmac and concrete, and a high level of police violence was meted out against them. As a result these shows offered an opportunity to get away from the site and enjoy some welcome relief.

One gig held at the Ainslie Hotel on Thursday 28 November featured Murri singer-songwriter Kev Carmody. Carmody's powerful songs regarding dispossession, inequality, struggle and hope were popular across Australia's First Nations communities and the left. On the day of the show his music was described in the *Canberra Times* as 'protest music that is powerful, absorbing and shocking' with the musician arguing 'I've never seen any Black performance that doesn't have some sort of questioning edge to the music.'

Many from the blockade took up the opportunity to see him play. Unfortunately, the performance was interrupted when police arrested an Aboriginal man outside the venue. People at the gig had previously suffered at the hands of the police, not least on that day and in those preceding, and as such were quick to respond.

The man in police custody was soon freed. A policeman who had another person on the ground, with a baton around their throat, was also disarmed. A stand-off ensued with dozens of police brought in, including the riot squad. An attempt by them to enter the venue was foiled before both groups dispersed and the gig restarted. Some audience members maintained a vigil however, with one remembering they 'spent the rest of the night out there because I wasn't sure that [the police] weren't going to cause some more trouble!'

The night before, a punk show at the Terrace Bar in Civic, featuring Sydney bands Tutti Parze and Deviant Kickback, and Melbourne folk-punks Mutiny, had, despite police lurking around, gone more smoothly. In this case the audience were only stirred by the music. One recalled, 'Everyone went in tired and worn out, but the bands played intense sets and fired us up to get out there and protest again the next day.'

Stop Aidex '91 punk gig poster, 1991

CHAPTER 64
WORKPLACE POLITICS AT THE WEST END BREWERY IN ADELAIDE
Phoebe Kelloway

Workers at Adelaide's West End Brewery manufactured the state's most popular beers until their employer closed the still-profitable plant in June 2021. A brewery was first established at the site in Thebarton in 1886, with the South Australian Brewing Company Ltd. buying it in 1938. It became the West End Brewery when the company's original Hindley Street site was closed in 1980, although for years it was also colloquially known by its previous name, Southwark. In a beer market traditionally divided along state lines, West End's products dominated in South Australia for decades. SA Brewing boasted in 1989 that its 'West End and Southwark beers hold approximately 80 per cent and 7 per cent' of the state and national markets respectively, a market share it maintained in the following few years. Red tins of West End draught, with a tiny map of the state and 'Born and Brewed SA' at the bottom of the logo, consistently made the company large profits.

West End Brewery workers on the picket line, 2020 (George Ivan Yankovich)

The plant's workers didn't often take industrial action in its last three decades, but when they did they made it count. Here are three stories of times when they stood up to the boss and won.

1991 – End of Beer Breaks

While other workers had smoke-oh or a tea break, brewery workers had beer-oh. At West End Brewery, workers could drink two free beers in their morning and afternoon breaks (that is, up to four a day). In September 1991, the fifty-year-old custom was about to be ended. SA Brewing said the move was prompted by state government occupational health and safety regulations. Its spokesperson also stated that it did not want to risk employees operating under the influence of alcohol, because if someone was injured in such circumstances, the company could face a lawsuit. Not everyone thought the practice was so hazardous. Terry Carroll, assistant state secretary of the Construction, Mining and Energy Union (which covered a minority of the plant's workers) told the *Advertiser*: 'My father worked at the brewery for 50 years and he was never drunk on the job … The company does not give the workforce enough credit for being able to handle alcohol responsibly.' Treating moderate alcohol consumption as potentially dangerous was a relatively new development. By 1991, random breath testing had been used to counter drink-driving for a decade, but SA's blood alcohol concentration limit was not reduced to 0.05 until July of that year (before it had been 0.08). However, the unions involved weren't against making it a dry workplace.

West End workers and their unions wanted a good trade-off for giving up the free beer. Initially, SA Brewing offered a five dollar discount on the four crates of beer per month that workers were entitled to buy at wholesale price. The workers didn't accept this – the Federated Liquor Trades Union (FLTU) called the offer 'stingy' – and on 3 September its 400 members joined a ban on working overtime that 50 maintenance workers had imposed a few days earlier.

They maintained the work ban, while management protested that its offer was a generous one. The company rejected the unions' demand that the proposed discount be increased to $10, or 50 per cent off. Two days into the FLTU's ban, SA Brewing improved its offer: $7.50 off each carton. It claimed this would cost twice as much as the current free beer provision, which it said amounted to $100 000 per year (bear in mind, the company's 1990/91 profit after tax was over $101 million). A mass meeting was called for 10 September for workers to consider the latest proposal.

At that meeting, a matter more serious than fair recompense was brought to light. Arguably the biggest problem with the company providing free beer was that a minority became dependent on it, although overall the workers consumed more non-alcoholic drinks like tea and cordial on their breaks. Union members were concerned that the end of the custom would lead to the victimisation of those who had become alcoholics. The FLTU estimated frankly that up to 60 people could be affected, that is, about ten percent of the 600-strong workforce. Already, there were two cases

West End Brewery, Hindley Street, Adelaide, 1982 (State Library of South Australia)

before the courts of workers seeking compensation from SA Brewing for developing alcoholism from free beer while working at the plant. Perhaps claims such as those, and the costs the company would be liable for, worried the management more than the potential for accidental injury claims. A rather defensive general manager, Glenn Wheatland, said that if drinking problems were more prevalent in his workforce than the average, 'it is not because we have been force-feeding them alcohol'. The workers demanded guarantees that none of them would be sacked, that instead those who needed it would receive rehabilitation at the company's expense. The management conceded to this, agreeing to examine rehabilitation programs with the unions. Workers accepted a discount of $30 off the wholesale price of two cartons of beer a month, and $2 off a further two cartons, as compensation for discontinuing the free beer, and ended their overtime ban. By standing together, West End workers ensured the minority who had industrial alcoholism were protected from victimisation and provided with treatment. Their solidarity meant the matter was dealt with, not swept under the rug. An echo of the tradition remained: years after beer-drinking during shift hours was stopped, the brewery workers still called their short break beer-oh.

Early 1990s – Against Secret Surveillance

This is a story that a participant in the event told me at the picket line in 2020 (more on that dispute next). Other longstanding workers there confirmed his account, but I've had no luck with finding documents from that time about it. As

West End Brewery, Hindley Street, Adelaide, 1982 (State Library of South Australia)

a historian, it bugs me that I haven't been able to verify the details, but as a unionist, I reckon it's too good a story not to share. If I've got anything wrong in retelling it, please accept my apologies.

The dispute started because, as strikers in 2020 alleged, one of their co-workers at the time was surreptitiously taking away some of the stout. He would stash it in the ceiling cavity above the locker room, then retrieve it later to take home. Somehow a manager got wind of this, and decided to use a video camera to catch him out. He secretly installed it in the locker room ceiling.

There was nothing illegal about the manager doing this. The use of video surveillance in the workplace was growing substantially in the early 1990s, but there were no laws to govern its use anywhere in the country. By August 1994, the NSW Labor Council was calling for legislation to regulate it and protect workers' rights, particularly in relation to covert surveillance. It said industrial disputes over spy cameras had already occurred in NSW, and warned they would likely become more prevalent if the issue was not addressed. A Privacy Committee report the following year agreed.

If the boss installed a surveillance camera without convincing their employees it was needed, it was almost guaranteed to cause resentment, and even more so if it was done in secret. Workers often pushed back, for instance some subverted the equipment by covering the lens, while others took stronger action. In June 1996, a Liquor, Hospitality and Miscellaneous Workers' Union (LHMU) spokesperson said that surveillance of staff had caused several big industrial disputes over the past year. The LHMU, the brewery workers' main union, saw video surveillance as 'a major threat to workers' privacy,' yet not necessarily a negative. Its monthly magazine in 1996 discussed the 'pros and cons' of video surveillance. An example of the former were the high-tech video cameras at Adelaide's casino. They could protect employees there, because the security team's real-time monitoring was able to detect cheating that the dealers missed. The magazine article listed NSW Privacy Committee recommendations, including: employers should consult their employees and union reps if they want to install cameras, monitoring work performance by video should be banned, and surveillance in toilets, locker rooms and so on should be banned. Laws restricting workplace surveillance were introduced in NSW in 1999, but in SA legislation regulating visual surveillance didn't come into effect until January 2003.

At West End, the manager's bright idea backfired bigtime. The next time that the worker who the camera was meant to detect went to hide some bottles, he found new wiring, and then the camera. Word quickly spread around the plant and prompted outrage: everyone walked out. What that manager hadn't factored in was that he was dealing with a well-unionised workforce, who weren't about to allow such a gross violation of their privacy. One striker recalled 600 furious blokes yelling 'Kill him!' With production ground to an indefinite halt, the covert surveillance effort had been wrecked. The strike ended when the offending manager was sacked.

In the twenty-first century, as newer technologies are providing employers with myriad means of monitoring workers and the prevalence of surveillance has grown further, it's worth remembering that strident collective action can switch it off.

2020 – Plant Closure

In mid-October 2020, six months into the pandemic closure of Australia's international borders, West End Brewery's owner Lion announced its plan to permanently close the plant in June 2021. This meant the company was set to destroy the livelihoods of most of the 94 people who worked there. It would keep producing West End draught, a beer long promoted as intrinsically South Australian, but interstate, at its Tooheys or XXXX breweries. Lion, which had bought the Thebarton plant from SA Brewing in 1993, had done the same thing to the Swan Brewery in WA in 2013: it shut it down, moved production of Swan beers to West End, and redeveloped the site. In the SA case, Lion carried out the closure in the middle of a global pandemic. West End workers, who were deemed essential, had continued working through pandemic lockdowns, putting the health of themselves and their families at risk. And this was how the company thanked them!

The United Workers' Union (UWU), which covered brewery technicians, most of the workforce, called it a 'massive betrayal.' It wasn't the case, the union contended, that West End Brewery was unprofitable. Indeed, a $70 million upgrade of the plant had been completed in 2015, supported by 'tens of millions of taxpayer money.' But for the multinational, the possibility of quick profits from selling off its prime inner-city land – which a valuation done for the UWU put at $80 million – and economies of scale, took precedence over local jobs. Adrian Radny, a brewery technician of 32 years, told the *Advertiser* that 'we could see it coming... because of the decline in production.' Lion's managing director said the plant was only operating at 50 per cent capacity. He blamed the closure decision on a decline in beer consumption, plus increased competition from craft breweries, claiming that 700 new ones had opened. Industry insiders acknowledged that tastes had changed, but didn't believe that smaller brewers had affected Lion's sales to such an extent.

Lion said it would pay its employees all of their entitlements and start a $1 million retraining fund for them. The UWU, however, argued that their redundancy payment (4 weeks' pay for each year with the company) wasn't adequate in the circumstances: West End workers were losing what many expected would be their job for life, during the unprecedented economic conditions of the Covid-19 pandemic. Hence the union called for Lion to give each employee an additional 52 weeks' pay, and to likewise compensate contractors, who had no redundancy entitlement. These were ambitious claims, but the UWU pointed to redundancies in 2009 as a precedent. When the New Zealand-based Lion was taken over by Japanese-headquartered Kirin, the workers made redundant were paid an extra 45 weeks' wages. It was clear the multinational could afford to make more generous payouts. As the union argued, its Australia-New Zealand arm had made a profit of over $540 million in the past year, with the boss taking $2.8 million. Moreover, the workers were prepared to fight.

Industrial action began with rolling four-hour stoppages on 12 November. A week later, workers declared they were willing to take 'an unlimited number of stoppages' of 'indefinite duration'. When the company wouldn't budge, they began an indefinite strike on 25 November and set up a 24/7 picket line, with picket shifts matching their work roster. The timing of their action – towards the end of the year, when demand for beer increased as the holiday season approached – strengthened their bargaining position. Strikers' placards called on Kirin to give them a 'fair end', not the 'worst end', and they got plenty of honks in support from passing traffic on Port Road. A solid majority of the workforce had walked out: as UWU food and beverage co-ordinator Mark Whenan commented to Channel 7, there was 'very, very little skill left to run the brewery.' He accurately predicted that management would try to continue production, but 'they're going to

West End Brewery workers on the picket line, 2020 (George Ivan Yankovich)

fail in producing very much at all.' Brewery technician Dylan Bingos told student newspaper *On Dit* that managers had said to him before 'that all I do is push buttons,' but now they found there was more to the job than they imagined. Each time machinery malfunctioned or bottles were smashed, the strikers replied by sounding an air-horn and jeering at those making pitiful attempts to do their work. Supporters joined the picket in solidarity: union officials and members came, and uni students, including a large socialist contingent, spent many hours with the brewery unionists, learning from their struggle. The West End workers were welcoming and generous, with some even offering their supermarket vouchers – which the union distributed as a relief measure since they were missing out on pay – to students as thanks.

After one week, strikers remained determined and escalated their action by hardening the picket. From 2 December, they took up the slogan 'nothing in, nothing out!' with gusto. Picketing of the four gates was now aimed at preventing vehicle access to the site. Some truck drivers turned around willingly, and most others couldn't get through. A manager tried to assert his authority, barking orders at the picketers to clear the way, but they didn't move. Cheers rang out as trucks were forced to turn back. One weakness was that a small minority of the plant's workforce (members of other unions and contractors – except for a few notable individuals) had not been convinced to join the action, so their scabbing undermined it. Nonetheless, a few days of harder picketing meant supplies were cut off, so production was forced to a standstill. Lion complained to the so-called 'Fair Work' Commission (the workplace relations tribunal) about the 'obstructive picketing'. The Commission duly made an order to restrain the UWU from blocking access to the brewery, which came into effect on 9 December. The union readily complied, calling off all picketing, but the strike continued.

Two days later, the UWU announced that their members at West End had won 'a minimum of $22,000 extra after 17 days on strike', made up of:

- 7 additional weeks pay on top of their redundancy
- A 2.4 per cent pay increase
- A $2000 sign on bonus, and
- A further bonus up to $7000 upon successful closure of the site.

These were significant gains, albeit less than they initially asked for. Perhaps they could have won more if the UWU leadership had advocated defying the Fair Work order, and therefore the law, to continue picketing. However, Australian union leaders have generally avoided defying industrial law, although it is stacked against the working class, for decades. Instead, they have presided over a decline in strike action since the Accord in the 1980s, and the union movement has been gravely weakened as a result. In this dire industrial context, the 2020 West End strike stands out all the more brightly.

West End workers proved their mettle by going on an indefinite strike and keeping it up for two-and-a-half weeks, until their employer conceded. Thousands wouldn't have had their courage. They faced a company that would soon shut the plant, so fears of a lockout (or even a precipitated shutdown) were reasonable. On top of that, it was less than a year into a global pandemic. They dared to struggle despite all of that: they took on a ruthless multinational, and won better redundancy pay – it was an impressive feat. One striker summed it up: 'To think all we took on and had a fair result against such a massive corporate giant is very satisfying.' This didn't undo the injustice of Lion axing their jobs, but the company didn't get everything its own way.

CHAPTER 65
ROCKHAMPTON ACCESSIBLE PUB CRAWLS, 1989–2022
Alex Ettling and Iain McIntyre

The Accessible Pub Crawl was first held in Rockhampton in the late 1980s, and has continued on a regular basis to this day. Organised by disability advocate Des Ryan, the event brings together people to travel by bus to a variety of venues. It plays an important role in local community building since, as Ryan argues, 'A lot of organisations' staff work all year but don't really get together socially, in a fun way. It's not like we're going to change the world but it's very good for morale and networking.' The event reaches beyond those directly involved in the disability community and regularly includes government figures such as the local mayor and MPs.

The pub crawl also serves as a practical test of the region's accessibility, with venues being assessed after each stop. 'After we leave the hotel we rate them on the noise levels, the accessibility, the staff, toilet facilities and the difficulty of ordering a drink,' Ryan explains. Feedback is later provided to the pub and those doing the right thing are rewarded through positive publicity.

The event is also used as a way to spotlight the oppression of disabled people via media coverage and the direct experience of those involved. It puts people in simulated situations where they may deepen their empathy for those who face barriers to engaging fully in public life. These include using wheelchairs, crutches, putting on blindfolds, and wearing goggles which simulate vision impairment. Attendees run through common activities for a night out such as browsing the menu, ordering a drink, and going to the toilet. One year, a pub's accessible toilet was found to be useless because it was being employed as a makeshift storage cupboard for toiletries. The next year it was shut altogether.

Rockhampton Accessible Pub Crawls, 2010s (Ryan)

Speaking on the ABC, Ryan explained his own journey of understanding through the pub crawls. 'The first time we did it we rated a certain hotel very highly, but the blind person who came along thought it was the worst,' he said. 'We were shocked, but he said it was because it was so noisy, he was isolated the whole time he was there because he couldn't hear anything.' It became clear that accessibility was not only about being able to physically enter and move around a space, but included a range of obstacles affecting different people.

For such commonly used civic spaces, it is disappointingly clear that there is no obligation for pub owners to act on recommendations or the concerns of pub-goers in their community. How feedback is received and considered is at the whim of business owners. These are often large multimillion dollar operations like Woolworths, who have a major stake in hundreds of pubs via the ALH group.

The question was put to Des Ryan, 'Do changes get made?' His cautious answer is an indication of the main challenge to achieving meaningful reform in this area: 'I'm not sure. They're in the business of making money.'

While costs are often used as an excuse to resist change, threats to profit, due to reputational damage or simply missing out on a segment of the market, can be used as a motivator. Although the Accessible Pub Crawl group have generally maintained a policy of using favourable publicity to encourage change, on one occasion they felt compelled to switch tactics. As Ryan recalls:

> We'd been to this venue three times over nearly 30 years and each time the same thing came up, there's no accessible toilet on the ground floor ... it was atrocious, no care for the consumer really. When we talked to the staff there they were most supportive, they'd lobbied the management [and heard] 'Gonna do it, gonna do it', and nothing happened. They gave us feedback that they'd lost some conferences because there was no ground floor accessible venue. We thought it was crazy, the management group must be so set back in their colonial attitude.

The group considered going to the Anti-Discrimination Commission but decided to try a more direct route first. Tracking down the venue's then owners, Wesfarmers, Ryan wrote an email to high level management. This stated that having provided multiple instances of private feedback to no avail, he would, as an individual consumer, be actively starting a boycott of the venue. Ryan took advantage of the competition between conglomerates by noting that the town's exemplary venue in regards to accessibility was owned by Wesfarmers' key rival, and that people could easily direct their custom there. His status as an Order of Australia medal recipient was included and mention made that the next pub crawl was happening in a week's time.

Initially there was no reply but come the morning of the event a response was received from the chairman of Wesfarmers. This requested that Ryan hold off from making any negative media statements as an accessible toilet would be promptly installed, which it duly was.

A subsequent celebration was held with the mayor at the pub. Joy soon changed to consternation however. Illustrating the difficulties of sustaining change when faced with blinkered attitudes, Ryan and friends found that the next time they attended the venue its accessible toilet was closed due to a blockage. A month had gone by as, rather than fix it immediately, the venue's manager had chosen to wait until an outsourced corporate maintenance firm next came by to replace a smoke detector. As Ryan says, 'There's just no hope for some people ... it just boggles your mind.' Needless to say he and his friends haven't been back for a drink since.

CHAPTER 66

CHOKE POINT: INSIDE A WILDCAT STRIKE IN THE MELBOURNE LIQUOR DISTRIBUTION CENTRE

Simon Burns in conversation with Alex Ettling

In 2014 **Simon Burns** started a job at the Melbourne Liquor Distribution Centre (MLDC) in Laverton. The warehouse is owned by Woolworths and is the point from which alcohol and other goods are supplied to the company's various retailers, including their supermarkets and the Dan Murphy's chain. Prior to this Simon had undergone a physical and political journey that had taken him to the Middle East, where at different points he witnessed a suicide bombing in Egypt, the Arab Spring in Syria, and resistance in Palestine. In Australia he moved through various groups before joining Socialist Alternative (SA).

At the time when Simon started at MLDC newcomers faced a high degree of job insecurity. Company practices and the use of invasive technology ensured constant pressure to work faster and compete with others, pushing workers into unsafe practices. Back and tendon injuries were endemic and it was common for employees to be placed under pressure to return to work before they were fully healed. Despite the cultivation of union delegates by management, and the use of a tiered employment system to divide workers, a core of activists built connections and solidarity to the point where they were able launch a major strike in 2015. In the following interview Simon discusses his experiences.

Alex Ettling: How did you come to take the job in the MLDC?
Simon Burns: I was unemployed and focusing a lot on activism basically. It was 2014, I was 29. When a young person is recruited to revolutionary socialism, there is that initial period of 'this is my life now and it's really exciting, and like everything is clicking and making sense', and you just want to get more involved. So I was in that stage, but I was a bit older than the average recruit. It was this awkward spot where I wasn't sure what I was going to do. I was hanging around the SA Melbourne Uni Club, and there was an expiry date on that perhaps (laughs). At a certain point, a comrade said why don't you try out some blue collar work, there's a chance in this warehouse where we've got history, with two comrades. It was just the thing I needed.

MLDC hire a couple of times a year. Their big, busy periods are Christmas and Easter for obvious reasons. Training was two weeks of classroom, and learning how to operate your basic machine which carries two pallets on the back, you stay on the front. And the job is called a 'pick packer'.

You're engaged as a casual, and at that time it was direct company casual. You're employed by Woolworths, or Woolstar, which is the company that actually owns the warehouse.

When you're casual you spend a year and half just picking, or if you stack on overtime you can do it quicker. And then you get trained on a forklift and your pay goes up. For the first time in my life I got into physical work, and blue collar work, and really enjoyed the different, I guess socially relaxed, atmosphere that prevailed there. Much more than academia. Just a lot of ordinary people, no bullshit much of the time. A pretty diverse workplace as well, there was no clear ethnic majority, or skin colour majority. There was a decent number of women, although not as many as you'd like to see hired there.

You're in this gigantic warehouse, the size of a couple of MCGs I think. And pallets are stacked in these gigantic metal shelves, going up 8 or 10 metres. A weird place to be in. You're basically driving this little machine through the aisles, as quick as you can, and as careful as you can, and you've got this headset on, and the headset tells you where to go and records your every move, and monitors your performance, your speed, gaps. If you have gaps where you talk, they can discipline you for that.

The place is like a prison. When you walk in, you have to go through this check point, guardhouse where they check your bag and if you have any products, like say a deodorant can or cigarettes, they put a staff sticker on it, because they check your bag when you come out. If you've got anything in your bag that's got no sticker on it, they'll assume you're stealing it.

I set about getting good at the work and being friendly and approachable, political, professional, kind, curious, interested in workmates and their opinions and their politics. I could talk union with people, could trust them, but I was also careful cos my comrade had given me an understanding that the place had rats in it.

Everyone is moving around constantly and mixing. By the time I'd been there six months, I pretty much knew everyone's name. I was really trying hard to do that and learn their politics and develop a relationship politically with them, but it wasn't that hard.

You're not around people all the time, sometimes you might spend half an hour by yourself in a little aisle picking. You're not allowed to listen to headphones, but there's a sneaky headphone underneath the headset, if you're lucky. If you'd see someone you knew, you'd stop and have a quick chat. And that's one of the good things about the place, you're mostly out of sight. You had to be a bit careful, they had a small army of team managers. They were at the lowest rung of management, recruited from the workers and then disciplining them. They would walk around and watch. Depending on who you were they would either hassle you or they'd leave you alone.

So I just got to know people and started to build a – probably sounds a bit self-important – but a bit of a base. I'd made a few points about who we should be pissed off with, and what we should do about it. And got a few 'fuck yeahs' from different people. There'd never been a strike in the warehouse but there was a general level of [feeling], especially amongst the less secure, that this place is a hell factory. But at the same time, there was a very, very social atmosphere.

I eventually got made part-time, which was a big win, because as a casual you're much more insecure and can be sacked more easily, or your shifts can be reduced. Once I was part-time I stepped up a bit. I could be a bit more relaxed about who I talked to and how much I would reveal.

AE: What sort of company were they like to work for?

SB: The first thing that comes into my head is the chant 'Woolies are Bullies', and like everything else I experienced, the strike underlined that. No regard for their workers at all, no real regard for the public, just making money off them. They had this whole empire of warehouses around the country, and their orientation was to protect their abuse, basically by ensuring, as much as they possibly could, that workers couldn't really organise in any serious way.

There was definitely not a culture of getting into the product. I suspect because there were cameras everywhere, and if you were caught you'd be gone. Obviously this didn't involve any human endangering accidents, but booze wasting accidents were hilarious. It's just a little bit of chaos, a bit of a break from the just sheer boredom. Sometimes someone would quite deliberately drop a box of wine or something in the middle of the aisle and block it up. Because the aisles are so thin you're then stuck in there until they clean it up. You could rearrange a pallet of booze, and have a chat to your mates, and appreciate that someone blocked up the aisle for a little while.

AE: How did the company try to make more money?
SB: The obvious one is the speed. There's an instant connection between injuries and profits. The reason you get injured is because they want you to go fast, all the time. And they've got the technology to monitor and surveil, to make sure you are going fast all the time. And there's a culture where everyone knows that if you work at a higher rate you're more likely to progress. So Woolworths just squeeze, squeeze more and more out of you by making you go faster. One of the ways that the company pressured you was casualisation. They'd hold your job security over your head to intimidate you.

There were fights around breaks. The piddly little breaks you had. They sacked one comrade for running upstairs, it would have taken him like three minutes, to grab a packet of chips. He didn't have a break on his shift and he was famished. When he got back onto the floor they sacked him. That's how intense it was.

MLDC workers, 2015 (*Red Flag*)

I really can't underline how alienating it is to have your entire human labour controlled by a computer. You're basically just an appendage for this computer. And that's all part of the strategy to make you go quicker and give you a feeling of powerlessness, undermine your sense of confidence and collectivity. Before they had that technology I think there was more of an ethic of 'get away with what you can'.

Whenever it came to an Enterprise Bargaining Agreement (EBA) they had their rat delegates in. They'd mobilise a lot of resources. There's quite a bit of socialising between low level management and the workers, and they'd be making the argument that 'Oh the company is very reasonable, blah blah blah. Don't want the company to go broke.'

AE: Did the union have any presence in the workplace?
SB: Yes, they did with National Union of Workers (NUW) delegates. For all intents and purposes it was a pretty well functioning delegate team. But to step back from it, there were some rat delegates who were less capable and less willing to stick their neck out. However, part of the whole rat cultivation strategy is that sometimes they can be successful. If the company recognises that me or other delegates are real troublemakers, they just dig their heels in. But if you go to the rats, then they have their own little networks of patronage and sometimes they can organise small concessions. So, the company built their rat delegates into semi-passable, functionaries. They were totally hostile to organising or making progress with our conditions, but had a nice cushy job and the promise of a nice managerial position at the end of it.

The company also worked on Health and Safety Representatives (HSRs) and did even better with them. I think they recognised that the HSRs had much more power to shut down work.

When Barnawartha, another Woolies warehouse, in NE Victoria, went on strike, our warehouse took the strike work, and the rat delegates came in on a Sunday to do the scab

MLDC picket line, 2015 (*Red Flag*)

work. I feel like Woolworths's strategy was always, if you don't have a rat in a delegate team, cultivate one.

When I came in the general attitude was, 'This union is fucking useless and it doesn't fight.' That was pretty much wall to wall, among the people I'm associating with. And I'm at the bottom rung with all the young casuals, people who might want to work here for another 10 years, or they might be passing through uni or whatever. But their conditions are harder than everyone else and they're pissed off that the union is not fighting around any of this stuff.

Sometimes the more angry people would be like 'fuck this union', let's quit or join another union like the Transport Workers Union (TWU). Internally I'd laugh and externally I'd say, 'The TWU or the Shop Distributive Association (SDA) is not going to fight harder than the NUW. They're going to fight against us. There's no way around it, we just have to build here, and I think that's with the union we have. I don't love them but the way to make them fight is not to shop around for a different union that's worse – it's to pressure the current one from within.' And that's what we did.

It was hard for management to partition us like other workplaces. But they did it in other ways, using not space but hierarchy. You start off as a casual, called Level 1, where you only pick. When you go to level 2 you get your forklift or your loader. Then you had another tier above called 'part-time', and another one above that called 'full-time'.

There was also a division between afternoon and the morning shifts. The warehouse was operating 19 hours a day and generally casuals would move between the two shifts. To keep your job you have to have open availability and say that you'll work anywhere between 5 am and 11 pm. Ultimately I went onto the afternoon shift.

The real thorn in our side was that there was a real fortress of reaction and anti-struggle in the day shift, and it was hard for us to do much about it. Whereas the afternoon shift was more our fortress as a comrade who had been there for years had fought for people. The afternoon delegates had been rats but they were rolled. My comrade's support base came from years and years of chipping away.

A lot of people were pissed off at the day shift and you'd have to be like, 'Yep management has its rats but the people in that shift are workers, and the only way we're going to get anything done here is by overcoming that division, not by entrenching it.' Honestly in hindsight, I don't think we ever managed to. Like the strike was an opening where it was dismantled a little bit. But the strike didn't last forever.

Before the strike the union didn't seem to have much of an orientation at all. They were pretty friendly towards us. Like, 'Oh here's a few Trots who want to help us organise. Good... to some extent.' They weren't red hot. You'd see the organiser every now and then, but they weren't running campaigns.

After the strike was a bit of a different story, the union started talking much bigger. They had a campaign that was called 'One Big Shed', which was, 'We're gonna get pattern bargaining for the entire Woolworths slash maybe entire supermarket chain.' And that did eventuate.

But earlier on, they weren't doing a hell of a lot to push things forward.

Pickets outside the MLDC warehouse, 2015 (*Red Flag*)

AE: What was the general awareness of the union in the workplace?
SB: Totally fine. I was knocked flat by it. For me that was an educational moment. To be in a blue collar workplace where you just need your fucking union to fight for you otherwise you're going to get hurt, or fucked over.

I was surprised and humbled, as a Trot going in there with highfalutin' ideas. All well and good, but I didn't know much about unionism, or only what I knew I'd learned in university and the NTEU, so very different. Old timers would tell stories about strikes and pickets in Kmart warehouses and Target warehouses, y'know Storeman and Packer days (the precursor union to the NUW). Unfortunately there was a tendency that the older people got, the more conservative they were. So I was lucky enough to get a couple of those little snippets. Y'know, 'It was the glory days, it was all a bit crazy but now we've moved on.'

Whereas the young people were less experienced, but less cynical and less blasé. There was a little bit of elitism cultivated by the company through their hierarchy of roles, but amongst the general population of pickers, even the way the older people would interact with you, it was just very egalitarian. The general ethic of solidarity was just woven into the life of the workers there, probably much like any warehouse. You're there for 40 hours a week, you get each other by with jokes and stories, and chats about sport and movies and shit like that. So even though there wasn't a lot of union experience there, there was a sense of, 'We know what a union does, or what it's meant to do.' And I think there was an underlying ethic, which was new to me, of 'We're ready to go if need be.'

AE: Did people know about the militant goings on at the Woolworths Broadmeadows warehouse?
SB: Yep, to the extent that a comrade could get the story out. I talked to people about it. And people do move around the Woolworths warehouse system a bit. People were like, 'Yeah, Broady (Broadmeadows) is a little bit harder than us.'

In terms of the wider warehouse industry, I think we were thereabouts when it came to wages. Like not great, not as good as Broady. And that was one of our arguments. 'The reason that Broadmeadows has better conditions is that they fought for it. They've been on four or five strikes in the last few years.' I don't think people had the sense that we had the greatest conditions. But it's not like there was a group of people running around the warehouse saying, 'Fuck Woolworths, we want more money.' And also you could also see the more conservative arguments go around, especially when Broady shut, like, 'See, that's what happens when you fight for better conditions.'

AE: What was your attitude to unions, in relation to your socialist politics?
SB: The watchword I'd always use was: 'I'm with the officials as long as they're with the workers, if the officials aren't with the workers I'm with the workers.' The main thing is building amongst workers, not currying favour with the officials or trying to appeal to them to fix things.

Obviously, that's without talking about when there's actually a revolutionary situation or whatever. Just normal union times. I did fuck up a lot of stuff. Just being a bit hot headed towards them. It's not an easy balance to strike when union officials are being hostile.

AE: So how did the strike start?
SB: It began with the announcement of outsourcing. They were going to bring in a labour hire agency to fulfil their casual labour requirements. That meant a complete lowering

of the security of everyone's work as well as insecurity in terms of you might not get told your shifts until 4 or 5 am each morning.

It was also the injury thing. If you're on labour hire, you have much less access to the same rights. You're not going to have the same support if you're injured at work. And the pressure to work harder and faster will be greater because you're insecure.

AE: After the announcement of the introduction of labour hire, how did you respond?
SB: There was good enough communication in the workplace that everyone soon knew about it. And there was a bit of an energy around it that, yep, not happy.

Under advice from a comrade in SA, I called the organiser and said this is happening and blah blah blah, and he said, 'There's not much we can do about it.' There was nothing in the Enterprise Bargaining Agreement (EBA) in terms of what was written down. But I believe the company had given an understanding during the previous EBA negotiations that they wouldn't do it. That was a part of why the workers were annoyed, because it was a kick in the face.

A group of us basically sat down and said, 'Well how are we going to build on this sentiment that's there, this anger?' And add that we should do something about it.

Our first objective was to get a mass meeting. We needed to get workers together, have some chanting, a few fiery speeches. I think the union, they were lukewarm about that. So, we had to operate under the radar.

We got cheapo sheets of fluro pink, fluro yellow, sticker paper. We got them printed to say 'No labour hire at MLDC'. We cut them out, and there were hundreds of them, and we gave them out one day. Secretive drops, bags in the locker room. Pretty soon, stickers popped up everywhere.

Maybe 60 per cent or 70 per cent of people had stickers on and it climbed up from there. Suddenly they were blanketing the warehouse, and that was a moment of victory for us. Management were pissed off, like really scared, and really angry that we'd done that.

I think the key point was that every worker in the warehouse knew that they weren't alone. There were heaps of good unionists in the place, but they'd all say pretty much the same thing: 'Oh, but everyone else here is shit.' That was the line that the industrially experienced people would say. But suddenly it's like, 'Oh, you're not wearing a sticker? But all these casuals are wearing these stickers… Oh you're not the *big union man* anymore. You better wear a sticker.' We got into it that way, and it was hard for anyone to disagree.

We did have to counter the arguments of 'Well, it doesn't affect us, so why would we care?' And we said, 'Well "Touch one, touch all", they're going to breed a new generation of workers to replace you – who are less secure, and they can use that to wedge down all our conditions.' It was a pretty basic union solidarity argument. We're all working in the same warehouse, y'know.

There were lots of late night calls and call lists. Lots of us just organising in the background, as the SA brains trust. More and more meetings were called, and the union was pulled into attending.

Eventually after meetings at the gate, in the tea room and what not, a lot of leafleting, me smuggling leaflets in etc, we had a meeting

Pickets outside the MLDC warehouse, 2015 (Kath Larkin)

of maybe 100 people outside on the road, including speeches by the delegates. People got fired up and then there was a strike vote.

I must underline that none of us agitating believed a strike would happen. We'd never been there before, but we were talking at the pub beforehand with some of the delegates and the idea was floated. 'Oh yeah, people have been talking about just blocking up the place, and just going all out.' And people were like, 'Nah probably won't happen, there's all these barriers to that.'

Nonetheless, we said 'fuck it', and floated it with one of our delegates and he got up at the meeting and gave this fiery argument about doing everything we had to do to win. And the vote went up for a strike, pretty much unanimously. Well there may have been some abstentions, but there were not a lot of nays. We were like 'What the fuck?' The vote on a Sunday was for an all-out strike and picket, starting after the weekend.

On the way home, I'm on Bell Street, and I saw Ezekiel Ox. I knew him through anti-fascist work and said 'We've got a picket tomorrow and I'm not sure how it's going to go, but could you come and help us MC. Because you can say all this mean shit about Woolworths that no one will say on the mic (laughs).' Just that picket line thing of trying to fill in time and keep people energised. So he brought his sound system down and blasted management with Ezekiel Ox hate and fury, it was so good.

On the Monday morning, which is a very important day for the warehouse, I got there at 4 or 5 am, barely slept. Not really knowing who was going to turn up, but enough people rocked up to have a presence. And pretty soon on the first day, suddenly this situation you didn't expect is unfolding. You're in a strike. And me and my comrade are leading it.

From early on it was good participation on all fronts and we blocked all the gates. We had people, mainly Maori and Islander people bringing in pallets. Another family brought drums and wood. Everyone was bringing wood.

We established a 24 hour presence. That was our argument. 'Are we doing a symbolic process, or are we here to stop things up and win?' So we were really feverishly doing that, this was our moment to shine.

I remember distinctly on the Monday, the organiser came down. And from the start it became apparent that his orientation was to hose things down. There was a meeting of the delegates, I wasn't a delegate at that stage. Our demands were pretty clear: no labour hire and no repercussions. The negotiators came out with some kind of compromise deal that didn't meet either of those.

Everything was poised on a knife's edge. It was getting late, people were not sure about anything. Some of the more conservative people were like, 'Yeah, maybe we are asking a bit too much, and what if the company is right?' And then one person spoke up and ripped it apart. I jumped in and backed him up. And we won a vote to basically say, 'Fuck off negotiators. We're going to stay here all night.' It was at that point that the same speaker took up the megaphone and started singing 'We're already winning' to the tune of 'We're Not Gonna Take It' on the megaphone.

AE: What did the bosses do to undermine the hard picket?
SB: We know they used a scab warehouse. Laverton North is just a sea of warehouses. But the thing is, they couldn't use their own warehouses. Logistics involves such intensive investment, and to get that competitive edge, there is no fat in the entire system. You save money by not having dead capital hanging around your business. Instead of having warehouses full of shit that just sits there, you only get it when you need it. It comes and it pretty much doesn't stop moving until it gets to the shop. And it doesn't go to a supermarket and sit out back in their storeroom. If they don't have it on the shelf, it's not there, and they're waiting for the next order.

These warehouses, they're operating at max capacity all the time. There's no empty space. That sort of environment abhors a vacuum. So during a strike they can't just go, 'Aw Broady, clear us an aisle for liquor.' I think there are contracted warehouses where they can get at least a few basic lines of high volume stuff through. But not enough to effect a strike.

AE: When did you become a delegate?
SB: It might have been the second day that I was elected. The organiser was like, 'You're having a lot of really heavy conversations here, you're at risk, so maybe you should back down'. 'Oh true. What if I was a delegate?' (laughs) There was a vote on the picket line and, again with maybe some abstentions, there was a pretty rousing unanimous vote in favour by the people there. Suddenly I was a delegate and I'm on the table witnessing the negotiations. I have access to megaphones, a responsibility to democratically lead the strike, and also to lead the more radical people, and I'm quite conscious of that.

Their strategy seemed to be attrition, just wear us down at the negotiating table. And from the start the officials' discussions with the delegates were not, 'How do we spread this struggle or intensify it until we win our demands, which have been given to us clearly by the workers?' It was, 'What concessions are we willing to accept? We have to be realistic.'

I was just disgusted by it all. And getting increasingly ragged. I probably spoke up a bit beyond my authority as a brand new delegate and shared a lot of open contempt to the big HR people that were around.

On the Wednesday there were more negotiations, more toing-and-froing, more of pretty much the same, keeping the fires burning. There were discussions about a union picnic day, 'Oh we're going to have a big solidarity march, get all the unions involved, send the call out brothers and sisters.' MUA people started coming. The real seafarer militant people.

There were big debates going on about whether we were having a hard picket line or not. And a lot of inexperienced people were like, 'Oh maybe we don't have to.' And so we, and other friendly local lefties, were burgeoning the argument, inoculating people against the bullshit.

Things were solid, and we knew our job was to keep morale up. The strategy from the officialdom, and I believe the company, was to keep the delegates away from the picket line. And away from where they needed to be, having conversations, in touch with the workers, the mood of the strike.

We had picket captains. We were playing games. I tried to get a game going of pretending someone was trying to get through the picket line and you had to stop them without being too violent (laughs).

I was sleeping when the scabs came, it was quite early. There was a certain detachment of people, quite independent of me, that managed to make it really, really difficult. Woolworths did get a few people through the gates, but not a lot. No trucks were getting in or out.

There were pictures of empty shelves at Dan Murphys and BWS that people were sending in. They were getting shared around. And messages of support from various people, especially people from SA networks, and union networks.

Sometime on the Wednesday I led a vote to withdraw our negotiators. It was increasingly hard to contain what looked like a really

Solidarity shown by other workers with MLDC strikers, 2015 (*Red Flag*)

concerted push, led by the officials, and carrying the more conservative or fearful delegates with them, towards selling out very clearly democratically voted demands. I'm trying to act like there's a strike committee. They're acting like we're a bunch of obedient little delegates who should be doing what we're told, and we're very much not that.

That's the moment when the red flags started being raised in the upper echelons of the union. On the Thursday all the brass were down there, all the nice solidarity stuff was called off. It was like, 'Nup we are hosing this shit down.' The lawyer came and gave this speech about how we could all lose our houses and cars, it was very doom and gloom.

Injunctions, that was their big thing. The argument was made that there was going to be an immediate court order for us all to pay a fine, personally, for illegal industrial action. Really? Think about the logic of Woolworths actually following through with that. How would they achieve industrial peace?

The officials would put these arguments out, and I said, 'Respectfully, I think it should be argued out politically, and democratically voted on by the workers.' I didn't know it at the time, but I was persona non grata for them, y'know the crazy Trot. 'We need to end this craziness.'

By the end of Thursday I'd lost my voice from yelling every day on the megaphone, and so had one of our angry dudes. The comrade who had been in the warehouse for years got to a point where he was so tired from just all the constant sparring at the negotiating table, dealing with bullshit, dealing with layers of extra bullshit from the bullshit, from not doing the things we needed to be doing.

I tried to get us out of that, and I guess it worked on one level, but it also brought the wrath of the union down on the strike. I was later chastised by leading SA comrades, who said, 'You had good instincts but you didn't understand a few things like this strike will be won at the negotiating table.' And in the end it was, because a union leader went in and got a settlement which, ultimately, I would say was a win. We eventually stopped labour hire coming in. The company dropped that after a while, quietly.

In the meantime there was a lot of organising between Broady and ourselves. We heard Broady was ready to strike in solidarity. They'd had a big meeting. We were getting so much support. The truckies supported us. Community support was coming in. They'd mentioned it in parliament.

Again I have to emphasise that all the SA people were like, 'Is this really happening? Three days ago we were in meetings thinking should we even raise a strike, or should we be talking about sick-offs or something? Now we were talking about going through the weekend, bringing the whole company to its knees.' But in the end a bigger campaign was not to be.

The problem was the officials. And me probably being a little hot headed at times fed into it. But they were always going to take control at some point and get an outcome at the negotiating table. Cos you know, all strikes short of a revolution end in a settlement, right. Which was apparent to many people in SA, but not me, for a while there. Because I was fucking injured and soul sore from just how bad it was.

On the Thursday there was toing-and-froing. It had been made clear to me by one comrade that I should stop speaking because there was a section of right-wing workers, where I was just throwing fuel on the fire of their red baiting. Another comrade was saying, 'If you don't make a speech, we'll never know what could have happened, and you'll regret it.'

I didn't even know what I was going to say, I just put my hand up. And a lot of people had already spoken and I made the case for how much we'd brought the company to its knees, and how much power we had, and how much our power was growing, and the answer was to spread out and keep fighting, we'd already sacrificed so much, blah blah blah.

And then the vote happened and it was two thirds to go back, and one third to continue. I pretty much remember every face of the people who wanted to keep going. The mood was relieved, and sorta disappointed, but sorta joyful. We all just said our goodbyes and drove off, had a few beers, went back to Trades Hall, and debriefed.

AE: What were things like after the strike?
SB: It was pretty bad going back. I was firing on all cylinders: 'We need a fight!' Everyone was more bruised and battered than I thought. I started building up a bit of a base around myself, especially with young casuals. I got in about every little thing that they got hassled or bullied about. Learning the ropes and making it so it would be hard to sack me.

Woolworths were on the prowl, they got their big dogs in from HR. One of them had his office in the front window, which you had to walk past every day when you went in. He put an NUW hat in his window. Like I'm here to take heads and it's going to be the ones that belong to the guys who wear these. I eventually went in and after a discussion I got the hat and gave it to someone who needed it.

MLDC picket line, 2015 (James Plested)

And they got their rats onto me. One of them made a bashing threat. A guy who'd been a picket captain. Didn't scab, but worse maybe.

One thing that happened after the strike is that the company had promised in the EBA that there'd be this thing called a forklift bonus, a couple of hundred bucks. And they somehow weaselled out of it. It was in the courts, and taking its time, and no one was pushing it. After we had the wildcat strike, suddenly things got pushed through to Fair Work Australia. I went there and heard the Commissioner say, 'I recommend that Woolworths use this bonus for the sake of peace.' So that was really sweet, we certainly played a part in that.

There was another campaign that came up and seemed like it had legs. A woman who was pretty well liked came to me incensed. She had a back injury and the doctor had instructed her to keep moving, play a bit of light sport. She was playing hockey one weekend and a manager rocked up and took photos of her to management. Suddenly she's in a 'disciplinary process', so called.

I was ropable. The first thing we always said as delegates was, 'Never, ever go to a meeting with the company without a delegate and always go to your own doctor.' It was known in the warehouse that if you went through company people they would not look after you. The company responded to that with, 'We're going to send people along to your doctors appointments.' So we said, 'What does that mean, do they sit outside, do they sit out in reception?' They said, 'No, they go into the appointment.' What business does management have to swoop in on our weekend lives and our doctors appointments?

We ran a campaign about management spying. I was running around campaigning and not working. Very obviously not working.

There had been a bit of a bitter mood after the strike as we sorted through the chaos of backed up product, just overtime for weeks and weeks. And eventually things got back to an even keel. And that's when the HR attack came again. Everything escalated and they were out for blood.

In the end, the lack of politics of the day sort of won out. A political attack on me came dressed up as a reasonable workplace management issue, and that was good enough to get people who were already a bit worn down to say, 'Oh yeah.' Things reached a point where the company felt they could get away with sacking me and they could.

What followed was a desperate campaign to save my job, and that of other comrades who were targeted, which involved a fluro green sticker saying 'Save the MLDC Three'. In the end we saved one job, but they did sack me.

AE: What role did Socialist Alternative and its members play in all this industrial activity?
SB: If I was talking to a fellow member of the far left, I'd say that one of the key lessons of the strike is that long term orientation to key workplaces can pay off, given the right circumstances and good luck. Strikes don't just happen like lightning bolts, they're made through organising, and the patient and tenacious efforts of socialists a lot of the time.

That was certainly the case with this strike. One comrade had been there for seven years before SA met him at a refugee rally. And then another ended up working there for six months. Then I came in. And then a year after that is when the strike happened.

The relationship between the long term employee and a leading SA member who was helping us with the brains trust, and who has spent years of being patient, humble, reading, going to picket lines, talking to workers, etc, was also central. Organisations at that level can afford to put resources into a full time industrial organiser.

Even though we weren't always confident it would happen, I don't think the strike would have happened without the intervention of organised socialists. And I reckon, if any one of the socialists in the picture were missing, it wouldn't have happened either. There were just moments where it could've all died. And there were moments where each of us had a key intervention and managed to push things forward. Rather than letting the circling wolves, the more conservative approach to unionism, stop things.

In regards to being a socialist in the workplace, that was something I thought about a lot. Whether there would come a time when someone would out me in front of meeting: 'Ah he's a dirty red!' or whatever. I was hiding who I was when I first went in there, for obvious reasons. And then I progressively revealed myself to people I trusted. And tried to camouflage myself from management, which I did successfully, basically up until the strike.

After a while it was just chill, I sold *Red Flag* to people, talked about articles I'd written for the paper. At the same time, and I think it is pretty important to note, my orientation in going into that workplace was not that we were going to recruit droves of warehouse workers to our organisation, at all. It was kind of an interesting line to walk.

For young SA members it gets emphasised: class, class, class, class, *class struggle*. You feel yourself standing on solid ground when you learn what workers did in the Russian Revolution, and Chile, and Iran, and in Australia with Clarrie O'Shea. It's SA, but it's the politics they represent more so. That politics isn't owned by SA, it's also the history of the working class. Of struggle. And having even a tiny fraction of that under my belt was the reason being a socialist made me, and us, able to operate in that situation.

I'd been so excited for these politics in an abstract way, and it just clicked in my intellect. But there was also a feeling, there was something akin to music, when suddenly the strike was happening, and it was like, 'Aw this all stacks up, it's not just a bunch of words, it works.'

CHAPTER 67

SPITTING IN A FASCIST'S BEER: THE FAR RIGHT AND PUBS

Alex Ettling and Iain McIntyre

The Irish Times front bar, Melbourne, 2023

In recent decades ultra-right groups and individuals have become increasingly emboldened, engaging in activities that glorify and epitomise hateful ideologies. Their ability to organise and operate has been challenged by those they seek to harm, as well as a range of allies.

Just as the left has long used pubs and other social spaces to meet, recruit, and build networks and connections, so have would-be genocidaires. As a result anti-fascists and others have campaigned to pressure publicans, club owners, and promoters to overcome greed and ignorance and end their support and enablement of hate based activities. Conscious that events celebrating Adolf Hitler's birthday and promoting mass murder are likely to draw opprobrium, fascists have often taken measures to operate under the radar. Investigative work in turn has exposed such gatherings, shutting them down and exposing organisers.

Venue staff and patrons have also had to push back against repugnant displays and bullying on a more everyday basis. A high-profile incident occurred in Melbourne bar The Irish Times in 2022, during which a staff member confronted and expelled neo-Nazis from their workplace. The following account is based on an interview with the bar worker involved, referred to here as J, and includes quotes regarding their experiences.

A Typical Day in a Contemporary Pub

Working in a pub has always been hard toil. As in other parts of the economy, increased casualisation, de-unionisation, and precarity has made hospitality work more difficult and demanding since the 1980s, as well as more poorly recompensed. If supportive management is present, along with easy going clientele and co-workers, then the job becomes a lot more attractive. But for many hotel workers much of their work is a grind. As J recalls:

> A general work day at the Irish Times would start off by going into the keg room and bringing out all the empty kegs and bringing in the new fresh ones to set us up for the day. I'd mainly be behind the bar pouring drinks. I might have to run food around depending on how many people that we had in.
>
> The clientele was mostly business types who come in from the neighbouring office buildings. Professionals tend to drink quite a lot. I remember there was this one guy who used to always come in and just get absolutely plastered Friday and Saturday night and it was always a bit of a nuisance. He was in a pretty high ranking position in the Australian Tax Office. So it was very interesting seeing that side of these professional types.
>
> Once, we had three business types come in on a week night and just get a bit too plastered. And one of them ended up stumbling into the back staff area, and threw up all over the staff toilet. I've had to clean up a lot of food spills working in kitchens and it's honestly a pretty similar principle once you get over the fact that this was at one point inside of someone's stomach.
>
> It never really occurred to me just quite how difficult, like annoying it is to deal with people who are extremely drunk when you are extremely sober. You get a lot of dickheads who come in, especially in the city, and you just kind of have to tell them to leave.
>
> On the weekends we'd have security guards but not on weekdays. I'd have to cut people off sometimes, and sometimes they'd get a bit upset about that. I have always been pretty good, I don't know, doing the whole conflict resolution thing.
>
> At the time of the incident there was a pretty high turnover rate in the bar. So when I got to a couple months there, I was one of the people they had on the longest.
>
> I was making a couple of dollars below what the general hospitality rate of pay was. It was maybe $23 an hour. Coming from washing dishes, that was a pay rise, but definitely not what I've gotten used to at other bar venues.
>
> There was no union presence. I was in talks with another co-worker who started around the same time to try to get a few of the crew together and go up to the boss and demand

The Irish Times, Melbourne, 2023

higher wages. But that was around the time that the whole incident kicked off.

Meeting the Neo-Nazis

A part of working in bars is maintaining safety for staff and patrons. This can include withdrawing service from overly intoxicated people, calming down belligerent drunks, and getting people to leave who pose a threat to others. Dealing with a group whose ideology revolves around the violent crushing of opponents presents a considerable escalation. J explains:

> Tuesday opening shift usually tends to be pretty dull. When it was quiet like that, we just got some basic tasks done, like cleaning the windows and stocking up.
>
> A group of blokey guys came in. I didn't really pay much attention to them until one of the group took off his jacket to reveal a tattoo on his shoulder which depicted a spiral symbol, called a sunwheel or a black sun or a Sonnenrad, used by a lot of fascist movements. I recognised it from what I'd seen online. A lot of the far right protests in America would be displaying that symbol pretty prominently on flags and that sort of thing. I got into left-wing online politics when I was a teenager. And so that was how I recognised it.

The Sonnenrad is one of many ancient symbols that have been misappropriated by far-right groups. While present in cultural groups with no connection to supremacist ideology, versions of it were also used by the SS and SA during the Nazi regime in Germany. Inspired by this, modern ultra-right groups have displayed the symbol on flags and patches, such as those used by the neo-Nazi Azov Brigade in Ukraine. Mass murderers who carried out atrocities in Aotearoa and the United States have also featured the symbol in statements and social media posts.

> It was definitely a big shock at first because I'd never been too used to dealing with these types of people in real life, you know. Like your classic garden variety Australian racists are a bit of a different thing from actual proper fascist neo-Nazis. I told my co-workers, one of whom was a woman of colour, to be careful around that group.

To further gauge the situation J approached the man with the Sonnenrad and asked him about his tattoo.

> He just sort of dismissively said, 'Oh it's a sun wheel.' Then the guy comes up and orders a pint of Heineken and asks me, 'Where have you seen that tattoo before?' I started pouring the pint and I mentioned, 'Well, I've seen that tattoo being worn by people who don't very much like queer people and immigrants and you know, as a queer person I just want to be careful of that.' I remember him saying, 'It's not that I don't like immigrants, I don't like multiculturalism', and then he said to me, very much directed at me, 'and if you're a faggot, then that's your problem.'
>
> That's a word that I've been called a few times in my life. Usually when someone is saying that to me it comes across as a threat of violence or an intention to do violence against me for being a queer person. So it was at that point that I spat in the drink that I was pouring. I put it up on the bar, and told him that he had to leave.
>
> It was very much an instinctual, I guess, fight or flight response. Which maybe wasn't the best decision when you're dealing with an extremely muscular guy, twice your size and three of his mates. So, when I realised what I'd done, I was sort of like, 'Holy shit. I can't believe I've done that. This guy's gonna kill me.'

The group began interrogating J, with one of them filming proceedings.

They became quite aggressive and started berating me, refusing to leave. They were trying to start a debate about how it's wrong and disrespectful to spit in someone's drink. I explained that, yes, the disrespect was definitely not unintentional.

I called them Nazis. And one of them responded and said, 'We're not Nazis, were *neo*-Nazis.' That was a pretty funny thing.

During the dispute one of the fascists argued, 'It makes me feel ill.' J quipped, 'If it makes you feel ill, the bathroom's upstairs.' At one point the man with the Sonnenrad pulled down his tank top to flash a tattoo of a swastika on his chest. They called J more homophobic slurs before finally exiting the pub.

They threw up a few Nazi salutes outside the front of the pub and then went on their way.

I was a bit shaken up naturally. I was the person working that day who had been there the longest. And so I just kind of figured, you know, have a break, cool down, have a cigarette and just get back to work.

I had taken a picture of the guy with the tattoo from behind the bar. I sent it to the work group chat, basically just being like, 'Fair warning, had a bit of an altercation with these guys. He's got a tattoo which represents a racist sort of thing, and they're not welcome back here.'

You get a lot of macho assholes in that sort of environment so I was thinking that these were just some random, unorganised dickheads. The next day, I got a text message from a friend of mine who's involved with left-wing politics and

The Irish Times, Melbourne, 2023

anti-fascism who was aware of these guys. One of them had uploaded the video of the altercation on his YouTube channel and they were members of this organisation called the National Socialist Network. They're fairly well known in that regard.

The Aftermath of the Event

The experience of work and work politics are now thoroughly enmeshed with online technologies and hand held devices. A mobile phone was used by the fascist to record the altercation as it was taking place. J used their phone to take and share a photo of the fascist's tattoo when they became aware of a threat. Social media shared the incident and was used to organise responses – both by fascists and those opposed to them.

> The bar started getting a lot of negative Google reviews. And we're getting phone calls from people just yelling down the phone. Homophobic slurs and people calling up with threats.
>
> When one of the fascist types called up, a co-worker defended my actions and then somehow they found out her name. She ended up also a target for these guys and lost her job, which was unfortunate.

The bar's owner was an Indian Australian man who runs multiple venues. The fascists located his personal phone number as well.

> The owner called me up, yelling. He was saying, 'We're getting all these negative Google reviews from people, what the fuck did you do?' He threatened to fire me and I said, 'Look, there's a lot more to the story. We need to have a chat about this.'
>
> The Nazis started demanding money. For 'emotional damages' I think was their line. I think they said they felt they had been 'disrespected' and 'emasculated' and they demanded a sum of $651 for emotional damages. And they wanted all the money that they'd spent there to be given back to them as well. The significance of the number 51 at the end is that that was the number of victims at the mass shooting at the Christchurch mosque. And so the number they gave was a little dog whistle.
>
> The bar owner had been receiving advice from lawyers. I tried to explain to him who the group was. I tried to explain, do not give them any quarter. From what I understand, at the start, he had left-wing anti-fascist types, reaching out to him and giving him advice regarding being a business owner who's being hounded by these guys.
>
> Despite this, he ended up completely caving to their demands. He paid the money and issued a public apology on the official Irish Times Facebook page, with an apology that had been clearly drafted by the Nazis and which they'd asked for him to post.

The day before the incident the man with the tattoo had been fined for pasting up anti-Semitic stickers featuring swastikas. His fellow drinkers all shared his history of menacing members of the public on and offline as well as of being egotistical publicity seekers. Conversations captured by anti-fascists revealed that the quartet had workshopped their campaign for financial gain before amplifying it via social media networks.

> These guys don't have any power, like political or otherwise, and I think a victory like this for them is quite rare, so they were definitely living it up for a bit there.
>
> I was just receiving the information secondhand, screenshots from Facebook groups and online message boards. There was the initial feeling of, 'Oh, fuck.' What with losing the job and getting threatened by political extremists and my face ending up on the news and all that kind of thing.

Since I got my last paycheck, I haven't heard anything from the managers or the owner. I tried reaching out to the manager as well as the owner, a few times, but just haven't received any response. Any sort of support from the business would have been nice.

I got a few people asking me, 'Should we like lay off on the business over their response because they're receiving a lot of hate from the Nazis as well?' And I think, honestly, fuck no. Just because the management are victims as well, doesn't doesn't mean they don't deserve a lot of criticism for how they handled the whole thing.

The original events became rapidly distorted with imputations that J had sneakily tried to serve unhygienic alcohol. In actuality, they had openly rendered the glass of beer undrinkable and ordered the men to leave. While fascists used social media to pile on the pressure, other people praised J's action. A representative comment read, 'If your bartender spits in a Nazi's beer, they deserve a pay rise and a bonus.'

Targets of hate-groups were able to broadly gain something positive from the situation. In recent times the far-right, including the neo-Nazis involved in this specific incident, have increased their attacks on LGBTIQA+ events and people. An online fundraiser was set up to show solidarity for J and their co-worker, and they chose to nominate queer housing mutual aid as the beneficiary.

A subsequent event was organised by the Community Union Defence League, in collaboration with the James Connolly Association. Held at left-wing venue Cafe Gummo, it featured an Irish folk singer and a number of punk, electronic and other bands, all brought together under the slogan of 'No Bar For Nazis'. In all over $5000 was raised with J remarking, 'It was a really huge turnout and the support was fantastic.'

Money was raised through an online appeal and a benefit gig in support of queer people in need of housing

FURTHER READING

Introduction   Alex Ettling and Iain McIntyre

Allen, Max, *Intoxicating: Ten Drinks that Shaped Australia*, Thames & Hudson, 2020.

Dingle, Anthony Edward, 'The Truly Magnificent Thirst': an Historical Survey of Australian Drinking Habits', *Historical Studies*, Vol 19 No.75, 1980.

Dunstan, David, 'Boozers and Wowsers', *Constructing A Culture: A People's History of Australia since 1788*, edited by Burgmann, Verity and Lee, Jenny, Penguin, 1988.

Fitzgerald, Ross, and Jordan, Trevor, *Under the Influence: A History of Alcohol in Australia*, HarperCollins, 2017.

Gilling, Tom, *Grog: A Bottled History of Australia's First 30 Years*, Hachette, 2016.

Kirkby, Diane, Luckins, Tanja and McConville, Chris. *The Australian Pub*, University of New South Wales Press, 2010.

Lloyd, David, 'Brewing in Early Australia', PhD, Australian National University, 1998.

Murphy, Matt, *Rum: A Distilled History of Colonial Australia*, HarperCollins, 2021.

Room, Robin, 'The Dialectic of Drinking in Australian Life: From the Rum Corps to the Wine Column', *Australian Drug and Alcohol Review*, vol: 7 no. 4, 1988.

Slingerland, Edward, *Drunk: How We Sipped, Danced, and Stumbled Our Way to Civilization*, Little, Brown Spark, 2021.

Wright, Clare, *Beyond the Ladies Lounge: Australia's Female Publicans*, Text Publishing, 2003.

Chapter 1   **'Grog For Me': Convicts and Alcohol**   Michael Quinlan and Hamish Maxwell-Stewart

Allen, Matthew, 'Policing a Free Society: Drunkenness and Liberty in Colonial New South Wales', *History Australia*, vol: 12 no. 2, 2015.

Hindmarsh, Bruce, 'Beer and Fighting: Some Aspects of Male Convict Leisure in Van Diemen's Land', *Journal of Australian Studies*, vol: 23 no. 63, 1999.

Maxwell-Stewart, Hamish and Quinlan, Michael, *Unfree Workers: Insubordination and Resistance in Convict Australia 1788-1860*, Palgrave, 2022.

Chapter 2   **Matthew Brady, Gentlemen Bushranger**   Alex Ettling

Butler, Richard. *And Wretches Hang : the True and Authentic Story of the Rise and Fall of Matt Brady, Bushranger*, Melbourne, Hyland House, 1977.

Calder, James Erskine and FitzSymonds, Eustace, *Brady: McCabe, Dunne, Bryan, Crawford, Murphy, Bird, McKenney, Goodwin, Pawley, Bryant, Cody, Hodgett's, Gregory, Tilley, Ryan, Williams, and their associates, bushrangers in Van Diemen's Land, 1824-1827 / from James Calder's text of 1873 together with newly discovered manuscripts*, Sullivan's Cove, 1979.

Juvenal, Pindar and Mackaness, George, *The Van Diemen's Land Warriors: with an Essay on Matthew Brady*, G. Mackaness, 1944.

von Stieglitz, K. R., *Matthew Brady: Van Diemen's Land Bushranger*, Fullers Book Shop, 1965.

Williams, Paul, *Matthew Brady and Ned Kelly: Kindred Spirits, Kindred Lives*, Arcadia North, 2007.

Chapter 3   **A Cheeky Few: Early Socialism and Alcohol**   Alex Ettling

Adams, J.D., 'Vogt, George Leonard (1848–1937)', *Australian Dictionary of Biography*, National Centre of Biography, 1990.

Bongiorno, Frank, 'Bernard O'Dowd's Socialism', *Labour History*, No. 77, 1999.

Bonnell, Andrew, 'From Saxony to South Brisbane: the German-Australian Socialist Hugo Kunze', *Labour History Canberra*, 2011.

Brown, Bruce W., 'The Machine Breaker Convicts from the Proteus and the Eliza', Masters thesis, University of Tasmania, 2004.

Burgmann, Verity, *In Our Time: Socialism and the Rise of Labor, 1885-1905*, Sydney, Allen & Unwin, 1985.

Coates, Roger, 'Socialism Next Time', *Australian Left Review*, vol. 1 no. 93, 1985.

Harris, Joe, *The Bitter Fight: a Pictorial History of the Australian Labor Movement*, University of Queensland Press, 1970.

James, Bob, Anarchism and State Violence in Sydney and Melbourne, 1886-1896: An Argument About Australian Labor History, James, 1986.

Mayer, Henry and Merrifield, Sam, 'The Democratic Association of Victoria and the "I" with Reply', *Labour History*, No. 8, 1965.

Mayer, Henry, *Marx, Engels, and Australia*, Melbourne, F. W. Cheshire, 1964.

McIlroy, Jim, *Australia's First Socialists*, Resistance Books, 2003.

Mellor, Suzanne, 'Ross, John (1833–1920)', *Australian Dictionary of Biography*, National Centre of Biography, 1976.

Merrifield, Sam, 'The 'Y' Club', *Recorder*, vol: 3 no. 3, 1968.

Merrifield, Sam, 'George Leonard Vogt', *Labour History*, No. 7, 1964.

Rainford, John, A Short History of Social Democracy: From Socialist Origins to Neoliberal Theocracy, Resistance Books, 2015.

Saunders, Malcolm, 'Harry Samuel Taylor, the 'William Lane' of the South Australian Riverland', *Labour History*, no. 72, 1997.

Strangio, Paul, *Neither Power Nor Glory: 100 Years Of Political Labor in Victoria,1856-1956*, Carlton, 2012.

Turner, Ian, 'Socialist Political Tactics, 1900-1920', *Bulletin of the Australian Society for the Study of Labour History*, vol: 2 no. 5, 1962.

Webb, John, 'A Critical Biography of Edwin James Brady 1869 - 1952', PhD thesis, University of Sydney, 1972.

Wehner, Volkhard, *Socialistischer Verein Vorwärts: Melbourne's Nineteenth Century German Socialist Association*, self-published, 2020.

Chapter 4   Pubs and the Formation of Unions in Australia   Iain McIntyre

Harris, Joe, *The Bitter Fight: a Pictorial History of the Australian Labor Movement*, University of Queensland Press, 1970.

Quinlan, Michael, *The Origins of Worker Mobilisation: Australia 1788-1850*. Routledge, 2017.

Chapter 5   Disturbing the Peace: The 1851 Rocks Riot   Iain McIntyre

Cahill, Rowan and Irving, Terry, *Radical Sydney: Places, Portraits and Unruly Episodes*, UNSW Press. 2010.

Swanston, Bruce, *The Police of Sydney: 1788-1862*, Australian Institute of Criminology, 1984.

Chapter 6   The Dunmore Arms and Brisbane's 'Blood or Bread' Riots, 1866   Iain McIntyre

Evans, Raymond & Ferrier Carole (eds), *Radical Brisbane: An Unruly History*, Vulgar Press, 2004.

Wilson, P. D. 'The Brisbane Riot of September 1866', *Queensland Heritage*, vol: 2 no. 4, 1971.

Chapter 7   Pay The Rent!: Wombeetch Puyuun   Alex Ettling

Neal, Matt, Wombeetch Puyuun, A Unique Friendship and the Push to Recognise A Monument Erected in His Honour, *Australian Broadcasting Corporation*, 10 Jul 2022, <abc.net.au/news/wombeetch-puyuun-james-dawson-camperdown-cemetery-memorial/101083712>.

Wright, Tony, 'Camperdown George's Voice from the Past: Pay the Rent', *Sydney Morning Herald*, August 26 2022.

Chapter 8   'Manhood... drowned out of them with liquor': William Lane's Teetotal Utopia   Jeff Sparrow

Allen, Matthew and Thomas, Natalie, 'Problem Substances: Temperance and the Control of Addictive Drugs in Nineteenth-Century Australia', *The Social History of Alcohol and Drugs*, vol: 35 no. 1, 2021.

Beresford, Quentin, 'Drinkers and the Anti-Drink Movement in Sydney, 1870-1930', PhD Thesis, Australian National University, 1984.

Blocker, Jack S., Fahey, David M. and Tyrrell, Ian R. (eds). *Alcohol and Temperance in Modern History: An International Encyclopedia*, ABC-CLIO, 2003.

Brown, J. B. 'The Pig or the Stye: Drink and Poverty in Late Victorian England', *International Review of Social History*, vol: 18 no. 3, 1973.

Burgmann, Verity, *In Our Time: Socialism and the Rise of Labor, 1885-1905*, Allen & Unwin, 1985.

Crouch, David, *Colonial Psychosocial: Reading William Lane*, Cambridge Scholars, 2014.

Dingle, A. E., '"The Truly Magnificent Thirst": An Historical Survey of Australian Drinking Habits', *Historical Studies*, vol: 19 no. 75, October 1980.

Doyle, Susan, 'Common Pleasures: Low Culture in Sydney 1887-1914', PhD Thesis, University of Technology Sydney, 2006.

Engels, Friedrich, *The Condition of the Working Class in England*. Oxford, Oxford University Press, 1993.

Fitzgerald, Ross, and Jordan, Trevor, *Under the Influence: A History of Alcohol in Australia*, HarperCollins, 2017.

Freudenberg, Norman Graham, *Cause for Power: The Official History of the New South Wales Branch of the Australian Labor Party*, Pluto Press, 1991.

Hannan, John Grant. 'The New Australia Movement', PhD Thesis, The University of Queensland, 1966.

Hoffrogge, Ralf, 'Booze and Socialism', *Jacobin*, 30 August 2018.

Kellett, John, '"William Lane and 'New Australia": A Reassessment', *Labour History*, no. 72, 1997.

Kiernan, Brian. '"Sydney or the Bush": Some Literary Images of Sydney', in *Twentieth Century Sydney: Studies in Urban and Social History*, Hale and Iremonger, 1980.

Lake, Marilyn, 'Historical Reconsiderations IV: The Politics of Respectability: Identifying the Masculinist Context'. *Historical Studies*, vol: 22 no. 86, April 1986.

Lane, William, *The Workingman's Paradise*, Sydney University Press, 1980.

Lawson, Henry, 'That Pretty Girl in the Army', in *Send Round the Hat*, Dodo Press, 2008.

Le Couteur, Howard, 'Of Intemperance, Class and Gender in Colonial Queensland: A Working-Class Woman's Account of Alcohol Abuse', *History Australia*, vol: 8 no. 3, January 2011.

McQueen, Humphrey, *A New Britannia*, Penguin, 1975.

Roberts, James S., *Drink, Temperance and the Working Class in Nineteenth Century Germany*, Routledge, 2019.

Room, Robin, 'The Dialectic of Drinking in Australian Life: From the Rum Corps to the Wine Column', *Australian Drug and Alcohol Review*, vol: 7 no. 4, 1988.

Ross, Lloyd, *William Lane and the Australian Labor Movement*, L. Ross, 1935.

Souter, Gavin, *A Peculiar People: William Lane's Australian Utopians in Paraguay*, Sydney University Press, 1981.

Stubbs, Ben, *Ticket to Paradise*, HarperCollins, 2012.

Walker, Samuel, 'Terence v. Powderly, Machinist: 1866–1877', *Labor History*, vol: 19 no. 2, 1978.

Whitehead, Anne, *Paradise Mislaid: In Search of the Australian Tribe of Paraguay*, University of Queensland Press, 1997.

Wilding, Michael, 'Introduction to 1980 Edition of The Workingman's Paradise', Sydney University Press, 1980.

Chapter 9 Alcohol and the Eight Hour Day Iain McIntyre

Scalmer, Sean, Remembering the Movement for Eight Hours: Commemoration and Mobilization in Australia, in *Remembering Social Movements*, Routledge, 2021.

Chapter 10 Anti-Chinese Racism and the life of publicans Jimmy and Evelina Ah Foo Alex Ettling and Iain McIntyre

Roberts, Mick, 'Chinese Publicans in Australia', 2015, <https://timegents.com/2015/12/06/chinese-pubs/amp>.

Ward, Liam, 'Radical Chinese Labour in Australian History', *Marxist Left Review*, issue 10, Winter 2017, <https://marxistleftreview.org/articles/radical-chinese-labour-in-australian-history>.

Chapter 11 'Stubborn Struggles': Beer Strikes in Western Australia, 1901-1925 Iain McIntyre

McIntyre, Iain, 'Beer Strikes', Labour History conference paper, 2022, <https://commonslibrary.org/beer-strikes-a-history-of-hotel-boycotts-in-australia-1900-1920>.

Chapter 12 'Champagne is Not Reserved for the Stomachs of the Rich': Chummy Fleming and a Donation to the Unemployed Iain McIntyre

James, Bob, 'Chummy Fleming: A Brief Biography (1863-1950)', *Libertarian Resources*, 1986. <http://www.takver.com/history/chummy.htm>.

Chapter 13 — **The Communists Meet The Bohemians: Drinking at the Margins, from the 1900s to the 1930s** Alex Ettling

Armstrong, Mick, 'Between Syndicalism and Reformism: Founding the Communist Party of Australia', *Marxist Left Review*, No.21, 2021.

Armstrong, Mick, '100 Years Since the Founding of Australia's Communist Party', *Red Flag*, 2020, <https://redflag.org.au/index.php/node/7428>.

Arnold, John, 'A night at Fasoli's ..', *Notes and Furphies*, vol: 6, 1981.

Burstall, Tim, with McPhee, Hilary and Standish, Ann, *The Memoirs of a Young Bastard: The Diaries of Tim Burstall, November 1953 to December 1954*, Melbourne University Publishing, 2012.

Cafe Petrushka, Langwarrin, McClelland Gallery, 1990.

Carter, David, *A Career in Writing: Judah Waten and the Cultural Politics of a Literary Career*, Association for the Study of Australian Literature, 1997.

Croll, Robert Henderson, *I Recall: Collections and Recollections*, Robertson & Mullens, 1939.

Davidson, Alistair, *The Communist Party of Australia: A Short History*, Hoover Institution Press, 1969.

Ferrier, Carole, 'A "Red Revolutionist and Ranter": Jean Devanny in the early 1930s', *Hecate*, vol: 24 no. 2, Nov 1998.

Fredman, L.E., 'Melbourne Bohemia in the Nineteenth Century', *Southerly*, vol: 18 no. 2, 1957.

Gollan, Robin, *Revolutionaries and Reformists: Communism and the Australian Labour Movement 1920-1955*, Australian National University Press, 1975.

Hudson, David, 'Walker, Bertha May (1912–1975)', *Australian Dictionary of Biography*, National Centre of Biography, Australian National University, 2002.

Inglis, Amirah, *The Hammer & Sickle and the Washing Up: Memories of an Australian Woman Communist*, Hyland House, 1995.

Irving, Terry, 'Modernity's Discontents: Esmonde Higgins and James Rawling as Labour Intellectuals', *Illawarra Unity*, vol: 11 no. 1, 2012.

Irving, Terry and Scalmer, Scalmer, 'Labour Intellectuals in Australia: Modes, Traditions, Generations, Transformations', *International Review of Social History*, vol:50 no1, 2005.

Jordan, Douglas, 'Conflict in the Unions: The Communist Party of Australia, Politics and the Trade Union Movement, 1945-1960', PhD thesis, Victoria University, 2011.

L.C.F. (likely pseudonym of Baracchi, Guido), 'Prohibition, Communism and the Joy of Life', *The Proletarian*, vol: 1 no 5, p 7, October 1920.

Macintyre, Stuart, *The Reds: The Communist Party of Australia from Origins to Illegality*, Allen & Unwin, 1998.

Moore, Tony, *Dancing with Empty Pockets: Australia's Bohemians Since 1860*, Pier 9, 2012.

Moore, Tony, 'Romancing the City: Australia's Bohemian Tradition' thesis, The University of Sydney, 1997 - 2007.

Macintyre, Stuart, *The Reds: The Communist Party of Australia from Origins to Illegality*, Allen & Unwin, 1998.

Morrison, Peter, 'The Communist Party of Australia and the Australian radical-socialist tradition, 1920-1939', PhD thesis, University of Adelaide, 1977.

O'Lincoln, Tom, *Into The Mainstream: The Decline of Australian Communism*, Stained Wattle Press, 1985.

Palmer, Vance, 'Australia and the Bohemian Ideal', 1907.

Penrose, Beris, 'The Communist Party and Trade Union Work in the Third Period 1928-1935', PhD thesis, University of Queensland, 1993.

Smith, Bernard, *Noel Counihan: Artist and Revolutionary*, Melbourne, Oxford University Press, 1993.

Sparrow, Jeff and Sparrow, Jill (eds), *Radical Melbourne*, Vulgar, 2001.

Sparrow, Jeff, *Communism: A Love Story*, Melbourne University Press, 2007.

Sullivan, Jane, 'A Stroll Around Melbourne's Lost Bohemia, *Sydney Morning Herald*, 12 September 2014, <https://www.smh.com.au/entertainment/books/a-stroll-around-melbournes-lost-bohemia-20140908-10drv4.html>.

Taylor, Alex, *Perils of the Studio: Inside the Artistic Affairs of Bohemian Melbourne*, Australian Scholarly Publishing, 2007.

Walker, Bertha, *Solidarity Forever!*, The National Press, 1972.

Watson, Don, *Brian Fitzpatrick, a Radical Life*, Hale & Iremonger, 1979.

Wills, Nancy, *Shades of Red*, Communist Arts Group, 1980.

Chapter 14 — The 1912 Broken Hill Hotel and Restaurant Strike Iain McIntyre

Kennedy, B., *Silver, Sin, and Sixpenny Ale: A Social History of Broken Hill, 1883-1921*, Melbourne University Press, 1978.

Chapter 15 — State Control of Liquor in the Northern Territory: A Brave but Unpopular Experiment Maggie Brady

Alcorta, F.X., *Darwin Rebellion 1911–1919*, NT Government Printer, 1984.

Harrison, Brian, *Drink and the Victorians. The Temperance Question in England 1815-1872*, Keele University Press, 1994.

Powell, Alan, *Far Country: A Short History of the Northern Territory*, Melbourne University Press, 1982.

Room, Robin, 'The Monopoly Option: Obsolescent or a "Best Buy"' in *Alcohol and Other Drug Control? The Social History of Alcohol and Drugs*, 2020.

Chapter 16 — 'Thirsty Days': The 1918 Brisbane Beer Strike Iain McIntyre

McIntyre, Iain, 'Beer Strikes: A History of Hotel Boycotts in Australia, 1901-1920', Commons Library, 2022, <https://commonslibrary.org/beer-strikes-a-history-of-hotel-boycotts-in-australia-1900-1920>.

Chapter 17 — Christmas and Beer Chris McConville

Bongiorno, Frank. *The Eighties: The Decade That Transformed Australia*, Black Inc., 2015.

Crawford, R., '"Anyhow.. Where D'yer Get It, Mate?" Ockerdom in adland Australia', *Journal of Australian Studies*, vol: 31 no. 90, 2007.

Darien-Smith, K., *On the Home Front: Melbourne in Wartime, 1939-1945*, Oxford University Press, 1990.

Davis, E.M., 'Trade Unions, Myth and Reality', *Journal of Australian Political Economy*, vol: 2, 1978.

Driscoll, R., *The Great Aussie Beer Book*, Gordon and Gotch, 1984.

Germov, J. and McIntyre, J., 'The Rise of Australia as a Wine Nation'. *The Conversation*, 5 June 2013, <https://theconversation.com/the-rise-of-australia-as-a-wine-nation-14875>.

Hewat, Tim, *The Elders Explosion*, Bay Books, 1988.

Kirkby, Diane, '"Beer, glorious beer": Gender politics and Australian popular culture', *Journal of Popular Culture*, vol: 37 no. 2, 2003.

Kirkby, Diane. and Luckins, Tanja, '"Winnies and Pats.. Brighten Our Pubs": Transforming the Gendered Spatial Economy of the Australian Pub, 1920–1970', *Journal of Australian Studies*, vol: 30 no. 87, 2006.

Pettigrew, Simone, 'A Grounded Theory of Beer Consumption in Australia', *Qualitative Market Research*, vol: 5 no. 2, 2002.

Chapter 18 — Pub Boycotts, Loyalism, and Unions in Queensland Iain McIntyre

Evans, Raymond, *The Red Flag Riots: A Study of Intolerance*, University of Queensland. 1988.

Hunt, Doug. *Labour in North Queensland: Industrial and Political Behaviour, 1900-1920*. VDM Verlag, 2010.

Chapter 19 — Cecilia Shelley: Feminist, Activist, Trailblazer Daniel Elias

Batterham, L., 'Cecilia M Shelley Western Australian Labour Activist 1893-1986.' *Papers in Labour History*, no. 14, 1994.

Brady, W., 'International Women's Day' in Layman, Lenore and Stannage, Tom (eds). 'Celebrations in Western Australia.' *Studies in Western Australian History*, no. 10, 1989.

Brady, W., '"Serfs of the Sodden Scone"?: Women Workers in the West Australian Hotel and Catering Industry', *Studies in Western Australian History*, no 7, 1983.

Fox, Charlie, Oliver, Bobbie, Layman, Lenore and Vassiley, Alexis (eds), *Radical Perth Militant Fremantle*, Interventions, 2019.

Popham, D. and Stokes, K.A. (eds). *Reflections: Profiles of 150 women Who Helped Make Western Australia's History*, Battye Library, 1978.

Shelley, Cecilia. 'Transcript: Oral History Programme an Interview with Cecilia Shelley', Battye Library, 1976.

Chapter 20 — Communist Jocka Burns and Grape Picking Alex Ettling and Iain McIntyre

Huelin, Frank, *Keep Moving*, Penguin Books, 1983.

Jocka Burns oral history interviewed by Wendy Lowenstein, Wendy Lowenstein 1930's Depression collection [sound recording] 1974, National Library of Australia, <https://nla.gov.au/nla.obj-582915641>.

Lowenstein, Wendy, *Weevils in the Flour: an Oral Record of the 1930s Depression in Australia*, Scribe, 1998.

Tully, John, 'John 'Jocka' Burns', *Green Left Weekly*, Issue 513, October 23 2002.

Chapter 21   **The Matteotti Club**   Iain McIntyre

Cresciani, G., 'The Proletarian Migrants: Fascism and Italian Anarchists in Australia', *Australian Quarterly*, vol: 51 no. 1, 1979.

Cresciani, G. 'Fascism, Anti-Fascism and Italians in Australia, 1922-1945', *Australian National University Press*, 1980.

Sparrow, Jeff and Sparrow, Jill (eds), *Radical Melbourne*, Vulgar, 2001.

Venturini, V.G., *Never Give In: Three Italian Antifascist Exiles in Australia, 1924-1956*, Search Foundation, 2007.

Chapter 22   **'What Should We Do…': Maritime Workers and Drinking**   Alex Ettling

Fitzpatrick, Brian & Cahill, Rowan, *The Seamen's Union of Australia, 1872-1972: a History*, Seamen's Union of Australia, 1981.

Kirkby, Diane, *Voices From The Ships: Australia's Seafarers and their Union*, UNSW Press Sydney, 2008.

LeftPress Collective, *After The Waterfront The Workers Are Quiet*, LeftPress Printing Society, 2007, <https://libcom.org/files/waq-whole-book-pdf-version.pdf>.

Chapter 23   **'Valour among the Vats': 1937 Castlemaine Brewery Dispute**   Carol Corless

Bowden Bradley and Rafferty, Cath, 'Independent Judgement: The History of the Queensland Industrial Relations Commission, 1916-2009', in *Work and Strife: The History of Labour Relations in Queensland 1859 to 2009*, Federation Press, 2009.

Brown, Ron, 'Your Wages-Hours and the Qld Beer Barons', Federated Liquor Trades Union, 1947.

Hayes, Jimmy, 'The Castlemaine "Stay In" Strike', unpublished manuscript (transcribed from handwriting), John Oxley Library, 1937.

Hunt, Doug, 'Evolution of the System: Industrial Relations Policy and Legislation, 1859-2009', in *Work and Strife: The History of Labour Relations in Queensland 1859 to 2009*, Federation Press, 2009.

Ryan, M.P., 'Queensland Government, Lessons from Brewery Workers' Strike' in 'Strikes: Brewery Strike – Brisbane', Item ID: 316929, Correspondence file – Police, Queensland State Archives.

Chapter 24   **The Battle of Australian Modernism**   Alex Ettling

Burstall, Tim, with McPhee, Hilary and Standish, Ann, *The Memoirs of a Young Bastard: The Diaries of Tim Burstall, November 1953 to December 1954*, Melbourne University Publishing, 2012.

Haese, Richard, *Rebels and Precursors: The Revolutionary Years of Australian Art*, Penguin, 1988.

Harris, Max, 'Nolan at St Kilda', *Art and Australia*, vo: 5 no. 2, 1967.

Knox, Alistair, *A Middle Class Man: An Autobiography*, Unpublished, Undated.

McLaren, John, *Free Radicals of the Left in Postwar Melbourne*, Australian Scholarly Publishing, 2003.

Turner, Ian, 'My Long March', in *Room For Manoeuvre: Writings on History, Politics, Ideas and Play*, Drummond, 1982.

Underhill, Nancy, *Sidney Nolan: A Life*, NewSouth Publishing, 2015.

Wills, Nancy, *Shades of Red*, Communist Arts Group, 1980.

Chapter 25   **Gold Diggings and Company Towns: From the Buckland Race Riot to the Rostrevor Hops Farm**   Alex Ettling and Iain McIntyre

Jokiranta, Miyuki, 'The Chinese Settler with a Hops Empire and a 'Visionary Idea' for Australian Beer', *The History Listen*, ABC Radio National, 2018.

Pipeclay-Brown, 'The Buckland River Riot: Victoria's Lambing Flat', *The Argus*, 5 March 1932.

'Victorian Goldfields Project Historic Gold Mining Sites In The North East Region Of Victoria Gazetteer: State & Regional Significant Sites', Department Of Natural Resources & Environment, 1999, <https://www.heritage.vic.gov.au/__data/assets/pdf_file/0020/512255/Historic-gold-mining-sites-in-the-north-east-region-of-Victoria-Bannear-1999.pdf>.

Ward, Liam, 'Radical Chinese Labour in Australian History', *Marxist Left Review*, issue 10, 2017, <https://marxistleftreview.org/articles/radical-chinese-labour-in-australian-history>.

Willard, Myra. *History of the White Australia Policy to 1920*, Melbourne University Press, 1967.

Chapter 26   **Folk, Jazz and Booze: Moral panics from 1940s–1970s**   Alex Ettling

Bell, Graeme and Mitchell, Jack. *Graeme Bell, Australian Jazzman: his autobiography*, Child & Associates, 1988.

Haese, Richard, *Rebels and Precursors: The Revolutionary Years of Australian Art*, Penguin, 1988.

Horne, Craig, *Roots: How Melbourne Became the Live Music Capital of the World*, Melbourne Books, 2019.

Piccini, Jon, '"Building their own scene to do their own thing": Imagining and contesting space/s in Brisbane's youth radicalisation 1968-1976', Honours Thesis, University of Queensland, 2009.

Sparrow, Jeff, *A Short History of Communist Jazz*, Overland, 20 June 2012, <https://overland.org.au/2012/06/a-short-history-of-communist-jazz/>.

Stein, Harry, *A Glance Over An Old Left Shoulder*, Hale & Iremonger, 1994.

Traynor, Mary, 'The Beginning of Traynor's', 2015, <http://www.franktraynors.net.au/the-beginning-of-traynors-1/the-beginning-of-traynors>.

Turnbull, Malcolm J., 'The Early Years Of The Folk Revival In Melbourne', *Trad & Now*, Issues 5, 6, 7, 9,10 & 11, 2003-2004, <https://www.warrenfahey.com.au/early-melbourne-1/>.

Vuleta, Thomas, 'Ups and Downs: Music Venues and Popular Music in Brisbane 1959-1989'. Honours Thesis, The University of Queensland, 2016.

Chapter 27 — Before, After and During Work: Alcohol and the Development of Noel Counihan as an Artist — Alex Ettling

Dimmack, Max, *Noel Counihan*, Melbourne University Press, 1974.

McKenzie, Janet, *Noel Counihan*, Kangaroo Press Kenthurst, 1986.

Noel Counihan oral history interviewed by James Gleeson, National Gallery of Australia collection, 1979.

Noel Counihan oral history interviewed by Hazel de Berg, National Library of Australia, 1961.

Noel Counihan oral history interviewed by Wendy Lowenstein, Wendy Lowenstein Collection. National Library of Australia, 1976.

Noel Counihan interviewed by Mark Cranfield, National Library of Australia, 1981.

Noel Counihan interviewed by Barbara Blackman, National Library of Australia, 1986.

Smith, Bernard, *Noel Counihan: Artist and Revolutionary*, Oxford University Press, 1993.

Chapter 28 — 'The Inns are Out': The Pub, the People and the Post-War New Order — Tanja Luckins

Brady, Maggie. 'The Reinvention of Sweden's "Gothenburg System" in Rural Australia: The Community Hotels Movement', *Journal of Australian Studies*, vol: 45 no. 1, 2021.

Cottle, Drew and Eather, Warwick. 'Middies, Schooners and Pints: The Newcastle unions, the Licensed Victuallers' Association and the 1943 beer black ban', *The Hummer*, vol: 7 no. 1, 2011.

Darian-Smith, Kate. *On the Homefront: Melbourne in Wartime 1939-1945*, (2nd ed) Oxford University Press, 2009.

Frappell, Samantha. 'Methodists and the Campaigns for Six O'clock Hotel Closing in New South Wales', *Aldersgate Papers*, no 10, 2012.

Kirkby, Diane. *Barmaids: A History of Women's Work in Pubs*, Cambridge University Press, Cambridge, 1997.

Kirkby, Diane, Luckins, Tanja and McConville, Chris. *The Australian Pub*, University of New South Wales Press, 2010.

Langhamer, Claire, '"A Public House is for all Classes, Men and Women Alike": Women, Leisure and Drink in Second World War England', *Women's History Review*, vol: 12 no. 3, 2003.

Luckins, Tanja. 'Pigs, Hogs and Aussie Blokes: The emergence of the Term "Six O'clock Swill"', *History Australia*, vol: 4 no. 1, 2007.

Luckins, Tanja. '"Satan Finds Some Mischief?": Drinkers' Responses to the Six O'clock Closing of Pubs in Australia, 1910s-1930s', *Journal of Australian Studies*, vol: 32 no. 3, 2008.

Macintyre, Stuart. *Australia's Boldest Experiment: War and Reconstruction in the 1940s*, NewSouth, 2015.

Samuelsson, Lauren. 'Six O'clock is Late Enough': The 1947 New South Wales Liquor Referendum, *History Australia*, vol: 15 no.4, 2018.

Wright, C. '"Doing the Beans": Women, Drinking and Community in the Ladies Lounge', *Journal of Australian Studies*, no. 77, 2003.

Chapter 29   **For Aboriginal Humanity: The Social Justice Agenda of the Woman's Christian Temperance Union in Australia** Alison Holland

Holland, Alison, 'To Eliminate Colour Prejudice: The WCTU and Decolonisation in Australia', *Journal of Religious History*, vol: 32 no. 2, June, 2008.

Pargeter, Judith, *For God, Home and Humanity: National Woman's Christian Temperance Union of Australia: centenary history 1891-1991*, National Woman's Christian Temperance Union, 1995.

Tyrrell, Ian, *Woman's World. Woman's Empire. The WCTU in International Perspective, 1880-1930*, University of North Carolina Press, 2014.

Chapter 30: Drink Deep: The Long Life of Jack Clancy by Alex Ettling.

McMenomy, Keith, Ned Kelly: The Authentic Illustrated History, Hardie Grant, 2001.

Chapter 31   **A Cold War Shirtfronting** Rowan Cahill

Fitzpatrick, Brian & Cahill, Rowan, *The Seamen's Union of Australia, 1872-1972: a History*, Seamen's Union of Australia, 1981.

Chapter 32   **George Seelaf: A Political Life Around Booze** Alex Ettling

Bartak, Felicity with Deery, Phillip, *A Unique Endeavour: A History of the Western Region Health Centre, 1964-2004*, Western Region Health Centre, 2004.

Davies, A. E., *The Meat Workers Unite*, Australasian Meat Industry Employees' Union (Victorian Branch), 1974.

Dawson, Mark and McKinnon, Libby, '"Hello, Fellow Slave": The Life and Times of George Seelaf' radio series, Footscray, Melbourne's Living Museum of the West, 1994.

George Seelaf oral history interviewed by Ken Mansell, Ken Mansell Collection, Oral history interviews with members of the Communist Party of Australia, Mitchell Library, State Library of New South Wales, 1983.

Healy, Chris, *The Lifeblood of Footscray: Working Lives at the Angliss Meatworks*, Melbourne's Living Museum of the West Footscray, 1986.

Hughes, John, *Is It Working?*, 1985.

Lack, John, *A History of Footscray*, Hargreen Publishing in conjunction with the City of Footscray, 1991.

Lack, John, 'Seelaf, George (1914–1988)', Australian Dictionary of Biography, National Centre of Biography, Australian National University, 2012.

Chapter 33   **Critical Drinking with the Sydney Push** Wendy Bacon

Appleton, Richard, *Appo*, Darlington Press, 2009.

Baranay, Inez, *Drink Against Drunkenness: The Life and Times of Sasha Soldatow*, Local Time Publishing, 2022.

Broadsheet, Sydney Libertarians, no. 1 [1957] - no. 96 [1979].

Coombs, Anne, *Sex and Anarchy: The Life and Death of the Sydney Push*, Viking, 1996.

Harrison, G. B., *Night train to Granada: from Sydney's Bohemia to Franco's Spain: an Offbeat Memoir*, Pluto Press, 2002.

Heraclitus. Darlinghurst, Published by some Sydney libertarians, pluralists and critical drinkers, no. 1 [1980] - no. 122 [2000].

Linn, Brenda and Manton, Marion (comps), 'Push Canon', The Sydney Realist, no. 39, 2020.

Milliken, Robert, *Mother of Rock. The Lillian Roxon Story*, Black Inc., 2002.

Moorehouse, Frank. *Days of Wine and Rage*, Penguin Books, 1980.

Perry, David. *Memoirs of a Dedicated Amateur*, Valentine Press, 2014.

The Sydney Realist. Glebe, Voluntary Committee of Sydney Realists, no. 1 [2005–].

Thoms, Albie. *My Generation*, Media 21 Publishing, 2012.

Chapter 34   **The 1962 Victorian Beer Ban** Iain McIntyre

Best, Alleyn, *The History of the Liquor Trades Union in Victoria*, Victorian Branch Federated Liquor and Allied Industries Employees Union of Victoria, 1990.

Chapter 35   **Education in Reverse? The Drinking Culture of Brisbane's Student Radicals** Alex Ettling

Anderson, Alan, 'The Foco Story', *Tribune*, 2 September 1970.

Armstrong, Mick, 'The radicalisation of the campuses, 1967-74', *Socialist Alternative*, 2001 <https://sa.org.au/interventions/students.htm>.

Beatson, Jim, 'The 4ZZZFM Story', *Radio Times*, Triple Zed, 1976.

Brisbane Discussion Circle, 'Remembering the University of Queensland Forum', <http://www.radicaltimes.info/PDF/Forum.pdf>.

Curr, Ian, 'Brisbane Radicals', Workers Bush Telegraph, 2020, <https://workersbushtelegraph.com.au/2020/11/12/brisbane-radicals/>.

Curr, Ian, 'Won't get fooled again?', Workers Bush Telegraph, 2014, <https://workersbushtelegraph.com.au/2014/04/18/pshift-on-we-wont-get-fooled-again/>.

David Darling Oral History interview by Phil Parker, State Library of Queensland, 2020, <https://vimeo.com/456745133>.

Diane Zetlin oral history interviewed by Peter Cross and Danielle Miller, Centre for the Government of Queensland, The University of Queensland, 2013, <www.queenslandspeaks.com.au/diane-zetlin>.

Evans, Raymond & Ferrier Carole (eds), *Radical Brisbane: An Unruly History*, Vulgar Press, 2004.

Geoff Wills interviewed by Wendy Lowenstein, Communists and the Left in the Arts and Community Oral History Project, National Library of Australia, 1995. <http://nla.gov.au/nla.obj-221196049>.

Gray, Peter with recollections by Neilsen, Frank, '"Australia's Most Evil and Repugnant Nightspot": Memories from those involved: The FOCO Club, Brisbane, 1968-69', <http://radicaltimes.info/PDF/FOCO.pdf>.

Jones, Anne and Whyte, Robert, *Eccentric Voices: A Scrapbook of Brisbane Cultural History 1965-1995*, 2019, <https://www.h-a-r-p-o.com.au/wp-content/uploads/2019/11/eccentric_voices.pdf>.

Knight, Alan, 'Radical Media in the Deep North: The Origins of 4ZZZ-FM', PhD thesis, University of Wollongong, 1998, <http://www.radicaltimes.info/PDF/origins4ZZZ.pdf>.

Piccini, Jon, '"Building their own scene to do their own thing": Imagining and Contesting Space/S in Brisbane's Youth Radicalisation 1968-1976', Honours Thesis, University of Queensland, 2009.

Piccini, Jon, 'A Group of Misguided Way Out Individuals': the Old Left and the Student Movement in Brisbane: 1966–70, *The Queensland Journal of Labour History*, no. 12, 2011.

Piccini, Jon, '"Up The New Channels": Student Activism in Brisbane During Australia's Sixties', *Crossroads*, 2011.

Piccini, Jon, '"Australia's Most Evil and Repugnant Nightspot", Foco Club and transnational politics in Brisbane's '68', *Dialogue e-Journal*, vol: 8 no. 1, 2010.

Piccini, Jon, 'Bacchanalian Carnival or Political Event? Remembering the Sixties in Australia', *Melbourne Historical Journal*, vol: 40 no. 1, 2012.

Piccini, Jon, 'Dangerous Spaces – Youth Politics in Brisbane, 1960s-70s',.

Queensland Historical Atlas, 2010. <https://www.qhatlas.com.au/content/dangerous-spaces-youth-politics-brisbane-1960s-70s>.

Prentice, James, 'The Brisbane Protests 1965-72', PhD thesis, Griffith University, 2005. <http://www.radicaltimes.info/PDF/Prentice.pdf>.

Richards, Anne, *A Book of Doors*, AndAlso Books, 2020.

Shaw, Edwina, *Bjelke Blues: Stories of Repression and Resistance in Joh Bjelke-Petersen's Queensland 1968 - 1987*, AndAlso Books, 2019.

Stuart, Roger, 'History of the Strike', *Semper Floreat*, vol: 41 no. 11, 1 September 1971, <http://radicaltimes.info/PDF/RogerStuart1971.pdf>.

Up the Right Channels, University of Queensland, 1970.

Vuleta, Thomas, 'Ups and Downs: Music Venues and Popular Music in Brisbane 1959-1989', Honours Thesis, The University of Queensland, 2016.

Young, Mark, 'A Historical Portrait of the New Student Left at the University of Queensland, 1966 - 1972', Honours Thesis, The University of Queensland, 1984.

Chapter 36   Colour bar – the Freedom Ride and the Walgett RSL   Lisa Milner

Curthoys, Ann, *Freedom Ride: A Freedom Rider Remembers*, Allen & Unwin Crows Nest, 2002.

Lawson, Sue, *Freedom Ride*, Black Dog Books, 2015.

Perkins, Charles, *A Bastard Like Me*, Ure Smith, 1975.

Rowley, Charles, *Outcasts in White Australia*, Penguin, 1972.

Read, Peter, 'Darce Cassidy's Freedom Ride', *Australian Aboriginal Studies*, no. 1, 1988.

1965 Freedom Ride website, <https://aiatsis.gov.au/explore/1965-freedom-ride>.

Chapter 37 **Balmain and the Politics of Draught** Terry Irving

Davidson, Bonnie and Hamey, Kath and Nicholls, Debby, *Called to the Bar: 150 years of Pubs in Balmain & Rozelle*, Balmain Association, 1991.

Greenland, Hall, *Red Hot: The Life and Times of Nick Origlass*, Wellington Lane Press, 1998.

Harris, Tony, *Basket Weavers and True Believers*, Leftbank Publishing, 2007.

Moorhouse, Frank, *Days of Wine and Rage*, Penguin, 1980.

Chapter 38: Jean Young, Kath Williams, and the Fight For Equal Pay by Iain McIntyre.

Best, Alleyn, *The History of the Liquor Trades Union in Victoria*, Victorian Branch Federated Liquor and Allied Industries Employees Union of Victoria, 1990.

D'Aprano, Zelda, *Kath Williams: The Unions and the Fight for Equal Pay*. Spinifex Press, 2001.

Kirkby, Diane, *Barmaids: A History of Women's Work in Pubs*, Cambridge University Press, 1997.

Lake, Marilyn. *Getting Equal : The History of Australian Feminism*, Allen & Unwin, 1999.

Smith, Yvonne, *Taking Time: A Women's Historical Data Kit*, Union of Australian Women (Victoria), 1988.

Chapter 39 **Counterculture Carlton and the Pubs** Alex Ettling

Cass, Adam, *La Mama*, Carlton, Miegunyah Press, 2017.

Garner, Bill, 'History and Myth of La Mama and the Pram Factory', *Arena*, no. 151, 2017.

Robertson, Tim, *The Pram Factory: The Australian Performing Group Recollected*, Melbourne University Press, 2001.

The Pram Factory: Australian Theatre History. The Australian Performing Group at the Pram Factory, website developed by Suzanne Ingleton <http://wayback.archive-it.org/10989/20180903014106/https://www.pramfactory.com/personalmemoirs.html\>.

Wolf, Gabrielle, *Make it Australian: the Australian Performing Group, the Pram Factory and New Wave Theatre*, Currency Press, 2008.

Yule, Peter, *Carlton: A History*, Melbourne University Publishing, 2004.

Chapter 40 **Black and White Solidarity in the Pubs of Brisbane** Alex Ettling

Anderson, Ian and Davis, Glyn, 'The Hard Conversation', *Meanjin*, Winter 2016, <https://meanjin.com.au/essays/the-hard-conversation/>.

Attwood, Bain and Markus, Andrew, *The 1967 Referendum: Race, Power and the Australian Constitution*, Aboriginal Studies Press, 2007.

Attwood, Bain and Markus, Andrew, *The Struggle for Aboriginal Rights: A Documentary History*, Allen & Unwin, 1999.

Bandler, Faith, *Turning the Tide: A personal history of the Federal Council for the Advancement of Aborigines and Torres Strait Islanders*, Aboriginal Studies Press for the Australian Institute of Aboriginal Studies, 1989.

'Black Panthers: Interview with Dennis (sic) Walker', *Direct Action*, no. 14, 7 Feb 1972.

Boughton, Bob, 'The Communist Party of Australia's Involvement in the Struggle for Aboriginal and Torres Strait Islander People's Rights, 1920-1970', in Markey, Ray (ed), *Labour and Community: Historical Essays*, University of Wollongong, 2001.

Dale David, '"Australia's Black Panther Woman": Marlene Cummins, Breaks Her Silence', *Sydney Morning Herald*, 26 October 2015, <https://www.smh.com.au/entertainment/tv-and-radio/australian-black-panthers-marlene-cummins-highlights-violence-against-women-20151026-gkj0d7.html>.

Dan O'Neill and Di Zetlin, 'Our Radical Past: Protest in 60s and 70s Brisbane' collection, State Library of Queensland, 2018, <https://vimeo.com/646242940>.

d'Avigdor, Lewis, 'Black Power and White Solidarity: The Action Conference on Racism and Education, Brisbane 1972', in *The Far Left in Australia Since 1945*, Routledge, 2018.

Dennis (sic) Walker and Sam Watson, 'Retrospective Discussion, Taking To The Streets', ToadShow, 2006, <https://vimeo.com/150077023?embedded=true&source=vimeo_logo&owner=6065502>.

Evans, Raymond & Ferrier Carole (eds), *Radical Brisbane: An Unruly History*, Vulgar Press, 2004.

Foley, Gary. 'Black Power in Redfern 1968–1972'. The Koori History Website, 2001, <http://www.kooriweb.org/foley/essays/essay_1.html>.

Goodall, Heather, *Invasion to Embassy: Land in Aboriginal politics in New South Wales, 1770-1972*, Allen & Unwin, 1996.

Harris, Stewart, *Political Football: The Springbok Tour of Australia 1971*, Gold Star, 1972.

'Indigenous Activist's Long Struggle for Justice', *Green Left Weekly*, 22 September 22 2004 <http://radicaltimes.info/PDF/samWatson.pdf>.

Moutzouris, Sofie, 'Abschol and the Politicisation of Australian University Students: The Arena of Aboriginal rights, 1950-1973', Honours Thesis, Macquarie University, 1990.

Osmond, Warren, 'Black Militancy and the White Left', *Arena*, issue 28, 1972.

Perkins, Rachel, *Black Panther Woman*, 2014.

Read, Peter, 'Cheeky, Insolent and Anti-white: The Split in the Federal Council for the Advancement of Aboriginal and Torres Strait Islanders - Easter 1971', *Australian Journal of Politics & History*, vol: 36 no. 1, 2008.

Shoemaker, Adam (ed), 'Oodgeroo, a tribute', *Australian Literary Studies*, vol: 16 no. 4, 1994.

Smith, Shirley, *Mum Shirl: An Autobiography*, Mammoth Publishing, 1992.

Taffe, Sue, *Black and White Together: FCAATSI The Federal Council for the Advancement of Aborigines and Torres Strait Islanders 1958-1973*, University of Queensland Press, 2005.

Tomlinson, John, *Community Work with the Aboriginal citizens of South Brisbane: an Account of A Successful Attempt by the South Brisbane Aboriginal community to Handle Some of the Most Pressing Difficulties Confronting Aborigines in this Suburb*, Wobbly Press, 1974.

Walker, Kath, 'Black–White Coalition Can Work', *Origin*, vol: 1 no. 4, 1969.

Walker, Kath, 'Coalition of Black and White', paper for executive of Federal Council for the Advancement of Aboriginal and Torres Strait Islanders, 1969.

Watson, Lilla, 'Richard Buckhorn and Lilla Watson', in *Australians Against Racism: Testimonies from the Anti-Apartheid Movement in Australia*, Pluto Press, 1995.

Chapter 41   'Alk!': Pubs, Communities, and a Brotherhood in its Cups   David Nichols

Aitken, Jonathan, *Land of Fortune: A Study of the New Australia*, Secker and Warburg, 1971.

Coupe, Stuart, *Gudinski: the Godfather of Australian Rock 'n' Roll*, Hachette, 2015.

Dunstan, Don, *Felicia*, Macmillan, 1981,.

Howard, Jack, *Small Moments of Glory*, Brolga, 2020.

Hutchings, Alan, 'Just a bit better', *Royal Australian Planning Institute Journal*, vol: 15 no. 4, 1977.

Kennedy, Graham, *Graham Kennedy's Melbourne*, Nelson, 1967.

Marshall, Victor, *Fraternity : Australian Pub Rock Pioneers*, Brolga Publishing, 2021.

Monarto Development Commission Annual Report, July 1975-June 1976.

Seymour, Mark, *Thirteen Tonne Theory*, Viking, 2008.

Studio Kazanski, Monarto City Centre, February 1975.

Chapter 42   Alcohol and the Law: The 1979 Frankston Riot and Other Stories
John Finlayson in conversation with Alex Ettling

Beyer, Lorraine, *Community Policing: Lessons from Victoria*, Australian Institute of Criminology, 1993, <https://www.aic.gov.au/sites/default/files/2020-05/community_policing.pdf>.

Cashman, P. K. and Neal, David. and Gardner, J. R. and Fitzroy Legal Service (eds), *Legal Resources Book*, Fitzroy Legal Service, 1977.

Chesterman, John, 'Law and the New Left: a History of the Fitzroy Legal Service, 1972- 1994', PhD thesis, The University of Melbourne, 1995.

History & Memories of Cardijn Movements in Australia website, <http://historyandmemories.cardijncommunityaustralia.org/p/the-developing-ycw.html >.

Neal, David, 'Delivery of Legal Services - The Innovative Approach of the Fitzroy Legal Service', *Melbourne University Law Review*, no. 427, 1978.

Neal, David, *On Tap, Not On Top*, Legal Service Bulletin, 1984.

Oliver, Bobbie, *Hell No! We Won't Go!: Resistance to Conscription in Postwar Australia*, Interventions, 2022.

Tatman, Christian, 'Frankston riot in 1979 paved way for improved community policing and pub security', *Herald Sun*, 18 June 2014, <https://www.heraldsun.com.au/leader/inner-south/frankston-riot-in-1979-paved-way-for-improved-community-policing-and-pub-security/news-story/721004e03d5d676f0ed07037ed8c89ad>.

| Chapter 43 | **Black Power and Alcohol: An Oral History with Gary Foley**
Gary Foley in conversation with Alex Ettling

Foley, Gary, 'Aboriginal Medical Service, Redfern 1971–1991: Twenty Years of Community Service', Aboriginal and Torres Strait Islanders Commission, 1991.

Foley, Gary, 'Black Power in Redfern 1968–1972'. The Koori History Website, 2001, <http://www.kooriweb.org/foley/essays/essay_1.html>.

Foley, Gary and Anderson, Tim, 'Land Rights and Aboriginal Voices', *Australian Journal of Human Rights*, vol: 12, 2006.

Goodall, Heather, *Invasion to Embassy: Land in Aboriginal Politics in New South Wales, 1770–1972*, Sydney University Press, 2008.

| Chapter 44 | **'We are going to blacklist this hotel': Alcohol and the Activism of Chicka Dixon** Alex Ettling

'Charles 'Chicka' Dixon: Docker, Trade Unionist, Aboriginal rights activist', 8 April 2010, <http://www.kooriweb.org/foley/heroes/biogs/chicka_dixon.html>.

Gilchrist, Catie, 'The Empress Hotel, Redfern', The Dictionary of Sydney, 2015, <https://dictionaryofsydney.org/entry/the_empress_hotel_redfern>.

Read, Peter and Sukovic, Suzana, 'A History of Aboriginal Sydney', University of Sydney, 2010 - 2013, <https://www.historyofaboriginalsydney.edu.au/central/1960s>.

Tatz, Colin (ed), *Black Viewpoints: The Aboriginal Experience*, New Zealand Book Co, 1975.

| Chapter 45 | **'Rough As Guts': The Summerhill and The Maoists** Alex Ettling

Anderson, Hugh, 'Edward Fowler (Ted) Hill (1915-1988)', *Australian Dictionary of Biography*, vol: 17, National Centre of Biography, Australian National University, 2007, <http://adb.anu.edu.au/biography/hill-edward-fowler-ted-12635>.

Edge, Gary, *Surviving The Six O'clock Swill: A History of Darebin's Hotels*. Darebin Libraries, 2004.

Hill, Ted, 'A Communist's Behaviour Must Be Exemplary At All Times', *The Australian Communist*, no. 63, 1974.

McCaskie, Gordon, 'Brian Boyd: A Biography of a Trade Unionist', Masters Thesis, Swinburne University of Technology, 2010.

Sparrow, Jeff, 'Mao and Then: Thirty Years of Melbourne Radicalism', in *Suburban Fantasies: Melbourne Unmasked*, Australian Scholarly Publishing, 2005.

York, York, 'Vale Ted Hill', *Blast*, vol: 6 no. 7, 1988.

York, York, 'The La Trobe Three, Fifty Years On', *Overland*, 3 August 2022.

York, York, *Student Revolt La Trobe University 1967-1973*, Nicholas Press, 1989.

York, York, '"Goddam The Pusherman!" Oppose The "Drug Culture"!', *A Communist (Marxist-Leninist) Publication*, Melbourne, October 1972.

| Chapter 46 | **Liberating The Public Bar For Women** Diane Kirkby

Curthoys, Ann, 'Doing it for Themselves: The Women's Movement Since 1970,' in *Gender Relations in Australia: Domination and Negotiation*, Harcourt Brace, 1992.

Kirkby, Diane, Luckins, Tanja and McConville, Chris. *The Australian Pub*, University of New South Wales Press, 2010.

Kirkby, Diane, '"From Wharfie Haunt to Foodie Haven": Modernity and Law in Changes to the Australian Working Class Pub', *Food Culture and Society*, vol: 11 no. 1, 2008.

Kirkby, Diane, '"This isn't a novel, it's a life!": Dymphna Cusack and Caddie, The Sydney Barmaid,' *Australian Literary Studies*, vol: 22 no. 4, 2006.

Kirkby, Diane. and Luckins, Tanja, '"Winnies and Pats.. Brighten Our Pubs": Transforming the Gendered Spatial Economy of the Australian Pub, 1920–1970', *Journal of Australian Studies*, vol: 30 no. 87, 2006.

Kirkby, Diane, 'Maxwell's Silver Hammer …':Licensing Laws, Liquor Trading and the. Maxwell Royal Commission in NSW, 1951-4', *Australia and New Zealand Law and History e-journal*, 2005.

Kirkby, Diane, '"In love with a café and what he could buy": Commodity, Desire and the Transformation of Dining Out in 1960s Melbourne', in *Go!: Melbourne in the Sixties*, 2005.

Kirkby,Diane, '"Beer, Glorious Beer': Gender Politics and Australian Popular Culture', *Journal of Popular Culture*, vol: 37 no. 2, 2003.

Kirkby, Diane, 'Barmaids, Feminists, Ockers and Pubs, 1950s-1970s,' in *Dealing With Difference: Essays in Gender, History and Culture*, Melbourne University Conference and Seminars Series, 1997.

Kirkby, Diane. *Barmaids: A History of Women's Work in Pubs*, Cambridge University Press, 1997.

Chapter 47 — A Sunken Ship and its Sunken Beer: The Tragedy of the Blythe Star — Alex Ettling

Beniuk, David, 'Blythe Star blind spot: 'We Weren't Rescued. We Had to Rescue Ourselves'', *The Mercury*, 1 May 2016, <https://www.themercury.com.au/news/tasmania/blythe-star-blind-spot-we-werent-rescued-we-had-to-rescue-ourselves/news-story/7ba048eadba75977d42698ffccf0579a>.

Jones, Ann, 'Shipwreck survivor Michael Doleman', ABC Radio National, 1 December 2016, <https://www.abc.net.au/radio/programs/conversations/conversations-michael-doleman/8056404>.

Lu, Donna, 'You can't be – they're all dead': the Miracle and Tragedy of Tasmania's Blythe Star Shipwreck, *The Guardian*, 20 May 2023, <https://www.theguardian.com/australia-news/2023/may/20/you-cant-be-theyre-all-dead-the-miracle-and-tragedy-of-tasmanias-blythe-star-shipwreck>.

Sadler, Rahni, 'The Last Survivor', *Sunday Night*, Channel 7, 2016, <https://vimeo.com/164933710>.

Stoddart, Michael, *The Blythe Star Tragedy: How Indifference and Neglect Sank a Ship and Cost Three Men Their Lives*, Forty South, 2022.

'The Blythe Star: The Last Mans Story of Survival', *The Docker Podcast*, 21 July 2017 <https://thedockerpodcast.libsyn.com/the-blythe-star-the-last-mans-story-of-survival>.

Chapter 48 — Whitlam and the Gurindji Land Rights Ceremony — Alex Ettling

Hardy, Frank. *The Unlucky Australians*, Nelson, 1968.

Ward, Charlie Russel. *A Handful of Sand: The Gurindji Struggle, After the Walk-off*, Monash University Publishing, 2016.

Chapter 49 — Farewell Frothies? Global Heating and Disappearing Kelp — Alex Ettling

Kean, Zoe, 'Remembering Tasmania's underwater forests: An ecosystem that once fizzed with life and supported a local industry has all but disappeared', *ABC Science*, 27 Feb 202.

Chapter 50 — 'We Found Our Own Way': Talking with Gay Liberation Activists — Bruce Carter

Cole, Shaun, *Don We Now Our Gay Apparel: Gay Men's Dress in the Twentieth Century*, Berg, 2000.

Coming Out in the 70s, State Library of New South Wales, 2020, <https://www.sl.nsw.gov.au/stories/coming-out-70s/introduction/1>.

Duffy, Michael and Hordern, Nick, *Sydney Noir: The Golden Years*, New South Publishing, 2017.

Jennings, Rebecca, 'A Room Full of Women: Lesbian Bars and Social Spaces in Post-War Sydney', *Women's History Review*, vol: 21 no. 5, 2012.

John Lee oral history interview by Robert French, April 16, 1990, Pride History Group (PHG) Sydney collection.

Johnston, Craig, *A Sydney Gaze: The Making of Gay Liberation*, Schiltron Press, 1999.

Portelli, Alesssandro, 'Living Voices: The Oral history Interview as Dialogue and Experience', *Oral History Review*, vol: 45 no. 2, 2018.

Reeves, Tony, *Mr Sin: The Abe Saffron Dossier*, Allen & Unwin, 2007.

Robinson, Sophie, 'Bar Dykes and Lesbian Feminists: Lesbian Encounters in 1970s Feminism', *Lilith*, no. 22, 2016.

Willett, Graham, *Living Out Loud: A History of Gay and Lesbian Activism in Australia*, Allen & Unwin, 2000.

Wotherspoon, Garry, *Gay Sydney: A History*, New South Books, 2016.

Oral Histories:

Terry Batterham oral history interview by Bruce Carter, March 4th, 2021, authors collection.

Ken (Kandy) Johnson oral history interview with Garry Wotherspoon, circa 1980. State Library of NSW collection [MLOH 448, Item 6].

Barry Charles oral history interview by Bruce Carter, 17 April, 2022, authors collection.

Ken Davis oral history interview with Bruce Carter, June 11, 2005, authors collection.

Garry Wotherspoon oral history interview with Bruce Carter, June 3, 2022, authors collection.

Penny Gulliver oral history interview with Bruce Carter, 28 April, 2022, authors collection.

Diane Minnis oral history interview with Bruce Carter, April 4, 2022, authors collection.

John Witte oral history interview with Bruce Carter, March 19, 2023, authors collection.

John Witte oral history interview with Bruce Carter, June 7, 2005, authors collection.

Ken Davis conversation with author, July 19, 2022.

Chapter 51   **Folk, Politics and the Law at The Rainbow Hotel** Alex Ettling

Horne, Craig, *Roots: How Melbourne Became the Live Music Capital of the World*, Melbourne Books, 2019.

Chapter 52   **Woolshed Kiss-In** Graham Willett

Willett, Graham, Mudoch, Wayne and Marshall, Daniel, *Secret Histories of Queer Melbourne*, Australian Lesbian and Gay Archives, 2011.

Chapter 53   **'Drink and Go To Work': The Saints and the Brisbane Punks** Alex Ettling

Ed Wreckage oral history interviewed by Phil Parker, State Library of Queensland, 2020.

Evans, Raymond & Ferrier Carole (eds), *Radical Brisbane: An Unruly History*, Vulgar Press, 2004.

Gorman, Joe, 'Looking For Johnny Burnaway: Punk, Pain and a Family Puzzle', *Griffith Review*, 6 Oct 2021, <https://www.griffithreview.com/articles/looking-for-johnny-burnaway-2/>.

Jiggens, John, Woodward, Linden, Finucan, Michael and Nunn, Graham, 'Personal Stories: Media Activism in Brisbane, 1970s and 1980s', *Queensland Review*, vol: 14 no. 1, 2007.

Jones, Anne and Whyte, Robert, *Eccentric Voices: A Scrapbook of Brisbane Cultural History 1965-1995*, 2019.

McMillan, Andrew. 'Club 76 and All That', *Meanjin*, vol: 65 no. 3, 2006.

'Misunderstood For Too Long: The Story Of Chris Bailey And The Saints',.

Foster Child, February 1998, <http://www.saintsmusic.com/electricsaintstory.htm >.

Nichols, David, *The Go-Betweens*, Allen & Unwin, 1997.

Piccini, Jon, '"Building their own scene to do their own thing": Imagining and Contesting Space/S in Brisbane's Youth Radicalisation 1968-1976', Honours Thesis, University of Queensland, 2009.

Razar, Young, Fast & Non-boring, Queensland Performing Arts Museum, Brisbane, QPAC, 2004.

Shaw, Barry (ed), *Brisbane: Relaxation, Recreation and Rock'n'Roll: Popular Culture 1890-1990*, Brisbane History Group, 2001.

Stafford, Andrew, *Pig City: From the Saints to Savage Garden*, University of Queensland Press, 2006.

Stafford, Andrew, *Andrew Stafford Collection*, Item: UQ FL440, Fryer Library, The University of Queensland.

Vuleta, Thomas, 'Ups and Downs: Music Venues and Popular Music in Brisbane 1959-1989', Honours Thesis, The University of Queensland, 2016.

Walker, Clinton, *Stranded: The Secret History of Australian Independent Music 1977-1991*, Macmillan, 1996.

Whitton, Evan, *The Hillbilly Dictator: Australia's Police State*, ABC Books, 1989.

Chapter 54   **The Star Hotel** Graham Willett

Benett, James, Cushy, Nancy, Eklund, Erik (eds), *Radical Newcastle*, NewSouth, 2015.

Coan Lyndall, Southgate, Erica, Wafer, Jim (eds), *Out in the Valley: Hunter Gay and Lesbian Histories*, Newcastle Region Library, 2000.

Chapter 55   **Triple Zed's Joint Efforts: Beer, Bands, and Breaking The News** Alex Ettling

Anderson, Alan, 'The Foco Story', *Tribune*, 2 September 1970.

Anderson, Heather, Backhaus, Bridget, Fox, Juliet and Bedford, Charlotte, 'Fifty Years of Resistance and Representation: A Historical Account of Australian Community Radio', Journal of Radio & Audio Media, vol: 27 no. 2, 2020.

Beatson, Jim, 'The 4ZZZFM Story', *Radio Times*, Triple Zed, 1976.

Beattie, Debra, '*Manufacturing Dissent* as part of a Masters Thesis, Queensland University of Technology, July 1997, <https://vimeo.com/96964409>.

Brisbane Discussion Circle, *Remembering the University of Queensland Forum*, <http://www.radicaltimes.info/PDF/Forum.pdf>.

Curr, Ian, 'Brisbane Radicals', Workers Bush Telegraph, 2020, <https://workersbushtelegraph.com.au/2020/11/12/brisbane-radicals/>.

Curr, Ian, 'Won't get fooled again?', Workers Bush Telegraph, 2014, <https://workersbushtelegraph.com.au/2014/04/18/pshift-on-we-wont-get-fooled-again/>.

Curr, Ian, 'Radical Radio – "One Hundred Steps"', Workers Bush Telegraph, 2020, <https://workersbushtelegraph.com.au/essays-2/analysis/pshift/radical-radio/>.

David Darling Oral History interview by Phil Parker, State Library of Queensland, 2020, <https://vimeo.com/456745133>.

Evans, Raymond & Ferrier Carole (eds), *Radical Brisbane: An Unruly History*, Vulgar Press, 2004.

Jiggens, John, Linden Woodward, Michael Finucan and Graham Nunn, 'Personal stories: media activism in Brisbane, 1970s and 1980s', *Queensland Review*, Vol: 14 no. 1, 2007.

Jones, Anne and Whyte, Robert, *Eccentric Voices: A Scrapbook of Brisbane Cultural History 1965-1995*, 2019, <https://www.h-a-r-p-o.com.au/wp-content/uploads/2019/11/eccentric_voices.pdf>.

Knight, Alan, 'Radical Media in the Deep North: The Origins of 4ZZZ-FM', PhD thesis, University of Wollongong, 1998, <http://www.radicaltimes.info/PDF/origins4ZZZ.pdf>.

Mockeridge, Tony, 'Rock'n'roll – What Future?', *Radio Times*, Triple Zed, March 1980.

Piccini, Jon, '"Building their own scene to do their own thing": Imagining and Contesting Space/S in Brisbane's Youth Radicalisation 1968-1976', Honours Thesis, University of Queensland, 2009.

Piccini, Jon, 'A Group of Misguided Way Out Individuals': the Old Left and the Student Movement in Brisbane: 1966–70, *The Queensland Journal of Labour History*, no. 12, 2011.

Piccini, Jon, '"Australia's Most Evil and Repugnant Nightspot", Foco Club and transnational politics in Brisbane's '68', *Dialogue e-Journal*, vol: 8 no. 1, 2010.

Piccini, Jon, 'Bacchanalian Carnival or Political Event? Remembering the Sixties in Australia', *Melbourne Historical Journal*, vol: 40 no. 1, 2012.

Piccini, Jon, 'Dangerous Spaces – Youth Politics in Brisbane, 1960s-70s',. *Queensland Historical Atlas*, 2010. <https://www.qhatlas.com.au/content/dangerous-spaces-youth-politics-brisbane-1960s-70s>.

Prentice, James, 'The Brisbane Protests 1965-72' PhD thesis, Griffith University, 2005. <http://www.radicaltimes.info/PDF/Prentice.pdf>.

Piccini, Jon, '"Up The New Channels": Student Activism in Brisbane During Australia's Sixties', *Crossroads*, 2011.

Shaw, Barry (ed), *Brisbane: Relaxation, Recreation and Rock'n'Roll: Popular Culture 1890-1990*, Brisbane History Group, 2001.

Stafford, Andrew, *Pig City: From the Saints to Savage Garden*, University of Queensland Press, 2006.

Stafford, Andrew, *Andrew Stafford Collection*, Item: UQ FL440, Fryer Library, The University of Queensland.

Stuart, Roger, 'History of the Strike', *Semper Floreat*, vol: 41 no. 11, 1 September 1971, <http://radicaltimes.info/PDF/RogerStuart1971.pdf>.

Vuleta, Thomas, 'Ups and Downs: Music Venues and Popular Music in Brisbane 1959-1989'. Honours Thesis, The University of Queensland, 2016.

Whitton, Evan, *The Hillbilly Dictator: Australia's Police State*, ABC Books, 1989.

Chapter 56 'A Pub of our Own!': The Kingston Hotel, Melbourne's Women's Pub Janey Stone

Berkovitch, Sheryl, 'Pat Longmore 1931-1992', *Lesbians*, August 1992.

Ross, Liz, *Revolution Is For Us*, Interventions, 2019.

Chapter 57 The Oxford Hotel 'Riot', Wollongong, 1981 Nick Southall

<https://revoltsnow.wordpress.com>.

Chapter 58 A Pub at the End of the World: Making Something Meaningful In Tasmania's Wild West Alex Ettling

Clarke, Renfrey, *The Picket: Tasmanian Mine Workers Defend Their Jobs*, Pathfinder Press, 1984.

Grigg, Angus, 'Digging In', Four Corners, Australian Broadcasting Corporation, 9 May 2022, <https://www.abc.net.au/4corners/digging-in:-why-powering-a-green-future-means-more/13873540>.

Hodder, Robert, 'Radical Tasmania: Rebellion, Reaction and Resistance - A Thesis in Creative Nonfiction', PhD thesis, University of Ballarat, 2010.

Howard, Patrick. *Pubs and Publicans of Tasmania's Old West: A History of the Hotels of the West Coast of Tasmania*, Forty South Publishing, 2017.

Jamieson, Ian (neé Andrew) a.k.a. "Jammo", 'A Contribution to Past Union Struggles Our Party Has Led', unpublished discussion bulletin *The Activist*, Perth Branch of the Democratic Socialist Perspective, Perth, 2005.

Maguire, Sarah, 'Mining a Lode of Cultural Pride, *Green Left Weekly*, Issue 353, 17 March 1999, <https://www.greenleft.org.au/content/mining-lode-cultural-pride>.

Rae, Lou, 'The Lost Province: Exploration, Isolation, Innovation And Domination In The Mount Lyell Region 1859-1935', PhD Thesis, University of Tasmania, 2005.

Vassiley, Alexis, 'Union Power in a Tasmanian Mining Town', *Red Flag*, 22 July 2019, <https://redflag.org.au/node/6849>.

Chapter 59 Confrontational Temperance Activism Among Indigenous Women Maggie Brady

Brady, Maggie, Byrne, Joe and Henderson, Grahame, '"Which bloke would stand up for Yalata?" The Struggle of an Aboriginal Community to Control the Availability of Alcohol', *Australian Aboriginal Studies*, Fall 2003.

Brady, Maggie, *Teaching "Proper" Drinking? Clubs and Pubs in Indigenous Australia*, Australian National University Press, 2017.

Schrad, Mark Lawrence, *Smashing the Liquor Machine: A Global History of Prohibition*, Oxford University Press, 2021.

Chapter 60 The Changing Face of Alcohol Consumption and Culture from the 1970s onwards Alex Ettling

Allen, Max, *Intoxicating: Ten Drinks that Shaped Australia*, Thames & Hudson, 2020.

Fitzgerald, Ross, and Jordan, Trevor, *Under the Influence: A History of Alcohol in Australia*, HarperCollins, 2017.

Fleckney, Paul, *Techno Shuffle: Rave Culture & The Melbourne Underground*, Melbourne Books Melbourne, 2018.

Harden, Michael, 'Unique and Deplorable: Regulating Drinking in Victoria', *Meanjin*, vol: 69 no. 3, 2010, <https://meanjin.com.au/essays/unique-and-deplorable-regulating-drinking-in-victoria/>.

Hawkins, Carolyn, 'Fun House: DIY House Venues and the Melbourne Underground', in *Music City Melbourne: Urban Culture, History and Policy*, Bloomsbury Academic, 2022.

Holsworth, Mark, 'Drinking & Melbourne's Culture', *Black Mark: Melbourne Art and Culture Critic*, 18 October 2014, <https://melbourneartcritic.wordpress.com/tag/nieuwenhuysen-report/>.

Homan, Shane, 'SLAM: the music city and cultural activism', *Law, Social Justice and Global Development Journal*, vol: 20, 2016.

Kirkby, Diane, Luckins, Tanja and McConville, Chris. *The Australian Pub*, University of New South Wales Press, 2010.

Moore, Timothy, 'How Melbourne Found its Laneways', *Broadsheet*, 25 July 2014, <https://www.broadsheet.com.au/melbourne/art-and-design/article/melbourne-laneways-bars-cafes-restaurants-six-degrees>.

Richards, Arielle, 'We Knew How Underground It Was': The Birth Of Melbourne's Rave Scene, *Vice*, 12 December 2022, <https://www.vice.com/en/article/epz9xm/we-knew-how-underground-it-was-the-birth-of-melbournes-rave-scene>.

Silvester, John, 'The night the wine flowed out their ears', *The Age*, 11 March 2022, <https://www.theage.com.au/national/victoria/the-night-wine-flowed-out-their-ears-20220309-p5a38t.html>.

Silvester, John and Rule, Andrew, 'We thirsted for European class, but got a hangover, '*The Age*, 11 September 2010, <https://www.theage.com.au/national/victoria/we-thirsted-for-european-class-but-got-a-hangover-20100910-15513.html>.

Strawhan, Peter, 'The Importance of Food and Drink in the Political and Private Life of Don Dunstan', Honours Thesis, University of Adelaide, 2004, <https://digital.library.adelaide.edu.au/dspace/bitstream/2440/37726/8/02whole.pdf>.

Taylor, Sarah, 'Local And/Or General: An Introductory Post Including Some Sample Maps of the Models and Melbourne in 1980', 2012, <https://fromstkildatokingscross.wordpress.com/2012/12/14/local-andor-general-an-introductory-post-including-some-sample-maps-of-the-models-and-melbourne-in-1980/>.

The Urbanist, 'Culture By Design: Can Melbourne's Laneway Infastructure be Replicated?', *Crikey*, 5 July 2013, <https://www.crikey.com.au/2013/07/05/culture-by-design-can-melbournes-laneway-infastructure-be-replicated/>.

Wilden, Necia, 'Here's cheers after 20 years', *The Age*, 21 March 2006, <https://amp.theage.com.au/lifestyle/heres-cheers-after-20-years-20060321-ge1yv8.html>.

Chapter 61 — Funding the Cause: Benefit Gigs at the Empress of India Hotel Iain McIntyre

Gazzo, Jane and Street, Andrew P., *Sound As Ever: A Celebration of the Greatest Decade in Australian Music, 1990-99*, Black Inc, 2022.

Chapter 62 — The Singing Syrup: Melbourne's Trades Hall Gets A Bar Alex Ettling

Burn, Ian and Kirby, Sandy, *Art: Critical, Political*, University of Western Sydney, 1996.

Doughty, Jacqueline, *State of the Union* exhibition catalogue, Ian Potter Museum of Art, The University of Melbourne, 2018.

Ettling, Alex, 'Vale Paddy Garritty', *Recorder*, Issue 300, 2021.

Garritty, Paddy, The Artful Socialist, unpublished memoir, 2009.

Garitty (sic), Paddy, 'Dockyard Daze: An Experiment With Art In Working Life in Williamstown Naval Dockyard 1983-85, *Overland*, issue 149, 1997.

Kellaway, Carlotta, *Melbourne Trades Hall Lygon Street Carlton: The Workingman's Parliament*, Victorian Trades Hall Council, 1988.

Kirby, Sandy. 'Artists and Unions: A Critical Tradition: A Report on the Art & Working Life Program', Australia Council: Community Cultural Development Unit, 1992.

Lack, John, 'Seelaf, George (1914–1988)', Australian Dictionary of Biography, National Centre of Biography, Australian National University, 2012.

Pearce, Marcella, *Melbourne Trades Hall Memories*, Victorian Trades Hall Council, 1997.

'The Artful Socialist', *The Age*, 19 July 2002, <https://www.theage.com.au/entertainment/art-and-design/the-artful-socialist-20020719-gdueqn.html>.

The Fabric of Labour: A Catalogue of Victorian Trades Hall Council's 125th anniversary Art Exhibition and Auction, Victorian Trades Hall Council, Carlton South, 1999.

Working Art: A Survey of Art in the Australian Labour Movement in the 1980s, Art Gallery of New South Wales and Australia Council Visual Arts Board, Sydney, 1985.

Wright, Tony, 'Arts Community Farewells Paddy Garritty, "a glory of a person"', *The Age*, 22 August 2020, <https://www.smh.com.au/national/arts-community-farewells-paddy-garrity-a-glory-of-a-person-20200821-p55o13.html>.

Chapter 63 — Stopping AIDEX '91 Iain McIntyre

Friends of the Hearings, *Piecing It Together: Hearing the Stories of AIDEX '91*, Penniless Press, 1995.

McIntyre, Iain, *Always Look on the Bright Side of Life: The AIDEX '91 Story*, Homebrew Press, 2018, <https://commonslibrary.org/always-look-on-the-bright-side-of-life-the-aidex-91-story/>.

Chapter 64: Workplace Politics at the West End Brewery in Adelaide by Phoebe Kelloway.

Bramble, Tom, 'Our Unions in Crisis: How Did it Come to This?', *Marxist Left Review*, no. 15, Summer 2018, <https://marxistleftreview.org/articles/our-unions-in-crisis-how-did-it-come-to-this/>.

Dynes, Emma, '"Nothing In, Nothing Out!": Adelaide Brewery Workers on Strike', *Red Flag*, 4 December 2020, <https://redflag.org.au/node/7478>.

Kapetanos, Stasi, 'Students, Strike. Solidarity!', *On Dit*, 24 December 2020, <https://onditmagazine.medium.com/students-strike-solidarity-c099655c21c9>.

Kurmelovs, Royce, '"What's happened is quite sad": What Brewery Closure Says About Australia's Drinking', *The Guardian*, 8 November 2020, <https://www.theguardian.com/food/2020/nov/08/whats-happened-is-quite-sad-what-brewery-closures-say-about-australias-drinking>.

Painter, Alison, 'South Australian Brewing Co. Ltd', *SA History Hub*, History Trust of South Australia, <https://sahistoryhub.history.sa.gov.au/organisations/south-australian-brewing-coltd>.

Chapter 65 **Rockhampton Accessible Pub Crawls, 1989–2022**
Alex Ettling and Iain McIntyre

McIntyre, Iain, 'Accessible Pub Crawls and Positive Change: An Interview with Des Ryan', *Commons Library*, 2023, <https://commonslibrary.org/accessible-pub-crawls-and-positive-change-an-interview/>.

Chapter 66 **Choke Point: Inside a Wildcat Strike in the Melbourne Liquor Distribution Centre** Simon Burns in conversation with Alex Ettling

Price, Steph, '"Nothing in, nothing out" at Woolworths Picket', *Red Flag*, 11 August 2015, <https://redflag.org.au/article/nothing-nothing-out-woolworths-picket>.

Stanton, Ryan, 'Workers Dare to Struggle', *Red Flag*, 16 August 2015, <https://redflag.org.au/article/workers-dare-struggle>.

Small, Jerome, 'Inside a Melbourne Warehouse Strike', *Red Flag*, 16 August 2015 <https://redflag.org.au/article/inside-melbourne-warehouse-strike>.

Small, Jerome, 'Showdown in the Supply Chain: Woolworths Workers Make Gains', *Red Flag*, 23 November 2017, <https://redflag.org.au/node/6123>.

Chapter 67 **Spitting In a Fascist's Beer: The Far Right and Pubs**
Alex Ettling and Iain McIntyre

Fox, Vashti, '"Never again": Fascism and Anti-Fascism in Melbourne in the 1990s', *Labour History*, vol: 116, 2019.

Fox, Vashti, Smith, Evan, Persian, Jayne (eds), *Histories of Fascism and Anti-Fascism in Australia*. New York, Taylor & Francis, 2022.

<https://slackbastard.anarchobase.com/>

CONTRIBUTORS

Alex Ettling (editor) is a social historian who takes a particular interest in the intersections of culture and politics. He has worked as a policy analyst for Creative Victoria, as well as being a co-founder of the Trades Hall Arts Studio. A former bar worker, throughout the 2010s Alex organised pub dance parties raising money for left-wing causes including strike funds, Palestine solidarity and LGBTIQ+ equality. Currently, he volunteers on the management committee of Interventions, and is developing an oral history program at Melbourne's Living Museum of the West.

Iain McIntyre (editor) is a Naarm/Melbourne based historian and community radio broadcaster who has written and edited a variety of books about political activism, music, literature and (un)popular culture. Recent publications include the Locus award winning *Dangerous Visions and New Worlds: Radical Science Fiction, 1950 to 1980* (PM Press, 2021) and *Environmental Blockades: Obstructive Direct Action and the History of the Environmental Movement* (Routledge, 2021). He is a regular contributor to the activist resource website commonslibrary.org

Wendy Bacon was part of the Sydney Push. In the 1960s and 70s, she was involved in fighting a high profile obscenity case. She became involved in prison activism and feminist struggles. She was part of the Green Ban movement. In the 1980s, she worked as a non-practicing lawyer and an investigative journalist for the *National Times*, *Sun Herald*, Channel's Nine's *Sunday* program and SBS's *Dateline*. From the early 1990s, she was a journalism academic at the University of Technology Sydney where she was the Director of the Australian Centre for Independent Journalism and a Professor of Journalism. She remains a radical activist and journalist.

Maggie Brady is an anthropologist based in Canberra at the Australian National University. Born in Bristol, England, Maggie moved to Australia in the early 1970s, and completed her PhD at the Australian National University. In the 1980s she worked for the Northern Land Council in Darwin and for the Royal Commission into British Nuclear Tests in Australia, but has since focused on health, drug and alcohol issues, undertaking fieldwork in different parts of Australia and in South Africa. She has published for both academic and community-based audiences, creating practical resources for community empowerment and for service providers. After holding two Australian Research Council Fellowships, she is now an Honorary Associate Professor at the Centre for Aboriginal Economic Policy Research.

Rowan Cahill is a graduate of the universities of Sydney, New England, and Wollongong. Prominent in the student, anti-war and New Left movements of the 1960s and 1970s, he was a Conscientious Objector during the Vietnam War. He has variously worked as a farmhand, teacher, freelance writer, and for the trade union movement as a publicist, historian, and rank and file activist. Currently an Honorary Fellow at the University of Wollongong, he has published widely in trade union, social movement, and academic publications. With Terry Irving he is co-author of *Radical Sydney* (2010), and *The Barber Who Read History* (2021).

Bruce Carter was born and has lived for most of his life on Gadigal country. He has cleaned pubs and offices, operated long distance calls for Telecom Australia and worked in a men's sex club. Training as a nurse he worked for many years in mental health, HIV and drug & alcohol community services. For the last 21 years Bruce has worked with communities on history projects. These have included oral history, exhibition curation, walking tours, writing and research. He was a founding member of Sydney's Pride History Group in 2005 and was co-curator on the exhibitions 'Coming Out in the 70s' in 2020-21 and 'Pride (R)evolution' in 2023, both at the State Library of NSW. His PhD – completed at UTS in 2019 – looked at the concept of 'memory activism' and the potential in personal memory and storytelling to challenge social inequity and dominant understandings of history and heritage.

Carol Corless graduated from UNE in 2016 with a Bachelor of Historical Inquiry and Practice. Carol has a long-term interest in labour history through her involvement in the union movement. Carol was a shop floor delegate at a food manufacturer in Brisbane until her role was made redundant after 28 years. Through her involvement in the union movement Carol held roles on the executive of her union, United Voice. Carol is a life member of United Voice, now the United Workers Union. Carol is currently studying for a Master of Philosophy through UNE.

Daniel A. Elias is a historian based in Fremantle, Western Australia. He is currently writing his PhD at the University of Western Australia on the historical development of the Australian nation-state, through the perspective of maritime workers. He, at present, works at the University of Notre Dame Australia, researching the disability sector – while acting as secretary of the local National Tertiary Education Union branch.

Gary Foley, actor, activist and academic historian, was a key member of the Aboriginal Black Power movement. He has been at the centre of major political activities in Australia for more than 40 years. Foley was involved in the establishment of some of the first Aboriginal community-controlled organisations including Redfern's Aboriginal Legal Service, the Aboriginal Health Service in Melbourne, and the National Black Theatre. His acting career began with the revue *Basically Black* (1972), and he appeared in the seminal films *Backroads* (1976) and *Dogs in Space* (1986). Since 2008, he has been an academic worker at Victoria University.

Alison Holland is an Associate Professor in the Department of History and Archaeology at Macquarie University. Her research focusses on the history of Indigenous-Settler relations in Australia, as well as histories of humanitarianism, human rights and race on which she has published in national and international journals. Her first monograph *Just Relations: The Story of Mary Bennett's Crusade For Aboriginal Rights* (UWA Publishing) was shortlisted for the NSW Premier's Australian history prize in 2016. With colleagues from the University of Technology, Sydney, she is a CI on an ARC Discovery Project titled 'Policy for Self-Determination. The Case Study of ATSIC.'

Terry Irving, radical historian and educator, was one of the founders of Sydney's Free University in the 1960s. He writes on colonial workers' movements, Australia's class structure, youth movements and policy, labour intellectuals, and radical democracy. With Rowan Cahill, he is the author of *Radical Sydney* (2010) and *The Barber Who Read History* (2021). He is currently an Honorary Professorial Fellow at the University of Wollongong. His writings can be found at terryirving.net

Phoebe Kelloway is a labour historian and socialist based in Adelaide, on Kaurna land. In 2020 she completed a PhD thesis about the three major industrial disputes in Australia at the start of the 1930s Depression. She has researched and written about rank-and-file involvement in strikes, anti-fascist activity in the interwar years, and the post-war development of the healthcare system.

Diane Kirkby is Professor of Law and Humanities at University of Technology Sydney. For many years she taught History at La Trobe University where she is now Research Professor (Emeritus). She is the author of two books and numerous articles on pubs, women's work, and drinking culture, including *Barmaids* (1996), and *The Australian Pub* (2010) co-authored with Tanja Luckins and Chris McConville. Since 2016 she has been the Editor of *Labour History*. Her current research concentrates on women maritime workers, following her latest book, *Maritime Men of the Asia-Pacific*, published by Liverpool University Press in 2022.

Tanja Luckins is a historian in the Department of Archeology and History, La Trobe University. Her books include (with Diane Kirkby and Chris McConville) *The Australian Pub* (2010) and (with Louise Johnson and David Walker) *The Story of Australia: A New History of People and Place* (2022).

Hamish Maxwell-Stewart is a professor of Heritage and Digital Humanities at the University of New England. He has authored several books including *Closing Hell's Gates* (Allen and Unwin, Sydney, 2007) and (with Michael Quinlan) *Unfree Workers: Insubordination and Resistance in Australia* (Palgrave Studies in Economic History, 2022). He has also co-designed several heritage site interpretations, including a digital convict memorial for the Penitentiary Chapel Hobart—a National Trust Tasmania Property. He lives in Hobart, Tasmania.

Chris McConville has written widely on Australian popular culture, urban environments and labour history. He has worked in the media and is currently lecturing at Victoria University. He is the co-author, with Diane Kirkby and Tanja Luckins, of *The Australian Pub* (2010).

Lisa Milner is a socialist and a recovering academic, has written extensively on left-wing and workers' culture, and is Vice-President of Interventions Publishing. Her current research addictions include an international comparative study of workers' theatre, screen representations of workers and unions, and labour history.

David Nichols is a historian of urban and/or popular culture focusing primarily on 20th century Australia. He lectures in Urban Planning at the University of Melbourne with a focus on history, culture, community and place. His previous books include a biography of *The Go-Betweens*, *The Bogan Delusion*, *Trendyville: the Battle for Australia's Inner Cities* (with Renate Howe and Graeme Davison), *Dig: Australian Rock and Pop Music 1960-1985*, and *Urban Australia and Post-Punk: Exploring Dogs in Space*.

Michael Quinlan PhD FASSA is emeritus professor of industrial relations at the University of New South Wales. In addition to his book *Unfree Workers* on convict worker resistance with Hamish Maxwell-Stewart he has published extensively on occupational health and safety and labour history including two books of worker mobilisation - *The Origins of Worker Mobilisation: Australia 1788-1850* (Routledge, New York, 2018) and *Contesting Inequality and Worker Mobilisation: Australia 1851-1880* (Routledge, New York, 2020). A third book covering the period 1881-1920 is in progress. He lives in Launceston, Tasmania.

Nick Southall grew-up in Wollongong and is currently casually employed by Wollongong University as an academic. For over forty years, he has helped to organise local radical and progressive political groups and social movements. His written work includes *Working for the Class: The Praxis of the Wollongong Out of Workers' Union*, *A Multitude of Possibilities: The Strategic Vision of Michael Hardt and Antonio Negri*, and with Mike Donaldson *Illawarra Cooperatives: The First One Hundred Years* and *Against Fascism and War: Pig Iron Bob and the Dalfram Dispute at Port Kembla*, as well as a wide-range of articles available via his blog – revoltsnow.wordpress.com

Jeff Sparrow is a writer, editor and broadcaster. A former editor of *Overland* literary journal, he now works at the Centre for Advancing Journalism at the University of Melbourne. His books include *Crimes Against Nature: Capitalism and Global Heating*, *Provocations: New and Selected Writing* and the forthcoming *Twelve Rules for Strife*, a collaboration with artist Sam Wallman.

Janey Stone became a socialist in 1962, participating in student and antiwar campaigns. She joined the Women's Liberation Movement in the US in 1969 and was very active in WLM in Australia in the 1970s. Janey has been a union delegate, political activist and frequent writer in many fields, including women workers, sexual politics and the Middle East. Her most recent field of research and publication is the radical Jewish tradition. Janey continues her activity in retirement as a leading member of Interventions.

Graham Willett is a historian of queer Australia. He is a recovering academic who in his post-university life has been promoting queer history to wide audiences. He has published chapters and articles and written and edited books. Graham is a long-time volunteer with the Australian Queer Archives which collects, preserves and celebrates queer lives. He curates exhibitions, writes and guides history walks, delivers talks and lectures, and is series editor of Queer Oz Folk publications. He is notoriously optimistic about things getting better.

Photographers and Illustrators

Alan Attwood is a Melbourne-based writer, journalist and photographer. He is a former New York correspondent for *The Age* and *The Sydney Morning Herald* newspapers and was editor of *The Big Issue* magazine between 2006 and 2016. See more of his work at alanattwood.com

Emmy Boudry was a big part of the Rave Production Company, Right On One productions. Founded in 1991 alongside Mark Hogan and Daniel Wittenberg, Emmy was a key figure in the emergence of the Melbourne rave scene. Emmy organised much of the logistics of a number of iconic early events, and took photos of the scene she was immersed in. Emmy continued organising rave events throughout the 1990s, up to 2001 and then went on to perform as a VJ playing at many well known events and festivals as well as running her own video production company. Emmy also organised numerous free Street Raves that took place in Brunswick Street, Fitzroy and St Kilda. Today, she lives in Northern NSW with her partner and two children.

Mark Chandler began taking photos of Brisbane bands in 1979. See his band photos on the Facebook page Bands of Brisbane.

John Corker is a public-interest lawyer and photographer who grew up in Melbourne but spent a decade in Alice Springs before moving to Sydney in 1990. He now lives in Thirroul just north of Wollongong and has worked for and with Aboriginal people for much of his life. Many Aboriginal Art books contain portraits of artists taken by him. In 2021, he published a book of photos taken in Gertrude Street Fitzroy where he lived in the 1970s. Copies can be found in the State Library of Victoria and the National Library. Instagram @johnnycorker

Gordon Curtis is one of the pioneers of Triple Zed radio station. In 1975, whilst in the beer garden of The Royal Exchange, Curtis learned that student radicals at the University of Queensland were going to build an FM radio station. At the time, Curtis was on the dole, as an unemployed camera operator (graphic reproducer). Curtis took part in the early meetings to establish community radio in Brisbane, and volunteered in the early period of the station's existence. On the basis of Curtis's printing industry experience he became the coordinator of the station publication *Radio Times* mailed to Double Zed subscribers. Curtis also assumed the role of taking photos during the early years at the station, a number of which feature in this book.

Audrey Eberhard is a socialist, and artist who lives in Melbourne. She paints and occasionally does some illustration work. Audrey has illustrated art for one other book published by interventions under a different name. She was very grateful for the opportunity to illustrate the cover art for this book and hopes that you enjoy it.   Instagram @boatgirlstoatgirl   audreyeberh@gmail.com

Juno Gemes, photographer and social justice activist, has spent much of her long career documenting and advocating for the rights and struggles of First Nations people. She has worked in collaboration with Indigenous political and cultural leaders and in communities to create visual narratives of empowerment. In 1984 she established Camera Future Photographers Cooperative Studio in Kings Cross. In 2003 the National Portrait Gallery exhibited her portraits of Aboriginal and Torres Strait Islander activists and leaders 'Proof: Portraits from the Movement 1978–2003.' Juno Gemes' photographs have been widely exhibited, and collected by the major Australian cultural institutions. She is working on a publication *Something Personal: Chronicles from The Movement 1976-2023*.

Jennifer Gow was born in Brisbane a member of the 'baby boomer' demographic. She grew up in a Catholic family in a stultifyingly conservative and corrupt Queensland when Brisbane was more a country town. By the late 1970s she was working as a freelance photographer mostly for *Nation Review*. The music culture was shaped by community radio 4ZZZ and the emergence of local bands such as the Saints who she photographed in 1978. After an academic career she transitioned to a ratbag video maker and activist.

Peter Gray is an international cinematographer and director of photography with a work history spanning 45-years and four continents: Australia, Asia, Europe and USA. He has accrued credits in hundreds of productions ranging from feature-film drama productions, commercials, television, and documentary films winning several awards for cinematography. He has taught film and television production techniques in workshops around the world, including a part-time lectureship at the University of Technology in Sydney (formerly NSWIT). In retirement, Peter founded and manages the Radical Times Archive: radicaltimes.info

Ross Gwyther retired recently after a career as a geophysicist at Qld University and CSIRO, followed by 10 years working as a union organiser with the National Tertiary Education Union. He has been actively involved in the labour, environment and peace movements for the past 50 years and is on the National Committee of the Independent and Peaceful Australia Network.

Ponch Hawkes is an Australian photographer whose work explores intergenerational relationships, queer identity and LGBTQI+ rights, the female body, masculinity, and women at work, capturing key moments in Australia's cultural and social histories.

Ruth Maddison's career spans more than 45 years of working in broad-ranging areas including lecturing; freelance, commissioned, and self-initiated works for publications and special projects; and many solo and group exhibitions since 1979. Her work explores themes of relationships, communities and families, offering the viewers glimpses into the daily lives and rituals of ordinary citizens within their homes, workplaces and neighbourhoods. Her most recent solo exhibition, 'It was the best of times, it was the worst of times', 2021 was a major survey show across all four galleries at the Centre for Contemporary Photography, Melbourne. Maddison's work is widely collected by major institutions throughout Australia.

Matt Mawson is a Brisbane cartoonist and designer, published since the late 1960s. He has contributed to 4ZZZ's *Radio Times*, *Semper*, and the *Cane Toad Times*. Many of his current drawings can be seen on Instagram @mattmawson1950

Frank Neilsen started taking photos in 1964, fresh out of high school, and turned this interest into a lifelong career. His great enthusiasm for music led to his spare-time work on *Go-Set* magazine. In 1975, Frank started his own studio in Melbourne which operated until 2002.

Syd Shelton studied fine in Yorkshire and began his photography practice in the early 1970s, following a move to Australia. In Sydney, Syd worked as a freelance photo-journalist for newspapers such as *Nation Review*, *Tribune*, and *Digger*. In 1975 he had a solo exhibition of his photographs, 'Working Class Heroes' at the Sydney Film-makers Cooperative. In 1976, Syd returned to London and became one of the key activists in the movement Rock Against Racism. He was the photographer and one of the designers of the RAR magazine *Temporary Hoarding* which was published between 1976 to 1981. His work has been widely published and exhibited and is in numerous collections including the V&A, The Tate Gallery and The National Portrait Gallery. Syd's photographs from the 1970s are featured in the touring exhibitions 'Facing Britain' and 'Syd Shelton: Rock Against Racism' and the accompanying monograph which was republished in March 2023 by Rare Bird Books in Los Angeles.

Bernadette Smith situates the 1979 Star Hotel riot in the context of Newcastle's history of class struggle, before placing the state in the frame and looking at local policing and power politics. She also explains the culture of the pub in a sociological way, challenging/undermining a whole lot of safe/traditional academic wisdom.

George Yankovich is an undergraduate law student living in Adelaide, South Australia. In 2021, he was the editor of *On Dit*, the University of Adelaide's student magazine, where he covered the West End brewery strikes, and also reported on student unionism and politics at large.

ACKNOWLEDGEMENTS

The editors thank everyone who contributed and made available images, stories, information and sources for this book. In addition we would also like to thank:

Emily Abbott, Mathew Abbott, Gary Adams, Paul Adams, Jon Altman, Rick Amor, Alan Anderson, Jim Anderson, Mick Armstrong, Margaret Bailey, Siena Balakrishnan, Balakrishnan-Webb clan, Greg Barr, Bernie Barnes, Scott Barrasford, Felicity Bartak, Louisa Bassini, Jim Beatson, Brendan Bennett, Aaron Billings, Andy Blunden, Julie Boaler, Irene Bolger, Emmy Boudry, Brian Boyd, John Braybrook, James Brennan, Phillip Brophy, David Brophy, Brunckton clan, Simon Burns, Gemma Cafarella, Steven Chang, Bruin Christensen, Renfrey Clarke, Paul Costigan, Mick Counihan, Joan Coxsedge, Bruin Cristensen, Ian Curr, Peter Curtis, Gordon Curtis, Steve Curtis, Glen Davis, Sam Davis, Ken Davis, Phillip Deery, Max Delany, Viraj Dissanayake, Barry Donovan, Judi Dransfield, Garry Dyson, Geraldine Earle, Audrey Eberhard, Sam Elkin, Jacinta Elliott, John Englart, Mary Ettling, Denis Evans, Naomi Evans, Ruby Evans-McIntyre, Evans clan, Nick Everett, Will Ewing, Jeltje Fanoy, John Finlayson, Bluey Fisher, Robert Forster, Charlie Fox, Adrian Gallagher, Bill Garner, The late Paddy Garritty, Juno Gemes, Grace Gorman, Angelo Grando, Peter Gray, Hall Greenland, Tom Griffiths, The late Peter Haffenden, Holly Hammond, Mark C Halstead, Adrian Hartland, Jon Hawkes, Ponch Hawkes, Kevin Healy, Merv Heers, Dan Hellier, Yolanda Hellier, Nick Henderson, Lou Hill, Mark Hosking, Jack Howard, Robert Hughes, Jack Hynes, Jammo, Erika Jellis, Anne Jones, Percy Jones, the extended Kalianan-Balakrishnan family, Sev Karantonis, Samson Keam, Haydn Keenan, Emma Kerin, Dave Kerin, Julie Kimber, Ed Kuepper, Matt Kunkel, Linzi Kurileff, Sandie la Gore, Orlando Labosco, Lyndsay Last, Brian Laver, Mary Leunig, Bill Liddy, Albert Littler, Richard Lowenstein, Martie Lowenstein, Doug Lucas, The late Stuart Macintyre, Ruth Maddison, Ken Mansell, Marlin, Mark Matcott, Matt Mawson, Tanya McConvell, Jackson McInerney, McIntyre clan, Jean McLean, Humphrey McQueen, Dean Mighell, Bruce Milne, Leigh Milward, Anthony Morgan, Manolya Moustafa, Cath Munckton, Chris Nash, Dale Nason, Tim Nelthorpe, Doug Nicholson, Leon Norster, Tom O'Lincoln, Dan O'Neill, Jack O'Toole, Bobbie Oliver, Michael Pearson, Eric Petersen, Jon Piccini, Rob Pyne, Rod Quantock, Vas Renn, Anne Richards, Jeff Rickertt, Jim Rimmer, Carla Rizio, Madeleine Roberts, Fergus Robinson, Tim Rogers, Liz Ross, Linda Rubinstein, Ben Russell, Dean Russell, The late Les Russell, Des Ryan, Charlie Sanders, Kim Sattler, Sean Scalmer, Zoë Scotland, John Sebesta, Carmel Shute, Paul Slape, Jerome Small, Terri Smeaton, Brian Smiddy, John Stanwell, Tess Stewart-Moore, Michael Stoddart, Simon Strong, Paul Sullivan, Joseph Tafra at CUDL, Fleur Taylor, Ann Taylor, Mike Thomas, Mitch Thompson, Neale Towart, Liz Turner, Alexis Vassiley, James Vigus, Alan Walker, Gritta Walker, Rob Walls, Uncle Larry Walsh, Felicity Watson, Dean Wharton, Phillip Whitefield, Luke Whitington, Ralph Williss, Carol Williss, John Willsteed, Mark Wilson, Roger Wilson, Clare Wright, Eileen Wright, Nick Wurlod, Wurlod clan, Barry York, Larry Zetlin, Rachelle Summers at Victoria Legal Aid, Melbourne's Living Museum of the West, Broken Hill Historical Society, Broken Hill City Library, Richmond Historical Society, Fitzroy Historical Society, Footscray Historical Society, Sydney Trades Hall, Commons Library, Radical Times Archive, Australian Queer Archives, Pride History Group, Radical History Archive, House Catastrophe, 3CR, 4ZZZ, Noel Butlin Centre, Australian National University, Fryer Library, University of Queensland, State Library of NSW, State Library of South Australia, State Library of Tasmania, State Library of Queensland, Australian Society for the Study of Labour History (ASSLH), ASSLH – Melbourne Branch, ASSLH – Perth Branch, ASSLH – Sydney Branch, ASSLH – Canberra Branch, Brisbane Labour History Association.

ABOUT INTERVENTIONS

At Interventions we believe radical ideas matter. We want our books to be part of the development of a critical and engaged Australian left.

Interventions is an independent, not-for-profit, incorporated publisher. We publish left-wing, radical and socialist books by Australian authors. We welcome books which for political or financial reasons are unlikely to be accepted by commercial publishers. Our books cover a wide range of topics including labour history, left-wing politics, radical cultural themes, and works about resistance to oppression.

By highlighting alternative voices, especially those that have been pushed to the margins, we hope to contribute to a greater insight and awareness of the injustices that exist in society, and the many efforts at the grassroots to right these wrongs.

We welcome publishing proposals. If you are interested in submitting one please check out the information for authors on our website.

Interventions has no independent source of income and is committed to keeping prices accessible. As bookshops and warehouses close around the world, our future hangs in the balance. By supporting us you will help us keep radical ideas alive and accessible to all.

If you would like to support radical publishing in Australia please consider donating, leaving a bequest, or supporting our Patreon: patreon.com/interventions

interventions.org.au

MORE BOOKS FROM INTERVENTIONS

The New Theatre: The people, plays and politics behind Australia's radical theatre

Editor: Lisa Milner

For the first time, this unique collection of essays brings the stories of New Theatre branches around Australia, filling a vital space in Australian cultural history. Radical left-wing theatre history tales, told by theatre practitioners, historians, academics and political ratbags, reveal a rich vein of Australia's hidden cultural heritage. New Theatre advocated for freedom and democracy, aiming to activate audiences politically, and create authentic, non-commercial Australian drama by telling the hidden stories about the real lives of working-class people.

Hell No! We Won't Go! Resistance to conscription in post war Australia

Author: Bobbie Oliver

Stories of the many young men who resisted the National Service schemes of 1951–59, and 1965–72. Some became well-known; others were known only to family and friends. The book describes their experiences in court, in prison and underground in hiding. In recounting these stories, Bobbie Oliver asks: What motivated them to take an unpopular stance – even to the extent of prison? What experiences and sufferings did they undergo? Did taking a stand against militarism and war make a difference to society or change their lives?

Without Bosses: Radical Australian Trade Unionism in the 1970s

Author: Sam Oldham

Without Bosses gives a fascinating insight into radical currents that developed in Australian trade unionism during the 1970s when rank-and-file trade unionists pushed the boundaries of action, in some cases setting global precedents. Some of the better-known events of the period include the almost complete neutralisation of anti-strike laws through mass strike action in 1969, and the famous green bans of the Builders Labourers' Federation. In some of the lesser-known actions of the period, the book details fascinating experiments with self-management and workers' control. Without Bosses overflows with incredible and inspiring stories from a critically important period in Australian history.

Radical Perth, Militant Fremantle

Edited by Charlie Fox, Alexis Vassiley, Bobbie Oliver, and Lenore Layman

Radical Perth, Militant Fremantle tells 34 fascinating stories of radical moments in the cities' past. This engaging, inspiring book charts Perth and Fremantle's radical history, uncovering the obscure and neglected, reframing the better known, opening new windows on former times while pointing to directions for the future.

The Crime of Not Knowing Your Crime: Ric Throssell Against ASIO

Author: Karen Throssell,
with a contextual essay by Phillip Deery

Karen Throssell is an award-winning writer and poet. In this book she tells the story of her grandmother Katharine Susannah Prichard, one of Australia's greatest novelists, her grandfather Hugo Throssell, the war hero who won the Victoria Cross for gallantry, and her father Ric Throssell, who was hounded all his life over allegations of espionage. A study of the psychology of spies and those who obsess about them, a narrative of guilt and innocence told through poetry, prose and historical documents.

Passionate Friends: Mary Fullerton, Mabel Singleton and Miles Franklin

Author: Sylvia Martin

A fascinating portrait of friendship, love, desire, politics and art – and the blurry, shape-shifting lines between them. 'What a story of it could be told' – wrote Mabel Singleton to Miles Franklin late in life, yet she could not bring herself to tell anything of the life she shared with author and poet Mary Fullerton. Rescued from near destruction, a box of Mary's manuscripts eventually made its way to the Mitchell Library. It contained poems she never sent to Mabel. These poignant poems trace a love story that sheds light on how women of the early twentieth century may have understood their love for each other.

Years of Rage: Social Conflicts in the Fraser Era

Author: Tom O'Lincoln

A furnace of social conflict forged resistance to the Fraser regime, on multiple fronts. The social temperature may have cooled since Fraser's time, but the outcomes of the stalemate are enduring. This new enhanced edition adds a wealth of visual material from the era. It also includes an Afterword by Rick Kuhn, outlining the main political events since 1983 and bringing together the main threads that continue today.

www.ingramcontent.com/pod-product-compliance
Lightning Source LLC
Chambersburg PA
CBHW051156290426
44109CB00022B/2481